Illinois and Federal Employment Law Manual

Volume 1

January 2011 Edition

For Reference

Not to be taken from this room

Published by
Ceridian Corporation
3311 East Old Shakopee Road
HQW01E
Bloomington, MN 55425-1640
800-643-5999
http://hrcompliance.ceridian.com

ISBN 0-923606-58-0
IL2011 (11-01)
Item # 1146-V1

Foreword

Objectives and Philosophy

This book is intended to provide a handy overview of the most important employment issues, from hiring and terminating through discrimination and electronic communications. It should help you make sense of the maze of federal and state laws that apply to all facets of the employment process and to help you determine if you are complying with fundamental employment laws and regulations. We have accomplished this by removing extraneous material and focused on those things you need to know to do your job effectively and efficiently.

Even with some pretty heavy and, we hope, judicious pruning of the material, there is still a lot of material here — and it is not simple material. Law is naturally complex and often difficult even for experts to understand fully. For the most part we have tried to present federal and state law in standard English, rather than in the all-too-familiar "legalese." Whenever possible we have rephrased especially obscure and confusing statements into something a bit more comprehensible. Where the legal language is particularly wordy and oblique we have tried to cut through the verbiage to find the germ of the section, the actual meaning lying beneath the often wordy and inflated prose. We have used as many bulleted lists as possible, presenting information in bite-size pieces in an easy-to-read and easy-to-remember format. In some instances, however, we have kept portions of the actual law, not necessarily because those portions were especially clearly written but because they contained essential information that could best be said in the particular legal phrasings used. We make no apologies for this, since eliminating essential information because it may be a little difficult to understand is not useful economy.

So we make some assumptions here. One is that you are not a lawyer and do not care to wade through the full law in all of its obscurity and unnatural English to find out the best way to deal with on-the-job matters. A competing assumption, however, is that although you may not be a legal expert you are an intelligent and informed professional who is willing to do a little thinking to understand some important and complex material. Indeed some serious thought is required to really understand all facets of employment law as it currently exists — and considerable effort will be required to keep up with the law as it changes, which it is always doing.

Organization

We have tried to provide an organizational approach that will help you approach the material easily and find specific topics quickly. We follow the same general pattern for each chapter, with some slight variation to accommodate the wide range of material covered. Each chapter has its own Introduction, indicating the specific topics treated under the general chapter topic.

General information and federal law are always handled first, and the material is broken down into subheadings indicating the specific aspects being discussed. You can use the chapter subheadings to skim through the manual as you seek specific information. Specific state law content is usually handled separately in the second part of the chapter, again with subheadings indicating specific aspects of the general law. Ordinarily, you can review the federal law — or the particular parts of it you need to review — and then go on to the state law or the parts of that you need to review.

Chapters

Table of Contents

Chapter 5

Background Checks 33

Chapter 6

Immigration 55

Chapter 7

New-Hire Reporting 95

Chapter 8
Employee Screening and Lie-Detector Tests.. 103

Chapter 9
Employee Handbooks 119

Chapter 10
Training 125

Chapter 11
Noncompetition Agreements and Trade Secrets 137

Chapter 12

Wages and Hours 145

Chapter 13
Payroll Taxes and Withholding 207

Chapter 14

Employment of Minors 223

Chapter 15
Discrimination in Employment 247

Chapter 16

Drug and Alcohol Testing in the Workplace ... 329

Chapter 17
Employee Performance Evaluations 351

Chapter 18
Personnel Files 359

Chapter 19
Discipline... 377

Chapter 20
Negligent Retention and Supervision 397

Chapter 21
Termination 401

Chapter 22

Plant Closings and Workforce Reduction 421

Chapter 23
Health Care Plans and COBRA........................439

Chapter 24
HIPAA **515**

Chapter 25
FMLA and Employee Leave 545

Chapter 26
Unemployment Compensation 601

Chapter 27
Workers' Compensation 611

Chapter 28
The NLRA and Labor Relations 645

Chapter 29
Alternative Dispute Resolution 677

Chapter 30
Independent Contractors 689

Chapter 31
Temporary Employees and Contingent Employment 705

Chapter 32
Workplace Flexibility 715

Chapter 33
Telecommuting 741

Chapter 34
Safety in the Workplace 763

Chapter 35

AIDS/Communicable Diseases in the Workplace 807

Chapter 36
Smoking in the Workplace 815

Chapter 37
Workplace Violence 827

Chapter 38
Whistleblower Protection................................. 855

Chapter 39
Privacy in the Workplace 879

Chapter 40
Electronic Information and Communications . 889

Chapter 41

Posting and Recordkeeping Requirements 905

Chapter 1

Snapshot

The following list of questions will provide a snapshot for employers to use in determining whether or not they are complying with fundamental employment laws and regulations. An employer should know the answer to every one of these questions. Although a "No" answer does not necessarily mean that the employer is in violation of any laws or regulations, the employer should understand why the answer is "No." The page number is provided for quick reference.

Yes	No		Page Reference
❏	❏	Does your employment application and your employee handbook contain "disclaimer" statements of any promise of job security?	123
❏	❏	Do you know what drug-testing laws apply to your organization?	329
❏	❏	Do you accommodate employees with AIDS?	807
❏	❏	Did you know to check your contracts with independent contractors against the tests used by the IRS to determine employment status?	690
❏	❏	Does your dress code potentially interfere with an employee's religious practices?	257
❏	❏	Do you have an employee handbook? If so, is it regularly updated and do you include a clear statement that continued employment is not guaranteed?	119
❏	❏	Do you know what questions you cannot ask job applicants and which ones you should?	16, 276
❏	❏	Do you give medical examinations to applicants only after the employment offer and are they given to all applicants in the job category?	19
❏	❏	Do you check all job and personal references before hiring?	33
❏	❏	Do you have a discipline policy, and do your supervisors understand it and apply it consistently?	377
❏	❏	Do you know when an organization can be sued for negligent retention or supervision of an employee?	397
❏	❏	Do you pay required overtime compensation to nonexempt employees, which can include salaried employees?	159

❑ ❑   Do you know if an employer can require job applicants
to be screened for drugs? 330, 333

❑ ❑   Do you use gender-neutral job titles when advertising position openings?............... 15

❑ ❑   Do you know if employee progress reviews are completed
on at least an annual basis for each employee? 354

❑ ❑   Do you know if adequate training has been given to supervisors on how to
plan, organize, and carry out effective progress reviews?......................... 133, 351, 357

❑ ❑   Do you know if the human resources department reviews performance appraisals
before final processing?.. 353

❑ ❑   Do you know if you have a written job description for all positions,
and are the areas covered on each employee's performance appraisal
related to it? 11, 12, 351

❑ ❑   Do you know your state's minimum wage, overtime, and wage payment laws?...... 173

❑ ❑   Do you know if all applicants are completing company application forms?............... 15

❑ ❑   Do you know if all interviews with applicants are conducted
in a structured format?.. 21

❑ ❑   Do you know if new employees are provided with copies
of appropriate handbooks and benefits booklets, and are they required
to sign handbook/booklet receipts? 119

❑ ❑   Do you know if new hires are informed of the "probationary period,"
if there is one?... 120

❑ ❑   Do you know if eligible full-time new hires have been properly enrolled
in all company group benefit plans?.. 439

❑ ❑   Do you know federal wage laws concerning employees
who serve jury duty?.. 172

❑ ❑   Do you know the employee's federal right to notice of plant closings?................... 421

❑ ❑   Do you know that the Employee Polygraph Protection Act (EPPA) prohibits
private employers from using lie-detector tests either for pre-employment
screening or during the course of employment?............................... 103, 882

❑ ❑   Do you know if the human resources department reviews all involuntary terminations
before they occur? 403

❑ ❑   Do you know if all objective guidelines are in place for evaluating
all job applicants? 15

Chapter 2

Compliance Thresholds

The following list does not include all federal and state employment laws, but it does provide an overview of how many employees an employer must have to be covered under these laws. Remember, however, that coverage for some of the laws also depends on requirements other than the number of employees. If the number places a business on the borderline, an employer should consult further in these materials for an explanation of those other requirements.

Federal Statutes	Minimum Employees
Age Discrimination in Employment Act (ADEA) of 1967 (29 U.S.C. § 621)	20
Americans with Disabilities Act (ADA) of 1990 (42 U.S.C. § 12101)	15
Civil Rights Act of 1964 — Title VII — Equal Employment Opportunities (42 U.S.C. §§ 2000e et seq.)	15
Civil Rights Act of 1991 (42 U.S.C. §§ 1981 – 1996b)	15
Consolidated Omnibus Benefits Reconciliation Act (COBRA) (29 U.S.C. §§ 1161 et seq.)	20
Consumer Credit Protection Act (15 U.S.C. §§ 1671 – 1677)	1
Drug-Free Workplace Act of 1988 (41 U.S.C. §§ 701 et seq.)	1
Electronic Communications Privacy Act of 1986 (ECPA) (18 U.S.C. §§ 2510 – 2522)	1
Employee Polygraph Protection Act (EPPA) of 1988 (29 U.S.C. §§ 2001 et seq.)	1
Employee Retirement Income Security Act (ERISA) (29 U.S.C. §§ 1001 et seq.)	1
Employee Right-to-Know Laws (Hazardous Chemicals in Workplace)	1
Equal Pay Act (EPA) (29 U.S.C. § 206)	1

Illinois Statutes	Minimum Employees

Access to Personnel Files

820 Ill. Comp. Stat. §§ 40/0.01 et seq. (Personnel Record Review Act) 5

Background Checks

220 Ill. Comp. Stat. § 5/8-501.5 (Public Utilities) .... N/A
225 Ill. Comp. Stat. § 10/4.1 (Child Care Facilities) .... N/A
225 Ill. Comp. Stat. §§ 46/1 – 46/99 (Healthcare Worker Background Check Act) .... N/A
705 Ill. Comp. Stat. § 405/5-915 (Expunged Juvenile Records) .... N/A
725 Ill. Comp. Stat. § 190/3 (School District Employees) .... N/A
745 Ill. Comp. Stat. §§ 46/1 – 46/99 (Employment Record Disclosure Act) .... N/A
775 Ill. Comp. Stat. § 5/2-103 (Use of Arrest History Information) 15

Child Labor

30 Ill. Comp. Stat. §§ 584/1 – 584/99 (State Prohibition of Goods from Child Labor Act) .... N/A
820 Ill. Comp. Stat. §§ 205/1 – 205/22 1

Discrimination

430 Ill. Comp. Stat. §§ 130/10 – 130/25 (Emergency Evacuation Plan for People w/ Disabilities) ...... N/A
745 Ill. Comp. Stat. §§ 70/5, 70/7, and 70/12 (Health Care Right of Conscience Act) .... N/A
775 Ill. Comp. Stat. §§ 5/1-101 et seq. (Human Rights Act) 15
775 Ill. Comp. Stat. § 30/3 (Rights of Disabled) .... N/A
820 Ill. Comp. Stat. § 55/5 (Use of Lawful Products) .... N/A
820 Ill. Comp. Stat. §§ 112/1 et seq. (Equal Pay) 4
820 Ill Comp. Stat. §§ 110/1 – 110/3 (Equal Wage) 6
820 Ill. Comp. Stat. § 260/10 (Nursing Mothers in the Workplace) 5

Drug and Alcohol Testing

30 Ill. Comp. Stat. §§ 580/1 – 580/11 (Drug-Free Workplace Act) 25
775 Ill. Comp. Stat. §§ 5/1-101 – 5/10-104 (Human Rights Act) 15
820 Ill. Comp. Stat. §§ 265/1 – 265/99 (Substance Abuse Prevention on Public Works Projects Act) .. N/A

Employee Leave

5 Ill. Comp. Stat. §§ 325/0.01 – 325/1.1 (Military Leave for State Employees) .... N/A
5 Ill. Comp. Stat. §§ 327/1 – 327/99 (Organ Donor Leave Act) .... N/A
5 Ill. Comp. Stat. §§ 335/1 – 335/3 (Disaster Services Leave for State Employees) .... N/A
10 Ill. Comp. Stat. § 5/17-15 (Voting Leave) .... N/A
20 Ill. Comp. Stat. §§ 1805/30.1 – 1805/30.30 and 1805/100 (National Guard Employment Rights Act) .... N/A
50 Ill. Comp. Stat. §§ 122/1 – 122/99 (Local Government Disaster Service Volunteer Act) .... N/A
105 Ill. Comp. Stat. § 5/24-6 (Full-Time Teachers) .... N/A
205 Ill. Comp. Stat. § 630/17 (Holiday Leave) .... N/A
215 Ill. Comp. Stat. § 5/368f (Military Service Member Insurance Reinstatement) .... N/A
330 Ill. Comp. Stat. §§ 60/1 – 60/7 (Service Member's Employment Tenure Act) .... N/A
705 Ill. Comp. Stat. §§ 305/4.1 and 310/10.1 (Jury Duty Leave) .... N/A
820 Ill. Comp. Stat. § 115/5 (Vacation Leave) .... N/A
820 Ill. Comp. Stat. §§ 147/1 – 147/49 (School Visitation Rights Act) 50
820 Ill. Comp. Stat. §§ 148/1 – 148/ (Civil Air Patrol Leave Act) 15-50
820 Ill. Comp. Stat. §§ 149/1 – 149/10 (Blood Donation Leave) 51
820 Ill. Comp. Stat. §§ 151/1 – 151/99 (Family Military Leave Act) .... Varies
820 Ill. Comp. Stat. §§ 180/1 – 180/999 (Victims' Economic Security and Safety Act) 15

820 Ill. Comp. Stat. §§ 260/1 – 260/99 (Nursing Mothers in the Workplace Act) 5
Ill. Admin. Code tit. 80, pt. 420.645 (Adoption and Child Care Leave) .... N/A

Employee Screening
225 Ill. Comp. Stat. §§ 430/0.01 – 430/32 (Polygraph Testing) .... N/A
410 Ill. Comp. Stat. §§ 513/1 – 513/45 (Genetic Testing) .... N/A

Immigration
820 Ill. Comp. Stat. §§ 55/12 and 55/15 (Employment Verification) .... N/A

Independent Contractors
820 Ill. Comp. Stat. §§ 185/1 – 185/999 (Employee Classification Act) .... N/A

Labor Relations
820 Ill. Comp. Stat. §§ 5/1 – 5/1.5 (Labor Disputes Act) .... N/A

New-Hire Reporting
820 Ill. Comp. Stat. § 405/1801.1 .... N/A

Plant Closing and Workforce Reduction
30 Ill. Comp. Stat. §§ 608/5-1 – 608/99-995 (State Facilities Closure Act) .... N/A
30 Ill. Comp. Stat. §§ 760/1 – 760/15 (Business Economic Support Act) 75
220 Ill. Comp. Stat. § 5/7-213 (Public Utilities Act) .... N/A
775 Ill. Comp. Stat. §§ 5/1-101 et seq. (Human Rights Act) .... N/A
820 Ill. Comp. Stat. §§ 65/1 – 65/99 (Worker Adjustment and Retraining Notification Act) 75

Privacy in the Workplace
820 Ill. Comp. Stat. §§ 55/1 – 55/20 (Right to Privacy in the Workplace Act) .... N/A

Safety and Health
430 Ill. Comp. Stat. §§ 130/10 – 130/25 (Emergency Evacuation Plan for People with Disabilities) .... N/A
820 Ill. Comp. Stat. §§ 225/.01 – 225/23 (Safety Inspection and Education) .... N/A
820 Ill. Comp. Stat. §§ 255/1 – 255/20 (Toxic Substances Disclosure to Employees Act) 5

Smoking in the Workplace
225 Ill. Comp. Stat. § 10/5.5 (Smoking in Child Care Facilities) .... N/A
410 Ill. Comp. Stat. §§ 82/1 – 82/75 (Smoke Free Illinois Act) 1

Termination
745 Ill. Comp. Stat. §§ 46/1 – 46/99 (Job Reference Liability) .... N/A

Wages and Hours
820 Ill. Comp. Stat. §§ 105/1 – 105/15 (Minimum Wage) .... N/A
820 Ill. Comp. Stat. §§ 115/1 – 115/16 (Wage Payment and Collection) .... N/A
820 Ill. Comp. Stat. §§ 130/1 – 130/12 (Prevailing Wage Act) .... N/A
820 Ill. Comp. Stat. §§ 140/1 – 140/9 (One Day Rest in Seven) .... N/A
820 Ill. Comp. Stat. §§ 260/1 – 260/99 (Illinois Nursing Mothers in the Workplace Act) .... N/A

Whistleblower Protection
5 Ill. Comp. Stat. §§ 430/1-1 – 430/99-99 (State Officials and Employees Ethics Act) .... N/A
175 Ill. Comp. Stat. §§ 175/1 – 175/8 (Whistleblower Reward and Protection Act) .... N/A
210 Ill. Comp. Stat. §§ 86/1 – 86/99 (Hospital Report Card Act) .... N/A
325 Ill. Comp. Stat. § 5/4.5 (Electronic and Information Technology) .... N/A
740 Ill. Comp. Stat. § 24/1 – 24/5 (Civil Rights Act) .... N/A

Workplace Violence

Note: N/A means application of the law is not dependent on the number of employees.

Chapter 3

Job Descriptions

Introduction

Job descriptions play an important role in minimizing employee-related liability. Along with employment policies and employment contracts, job descriptions define the employment relationship. Job descriptions often become critical evidence in employment disputes. In particular, job descriptions play an important role in disability discrimination cases and the determination of which employees are exempt from the requirements of wage and hour laws. Thus, employers need to take great care when preparing and updating job descriptions.

Roles of Job Descriptions

Disability Discrimination Cases

The disability discrimination laws prohibit discrimination against a qualified individual on the basis of disability. ***Qualified individuals with disabilities*** are those who can perform the essential functions of a job — with or without reasonable accommodation. The federal Americans with Disabilities Act (ADA) and state-created disability protection laws provide that it is illegal for an employer to discriminate against a qualified individual on the basis of disability in any of the following areas:

◆ Job application procedures.

◆ The hiring, advancement, or discharge of employees.

◆ Employee compensation.

◆ Job training.

◆ Other terms, conditions, and privileges of employment.

Disability discrimination cases examine the essential functions of the job to determine whether the complaining employee or former employee is protected as a qualified individual with a disability — under federal and state law — from the employer's allegedly discriminatory actions. Written job descriptions are not required by the ADA or any other federal law. However, the ADA expressly recognizes that a written job description will be considered evidence of the essential functions of the job in ADA cases. Although determining the essential functions of a job involves many factors, the construction of a specific, detailed job description is the first step in any such definition. The ADA expressly recognizes that a written job description will be considered evidence of the essential functions of the job in ADA lawsuits. Employers have been successful in ADA cases where courts have held that an employee could not perform the essential functions of the job shown in the job description.

Conversely, employers have been unsuccessful in ADA cases because the job description failed to include the essential job duties of which, according to the employer, the employee could not perform. It is difficult for an employer to argue that a job duty is an essential function when that duty, which the employer claimed to be an essential one and the employee could not perform, is not included in the employer-prepared job description. These cases underscore the importance of carefully preparing job descriptions. Additionally, job descriptions must clearly state that the employee might be asked to perform duties not listed in the job description, but which are also considered to be essential to the employment position.

Exemption from Wage and Hour Laws

An employee's job description also plays a role in determining whether an employee is exempt from the overtime compensation and minimum wage requirements of wage and hour laws. For example, an employee who is paid a salary like an exempt employee is not necessarily exempt unless the employee has exempt duties involving the level of responsibility required by the U.S. Department of Labor regulations.

Similar to disability discrimination cases, a court or administrative agency will likely find that the employee's job description provides significant evidence of the employee's job duties. In Department of Labor investigations and court cases involving exemption issues, employees may attempt to minimize the importance of their duties so as to qualify for the nonexempt status and be eligible for overtime compensation. Current and accurate job descriptions provide the employer with evidentiary protection against an employee's claim in the form of an irrefutable written record that clearly establishes an employee's duties and exempt status.

Performance Expectations

Almost any employment dispute where the employer has found the employee's job performance to be inadequate will require a determination, similar to such determination in discrimination and exempt status claims, of the employee's actual job duties. Employers are more likely to be successful in defending a claim where the employee had clear notice of the job expectations and failed to meet them. Job descriptions are the catalyst in providing employees with both the essential functions of a job and clear notice of employer expectations. Employers who are unable to prove that an employee was provided notice of the employer's expectations are at a disadvantage in attempting to resolve a dispute.

Preparation of Job Descriptions

The preparation of job descriptions requires a thorough analysis of all of, but not limited to, the following:

- ◆ Essential tasks of the position and elements required for the position.
- ◆ Individual and professional qualifications needed from an employee to fulfill the essential tasks, for example:
  - • Experience.
  - • Education.
  - • Physical ability.
  - • Language proficiency.
- ◆ Employer expectations in regard to the employment position, employee output, employee conduct, and any other applicable issues.

In creating an accurate and clear job description, an employer may opt to use any of the following methods:

- **Obtain Employee Input.** A current employee's first hand knowledge of a job is a valuable tool in understanding the intricacies of a position. With the addition of an employee's input, a job description may provide insight as to elements of the job that only a person actually performing the tasks would know.

  Although employees should not be permitted to create their own job descriptions, obtaining an employee's input in regard to the position provides employers with protections against any future employee-based claim that the job description does not accurately reflect the duties.

- **Maintain Current Job Descriptions.** Job descriptions must accurately and clearly reflect the expectations, qualifications, and other applicable information in relationship to the employment position to be effective.

  A job description loses value and the employer loses the job description protections against employee claims where the information becomes outdated or fails to provide information about an essential task. Employers must regularly review employment positions and ensure that the applicable job description accurately reflects the requirements of the position.

- **Provide Employees with Regular Updates.** In an effort to keep employees aware of any job description changes or updates, employers should periodically distribute job descriptions to employees. For example, employees who do not review their job descriptions for a long time may allege that that the job has changed; thus, periodically distributing information avoids that problem.

  Employees should be required to identify any changes in their job duties since the descriptions were last reviewed. Additionally, employers may ask that employees conduct a review of the position as part of the performance-evaluation process.

- **Include Essential Information.** Employers need to maintain a balance between too much and too little information in job descriptions yet should include as many job duties and expectations as possible. Employers should be particularly careful to include any physical requirements for the job, such as lifting, standing, walking, working frequent overtime, working weekends, rotating shifts, and exposure to particular conditions such as weather and chemicals.

  The job description should also include unexpected job duties and should state that the employee may be asked to perform other duties as required by business needs.

  Employers should be careful not to include job duties that the employee will not perform. The more duties in a job description that the employee does not perform, the less likely the employer can persuade a judge or jury that the job description is a reasonable measure of the employee's job responsibilities.

  Overall, job descriptions should reflect the reality of the employee's job as accurately as possible. Business needs may also change on a daily basis, so job descriptions should specifically provide for this flexibility in a properly drafted description.

- **Include Special Attendance Requirements.** Employers covered by the federal Family and Medical Leave Act (FMLA) must provide employees with 12 weeks of leave for serious health conditions per 12-month period. However, organizations may incur an unreasonable burden and be unable to function if certain positions are vacant for 12 weeks per year. If a particular job has unusual attendance requirements, the job description should include those requirements. However, an employee still might be entitled to be absent from work under the FMLA, notwithstanding such requirements.

♦ **Include Unusual Job Stress.** Job-related stress can become an issue in disability discrimination litigation. Therefore, job stress should be addressed in the job description so that applicants and employees have advance notice of special circumstances they may be required to handle.

♦ **Use Descriptions in the Application Process.** Employers will benefit most from job descriptions when used during the application process as a foundation for the position and guideline for the type of individual who would best fit the position.

Applicants should be asked to review the job description for each job they are seeking and to certify, by signature, that they understand the job requirements and are able to perform that job. Such preventive measures may protect the employer from future assertions of an individual's inability to perform an essential job function. For example, if an employee later asserts a disability that limits ability to perform the job and the disability was known to the employee at the time of application, the employer may be able to assert that the employee falsified the application. Note, however, that termination of an employee for this reason should be carefully reviewed. Intentional falsification or the reason why the employee did not disclose a disability that would interfere with the essential job functions will not always be provable.

Some employees who have performed similar work for another employer may honestly believe they can perform the present job as well, only to discover there are some differences not readily discernible from the job description that render them a bad fit for the job. For example, the job may require operating a truck that is unlike the truck the employee used on a previous job. If the employee's disability precludes using the gearshift, the employee will not be able to do this particular job, but was not dishonest on the initial application.

♦ **Measures of Satisfactory Performance.** Performance evaluations should help both supervisors and employees measure how well the employee is performing their job. A carefully drafted job description that identifies the essential functions of the job and clearly describes the employer's qualitative and quantitative expectations for each function should serve as the cornerstone of the performance evaluation process.

Chapter 4

Recruiting and Hiring

Introduction

The hiring process is one of an employer's most important activities. It is also a process full of traps for the unwary. Effective hiring policies and procedures will help avoid potential liabilities and improve the quality of an employer's workforce, thus improving productivity.

Advertising for Employees

Good advertising can help employers hire and retain the best employees and can protect against negligent hiring claims from applicants, employees, and others. Bad advertising can lead to lawsuits from applicants who were not hired and could result in a poorly qualified and unmotivated workforce.

Except when based on a bona fide occupational qualification (BFOQ), it is unlawful to print or publish a notice or advertisement for employment that suggests any preference, limitation, specification, or discrimination based on legally protected characteristics such as race, color, creed, religion, national origin or citizenship, sex or sexual orientation, marital status, disability, status with regard to public assistance, age, or any other protected category listed under federal, state, or local law.

Employment Applications

The first step in the hiring process is the creation of an effective employment application. Applications and the application process make up a mutual introduction — the applicant gets a first impression of the organization and the organization gets to know something about the applicant. Applications allow employers and interviewers to compare applicants on some uniform basis, since all the applications are the same blank-form sort of document. Thus, all candidates should be required to complete applications even if they have submitted résumés.

Pre-Employment Inquiries

Except when based on a BFOQ, it is unlawful for an employer, prior to employment, to require or request information from an applicant or from any source pertaining to the applicant's race, color, religion, citizenship status, sex or sexual orientation, national origin, marital status, disability, status with regard to public assistance, age, or other protected status under any federal, state, or local law. This is true in employment applications as well as interviews.

Exception: The one exception to the prohibition on seeking this information is where an employer is required to maintain certain applicant information as part of an affirmative action plan.

Employers and employees involved in designing and reviewing applications, interviewing applicants, and hiring must be aware of the requirements of the law in this area. As a general rule, pre-employment inquiries that relate to job qualifications will be lawful, while inquiries that are not job related could be relied upon to suggest unlawful discrimination.

Employee Screening

EEOC Regulated Employment Tests and Selection Procedures

The U.S. Equal Employment Opportunity Commission (EEOC) governs Title VII of the Civil Rights Act (Title VII), the Americans with Disabilities Act (ADA), and the Age Discrimination in Employment Act (ADEA), which prohibit the use of discriminatory employment tests and selection procedures.

Employers often use tests and other selection procedures to screen applicants for hire and employees for promotion. There are many different types of tests and selection procedures, including cognitive tests, personality tests, medical examinations, credit checks, and criminal background checks.

The use of tests and other selection procedures can be a very effective means of determining which applicants or employees are most qualified for a particular job. However, the use of these tools can violate the federal antidiscrimination laws if an employer intentionally uses them to discriminate based on race, color, sex, national origin, religion, disability, or age (40 or older). Use of tests and other selection procedures can also violate the federal antidiscrimination laws if they disproportionately exclude people in a particular group by race, sex, or another covered basis, unless the employer can justify the test or procedure under the law.

In-depth information regarding employment tests and selection procedures may be found in the chapter entitled **Employee Screening and Lie-Detector Tests**.

Problem Areas and Possible Questions

The following list is a general outline of particularly difficult areas of pre-employment inquiry (please note that these are only general guidelines and employers should not interpret them as representing the law of any one state or municipality):

- **Age.**
  - Any inquiry about an applicant's age must be limited to establishing that the applicant meets minimum age requirements.
  - Employers **may not** ask the dates of attendance at elementary, junior high, high school, or college.
- **National Origin.**
  - Employers **may** ask if the applicant can furnish proof of employment authorization that the applicant is eligible to work in the United States. This proof must be in a form acceptable to the U.S. Citizenship and Immigration Services (USCIS).
  - Employers **may not** ask an applicant's national origin or that of any relatives.
  - Employers **may not** ask an applicant's place of birth or that of any relatives.
  - Employers **may not** ask about any foreign addresses, which might indicate national origin.
  - Employers **may not** ask about languages spoken by an applicant unless it is job related.

♦ **Race/Color.**

- Employers **may not** inquire into race or color.

- Employers **may not** ask any questions that might reveal race or color.

- Employers **may not** ask questions particular to applicants of only one race or color.

♦ **Sex.**

- Employers **may not** ask questions that might reveal an applicant's sex.

- Employers **may not** ask questions applicable to only one sex, for example, asking if the applicant plans on having children.

- Employers **may not** ask about child care arrangements.

♦ **Religion.**

- Employers **may not** ask about an applicant's religious denomination or religious customs.

- Employers may not tell an applicant the employer's religion or religious preference.

♦ **Disability.**

- Employers **may ask** questions needed to determine an applicant's ability to perform specific essential job tasks.

  Questions in this area should be phrased positively, demonstrated as follows:

  RIGHT: Is the applicant able to lift a box weighing over 20 pounds with or without reasonable accommodation?

  WRONG: Is there any reason why the applicant would not be able to lift a box weighing over 20 pounds?

- Employers **may not** ask about disabilities.

- Employers **may not** ask any questions that may reveal disabilities.

- Employers **may not** ask about workers' compensation history or claims.

- Employers **may not** ask about past or current medical conditions.

♦ **Arrests/Convictions.**

- Employers **may** ask whether an applicant has been convicted of or pled guilty to a felony. (Employers must make it clear that a "Yes" answer will not automatically disqualify the applicant from employment).

- Employers **may** ask about convictions of special crimes related to qualifications for the job.

- Employers **may not** ask about any prior arrests.

♦ **Education.**

- Employers **may** ask about an applicant's education to the extent that such inquiry is job related.

- Employers **may** ask about an applicant's foreign language skills if the question is job related.

- Employers **may not** ask when an applicant graduated.

- Employers **may not** ask how an applicant acquired foreign language skills.

◆ **Military Service.**

- Federal law states that employers **may** ask about service in the U.S. Armed Forces, when such service is a qualification for the job.

- Employers **may not** ask about foreign military service.

- Employers **may not** ask about the type of discharge an applicant received.

- Employers **may not** request military service records.

◆ **Organizations.**

- Employers **may** ask about job-related membership in professional clubs or organizations and positions held.

- Employers **may not** ask about membership in any organizations that would reveal the person's protected status.

- Employers **may not** ask an applicant to name every organization to which the person belongs.

◆ **Work Schedule.**

- Employers **may** ask whether an applicant is willing to work the required work schedule.

- Employers **may** ask whether the applicant is willing to work overtime.

- Employers **may not** ask if there is any reason why the applicant would not be able to work the required work schedule.

- Employers **may not** ask whether there are any religious holidays on which an applicant would be unable to work.

◆ **References.**

- Employers **may** ask for general personal and work references that do not reveal the applicant's protected status.

- Federal defense contractors **may** make such inquiries as might be required by federal law or regulation for security purposes.

- Employers **may not** request references specifically from clergy.

◆ **Photographs.**

- Employers **may** require photographs after hiring for identification purposes.

- Employers **may not** require pre-employment photographs.

Nondiscriminatory Practices

Several exemptions in discrimination law specify the following:

◆ The protected classifications do not apply when an individual is employed by a parent, grandparent, spouse, child, or grandchild or in the domestic service of any person.

◆ It is lawful for religious organizations to consider religion where religion is a bona fide occupational requirement.

♦ It is lawful for an employer to observe a bona fide seniority or merit system if it is not used as an excuse to discriminate unlawfully or there has not been a past pattern of discrimination.

♦ In accordance with the EEOC's equal-cost, equal-benefit regulations, it may be unlawful to reduce benefit levels for older workers, to the extent necessary to achieve approximate equivalency in cost for older and younger workers.

♦ It is lawful for a public entity to establish a maximum age for beginning employment as a peace officer or firefighter.

♦ It is lawful for an employer to require an applicant to undergo a physical examination to test the applicant's ability to perform essential job-related tasks, but only after the applicant has received a conditional offer of employment and only if all individuals who are conditionally offered the position are required to undergo the examination.

♦ It is lawful for an employer to administer pre-employment tests that measure essential job-related abilities if such tests provide an accurate measurement of these abilities and are required of all applicants for the same position.

Introductory Language

Certain information and disclaimers should be included either in the introduction to the job application or in an acknowledgement section the applicant must sign.

These items can include the following:

♦ A statement that the employer is an equal employment opportunity employer.

♦ A statement of nondiscrimination.

♦ A reminder that if the applicant is hired, it will be on an *employment-at-will* basis. This means that the employee may terminate employment at any time for any reason with or without notice and that the employer may terminate the employee's employment at any time for any reason.

♦ A statement that the application is not a contract or guarantee of employment.

♦ An indication that by completing the application, the applicant represents that all information presented in the application is complete and accurate.

♦ A statement that if information in the application is found to be false or to have been intentionally omitted, adverse employment action, including termination, may occur.

Information Requested

Employers should seek information describing the applicant's qualifications for the job for which the individual is applying.

This section lists suggested informational items. These are not all inclusive and may vary depending on the type of job the employer is trying to fill.

General

Basic information to be requested on all employment applications includes the following:

♦ Name, address, and telephone number.

♦ Confirmation that applicant, at time of hire, will be lawfully eligible to work in the United States.

♦ Identification of position sought.

♦ Identification of hours/shift sought if appropriate.

♦ Pay expectations.

Professional

Employers should ask for at least the following professional information from applicants:

- ◆ Work experience, including the following:
  - Current and previous employer's name, address, and telephone number.
  - Dates of employment.
  - Starting and ending wage/pay rate.
  - Supervisor's name and title.
  - Job title and duties.
  - Reason for leaving.
- ◆ Educational background, such as the following:
  - School name.
  - Last grade completed (not specific dates of graduation).
  - Fact of graduation, but only if job related.
  - Major or course of study, as it relates to position sought.
  - Training and special skills.
- ◆ Other knowledge, skills, or abilities as required by the position, including the following:
  - Equipment certification or experience.
  - Licenses.
  - Typing, computer, or other office skills.
  - Professional affiliations and memberships.
  - Languages.
  - Other training and special skills (including military training).
- ◆ References.

Note: Employers should not require applicants to provide references from religious figures.

Interviews

Conducting interviews is a good way to improve recruitment and avoid potential liability. Interviews are, however, basically subjective predictors of how candidates will perform a job. Although an interviewer can assess the objective data provided by a candidate during an interview, often the interviewer will also rely on subjective indicators such as body language, tone of voice, and mannerisms, and may fall into the trap of relying upon "gut feeling."

An interview is the appropriate time to review the job descriptions with the candidate to ensure that the candidate is aware of the job requirements, and indicates that the person is qualified to perform the job. If it is disclosed during the interview that the candidate may be unable to perform the job because of a known disability or religious beliefs, the interviewer should ask about any accommodation the candidate believes would permit the individual to meet the essential requirements of the job in order to perform the work. The interviewer should make no decisions or assessment regarding the feasibility or reasonableness of a requested accommodation during the interview.

Patterned Interview Form

An effective way to minimize potential liability based on interviews is to develop an objective, patterned interview form for each position. This forces the interviewer to remain focused on the essential job functions and to deal with each candidate in the same way. The form should be used as follows:

♦ Identify the job functions or goals based on information contained in the job description.

Example: Word Processing Supervisor — Supervise and coordinate word-processing staff to ensure timely processing of work orders.

♦ List the essential knowledge, skills, and abilities that will enable a successful candidate to effectively perform each job function.

Example: Interpersonal skills, supervisory experience or training, ability to delegate tasks, and ability to work with required equipment.

♦ Develop interview questions that address knowledge, skill, or ability in a nondiscriminatory way. Focus on previous experiences or incidents that will serve as indicators of future on-the-job behavior. Be prepared to follow up each question with additional questions that look further into a candidate's answer.

Example: In your previous job, what types of problems did your subordinates bring to you for resolution? How often? What decisions did you make regarding these problems? What types of decisions did you refer to your manager for resolution?

Things to Avoid

Avoid excessive "chit chat" before and during the interview. This will help avoid topics that could cross over into unlawful areas (for example, age or marital status).

Avoid interviewing from the application form. Take a moment to review the candidate's application before the interview and to frame questions based on the patterned interview.

General Interview Questions

The following bulleted lists offer suggested general interview questions that an employer may choose to utilize during an initial or follow-up interview. Importantly, interviewers must always remain in compliance with all federal and applicable state laws regulating the interview process.

Targeting Integrity, Honesty, and Trustworthiness

♦ Discuss a time when your integrity was challenged. How did you handle the situation?

♦ What would you do if someone asked you to do something unethical?

♦ Have you ever experienced a loss for doing what is right?

♦ In what business situations do you feel honesty would be inappropriate?

♦ If you saw a co-worker doing something dishonest, would you tell your manager? What would you do about the situation?

Targeting Personality, Temperament, and the Ability to Work with Others

- If you took out a full-page ad in a major publication and had to describe yourself in only three words, what would those words be?

- How would you describe your personality?

- What motivates you the most?

- If I call your references, what will they say about you?

- Do you consider yourself a risk taker? Describe a situation in which you had to take a risk.

- What kind of environment would you like to work in?

- What type of people would you rather not work with?

- What type of responsibilities would you like to avoid in your next job?

- Give me two or three examples of tasks that you do not particularly enjoy doing. Indicate how you remain motivated to complete those tasks.

- What types of people annoy you?

- Tell me about a work situation that irritated you.

- Have you ever had to resolve a conflict with a co-worker or client? How did you resolve the conflict?

- Describe the appropriate relationship between a supervisor and subordinates.

- What sort of relationships do you have with your business associates, both at the same level and above and/or below you?

- How have you worked as a member of a team in the past?

- What is your management style? How do you think your subordinates perceive you?

- As a manager, have you ever had to fire anyone? If so, what were the circumstances, and how did you handle the situation?

- Have you ever been in a situation where a project was returned for errors? What effect did this have on you?

- What previous job was the most satisfying and why?

- What job was the most frustrating and why?

- Tell me about the best boss you ever had. Now tell me about the worst boss. What made it tough to work for that person?

Targeting Past Mistakes

- Tell me about an objective in your last job that you failed to meet and why.

- When is the last time you were criticized? How did you deal with the criticism?

- What have you learned from your mistakes?

- Tell me about a situation where you "blew it." How did you resolve or correct your mistake so as to save face?

♦ Tell me about a situation where you abruptly had to change what you were doing.

♦ If you could change one (managerial) decision you made during the past two years, what would that be?

♦ Tell me of a time when you had to work on a project that did not work out the way it should have. What did you do?

♦ If you had the opportunity to change anything in your career, what would you have done differently?

Targeting Creativity, Creative Thinking, and Problem Solving

♦ When was the last time you "thought outside the box," and how?

♦ What have you done that was innovative?

♦ What was the wildest idea you had in the past year? What did you do about your idea?

♦ Give me an example of when someone brought you a new idea, particularly one that was odd or unusual. What did you do?

♦ If you could do anything in the world, what would you do?

♦ Describe a situation in which you had a difficult (management) problem. How did you solve the problem?

♦ What is the most difficult decision you have made on the job? How did you arrive at your decision?

♦ Describe some situations in which you worked under pressure or met deadlines.

♦ Were you ever in a situation where you needed to meet two different deadlines given to you by two different people and you could not meet both deadlines? What did you do?

♦ What type of approach to solving work problems seems to work best for you? Give me an example of when you solved a tough problem.

♦ When taking on a new task, do you like to have a great deal of feedback and responsibility at the outset or do you like to try your own approach?

♦ You are on the phone with another department resolving a problem. The intercom pages you for a customer on hold. Your manager returns your monthly report with red pen markings and demands corrections within the hour. What do you do?

♦ Describe a sales presentation when you had the right product/service, and the customer wanted the product/service but would not buy the product/service. What did you do next?

Miscellaneous Questions

♦ How do you measure your own success?

♦ What is the most interesting thing you have done in the past three years?

♦ What are your short-term or long-term career goals?

♦ Why should we hire you?

♦ What responsibilities do you want, and what kinds of results do you expect to achieve in your next job?

- What do you think it takes to be successful in a company like ours?

- How did the best manager you ever had motivate you to perform well? Why did that method work?

- What is the best thing a previous employer did that you wish everyone did?

- What are you most proud of?

- What is important to you in a job?

- What do you expect to find in our company that you do not have now?

- Is there anything you wanted me to know about you that we have not discussed?

- Do you have any questions for me?

Offer Letters

Employers may provide written offers of employment verifying the terms agreed to by the employer and the prospective employee. These letters may be construed as a contract. Therefore, give the necessary details but be cautious; do not make long-term promises or implications regarding job security. To avoid implying that employment is for a yearlong period, quote salary as an hourly, weekly, or monthly equivalent rather than an annual figure.

Form I-9

Employers in the United States may not knowingly recruit, hire, or continue to employ an alien not authorized to work in the United States. The U.S. Immigration Reform and Control Act of 1986 (IRCA) requires all employers to verify the immigration status of employees hired after November 6, 1986, and ensure that each employee is a U.S. citizen or an alien legally authorized to work in the United States.

To accomplish this, all employees must present documentation to their employer that establishes their identity and their authorization to work in the United States. Employers must review the documents, check their validity, and jointly complete Form I-9, *Employer Eligibility Verification Form*, with their employees within three days of hire. Employers are only required to ensure that the documents submitted by the employees reasonably appear to be genuine. Acceptable documents are listed on Form I-9. Employers who violate the IRCA are subject to civil and criminal penalties including imprisonment for up to six months.

Notification of New Hires

In an effort to improve collection of unpaid child support, state and federal regulations have been enacted that require employers to report new hires. Effective since July 1, 1996, employers must report to state agencies the hiring or rehiring of employees who live or work in the state.

The report must be provided within 20 days of the hiring date and must include the following:

- The employer's name, address, and federal Employer Identification Number (EIN).

- ♦ The employee's name, address, and Social Security number.

- ♦ The date of hire.

- ♦ The state of hire.

An employer may report the information by magnetic tape, cartridge tape, diskette, Web site, email, bulletin board (BBS), FTP, and EFT. However, all states do not use all methods. The information may be included and delivered on an employee's Form W-4 or W-9, a printed list produced by the employer's computer system, or on a new-hire reporting form available from the state reporting agency. If the employer submits the employee's Form W-4 or W-9, the employee's date of birth can be added to the form. Employers who do not comply may receive a written notice of noncompliance. Federal law sets a limit of $25 per newly hired employee. If there is a conspiracy between the employer and the employee not to report, the penalty may not exceed $500. States may also impose nonmonetary civil penalties under state law for noncompliance.

Avoiding Negligent Hiring Claims

In recent years, there have been many claims related to the hiring and retention of employees. To guard against such claims, employers should review their standard applications, their interview procedures, and their pre-employment screening practices. Courts will examine employers' actions and knowledge from the point at which the initial hiring decision was made. Thus, whether an employer failed to exercise reasonable care in hiring will be determined by examining the employer's actions at the time of the hiring decision.

For more information, please see the **Negligent Retention and Supervision** chapter.

Contracts

In the past, the law assumed that when an employer hired an employee, the employee was being hired for a full year, unless the employer and the employee reached a different agreement. Today, however, this assumption has changed and employment is ordinarily based on contractual relationships that are usually found to arise out of collective-bargaining agreements, express written or oral contracts, or sometimes implied contracts. Such contracts can restrict the employer's ability to discipline or discharge employees.

An employment relationship based on no contract at all or for a nonspecific period is known as employment-at-will. Either the employer or the employee may terminate such employment at any time for any reason. In other words, the job will last just as long as both parties want it to last and will end when either party wants it to end. The contractual types of employment previously listed are exceptions to employment-at-will relationships. Additionally, many restrictions to employment-at-will exist and are further discussed in the **Termination** chapter.

Collective-Bargaining Agreements

Where a union has been recognized as the exclusive collective-bargaining agent for employees, the respective rights and obligations of the employer and its employees are defined by the terms of the written contract between the employer and the union. Such contracts, called *collective-bargaining agreements*, normally supersede individual contract rights or common law rights of employees covered by the agreement. They do not, however, supersede other rights provided by federal, state, or local laws, such as nondiscrimination laws or whistleblower laws.

Express Contracts

The terms and conditions of employment for employees not covered by collective-bargaining agreements may be governed by written or oral individual employment contracts. Written contracts are most common with executive-level employees. Typically, individual contracts define current and deferred compensation arrangements, benefits, the period of employment, and the rights of the parties with respect to termination and resignation.

Express Written Contracts

Express written contracts can be, by definition, an exception to the employment-at-will understanding. In express written contracts, both the employer and the employee can indicate at the beginning of the employment that the employment will not be at-will.

Like any contract, express written contracts require the following:

♦ An offer by one party.

♦ Acceptance of the offer by the other party.

♦ Sufficient consideration (for example, salary, benefits, or performance of work) to support the contract.

The terms of the contract may include as little as one or two concepts or a comprehensive and detailed description of the employment relationship.

The parties in such contracts generally intend to create an exception to employment-at-will because they perceive, at least at the time they enter into the contract, some advantage to abandoning the benefits of employment-at-will. An employer, for instance, may give up the right to fire the employee at any time for almost any reason because the employer feels it is more important to keep the employee for a fixed period (and, perhaps, to prevent the employee from going to work for a competitor after the term of employment) than it is to reserve the right to terminate at-will. Similarly, an employee in such a situation may decide that the extra salary in exchange for a promise to not resign is worth giving up the right to leave at any time.

Express Oral Contracts

Express oral contracts might create an exception to employment-at-will in certain jurisdictions in the event employees allege that they were promised a specific term of employment sometime during the hiring process. The lack of documentation of the parties' bargain makes it difficult to tell whether the parties have intended to form a contract and thereby create an exception to employment-at-will. As with express written contracts, the party alleging the existence of the contract must prove that there was intent to enter into a contract by demonstrating the existence of an offer, the acceptance of that offer, and some consideration sufficient to support the agreement.

For the employer, the most troublesome oral contracts arise out of employer statements made during the hiring process that the prospective employee perceives as promises about the terms of employment. In such a case, the prospective employee does not verbally accept these perceived promises but merely accepts employment with the employer. The employee then claims at termination that the contract for employment contained certain terms and conditions, which the employee accepted by coming to work for the employer. A court evaluating a claim of oral contract in such a situation might look at facts such as how definite was the promise and whether additional considerations, above and beyond an agreement, to forego other employment were supplied by the employee to support the alleged contract.

Whether an express oral contract has been formed in any given case is highly dependent upon the specific facts of the case. Employers should put procedures in place during the hiring process to minimize the chances that statements will be mistaken for offers regarding the particular conditions of employment. These procedures could include the use of a form signed by the employee acknowledging that the employment is at-will. Such a document would help to demonstrate that the parties did not intend to create an exception to employment-at-will. Similarly, the form can clearly disclaim any reliance on oral promises made during the application process.

Implied Contracts

Some courts have recognized certain implied contract rights governing the employment relationship, even when employers make no specific promises. In certain jurisdictions, courts sometimes restrict an employer's right to discharge an employee if, after examining the facts and circumstances of the employment arrangement, the court concludes that the parties intended a continuing employment relationship, terminable only for *just cause* (for a good reason). Examples might include an implied right to certain disciplinary or evaluation procedures before termination, or a specified list of grounds for termination of employment.

In determining whether an implied contract existed and an employer had created a reasonable expectation that an employee would not be discharged, courts may consider facts and circumstances such as the following:

- The nature and type of the employment.
- The custom or practice in the industry (for example, treating employees fairly and discharging them only for just cause).
- The employer's regular practice of only discharging employees for just cause.
- The course of dealing between the parties.
- The employer's personnel handbook or employee manual, especially statements about an initial probationary period.
- Statements appearing on the job application form.
- Oral representations made by the employer.
- Disciplinary policies that state employees will only be discharged for specific offenses.
- Progressive disciplinary policies that give employees chances to improve their performance, when such chances were not given an employee.
- Statements that special consideration will be given to employees due to longevity or seniority.
- An employee's work history that reflects regular merit raises, good performance evaluations, praise, and promotions.

Employee Handbooks

Employee handbooks may create binding contracts in some circumstances, such as the following:

- The provisions of the handbook identified as the terms of the contract are definite.
- The terms are communicated to the employee.
- The employee accepts the offer.
- The employee furnishes adequate consideration by continuing to work while retaining freedom to quit.

As with interpretation of an express oral contract, the employee does not have to verbally reply to the terms of an offer made through an employee handbook. The employee may accept the offer simply by beginning and/or continuing employment. Therefore, whether an employee handbook creates an implied contract depends primarily on the definiteness of the terms of the handbook.

Unlike an express oral contract, there is not likely to be great dispute about the alleged terms of the contract implied by the employee handbook because those terms have been written down. Although this difference alone will not protect an employer from a court finding that the handbook has created a contract, it will probably turn the issue from a factual one to a legal one, thereby allowing the court to resolve the matter at a preliminary stage of litigation.

As with oral contracts, the easiest way to prevent forming a contract with the employee handbook is to include language that the handbook is not intended to be a contract or to modify the employment-at-will relationship. Unlike the oral contract, the written handbook makes it easy for an employer to include such a disclaimer. For employers whose handbooks have no such disclaimers and have been distributed to employees, any risk that the handbook will create an implied contract can be reduced by distributing an amendment to the handbook including the appropriate disclaimer.

Note that in situations where a handbook sets forth a policy on vacation days, a contractual obligation in effect is established, which cannot be disclaimed by an employer.

Promissory Estoppel

Although it cannot be used when a contract exists — again reinforcing the wisdom of a written offer of employment confirming that the employment is at-will — the courts can use the theory of promissory estoppel to determine that a contract has been made even when the parties do not intend to form such an agreement.

Promissory estoppel exists when:

- ◆ A promise has been made.
- ◆ The person making the promise reasonably expected to induce an action in reliance on the promise.
- ◆ Action is actually taken in reliance on the promise.
- ◆ Failure to fulfill the promise would create an injustice and/or economic harm.

The theory of promissory estoppel is used most often in cases where an employer extends an offer of employment to a prospective employee, and based on the offer, the prospective employee quits a current job or rejects another job offer. When the employer subsequently withdraws the offer or terminates the employee shortly after the employment begins, the employee can rely on this theory to establish a claim. For example, a court may hold that a hired-then-fired employee is entitled to damages reflecting a reasonable period of employment.

No Contracts

Employees that are subject to neither a collective-bargaining agreement nor an individual employment contract generally have only those rights to employment as are conferred by statute or recognized by common law. There may also be specific state statutes generally governing the employment relationship or prohibiting the discharge of an employee without just cause.

The nature of common law employment rights has been the subject of much recent court interpretation and expansion. Historically, common law has put employees without written contracts into one of two categories:

- ◆ Those employed for a definite term.
- ◆ Those employed for an indefinite term.

Employment for a Definite Term

Employees may be hired for a definite term, such as month-to-month, year-to-year, or until some specified date. These employees may only be terminated for just cause until the expiration of the employment period. Employment for a definite term may commonly be handled by a written contract.

Either party may terminate the employment relationship at the end of the term. If the employment relationship is continued after the end of the term, unless otherwise specified, it is considered to be renewed for the same period as the original term. If there is a contract, and it requires notice before termination of employment, the contractual notice must be given or a breach of contract will exist. Courts will generally find the employer has the same notification requirements as the employee in terms of terminating and quitting.

Employment for an Indefinite Term

Employment for an indefinite term is the employment-at-will relationship discussed earlier in this chapter in which either the employer or the employee may terminate the employment relationship at any time for any or no reason. The employment-at-will relationship has all of the exceptions previously described and all of the restrictions that are noted in the **Employment of Minors** chapter.

Avoiding Employment Contract Claims

While it is impossible to avoid all employment contract claims, employers may minimize the number of such claims and improve their ability to defend against these claims by taking some preventive measures in their policies and procedures, such as the following:

- ♦ Include in applications for employment a statement indicating that the employment is at-will and defining employment-at-will.

- ♦ Include in offer letters a statement indicating that the employment is at-will and defining the term.

- ♦ Include a similar statement in the employee handbook. Likewise, the employer can state in the handbook that it should not be construed as a contract of employment for any duration. Further, employee handbooks should also contain a carefully written section on discharge, specifying that an employee can be discharged at any time and with or without cause or notice.

- ♦ Train personnel involved in hiring not to make statements that can be construed as altering the employment-at-will relationship.

- ♦ Train supervisors to avoid such statements after hiring.

- ♦ Include an employment-at-will reminder in all significant employment documents (for example, performance reviews, performance improvement plans, and warnings).

- ♦ Review all of the documents with an attorney to ensure that contractual disclaimers are in place and effective and that the documents do not contain other language that might create a "for cause" employment relationship.

- ♦ Replace all older employee documents with newer versions and retrieve the older documents from employees.

These precautions will not guarantee victory in every employment contract case, but if followed they may help an employer defend against contractual types of claims arising out of employment relationships.

Employment Agreements

Employers should consider using carefully written employment agreements to avoid employment contract and promissory estoppel claims and to gain valuable protections and benefits. In particular, employers commonly use employment agreements to implement noncompetition restrictions, protections for confidential information and trade secrets, conflict-of-interest restrictions, and mandatory arbitration clauses. Additionally, some employers use employment agreements to eliminate uncertainty by specifically defining terms and conditions of employment, job duties, and compensation and benefits.

To provide themselves with job security, applicants for professional or executive positions may sometimes require employment agreements setting forth specific lengths of employment or separating benefits as a condition of accepting an offer of employment.

To decide whether to use an employment agreement, consider the following factors:

- ♦ Employment agreements can establish certainty in the employment relationship by providing specifically agreed upon grounds and procedures for termination if the employment relationship deteriorates.

- ♦ Employment agreements can specifically define the employee's job duties, compensation, and benefits to clarify the employment relationship. Employment agreements let the employer specifically define terms and conditions of employment unique to a particular position.

- ♦ Confidentiality provisions and other restrictions defined in the employment agreement on the ability of former employees to compete with the employer can provide contractual protection to employers in highly competitive businesses that depend on customer goodwill and involve the use of confidential information.

- ♦ Employment agreements can provide mandatory arbitration or other alternative dispute-resolution methods to address potential discrimination, wrongful termination, and/or other employee claims. This helps employers manage litigation costs and expenses for employment related claims.

Although the benefits of employment agreements are considerable, employers who decide to use them must be willing to live with the terms they create. Employers must also decide if it is worthwhile to invest the time and money necessary to draft and implement effective employment agreements and to enforce them if employees fail to abide by the terms of the agreement.

Hiring Suggestions

Employment-at-Will

Where a particular position does not require a specified length of employment as a hiring condition, an employer may choose to hire an employee under an employment-at-will agreement in which either the employer or the employee may terminate the relationship at any time and for any reason, with or without prior notice.

Definite Term of Employment

When an employee or employer requires the use of an employment agreement to specify the length of employment, the employer cannot use the employment-at-will doctrine to justify termination.

Employment agreements defining an exact term of employment must be carefully written to express very specific, defined reasons and procedures for termination, along with any notification requirements. If the employment relationship breaks down, the employer must then follow the stated procedure for termination. It is, therefore, important to describe the grounds for termination in the most flexible way possible.

Mandatory Arbitration

Employers are increasingly implementing mandatory arbitration agreements with their employees as an effective and cost-saving alternative to litigation. Arbitration agreements can reduce the time needed to process and resolve a claim, minimize litigation costs, and eliminate the possibility of an unpredictable jury verdict. Arbitration agreements generally mandate that any potential claims by employees, including discrimination claims, be addressed by a panel of arbitrators rather than by a judge or jury.

Most employment discrimination claims and other employment-related statutory claims as well as wrongful termination claims are now subject to jury trials, prompting many employers to implement arbitration agreements in an effort to avoid litigation. Although there is currently some conflict in the courts about which claims can be arbitrated, employers are increasingly implementing such agreements as effective strategic tools.

Employers who decide to include a mandatory arbitration clause in their employment agreements should list the specific types of claims that are subject to arbitration, including wages, contract, discrimination, employee benefits, and any other claims for violation of federal, state, or local law or ordinance.

To avoid ambiguity, employers should also describe in the coverage clause the specific types of discrimination claims that are subject to arbitration. Employers should also specify applicable state law applying in arbitration and whether the arbitration would be binding. Employers should not try to alter the established rights of employees in these provisions, such as by limiting the damages available, since such restrictions can invalidate the arbitration agreement.

Other Terms and Conditions

Employers can also use employment agreements to define other important terms and conditions of employment, including the job duties or expectations of the employee, and compensation and benefits such as stock options, bonuses, travel and entertainment expenses, and participation in employee benefit plans. Employers may also use employment agreements to protect trade secrets and confidential information.

Frequently Asked Questions About Employment Eligibility

Q **Do citizens and nationals of the United States need to prove to their employers that they are eligible to work?**

A Yes. While citizens and nationals of the United States are automatically eligible for employment, they too must present proof of employment eligibility and identity and complete an *Employment Eligibility Verification* form (Form I-9). U.S. citizens include persons born in Puerto Rico, Guam, the U.S. Virgin Islands, and the Northern Mariana Islands. Nationals of the United States include persons born in American Samoa, including Swains Island.

Q **Do employers need to complete Form I-9 for everyone who applies for a job with an organization?**

A No. An employer needs to complete Form I-9 only for people who are actually hired. For purposes of the Form I-9 rules, a person is hired when the employee begins to work for wages or other compensation.

Q **An employer must complete Form I-9 for anyone hired to perform labor or services in return for wages or other remuneration. What is "remuneration"?**

A *Remuneration* is anything of value given in exchange for labor or services rendered by an employee, including food and lodging.

Q **Can an employer fire an employee who fails to produce the required document(s) within three business days?**

A Yes. An employer can terminate an employee who fails to produce the required document(s), or a receipt for a replacement document (in the case of lost, stolen, or destroyed documents), within three business days of the date employment begins. However, the employer must apply these practices uniformly to all employees. If an employee has presented a receipt for a replacement document, the individual must produce the actual document within 90 days of the date employment began.

Q **What happens if an employer properly completes Form I-9 and the DHS discovers that an employee is not actually authorized to work?**

A The employer cannot be charged with a verification violation; however, the employer cannot knowingly continue to employ this individual. The employer will have a good faith defense against the imposition of employer sanctions penalties for knowingly hiring an unauthorized alien unless the government can prove the employer had actual knowledge of the unauthorized status of the employee.

Q **What is an employer's responsibility concerning the authenticity of documents?**

A The employer must examine the documents and, if they reasonably appear on their face to be genuine and to relate to the person presenting them, must accept them. To do otherwise could be an unfair immigration-related employment practice. If a document does not reasonably appear on its face to be genuine and to relate to the person presenting it, the employer must not accept it. An employer may contact a local USCIS office for assistance.

Q **May an employer accept a photocopy of a document presented by an employee?**

A No. Employees must present original documents. The only exception is an employee may present a certified copy of a birth certificate.

Contact Information

Equal Employment Opportunity Commission

131 M Street, NE
Washington, DC 20507

Telephone: 202-663-4900
Toll-Free: 800-669-4000
Internet: *www.eeoc.gov*

Chapter 5

Background Checks

Introduction

Pre-employment investigations and background checks are important to verify the accuracy of information provided by an applicant for employment and to ensure that an applicant is the best-qualified individual for a position. A thorough pre-employment investigation is also a preventive measure that enables employers to determine if a candidate's background indicates a possible safety threat of injury to other employees.

General Guidelines

If conducted with inappropriate planning and training, a pre-employment investigation can be a potential source of liability. Pre-employment investigations should not be used as fishing expeditions into an applicant's background.

Therefore, when conducting pre-employment investigations, employers should consider the following general guidelines:

♦   Employers should use pre-employment investigation tools that are reasonable, appropriate, and relevant to the position for which the applicant is applying.

♦   Pre-employment investigations should be consistently implemented with all candidates, regardless of class or position.

♦   Pre-employment investigations should be conducted by persons with special training such as a reputable investigative service.

♦   All information must be evaluated in compliance with the Fair Credit Reporting Act (FCRA), the Americans with Disabilities Act (ADA), Title VII of the Civil Rights Act (Title VII), and any other applicable state and federal law. The FCRA is discussed later in this chapter. For information on Title VII and the ADA, please consult the chapter entitled **Discrimination in Employment**.

Additionally, the U.S. Equal Employment Opportunity Commission (EEOC) governs Title VII, the ADA, and the Age Discrimination in Employment Act (ADEA), which prohibit the use of discriminatory employment tests and selection procedures. Employers often use tests and other selection procedures to screen applicants for hire and employees for promotion. There are many different types of tests and selection procedures, including cognitive tests, personality tests, medical examinations, credit checks, and criminal background checks.

The use of tests and other selection procedures can be a very effective means of determining which applicants or employees are most qualified for a particular job. However, the use of these tools can violate the federal antidiscrimination laws if an employer intentionally uses them to discriminate based on race, color, sex, national origin, religion, disability, or age (40 or older).

Use of tests and other selection procedures can also violate the federal antidiscrimination laws if they disproportionately exclude people in a particular group by race, sex, or another covered basis, unless the employer can justify the test or procedure under the law. In-depth information regarding employment tests and selection procedures may be found in the chapter entitled **Employee Screening and Lie-Detector Tests**.

With these guidelines in mind, employers should consider which background checks are appropriate given the nature and scope of the position sought. Many employers request criminal background checks to be completed by an outside consumer-reporting agency to reduce their exposure to negligent hiring claims because employers must exercise reasonable care in hiring an applicant and pursue reasonable effort to properly investigate an applicant's background. Employers who fail to conduct proper background checks may be held liable for the employee's actions. Such agencies can conduct background investigations both internally and through contacting references provided by job applicants.

Note: Many states require employers to perform background checks within certain industries. For example, most states require background checks on education and banking personnel.

Employer Tools

Employers have several tools that they can use to find information about employees and potential employees.

Consumer Reports

Consumer reports are reports an employer obtains from a consumer-reporting agency. Employers typically use the information obtained from a consumer-reporting agency for verifying the following information:

- ◆ Criminal history.
- ◆ Driving records.
- ◆ Employment history.
- ◆ An individual's education.
- ◆ Social Security numbers.
- ◆ Professional licenses.

Credit Checks

Credit checks are permissible when there is a close relationship between credit information and job performance. For example, when hiring for a bank teller position, an employer may want to conduct a credit check on the applicant to determine the applicant's credit history because the position will directly deal with money and financial information. When conducting a credit check on a potential applicant, companies must be careful because neutral decisions, such as the rejection of an applicant solely on the basis of a poor credit rating, may have a disparate impact on minority groups.

Investigation of Criminal Records

An employer may investigate an applicant's criminal conviction record because the information might be job related and consistent with a business necessity. With exception, criminal record searches may retrace the past seven years. Before rejecting an applicant, the employer should consider the relationship between the conviction, the nature of the conviction, the number of convictions, rehabilitation efforts, and the applicant's fitness for the job.

Employment Verification

In performing an employment verification check, employers may verify information about an applicant from former employers. Employers may obtain references to confirm and supplement information in the résumé or application.

Additionally, employers may seek confirmation of background data (such as dates of employment, salary, position and duties, education, and professional licenses) and competency with respect to certain job-related skills (such as attendance, dependability, judgment, and initiative).

Obtaining a Release

Before conducting a reference check, it is prudent for employers to obtain a release from the applicant. A release signed by the applicant can be a useful tool to facilitate obtaining information from the applicant's former associates, schools, and employers. A release should generally acknowledge that the information obtained by the prospective employer may not all be positive, and that the persons making statements about the applicant are discharged from any legal liability. The release may be included in the disclaimer language on the application or as a separate document.

Obtaining References

A reference check should consist of contacting people with knowledge of the applicant's actual work performance rather than a person in the organization's general human resources department. If possible, an applicant's former supervisor should be contacted. Other individuals with knowledge of the applicant's work performance may include an applicant's associates, team members, or peers, as well as any subordinates. Depending on the nature of the job, former clients or customers may also be knowledgeable sources of information about the applicant.

Content of Conversation

When conducting an interview of a reference, employers should adhere to the following guidelines:

- Confirm the information provided on the application or résumé.

- Focus on work performance questions. These questions are crucial for obtaining the most useful information and include areas such as former job responsibilities, description of work performance, strengths and weaknesses of the applicant, reasons for leaving the job, and eligibility for rehire.

- Avoid questions that go beyond work performance and job-related issues. As with interviewing, questions regarding race, age, disability, or other protected characteristics should be avoided.

- Offer to mail or fax the reference form along with the release signed by the applicant if the reference giver is unwilling to discuss the former employee over the phone.

- Document nonresponses such as, "Our company does not give references," or if the company only provides a neutral reference, such as confirming dates of employment.

The Fair Credit Reporting Act

Employers who make the decision to use pre-employment investigations and background checks must have an understanding of the federal Fair Credit Reporting Act (15 U.S.C. §§ 1681 et seq.). The purpose of the FCRA is to promote the accuracy, fairness, and privacy of the information obtained by consumer reporting agencies. A *consumer-reporting agency* is an entity that regularly assembles or evaluates certain types of information for the purpose of providing consumer reports to third parties for a fee or on a cooperative nonprofit basis. The FCRA and applicable state law requirements apply when an employer seeks to obtain a consumer or investigative consumer report for employment purposes.

General Rights Under the FCRA

The FCRA grants many rights to those individuals whose information is used by consumer reporting agencies. These rights are outlined in the Federal Trade Commission's (FTC) *A Summary of Your Rights Under the Fair Credit Reporting Act* (*www.ftc.gov/os/2004/11/041119factaappf.pdf*). The following is an overview of the major rights individuals have under the FCRA:

♦ **Individuals must be told if information has been used against them.** Anyone who uses a credit report or other type of consumer report to deny a person's application for credit, insurance, or employment — or to take another adverse action against a person — must tell the person the name, address, and phone number of the agency that provided the information.

♦ **Individuals have the right to know what is in their file.** Any person may request and obtain all the information about the person kept in the files of a consumer-reporting agency. The person is required to provide proper identification, which may include the person's Social Security number. In many instances, disclosure will be free. Individuals are entitled to a free file disclosure if the following apply:

• A person has taken adverse action against an individual because of the information in a report.

• An individual is the victim of identity theft and the individual places a fraud alert in the file.

• An individual's file contains inaccurate information as a result of fraud.

• An individual is on public assistance.

• An individual is unemployed, but is expected to apply for employment within 60 days.

♦ **Individuals have the right to ask for their credit score.** Credit scores are numerical summaries of an individual's credit-worthiness based on information from credit bureaus. Individuals may request a credit score from consumer-reporting agencies that create scores or distribute scores used in residential real property loans, but will have to pay for it. In some mortgage transactions, individuals will receive credit score information for free from the mortgage lender.

♦ **Individuals have the right to dispute incomplete or inaccurate information.** If an individual identifies information in their file that is incomplete or inaccurate and reports it to the consumer-reporting agency, the agency must investigate unless the individual's dispute is frivolous.

♦ **Consumer-reporting agencies must correct or delete inaccurate, incomplete, or unverifiable information.** Inaccurate, incomplete, or unverifiable information must be removed or corrected, usually within 30 days. However, a consumer-reporting agency may continue to report information it has verified as accurate.

♦ **Consumer-reporting agencies may not report outdated negative information.** In most cases, a consumer-reporting agency may not report negative information that is more than seven years old or bankruptcies that are more than 10 years old.

♦ **Limited access to files.** A consumer-reporting agency may only provide information about an individual to a person or entity with a valid need — usually to consider an application with a creditor, insurer, employer, landlord, or other business.

♦ **Individuals must consent for reports to be provided to employers.** A consumer-reporting agency may not give information about an individual to an individual's employer or potential employer without the written consent of the individual. Written consent is generally not required in the trucking industry.

♦ **Individuals may seek damages from violators.** If a consumer-reporting agency or, in some cases, a user of consumer reports or a furnisher of information to a consumer-reporting agency violates the FCRA, an individual may be able to bring an action for damages in state or federal court.

Obligations of Furnishers of Information

The FCRA imposes responsibilities on all persons who furnish information to consumer-reporting agencies. State law may impose additional requirements on furnishers. All furnishers of information to consumer-reporting agencies should become familiar with the applicable laws and may want to consult with their counsel to ensure they are in compliance. The following is a summary of some of the general requirements set forth by the FCRA on furnishers of information:

♦ **General prohibition on reporting inaccurate information.** The FCRA prohibits information furnishers from providing information to a consumer-reporting agency that they know or have reasonable cause to believe is inaccurate. However, the furnisher is not subject to this general prohibition if it clearly and conspicuously specifies an address to which consumers may write to notify the furnisher that certain information is inaccurate.

♦ **Duty to correct and update information.** If at any time a person who regularly and in the ordinary course of business furnishes information to one or more consumer-reporting agencies determines that the information provided is not complete or accurate, the furnisher must promptly provide complete and accurate information to the consumer-reporting agency. In addition, the furnisher must notify all consumer-reporting agencies that received the information of any corrections and must thereafter report only the complete and accurate information.

♦ **Duties after notice of dispute from consumer.** If a consumer notifies a furnisher, at an address specified for the furnisher for such notices, which specific information is inaccurate, and the information is, in fact, inaccurate, the furnisher must thereafter report the correct information to the consumer-reporting agencies. If a consumer notifies a furnisher that the consumer disputes the completeness or accuracy of any information reported by the furnisher, the furnisher may not subsequently report that information to a consumer-reporting agency without providing notice of the dispute.

♦ **Duties after notice of dispute from consumer-reporting agency.** If a consumer-reporting agency notifies a furnisher that a consumer disputes the completeness or accuracy of information provided by the furnisher, the furnisher has a duty to follow certain procedures. The furnisher must:

• Conduct an investigation and review all relevant information provided by the consumer-reporting agency, including information given to the consumer-reporting agency by the consumer.

• Report the results to the consumer-reporting agency that referred the dispute, and, if the investigation establishes that the information was, in fact, incomplete or inaccurate, report the results to all consumer-reporting agencies to which the furnisher provided the information.

• Complete the steps within 30 days from the date the consumer-reporting agency received the dispute (or 45 days, if the consumer later provides relevant additional information to the consumer-reporting agency).

• Promptly modify or delete the information or block its reporting.

- ◆ **Duty to report voluntary closing of credit accounts.** If a consumer voluntarily closes a credit account, any person who regularly and in the ordinary course of business furnishes information to one or more consumer-reporting agencies must report this fact when it provides information to consumer-reporting agencies for the time period in which the account was closed.

- ◆ **Duty to report dates of delinquencies.** If a furnisher reports information concerning a delinquent account placed for collection, charged to profit or loss, subject to any similar action, the furnisher must, within 90 days after reporting the information, provide the consumer-reporting agency with the month and the year of the commencement of the delinquency that immediately preceded the action, so that the agency will know how long to keep the information in the consumer's file.

- ◆ **Duties of financial institutions when reporting negative information.** Financial institutions that furnish information to nationwide consumer-reporting agencies must notify consumers in writing if they may furnish or have furnished negative information to a consumer-reporting agency.

- ◆ **Duties when furnishing medical information.** A furnisher whose primary business is providing services, products, or devices (and such furnisher's agents or assignees) is a medical information furnisher for purposes of the FCRA and must notify all consumer-reporting agencies to which it reports of this fact.

Employer Obligations Under the FCRA

For employers, the most important parts of the FCRA concern the obligation of those who use the information provided by consumer-reporting agencies. This section provides a brief summary of the responsibilities imposed by the FCRA on all users of consumer reports.

Users Must Have a Permissible Purpose

Congress has limited the use of consumer reports in order to protect consumers' privacy. In order to obtain a consumer report, an employer must have a permissible purpose. The following are listed as **permissible** purposes under the FCRA:

- ◆ If ordered by a court or federal grand jury subpoena.

- ◆ If instructed by the consumer in writing.

- ◆ For the extension of credit as a result of an application from a consumer or the review or collection of a consumer's account.

- ◆ For employment purposes, including hiring and promotion decisions, where the consumer has given written permission.

- ◆ For the underwriting of insurance as a result of an application from a consumer.

- ◆ Where there is a legitimate business need in connection with a business transaction that is initiated by the consumer.

- ◆ To review a customer's account to determine whether the consumer continues to meet the terms and conditions of the account.

- ◆ To determine a consumer's eligibility for a license or other benefit granted by a governmental instrumentality required by law to consider an applicant's financial responsibility or status.

♦ For use by a potential investor or current insurer in a valuation or assessment of the credit or prepayment risks associated with an existing credit obligation.

♦ For use by state and local officials in connection with child support payments, modifications, and enforcement.

Disclosure and Authorization Required for Consumer Reports

Before an employer may obtain a consumer report or cause one to be prepared, it must disclose to that person in writing that such a report may be obtained and secure the person's written authorization. This written disclosure must be contained in a separate document used solely for that purpose, and it may not simply be included on an employment application or in an employee handbook.

Before a consumer-reporting agency may provide or prepare a consumer report for an employer, it must obtain certification from the employer that the employer has performed and/or agreed to the following:

♦ Provided the required disclosure to the applicant/employee.

♦ Received written permission to obtain the report.

♦ Will not use the information in violation of any applicable equal employment opportunity law or regulation.

♦ Will abide by the requirements stated before taking any adverse employment action.

Investigative Consumer Reports

Investigative consumer reports are a special type of consumer report in which information about a consumer's character, general reputation, personal characteristics, and mode of living is obtained through personal interviews by an entity or person that is a consumer-reporting agency. Consumers who are the subjects of such reports are given special rights under the FCRA.

If a user intends to obtain an investigative consumer report, the FCRA requires the following:

♦ The user must disclose to the consumer that an investigative consumer report may be obtained. The disclosure must be in writing and be mailed or otherwise delivered to the consumer at some time before or not later than three days after the date on which the report was first requested. The disclosure must include a statement informing the consumer of the right to request additional disclosures of the nature and scope of the investigation and the summary of consumer rights.

♦ The user must certify to the FCRA that the disclosures have been made and that the user will make the disclosure.

Upon written request of a consumer made within a reasonable period of time after the disclosures required, the user must make a complete disclosure of the nature and scope of the investigation. This must be made in a written statement that is mailed or otherwise delivered to the consumer no later than five days after the date on which the request was received from the consumer or the report was first requested — whichever is later.

Indirect and Direct Disputes

Under the FCRA, employers that furnish information to consumer reporting agencies are required to investigate both indirect and direct employee disputes. *Indirect disputes* are disputes the current or former employee presents directly to the consumer reporting agency to relay to the employer.

If the employer discovers that inaccurate or incomplete information about an employee was furnished to a consumer reporting agency, the employer has an affirmative duty to provide any recipient with complete and accurate information.

Direct disputes occur when an employee challenges the accuracy or completeness of information contained in a consumer report by directly contacting their current or prior employer, rather than going through the consumer agency. Upon receipt of a direct dispute, employers are required to conduct a reasonable investigation to determine the validity of the employee's dispute.

Although only specific situations trigger a furnisher's obligation to investigate a direct dispute (for example, those in relation to credit accounts or debts) an individual or entity must investigate a dispute if it relates to any other information contained in a consumer report regarding an account or other relationship with the furnisher that bears on the consumer's:

- ♦ Creditworthiness, credit standing, or credit capacity.

- ♦ Character or general reputation.

- ♦ Personal characteristics or mode of living.

Consequently, information that employers furnish to consumer reporting agencies (information about the employee's work or work history, such as the employee's current or former position, compensation, dates of employment, and the reason the employment relationship ended) is covered by the regulations allowing a direct dispute. As a result, if a current or former employee disputes any of this type of information, the employer must conduct an investigation.

Direct Dispute Procedure

In processing a direct dispute, an employee must provide the employer with all of the following:

- ♦ Sufficient information to prove that the employee has or had an employment relationship with the employer.

- ♦ An explanation for the employee's belief that the information is inaccurate or incomplete.

- ♦ Supporting documentation regarding the dispute, if any.

Upon receiving the notice, the employer must conduct a reasonable investigation, which means at a minimum reviewing the submitted information and determining the validity of the employee's dispute. The employer must complete the investigation and report back to the employee within 30 days of receiving notice of the dispute (with a possible extra 15 days if the employee provides new information). If the employer determines that the employee information reported was inaccurate, the furnisher must also promptly notify each consumer reporting agency that received the information and provide any correction necessary to make the information accurate.

Note: Employers are not required to investigate direct disputes that are frivolous or irrelevant. Employers must provide written notification to employees within five business days of the choice to not investigate. The notice must inform the employee of the reason for the employer's determination that the dispute is frivolous or irrelevant and, therefore, will not be investigated, and should include a description of the type of information necessary to proceed with the investigation, if any.

Policies and Procedures

Employers that furnish information to consumer reporting agencies are required to establish and implement reasonable written policies and procedures to ensure the accuracy and integrity of information reported about its employees. Additionally, an employer's policies and procedures must be appropriate to the nature, size, complexity, and scope of its actual activities.

Adverse Action

Before taking any adverse action based in whole or in part on a consumer report, an employer must provide the affected person with a copy of the report and a written description of that person's rights under the FCRA. The term *adverse action* includes a denial of employment or any other decision for employment purposes that adversely affects a current or prospective employee.

Subsequent to taking any adverse action, the employer again must notify the consumer that adverse action has been taken based in whole or in part on a consumer report. Further, the employer must provide the individual with the following:

♦ The name, address, and telephone number of the consumer-reporting agency (including a toll-free telephone number, if it is a nationwide consumer-reporting agency) that provided the report.

♦ A statement that the consumer-reporting agency did not make the adverse decision and it is not able to explain why the decision was made.

♦ A statement setting forth the consumer's right to obtain a free disclosure of the consumer's file from the consumer-reporting agency if the consumer makes a request within 60 days.

♦ A statement setting forth the consumer's right to dispute directly with the consumer-reporting agency the accuracy or completeness of any information provided by the agency.

Adverse Action Based on Information Obtained from Affiliates

If a person takes an adverse action involving insurance, employment, or a credit transaction initiated by the consumer, based on information of the type covered by the FCRA, and this information was obtained from an entity affiliated with the user of the information by common ownership or control, the user is required to notify the consumer of the adverse action.

The notice must inform the consumer that a disclosure may be obtained of the nature of the information relied upon by making a written request within 60 days of receiving the adverse action notice. If the consumer makes such a request, the user must disclose the nature of the information not later than 30 days after receiving the request. If consumer information is shared among affiliates and then used for an adverse action, the user must make an adverse action disclosure as set forth by law.

Disposing of Records

The FCRA requires that all users of consumer report information have procedures to properly dispose of records containing this information. The FTC, the Securities and Exchange Commission, and the banking and credit union regulators have issued regulations covering disposal.

Special Procedures for Employee Investigations

Section 603(x) provides special procedures for investigations of suspected misconduct by an employee or for compliance with federal, state, or local laws and regulations or rules of a self-regulatory organization and compliance with an employer's written policies. These investigations are not treated as consumer reports as long as the employer complies with the procedures set forth in § 603(x), and a summary describing the nature and scope of the inquiry is made to the employee if adverse action is taken based on the investigation.

In addition, according to the Fair and Accurate Credit Transactions Act of 2003 (FACTA), which added new sections to the FCRA, employers are not required to notify an employee or obtain an employee's consent prior to using a consumer-reporting agency to investigate suspected employment-related misconduct by the employee or compliance with the law or any pre-existing employer policies.

If the employer takes adverse action based in whole or in part upon a consumer report obtained for one of these purposes, the employer must disclose a summary of the report upon which the adverse action was based. The employer is not required to disclose the source of the information, such as the identity of a co-worker who was interviewed during the investigation. The employer **must not** disclose the report to outside parties other than law enforcement, governmental, or self-regulatory agencies (such as the Securities and Exchange Commission). If part of the investigation includes an investigation of the employee's creditworthiness or credit standing, the regular rules relating to disclosure and consent apply.

Obligations of Users of Medical Information

The FCRA limits the use of medical information obtained from consumer-reporting agencies (other than payment information that appears in a coded form that does not identify the medical provider). If the information is to be used for an insurance transaction, the consumer must give consent to the user of the report or the information must be coded. If the report is to be used for employment purposes or in connection with a credit transaction (except as provided in regulations issued by the banking and credit union regulators), the consumer must provide specific written consent and the medical information must be relevant. Any user who receives medical information **may not** disclose the information to any other person except where necessary to carry out the purpose for which the information was disclosed or as permitted by statute, regulation, or order.

Penalties

Employers who fail to obtain an applicant's permission before requesting a consumer report or fail to provide pre-adverse action disclosures and adverse action notices pay legal consequences. The FCRA allows individuals to sue employers for damages in federal court. A person who successfully sues is entitled to recover court costs and reasonable legal fees from the employer. The law also allows individuals to seek punitive damages for deliberate violations. In addition, the FTC, other federal agencies, and the states may sue employers for noncompliance for civil penalties of up to $2,500 per violation. Notwithstanding the civil penalties, any person who knowingly and willfully obtains a consumer report under false pretenses may face criminal prosecution.

Note: In *Safeco Ins. Co. of America v. Burr*, 127 S.Ct. 2201, 2208-2210, (2007), the U.S. Supreme Court held that in order for a violation of the FCRA to be willful, it must have been committed knowingly and recklessly. In its decision, the court expressly rejected the argument that "willfulness" is limited to knowing violations, but held that an action is only reckless if it is "objectively unreasonable."

Contact Information

Federal Trade Commission, Consumer Response Center

600 Pennsylvania Avenue, NW
Washington, DC 20580

Telephone: 202-326-2222
Toll-Free: 877-FTC-HELP (382-4357)
Internet: *www.ftc.gov*

Illinois Law

The Illinois Human Rights Act

Pursuant to 775 Ill. Comp. Stat. § 5/2-103 and unless otherwise authorized by law, it is a civil rights violation for an employer, employment agency, or labor organization to inquire into or to use the fact of an arrest or criminal history record information ordered expunged, sealed, or impounded as a basis to refuse to hire, to segregate, or to act with respect to any of the following:

♦ Recruitment, hiring, and promotion.

♦ Renewal of employment and selection for training or apprenticeship.

♦ Discharge, discipline, and tenure.

♦ Terms, privileges, and conditions of employment.

The Illinois Human Rights Act applies to the following employers:

♦ Those employing 15 or more employees within Illinois during 20 or more calendar weeks in the calendar year of or preceding an alleged violation.

♦ The state and any political subdivision, municipal corporation, or other governmental unit or agency, without regard to the number of employees.

♦ Any party to a public contract, without regard to the number of employees.

♦ A joint apprenticeship or training committee, without regard to the number of employees.

Exceptions

Although the use of the fact of an arrest is generally prohibited, an employer, employment agency, or labor organization **may** obtain or use other information that indicates that a person actually engaged in the conduct for which the person was arrested.

A state agency, unit of local government, school district, or private organization may utilize conviction information obtained from the Illinois Department of State Police (according to the Criminal Identification Act, or other state or federal laws or regulations) in evaluating the qualifications and character of an employee or a prospective employee.

Illinois Employee Credit Privacy Act

According to the Illinois Employee Credit Privacy Act and effective January 1, 2011, Illinois employers are prohibited from using a person's credit history to determine employment, recruiting, discharge, or compensation. The act specifically prohibits an employer from:

♦ Failing or refusing to hire or recruit, discharge, or otherwise discriminating against an individual with respect to employment, compensation, or a term, condition, or privilege of employment because of the individual's credit history or credit report.

♦ Inquiring about an applicant's or employee's credit history.

♦ Ordering or obtaining an applicant's or employee's credit report from a consumer reporting agency.

Credit history is an individual's past borrowing and repaying behavior, including paying bills on time and managing debt and other financial obligations. ***Credit report*** is any written or other communication of any information by a consumer reporting agency that bears on a consumer's creditworthiness, credit standing, credit capacity, or credit history.

However, the act does not prohibit employers from conducting a thorough background investigation, which may include obtaining a report without information on credit history or an investigative report without information on credit history, or both, as permitted under the federal Fair Credit Reporting Act. Such information may be used for employment purposes only.

Additionally, the act does not prevent an employer from inquiring or taking employment action if a satisfactory credit history is an established bona fide occupational requirement of a particular position or a particular group of employees. A satisfactory credit history is not a bona fide occupational requirement unless at least one of the following circumstances is present:

♦ State or federal law requires bonding or other security covering an individual holding the position.

♦ The duties of the position include custody of or unsupervised access to cash or marketable assets valued at $2,500 or more.

♦ The duties of the position include signatory power over business assets of $100 or more per transaction.

♦ The position is a managerial position that involves setting the direction or control of the business.

♦ The position involves access to personal or confidential information, financial information, trade secrets, or state or national security information.

♦ The position meets criteria in administrative rules, if any, that the U.S. Department of Labor or the Illinois Department of Labor has promulgated to establish the circumstances in which a credit history is a bona fide occupational requirement.

♦ The employee's or applicant's credit history is otherwise required by or exempt under federal or state law.

Exceptions

The act does not apply to any of the following:

♦ Any bank holding company, financial holding company, bank, savings bank, savings and loan association, credit union, or trust company, or any subsidiary or affiliate thereof, that is authorized to do business under Illinois or U.S. laws.

♦ Any company authorized to engage in any kind of insurance or surety business, including any employee, agent, or employee of an agent acting on behalf of a company engaged in the insurance or surety business.

♦ Any state law enforcement or investigative unit, including, without limitation, any such unit within the office of any Executive Inspector General, the Department of State Police, the Department of Corrections, the Department of Juvenile Justice, or the Department of Natural Resources.

♦ Any state or local government agency that otherwise requires use of the employee's or applicant's credit history or credit report.

♦ Any entity that is defined as a debt collector under federal or state statute.

Waiver Prohibited

An employer may not require an applicant or employee to waive any right under the act. An agreement by an applicant or employee to waive any right under the act is invalid and unenforceable.

Retaliation and Discrimination

Employers may not retaliate or discriminate against a person because the person has done or was about to do any of the following:

- File a complaint under the act.
- Testify, assist, or participate in an investigation, proceeding, or action concerning a violation of the act.
- Oppose a violation of the act.

Enforcement and Penalties

A person who is injured by a violation of the act may bring a civil action in circuit court to obtain injunctive relief, damages, or both. The court will award costs and reasonable attorney's fees to a person who prevails as a plaintiff in an action.

Expunged Juvenile Record

Pursuant to 705 Ill. Comp. Stat. § 405/5-915, an expunged juvenile record **may not** be considered by any private or public entity in employment matters, certification, licensing, revocation of certification or licensure, or registration.

Applications for employment must contain specific language stating that the applicant is not obligated to disclose expunged juvenile records of conviction or arrest. Additionally, employers are prohibited from asking if an applicant has had a juvenile record expunged.

Employment Record Disclosure Act

Under the Illinois Employment Record Disclosure Act, located at 745 Ill. Comp. Stat. §§ 46/1 – 46/99, any employer or authorized employee or agent acting on behalf of an employer who, upon inquiry by a prospective employer, provides truthful written or verbal information or information believed in good faith to be truthful about a current or former employee's job performance is presumed to be acting in good faith and is immune from civil liability for the disclosure and the consequences of the disclosure.

The presumption of good faith may be rebutted by a preponderance of evidence that the information disclosed was known to be false or in violation of a civil right of the employee or former employee.

Health Care Worker Background Check Act

The Health Care Worker Background Check Act, located at 225 Ill. Comp. Stat. §§ 46/1 – 46/99, was enacted to protect the most frail and disabled citizens of Illinois from possible harm through a criminal background check of certain health care workers.

Covered Health Care Workers

Health care workers covered by the act include, but are not limited to, the following:

♦ All individuals employed or retained by a health care employer as home health care aides, nurse aides, personal care assistants, private duty nurse aides, day training personnel, or an individual working in any similar health-related occupation where the individual provides direct care or has access to long-term care residents or the living quarters or financial, medical, or personal records of long-term care residents.

Direct care is the provision of nursing care or assistance with feeding, dressing, movement, bathing, toileting, or other personal needs, including home services (as defined in the Home Health, Home Services, and Home Nursing Agency Licensing Act).

♦ All employees of licensed or certified long-term care facilities who have or may have contact with residents or access to the living quarters or the financial, medical, or personal records of residents.

A long-term care facility is a facility licensed by the state, certified under federal law as a long-term care facility, a supportive living facility, an assisted living establishment, or a shared housing establishment, or registered as a board and care home.

Exceptions

The Health Care Worker Background Check Act **does not apply** to any of the following:

♦ An individual who is licensed by the Department of Financial and Professional Regulation or the Department of Public Health under another Illinois law.

♦ An individual employed or retained by a health care employer for whom a criminal background check is required by another Illinois law.

♦ A student in a licensed health care field including, but not limited to, a student nurse, a physical therapy student, or a respiratory care student, unless the student is employed by either:

• A health care employer in a position with duties involving direct care for clients, patients, or residents.

• A long-term care facility in a position that involves or may involve contact with resident or access to the living quarters or the financial, medical, or personal records of residents.

Covered Health Care Employers

Health care employers covered by the act include the following:

♦ The owner or licensee of any of the following:

• A community living facility.

• A life care facility.

• A long-term care facility.

• A home health agency.

• A hospice care program or volunteer hospice program.

• A hospital.

• A nurse agency.

• A respite care provider.

• An establishment licensed under the Assisted Living and Shared Housing Act.

- A supportive living program.

- Early childhood intervention programs.

- The University of Illinois Hospital, Chicago.

- Programs funded by the Department on Aging through the Community Care Program.

- Programs certified to participate in the Illinois Supportive Living Program.

- Programs listed by the Emergency Medical Services (EMS) Systems Act as freestanding emergency centers.

- Locations licensed under the Alternative Health Care Delivery Act.

♦ A day training program certified by the Department of Human Services.

♦ A community integrated living arrangement operated by a community mental health and developmental service agency.

♦ The State Long Term Care Ombudsman Program, including any regional long-term care ombudsman programs, only for the purpose of securing background checks.

Ineligibility for Employment with Health Care Employers and Long Term Facilities

No health care employer may knowingly hire, employ, or retain any individual in a position with duties involving direct care for clients, patients, or residents and no long-term care facility may knowingly hire, employ, or retain any individual in a position with duties that involve or may involve contact with residents or access to the living quarters or the financial, medical, or personal records of residents, if the individual has been convicted of committing or attempting to commit one or more of the following offenses, unless the employee obtains a waiver:

♦ Illinois Criminal Code Offenses, such as, but not limited to, the following:
  - Inchoate offenses, such as solicitation, conspiracy, and attempt.
  - Offenses against the person, such as homicide, kidnapping, bodily harm, and endangering the life or health of a child.
  - Offenses directed against property, such as theft, deception, robbery, burglary, and arson.
  - Offenses affecting public health, safety, and decency, such as, use of deadly weapons.

♦ Cruelty to children offenses.

♦ Offenses relating to the manufacturing, trafficking, criminal drug conspiracy, and involvement with minors under the Illinois Cannabis Control Act.

♦ Offenses relating to the manufacturing, trafficking, delivery, criminal drug conspiracy, look-alike substances, and involvement of minors under the Illinois Controlled Substances Act.

♦ Aggravated domestic battery or aggravated battery with a machine gun or firearm equipped with a silencer.

♦ Theft of lost or mislaid property.

♦ Identity theft or aggravated identity theft.

♦ Aggravated robbery or residential arson.

♦ Specific deadly weapon offenses.

♦ Specific violations of the Illinois Credit Card and Debit Card Act.

♦ Permitting sexual abuse of a child as prohibited by the Illinois Wrongs to Children Act.

♦ The individual has violated the prohibited acts of the Illinois Nursing and Advanced Practice Nursing Act.

No health care employer is required to retain an individual in a position with duties involving direct care for clients, patients, or residents, and no long-term care facility is required to retain an individual in a position with duties that involve or may involve contact with residents or access to the living quarters or the financial, medical, or personal records of residents if the individual has been convicted of committing or attempting to commit one or more of the aforementioned offenses.

Additionally, a health care employer may not hire, employ, or retain any individual with duties involving direct care of clients, patients or residents, and no long-term care facility may knowingly hire, employ, or retain any individual in a position with duties that involve or may involve contact with residents or access to the living quarters or the financial, medical, or personal records of residents if the employer becomes aware that the individual has been convicted in another state of committing or attempting to commit an offense that has the same or similar elements as an offense previously listed, as verified by court records, records from a state agency, or a Federal Bureau of Investigation (FBI) criminal history record check, unless the applicant or employee obtains a waiver. However, health care employers are **not** obligated to conduct a criminal history records check in other states in which an employee has resided.

Offense

Any person whose profession is job counseling who knowingly counsels any person who has been convicted of committing or attempting to commit any of the aforementioned to apply for a position with duties involving direct contact with a client, patient, or resident of a health care employer or a position with duties that involve or may involve contact with residents or access to the living quarters or the financial, medical, or personal records of residents of a long-term care facility may be charged with a Class A misdemeanor unless a waiver is granted.

Fingerprint-Based Criminal History Records Check

A *fingerprint-based criminal history records* check is a livescan fingerprint-based criminal history records check submitted as a fee applicant inquiry in the form and manner prescribed by the Department of State Police. A *livescan vendor* is an entity whose equipment has been certified by the Department of State Police to collect an individual's demographics and inkless fingerprints and, in a manner prescribed by the Department of State Police and the Department of Public Health, electronically transmit the fingerprints and required data to the Department of State Police and a daily file of required data to the Department of Public Health.

Health Care Worker Registry

As of October 1, 2007 or as soon as reasonably practical and at the discretion of the Director of Public Health, any student, applicant, or employee who desires to be included on the Department of Public Health's Health Care Worker Registry must authorize the Department of Public Health or its designee to request a fingerprint-based criminal history records check to determine if the individual has a conviction for a disqualifying offense. This authorization allows the Department of Public Health to request and receive information and assistance from any State or local governmental agency.

Each individual must submit their fingerprints to the Department of State Police in an electronic format and then these fingerprints are then checked against the fingerprint records contained in the Department of State Police criminal history record databases. The Department of State Police will provide information concerning any criminal convictions against the individual. The Department of State Police charges a fee for conducting the criminal history records check, which may not exceed the actual cost of the records check.

Educational Entity and Health Care Employer

As of October 1, 2007 or as soon as reasonably practical and at the discretion of the Director of Public Health:

♦ An educational entity, other than a secondary school, conducting a nurse aide training program must initiate a fingerprint-based criminal history records check requested by the Department of Public Health prior to entry of an individual into the training program.

♦ A health care employer who makes a conditional offer of employment to an applicant for a position as an employee must initiate a fingerprint-based criminal history record check, requested by the Department of Public Health, on the applicant, if such a background check has not been previously conducted.

To *initiate* is to:

♦ Obtain from a student, applicant, or employee their Social Security number, demographics, a disclosure statement, and an authorization for the Department of Public Health or its designee to request a fingerprint-based criminal history records check.

♦ Transmit this information electronically to the Department of Public Health.

♦ Conduct Internet searches on certain Web sites, including, without limitation, all of the following to determine if the applicant has been adjudicated a sex offender, has been a prison inmate, or has committed Medicare or Medicaid fraud:

- Illinois Sex Offender Registry.

- Department of Corrections' Sex Offender Search Engine.

- Department of Corrections' Inmate Search Engine.

- Department of Corrections' Wanted Fugitives Search Engine.

- National Sex Offender Public Registry.

- Web site of the Health and Human Services Office of Inspector General.

♦ Collect and transmit the student, applicant, or employee's fingerprints electronically to the Department of State Police.

When initiating a background check requested by the Department of Public Health, an educational entity or health care employer must electronically submit to the Department of Public Health the student's, applicant's, or employee's Social Security number, demographics, disclosure, and authorization information within two working days after the authorization is secured. The student, applicant, or employee must have their fingerprints collected electronically and transmitted to the Department of State Police within 10 working days. The educational entity or health care employer must transmit all necessary information and fees to the livescan vendor and Department of State Police within 10 working days after receipt of the authorization. This information and the results of the criminal history record checks are maintained by the Department of Public Health's Health Care Worker Registry.

Direct Care Employer

A direct care employer may initiate a fingerprint-based background check requested by the Department of Public Health for any of its employees, but may not use this process to initiate background checks for residents. The results of any fingerprint-based background check that is initiated with the Department as the requestor is entered in the Health Care Worker Registry.

Frequency

As long as the employee has had a fingerprint-based criminal history record check requested by the Department of Public Health and stays active on the Health Care Worker Registry, no further criminal history record checks are necessary, as the Department of State Police will notify the Department of Public Health of any additional convictions associated with the fingerprints previously submitted.

Health care employers are required to check the Health Care Worker Registry before hiring an employee to determine that the individual has had a fingerprint-based record check requested by the Department of Public Health and has no disqualifying convictions or has been granted a waiver. If the individual has not had such a background check or is not active on the Health Care Worker Registry, then the health care employer must initiate a fingerprint-based record check requested by the Department of Public Health.

If an individual is inactive on the Health Care Worker Registry, that individual is prohibited from being hired to work as a certified nurse aide if, since the individual's most recent completion of a competency test, there has been a period of 24 consecutive months during which the individual has not provided nursing or nursing-related services for pay. If the individual can provide proof of having retained certification by not having a 24 consecutive month break in service for pay, the individual may be hired as a certified nurse aide and that employment information will be entered into the Health Care Worker Registry.

Notifications

As of October 1, 2007 or as soon as reasonably practical and at the discretion of the Director of Public Health:

- If the Department of State Police notifies the Department of Public Health that an employee has a new conviction of a disqualifying offense, based upon the fingerprints that were previously submitted, then:

  - The Health Care Worker Registry will notify the employee's last known employer of the offense.

  - A record of the employee's disqualifying offense will be entered on the Health Care Worker Registry.

  - The individual is no longer eligible to work as an employee unless the individual obtains a waiver.

- Each direct care employer or its designee must provide an employment verification for each employee no less than annually. The health care employer or its designee must indicate employment and termination dates within 30 days after hiring or terminating an employee, as well as the employment category and type. Failure to comply with this requirement to indicate employment and termination dates constitutes a licensing violation. For health care employers that are not licensed or certified, a fine of up to $500 may be imposed for failure to maintain these records. This information will be used by the Department of Public Health to notify the last known employer of any disqualifying offenses that are reported by the Department of State Police.

The Department of Public Health will notify each health care employer or long-term care facility inquiring as to the information on the Health Care Worker Registry if the applicant or employee listed on the registry has a disqualifying offense and is therefore ineligible to work or has a waiver.

Exceptions

A fingerprint-based criminal history records check is not required for health care employees who have:

- ◆ Been continuously employed by a health care employer since October 1, 2007.

- ◆ Met the requirements for criminal history background checks prior to October 1, 2007.

- ◆ No disqualifying convictions or requested and received a waiver of those disqualifying convictions.

These employees are retained on the Health Care Worker Registry as long as they remain active. However, a health care employer is not prohibited from initiating a criminal history records check for these employees. Should these employees seek a new position with a different health care employer, then a fingerprint-based criminal history records check is required.

Required Notification of Student, Applicant, or Employee

The student, applicant, or employee must be notified of each of the following whenever a fingerprint-based criminal history records check is required:

- ◆ That the educational entity, health care employer, or long-term care facility will initiate a fingerprint-based criminal history record check requested by the Department of Public Health of the student, applicant, or employee.

- ◆ That the student, applicant, or employee has a right to obtain a copy of the criminal records report that indicates a conviction for a disqualifying offense and challenge the accuracy and completeness of the report through an established Department of State Police procedure of Access and Review.

- ◆ That the applicant, if hired conditionally, may be terminated if the criminal records report indicates that the applicant has a record of a conviction of any of the aforementioned criminal offenses, unless the applicant obtains a waiver.

- ◆ That the applicant, if not hired conditionally, will not be hired if the criminal records report indicates that the applicant has a record of a conviction of any of the aforementioned criminal offenses, unless the applicant obtains a waiver.

- ◆ That the employee will be terminated if the criminal records report indicates that the employee has a record of a conviction of any of the aforementioned criminal offenses.

- ◆ If, after the employee has originally been determined not to have disqualifying offenses, the employer is notified that the employee has a new conviction(s) of any of the aforementioned criminal offenses, then the employee will be terminated.

A health care employer or long-term care facility may conditionally employ an applicant for up to 3 months pending the results of a fingerprint-based criminal history record check requested by the Department of Public Health.

Waiver

Any student, applicant, or employee listed on the Health Care Worker Registry may request a waiver of the prohibition against employment by:

- ◆ Completing a waiver application on a form prescribed by the Department of Public Health.

- ◆ Providing a written explanation of each conviction describing all of the following:

- What happened.
- How many years have passed since the offense.
- The identity of the individuals involved.
- The age of the applicant at the time of the offense.
- Any other circumstances surrounding the offense.
- Providing official documentation showing that all fines have been paid, if applicable, and the date probation or parole was satisfactorily completed, if applicable.

The applicant may, but is not required to, submit employment and character references and any other evidence demonstrating the ability of the applicant or employee to perform the employment responsibilities competently and evidence that the applicant or employee does not pose a threat to the health or safety of residents, patients, or clients.

The Department of Public Health must inform health care employers if a waiver is being sought by entering a record on the Health Care Worker Registry that a waiver is pending and must act upon the waiver request within 30 days of receipt of all necessary information. Except in cases where a rehabilitation waiver is granted, a letter will be sent to the applicant notifying the applicant that they have received an automatic waiver.

An individual may not be employed from the time that the employer receives a notification from the Department of Public Health based upon the results of a fingerprint-based criminal history records check containing disqualifying conditions until the time that the individual receives a waiver. A health care employer is not obligated to employ or offer permanent employment to an applicant, or to retain an employee who is granted a waiver. Additionally, the entity responsible for inspecting, licensing, certifying, or registering the health care employer and the Department of Public Health are immune from liability for any waivers granted.

Recordkeeping

The health care employer must retain on file for a period of five years records of criminal records requests for all employees. The health care employer must retain a copy of the disclosure and authorization forms, a copy of the livescan request form, all notifications resulting from the fingerprint-based criminal history records check and waiver, if appropriate, for the duration of the individual's employment. These files are subject to inspection by the agency responsible for inspecting, licensing, or certifying the health care employer and a fine of up to $500 may be imposed by the appropriate agency for failure to maintain these records.

The Department of Public Health must keep an electronic record of criminal history background checks for an individual for as long as the individual remains active on the Health Care Worker Registry.

Liability

A health care employer will not be liable for the failure to hire or to retain an applicant or employee who has been convicted of committing or attempting to commit one or more of the offenses enumerated by the Health Care Worker Background Check Act. However, if an employee is suspended from employment based on the results of a criminal background check conducted under the Health Care Worker Background Check Act and the results prompting the suspension are subsequently found to be inaccurate, the employee is entitled to recover backpay from the employer for the suspension period, provided that the employer is the cause of the inaccuracy.

No health care employer will be liable for any benefit charges that result from the payment of unemployment benefits to any claimant when the claimant's separation occurred because the claimant's criminal background included an offense previously enumerated, or the claimant's separation from that employer occurred as a result of the claimant violating a policy that the employer was required to maintain pursuant to the Drug-Free Workplace Act.

The Department of Public Health or an entity responsible for inspecting, licensing, certifying, or registering the health care employer or long-term care facility is immune from liability for notices given based on the results of a fingerprint-based criminal history record check.

School District Employees

According to 725 Ill. Comp. Stat. § 190/3, when a criminal sexual offense is committed or alleged to have been committed by a school district employee or any individual contractually employed by a school district, a copy of the criminal history record information relating to the investigation of the offense or alleged offense will be transmitted to the superintendent of schools of the district immediately upon request. Additionally, if the law enforcement agency knows that a school district employee or any individual contractually employed by a school district has committed or is alleged to have committed a criminal sexual offense, the superintendent of schools of the district will be immediately provided a copy of the criminal history record information.

Criminal history record information is any of the following:

♦ Chronologically maintained arrest information, such as traditional arrest logs or blotters.

♦ The name of a person in the custody of a law enforcement agency and the charges for which that person is being held.

♦ Public court records.

♦ Records otherwise available under state or local law.

♦ Records in which the requesting party is the individual identified, except as provided the Freedom of Information Act.

Superintendents are restricted from specifically revealing the name of the victim without written consent of the victim or victim's parent or guardian. A court may prohibit such disclosure only after giving notice and a hearing to all affected parties.

Note: According to 105 Ill. Comp. Stat. § 5/10-21.9, in order to student teach in the public schools, a person is required to authorize a fingerprint-based criminal history records check and checks of the Statewide Sex Offender Database and Statewide Child Murderer and Violent Offender Against Youth Database prior to participating in any field experiences in the public schools. Authorization for and payment of the costs of the checks must be furnished by the student teacher. Results of the checks must be furnished to the higher education institution where the student teacher is enrolled and the superintendent of the school district where the student is assigned.

Child Care Facilities

According to 225 Ill. Comp. Stat. § 10/4.1, the Department of Children and Family Services requires that each child care facility license applicant as part of the application process, and each employee of a child care facility as a condition of employment, must authorize an investigation to determine if such applicant or employee has ever been charged with a crime, and if so, the disposition of those charges. This authorization must indicate the scope of the inquiry and the agencies that may be contacted. Upon the authorization, the director will request and receive information and assistance from any federal, state, or local governmental agency as part of the investigation.

Each applicant must submit a set of fingerprints to the Department of State Police, which will be checked against the fingerprint records in the Department of State Police and FBI criminal history records databases. The Department of State Police must provide information concerning any criminal charges and their disposition against an applicant or child care facility employee upon request of the Department of Children and Family Services when the request is made as required.

Confidentiality

Information concerning convictions of a license applicant investigated under this section must be provided, upon request, to the applicant prior to final action by the department on the application. State conviction information provided by the Department of State Police regarding employees or prospective employees of child care facilities licensed under the Child Care Act of 1969 must be provided to the operator of the facility, and, upon request, to the employee or prospective employee. Any information concerning criminal charges and the disposition of such charges obtained by the department is confidential and may not be transmitted outside the department, except as outlined, and may not be transmitted to anyone within the department except as needed for the purpose of evaluating an application or a child care facility employee. Only information and standards that bear a reasonable and rational relation to the performance of a child care facility may be used by the department or any licensee.

Any employee of the Department of Children and Family Services, Department of State Police, or a child care facility receiving confidential information under this section who gives or causes to be given any confidential information concerning any criminal convictions of a child care facility applicant or child care facility employee may be charged with a Class A misdemeanor unless release of such information is authorized in accordance this section.

Probationary Status

A child care facility may hire, on a probationary basis, any employee authorizing a criminal background investigation under the law, pending the result of such investigation. Employees must be notified prior to hiring that employment may be terminated on the basis of criminal background information obtained by the facility.

Public Utilities

According to 220 Ill. Comp. Stat. § 5/8-501.5, before hiring an employee or independent contractor to perform work involving facilities used for the distribution of natural gas to customers, a public utility must require the proposed employee or independent contractor to complete a certificate listing the proposed employee's or contractor's violations of pertinent safety or environmental laws.

Contact Information

Illinois Department of Public Health

535 West Jefferson Street
Springfield, IL 62761

Telephone: 217-782-4977
Fax: 217-782-3987
Internet: *www.idph.state.il.us*

Illinois State Police

801 South Seventh Street
Springfield, IL 62794-9461

Internet: *www.isp.state.il.us/isphome.cfm*

Chapter 6

Immigration

Introduction

Under immigration laws and regulations, employers may legally hire workers only if they are U.S. citizens or aliens authorized to work in the United States. This chapter addresses the federal rules that govern documentation of eligible employees, antidiscrimination enforcement, and temporary and permanent employment of foreign nationals. Per §§ 274A – 274C of the Immigration and Naturalization Act (INA), all U.S. employers are required to verify that their employees are authorized to work in the United States. Verification is completed upon the submission of Form I-9, *Employer Eligibility Verification Form*, by all new hires, accompanied by documentation confirming identity and authorization to work in the United States.

While the purpose of Form I-9 requirements is to eliminate the employment of unauthorized aliens, the laws also include provisions that prohibit discrimination on the basis of citizenship and national origin. As a result, employers may be penalized if they engage in activities, such as demanding specific documents or more documents than required by Form I-9, which could have a disparate impact upon one of the protected classes of job applicants. An employer who demands more documents than required or rejects documents that appear to be genuine may be subject to civil penalties for each individual discriminated against. Employers found to have engaged in any unfair immigration-related employment practices (UIREPs) may also be subject to penalties for each individual discriminated against.

UIREPs include any of the following:

♦ Refusing to hire or discharging a protected individual because of national origin or citizenship.

♦ Requesting specific documents.

♦ Rejecting apparently valid documents during employment eligibility verification for the purpose or with the intent of discriminating on the basis of citizenship or national origin.

Form I-9

The Form I-9 assists employers in verifying individuals who are authorized to work in the United States. Employers must complete a Form I-9 for every new employee hired after November 6, 1986. An individual is deemed as *hired* upon the commencement of employment. Job applicants need not complete Form I-9. Employers who request more or different documentation than the minimum necessary to meet Form I-9 requirements may constitute an UIREP as previously mentioned. Employers **must** complete a Form I-9 for all newly hired employees to verify their identity and authorization to work in the United States.

In April 2009, the USCIS revised the Form I-9 requirements to no longer allow an employer to accept expired documents to verify employment authorization on the Form I-9. The USCIS also added a new document to the list of acceptable documents that evidence both identity and employment authorization and made several technical corrections and updates. Effective August 31, 2009, the USCIS announced that the Office of Management and Budget extended its approval of the Form I-9 to August 31, 2012. Consequently, the USCIS amended the form to reflect a new revision date of August 7, 2009. However, employers may use the Form I-9 with the revision date of either August 7, 2009 or February 2, 2009. The revision dates are located on the bottom right-hand portion of the form.

Completing the Form

With exception, a Form I-9 must be completed for every employee hired to perform labor or services in return for wages or other remuneration on or after November 6, 1986. However, the completion of a Form I-9 is not required for persons who are:

- ♦ Hired before November 7, 1986, who are continuing in their employment and have a reasonable expectation of employment at all times.

- ♦ Employed for casual domestic work in a private home on a sporadic, irregular, or intermittent basis.

- ♦ Independent contractors.

- ♦ Providing labor but are employees of a contractor providing contract services (for example, employee leasing or temporary agencies).

- ♦ Not physically working on U.S. soil.

Note: Employers cannot contract for the labor of an alien if the employer knows the alien is not authorized to work in the United States.

Employee's Responsibility

New employees must complete Section 1 of a Form I-9 at the time of hire, but no later than the close of business on the first day of employment. The employee is held responsible for the accuracy of the information provided via signature.

Someone may assist the employee if the employee cannot complete Section 1 without assistance or if the employee needs the Form I-9 translated. The preparer or translator must read the form to the employee, assist the employee in completing Section 1, and have the employee sign or mark the form in the appropriate place. The preparer or translator must then complete the Preparer/Translator Certification block on the Form I-9. The employee must be given Form I-9 by the employer and asked to provide either one original document on List A or one original document on each of Lists B and C (*see* the section entitled **List of Acceptable Documents**) within three business days of the date employment began. The employee can choose which documents they want to present from the List of Acceptable Documents.

Note: There is no filing fee associated with the Form I-9.

Employer's Responsibility

Employers are responsible for ensuring the completion of the entire Form I-9, including ensuring that the employee completes Section 1 in full when the employee begins to work. The employer should immediately examine all documents establishing each employee's identity and eligibility to work.

Employers must accept any document(s) (from the List of Acceptable Documents) presented by the individual, which reasonably appear on their face to be genuine and to relate to the person presenting them. Employers may not specify which document(s) an employee must present. However, employers who participate in the USCIS E-Verify Program may only accept List B documents that have a photograph.

Employers may also require that employees make any necessary corrections so as to ensure proper completion of the form. Employers need not receive any documentation to substantiate the employee-provided information in Section 1. Additionally, and pursuant to § 7 of the Privacy Act (8 U.S.C.A. § 552a), providing a Social Security number on the Form I-9 is voluntary for all employees unless the employer participates in the E-Verify Program, which requires an employee's Social Security number for employment eligibility verification.

The employer must complete Section 2 of the form no later than the close of business on the new employee's third day of employment. If an individual is hired for less than three business days, then Sections 1 and 2 of the Form I-9 must be fully completed at the time of the hire, when the employee begins work. To ensure consistency and accuracy, employers should review the information provided in Section 1 against the documents produced by the employee for Section 2. If there is a discrepancy between the two sections, the employee should be given an opportunity to make necessary corrections.

Employers are not required to make copies of the documents that are produced for Section 2. However, employers may attach photocopies of documentation submitted to satisfy Form I-9 requirements to the employee's Form I-9. This must be consistently applied to every employee, without regard to citizenship or national origin, should employers choose to make and attach photocopies.

In certain circumstances, employers must accept a receipt in lieu of a List A, List B, or a List C document if one is presented by an employee. Examples of receipts and other documents that serve as proof of temporary employment eligibility that employers can accept are the following:

- All employees may provide receipts for the application of a replacement document where the document was lost, stolen, or destroyed, which can be a List A, List B, or List C document. The employee must present the actual document for which the receipt was issued within 90 days from the date of hire, or for reverification, within 90 days from the date employment authorization expires.

- Lawful permanent residents may provide the arrival portion of a Form I-94 or I-94A containing a temporary I-551 stamp and photograph as a receipt for a List A document. When the stamp expires, or if the stamp has no expiration, one year from date of issue the employee must present the actual Form I-551 (*Permanent Resident Card*, or green card).

- Refugees may provide the departure portion of Form I-94 or I-94A with an unexpired refugee admission stamp, as a receipt for a List A document. Within 90 days from the date of hire or for reverification, the employee must present an unexpired *Employment Authorization Document* (Form I-766), or combination of a valid List B document and an unrestricted Social Security card.

A receipt indicating that an individual has applied for initial work authorization or for an extension of expiring work authorization is **not** acceptable proof of employment eligibility on the Form I-9. Additionally, receipts are never acceptable if employment lasts less than three business days.

List of Acceptable Documents

All acceptable documents must be unexpired.

List A

The following documents are included in List A, which establish both identity and employment authorization:

♦ U.S. Passport or U.S. Passport Card.

♦ *Permanent Resident Card* or *Alien Registration Receipt Card* (Form I-551).

♦ Foreign passport that contains a temporary I-551 stamp or temporary I-551 printed notation on a machine-readable immigrant visa.

♦ *Employment Authorization Document* that contains a photograph (Form I-766).

♦ In the case of a nonimmigrant alien authorized to work for a specific employer incident to status, a foreign passport with Form I-94 or Form I-94A bearing the same name as the passport and containing an endorsement of the alien's nonimmigrant status, as long as the period of endorsement has not yet expired and the proposed employment is not in conflict with any restrictions or limitations identified on the form.

♦ Passport from the Federated States of Micronesia (FSM) or the Republic of the Marshall Islands (RMI) with Form I-94 or Form I-94A indicating nonimmigrant admission under the Compact of Free Association Between the United States and the FSM or RMI.

List B

The following documents may also be used to establish identity:

♦ Driver's license or ID card issued by a state or outlying possession of the United States provided it contains a photograph or information such as name, date of birth, gender, height, eye color, and address.

♦ ID card issued by federal, state, or local government agencies or entities, provided it contains a photograph or information such as name, date of birth, gender, height, eye color, and address.

♦ School ID card with a photograph.

♦ Voter's registration card.

♦ U.S. military card or draft record.

♦ Military dependent's ID card.

♦ U.S. Coast Guard Merchant Mariner Card.

♦ Native American tribal document.

♦ Driver's license issued by a Canadian government authority.

♦ For individuals under age 18 who are unable to present any of the aforementioned documents:

  • School record or report card.

  • Clinic, doctor, or hospital record.

  • Day care or nursery school record.

List C

The following documents may be used to establish employment authorization:

♦ Social Security account number card other than one that specifies on the face that the issuance of the card does not authorize employment in the United States.

♦ *Certification of Birth Abroad* issued by the Department of State (Form FS-545).

♦ *Certification of Report of Birth* issued by the Department of State (Form DS-1350).

♦ Original or certified copy of a birth certificate issued by a state, county, municipal authority, or outlying possession of the United States bearing an official seal.

♦ Native American tribal document.

♦ *U.S. Citizen ID Card* (Form I-197).

♦ *Identification Card for use of a Resident Citizen in the United States* (Form I-179).

♦ Employment authorization document issued by the DHS.

Employee's Failure to Produce Documents

Employers should terminate an employee who fails to produce the required documents for employment within three business days of the date employment begins.

An employee may present a receipt for a replacement document (in the case of lost, stolen, or destroyed documents) as a temporary solution. However, if an employee has presented a receipt for a replacement document, the employee must produce the actual document within 90 days of the start of employment. Employers must apply these practices uniformly to all employees because without uniformity a termination may be grounds for a discrimination lawsuit.

Reverifying Employment Authorization for Current Employees

Employers must reverify the employment eligibility no later than when an employee's work authorization expires. For reverification, Section 3 of the Form I-9 may be used; however, if Section 3 has already been used for a previous reverification or update, a new Form I-9 must be used. If a new form is used, the employee's name should be written in Section 1, Section 3 must be completed, and employers must retain the new form with the original.

Employee Requirements

The employee must present a document that shows either an extension of the employee's initial employment authorization or new work authorization. If the employee cannot provide proof of current work authorization (for example, any document from List A or List C, including an unrestricted Social Security card), then such individual cannot continue to be employed.

Employer Requirements

If an employer rehires an employee who previously completed a Form I-9, the employer may **reverify** on the employee's original Form I-9 (or on a new Form I-9 if Section 3 of the original was used) if both of the following apply:

♦ The employer rehires the employee within three years of the initial date of hire.

♦ The employee's previous grant of work authorization expired, but the employee is currently eligible to work on a different basis or under a new grant of work authorization than when the original Form I-9 was completed.

To reverify, employers must:

♦ Record the date of rehire.

♦ Record the document title, number, and expiration date (if any) of any document(s) presented.

♦ Sign and date Section 3.

♦ If using a new Form I-9, write the employee's name in Section 1.

If an employer rehires an employee who has previously completed a Form I-9, the employer may **update** on the employee's original Form I-9 or on a new Form I-9 if both:

♦ The employee is rehired within three years of the initial date of hire.

♦ The employee is still eligible to work on the same basis as when the original Form I-9 was completed.

To update, employers must:

♦ Record the date of rehire.

♦ Sign and date Section 3.

♦ If using a new Form I-9, write the employee's name in Section 1.

Employers always have the option of completing Sections 1 and 2 of a new Form I-9 rather than completing Section 3 when rehiring employees.

Retaining Forms

Employers must retain completed Forms I-9 for all employees for three years from the date of hire or one year after the date employment is terminated, whichever is later. These forms may be retained in paper, microfilm, microfiche, or electronically.

To store Form I-9 electronically, employers may use any electronic recordkeeping, attestation, and retention system that complies with the DHS standards, which includes most off-the-shelf computer programs and commercial automated data processing systems. However, the system must not be subject to any agreement that would restrict access to and use of it by an agency of the United States.

Note: The form must be available for inspection by authorized U.S. government officials (for example, authorized officers of the DHS, the U.S. Department of Labor, or the Office of Special Counsel for Immigration Related Unfair Employment Practices). Employers will be provided with three business days' notice prior to an inspection of the employers' retained Forms I-9.

Paper Retention

The Form I-9 can be signed and stored in paper format. However, employers must reproduce a complete, blank Form I-9 and ensure that the employee receives the instructions for completing the form. When copying or printing the paper Form I-9, employers may reproduce the two-sided form by making either double-sided or single-sided copies. Employers may retain completed paper forms onsite or at an off-site storage facility for the required retention period, as long as the employer is able to present the Form I-9 within three days of an audit request from the DHS, the Office of Special Counsel for Immigration Related Unfair Employment Practices, or the Department of Labor officers.

Microform Retention

Employers may store Form I-9 on microfilm or microfiche. To do so, employers should:

♦ Select film stock that will preserve the image and allow accessibility and usability for the entire retention period, which in certain circumstances could be upward of 20 years, depending on the employee and the business.

♦ Use well-maintained equipment to create and view microfilms and microfiche that provides a high degree of legibility and readability, and has the ability to reproduce legible and readable paper copies. The DHS officers must have immediate access to clear, readable documents should they need to inspect the forms.

♦ Place the required indexes either in the first frames of the first roll of film or in the last frames of the last roll of film of a series. For microfiche, place them in the last frames of the last microfiche or microfilm jacket of a series.

Retaining Copies of Documentation Provided by Employee

Employers may choose to copy or scan documents presented by an employee, which the employer must retain with the employee's Form I-9. However, retaining copies of documentation does not relieve the employer from the requirement to fully complete Section 2 of the Form I-9. If an employer chooses to retain copies of employee documentation, the employer may not just do so for employees of certain national origins or citizenship statuses, or the employer may be in violation of antidiscrimination laws.

Electronic Methods

Employers must utilize electronic completion, retention, and electronic signatures so long as they abide by specific stipulations.

Electronic Retention

Employers may complete or retain the Form I-9 in an electronic generation or storage system that includes all of the following:

♦ Reasonable controls to ensure the integrity, accuracy, and reliability of the electronic storage system.

♦ Reasonable controls designed to prevent and detect the unauthorized or accidental creation of, addition to, alteration of, deletion of, or deterioration of an electronically completed or stored Form I-9, including the electronic signature if used.

♦ An inspection and quality assurance program evidenced by regular evaluations of the electronic generation or storage system, including periodic checks of electronically stored Form I-9, including the electronic signature if used.

♦ A retrieval system that includes an indexing system that permits the identification and retrieval for viewing or reproducing of relevant documents and records maintained in an electronic storage system. The requirement to maintain an indexing system does not require that a separate electronically stored documents and records description database be maintained if comparable results can be achieved without a separate description database.

♦ The ability to reproduce legible and readable hardcopies.

An employer that completes or retains Forms I-9 electronically may use one or more electronic generation or storage systems so long as the systems meet the aforementioned requirements and remain available as long as legally required. Additionally, employers may implement new electronic storage systems provided those new systems are consistent with the law and existing Forms I-9 are retained in a system that remains fully accessible.

Note: The USCIS provides a fillable-printable Form I-9 from its Web site, which may be electronically generated or retained.

Electronic Signatures

Employers and employees may choose to fill out a paper Form I-9 and scan and upload the signed form to retain it electronically. Once the employer has securely stored the Form I-9 in electronic format, the employer may destroy the original paper Form I-9. If the Form I-9 is completed electronically using an electronic signature, the employer must implement a system for capturing electronic signatures that allows signatories to acknowledge that they have read the attestation, and that can associate an electronic signature with an electronically completed Form I-9. In addition, the system must:

- Affix the electronic signature at the time of the transaction.

- Create and preserve a record verifying the identity of the person producing the signature.

- Upon request of the employee, provide a printed confirmation of the transaction to the person providing the signature.

If an employer chooses to use an electronic signature to complete Form I-9, but does not comply with the aforementioned standards, the DHS will determine that the Form I-9 has not been properly completed and is in violation of the law.

Electronic Copies

An employer may, but is not required to, copy or make an electronic image of a document presented by an individual solely for the purpose of complying with the verification requirements. If a copy or electronic image is made, it must either be retained with the Form I-9 or stored with the employee's records and be retrievable.

System Documentation and Inspection

For each electronic generation or storage system used, an employer must maintain, and make available upon request, complete descriptions of all of the following:

- The electronic generation and storage system, including all procedures relating to its use.

- The indexing system, which permits the identification and retrieval for viewing or reproducing of relevant records maintained in an electronic storage system.

- The business processes that create, modify, and maintain the retained Form I-9, and establish the authenticity and integrity of the forms, such as audit trails.

Note: Insufficient documentation is a violation of the law.

At the time of an inspection by a U.S. agency, the person or entity required to retain completed Forms I-9 must:

- Retrieve and reproduce (including printing copies on paper, if requested) only the Forms I-9 electronically retained in the electronic storage system and supporting documentation specifically requested by a U.S. agency, along with associated audit trails. Generally, an *audit trail* is a record showing who has accessed a computer system and the actions performed within or on the computer system during a given period of time.

♦ Provide a requesting U.S. agency with the resources (for instance, the appropriate hardware and software, personnel, and documentation) necessary to locate, retrieve, read, and reproduce (including paper copies) any electronically stored Forms I-9, any supporting documents, and their associated audit trails, reports, and other data used to maintain the authenticity, integrity, and reliability of the records.

♦ Provide, if requested, any reasonably available or obtainable electronic summary file(s), such as a spreadsheet, containing all of the information fields on all of the electronically stored Forms I-9 requested by the U.S. agency.

Security

If an employer retains Forms I-9 electronically, the employer must implement a records security program that:

♦ Ensures that only authorized personnel have access to electronic records.

♦ Provides for backup and recovery of records to protect against information loss.

♦ Ensures that employees are trained to minimize the risk of unauthorized or accidental alteration or erasure of electronic records.

♦ Ensure that whenever the electronic record is created, completed, updated, modified, altered, or corrected, a secure and permanent record is created that establishes the date of access, the identity of the individual who accessed the electronic record, and the particular action taken.

If an employer's action or inaction results in the alteration, loss, or erasure of electronic records and the employer knew or reasonably should have known that the action or inaction could have that effect, the employer is in violation the law.

Penalties

The DHS is authorized to enforce the employment eligibility verification requirements. Employers who fail to properly complete, retain, and/or make available for inspections Forms I-9 may incur civil penalties between $110 and $1,100 for each employee for which the form was incorrect.

Knowingly Hire

Employers who knowingly hired unauthorized aliens or knowingly continue to employ aliens who have become unauthorized to work in the United States may be ordered to cease and desist from such activity and pay the following for each unauthorized alien:

♦ **First Offense:** Between $375 and $3,200.

♦ **Second Offense:** Between $3,200 and $6,500.

♦ **Subsequent Offenses:** Between $4,300 and $11,000.

The DHS will consider an employer to have ***knowingly hired*** an unauthorized alien if the employer uses a contract, subcontract, or exchange, which is entered into, renegotiated, or extended to obtain the labor of an alien and knows the alien is not authorized to work in the United States.

Liability is also imposed when an employer uses a contract or subcontract — renegotiated or extended — to obtain the labor of an alien and knew the alien was not authorized to work in the United States.

Criminal Penalties

Criminal penalties of up to $3,000 in fines and imprisonment for up to six months are possible when a pattern or practice of knowingly employing unauthorized workers is demonstrated. People who use fraudulent identification or employment eligibility documents or documents that were lawfully issued to another person, or those who make a false statement or attestation for purposes of satisfying the employment eligibility verification requirements may be fined, imprisoned for up to five years, or both.

Document Fraud

If a DHS investigation reveals that an individual has knowingly committed or participated in acts relating to document fraud, the DHS may take action. The DHS will issue a *Notice of Intent to Fine* when it intends to impose penalties and persons who receive this notice may request a hearing before an administrative law judge. If the DHS does not receive a request for a hearing within 30 days, it will impose the penalty and issue a Final Order, which is final and cannot be appealed.

Individuals found by the DHS or an administrative law judge to have violated § 274C of the Immigration and Nationality Act (INA) may be ordered to:

- Cease and desist from such behavior.

- Pay a civil penalty as follows:

  - **First Offense:** Between $375 and $3,200 for each fraudulent document that is the subject of the violation.

  - **Subsequent Offenses:** Between $3,200 and $6,500 for each fraudulent document that is the subject of the violation.

Good Faith Defense

If an employer can demonstrate that they have, in good faith, complied with the Form I-9 requirements, then the employer has established a good faith defense with respect to a charge of knowingly hiring an unauthorized alien, unless the government can show that the employer had actual knowledge of the unauthorized status of the employee.

A good faith attempt to comply with the paperwork requirements of the law may be adequate notwithstanding a technical or procedural failure to comply, unless the employer has failed to correct the violation within 10 days after notice from the DHS, or the employer is engaging in a pattern or practice of violations.

SAVE Program

The Systematic Alien Verification for Entitlements (SAVE) Program is an intergovernmental, information-sharing initiative designed to aid federal, state, and local benefit-issuing agencies and licensing bureaus in verifying a noncitizen applicant's immigration status, thus ensuring that only eligible noncitizens receive public benefits and licenses. The SAVE Program is responsible for administering programs involving customer access to information contained in the Verification Information System (VIS) database. The VIS database is a nationally accessible database of selected immigration status information on over 60 million records.

The SAVE Program also administers employment verification pilot programs that enable employers to quickly and easily verify the work authorization of their newly-hired employees. The USCIS is the DHS agency responsible for administering the SAVE Program.

The SAVE Program is the **only** means available for employers to verify the information that their newly-hired employees have provided on the Form I-9 attesting that they are authorized to work in the United States.

Form I-9 Frequently Asked Questions

Q   Why was a revised Form I-9 released?

A   The revised Form I-9 reflects changes made to the list of documents acceptable for Form I-9 in accordance with the DHS recent interim final rule. The rule furthers DHS's ongoing effort to increase the security of the employment authorization verification process. The new rule:

- Required that all documents presented during the verification process be unexpired.

- Eliminated List A identity and employment authorization documentation Forms I-688, I-688A, and I-688B (*Temporary Resident Card* and outdated *Employment Authorization Card*).

- Added foreign passports containing certain machine-readable immigrant visas to List A.

- Added to List A as evidence of identity and employment authorization valid passports for citizens of the Federated States of Micronesia (FSM) and the Republic of the Marshall Islands (RMI), along with Form I-94 or Form I-94A indicating nonimmigrant admission under the Compact of Free Association Between the United States and the FSM or RMI.

- Made technical updates.

Q   What is the difference between the revised Form I-9 and the prior form?

A   The biggest difference in the revised Form I-9 is that all documents presented during the verification process must be unexpired. Other than several technical updates, the following documents have been added or removed:

Two documents were added to List A (Documents that Establish Both Identity and Employment Authorization) on the List of Acceptable Documents:

- A temporary I-551 printed notation on a machine-readable immigrant visa in addition to the foreign passport with a temporary I-551 stamp.

- A passport from the Federated States of Micronesia (FSM) or the Republic of the Marshall Islands (RMI) with a valid Form I-94 or Form I-94A indicating nonimmigrant admission under the Compact of Free Association Between the United States and the FSM or RMI.

Although prior regulations refer to temporary I-551 stamps, the Department of State for several years has been affixing machine-readable immigrant visas (MRIVs) that contain a pre-printed temporary I-551 notation in the foreign passports of aliens immigrating to the United States. DHS therefore is updating the regulations to reflect this alternate temporary I-551 document with the pre-printed temporary I-551 notation on MRIVs.

Additionally, under both the pre-existing compacts with the FSM and the RMI, and the compacts as amended, most citizens of the FSM and RMI are eligible for admission to the United States as nonimmigrants. Such citizens of the FSM and RMI have the privilege of residing and working in the United States. Amendments to the compacts include provisions that eliminated the need for citizens of the FSM and RMI to obtain an *Employment Authorization Document* (Form I-766). By adding to List A the FSM and RMI passports, with a valid Form I-94 or I-94A, citizens of the FSM and RMI will be able to use their passports in the I-9 process without the need to obtain a separate Form I-766.

Three documents were removed from List A of the List of Acceptable Documents:

- Form I-688, *Temporary Resident Card.*

- Form I-688A, *Employment Authorization Card.*

- Form I-688B, *Employment Authorization Card.*

Q Where may employers obtain a copy of the revised Form I-9?

A An informational copy of the revised Form I-9 and the interim final rule can be found in the Federal Register. The revised Form I-9 for use by the public can also be downloaded from the USCIS Web site. Paper copies of Form I-9 can be ordered by calling USCIS at 800-870-3676.

Q Why are expired documents not permitted to be presented?

A The DHS wants to ensure that documents presented for use in the Form I-9 process are valid and reliably establish both identity and employment authorization. Expired documents may not portray a valid status, and are also prone to tampering and fraudulent use. This change takes into account the limits placed on these documents by their issuing authorities. If a document does not contain an expiration date, such as a Social Security card, it is considered unexpired.

Q Why is only one type of Employment Authorization Document left in List A?

A Forms I-688, I-688A, and I-688B are older employment authorization documents. These are no longer issued and have now expired.

Q In Section 1 (Employee Information and Verification) of the revised Form I-9, an employee can now attest to being either a citizen or noncitizen national of the United States. Who is a noncitizen national?

A *Noncitizen nationals* are persons born in American Samoa, certain former citizens of the former Trust Territory of the Pacific Islands, and certain children of noncitizen nationals born abroad.

Q Where can the revised Form I-9 and the employer handbook (M-274) be obtained?

A An informational copy of the revised Form I-9 and the interim final rule are available online through the Federal Register and on the Immigration Forms page of the USCIS Web site. The *Handbook for Employers, Instructions for Completing the Form I-9* (M-274) is being updated to reflect the revision to the Form I-9 and will be available on the USCIS Web site in the near future. Employers who do not have computer access can order USCIS forms by calling the toll-free forms line at 800-870-3676. USCIS forms and information on immigration laws, regulations, and procedures are also available by calling the National Customer Service Center toll-free at 800-375-5283.

Q May employers accept documents that were on the Form I-9 but are not now?

A No. As of April 3, 2009, employers may only accept documents listed on the List of Acceptable Documents on the revised Form I-9. When an employee must be reverified because their employment authorization has expired, employers should ensure that they use the revised Form I-9 with its new List of Acceptable Documents. An employer may not reverify the employee by completing Section 3 – Updating and Reverification, on a previous version of the Form I-9.

Q Are there any changes in the way the revised Form I-9 is completed?

A No. The revised form should be completed in exactly the same way as the old one. Employers should be mindful of changes to the types of documents that they may accept in Section 2 – Employer Review and Verification.

Q Is the Form I-9 available in different languages?

A Form I-9 is available in English and Spanish. However, only employers in Puerto Rico may have employees complete the Spanish version for their records. Employers in the 50 states and other U.S. territories may use the Spanish version as a translation guide for Spanish-speaking employees, but must complete the English version and keep it in their records. Employees may also use or ask for a translator/preparer to assist them in completing the form.

Q **Are employers in Puerto Rico required to use the Spanish version of the Form I-9?**

A No. Employers in Puerto Rico may use either the Spanish or the English version of the revised Form I-9 to verify employees.

Q **When should employers begin using the revised version of the Form I-9?**

A Employers must use the revised Form I-9 for all new hires (and reverifications). Employers may use the Form I-9 with the revision date of either August 7, 2009 or February 2, 2009. The revision dates are located on the bottom right-hand portion of the form.

Q **Must employers complete the revised version of the Form I-9 for all employees or just the new ones?**

A Employers only need to complete the revised version of the Form I-9 for new employees. Employers should not be completing Forms I-9 for existing employees. However, employers must use Form I-9 when their employees require reverification.

E-Verify

E-Verify (formerly known as the Basic Pilot Employment Eligibility Verification Program) is an Internet based system operated by the Department of Homeland Security (DHS) in partnership with the Social Security Administration (SSA) that allows participating employers to electronically verify the employment eligibility of the newly hired employees and the validity of their Social Security numbers. E-Verify electronically compares information contained on the Form I-9 with records contained in the SSA and DHS databases to help employers verify identity and employment eligibility of newly hired employees.

Methods of Access

E-Verify offers the following four possible access methods:

- ♦ **Employer Access.** This access method allows a company to electronically verify the employment eligibility of its own newly hired employees.

- ♦ **Designated Agent.** The Designated Agent access method allows an individual or company to act on behalf of other companies to verify the employment eligibility of newly hired employees.

- ♦ **Corporate Administrator.** The Corporate Administrator access method allows companies to create, manage, and oversee E-Verify accounts for multiple offices or locations. This access method is designed for companies that have a need to oversee multiple locations.

- ♦ **Web Services Access for Designated Agents or Employers.** The Web Services Designated Agents access method requires a company to develop software that interfaces with E-Verify to perform employment eligibility verifications of newly hired employees. The company's software will extract data from its existing system or an electronic Form I-9 and transmit the information to government records. If a company chooses this option, the company is sent the Web Services Interface Control Agreement (ICA). The ICA contains the information used to develop and test the software interface. Both Designated Agents and Employers are eligible to use this access method.

Registration

Unless required by state law, an employer's participation in E-Verify is voluntary. Registration for E-Verify can be completed at *https://e-verify.uscis.gov/enroll*, which provides instructions for completing the registration process. Users may access the Web-based access methods using any Internet-capable Windows-based personal computer and a Web browser of Internet Explorer 5.5, Netscape 4.79 or higher (with the exception of Netscape 7.0), or Mozilla Firefox 1.0 or higher. To participate, an employer must also register online and accept the electronic *E-Verify Memorandum of Understanding* (MOU) that details the responsibilities of the SSA, the DHS, and the employer.

Rules of Use

All employers participating in E-Verify **must**:

- ◆ Follow E-Verify procedures for all new hires while enrolled/participating in E-Verify.

- ◆ Notify all job applicants of E-Verify participation.

- ◆ Clearly display both the English and Spanish *Notice of E-Verify Participation* and the *Right to Work* poster(s).

- ◆ Complete the Form I-9, *Employment Eligibility Verification*, for each newly hired employee before creating a case in E-Verify.

- ◆ Ensure that all Form I-9 List B identity documents have a photograph.

- ◆ Create a case for all newly hired employees no later than the third business day after they start work for pay.

- ◆ Obtain a Social Security number from all newly hired employees.

- ◆ Provide employees the opportunity to contest a Tentative Nonconfirmation (TNC).

- ◆ Allow newly hired employees to start and continue working during the E-Verify verification process, even if they receive a TNC.

- ◆ Ensure that all personally identifiable information is safeguarded.

All employers participating in E-Verify **must not**:

- ◆ Use E-Verify to prescreen applicants for employment.

- ◆ Check employment eligibility for employees hired before their company signed the MOU.

- ◆ Take any adverse action against an employee based upon a case result unless E-Verify issues a Final Nonconfirmation.

- ◆ Specify or request which Form I-9 documentation a newly hired employee must use.

- ◆ Use E-Verify to discriminate against any job applicant or new hire on the basis of national origin, citizenship, or immigration status.

- ◆ Selectively verify work authorization for newly hired employees.

- ◆ Share any user ID and/or password.

Verification Process

The verification process consists of a series of steps, including:

- Entering Form I-9 information.

- Creating a case and receiving results.

- Photo matching.

- Ensuring that the information found in E-Verify matches with the employee's Form I-9.

- Closing the case.

Once a newly hired employee has completed the Form I-9, the employer may create a case in E-Verify by entering the information on the Form I-9 in E-Verify. An E-Verify case must be created no later than the end of three business days after the employee begins work for pay (the three-day rule). The date entered into the hire date field in E-Verify is usually the date the employee began work for pay. This is also the date that was entered into the Section 2 Certification on Form I-9.

The E-Verify case can be created before the employee begins work for pay as long as the employee has accepted an offer of employment and Form I-9 is complete. In these situations, the date entered into the hire date field in E-Verify is the date the case in E-Verify is created. A future date cannot be entered in the hire date field.

The information entered into E-Verify is checked against SSA and DHS records. Once a case is created, a result is displayed. If the information entered does not immediately match SSA or DHS records, users must check the information to confirm if the information entered is correct. The initial case result depends on the information retrieved from SSA and DHS records.

There are three possible initial case results:

- **Employment Authorized.** An initial case result of 'Employment Authorized' means that the information entered into E-Verify matched DHS and/or SSA records and that E-Verify verified the work eligibility for the employee entered. However, a case that is 'Employment Authorized' is incomplete until it is closed. In some cases E-Verify generates a case result of 'Employment Authorized,' but the name returned in E-Verify does not match exactly with the name on Form I-9. This happens when the information matches but there are name variations in the DHS records. The employee's name must be reviewed before a final case result can be determined to ensure that the case result belongs to the intended employee. E-Verify allows for a name review by requesting a name review.

- **SSA Tentative Nonconfirmation (SSA TNC).** An SSA TNC indicates that the employee's Social Security information could not be verified. A TNC does not mean that the employee is not authorized to work; therefore, the employee should continue to work during the verification process. Employers must privately notify an employee of the TNC as soon as possible and refer the employee to the SSA so the employee may contest the response. Employers must print, sign, and date the SSA TNC Notice and likewise, instruct the employee to sign and date the notice. Employers must then:

  - Keep the original signed SSA TNC Notice on file with Form I-9.

  - Provide a copy of the signed SSA TNC Notice to the employee.

  - Take action based on whether the employee decides to contest or not contest the SSA TNC.

The employee has eight federal government workdays from the date of referral to SSA through E-Verify to contest their case by visiting a local SSA office. If an employee decides to contest the case, employers must refer the employee to an SSA field office through specific steps provided for in E-Verify. Employers may not terminate, suspend, delay training, withhold or lower pay, or take any other adverse action against an employee based on the employee's decision to contest a TNC or while the case is still pending with the SSA.

♦ **DHS Verification in Process.** A case result of 'DHS Verification in Process' indicates that the information provided information does not match DHS records. The case is automatically referred to DHS for further verification but no action is required by the user. DHS will respond to most of these cases within 24 hours, although some responses may take up to three federal government workdays.

An employee must be notified as soon as possible if a DHS TNC results, which occurs when the information submitted to E-Verify does not initially match with DHS records. By agreeing to participate in E-Verify, employers must also:

- Provide the employee with a copy of the notice (signed and dated).

- Review the notice with the employee and explain the right to contest or not contest the DHS TNC.

If the employee contests the DHS TNC, the employer must confirm through E-Verify the employee's decision to contest or not contest the case. An employee that chooses to contest the case must be referred to the DHS. E-Verify generates a DHS Referral Letter that must be provided to the employee. Employers must also instruct the employee that they have eight federal government workdays to contact DHS. A DHS Referral will provide one of the following case results:

- Employment authorized.

- DHS final nonconfirmation.

- DHS case in continuance.

- DHS no show.

Each case result requires different actions or steps to continue or close the case.

Employers may not terminate, suspend, delay training, withhold or lower pay, or take any other adverse action against an employee based on the employee's decision to contest a TNC or while a case is still pending with the DHS.

Employers must close every case created in E-Verify. Each case is closed by using a Close Case Statement as provided by E-Verify.

Note: Employers have additional responsibilities depending upon the result of the initial verification. For example, some employers may be required to review and update employee data where the SSA found a discrepancy in the information received in the E-Verify referral. Further information may be obtained from the E-Verify Web site located within the USCIS Web site (*www.uscis.gov*).

Three-Day Rule

An E-Verify case is considered late if it is created later than the third business day after the employee first started work for pay. If the case is created late, the redesigned E-Verify will ask why, and employers can either select one of the reasons provided or enter their own. The reasons provided are:

- ♦ Awaiting Social Security Number.
- ♦ Technical Problems.
- ♦ Audit Revealed that New Hire Was Not Run.
- ♦ Federal Contractor with FAR E-Verify Clause verifying an existing employee (this reason is displayed only to an organization enrolled in E-Verify as a "Federal Contractor with FAR E-Verify Clause").
- ♦ Other.

Employers that select "other" must provide a reason, which must be 200 or fewer characters and should not include any personally identifiable or sensitive information (such as Social Security numbers).

Because there is overlap between Form I-9, *Employment Eligibility Verification*, and E-Verify requirements, the following charts identify compliance with the three-day rule as it applies to E-Verify.

Completing Form I-9 and E-Verify

Completing Form I-9 and E-Verify		
To comply with the law	**Complete Form I-9**	**Create a Case in E-Verify**
The earliest an employer may:	The employee has accepted an offer of employment.	♦ The employee has accepted an offer of employment; and ♦ Form I-9 is complete.
The latest an employer may:	The third business day after the employee started work for pay.	♦ The third business day after the employee started work for pay; and ♦ Form I-9 is complete.

If the employee starts work for pay on Monday, the third business day after the employee started work for pay is Thursday (assuming all days were business days for the employer). The first day the employee starts work for pay is not included in the three business day calculation.

Determining the E-Verify Hire Date

The term *hire date* in E-Verify may be confusing because its meaning can vary depending on:

- ♦ When the employee starts work for pay.
- ♦ The date the case is created in E-Verify.

Determining the E-Verify Hire Date	
If an employer creates the case in E-Verify:	**Then the E-Verify hire date is:**
Before the employee starts work for pay.	The date the case in E-Verify is created.
On or after the employee starts work for pay.	The date the employee started work for pay.

E-Verify does not allow employers to select a future date as the hire date, so if the employee has not yet started work for pay, the E-Verify hire date is always the date the case was created in E-Verify. The reason for this is because the three-day rule for E-Verify purposes is associated with the date the employee starts work for pay. An E-Verify case is not late as long as it is created no later than the third business day after the employee started work for pay — it does not matter how many days have passed between the employee completing Form I-9 and the employer creating the case in E-Verify.

For federal contractors with the FAR E-Verify clause and that are creating a case for an existing employee, the hire date is always the date the employee first started work for pay. It does not matter if the employee completes a new Form I-9 — the hire date is always the Section 2 certification date of the original Form I-9.

Federal Contractors

As of September 8, 2009, federal contractors and subcontractors who are awarded a new contract that includes the Federal Acquisition Regulation (FAR) E-Verify clause are required to use E-Verify to verify the employment of:

- All persons hired during the contract term by the contractor to perform employment duties within the United States. For purposes of E-Verify, the *United States* is defined as the 50 states, the District of Columbia, Guam, Puerto Rico, and the U.S. Virgin Islands.

- All current employees of the federal contractor who perform contract services for the federal government within the United States.

The E-Verify clause must be placed in prime federal contracts with a period of performance that is 120 days or more and a value that exceeds the simplified acquisition threshold ($100,000). Additionally, at least some portion of the work under the contract must be performed in the United States. The rule only covers subcontractors if a prime contract includes the clause. For subcontracts that flow from those prime contracts, the rule extends the E-Verify requirement to subcontracts for services or for construction with a value over $3,000.

All employers, including federal contractors, may enroll in E-Verify at any time without waiting for the applicability date. However, when a contractor wins the bid on a federal contract that contains the FAR E-Verify clause, the contractor and any covered subcontractors on the project are required to enroll in the E-Verify Program within 30 calendar days of the contract or subcontract award date.

Exemptions

All of the following prime contracts are exempt from the E-Verify requirement:

- Contracts that include only commercially available off-the-shelf (COTS) items (or minor modifications to a COTS item) and related services.

- Contracts valued at less than the simplified acquisition threshold ($100,000).

- Contracts less than 120 days.

- Contracts where all work is performed outside the United States.

Photo Matching

Photo matching is an automatic part of creating a case in E-Verify that prompts users to compare an employee's photo ID with a photo displayed on the E-Verify screen. This helps ensure that the documents provided are valid.

The photo matching step occurs automatically when a case is created for an employee who has presented a *Permanent Resident Card* (Form I-551) or an *Employment Authorization Document* (Form I-766) for their Form I-9 documentation. When the employee presents either of these two documents and the Form I-9 information entered by the employer matches DHS records, the employee's photo automatically displays on the E-Verify screen. A copy of the employee's document must be obtained in order to match the photos.

Posting Requirements

Upon enrollment, all employers are required to clearly display both the English and Spanish *Notice of E-Verify Participation* and the *Right to Work* poster(s). Notices that cannot be displayed must be printed and distributed to every job applicant.

Frequently Asked Questions

Q Why should employers consider participating in E-Verify?

A E-Verify is an easily accessible means for employers to electronically verify the employment eligibility of their newly hired employees. E-Verify helps eliminate Social Security mismatch letters, improves the accuracy of wage and tax reporting, protects jobs for authorized U.S. workers, and assists U.S. employers in maintaining a legal workforce.

Q How do employers register for participation in E-Verify?

A Employers can register for E-Verify at *https://e-verify.uscis.gov/enroll*, which provides instructions for completing the registration process. At the end of the registration process, the employer will be required to sign a MOU that provides the terms of agreement between the employer, the SSA, and the USCIS. An employee who has signatory authority for the employer can sign the MOU.

Q Can one site verify every new hire where an employer has multiple hiring sites?

A Yes. One site may verify new hires at all sites. When registering, the individual at the site that will be verifying new hires should select "multiple site registration" and give the number of sites per states it will be verifying.

Q Are employers with multiple hiring sites required to enroll every site in E-Verify?

A No. Employers with multiple hiring sites may choose which sites to enroll.

Q What is the required timeframe for conducting an employment eligibility check on a newly hired employee?

A The earliest the employer may initiate a query is after an individual accepts an offer of employment and after the employee and employer complete the Form I-9. The employer must initiate the query no later than the end of three business days after the new hire's actual start date. An employer may initiate the query before a new hire's actual start date. However, the employer may not prescreen applicants and may not delay training or an actual start date based upon a tentative nonconfirmation or a delay in the receipt of a confirmation of employment authorization. An employee should not face any adverse employment consequences based upon an employer's use of E-Verify unless a query results in a final nonconfirmation. In addition, an employer cannot use an employment authorization response to speed up an employee's start date. This would be unfair treatment to use E-Verify results to accelerate employment for this employee compared to another who may have received a tentative nonconfirmation. Employers must verify employees in a nondiscriminatory manner and may not schedule the timing of queries based upon the new hire's national origin, citizenship status, race, or other characteristic that is prohibited by U.S. law.

Q **My company was just awarded a federal contract and the E-Verify rule is now in effect. When is my company required to enroll in E-Verify?**

A When a contractor wins the bid on a federal contract that contains the FAR E-Verify clause, the contractor and any covered subcontractors on the project are required to enroll in the E-Verify Program within 30 calendar days of the contract or subcontract award date.

Q **The FAR rule requires federal contractors to use E-Verify for both new hires and existing employees who work on a new federal contract. Does the federal government use E-Verify (or otherwise verify work authorization) for both new hires and existing employees?**

A Yes. Federal agencies verify employment eligibility of new and existing employees. In most instances, the federal government goes well beyond an E-Verify check to confirm work eligibility as part of a variety of suitability and other background checks that are required to be performed on federal employees. These background checks may include, but are not limited to:

- FBI fingerprint and name check.

- Checks against local law enforcement databases.

- Written inquiries to educational institutions, previous employers, and neighbors.

- Credit check.

- Checks to verify name, Social Security number, date of birth, and citizenship.

- Checks against other federal and private data sources.

For all new hires, federal agencies are required to use E-Verify to verify their employment eligibility. Additionally, many new hires also subsequently undergo background investigations and an FBI fingerprint and name check.

For both new and existing employees, federal agencies are required by Homeland Security Presidential Directive – 12, "Policy for a Common Identification Standard for Federal Employees and Contractors" to follow certain credentialing standards prior to issuing personal identity verification cards. These standards include conducting a background investigation which includes verification of name, date of birth, and Social Security number (among other data points) against federal and private data sources. This includes a check against SSA records to validate Social Security numbers. Additionally, these standards require verification of work authorization for non-U.S. citizens against federal immigration databases.

Antidiscrimination Enforcement

Employers are prohibited from discriminating when hiring or promoting on the basis of national origin citizenship status. If an investigation reveals that an employer has engaged in unfair immigration-related employment practices under the Immigration and Nationality Act (INA), the Office of Special Counsel for Immigration-Related Unfair Employment Practices may take action. An employer will be ordered to stop the prohibited practice and may be ordered to take one or more corrective steps, including:

♦ Hire or reinstate, with or without backpay, individuals directly injured by the discrimination.

♦ Post notices to employees about their rights and about employers' obligations.

♦ Educate all personnel involved in hiring and in complying with the employer sanctions and antidiscrimination laws about the requirements of these laws.

The court may award attorney's fees to prevailing parties, other than the United States, if it determines that the losing parties' argument is without foundation in law and fact. Employers who commit citizenship status or national origin discrimination in violation of the antidiscrimination provisions of the INA may also be ordered to pay a civil penalty as follows:

♦ **First Offense:** Between $375 and $3,200 for each individual discriminated against.

♦ **Second Offense:** Between $3,200 and $6,500 for each individual discriminated against.

♦ **Subsequent Offenses:** Between $4,300 and $16,000 for each individual discriminated against.

Employers who commit document abuse in violation of the antidiscrimination provisions of the INA may similarly be ordered to pay between $110 and $1,100 for each individual discriminated against.

If an employer is found to have committed national origin discrimination under Title VII of the Civil Rights Act of 1964 (Title VII), the employer may be ordered to stop the prohibited practice and to take one or more corrective steps, including:

♦ Hire, reinstate, or promote with backpay and retroactive seniority.

♦ Post notices to employees about their rights and about the employer's obligations.

♦ Remove incorrect information, such as a false warning, from an employee's personnel file.

Under Title VII, compensatory damages may also be available where intentional discrimination is found. Damages may be available to compensate for actual monetary losses, for future monetary losses, and for mental anguish and inconvenience. Punitive damages may be available if the employer acted with malice or reckless indifference. The employer may also be required to pay attorneys' fees, expert witness fees, and court costs.

Employment of Non-U.S. Citizens

Temporary Employment
H-1B Classification

The H-1B is a nonimmigrant classification used by an alien and provides temporary admission to the United States for professionals in specialty occupations. A *specialty occupation* is an occupation that requires theoretical and practical application of a body of highly specialized knowledge. The individual must posses at the minimum a bachelor's degree in the specific specialty prior to consideration for entry into the occupation.

For example, mathematics, physical sciences, medicine, health, and the arts are recognized specialty occupations. With exceptions, an alien may hold H-1B status for a maximum of six consecutive years. H-1B status will be initially granted for a term of three years and may be renewed for an additional three years. After six years, an alien must remain outside the United States for one year before another H-1B petition may be approved. Certain aliens working on Department of Defense projects may remain in H-1B status for 10 years.

H-1B status requires a sponsoring U.S. employer. To obtain the H-1B work visa employers must file a *Labor Condition Application* (LCA) with the U.S. Department of Labor through the department's LCA online system. Employers with physical disabilities that prohibit them from filing electronic applications may submit a written request to file their labor condition applications by U.S. Mail. Employers must then file the certified LCA with a Form I-129, *Petition for Nonimmigrant Worker*, plus an accompanying fee.

An LCA certifies the following:

♦ The employer is offering the position at the higher of the actual wage or the prevailing wage and with working conditions that will not adversely affect similarly employed U.S. workers.

♦ The employer will offer benefits to H-1B employees on the same basis as similarly employed U.S. workers.

♦ There is not a strike or lockout involving the position at the place of employment.

♦ The employer has provided notice of the petition to any bargaining representative or has posted notice of the petition in conspicuous locations at the place of employment if there is no bargaining representative.

♦ The employer will provide a copy of the completed, required application to the H-1B workers.

Complaints

The U.S. Department of Labor has established procedures for receipt, investigation, and disposition of complaints filed by any party.

If the department finds the complaints to be justified, it may sanction the employer in the following ways:

♦ Impose a civil monetary fine from $1,000 to $35,000 per violation, depending upon the type and severity of the violation.

♦ Bar the employer from having H-1B petitions approved for at least one year.

♦ Impose possible reinstatement and backpay awards.

Note: Only 65,000 aliens may be issued a visa or otherwise provided H-1B status for fiscal years 2004 and beyond.

Employ American Workers Act and H-1B Certification

Employers who receive funds through the Troubled Asset Relief Program (TARP) or under § 13 of the Federal Reserve Act (covered funding) are required to abide by additional requirements before they may hire a foreign national to work in the H-1B specialty occupation category. The Employ American Workers Act (EAWA), signed into law by President Obama as part of the American Recovery and Reinvestment Act on February 17, 2009, was enacted to ensure that companies receiving covered funding do not displace U.S. workers. Under this legislation, any company that received covered funding and seeks to hire new H-1B workers is considered an H-1B dependent employer. All H-1B dependent employers must make additional attestations to the U.S. Department of Labor when filing the Labor Condition Application (LCA).

The EAWA applies to any LCA and/or H-1B petition filed on or after February 17, 2009 involving any employment by a new employer, including concurrent employment and regardless of whether the beneficiary is already in H-1B status. The EAWA also applies to new hires based on a petition approved before February 17, 2009 if the H-1B employee had not actually commenced employment before that date.

The EAWA does not apply to either of the following:

♦ H-1B petitions seeking to change the status of a beneficiary already working for the employer in another work-authorized category.

♦ H-1B petitions seeking an extension of stay for a current employee with the same employer.

Employers are advised to comply with either of the following in order to avoid processing delays:

♦ Use a version of Form I-129, *Petition for a Nonimmigrant Worker*, with a revision date of March 11, 2009 or later and ensure that Question A.1.d on the H-1B *Data Collection and Filing Fee Exemption Supplement* has been properly answered.

♦ Submit page 13 of Form I-129 with a revision date of March 11, 2009 or later and answer Question A.1.d. if using a version of Form I-129 with a revision date earlier than March 11, 2009.

A valid LCA must be on file with U.S. Department of Labor at the time the H-1B petition is filed with the USCIS. Consequently, if the petitioner indicates on its petition that it is subject to the EAWA, but the Labor Condition Application does not contain the proper attestations relating to H-1B dependent employers, the USCIS will deny the H-1B petition.

EAWA and H-1B Frequently Asked Questions

Q **What does the EAWA do?**

A The EAWA prevents a company from displacing U.S. workers when hiring H-1B specialty occupation workers if the company received funds through the TARP, Pub. L. 110-343, Div. A, Title I, or under § 13 of the Federal Reserve Act (covered funding). Under the EAWA, any company that has received covered funding and seeks to hire H-1B workers is considered to be an H-1B dependent employer. An H-1B dependent employer must make all of the following additional attestations to the U.S. Department of Labor when filing an LCA:

- It has taken good faith steps to recruit U.S. workers (workers other than nonimmigrant aliens) using industry-wide standards and offering compensation that is at least as great as those offered to the H-1B nonimmigrant. U.S. workers are U.S. citizens or nationals, lawful permanent resident aliens, refugees, asylees, or other immigrants authorized to be employed in the United States.

- It has offered the job to any U.S. worker who applies and is equally or better qualified for the job that is intended for the H-1B nonimmigrant.

- It has not displaced any U.S. worker employed within the period beginning 90 days prior to the filing of the H-1B petition and ending 90 days after its filing. A U.S. worker is displaced if the worker is laid off from a job that is essentially the equivalent of the job for which an H-1B nonimmigrant is sought.

- It will not place an H-1B worker to work for another employer unless it has inquired whether the other employer has displaced or will displace a U.S. worker within 90 days before or after the placement of the H-1B worker.

Q **Are the EAWA requirements permanent?**

A No. The EAWA took effect on Feb. 17, 2009, and will sunset two years from the date of enactment.

Q **Which specific U.S. companies are affected?**

A The USCIS is working with the Department of the Treasury and other relevant agencies to identify companies that have received covered funding. However, the USCIS expects companies seeking to hire H-1B workers to know whether or not they have received covered funding and act accordingly with respect to hiring an H-1B nonimmigrant. The EAWA only applies to U.S. companies that received covered funding and want to hire new H-1B workers. The normal exception to the H-1B dependent employer requirements that an H-1B nonimmigrant is exempt from the dependency calculation if the individual earns a salary of at least $60,000 or has a master's degree or higher is not available to companies that have received covered funding.

Q   What is an H-1B nonimmigrant?

A   An H-1B nonimmigrant is a foreign national who comes to the United States temporarily to work in a specialty occupation. A specialty occupation position is one that generally requires a bachelor's or higher degree and specialized knowledge. A U.S. employer seeking to hire H-1B workers must file an LCA with the Department of Labor and submit the certified LCA with the H-1B petition with the USCIS. There also is an annual limit of 65,000 on H-1B workers, subject to certain exceptions. Additionally, the first 20,000 H-1B petitions filed on behalf of aliens who have earned a U.S. master's degree or higher are exempt from the fiscal year cap.

Q   To which H-1B hires does the EAWA apply?

A   The EAWA applies to any hire taking place on or after February 17, 2009 and before February 17, 2011. The EAWA defines *hire* as an employer permitting a new employee to commence a period of employment; specifically, the introduction of a new employee to the employer's U.S. workforce.

The EAWA applies to:

- Any LCA or petition filed on or after February 17, 2009 involving any employment by a new employer, including concurrent employment and regardless of whether the beneficiary is already in H-1B status.

- New employment (for instance, hires) based on a petition approved before February 17, 2009, if the H-1B employee had not actually commenced employment before that date.

The EAWA does not apply to:

- A petition to extend the H-1B status of a current employee with the same employer.

- A petition seeking to change the status of a current U.S. work-authorized employee to H-1B status with the same employer.

Q   How is the USCIS implementing the EAWA?

A   The EAWA affects the current LCA process administered by the Department of Labor and the USCIS petition process for companies seeking H-1B workers. Companies subject to the EAWA will now need to make new statements regarding recruitment and hiring of U.S. workers.

H-2A Certification

The H-2A Program allows U.S. employers to bring foreign nationals to the United States to fill temporary agricultural jobs for which U.S. workers are not available. An ***employer*** is a person (including any individual, partnership, association, corporation, cooperative, firm, joint stock company, trust, or other organization with legal rights and duties) that:

- Has a place of business (physical location) in the U.S. and a means by which it may be contacted for employment.

- Has an employer relationship (such as the ability to hire, pay, fire, supervise, or otherwise control the work of an employee) with respect to an H-2A worker or a worker in corresponding employment.

- Possesses, for purposes of filing an *Application for Temporary Employment Certification*, a valid federal Employer Identification Number (EIN).

H-2A nonimmigrant classification applies to aliens seeking to perform agricultural labor or services of a temporary or seasonal nature in the United States on a temporary basis. A U.S. employer (or an association of U.S. agricultural producers named as a joint employer) must file a Form I-129, *Petition for Nonimmigrant Worker* on a prospective worker's behalf.

To qualify for H-2A nonimmigrant classification:

♦ The job offered must be of a temporary or seasonal nature.

♦ The employer must demonstrate that there are not sufficient U.S. workers who are able, willing, qualified, and available to do the temporary work.

♦ The employer must show that the employment of H-2A workers will not adversely affect the wages and working conditions of similarly employed U.S. workers.

♦ Generally, a single, valid temporary labor certification from the U.S. Department of Labor must be submitted with the H-2A petition; however, a limited exception to this requirement exists in certain emergent circumstances.

H-2A petitions may only be approved for nationals of countries that the Secretary of Homeland Security has designated, with the concurrence of the Secretary of State, as eligible to participate in the H-2A Program. The list of H-2A eligible countries is published in a notice in the Federal Register by the DHS on a rolling basis. Designation of countries on the H-2A list of eligible countries will be valid for one year from publication.

Effective January 19, 2010, nationals from the following countries are eligible to participate in the H-2A Program: Argentina, Australia, Belize, Brazil, Bulgaria, Canada, Chile, Costa Rica, Croatia, Dominican Republic, Ecuador, El Salvador, Ethiopia, Guatemala, Honduras, Indonesia, Ireland, Israel, Jamaica, Japan, Lithuania, Mexico, Moldova, the Netherlands, New Zealand, Nicaragua, Norway, Peru, Philippines, Poland, Romania, Serbia, Slovakia, South Africa, South Korea, Turkey, Ukraine, United Kingdom, and Uruguay.

A national from a country not on the list may only be the beneficiary of an approved H-2A petition if the Secretary of Homeland Security determines that it is in the U.S. interest for that alien to be the beneficiary of such a petition.

Rate of Pay

Employers must pay all covered workers at least the highest of the following applicable wage rates in effect at the time work is performed:

♦ The adverse effect wage rate (AEWR).

♦ The applicable prevailing wage.

♦ The agreed-upon collective bargaining rate.

♦ The federal or state statutory minimum wage.

Wages may be calculated on the basis of hourly or piece-rates of pay. The piece-rate must be no less than the piece-rate prevailing for the activity in the area of intended employment and on a pay period basis must average no less than the highest required hourly wage rate.

Period of Stay

Generally, the USCIS may grant H-2A classification for the period of time authorized on the temporary labor certification (usually authorized for no longer than one year) and the H-2A classification may be extended for qualifying employment in increments of up to one year. The maximum period of stay in H-2A classification is three years.

An individual who has held H-2A nonimmigrant status for a total of three years is required to depart and remain outside the United States for an uninterrupted period of three months before seeking readmission as an H-2A nonimmigrant.

Family of H-2A Workers

Any spouse and unmarried children under 21 years of age of an H-2A worker may seek admission in H-4 nonimmigrant classification. Family members in H-4 nonimmigrant classification may not engage in employment in the United States.

Employer Requirements

Three-Fourths Guarantee

H-2A employers must provide a three-fourths guarantee to offer each covered worker. A three-fourths guarantee is a guarantee of employment for a total number of hours equal to at least 75 percent of the workdays in the contract period. For example, if a contract is for a 10-week period, during which a normal workweek is specified as 6 days a week, 8 hours per day, the worker would need to be guaranteed employment for at least 360 hours (10 weeks x 48 hours/week = 480 hours x 75 percent = 360).

If during the total work contract period the employer does not offer sufficient workdays to the H-2A or corresponding workers to reach the total amount required to meet the three-fourths guarantee, the employer must pay such workers the amount they would have earned had they actually worked for the guaranteed number of workdays. Wages for the guaranteed 75 percent period will be calculated at no less than the rate stated in the work contract.

Housing, Meals, Transportation, and Expenses

Employers must provide:

- ◆ Housing at no cost to H-2A workers and to workers in corresponding employment who are not reasonably able to return to their residence within the same day. If the employer elects to secure rental (public) accommodations for such workers, the employer is required to pay all housing-related charges directly to the housing's management. Employer-provided or secured housing must meet all applicable safety standards.

- ◆ Each covered worker with three meals per day, at no more than a Department of Labor-specified cost, or to furnish free and convenient cooking and kitchen facilities where workers can prepare their own meals.

- ◆ Daily transportation between the workers' living quarters and the employer's worksite at no cost to covered workers living in employer-provided housing. Employer-provided transportation must meet all applicable safety standards, be properly insured, and be operated by licensed drivers.

Additionally, if not previously advanced or otherwise provided, the employer must reimburse workers for reasonable costs incurred for inbound transportation and subsistence costs once the worker completes 50 percent of the work contract period.

Note: The FLSA applies independently of H-2A and prohibits covered employees from incurring costs that are primarily for the benefit of the employer if such costs take the employee's wages below the FLSA minimum wage. Upon completion of the work contract, the employer must either provide or pay for the covered worker's return transportation and daily subsistence.

Written Disclosure

No later than the time at which an H-2A worker applies for a visa and no later than on the first day of work for workers in corresponding employment, the employer must provide each worker a copy of the work contract — in a language understood by the worker — which describes the terms and conditions of employment. In the absence of a separate written work contract, the employer must provide each worker with a copy of the job order that was submitted to and approved by the Department of Labor. The work contract must include all of the following:

♦ The beginning and ending dates of the contract period as well as the location(s) of work.

♦ Any and all significant conditions of employment, including payment for transportation expenses incurred, housing and meals to be provided (and related charges), specific days workers are not required to work (i.e., Sabbath, federal holidays).

♦ The hours per day and the days per week each worker will be expected to work.

♦ The crop(s) to be worked and/or each job to be performed.

♦ The applicable rate(s) for each crop/job.

♦ That any required tools, supplies, and equipment will be provided at no charge.

♦ That workers' compensation insurance will be provided at no charge.

♦ Any deductions not otherwise required by law. All deductions must be reasonable. Any deduction not specified is not permissible.

Required Notification

Petitioners of H-2A workers must notify the USCIS within two workdays in the case of any of the following:

♦ **No show:** An alien who fails to report to work within five workdays of the employment start date on the H–2A petition or within five workdays of the start date established by the petitioner, whichever is later.

♦ **Absconder:** An H-2A worker who fails to report for work for a period of five consecutive workdays without the consent of the employer.

♦ **Termination:** An H-2A worker who is terminated prior to the completion of agricultural labor or services for which the worker was hired.

♦ **Early Completion:** An H-2A worker who completes the agricultural labor or services for which the worker was hired more than 30 days earlier than the date specified in the H-2A petition.

A *workday* is the period between the time on any particular day when an employee commences their principal activity and the time on that day at which the employee ceases such principal activity or activities.

Posting and Recordkeeping Requirements

Employers must post and maintain in a conspicuous location at the place of employment, a poster provided by the Secretary of Labor in English, and, to the extent necessary, any language common to a significant portion of the workers if they are not fluent in English, which sets out the rights and protections for workers.

Employers must keep accurate records of the number of hours of work offered each day by the employer and the hours actually worked each day by the worker. On or before each payday (which must be at least twice monthly), each worker must be given an hours and earnings statement showing:

♦ Hours offered.

♦ Hours actually worked.

♦ Hourly rate and/or piece-rate of pay. If piece-rates are used, the units produced daily.

♦ Total earnings for the pay period and all deductions from wages.

H-2A Labor Contractors

An H-2ALC is a person who meets the definition of an employer under the H-2A Program and does not otherwise qualify as a fixed-site employer or an agricultural association (or an employee of a fixed-site employer or agricultural association) and who is engaged in any one of the following activities in regards to any worker subject to the H-2A regulations:

♦ Recruiting.

♦ Soliciting.

♦ Hiring.

♦ Employing.

♦ Furnishing.

♦ Housing.

♦ Transporting.

While H-2A does not require labor contractors to register as such with the Department of Labor, any person who is subject to the Migrant Seasonal Protection Act (MSPA) as a Farm Labor Contractor (FLC) must register with the department and be issued an FLC Certificate of Registration prior to engaging in any farm labor contracting activity. In their H-2A applications, H-2ALCs required to be registered under MSPA are obligated to provide their respective MSPA FLC Certificate of Registration number and to identify the farm labor contracting activities they are authorized to perform.

In addition to meeting the same assurances and obligations as any other H-2A employer, H-2ALCs must fulfill the following requirements:

♦ List the name and location of each fixed-site agricultural business to which they expect to provide H-2A workers, the dates of each employment opportunity, and a description of the crops and activities the workers are expected to perform at each area of intended employment.

♦ Submit a copy of each work contract agreement between the H-2ALC and the agricultural business to which they expect to provide workers.

♦ Provide proof that all housing and transportation if provided or secured by the fixed-site employer complies with applicable safety and health standards.

♦ Obtain and submit the original surety bond with the H-2A application.

The surety bond must be written to cover liability incurred during the term of the work contract period listed on the H-2A application and must remain in effect for a period of at least two years from the expiration date of the labor certification. H-2ALCs must obtain the surety bond in the following amounts:

♦ $5,000 for a labor certification with fewer than 25 employees.

♦ $10,000 for a labor certification with 25 to 49 employees.

♦ $20,000 for a labor certification with 50 to 74 employees.

♦ $50,000 for a labor certification with 75 to 99 employees.

♦ $75,000 for a labor certification with 100 or more employees.

H-2B Certification

The H-2B certification allows employers to hire foreign workers to temporarily come to the United States and perform temporary nonagricultural work. Typically, H-2B workers fill labor needs in occupational areas such as construction, health care, landscaping, lumber, manufacturing, food service/processing, and resort/hospitality services. This temporary employment may be one-time, seasonal, peak load, or intermittent, and the job must be for a year or less, although there may be extraordinary circumstances where the temporary services or labor might last longer than one year. If there are unforeseen circumstances where the employer's need exceeds one year, a new application for temporary labor certification is required for each period beyond one year. However, an employer's seasonal or peak load need of longer than 10 months, which is not of a recurring nature, will not be accepted.

A job opportunity is considered temporary under the H-2B classification if the employer's need for the duties to be performed is temporary, whether or not the underlying job is permanent or temporary. It is the nature of the employer's need, not the nature of the duties, which is controlling. Additionally, part-time employment does not qualify as employment for temporary labor certification under the H-2B Program. Only full-time employment can be certified.

A temporary labor certification is valid only for the number of aliens, the area of intended employment, the specific occupation and duties, the period of time, and the employer specified on Form ETA 750. The total number of employees who may be issued H-2B visas per fiscal year **may not** exceed 66,000.

Application

Every H-2B application must include both of the following:

♦ An original ETA Form 9142 and Appendix B.1, signed and dated by the employer, which includes a detailed statement of the employer's temporary need.

♦ A Recruitment Report.

Recruitment Report and Further Processing

Effective October 1, 2009, and according to 8 C.F.R. 655 Subpart A, employers must conduct pre-filing recruitment. However, in order to do so, the employer must first obtain a prevailing wage by filing ETA Form 9141 with the National Processing Center (NPC). Prefiling recruitment includes all of the following:

♦ Submitting a job order to the State Workforce Agency (SWA) serving the area of intended employment.

♦ Publishing two print advertisements, one of which must be on a Sunday.

♦ Contacting the local union as a recruitment source if the employer is a party to a collective-bargaining agreement in the occupation in which H-2B workers are sought.

The job order must be posted at the SWA for no less than 10 days. Applicants must be considered for no fewer than two calendar days after the last date on which the job order was posted and no fewer than five calendar days after the last newspaper advertisement appeared.

Employers must also prepare and sign a recruitment report summarizing the results of the effort. The report must include all of the following information:

♦ Identification of each recruitment source by name.

♦ The name, address, and telephone number of each U.S. worker who applied for the job.

♦ Explanation of the lawful job-related reasons for not hiring each U.S. worker.

The U.S. Department of Labor's Wage and Hour Division is responsible for enforcement of this program.

If the Department of Labor denies certification, the employer may appeal to the Board of Alien Labor Certification Appeals.

Employee Rights

Employers seeking to employ H-2B workers must attest that the workers will be paid at least the prevailing wage for the occupation in the area of intended employment. Additionally, worker-protection provisions that apply to U.S. workers (such as the Fair Labor Standards Act) cover nonimmigrant H-2B workers.

If the employer terminates the H-2B worker's employment prior to the end of the contract period, the employer is liable for the H-2B worker's return transportation.

Recordkeeping and Reporting

Employers must retain, for a period of three years, the recruitment report, resumes (if any) of H-2B workers, and evidence of contact with each U.S. worker who applied or was referred.

Employers are also obligated to report, to both the Office of Foreign Labor Certification and DHS, the early termination of an H-2B worker or that worker's abscondment or abandonment prior to the end date of the contract period. The report must be made within two days of termination or discovery of the abandonment or abscondment.

E-1 (Trader) and E-2 (Investor)

E-1 and E-2 visas allow foreign nationals to come to the United States to conduct trade or to manage substantial investments. Treaty traders or investors are individuals from a country with a treaty of commerce and navigation or equivalent agreement with the United States.

The requirements for traders to conduct business in the United States are as follows:

- The applicant must be a national of a treaty country.
- The trading firm for which the applicant is coming to the United States must have the nationality of the treaty country.
- The international trade must be "substantial" in the sense that there is a sizable and continuing volume of trade.
- The trade must be principally between the United States and the treaty country, which is defined to mean that more than 50 percent of the international trade involved must be between the United States and the country of the applicant's nationality.
- Trade means the international exchange of goods, services, and technology. Title of the trade items must pass from one party to the other.
- The applicant must be employed in a supervisory or executive capacity, or possess highly specialized skills essential to the efficient operation of the firm. Ordinary skilled or unskilled workers do not qualify.

The requirements for investors to conduct business in the United States are as follows:

- The investor, either a real or corporate person, must be a national of a treaty country.
- The investment must be substantial. It must be sufficient to ensure the successful operation of the enterprise. The percentage of investment for a low-cost business enterprise must be higher than the percentage of investment in a high-cost enterprise.

- The investment must be a real operating enterprise. Speculative or idle investment does not qualify. Uncommitted funds in a bank account or similar security are not considered an investment.

- The investment may not be marginal. It must generate significantly more income than just to provide a living to the investor and family, or it must have a significant economic impact in the United States.

- The investor must have control of the funds, and the investment must be at risk in the commercial sense. Loans secured with the assets of the investment enterprise are not allowed.

- The investor must be coming to the United States to develop and direct the enterprise. If the applicant is not the principal investor, then they must be employed in a supervisory, executive, or highly specialized skill capacity. Ordinary skilled and unskilled workers do not qualify.

L-1 Intra-Company Transferee

The L-1 visa category is for intra-company transferee.

L-1A Managerial or Executive Transferee

The L-1A nonimmigrant classification enables a U.S. employer to transfer an executive or manager from one of its affiliated foreign offices to one of its offices in the United States. This classification also enables a foreign company which does not yet have an affiliated U.S. office to send an executive or manager to the United States with the purpose of establishing one. The employer must file Form I-129, *Petition for a Nonimmigrant Worker*, on behalf of the employee.

General Qualifications of the Employer and Employee

To qualify for L-1A Intra-Company Transferee classification, the employer must meet both of the following:

- Have a qualifying relationship with a foreign company (parent company, branch, subsidiary, or affiliate, collectively referred to as qualifying organizations).

- Currently be, or will be, doing business as an employer in the United States and in at least one other country directly or through a qualifying organization for the duration of the beneficiary's stay in the United States as an L-1. While the business must be viable, there is no requirement that it be engaged in international trade.

Doing business means the regular, systematic, and continuous provision of goods and/or services by a qualifying organization and does not include the mere presence of an agent or office of the qualifying organization in the United States and abroad.

Also to qualify, the named employee must meet both of the following:

- Generally have been working for a qualifying organization abroad for one continuous year within the three years immediately preceding his or her admission to the United States.

- Be seeking to enter the United States to render services in an executive or managerial capacity to a branch of the same employer or one of its qualifying organizations.

Executive capacity generally refers to the employee's ability to make decisions of wide latitude without much oversight. *Managerial capacity* generally refers to the ability of the employee to supervise and control the work of professional employees and to manage the organization, or a department, subdivision, function, or component of the organization. It may also refer to the employee's ability to manage an essential function of the organization at a high level, without direct supervision of others.

L-1B Specialized Knowledge

The L-1B nonimmigrant classification enables a U.S. employer to transfer a professional employee with specialized knowledge relating to the organization's interests from one of its affiliated foreign offices to one of its offices in the United States. This classification also enables a foreign company which does not yet have an affiliated U.S. office to send a specialized knowledge employee to the United States to help establish the office. The employer must file Form I-129, *Petition for a Nonimmigrant Worker*, on behalf of the employee.

General Qualifications of the Employer and Employee

To qualify for L-1B Specialized Knowledge classification in this category, the employer must meet both of the following:

♦ Have a qualifying relationship with a foreign company (parent company, branch, subsidiary, or affiliate, collectively referred to as qualifying organizations).

♦ Currently be, or will be, doing business as an employer in the United States and in at least one other country directly or through a qualifying organization for the duration of the beneficiary's stay in the United States as an L-1. While the business must be viable, there is no requirement that it be engaged in international trade.

Doing business means the regular, systematic, and continuous provision of goods and/or services by a qualifying organization and does not include the mere presence of an agent or office of the qualifying organization in the United States and abroad.

Also to qualify, the named employee must meet both of the following:

♦ Generally have been working for a qualifying organization abroad for one continuous year within the three years immediately preceding his or her admission to the United States.

♦ Be seeking to enter the United States to render services in a specialized knowledge capacity to a branch of the same employer or one of its qualifying organizations.

Specialized knowledge means special knowledge possessed by an individual of the petitioning organization's product, service, research, equipment, techniques, management, or other interests and its application in international markets, or expertise in the organization's processes and procedures. Such knowledge is beyond the ordinary and not commonplace within the industry or the petitioning organization — the employee must be more than simply skilled or familiar with the employer's interests.

Individual L Petitions

Requirements for an individual L petition are as follows:

♦ The employer abroad and the petitioning U.S. organization must be properly related (for example, a parent-subsidiary, sibling, joint venture, or affiliate relationship).

♦ The transferee must have worked in a managerial, executive, or specialized knowledge capacity for the employer abroad for at least one continuous year within the three years immediately preceding entry into the United States.

♦ The transferee must be coming to work for the U.S. employer in a managerial, executive, or specialized knowledge capacity for a temporary period.

In addition, to obtain an L-1B visa for specialized personnel continuing employment with an international firm or corporation, the employer must justify its need for the transferee's specialized knowledge in the United States.

Blanket L Petitions

A blanket L petition simplifies the process of later filing for individual L-1A and L-1B workers. A U.S. employer, who will be the single representative between the USCIS and the qualifying organizations, must file the blanket L petition.

Requirements for a blanket L petition are as follows:

- ◆ The employer and each of the entities must be engaged in commercial trade or services.
- ◆ The employer has an office in the United States conducting business for at least one year.
- ◆ The employer has three or more domestic and foreign branches, subsidiaries, or affiliates.
- ◆ The employer meets one of the following:
  - Has obtained at least 10 L-1 approvals during the previous 12 months.
  - Has U.S. subsidiaries or affiliates with combined annual sales of at least $25 million.
  - Has a U.S. workforce of at least 1,000 employees.

O-1 Extraordinary Ability Nationals

An O-1 nonimmigrant visa is for the individual who possesses extraordinary ability in the sciences, arts, education, business, or athletics or who has a demonstrated record of extraordinary achievement in the motion picture or television industry and has been recognized nationally or internationally for those achievements.

The O nonimmigrant classification is commonly referred to as:

- ◆ **O-1A:** individuals with an extraordinary ability in the sciences, education, business, or athletics (not including the arts, motion pictures, or television industry).
- ◆ **O-1B:** individuals with an extraordinary ability in the arts or extraordinary achievement in motion picture or television industry.
- ◆ **O-2:** individuals who will accompany an O-1 artist or athlete to assist in a specific event or performance. For an O-1A, the O-2's assistance must be an "integral part" of the O-1A's activity. For an O-1B, the O-2's assistance must be "essential" to the completion of the O-1B's production. The O-2 worker has critical skills and experience with the O-1 that cannot be readily performed by a U.S. worker and which are essential to the successful performance of the O-1.
- ◆ **O-3:** individuals who are the spouse or children of O-1's and O-2's.

The O visa may be issued for three years; thereafter the USCIS will determine time necessary to accomplish the initial event or activity in increments of up to one year.

Permanent Employment

The Immigration and Naturalization Act (INA) provides a yearly minimum of 140,000 employment-based immigrant visas divided into five preference classifications.

The first, second, and third priority workers receive 28.6 percent of the yearly worldwide limit of visas.

- ◆ **Employment First Preference (E1): Priority Workers.** The subcategories of priority workers are as follows:
  - Persons of extraordinary ability.

- Outstanding professors and researchers.

- Certain multinational executives and managers.

♦ **Employment Second Preference (E2): Professional Holding Advanced Degrees and Persons of Exceptional Ability.** Qualified employees must be members of the professions holding advanced degrees (or the equivalent) or have exceptional ability in sciences, arts, professions, or business that will substantially benefit the national economy of the United States. The requirements of a job offer and labor certification may be waived if a determination is made that it would be in the national interest to admit an applicant for lawful permanent residence.

♦ **Employment Third Preference (E3): Skilled Workers, Professionals, and Other Workers.** This category includes the following:

- *Skilled workers* are persons capable of performing a job requiring at least two years of experience or training.

- *Professionals* are members of professions who hold baccalaureate degrees (for example, bachelors' degrees in engineering, computer science, or economics) and are members of a profession.

- *Unskilled workers* are persons petitioning for classification as unskilled labor that requires less than two years of training or experience.

♦ **Employment Fourth Preference (E4): Certain Special Immigrants.** Fourth Preference applicants must be the beneficiary of an approved *Petition for Amerasian, Widow(er), or Special Immigrant*, Form I-360, with the exception of the category Certain Employees or Former Employees of the U.S. Government Abroad. Labor certification is not required for any of the Certain Special Immigrants subgroups. Special Immigrants receive 7.1 percent of the yearly worldwide limit of employment-based immigrant visas. -This category includes, but is not limited to, the following subgroups:

- Broadcasters in the United States employed by the International Broadcasting Bureau of the Broadcasting Board of Governors or a grantee of such organization.

- Religious workers coming to carry on the vocation of a minister of religion, to work in a professional capacity in a religious vocation, or to work for a tax-exempt organization affiliated with a religious denomination.

- Overseas employees of the U.S. government, consulate, and embassy offices.

- Former employees of the Panama Canal Company and their families.

- Iraqi and Afghan interpreters/translators who have worked directly with the U.S. Armed Forces or under Chief of Mission authority as a translator/interpreter for a period of at least 12 months and meet requirements.

- Foreign medical graduates.

- Retired employees of international organizations and their family members.

- Certain members of the U.S. Armed Forces.

♦ **Employment Fifth Preference (E5): Immigrant Investors.** A Fifth Preference applicant must file an *Immigrant Petition by Alien Entrepreneur*, Form I-526, with USCIS. Labor certification is not required for Immigrant Investors. To qualify as an Immigrant Investor, a foreign citizen must invest between U.S. $500,000 and $1,000,000, depending on the unemployment rate in the geographical area, in a commercial enterprise in the United States which creates at least 10 new full-time jobs for U.S. citizens, permanent residents, or other lawful immigrants, not including the investor and the investor's family. Immigrant Investors receive 7.1 percent of the yearly worldwide limit of employment-based immigrant visas.

Wages

Wages offered to the alien must meet or exceed the prevailing wage for that occupation. All job requirements must be reasonable and minimum, as provided by federal and applicable state laws.

Recruiting

The employer must demonstrate to the U.S. Department of Labor the attempts to recruit U.S. workers. The recruiting attempts must also adhere to the following requirements:

♦ A job order must run for a minimum of 30 days through the National Employment Service recruitment system.

♦ The employer must conspicuously post the job opening on the premises for at least 10 days.

♦ The employer must place an advertisement for the job in a newspaper of general circulation or in a professional, trade, or ethnic publication — whichever will elicit responses from U.S. workers as follows:

• If published in a newspaper of general circulation, the advertisement must be published for at least three consecutive days.

• If published in a professional, trade, or ethnic publication, the advertisement must be published in the next published edition.

An employer may request a reduction in recruitment efforts upon the demonstration of the employer's adequate testing of the labor market with no success at recruiting a U.S. worker. An employer's request for a reduction in recruitment must contain the following:

♦ Evidence that the employer conducted substantial recruitment during the six months immediately prior to the filing of the labor certification.

♦ The employer has made good faith efforts to recruit U.S. workers for the job.

If a union represents the organization's employees in the occupational classification and geographical areas for which aliens are sought, employers are required to notify a union representative or bargaining agent that such alien labor certification application has been filed.

If no such bargaining agent or representative exists, the employer must post a notice conspicuously on the premises informing all employees that an alien labor certification application has been filed.

No-Match Letters and Safe Harbor

The No-Match Rule and safe harbor procedures were rescinded by the DHS on October 7, 2009 (the final rule became effective November 6, 2009). The No-Match Rule attempted to establish procedures that employers could follow if they received a SSA no-match letter or notice from the DHS that call into question work eligibility information provided by employees.

Contact Information

Office of the Citizenship and Immigration Services Ombudsman

Department of Homeland Security
245 Murray Lane
Mail Stop 1225
Washington, DC 20528

Internet: *www.dhs.gov/xabout/structure/editorial_0482.shtm*

Systematic Alien Verification for Entitlements Program

USCIS, SAVE Program
490 L'Enfant Plaza East SW, Suite 7112
Washington, DC 20529-2620

Telephone: 888-464-4218 or 800-741-5023
Fax: 202-358-7867

U.S. Citizenship and Immigration Services

National Customer Service Center (NCSC)
Toll-Free: 800-375-5283
Forms Line (Toll-Free): 800-870-3676
Internet: *www.uscis.gov*

USCIS Office of Business Liaison

111 Massachusetts Avenue, NW, 6th Floor
Washington, DC 20539

Telephone (Toll-Free): 800-357-2099
Fax: 202-272-1865

U.S. Department of Homeland Security

245 Murray Lane, SW
Washington, DC 20528

Citizen Line: 202-282-8000
Internet: *www.dhs.gov*

U.S. Immigration and Customs Enforcement

500 12th Street, SW
Washington, DC 20536

Telephone: 866-DHS-2-ICE
Internet: *www.ice.gov*

Illinois Law

Right to Privacy in the Workplace Act

According to the Illinois Right to Privacy in the Workplace Act, located at 820 Ill. Comp. Stat. §§ 55/12 and 55/15, prior to choosing to voluntarily enroll in any Employment Eligibility Verification System, including the federal E-Verify program and the Basic Pilot program, employers are urged to consult the Illinois Department of Labor's Web site for current information on the accuracy of E-Verify and to review and understand an employer's legal responsibilities relating to the use of the voluntary E-Verify program.

The Illinois Department of Labor (IDOL) will post on its Web site information or links to information from the U.S. Government Accountability Office, Westat, or a similar reliable source independent of the Department of Homeland Security (DHS) regarding all of the following:

♦ The accuracy of the E-Verify databases.

♦ The approximate financial burden and expenditure of time that use of E-Verify requires from employers.

♦ An overview of an employer's responsibilities under federal and state law relating to the use of E-Verify.

Upon initial enrollment in an Employment Eligibility Verification System, an employer enrolled in E-Verify or any other Employment Eligibility Verification System must attest to both of the following under penalty of perjury:

♦ The employer has received the Basic Pilot or E-Verify training materials from the DHS, and all employees who will administer the program have completed the Basic Pilot or E-Verify Computer Based Tutorial (CBT).

♦ The employer has posted the notice from DHS indicating that the employer is enrolled in the Basic Pilot or E-Verify program and the antidiscrimination notice issued by the Office of Special Counsel for Immigration-Related Unfair Employment Practices (OSC), Civil Rights Division, U.S. Department of Justice in a prominent place that is clearly visible to both prospective and current employees.

The required attestation form is prescribed by the IDOL and is available on the IDOL Web site. Employers must maintain the signed original of the attestation form prescribed by the IDOL, as well as all CBT certificates of completion, and make them available for inspection or copying by the IDOL at any reasonable time.

Violations

It is a violation of the act for an employer enrolled in an Employment Eligibility Verification System, including the E-Verify program and the Basic Pilot program, to:

♦ Fail to display the notices supplied by the DHS and OSC in a prominent place that is clearly visible to both prospective and current employees.

♦ Allow any employee to use an Employment Eligibility Verification System prior to having completed the CBT.

♦ Fail to take reasonable steps to prevent an employee from circumventing the requirement to complete the CBT by assuming another employee's E-Verify or Basic Pilot user identification or password.

- Use the Employment Eligibility Verification System to verify the employment eligibility of job applicants prior to hiring or to otherwise use the Employment Eligibility Verification System to screen individuals prior to hiring and prior to the completion of a Form I-9.

- Terminate an employee or take any other adverse employment action against an individual prior to receiving a final nonconfirmation notice from the Social Security Administration or the DHS.

- Fail to notify an individual, in writing, of the employer's receipt of a tentative nonconfirmation notice, of the individual's right to contest the tentative nonconfirmation notice, and of the contact information for the relevant government agency or agencies that the individual must contact to resolve the tentative nonconfirmation notice.

- Fail to safeguard the information contained in the Employment Eligibility Verification System, and the means of access to the system (such as passwords and other privacy protections). An employer must ensure that the system is not used for any purpose other than employment verification of newly hired employees and must ensure that the information contained in the system and the means of access to the system are not disseminated to any person other than employees who need such information and access to perform the employer's employment verification responsibilities.

Any claim that an employer refused to hire, segregated, or acted with respect to recruitment, hiring, promotion, renewal, or employment, selection for training or apprenticeship, discharge, discipline, tenure, or terms, privileges, or conditions of employment without following the procedures of the Employment Eligibility Verification System, including the Basic Pilot and E-Verify programs, may be brought under the Illinois Human Rights Act.

Additionally, it is a violation for an individual to falsely pose as an employer in order to enroll in an Employment Eligibility Verification System or for an employer to use an Employment Eligibility Verification System to access information regarding an individual who is not an employee of the employer.

Additional Provisions

Neither the state, any of its political subdivisions, nor any unit of local government, including a home rule unit, may require any employer to use an Employment Eligibility Verification System:

- As a condition of receiving a government contract.
- As a condition of receiving a business license.
- As a penalty for violating licensing or other similar laws.

These stipulations are tantamount to a denial and limitation of home rule powers and functions under the Illinois Constitution.

Retaliation Prohibited

Any employer or prospective employer, or the officer or agent of any employer or prospective employer, who discharges or in any other manner discriminates against any employee or applicant for employment based on any of the following is guilty of a petty offense:

- The employee or applicant for employment has made a complaint related to the act to the employer or to the Illinois Director of Labor.

- The employee or applicant for employment has caused to be instituted or is about to cause to be instituted any proceeding under or related to the act.

- The employee or applicant for employment has testified or is about to testify in an investigation or proceeding under the act.

Enforcement and Penalties

The Illinois Director of Labor, or an authorized representative, is responsible for administering and enforcing the Illinois Right to Privacy in the Workplace Act.

If an employee or applicant for employment alleges that they were denied their rights under the act, they may file a complaint with the Illinois Department of Labor. The department will investigate the complaint and may request the issuance of a search warrant or subpoena to inspect the files of the employer or prospective employer, if necessary. The department will attempt to resolve the complaint by conference, conciliation, or persuasion. However, if the complaint is not so resolved and the department finds the employer or prospective employer has violated the act, the department may commence an action in the circuit court to enforce the act, including an action to compel compliance.

If an employer or prospective employer violates the act, an employee or applicant for employment may commence an action in the circuit court to enforce the act, including actions to compel compliance, where efforts to resolve the employee's or applicant for employment's complaint concerning the violation by conference, conciliation, or persuasion have failed and the department has not commenced an action in circuit court to redress the violation.

Failure to comply with an order of the court may be punished as contempt. Additionally, the court will award an employee or applicant for employment prevailing in an action under the act the following damages:

- ♦ Actual damages plus costs.
- ♦ For a willful and knowing violation of the act, $200 plus costs, reasonable attorney's fees, and actual damages.
- ♦ For the following willful and knowing violations, $500 per affected employee plus costs, reasonable attorneys' fees, and actual damages:
  - Where an employer refused to hire, segregated, or acted with respect to recruitment, hiring, promotion, renewal, or employment, selection for training or apprenticeship, discharge, discipline, tenure, or terms, privileges, or conditions of employment without following the procedures of the Employment Eligibility Verification System, including the Basic Pilot and E-Verify programs.
  - Where an individual falsely posed as an employer in order to enroll in an Employment Eligibility Verification System or for an employer to use an Employment Eligibility Verification System to access information regarding an individual who is not an employee of the employer.

Any employer, prospective employer, or employer's agent who violates the provisions of the act is guilty of a petty offense.

Contact Information

Illinois Department of Labor

1 West Old State Capitol Plaza, Room 300
Springfield, IL 62701

Telephone: 217-782-6206
Fax: 217-782-0596
Internet: *www.state.il.us/agency/idol*

Chapter 7

New-Hire Reporting

Introduction

All employers must report the hiring, rehiring, and return to work of all paid employees. A few of the many procedural goals of reporting are to detect fraud, help locate individuals for establishing paternity, and/or establishing, notifying, and enforcing child support orders. New-hire reports are matched against child support records at the state and national levels to locate parents that owe child support.

Federal law, located at 42 U.S.C.A. § 653a, requires each state to establish an automated directory (known as the State Directory of New Hires) which will contain specific information supplied by employers on each newly hired employee.

Reporting Process

Information to Be Reported

Federal law requires employers to collect and transmit several data elements to fulfill their new-hire reporting responsibilities. However, if a returning employee had not been formally terminated or removed from payroll records, there is no need to report that individual as a new hire.

Required information to be reported includes the following:

♦ **Employee Information.** The following employee information must be reported upon the hiring, rehiring, or return to work for all employees:

  • Name.

  • Address.

  • Social Security number.

  • Date of hire, rehire, or return to work.

♦ **Employer Information.** The following employer information must be reported upon the hiring, rehiring, or return to work for all employees:

  • Name.

  • Address.

  • Employer Identification Number (EIN).

Employers are not required to report an individual if the work performed is based on a contract rather than an employer/employee relationship. However, some states have laws requiring new-hire reporting of independent contractors. In either case, the contractor is responsible for the reporting of their employees.

Any department, agency, or instrumentality of the United States must comply with the reporting requirements by transmitting the report to the National Directory of New Hires. Reporting is not required for an employee of a federal or state agency performing intelligence or counterintelligence functions if the head of such agency has determined that the new-hire reporting, with respect to the employee, could endanger the safety of the employee or compromise an ongoing investigation or intelligence mission.

Means of Reporting

Employers may submit any of the following items via first class mail, fax, interactive telephone systems, email, state Web sites, other electronic or magnetic media:

♦ A copy of the employee's Form W-4 or an equivalent form.

♦ Any other hiring document, data storage device, or mechanism authorized by state law.

Employers Operating in Two or More States

An employer with employees in more than one state has two options in fulfilling new-hire reporting requirements.

Multistate employers may choose either of the following:

♦ Abide by the new-hire reporting program of each state and report newly hired employees to the various states in which employees are working.

♦ Select one state where employees are working and report all new hires to that state's designated new-hire reporting office.

Multistate employers who opt to report to only one state must submit new-hire reports electronically or magnetically. Such employers must also notify the federal Department of Health and Human Services as to which state they have designated to receive all their new-hire information. The National Directory of New Hires then maintains a list of multistate employers who have elected to use single-state notification.

When notifying the department, the multistate employer must include all generally required reporting information along with the following:

♦ The specific state selected for reporting purposes.

♦ Other states in which the company has employees.

♦ A corporate contact person.

♦ A list of the names, EINs, and the states where the employees are located if the company is reporting new hires on behalf of subsidiaries operating under different names and EINs.

Deadlines

Unless the submission is made electronically or magnetically, employers must submit information concerning every new hire within 20 days of the date of hire. States have the option of establishing reporting time frames shorter than 20 days. An employer reporting electronically or by magnetic medium is required to submit two transmissions each month (if necessary, based on the volume of hiring) at least 12 to 16 days apart. Employers must abide by new-hire reporting requirements for employees who quit before the reporting deadline because an employer/employee relationship existed and wages were earned. Employers need to report all new hires regardless of the short duration of employment.

Additional Information

Penalties

An employer who fails to make a report as indicated by law may be liable for up to $25 for each newly hired employee. Additionally, if the failure to make a report is the result of a conspiracy between the employer and the employee not to supply the report or to supply a false or incomplete report, the employer will be required to pay a fine of up to $500 for each such failure. Under state law, civil penalties for noncompliance with new-hire reporting may be either monetary or nonmonetary.

Contact Information

Office of Child Support Enforcement

370 L'Enfant Promenade SW
Washington, DC 20447

Telephone: 202-401-9373
Internet: *www.acf.hhs.gov/programs/cse*

Illinois Law

The federal Personal Responsibility and Work Opportunity Reconciliation Act of 1996 (PRWORA) requires all states to adopt laws requiring employers to report information on newly-hired employees to the state child support agency. Illinois new-hire reporting law is located at 820 Ill. Comp. Stat. § 405/1801.1. Pursuant to the law, Illinois employers must report newly hired or rehired employees to the Illinois Directory of New Hires within 20 days of hiring or rehiring.

Covered Employers

The Illinois new-hire reporting regulations **apply** to all Illinois employers, including all of the following:

♦ Private firms.

♦ Unions.

♦ Nonprofit and religious organizations.

♦ Hiring halls.

♦ Government agencies.

Generally, an *employer* is the person for whom an individual performs or performed any service as an employee. The term employer also includes any person acting as an agent of an employer — directly or indirectly — but does **not** include any of the following:

♦ U.S. departments, agencies, instrumentalities, or any wholly owned government corporation.

♦ Any Federal Reserve Bank.

♦ Any state or political subdivision.

♦ Any person subject to the Railway Labor Act.

♦ Any labor organization (other than when acting as an employer) or anyone acting in the capacity of officer or agent of a labor organization.

Covered Employees

Employers are required to report all of the following employees:

- ◆ Full-time employees.
- ◆ Part-time employees.
- ◆ Temporary and seasonal employees.
- ◆ Student workers.
- ◆ Any employee returning to work who has been off the payroll for 180 days or more within the same company due to any of the following:
  - Lay-off.
  - Furlough.
  - Medical leave.
  - Leave of absence.
  - Separation from work.

Note: As a general rule, if an employee fills out a Form W-4, the employer must report the employee.

Information to Be Reported

Employers must submit the following information for each newly hired employee:

- ◆ The employee's name, address, and Social Security number.
- ◆ The employer's name, address, federal Employer Identification Number (EIN) as assigned by the Internal Revenue Service, and any other information that may be required by federal law or regulation.

Employers may voluntarily submit the date of new hire and the address to which the employer wants income withholding orders to be mailed, if the address is different from the one given on the EIN. Employers may also voluntarily submit information regarding rehired employees in the same manner as newly hired employees.

Reporting Methods

Illinois employers may report new hires using one of the following methods:

- ◆ Completing and submitting the new-hire reporting form provided by the Illinois Department of Employment Security (via first-class mail or fax).
- ◆ Submitting copies of the employee's Form W-4, with all information completed legibly, including the employer information (via first-class mail or fax).
- ◆ Submitting a separate listing of new employees, with the required data (via first-class mail, fax, or email).

♦ Using magnetic (excluding tape) submission of data, reported twice monthly, not less than 12 or more than 16 days apart (cartridge or diskette).

♦ Registered employers can login to the new-hire reporting Web site and complete an online new-hire reporting Web form.

Reports must be submitted on either an IRS Form W-4 or an equivalent form and may be transmitted by first class mail, telefax, magnetically, or electronically. Employers must report within 20 days of the date of hire or, if employers transmit reports magnetically or electronically, by two monthly transmissions between 12 and 16 days apart.

Multistate Employers

Multistate employers have two options for reporting their new hires:

♦ Report newly hired employees to the state in which they are working, following the new-hire regulations of each state to which the employer will report.

♦ Select one state where the employer has employees working and report all new hires to that state electronically.

Under the second option, employers are required to follow the new-hire regulations of the selected state. In addition, the employer must inform the Secretary of the U.S. Department of Health and Human Services as to which state the employer has designated to receive all of the new-hire information.

Employers may notify the secretary either by mail or electronically via the secretary's Web site at *www.acf.hhs.gov/programs/cse/newhire*. The following information must be included in the notification:

♦ The employer's name, address, federal EIN, and telephone number.

♦ The state to which the employer will be reporting.

♦ Other states in which the company has employees.

♦ Corporate point of contact and phone number.

Penalties

Employers that knowingly fail to comply with the new-hire reporting requirements will be subject to a civil penalty of $15 for each individual they fail to report.

Employers are considered to have knowingly failed to comply with the Department of Employment Security's reporting requirements if both of the following apply:

♦ The department notified the employer of the failure to comply with the reporting requirements.

♦ The employer fails, without reasonable cause, to supply the required information to the department within 21 days of the date the notice was mailed.

Any individual who knowingly conspires with a newly hired employee to cause the employer to fail to report new-hire information or to cause the employer to file a false or incomplete report will be guilty of a Class B misdemeanor with a fine of up to $500 for each employee with whom the individual conspires.

Frequently Asked Questions

Q What is the New-Hire Reporting Program?

A The New-Hire Reporting Program is part of the federal welfare reform law. The law includes strict work requirements for custodial parents receiving public assistance and stepped up efforts to locate absent parents who are not supporting their children.

All employers are required to report new employees to their state's New-Hire Directory within 20 days of the employee's first day on the payroll (twice monthly if reporting magnetically). The agency selected to receive this information in Illinois is the Illinois Department of Employment Security.

Q **How is new-hire information used?**

A States will match new-hire reports against their child support records to locate parents, establish a support order, or enforce an existing order. This information will also be fed into a national directory to provide more current information for locating out-of-state noncustodial parents.

Each state will have access to this directory; therefore up-to-date information will be available regardless where the parent is located in the United States. Nearly one-third of child support cases involve parents who do not live in the same state as their children.

Q **Why not just use the information on the quarterly wage reporting?**

A Quicker notification is needed to enable child support officials to locate individuals and enforce child support orders. New-hire reporting provides up-to-date employment information that can be used to collect child support from individuals who move from job to job. Quarterly data is often out of date before the child support office receives the information. There can be as much as a six-month lag between the time the data is submitted and when it is available to child support officials. Since the data will be significantly more current under new-hire reporting, noncustodial parents can be located more quickly, allowing child support orders to be established and/or enforced more quickly.

Q **Which employers need to report new employees under the New-Hire Reporting Program?**

A All employers, including private firms, unions, nonprofit and religious organizations, and government agencies, must report all new employees.

Q **What is the definition of an employer?**

A This federal legislation defines an employer for new-hire reporting purposes the same as for federal income tax purposes (I.R.C. § 3401(d)).

Q **Which employees must be reported?**

A All new employees who are required to fill out federal wage withholding Forms W-4 must be reported. This includes all of the following:

- Full-time, part-time, seasonal, and temporary employees.
- Student workers.
- Employees rehired after a separation of 180 days or more.

Q **Do employees who return from leave or who are rehired after layoff need to be reported?**

A Yes. The employer must submit a report if an employee is reinstated after any lapse of pay of 180 days or more. However, if the employee remains on the payroll while away from the job, the employer need not submit a report when the employee returns to work.

Q **Do new-hire reports need to be submitted for independent contractors and subcontractors?**

A The business/organization must first determine whether there is an employer/employee relationship. If the relationship meets the Internal Revenue Service test for an independent contractor relationship, the business/organization is not required to report. In this case, the contractors are responsible for reporting their employees.

Q   What about temporary or seasonal employees?

A   Temporary and seasonal employees are required to be reported. One exception, however, is temporary employees that are sent to the jobsite by a temporary employee agency. In these situations, it is the responsibility of the temporary agency, not the business in which the employee is working temporarily, to report the individual.

Q   Must temporary employment agencies report each individual placed by their agency?

A   If the agency is paying wages to the individual, they must submit a new-hire report. The individual needs to be reported only once, except when there is a break in service with the agency of 180 days or more.

If the agency simply refers individuals for employment and does not pay salaries, the agency does not need to file new-hire reports.

However, the employer who actually hires and pays the individual, whether on a part-time or full-time basis, is required to report the new-hire information.

Q   Are labor organizations and hiring halls required to report members under the New-Hire Reporting Program?

A   Labor organizations and hiring halls must report their own employees (individuals who work directly for the labor organization or hiring hall). If the labor organization or hiring hall simply refers individuals for employment, a new-hire report does not need to be filed by the labor organization or hiring hall. The employer who puts them on the payroll must report the employee information.

Q   What information must be reported?

A   The following information is to be reported:

- Employee data as follows:

  - Employee name.
  - Home address.
  - Social Security number.
  - Date of hire, that is, the date the employee started working. (This is optional, but employers are encouraged to provide the date because it will be used to prevent unemployment insurance overpayments and fraud.)

- Employer data as follows:

  - Name of business/employer.
  - Address of employer.
  - Federal EIN.
  - Address where income withholding orders should be sent, if different from the EIN address (optional data that can be added by employers who want withholding orders directed to a specific address other than their regular EIN address).

Q   When is the date of hire?

A   The date of hire is the employee's first day of work for pay.

Q   Are there different reporting time frames for employers who will submit new-hire reports magnetically?

A Employers who file these reports magnetically or electronically must submit these reports twice each month, not less than 12 or more than 16 days apart.

Q **What about employers with employees in several states?**

A Multistate employers who report magnetically or electronically may either report in each of the states separately or designate a single state in which to report all new hires.

Multistate employers who choose to report to one state must notify the Secretary of the Department of Health and Human Services in writing which state they have chosen.

The National Directory of New Hires will maintain a list of multistate employers and their designated reporting locations. This data will be made available to all states.

Q **How will new-hire reporting benefit employers?**

A All taxpayers will benefit from the reduced tax burden when parents who have not been supporting their children begin paying their obligations for child support. Employers in particular will benefit through the cost savings that come with the reduction and prevention of fraudulent unemployment insurance payments. Timely receipt of new-hire data allows each state to cross-match this data against its active unemployment claimant files — either stopping payments or recovering erroneous payments. In addition, it should promote more stability in the workforce because employees will have less incentive to job-hop in order to avoid paying child support since officials will be able to quickly track their movement from job to job. Employees who are due child support will have the additional resources they need to stabilize their home lives so they can maintain their focus on work.

Contact Information

Illinois New-Hire Directory

P.O. Box 19473
Springfield, IL 62794-9473

Telephone (Toll-Free): 800-327-HIRE
Fax: 217-557-1947
Internet: *www.ides.state.il.us/employer/new-hire.asp*

Chapter 8

Employee Screening and Lie-Detector Tests

Introduction

Congress and various state legislatures have regulated the use of polygraph tests in the workplace. Congress believed that employees and applicants should not be required to answer intrusive questions, and inaccurate test results may unfairly victimize honest employees and applicants. Consequently, employers cannot use polygraph tests **unless** they meet certain narrow exceptions and follow a complex set of procedures. This chapter details the law on the use of polygraph and other types of tests used to determine an individual's honesty.

The U.S. Equal Employment Opportunity Commission (EEOC) governs the application of federal antidiscrimination laws to employer tests and other selection procedures to screen applicants for hire and employees for promotion. There are many different types of tests and selection procedures, including cognitive tests, personality tests, medical examinations, credit checks, and criminal background checks. The use of tests and other selection procedures can be a very effective means of determining which applicants or employees are most qualified for a particular job. However, use of these tools can violate the federal antidiscrimination laws if an employer intentionally uses them to discriminate based on race, color, sex, national origin, religion, disability, or age (40 or older). Use of tests and other selection procedures can also violate the federal antidiscrimination laws if they disproportionately exclude people in a particular group by race, sex, or another covered basis, unless the employer can justify the test or procedure under the law. This chapter provides assistance on some common issues relating to the federal antidiscrimination laws and the use of tests and other selection procedures in the employment screening process.

The Employee Polygraph Protection Act

The federal Employee Polygraph Protection Act of 1988 (EPPA), located at 29 U.S.C.A. §§ 2001 – 2009 and 29 C.F.R. 801 – 801.75, prohibits most private employers from using lie-detector tests either for pre-employment screening or during the course of employment. Employers generally may not require or request any employee or job applicant to take a lie-detector test or discharge, discipline, or discriminate against an employee or job applicant for refusing to take a test or for exercising other rights under the EPPA.

The EPPA regulates not only polygraph tests but also voice-stress analyses and other tests designed to determine honesty by measuring a person's physiological responses. The EPPA also prohibits deceptographs, psychological stress evaluators, and any similar devices — whether mechanical or electrical — used to determine the honesty or dishonesty of an individual.

A *lie detector* includes a polygraph, deceptograph, voice stress analyzer, psychological stress evaluator, or similar device (whether mechanical or electrical) used to render a diagnostic opinion as to the honesty or dishonesty of an individual. A *polygraph* is an instrument that records continuously, visually, permanently, and simultaneously changes in cardiovascular, respiratory, and electrodermal patterns as minimum instrumentation standards and is used to render a diagnostic opinion as to the honesty or dishonesty of as individual.

Pre-Emption

The EPPA does not pre-empt any provision of a state or local law or any provision of a collective-bargaining agreement that prohibited lie-detector tests or is more restrictive with respect to the use of lie-detector tests. For example:

- If a state prohibits the use of polygraphs in all private employment, then polygraph examinations could not be conducted.

- A collective-bargaining agreement that provides greater protection to an examinee would apply in addition to the protections provided in the EPPA.

- More stringent licensing or bonding requirements in a state law would apply in addition to the federal bonding requirement.

However, industry exemptions and applicable industry restrictions, provided in the EPPA, would pre-empt less restrictive exemptions established by state law for the same industry. For example, the random testing of current employees in the drug industry is not prohibited by state law, but is limited by the EPPA to tests administered in connection with ongoing investigations. Thus, employers must comply with **both** federal and state laws.

Covered Employers

The EPPA generally prevents employers engaged in interstate commerce from using lie-detector test either for pre-employment screening or during the course of employment, with certain exemptions. Consequently, the EPPA applies to most private employers. However, the law does not cover federal, state, and local governments. Additionally, the EPPA broadly defines an *employer* as any person acting directly or indirectly in the interest of an employer in relationship to an employee or prospective employee.

Exemptions

Federal, state, and local governments are excluded from EPPA coverage. Additionally, lie-detector tests administered by the federal government to employees of federal contractors engaged in national security intelligence or counterintelligence functions are exempt. The EPPA also includes limited exemptions where polygraph tests (but no other lie-detector tests) may be administered in the private sector, subject to certain restrictions:

- To employees who are reasonably suspected of involvement in a workplace incident that results in economic loss to the employer and who had access to the property that is the subject of an investigation.

- To prospective employees of armored car, security alarm, and security guard firms who protect facilities, materials, or operations affecting health or safety, national security, or currency and other like instruments.

- To prospective employees of pharmaceutical and other firms authorized to manufacture, distribute, or dispense controlled substances that will have direct access to such controlled substances, as well as current employees who had access to persons or property that are the subject of an ongoing investigation.

Prohibitions

Per EPPA protections, covered employers are prohibited from all of the following:

♦ Directly or indirectly requiring, requesting, suggesting, or causing an employee or prospective employee to take or submit to any lie-detector test.

♦ Using, accepting, referring to, or inquiring about the results of any lie-detector test of an employee or prospective employee.

♦ Discharging, disciplining, discriminating against, denying employment or promotion, or threatening to take any such action against an employee or prospective employee for their refusal or failure to take a test, on the basis of the results of a test, for filing a complaint, for testifying in any proceeding or for exercising any rights afforded by the EPPA.

Former Employees

The EPPA prohibitions against discrimination also apply to former employees of an employer. For example, an employee may quit rather than take a lie-detector test. The employer cannot discriminate or threaten to discriminate in any manner against that person (such as by providing bad references in the future) because of that person's refusal to be tested, or because that person files a complaint, institutes a proceeding, testifies in a proceeding, or exercises any right under the EPPA.

Waivers

The rights and procedures provided by the EPPA may not be waived by contract or otherwise, unless such waiver is part of a written settlement agreed to and signed by the parties to the pending action or complaint under the EPPA.

Testing Procedures

Where polygraph examinations are allowed, they are subject to strict standards for the conduct of the test, including the pretest, testing, and post-testing phases.

Qualified Examiners

An examiner must have a valid and current license if required by a state in which the test is to be conducted, and must maintain a minimum of $50,000 bond or professional liability coverage.

Employee Rights and Required Notice

An employee or prospective employee must be given a written notice explaining the employee's or prospective employee's rights and the limitations imposed, such as prohibited areas of questioning and restriction on the use of test results. Additionally, an employee or prospective employee may:

♦ Refuse to take a test.

♦ Terminate a test at any time.

♦ Decline to take a test if they suffer from a medical condition.

Employees or prospective employees also have the right to not be asked questions concerning any of the following:

- Religious or political beliefs and affiliations.

- Any matters relating to sexual behavior.

- Beliefs or opinions on racial matters.

- Beliefs, affiliations, opinions, or lawful activities regarding unions or labor organizations.

The results of a test alone cannot be disclosed to anyone other than the employer or employee/prospective employee without their consent or, pursuant to court order, to a court, government agency, arbitrator, or mediator.

Under the exemption for ongoing investigations of workplace incidents involving economic loss, a written or verbal statement must be provided to the employee prior to the polygraph test that explains the specific incident or activity being investigated and the basis for the employer's reasonable suspicion that the employee was involved in such incident or activity.

Where polygraph examinations are permitted under the EPPA, they are subject to strict standards concerning the conduct of the test, including the pretest, testing, and post-test phases of the examination.

Prohibition Against Disclosure

The EPPA strictly prohibits the unauthorized disclosure of any information obtained during a polygraph test by any person other than the examinee, directly or indirectly, except as follows:

- A polygraph examiner or an employer may disclose information acquired from a polygraph test only to the following:

  - The examinee or an individual specifically designated in writing by the examinee to receive such information.

  - The employer that requested the polygraph test (including management personnel of the employer where the disclosure is relevant to the carrying out of their job responsibilities).

  - Any court, governmental agency, arbitrator, or mediator pursuant to an order from a court of competent jurisdiction requiring the production of such information.

  - The Secretary of Labor or the secretary's representative, when specifically designated in writing by the examinee to receive such information.

- An employer may disclose information from the polygraph test at any time to an appropriate governmental agency without the need of a court order only where the information disclosed is an admission of criminal conduct.

- A polygraph examiner may disclose test charts without identifying information (but not other examination materials and records) to another examiner(s) for examination and analysis, provided that such disclosure is for the sole purpose of consultation and review of the initial examiner's opinion concerning the indications of truthfulness or deception. Such action would not constitute disclosure under the EPPA provided that the other examiner has no direct or indirect interest in the matter.

Posting and Recordkeeping

Every employer subject to the EPPA is required to post and keep posted on its premises a notice explaining the EPPA, as prescribed by the U.S. Secretary of Labor. The notice must be posted in a prominent and conspicuous place in every establishment of the employer where it can readily be observed by employees and applicants for employment. Copies of this required poster may be obtained from local offices of the Wage and Hour Division or on their Web site.

The following records must be kept for at least three years from the date a polygraph examination was conducted (or from the date the examination was requested if no examination was conducted):

- ◆ Each employer who requests an employee to submit to a polygraph examination in connection with an ongoing investigation involving economic loss or injury must retain a copy of the statement that sets forth the specific incident or activity under investigation and the basis for testing that particular employee.

- ◆ Each employer who administers a polygraph examination under the exemption in connection with an ongoing investigation of criminal or other misconduct involving, or potentially involving, loss or injury to the manufacture, distribution, or dispensing of a controlled substance, must retain records specifically identifying the loss or injury in question and the nature of the employee's access to the person or property that is the subject of the investigation.

- ◆ Each employer who requests an employee or prospective employee to submit to a polygraph examination pursuant to any of the exemptions must retain a copy of the written statement that sets forth the time and place of the examination and the examinee's right to consult with counsel.

- ◆ Each employer must identify in writing to the examiner persons to be examined pursuant to any of the exemptions and must retain a copy of such notice.

- ◆ Each employer who retains an examiner to administer examinations pursuant to any of the exemptions must maintain copies of all opinions, reports, or other records furnished to the employer by the examiner relating to such examinations.

- ◆ Each examiner retained to administer examinations to persons identified by employers under any exemption must maintain all opinions, reports, charts, written questions, lists, and other records relating to polygraph tests of such persons. Additionally, the examiner must maintain records of the number of examinations conducted during each day in which one or more tests are conducted and, with regard to tests administered to persons identified by their employer under an exemption, the duration of each test period.

Both employers and examiners must keep these required records safe and accessible at the place(s) of employment/business or at one or more established central recordkeeping offices where employment/examination records are customarily maintained. If the records are maintained at a central recordkeeping office other than in the place or places of employment/business, such records must be made available within 72 hours following notice from the secretary or an authorized representative.

All records must be available for inspection and copying by the secretary or an authorized representative. Information for which disclosure is restricted must be made available to the secretary or the secretary's representative where the examinee has designated the secretary, in writing, to receive such information, or by order of a court of competent jurisdiction.

Enforcement

The Wage and Hour Division of the Department of Labor administers and enforces the EPPA. The U.S. Secretary of Labor can bring court action to restrain violators and assess civil money penalties up to $10,000 per violation. Civil actions may be brought by an employee or prospective employee in federal or state court against employers who violate the EPPA for legal or equitable relief such as employment reinstatement, promotion, and payment of lost wages and benefits. The action must be brought within three years of the date of the alleged violation.

Any person against whom a civil money penalty is assessed may, within 30 days of the notice of assessment, request a hearing before an Administrative Law Judge. If dissatisfied with the Administrative Law Judge's decision, such person may request a review of the decision by the Secretary of Labor. Final determinations on violations are enforceable through the courts.

Other Types of Testing

The passage of the EPPA created a new mandate for employee testing. Except in limited circumstances, private employers were prohibited from using a pre-employment polygraph to screen applicants. With the polygraph no longer available, employers have implemented alternative types of testing, such as integrity tests, to perform the screening function.

Although there is currently no federal regulation of integrity testing, several states have restricted their use under their antipolygraph statutes. For example, the Rhode Island statute does not ban integrity tests, but it requires that such tests not constitute the "primary basis" of an employment decision. Massachusetts forbids the use of any written technique that provides a diagnostic opinion of honesty, a proscription so broad that it may prohibit not only integrity tests but also the use of application blanks, reference checks, structured interviews, and the validity scales of most psychological tests.

The three basic types of integrity tests are as follows:

- **Overt Integrity Tests.** These tests are specifically designed to predict the predisposition of job applicants to engage in on-the-job theft and other counterproductive job behavior. The tests typically include questions about beliefs regarding theft as well as requests for admission regarding theft and other wrongdoing.

- **Personality-Oriented Measures.** These tests try to predict a broad range of counterproductive work behaviors by measuring personality dimensions such as reliability, conscientiousness, adjustment, trustworthiness, and sociability.

- **Clinical Measures.** These tests were developed for other uses, such as identifying psychopathology. These measures can also be used by a trained psychologist to form a diagnostic opinion about an applicant's integrity.

Prohibitions

Title VII of the Civil Rights Act (Title VII) does not prohibit employers from using personality or integrity tests in the workplace. However, Title VII is implicated when either of the following applies:

- An employer uses tests to intentionally discriminate against a protected group.

- The tests have an adverse impact on a protected group and are not job related for the position in question and consistent with business necessity.

EEOC Regulated Employment Tests and Selection Procedures

Employers often use tests and other selection procedures to screen applicants for hire and employees for promotion.

There are many different types of tests and selection procedures, including the following:

- Cognitive tests.

- Personality tests.

- Medical examinations.

- Credit checks.

- Criminal background checks.

The use of tests and other selection procedures can be a very effective means of determining which applicants or employees are most qualified for a particular job. However, use of these tools can violate the federal antidiscrimination laws if an employer intentionally uses them to discriminate based on race, color, sex, national origin, religion, disability, or age (40 or older).

Use of tests and other selection procedures can also violate the federal antidiscrimination laws if they disproportionately exclude people in a particular group by race, sex, or another covered basis, unless the employer can justify the test or procedure under the law.

The EEOC governs Title VII, the Americans with Disabilities Act (ADA), and the Age Discrimination in Employment Act (ADEA), which prohibit the use of discriminatory employment tests and selection procedures.

Types of Tests and Selection Procedures

Many employers use the following employment tests and other selection procedures in making employment decisions:

- Cognitive tests assess reasoning, memory, perceptual speed and accuracy, and skills in arithmetic and reading comprehension as well as knowledge of a particular function or job.

- Physical ability tests measure the physical ability to perform a particular task or the strength of specific muscle groups as well as strength and stamina in general.

- Sample job tasks (for example, performance tests, simulations, work samples, and realistic job previews) assess performance and aptitude on particular tasks.

- Medical inquiries and physical examinations, including psychological tests, assess physical or mental health.

- Personality tests and integrity tests assess the degree to which a person has certain traits or dispositions (for example, dependability, cooperativeness, or safety) or aim to predict the likelihood that a person will engage in certain conduct (for example, theft or absenteeism).

- Criminal background checks provide information on arrest and conviction history.

- Credit checks provide information on credit and financial history.

- Performance appraisals reflect a supervisor's assessment of an individual's performance.

- English proficiency tests determine English fluency.

Title VII and Employment Tests

Title VII prohibits employment discrimination based on race, color, religion, sex, or national origin. According to 42 U.S.C.A. § 703 and with respect to tests in particular, Title VII permits employment tests as long as the tests are not designed, intended, or used to discriminate because of race, color, religion, sex, or national origin. Title VII also imposes restrictions on how to score tests. For example, employers are not permitted to adjust the scores of, use different cutoff scores for, or otherwise alter the results of employment-related tests on the basis of race, color, religion, sex, or national origin.

Disparate Treatment and Disparate Impact Discrimination

Title VII prohibits both disparate treatment and disparate impact discrimination. Title VII disparate treatment discrimination occurs where the discrimination is intentional and based on race, color, religion, sex, or national origin. For example, Title VII forbids a covered employer from testing the reading ability of African American applicants or employees but not testing the reading ability of their Caucasian counterparts.

Disparate treatment cases typically involve the following issues:

♦ Whether people of a different race, color, religion, sex, or national origin are treated differently.

♦ Whether there is any evidence of bias, such as discriminatory statements.

♦ The employer's reason for the difference in treatment.

♦ Whether the evidence demonstrates that the employer's reason for the difference in treatment is untrue, and that the actual reason for the different treatment is race, color, religion, sex, or national origin.

Title VII disparate impact discrimination occurs where employers use neutral tests or selection procedures that have the effect of disproportionately excluding persons based on race, color, religion, sex, or national origin where the tests or selection procedures are not job related and consistent with business necessity.

Disparate impact cases typically involve the following issues:

♦ Whether the employer implements a particular employment practice that has a disparate impact on the basis of race, color, religion, sex, or national origin. For example, if an employer requires that all applicants pass a physical agility test, the test may disproportionately screen out women or another group. Determining whether a test or other selection procedure has a disparate impact on a particular group ordinarily requires a statistical analysis.

♦ Whether the selection procedure has a disparate impact based on race, color, religion, sex, or national origin, and whether the employer can demonstrate that the selection procedure is job related and consistent with business necessity. An employer can meet this standard by showing that it is necessary to the safe and efficient performance of the job. The challenged policy or practice should therefore be associated with the skills needed to perform the job successfully. In contrast to a general measurement of applicants' or employees' skills, the challenged policy or practice must evaluate an individual's skills as related to the particular job in question.

♦ Whether the employer can demonstrate that the selection procedure is job related and consistent with business necessity, and whether the person challenging the selection procedure can demonstrate that there is a less discriminatory alternative available; for example, whether there is another test available that would be equally effective in predicting job performance but would not disproportionately exclude the protected group.

Note: In 1978, the EEOC adopted the Uniform Guidelines on Employee Selection Procedures (UGESP) under Title VII. The UGESP provided uniform guidance for employers about how to determine if their tests and selection procedures were lawful for purposes of Title VII disparate impact theory. The UGESP outlines three different ways employers can show that their employment tests and other selection criteria are job related and consistent with business necessity. These methods of demonstrating job-relatedness are test validation. The UGESP provides detailed guidance about each method of test validation.

EEOC Enforcement Actions and Employment Testing

Title VII and Cognitive Tests

EEOC v. Ford Motor Co. and United Automobile Workers of America involved a court-approved settlement agreement on behalf of a nationwide class of African Americans who were rejected for an apprenticeship program after taking a cognitive test known as the Apprenticeship Training Selection System (ATSS). The ATSS was a written cognitive test that measured verbal, numerical, and spatial reasoning in order to evaluate mechanical aptitude. Although it had been validated in 1991, the ATSS continued to have a statistically significant disparate impact by excluding African American applicants.

Less discriminatory selection procedures were subsequently developed that would have served Ford's needs, but Ford did not modify its procedures. In the settlement agreement, Ford agreed to replace the ATSS with a selection procedure to be designed by a jointly-selected industrial psychologist that would predict job success and reduce adverse impact. Additionally, Ford paid $8.55 million in monetary relief.

Title VII and Physical Strength Tests

In *EEOC v. Dial Corp.*, women were disproportionately rejected for entry-level production jobs because of a strength test. The test had a significant adverse impact on women — prior to the use of the test, 46 percent of hires were women; after use of the test, only 15 percent of hires were women. Dial defended the test by noting that it looked like the job and use of the test had resulted in fewer injuries to hired workers. However, the EEOC established through expert testimony that the test was considerably more difficult than the job and that the reduction in injuries occurred two years before the test was implemented, most likely due to improved training and better job rotation procedures.

On appeal, the Eighth Circuit upheld the trial court's finding that Dial's use of the test violated Title VII under the disparate impact theory of discrimination.

The Americans with Disabilities Act

The ADA prohibits private employers and state and local governments from discriminating against qualified individuals on the basis of disability. The ADA specifies when an employer may require an applicant or employee to undergo a medical examination — specifically, a procedure or test that seeks information about an individual's physical or mental impairments or health. The ADA also specifies when an employer may make disability-related inquiries, which are inquiries that are likely to elicit information about a disability.

The ADA regulates the following:

♦ When hiring, an employer may not ask questions about disability or require medical examinations until after the employer makes a conditional job offer to the applicant.

♦ After making a job offer (but before the person starts working), an employer may ask disability-related questions and conduct medical examinations as long as it does so for all individuals entering the same job category.

♦ With respect to employees, an employer may ask questions about disability or require medical examinations only if doing so is job related and consistent with business necessity. For example, an employer could request medical information when the employer has a reasonable belief — based on objective evidence — that a particular employee will be unable to perform essential job functions or will pose a direct threat because of a medical condition, or when an employer receives a request for a reasonable accommodation and the person's disability and/or need for accommodation is not obvious.

The ADA also makes it unlawful to:

♦ Use employment tests that screen out or tend to screen out an individual with a disability or a class of individuals with disabilities unless the test, as used by the employer, is shown to be job related and consistent with business necessity.

♦ Fail to select and administer employment tests in the most effective manner to ensure that test results accurately reflect the skills, aptitude, or whatever other factor that such test purports to measure, rather than reflecting an applicant's or employee's impairment.

♦ Fail to make reasonable accommodations, including in the administration of tests, to the known physical or mental limitations of an otherwise qualified individual with a disability who is an applicant or employee, unless such accommodation would impose an undue hardship.

EEOC Enforcement

The EEOC settled *EEOC v. Daimler Chrysler Corp.*, a case brought on behalf of applicants with learning disabilities who needed reading accommodations during a pre-employment test given for hourly unskilled manufacturing jobs. The resulting settlement agreement provided monetary relief for 12 identified individuals and the opportunity to take the hiring test with the assistance of a reader.

The settlement agreement also required that the employer provide a reasonable accommodation on this particular test to each applicant who requested a reader and provided documentation establishing an ADA disability. The accommodation consisted of either a reader for all instructions and all written parts of the test, or an audiotape providing the same information.

Age Discrimination in Employment Act

The ADEA prohibits discrimination based on age (40 and over) with respect to any term, condition, or privilege of employment. Under the ADEA, covered employers may not select individuals for hiring, promotion, or reductions in force in a way that unlawfully discriminates on the basis of age. The ADEA also prohibits disparate treatment discrimination (intentional discrimination based on age). For example, the ADEA forbids an employer from giving a physical agility test only to applicants over age 50, based on a belief that they are less physically able to perform a particular job, but not testing younger applicants.

The ADEA also prohibits employers from using neutral tests or selection procedures that have a discriminatory impact on persons based on age (40 or older), unless the challenged employment action is based on a reasonable factor other than age. Consequently, if a test or other selection procedure has a disparate impact based on age, the employer must show that the test or device chosen was a reasonable one.

Employer Best Practices

Employers must:

- ◆ Administer tests and other selection procedures without regard to race, color, national origin, sex, religion, age (40 or older), or disability.

- ◆ Ensure that employment tests and other selection procedures are properly validated for the positions and purposes for which they are used. The test or selection procedure must be job related and its results appropriate for the employer's purpose. While a test vendor's documentation supporting the validity of a test may be helpful, the employer is still responsible for ensuring that its tests are valid under the UGESP.

If a selection procedure screens out a protected group, the employer should determine whether there is an equally effective alternative selection procedure that has less adverse impact and, if so, adopt the alternative procedure. For example, if the selection procedure is a test, the employer should determine whether another test would predict job performance but not disproportionately exclude the protected group.

To ensure that a test or selection procedure remains predictive of success in a job, employers should keep abreast of changes in job requirements and should update the test specifications or selection procedures accordingly.

Employers should also ensure that tests and selection procedures are not adopted casually by managers who know little about these processes. A test or selection procedure can be an effective management tool, but no test or selection procedure should be implemented without an understanding of its effectiveness and limitations for the organization, its appropriateness for a specific job, and whether it can be appropriately administered and scored.

Contact Information

Department of Labor

Wage and Hour Division

Frances Perkins Building
200 Constitution Avenue, NW
Washington, DC 20210

Telephone: 866-4-USWAGE or 866-4-USA-DOL
Internet: *www.dol.gov/whd*

Equal Employment Opportunity Commission

131 M Street, NE
Washington, DC 20507

Telephone: 202-663-4900
Toll-Free: 800-669-4000
Internet: *www.eeoc.gov*

Illinois Law

Polygraph Testing

Illinois law regarding polygraph testing falls within the realm of Illinois' Detection of Deception Examiners Act, located at 225 Ill. Comp. Stat. §§ 430/0.01 – 430/32.

Coverage

According to the act, the prohibited areas of inquiry apply to all detection-of-deception examinations used as pre-employment and periodic employment examinations. However, examiners may inquire into some of the prohibited areas if the area is directly related to the employment.

A *detection of deception examination* means any examination in which a device or instrument is used to test or question individuals for the purpose of evaluation truthfulness or untruthfulness.

Basic Provisions

Under Illinois law, employers **may not** inquire into any of the following areas during pre-employment or periodic employment examinations, unless the area is directly related to the employment:

- Religious beliefs or affiliations.
- Beliefs or opinions regarding racial matters.
- Political beliefs or affiliations.
- Beliefs, affiliations, or lawful activities regarding unions or labor organizations.
- Sexual preferences or activities.

Exemption

The Illinois Detection of Deception Examiners Act does not prohibit the use of a voice stress analyzer by any fully trained full time certified law enforcement officer of a law enforcement agency in the course of its duties as an investigative aid in a criminal investigation.

A *voice stress analyzer* is an investigative tool that records voice stress factors related to frequency modulations in the human voice.

Genetic Testing

Illinois' Genetic-Information Privacy Act, located at 410 Ill. Comp. Stat. §§ 513/1 – 513/45, requires that employers treat genetic-testing information in such a manner that is consistent with the requirements of federal law, including, but not limited to, the Genetic Information Nondiscrimination Act (GINA), the Americans with Disabilities Act (ADA), Title VII of the Civil Rights Act (Title VII), the Family and Medical Leave Act (FMLA), the Occupational Safety and Health Act (OSH Act), the Federal Mine Safety and Health Act, or the Atomic Energy Act. Additionally, employers may release genetic-testing information **only** in accordance with the provisions set forth in the act.

As used in the act:

- *Genetic information* means, with respect to any individual, information about:
  - The individual's genetic tests.

- The genetic tests of a family member of the individual.
- The manifestation or possible manifestation of a disease or disorder in a family member of the individual.

Note: Genetic information **does not** include information about the sex or age of any individual.

♦ *Genetic testing* and *genetic test* means a test or analysis of human genes, gene products, DNA, RNA, chromosomes, proteins, or metabolites that detect genotypes, mutations, chromosomal changes, abnormalities, or deficiencies, including carrier status, that:

- Are linked to physical or mental disorders or impairments.
- Indicate a susceptibility to illness, disease, impairment, or other disorders, whether physical or mental.
- Demonstrate genetic or chromosomal damage due to environmental factors.

Note: Genetic testing and genetic tests **do not** include routine physical measurements; chemical, blood, and urine analyses that are widely accepted and in use in clinical practice; tests for use of drugs; tests for the presence of HIV; analyses of proteins or metabolites that do not detect genotypes, mutations, chromosomal changes, abnormalities, or deficiencies; or analyses of proteins or metabolites that are directly related to a manifested disease, disorder, or pathological condition that could reasonably be detected by a health care professional with appropriate training and expertise in the field of medicine involved.

Coverage

Illinois' Genetic-Information Privacy Act applies to the state of Illinois, any unit of local government, and any board, commission, department, institution, school district, party to a public contract, joint apprenticeship, or training committee within the state, and every other person employing employees within the state.

Prohibited Conduct

An employer, employment agency, labor organization, and licensing agency may not — directly or indirectly — do any of the following:

♦ Solicit, request, require, or purchase genetic testing or genetic information of a person or a family member of the person, or administer a genetic test to a person or a family member of the person as a condition of employment, pre-employment application, labor organization membership, or licensure.

♦ Affect the terms, conditions, or privileges of employment, pre-employment application, labor organization membership, or licensure, or terminate the employment, labor organization membership, or licensure of any person because of genetic testing or genetic information with respect to the employee or family member, or information about a request for or the receipt of genetic testing by such employee or family member of such employee.

♦ Limit, segregate, or classify employees in any way that would deprive or tend to deprive any employee of employment opportunities or otherwise adversely affect the status of the employee as an employee because of genetic testing or genetic information with respect to the employee or a family member, or information about a request for or the receipt of genetic testing or genetic information by such employee or family member of such employee.

♦ Retaliate through discharge or in any other manner against any person alleging a violation of the Genetic-Information Privacy Act or participating in any manner in a proceeding under the act.

Unlawful Agreements

An agreement between a person and an employer, prospective employer, employment agency, labor organization, or licensing agency, or its employees, agents, or members offering the person employment, labor organization membership, licensure, or any pay or benefit in return for taking a genetic test is prohibited.

Workplace Wellness Programs

Employers may not use genetic information or genetic testing in furtherance of a workplace wellness program benefiting employees unless the following occur:

♦ Health or genetic services are offered by the employer.

♦ The employee provides written and informed consent in accordance with § 30 of the act.

♦ Only the employee — or family member if the family member is receiving genetic services — and the licensed health care professional or licensed genetic counselor involved in providing such services receive individually identifiable information concerning the results of such services.

♦ Any individually identifiable information is only available for purposes of such services and may not be disclosed to the employer except in aggregate terms that do not disclose the identity of specific employees.

Exceptions

Requesting a Genetic Test

Nothing in the act prohibits genetic testing of an employee who requests a genetic test and who provides written and informed consent for taking a genetic test for the purpose of initiating a workers' compensation claim under the Workers' Compensation Act.

Public Documents

The purchase of commercially and publicly available documents, including newspapers, magazines, periodicals, and books, but not including medical databases or court records or inadvertently requesting family medical history by an employer, employment agency, labor organization, and licensing agency **is not** a violation of the act.

Law Enforcement

Nothing in the law prohibits an employer that conducts DNA analysis for law enforcement purposes as a forensic laboratory and that includes such analysis in the Combined DNA Index System pursuant to the federal Violent Crime Control and Law Enforcement Act of 1994 from requesting or requiring genetic testing or genetic information of such employer's employees, but only to the extent that such genetic testing or genetic information is used for analysis of DNA identification markers for quality control to detect sample contamination.

Genetic Monitoring

Employers are not prohibited from requesting or requiring genetic information to be used for genetic monitoring of the biological effects of toxic substances in the workplace if the following requirements are met:

♦ The employer provides written notice of the genetic monitoring to the employee.

♦ The employee provides written and informed consent or the genetic monitoring is required by federal or state law.

♦ The employee is informed of individual monitoring results.

- The monitoring is in compliance with any federal genetic monitoring regulations or state genetic monitoring regulations under the authority of the federal OSH Act.

- The employer, excluding any licensed health care professional or licensed genetic counselor that is involved in the genetic monitoring program, receives the results of the monitoring only in aggregate terms that do not disclose the identity of specific employees.

Genetic monitoring means the periodic examination of employees to evaluate acquired modifications to their genetic material, such as chromosomal damage or evidence of increased occurrence of mutations that may have developed in the course of employment due to exposure to toxic substances in the workplace in order to identify, evaluate, and respond to effects of or control adverse environmental exposures in the workplace.

Lawful Acquisition

Despite lawful acquisition of genetic testing or genetic information, an employer, employment agency, labor organization, and licensing agency still **may not** use or disclose the genetic test or genetic information in violation of the act.

Except as previously provided, a person **may not** knowingly sell to or interpret for an employer, employment agency, labor organization, or licensing agency, or its employees, agents, or members, a genetic test of an employee, labor organization member, or license holder or of a prospective employee, member, or license holder.

Identity of Person Tested

No person may disclose or be compelled to disclose the identity of any person upon whom a genetic test is performed or the results of a genetic test in a manner that permits identification of the subject of the test, **except** to the following:

- The subject of the test or the subject's legally authorized representative.

- Any person designated in a specific, written, legally effective release of the test results executed by the subject of the test or the subject's representative.

- An authorized agent or employee of a health facility or health care provider if the following apply:

  - The facility or provider is authorized to obtain the test results.

  - The agent or employee provides patient care.

  - The agent or employee has a need to know the information to conduct the tests or provide care or treatment.

- A heath facility or health care provider that procures, processes, distributes, or uses either of the following:

  - A human body part from a deceased person with respect to medical information regarding that person.

  - Semen provided before January 1, 1998, for the purpose of artificial insemination.

- Health facility staff committees for the purposes of conducting program monitoring, program evaluation, or service reviews.

- In the case of a minor under 18, the health care provider who ordered the test must make a reasonable effort to notify the minor's parent or guardian if, in the professional judgment of the health care provider, notification would be in the best interest of the minor and either:

  - The health care provider has first sought unsuccessfully to persuade the minor to notify the parent or legal guardian.

  - A reasonable time has passed since the minor agreed to notify the applicable parent or legal guardian, and the health care provider has reason to believe the minor has not done so.

All information and records held by a state agency or local health authority pertaining to genetic information must be strictly confidential and exempt from copying and inspection under the Freedom of Information Act.

Confidentiality

Genetic testing and information derived from genetic testing is confidential and privileged and may be released only to the individual tested and to persons specifically authorized, in writing, by that individual to receive the information. In addition, except as previously provided, this information is not admissible as evidence, nor discoverable in any action of any kind in any court, or before any tribunal, board, agency, or person pursuant to Part 21 of Article VIII of the Code of Civil Procedure. No liability may attach to any hospital, physician, or other health care provider for compliance with the provisions of the law, including a specific written release by the individual in accordance with the law.

Genetic testing and genetic information derived thereof may be admissible as evidence and discoverable, subject to a protective order, in any actions alleging a violation of Genetic Information Privacy Act, seeking to enforce § 30 of the act through the Illinois Insurance Code, alleging discriminatory genetic testing or use of genetic information under the Illinois Human Rights Act or the Illinois Civil Rights Act of 2003, or requesting a workers' compensation claim under the Workers' Compensation Act.

Home Rule

Any home rule unit of local government, any nonhome rule municipality, or any nonhome rule county within the unincorporated territory of the county may enact ordinances, standards, rules, or regulations that protect genetic information and genetic testing in a manner or to an extent equal to or greater than the protection provided in the Genetic-Information Privacy Act.

Penalties

Any person aggrieved by a violation of Illinois' Genetic-Information Privacy Act has a right of action in a state circuit court or as a supplemental claim in a federal district court against an offending party. A prevailing party may recover for each violation:

- Liquidated damages of $2,500 or actual damages — whichever is greater — against any person who negligently violates a genetic testing provision.

- Liquidated damages of $15,000 or actual damages — whichever is greater — against any person who intentionally or recklessly violates a genetic-testing provision.

- Reasonable attorneys' fees and costs, including expert witness fees and other litigation expenses.

- Such other relief, including an injunction, as the state or federal court may deem appropriate.

In addition, any person alleging a violation of the disclosure provisions of the law may seek a preliminary injunction preventing the release or disclosure of genetic testing or genetic information pending the final resolution of any action under the law.

Chapter 9
Employee Handbooks

Introduction

Employee handbooks — sometimes referred to as "personnel policies," "personnel statements," "employee manuals," or "personnel handbooks" — are an integral part of the employment relationship. Employers often use employee handbooks to inform employees of company disciplinary policies, office procedures, evaluation procedures, or to list grounds for employee discharge. In addition, employers may use handbooks to inform employees of their rights provided by the law.

Advantages and Disadvantages of Employee Handbooks

Advantages

Some advantages of employee handbooks are as follows:

♦ Information is distributed clearly to all employees.

♦ Supervisors can apply company policy more consistently.

♦ Supervisors have a definite plan of action allowing them to operate more confidently when issues arise.

♦ In litigation, a well-considered, carefully drafted employee handbook can provide an employer's best defense in showing that employees were treated consistently by company policy.

♦ A well-drafted employee handbook can help an organization avoid unions.

Disadvantages

Employee handbooks also have some disadvantages, such as the following:

♦ If the employee handbook is not carefully drafted, it may support a claim that the employer created an express or implied contract modifying the employee's at-will status.

♦ Treating the employee inconsistently with the employee handbook may be evidence of disparate or discriminatory treatment.

♦ Losing track of when handbooks were revised or specific policies were amended can play havoc in litigation.

♦ A poorly drafted employee handbook can lead to employee dissatisfaction and encourage unionizing.

Important Considerations When Preparing Employee Handbooks

When preparing an employee handbook, consider the following:

♦ Use clear and concise language. Avoid using phrases and terms that suggest a change in the at-will status. For example, avoid phrases such as: "Upon completing the probationary period, you become entitled to all the rights and privileges of a permanent employee in reference to at-will employees in the handbook."

♦ Use positive language in policies to help employee morale.

♦ Have the employee sign an acknowledgment form stating that the employee has received the handbook and understands the at-will nature of the employment.

♦ In addition to the employee acknowledgment form, it is recommend that the employer insert a disclaimer provision in the employee handbook as follows:

• The disclaimer must be worded to convey the fact that the employee handbook does not form a contract or alter the at-will terms and conditions of the employment relationship.

• Place the disclaimer in a prominent place (such as the front page) in the employee handbook, set off by a border, contrasting print, or capitalized letters.

• The disclaimer should advise the employee that statements made by management or supervisors — especially those that contradict the employee's at-will status — are not binding on the employer.

• Insert a provision in the disclaimer stating that the organization reserves the right to alter, amend, or suspend the terms of the handbook at its sole discretion.

Note: After the employee signs the acknowledgment form and disclaimer, it is advisable that the employer place a copy of both signed documents in the employee's personnel file (for more information, *see* the section entitled **Disclaimers** later in this chapter).

♦ If a revised employee handbook replaces an older version, the employer should ensure that the employee is aware the revised version supersedes all previous versions. The employee should sign a statement acknowledging this fact.

♦ All employee handbooks should be dated and versions numbered where appropriate. The employer should keep dated or numbered versions of the handbook on file.

♦ Employers need to inform their managers and supervisors not to make oral representations to employees having anything to do with permanent employee status.

♦ Employment law counsel should review employee handbooks before they are distributed and their policies implemented.

♦ Termination policies specifying causes for discharge should also contain a disclaimer stating that such causes are illustrative only and the employer reserves the right to terminate with or without cause at any time.

Types of Policies

The following are examples of certain types of policies an employer should include in an employee handbook. This is not an exhaustive list of policies and is only a general overview of particular areas.

Employment-at-Will Statements

Most employees in the United States are considered to be employed at-will.

Typically, *employment-at-will* means that in the absence of an express contract of employment, no contractual or similar obligation is implied or inferred from the employment relationship. Nonetheless, unless care is taken in drafting the language used in employee handbooks, they may be interpreted to create an implied contract. Although courts have traditionally been reluctant to alter the at-will employment relationship, specific representations and promises that employers make in employee handbooks can be viewed as contractual provisions if employees rely on the promises to their detriment. Therefore, a clear statement should be made at the beginning of an employee handbook that informs the employee that the handbook is not a contract of employment and it does not guarantee employment for any length of time or any specific duration.

Harassment Policies

In *Faragher v. The City of Boca Raton*, 524 U.S. 775 (1998) and *Burlington Industries Inc. v. Ellerth*, 524 U.S. 742 (1998), the Supreme Court held that if an employer is harassed by a supervisor and suffers an adverse employment action, then the employer is liable for harassment. These cases also held that if an employee is harassed by a supervisor but does not suffer adverse employment action, then the employer is liable for harassment unless the employer can establish an affirmative defense.

To establish the affirmative defense, the employer must prove that:

♦ The employer took reasonable steps to protect employees from harassment.

♦ The aggrieved employee did not avail himself or herself of those steps or take steps to avoid harm otherwise.

This affirmative defense is the reason it is necessary for employers to have harassment policies.

Harassment Policy Requirements

Employer policies regarding harassment need to include the following:

♦ A definition of harassment and conduct that may constitute harassment.

♦ A statement that the employer will not tolerate harassment.

♦ A mechanism for reporting harassment. The mechanism should provide the following:

• The name of two persons (one male and one female) to which a person may report harassment.

• A bypass option for reporting harassment in the event that the alleged harasser is the employee's supervisor.

• Guidance on what to do if the harasser is a customer or independent contractor.

♦ A statement offering a degree of confidentiality and support for an employee reporting harassment.

♦ A statement that promises an employee will not be retaliated against for reporting harassment.

♦ A statement regarding potential disciplinary procedures.

Employers should be cautious of the way they define harassment. Many employers operate under the assumption that harassment policies only need to cover sexual harassment; however, under Title VII an employer may be held liable for sexual harassment **and/or** harassment based on race, national origin, ethnicity, religion, or gender. Employers should also be cautious about attempting to list specific types of behavior that constitute harassment. Instead, employers should use broad language that covers many types of conduct.

For example, harassment can be described as either of the following:

- ◆ Verbal or physical conduct that denigrates or shows hostility or aversion toward an individual because of the individual's race, color, gender, religion, age, national origin, disability, sexual orientation, veteran status, or other characteristic protected by law.

- ◆ Conduct that has the purpose or effect of:

  - Creating an intimidating, hostile, or offensive work environment.

  - Unreasonably interfering with the individual's work performance.

  - Otherwise adversely affecting an individual's employment opportunities.

Equal Employment Opportunity Statement

In addition to a harassment policy, an employer should include an equal employment opportunity statement, which affirms the employer's commitment to a nondiscriminatory workplace as well as nondiscriminatory hiring practices. This statement may be viewed as evidence of an employer's good faith intent to comply with employment laws that prohibit harassment, discrimination, and retaliation.

Leave Policies

Employers should develop a set of written policies governing absenteeism, leave, and return to work. Other than the federal Family and Medical Leave Act (FMLA) and any applicable state law, there is no specific requirement to have a written policy regarding employee leave. Nonetheless, written policies are recommended because they help ensure consistent application of the policy and provide employees with information on what types of leaves are available as well as procedures for requesting leave. Additionally, a written policy that coordinates FMLA leave with other types of leave is absolutely necessary if the employer intends to require, where the law allows, that employees substitute various types of paid leave available under the employer's policies for unpaid FMLA leave.

FMLA Policy Requirements

Pursuant to FMLA regulations, employers that are covered by the FMLA must have a policy that includes a brief description of the following:

- ◆ Reasons an employee may take FMLA leave, including military family leave.

- ◆ The entitlement to 12 weeks of unpaid leave in a 12-month period, with a definition of the 12-month period.

- ◆ Employee notice requirements.

- ◆ Substitution of paid leave, or current running of such leave.

- ◆ Intermittent or reduced schedule leave.

- ◆ Job restoration rights.

- ◆ Benefit protection and premium payment.

- ♦ Requirement for medical certification, recertification, and fitness for duty and consequences for failure to provide.

- ♦ Whether short-term disability and workers' compensation leave will count as FMLA leave due to an employee's own serious health condition.

Depending on the employer, a brief description of the following may also be appropriate:

- ♦ Leave available to spouses working for the same employer.

- ♦ Transfer to alternate equivalent position when employee takes intermittent or reduced scheduled leave.

- ♦ The key employee exemption.

Medical Leave Policy Suggestions

Any medical leave policy drafted by an employer should define the circumstances under which an employee can take medical leave and should reference the following:

- ♦ Length and purpose of leave.

- ♦ Job protection and restoration rights.

- ♦ Benefit continuation.

- ♦ Employee notice requirement.

- ♦ Employee eligibility requirements.

- ♦ Duty to return to work at the expiration of leave.

- ♦ A cross reference to the FMLA.

Wage and Hour Policies

Employers should act proactively to avoid violations of the Fair Labor Standards Act (FLSA) and state labor laws. In order to avoid common wage and hour problems, such as employees working overtime but not recording it, employers should include the following provisions in their employee handbook:

- ♦ Employees must seek and receive approval before working overtime.

- ♦ Employees must record all time worked.

- ♦ Employees may not work through lunch or meal periods.

- ♦ Employees may not clock in or complete timecards for other employees.

- ♦ Exempt employees will be subjected to suspensions without pay in weekly increments only.

- ♦ Employees will be subject to discipline for failing to comply with the employer's wage and hour policy.

Disclaimers

Employers often insert disclaimer provisions into employee handbooks. Typically, disclaimers are worded and designed to inform employees that the employee handbook does not form an employment contract or alter the at-will employment relationship.

Disclaimers serve a useful purpose because when a disclaimer is well drafted the scope and potential liability arising from representations made in an employee handbook is limited. However, employers must be careful due to the fact that poorly drafted or ambiguously worded disclaimers sometimes fail in litigation.

Despite the disclaimers, where there is ambiguity and inconsistency between the disclaimer and the contents of the handbook courts have examined whether an employment contract existed between employer and employee. In many cases, contract liability arising from an employee handbook has been imposed although a disclaimer was present due to a conflict with the disclaimers and other sections of the handbook.

Frequently Asked Questions

Q **Does an employee handbook create an employment contract limiting an employer's right to discharge an at-will employee without cause?**

A Usually, no. In most jurisdictions, unless the parties enter into an explicit employment contract, the employee handbook cannot be deemed to be a valid employment contract. However, some courts have interpreted overly contractual, inconsistent, or ambiguous handbook language as an employment contract that may create limitations on an employer's right to discharge an employee.

Q **Must the employer follow the provisions of the employee handbook?**

A Lacking an express provision stating that the employer may exercise its discretion in implementing the employee handbook, courts have held that the employer must follow the provisions of the handbook.

Q **Is the employee bound by a second employee handbook if the employee refuses to sign the handbook and writes on the handbook that the employee "does not agree with, nor agree to abide by the terms of the second handbook"?**

A In such cases, some courts have held that the first employee handbook is the one that governs if the employee continues in the employment relationship, because the first handbook is the one to which the employee assented. Courts require that both the employee and employer agree on the employee handbook. However, if an employee refuses to be bound by the terms of a new employment handbook, the employer may be free to terminate the employment relationship.

Q **Does the disclaimer have to appear in the front of the employee handbook?**

A The disclaimer may appear anywhere in the employee handbook. However, the disclaimer should be visible, conspicuous, and clear. The placement of the disclaimer should be noticeable to the average person. The most advantageous location is at the front of the handbook. Some jurisdictions demand placement at the beginning to accord full weight to the disclaimer.

Q **Does the employee have to read the employee handbook to be bound by its provisions and disclaimers?**

A An employee cannot escape the provisions of an employee handbook, especially the disclaimer provision, on the basis of not having fully read the handbook. Providing the employee with a carefully drafted handbook should be enough. Conscientious employers, however, will take the extra step of obtaining a signed acknowledgment from the employee stating that the employee has received and read the handbook.

Chapter 10

Training

Introduction

As the frequency of employment-related lawsuits and costs of defense continue to rise, investing in effective training of supervisors and employees can generate substantial savings for employers. Adequate and effective training reduces the number of claims, and assists in lowering the risk of an adverse outcome for the employer as courts and juries respond more favorably to employers who invest in training. Moreover, training can enhance job satisfaction and increase productivity.

Legal Duty to Train

Sexual Harassment and Discrimination Prevention

Training has long been recognized by human resource (HR) professionals as an important activity. In 1998, the U.S. Supreme Court decided several landmark decisions, which caused training to take on a new, more important meaning. Although the Supreme Court's decisions simplified the employee's capacity to sue their employer for sexual harassment, the decisions also provided employers with insight as to methods in harassment avoidance and rectifying harassment before the illegal measures became an actionable offense.

The Supreme Court's decisions established the legal principle of tangible employment loss. Examples of tangible employment loss are firing, failure to promote, inappropriate reassignment with different responsibilities, and change of benefits.

Where the victim of sexual harassment has not suffered a tangible employment loss, an employer may successfully defend against a harassment lawsuit by proving that the employer took both of the following steps:

♦ Exercised reasonable care to prevent and promptly correct sexual harassment.

♦ Offered preventive or corrective opportunities and the employee unreasonably failed to take advantage of such opportunities.

The development of an employer's defense against a harassment claim requires planning and preparation. However, such planning and preparation should occur before any harassment claims are filed. Employers must take all necessary precautions and steps to fashion a work environment free from harassment.

For example, an employer may demonstrate the exercise of reasonable care to prevent and promptly correct sexual harassment by implementing the following steps, at a minimum:

♦ Developing both a policy that explains the types of behavior prohibited and a legally effective complaint procedure to address concerns.

♦ Timely distribution of the company policy to all supervisors and employees.

♦ Educating and training employees about their rights and responsibilities under the policy and complaint procedures.

♦ Educating and training supervisors about how they should respond to inappropriate behavior from others and their own responsibilities for complying with and enforcing the policy.

♦ Training those who are charged with receiving and investigating complaints on how to properly conduct investigations, document results, and take corrective action.

Moreover, the Supreme Court continued to emphasize the importance of training and essentially ruled in a 1999 decision that punitive damages cannot be awarded against an employer who has taken all the preventive steps in discrimination and harassment. Thus, harassment prevention training has become almost mandatory for employers to prevent the prohibited acts and avoid liability.

Oftentimes, in sexual harassment litigation, the plaintiff will try to demonstrate that the employer failed to provide the plaintiff with proper training on the employer's harassment policy and/or that the training was ineffective. Subsequently, HR directors and administrators may be subject to extensive questioning, in depositions and at trial, on the training issue. Additionally, courts have continued to expand an employer's legal duty to prevent and avoid harassment targeting any protected class, such as that based on race, national origin, or disability status.

Safety and Health

The employer's duty to train is an important element of several Occupational Safety and Health Administration (OSHA) safety and health regulations.

For example, OSHA requires that employers implement the following safety procedures:

♦ Every employer must either provide portable fire extinguishers throughout the workplace and train all employees on their use or implement an Emergency Action Plan and a Fire Prevention Plan that covers every employee who is not expected to fight fires.

♦ Any employees expected to use portable fire extinguishers to fight incipient fires must be trained pursuant to 29 C.F.R. 1910.157(g)(l) – (4).

♦ Where the employer has provided portable fire extinguishers for employee use in the workplace, the employer must also provide an educational program to familiarize employees with the general principles of fire extinguisher use and the hazards involved with incipient stage fire fighting. The education is required upon initial employment and at least annually thereafter.

♦ Employers must provide employees who have been designated to use fire-fighting equipment as part of an emergency action plan with training in the use of the appropriate equipment. Such training is required upon initial assignment to the designated group of employees and at least annually thereafter.

♦ Employers in the construction industry must provide safety training for each employee in the recognition and avoidance of unsafe conditions and the regulations applicable to the work environment to control or eliminate any hazards or other exposure to illness or injury.

In addition to the training and information requirements, OSHA might require that housekeeping and/or sanitation employees be trained under the Bloodborne Pathogens (BBP) Standard and the Hazard Communication (HazComm) Standard. To require BBP training, OSHA presumes that those employees have "reasonably anticipated" occupational exposure to blood or other potentially infectious materials. To require HazComm training, OSHA assumes that the housekeeping/sanitation employees use hazardous consumer products (such as cleaners) in a manner that results in a duration and frequency of exposure which is greater than the range of exposures that could reasonably be experienced by consumers when the product is used for its intended purpose.

The Occupational Safety and Health Review Commission has also provided guidance on other suggested training programs, such as guidelines for preventing workplace violence. Failure to comply with OSHA's regulations covering training may create liability for the employer.

Tort Claims

Plaintiffs may also file lawsuits claiming that during employment they were personally injured as a result of the employer's failure to properly train co-workers or supervisors on proper techniques to accomplish job duties and responsibilities. For example, inadequacy of police training may serve as a basis for a municipality being liable for a constitutional violation when the failure to adequately train a police officer results in injury to a citizen.

Effective Training Characteristics

Effective training requires thorough planning and preparation. Planning requires that employers establish both training goals and strategies as the foundation to the training program. The following are critical elements of effective programs:

- ♦ Training classes should be conducted by qualified instructors. The qualification of the instructor not only extends to training ability, but also to the subject matter and the employer's industry and policies.

- ♦ Training should be accomplished in a reasonable amount of time and sessions should be tailored to accommodate the employee's attention span and concentration levels. Employees should not be required to endure lengthy hours of instruction but rather reasonable sessions of intricately planned education that is easily retainable.

- ♦ Trainers should employ effective teaching methods so as to maintain the audience's attention and interest, such as the following:

  - Use humor, war stories, and examples to teach.

  - Use hands-on problem solving techniques to get participants to be actively involved in the class.

  - Use visual aids.

- ♦ Training should be evaluated for effectiveness and usefulness in the targeted employment area.

The training of a large workforce on a subject such as harassment can be expensive, and some large employers are using computer programs to accomplish the task. The use of computer programs may be efficient, but should also be reviewed by counsel to ensure that the training material is legally current and defensible.

A collective approach to training can involve any combination of classroom training, self-paced instruction accessed via the Internet, live classroom training, CD-ROMs, or printed material. Importantly, the content of the training material may be the subject of a challenge in subsequent litigation. Trainers should customize the educational content of each training session to the employer's culture, ensuring that the employer's policies are being taught. Regardless of the training format, careful documentation must be kept of those who attended the sessions and the curriculum material that was used during the sessions. If an employee misses a particular session, management should provide for make-up training at a later date.

Suggestions for Training Topics

Each employer's training needs differ based on the company's area of employment. For example, depending on the size, industry, and organizational structure of the entity, the training topics will differ. The following sets forth a description of suggested topics applicable to most employers.

Orientation

Training begins with new employee orientation. New employee orientation training is crucial because it sets the tone for an employee's career with the employer. Orientation serves as an excellent time to introduce the organization to the employee in terms of culture, values, and goals, as well as to outline expectations and policies.

While some employers wait until they have a group of new employees before running an orientation session, such an approach may be a mistake, as delays can result in misconceptions and lack of productivity. Therefore, it is generally recognized that orientation should be conducted as soon as possible and on a personal level.

The following is a list of topics an employer may want to address in a new employee orientation program:

- Company history, philosophy, and an overview of the company's purpose.

- Organizational charts.

- Industry overview.

- Review of benefits package, including health insurance, vacation time, sick leave, Family and Medical Leave Act (FMLA) leave, tuition reimbursement, and retirement.

- Summary of performance appraisal system such as how, when, and by whom employees are evaluated.

- Review of compensation procedures, including pay periods, direct deposit, and how and where to punch timecards or complete time sheets.

- How to schedule and what to expect during an employee physical, if required.

- Career development information, such as an overview of possible career paths and resource library offerings.

- Distribution of employee handbook, policies and procedures, medical provider books, company newsletter, and credit union brochures.

- Information on confidentiality and security.

♦ How and where to obtain required items, such as identification badge, email account, computer password, pager, telephone, office supplies, and parking pass.

♦ A tour of the facility and an introduction to supervisor and co-workers.

♦ Technical and job-specific training, or how to schedule such training with appropriate supervisor.

As with all training, the orientation session should be well documented. For example, a checklist may be used to indicate what was addressed during the session. The checklist should be dated and signed by the individual responsible for the training, as well as the employees in attendance.

Workplace Safety/Risk Management

Training is one of the key elements in reducing workplace accidents and the costs associated with such accidents.

Examples of the costs associated with workplace accidents include, but are not limited to, the following:

♦ Increasing workers' compensation rates.

♦ Heavy fines levied by OSHA for failure to comply with training requirements.

♦ Indirect costs related to turnover and loss of productivity.

Employers can alleviate the burden of such costs, fees, and fines by implementing training programs. However, employers must assess the areas of employment that require training before creating a program. In assessing training needs, it is recommended that employers conduct a safety training needs analysis. For example, employers should determine the types of workers' compensation losses the organization has experienced in the past, and what types of losses should have been expected based on industry norms. To help with the assessment employers may examine company insurance carrier records, OSHA records, and internal accounts payable records. In addition, employers should be cognizant of any OSHA training requirement for the organization's specific industry. OSHA identifies its training requirements in OSHA Publication 2254, entitled *Training Requirements in OSHA Standards and Training Guidelines*.

Workplace safety training also includes courses that teach an employee how to recognize and respond to potential workplace violence situations. This training should include a review of the company policies that provide supervisors with the necessary tools to address volatile circumstances, including, but not limited to, policies on the following topics:

♦ Performance management.

♦ Substance abuse, weapons, and other dangerous devices.

♦ Workplace searches.

♦ Termination.

Workplace violence training should also emphasize the resources available to employees in seeking a nonviolent solution to problems, such as the following:

♦ Internal agreements or complaint resolution processes.

♦ Employee assistance programs (EAPs).

♦ Counseling services available through the group health coverage.

Equal Employment Opportunity and Diversity

A well-developed equal employment opportunity and diversity training program is important for all employers. Such training is seen by civil rights agencies as a benchmark for the employer's equal employment opportunity compliance. It also is essential to effectively communicate the company's commitment to equal opportunity because every workforce is built on people from varied racial, ethnic, religious, cultural, social, and political backgrounds. Supervisor training in how to effectively motivate a diverse workforce to cooperate and collaborate is essential to meet all business goals, as well as reduce legal risks.

Harassment

The Supreme Court's emphasis on prevention and prompt corrective action indicates that in order to manage workplace harassment, employers must:

- Develop a policy prohibiting harassment (based on sex, national origin, age, and all other protected characteristics).

- Broadly distribute and communicate the policy among the entire workforce.

- Educate the entire workforce regarding the policy.

The fact that an employee may receive a copy of the policy does not mean that the employee understands the policy or knows how to comply with the procedures set forth in the policy. Thus, it becomes critical that employers not only distribute procedures, but that they also educate their workforce. Education should go beyond the hourly employee, and most importantly should ensure that supervisors understand the policies and procedures and know how to react to complaints of harassment when they occur. Employers should develop and provide regular training to managers and employees, and carefully document the training.

Elements of Harassment Policy and Training

Education of employees usually focuses on somewhat different points than that of supervisors. Before reviewing the elements of effective harassment training, the employer should ensure that the company harassment policy adequately addresses the issue. The following list contains the prominent elements of an effective harassment policy:

- Design the policy to specifically target the issue of sexual harassment and other kinds of unlawful harassment (such as race, ethnicity, age, or disability).

- Include practical examples (as opposed to legal descriptions).

- Focus on inappropriateness, not illegality.

- Clarify the policy's application to electronic mail (email) and Internet usage.

- Provide a clear complaint procedure, ensuring its application to all types of unlawful harassment and discrimination, and that the procedure addresses conduct by employees and nonemployees alike.

- Specify the people or departments who represent points of contact where an employee may file a complaint. Ensure the procedure includes a by-pass provision where the employee is not required to directly contact a supervisor who was a party to the harassment. Moreover, the employee should be offered diverse options for points of contact.

- Include a nonretaliation provision for complainants and witnesses.

- Include a provision that a complainant's identification will not be disclosed to those who do not have a need to know.

- Provide reference information as to the discipline procedures for inappropriate (as opposed to illegal) behavior and violation of company policy.

Employee training should focus on the following:

- Review of the company policy, including complaint procedure.

- Provide a description of behavior that employees must avoid.

- Emphasize the employee's responsibility to use the complaint procedure if the employee feels uncomfortable or offended.

- With regard to responding to inappropriate behavior, explain that direct confrontation of the perpetrator is an option but not a requirement, and offer strategies.

- Stress the nonretaliation portion of policy.

- Discuss forms of corrective actions and steps that may be taken to remedy claims of harassment.

Managers and supervisors are the keys to preventing harassment, so they must be trained to understand their legal obligations. In addition to the points covered in employee training, the training of managers and supervisors should:

- Emphasize the following legal obligations:

  - Managers and supervisors must refrain from engaging in quid pro quo or hostile environment harassment. Explain how the manager or supervisor's behavior may create strict liability for the employer and how their authority in the workplace affects how their behaviors are perceived by others.

  - Managers and supervisors must respond proactively when witnessing inappropriate behavior, regardless of whether a complaint was filed.

  - Managers and supervisors must ensure that no employee engages in prohibited retaliation.

- Provide the following information:

  - Dissuade supervisory/subordinate dating.

  - Offer guidance on how to respond to complaints of harassment. All complaints should be reported to management, whether or not the employee requests action.

  - Offer an overview of how management will investigate a claim and how inappropriate behavior may be remedied by management.

Those who are charged with investigating and resolving claims of harassment should also be well trained. Investigatory guidelines should address, among other issues, the following:

- When to investigate.

- Who should investigate.

- To whom questions should be addressed, such as the following individuals:

  - Complainant.

- Accused.

- Witnesses.

♦ How to document the investigation, focusing on inappropriateness of conduct in violation of policy, not illegality of conduct.

♦ How to take decisive disciplinary and other corrective actions, if applicable.

♦ Importance of follow-up and documentation.

Overview of Employment Laws

Supervisors should be required to attend a course that provides a general overview of the many and varied laws and principles applicable to employment relationships. An overview class is a good opening session as part of a series of classes, or it can be a stand-alone fundamental class. An overview course may also be an effective means of highlighting the legal issues of HR in working with supervisors to manage the company's legal compliance and limit exposure to employment claims. Such classes should, at a minimum, cover the following federal laws:

♦ Title VII of the Civil Rights Act.

♦ The Americans with Disabilities Act (ADA).

♦ The Age Discrimination in Employment Act (ADEA).

♦ The Pregnancy Disability Act.

♦ The Equal Pay Act (EPA).

♦ The Fair Labor Standards Act (FLSA).

♦ The Family and Medical Leave Act (FMLA) — if applicable.

♦ Applicable state civil rights statutes.

♦ Applicable whistleblower statutes.

♦ Workers' compensation retaliation provisions.

♦ Common law torts of assault, battery, and invasion of privacy, as well as negligent hiring, supervision, and retention.

Hiring and Promoting

All supervisors and employees who are involved in making hiring decisions or in interviewing applicants should be provided with fundamental rules of hiring. For example, the fundamental rules and applicable training would provide the individual responsible for conducting an interview with the following:

♦ Examples of impermissible questions that must be avoided in the interview process.

♦ A list of questions that can and should be asked in an interview.

♦ How to ask questions aimed at assessing the applicant's reliability, interpersonal skills, and teamwork skills, not just technical skills.

- The benefits of having a uniform list of job-related questions for each applicant.

- Role-playing examples, including proper listening techniques and follow-up questioning.

- How to manage voluntary disclosures of past, current, or prospective medical or emotional conditions.

- Pluses and minuses of note taking during the interview.

- Emphasis on considering only job-related, nondiscriminatory factors when making hiring and promotion decisions.

- The employer's policy on providing the unsuccessful applicant with a reason for the employment choice.

Performance Evaluations

Providing training to every person who is responsible for conducting performance appraisals is critical. Such training must provide instruction as to the proper procedure for performance evaluations and the potential consequences to the employer if the appraisals are inflated. Courts have commented positively on workplace evaluation systems where evaluators received training to avoid common mistakes and/or biases in evaluations. Conversely, courts have criticized workplace evaluation systems where training of evaluators is not provided. From a practical perspective, training should include a discussion of the evaluation instrument, the employer's policy behind the characteristics reviewed, and evaluation grading system. In providing training for performance appraisals, points to stress from a legal perspective include recording factual observations, not conclusory judgments, and the following:

- Addressing performance problems when they occur, not months later in the annual review.

- Providing the employee with an opportunity for both self-evaluation and to respond to the supervisor's evaluation.

- Providing regular follow-up on areas for performance improvement.

Supervisor Training
New Supervisors

Many employers promote employees based on their technical expertise — not on their leadership skills — and do not teach the promoted employees how to adapt to their new supervisory role. Similar to new employee orientation, new supervisors should receive training that eases and facilitates the transition from employee to management. In fact, a study by Hewitt Associates found a commonality in top companies (based on factors such as net income and reputation) was that the companies all executed formal leadership development programs for employees. In addition to other training topics (previously addressed), new manager training may include effective coaching and negotiating skills, conflict resolution, and effective delegation. Generally, training for new supervisors should be gradual so that the training does not overwhelm the newly-promoted employee.

Discipline and Termination

Supervisor training programs should unquestionably emphasize guidelines for appropriate discipline and termination actions. While an employer may operate in an at-will employment state, the number of exceptions to the legal principle of at-will employment is sizeable. Supervisors need to understand how to adequately frame corrective action for unsatisfactory performance or unacceptable behavior so that the supervisor can credibly testify that the employee was warned about the problem and that despite such warning the employee finally left the supervisor no other alternative but termination.

Training Guidelines

Providing supervisors with guidelines for taking disciplinary action, including terminations, must consist of practical and legal information.

Such training may include the following:

- Understanding why pretermination notice and corresponding documentation is important — emotionally and legally.

- Steps to take for pretermination notice, as follows:

  - Progressive discipline.

  - Exceptions to progressive discipline for new hires and summary offenses.

- Focusing on workplace behavior or performance.

- Appropriate responses to a voluntary disclosure of physical or emotional conditions, such as the following:

  - Possible duty to accommodate.

  - Report to management (without trying to resolve).

- Ensuring consistency, including the following:

  - How inconsistency happens, such as favoritism or avoidance of difference.

  - Documenting basis for exceptions in consistency.

- Timing, veracity, and dignity to use during disciplinary proceedings.

- Avoiding delays.

- Compliance to ensure true and legitimate reasons for termination.

- Learning the principles of confidentiality and impartiality.

Documentation

Included in a discipline and termination course should be a thorough discussion on documentation. While supervisors should be instructed on the importance and elements of proper documentation for good and bad behavior, training should also remind supervisors that there is such a thing as too much documentation and that consistency is critical. Training should include what and how to document.

Managing Leave

One of the most complicated areas (and biggest frustrations) for supervisors is managing attendance problems. Often, HR is the last department to know the reason for an employee's absence because the supervisor did not understand the inter-relationship of workers' compensation, FMLA, and routine illnesses. It is imperative that HR train supervisors on the overlap in conflict in these areas of the law, and the need to keep HR abreast of the reasons employees take a leave of absence.

Union Organizing Efforts and Contract Administration

Employers who do not have a unionized workforce must remain vigilant to sophisticated union organizing efforts. Indeed, employers cannot afford to wait until the first signs of an organizing campaign appear before training supervisors in the area of unions and contract administration.

Supervisors should receive expert guidance on how to recognize signs of union organizing, when and where to report such activity, and the fundamental rules of campaigning.

Training on contract administration should include the following:

♦ Analysis of the grievance and arbitration procedures.

♦ Any rights and restitutions union stewards or representatives have to appear and address grievances or conduct business.

♦ The rights employees have to union representation at a disciplinary meeting.

♦ Management rights provisions of the agreements.

Supervisors must have a working knowledge of their authority to manage in a union environment and how collective-bargaining agreements affect the supervisory relationships with bargaining-unit employees.

Additional Information

Training should be initiated for a variety of reasons, including performance improvement, overall professional development, succession planning, and risk management. HR's role in contributing to the success of the business must include leading the way in fostering a trained workforce.

Efforts in this regard will prove lucrative, not only by serving as the defense to employment-related lawsuits, but most importantly by ensuring a motivational and healthy employment practices environment.

Compensability of Training Time
Independent School and Training Programs

According to federal regulations, if an employee attended an independent school, college, or trade school after normal working hours (on the employee's own initiative and not due to the employer's prompting), the time while in school **does not** constitute hours worked and is not compensable. Moreover, the hours are **not** compensable regardless of whether the schooling was directly related to the employee's job.

Employment Related Training Programs

Employer-Sponsored Training Programs

Generally, time spent attending employer-sponsored training programs is compensable for nonexempt employees.

However, when the activity meets all of the following four criteria, an exception applies to required compensation:

♦ Attendance is outside of the employee's regular working hours.

♦ Attendance is voluntary.

♦ The course, lecture, or meeting is not directly related to the employee's job.

♦ The employee does not perform any productive work during such attendance.

According to the U.S. Department of Labor, attendance at training programs is **involuntary** if any of the following apply:

♦ The employer requires attendance.

♦ It is the employee's understanding, or the employee is lead to believe, that present working conditions or continuance of employment would be adversely affected by nonattendance.

Training is directly related to an employee's job if it is designed to make the employee more effective in their current position in the workplace, as distinguished from training that an employee receives for another job or for a new or additional skill.

For example, when a training program is designed to prepare an employee for advancement or promotion, rather than make the employee more effective in their current position, the training is **not** considered to be directly related to the employee's job.

First-Day Training Programs

Hours spent by employees attending a first-day training program (new employee orientation) have been held to be compensable by the Wage and Hour Division of the Department of Labor.

Note: In most cases, the time an employee spends in the training suggested in this chapter would be compensable by the employer.

Discriminatory Training Claims

Many lawsuits are filed each year contending that employers unlawfully discriminated against workers in protected classifications by refusing to provide the workers with training opportunities while simultaneously providing training to nonminorities.

Failure-to-train cases can be avoided through a policy of consistently training employees without respect to age, race, national origin, sex, or other protected characteristics, and careful documentation of all training opportunities.

Chapter 11

Noncompetition Agreements and Trade Secrets

Introduction

Whenever an employer hires a new employee, the employer provides that person with access to the organization's most valuable assets: its people, its customers, and its way of doing business. Given that the average American will change jobs seven times over a work life, chances are high that some of that information will eventually find its way to a competitor. More frequently than ever, companies are trying to protect themselves and their assets from the damage that can result when employees depart to work for a competing business or set up a competing enterprise.

There is no easy way to prevent such conduct, especially if precautions have not been taken in advance. An employer should require employees to sign employment agreements wherein they agree to maintain the secrecy for all of the organization's trade secrets. In addition, an employer may consider a covenant not to compete that has geographic, scope, and duration limitations. Such terms should be included in an initial employment agreement entered into at the start of the employment relationship. While it may not be easy to go back and add these terms, because there must be adequate consideration in exchange for these post-employment obligations, if an employer will be paying the employee anything more than absolutely legally owed, the employer may be able to condition the bonus on having signed an agreement to maintain the trade secret as confidential and to provide the employer with written assurances that the employee no longer has any proprietary or trade secret material.

Please note, however, that state law governs restrictive covenants, trade secrets, and other noncompetition agreements discussed in this chapter. While many of the general legal principals set forth in this chapter apply universally, there can be significant differences among states. The most obvious distinction is that some states, notably California, prohibit restrictive covenants that inhibit an employee's ability to find new employment. Other distinctions among the laws of various states may be less dramatic but, under certain circumstances, no less important. Such differences are particularly critical if the agreement is intended to apply to employees who may be located in different states, such as a sales force. The substance of individual state laws is beyond the scope of this chapter, which is intended to offer a general understanding of the concepts involved. Individual state laws should be reviewed before any agreement discussed in this chapter is drafted.

General Protections

Employers have certain limited protections, recognized by the law under a variety of theories, against unfair competition, disloyal employees, and overreaching competitors. Turning legal theory into meaningful remedies requires attention to detail and an appreciation for conflicting public policies.

The Duty of Loyalty

An organization's current employees are under a "duty of loyalty" to the organization. Each state defines that duty a bit differently. In general, employees are not permitted to induce current customers, suppliers, or other employees to leave the organization, nor are they allowed to operate a competing business while still employed by the organization. When that duty is breached, the employer may be entitled to collect lost profits, punitive damages, and out-of-pocket costs incurred to train replacements. Offending employees may be forced to forfeit their salaries and to give up any profits they made as a result of the disloyal conduct. In addition, courts may issue injunctions forbidding the employees to engage in similar conduct for a specified period. Under the duty of loyalty, the law generally prevents an individual from using trade secrets or proprietary information of a current or former employer to the detriment of that employer.

An employer need not do anything special to create this duty, and the employee need not sign any agreement to be covered by it. The law recognizes the duty of loyalty and the value of proprietary information. When wrongful conduct has been proven, the law provides a remedy. It will, however, be up to the employer to prove in court that the information it seeks to protect meets standards for trade secrets and that it did everything it could to safeguard the secret nature of the information.

Trade Secrets

What Is a Trade Secret

A trade secret can be any information that derives independent economic value from not being generally known or readily ascertainable. Among the things that can be trade secrets are formulas, patterns, compilations, programs, devices, methods, techniques, or processes. Among things courts have found to be trade secrets are machining processes, blueprints, stock-picking formulae, customer lists, pricing information, and nonpublic financial data. On the other hand, information such as overhead rates and profit margins that help define a price may be found to be a trade secret even if the price itself is known.

Legal Tests

Forty-two states and the District of Columbia have adopted in whole or in part the Uniform Trade Secrets Act (UTSA). The UTSA codifies the basic principles of common law trade secret protection and may afford employers protection even in those states, like California, where restrictive covenants are generally not enforceable. The UTSA protects an employer from misappropriation and misuse of actual trade secrets, which are defined as information, including a formula, pattern, compilation, program, device, method, technique, process, drawing, data, or customer list that:

- Derives independent economic value — actual or potential — from not being generally known to or readily ascertainable (by proper means) by other persons who can obtain economic value from its disclosure or use.

- Is the subject of efforts that are reasonable under the circumstances to maintain its secrecy.

An employer must take reasonable measures to maintain the confidentiality of trade secrets. In determining whether reasonable steps have been taken, courts balance the costs and benefits on a case-by-case basis. Even states that have not adopted the UTSA generally accord similar protection to trade secrets under the Restatement (Second) of Torts, § 757.

To determine whether a piece of information is a trade secret, states following the Restatement will generally examine the following factors:

♦ Whether the information was known outside the organization.

♦ The savings affected and the value to the holder in having the information as against competitors.

♦ The value of the information and the amount of money or effort spent to develop it.

♦ The efforts the employer made to limit the number of people having access to the information.

♦ What other efforts were made to keep the information secret.

♦ The relative difficulty required in obtaining or duplicating the information using proper means.

Restrictive Covenants

Definition

Restrictive covenants, also known as noncompetition/noncompete agreements, are contractual arrangements that restrict employees' rights to compete with their employers for a period of time following termination of employment. Once reserved for the highest-level executives, researchers, and outside sales personnel, noncompete agreements are being increasingly used with midlevel managers, technical staff, and any other employee whose departure could create a competitive disadvantage. Unlike the common law duty of loyalty, an agreement not to compete prohibits conduct that takes place after the employment relationship has ended and is not limited to "wrongful conduct," such as stealing client lists.

Other agreements are more narrow, restricting only contact with customers. Such an agreement is referred to as a nonsolicitation agreement. Through the use of noncompete, nonsolicitation, and nondisclosure agreements, employers try to prevent employees from cashing in on opportunities gained during the employment relationship.

What Restrictive Covenants Protect

Restrictive covenants provide protection by preventing former employees from alienating long-standing customers and disclosing or using confidential information acquired from the employer.

Note, however, that with professionals such as doctors, accountants, and certain others, where a personal relationship has developed, courts will frequently refuse to enforce a noncompetition agreement that would result in patients not being able to see their own doctor or clients not being able to use the accountant they have dealt with for years.

Employers can protect confidential information that may be helpful to a competitor or to an employee who decides to go into private business. Courts will enforce this protection if an employee has signed a restrictive covenant and the covenant is reasonable in all other important aspects. This is distinct from the general provision provided by the law of trade secrets and is a way for employers to protect themselves against disclosure of information that may not otherwise qualify as a trade secret. An employer must, however, be able to show that the information was indeed treated as confidential.

Restrictions on Noncompete Agreements

Before embarking on a campaign to have employees sign noncompete agreements, companies should consider a few cautionary points. Considering these points will also help companies draft workable agreements.

Courts in all states dislike noncompete agreements and welcome the opportunity to limit or eliminate them. Their sentiment is largely based on a desire to allow individuals to earn a living in the field of their choice. Agreements that are too broad are likely to be tossed out or at least rewritten by a judge in those states that allow for such an option.

As a general rule, courts will consider the following factors in determining whether to enforce a restrictive covenant:

- ◆ **Does the employer have a legitimate interest in being protected from this employee's competitive activity?** A court may refuse to enforce a restriction that is too broadly drafted even though the employer may be able to demonstrate a legitimate business interest worthy of protection.

- ◆ **Is the restriction reasonable in light of all the circumstances?** By reasonable, the courts would mean that the agreement is no more restrictive upon an employee than necessary to protect the employer's legitimate business interests.

- ◆ **Is the restriction reasonably limited in time and geography?** The agreement must contain a reasonable time restriction. Such a time restriction would be based on such factors as the time it would take to train a new employee and for customers to become familiar with this employee and eliminate the identification between the employer's business and the former employee. The geographical scope of the restriction must be limited to areas necessary to protect the employer's interests.

- ◆ **Will enforcing the restriction harm the public interest? Will any aspect of public policy be affected if the agreement is enforced?** This factor tends to be the least definitive. However, the following example may illustrate this factor. An employer-hospital requires a restrictive covenant with the only cardiac surgeon in a 500 hundred mile radius and that surgeon then leaves the hospital. If the restrictive covenant were to require the surgeon to not compete within a 200 mile radius, the public would be severely harmed by this restrictive covenant.

- ◆ **Was there reasonable consideration given in return for the restrictive covenant being signed?** Most states require an employee's agreement to noncompetition restrictions to be in exchange for receiving something of value, such as the initial job offer, a raise or promotion, or extra benefits upon leaving the organization.

- ◆ **When will the noncompetition restriction be triggered?** Some agreements apply automatically, whether the employee's termination was for cause, without cause, or as part of a layoff. Some agreements apply only if the employee resigns or is terminated for cause. Other agreements limit the period of restricted activity to the time severance benefits are being paid. Where the period of restricted activity is limited to the duration of severance benefit payments, the employee is free to forego severance payments to accept employment. Note that some employers include an agreed-upon fee that the employee will pay if the employee engages in the prohibited activity during the restricted period.

Enforcement

The best noncompete agreements are narrowly tailored to meet the most important needs of the organization, judiciously applied to only individuals in sensitive positions, and vigorously invoked when violated.

In many cases, merely having a noncompete agreement in place will discourage most employees from leaving the organization to work for a competitor. When an employee does leave, however, the agreement allows the employer to have some control over the timing, terms, and effect of the departure.

Companies must fight to enforce their noncompete agreements. If the potential harm is sufficient to justify a restrictive covenant, it is serious enough to do something about when that covenant is violated.

Violation of noncompete agreements may allow employers to obtain, in addition to monetary damages, nonmonetary relief such as a restraining orders and injunctions to protect the organization's interests. Companies that fail to enforce their noncompete agreements often find that their former employees' attorneys can argue that there was no need for the restriction in the first place since the organization has not bothered to enforce it in the past.

Nondisclosure, No-Solicitation, and No-Raid Agreements

Employers can have employees sign even more limited agreements — for example, nondisclosure, no-solicitation, and no-raid agreements — which do not limit their ability to work in the field but do prevent them from causing harm to the old employer in their new job. These more limited agreements are usually more easily enforced than a true noncompete agreement. One difficulty with these agreements, however, is the difficulty of proving they have been violated.

A *nondisclosure agreement* can prevent an employee from using or disclosing an employer's confidential information in the new job. An advantage of this sort of agreement is that the employer can define confidential information so that more things are included than would qualify as trade secrets under common law. In addition, such a signed agreement would prevent employees from pleading ignorance as an excuse for sharing confidential information. It would, of course, be difficult to prove a violation of this sort of agreement when the employer's confidential information could arguably be ascertained from sources other than the employee.

A *no-solicitation agreement* prohibits the employee from going after the organization's customers or suppliers.

A *no-raid agreement* prohibits the employee and a new employer from inducing other employees to leave the original employer to work for the new one, at least for some specific time after the former employee leaves employment. While employee raiding is not recognized as a cause of action in most states, employers may be able to pursue a remedy for raiding of employees based on a claim of intentional interference with contractual relations or prospective economic advantage. These agreements tend to be viewed more favorably by the courts since they do not actually keep anyone from working.

Conflict-of-Interest Clauses

Many employers also include a conflict-of-interest clause in their noncompetition agreements. This provision generally requires employees to devote their entire productive time and full attention to the employer as a condition of employment.

A conflict-of-interest clause may also contain an agreement by employees to refrain from directly or indirectly engaging in any outside employment, consulting, or other business activities while employed by the employer. Employees can additionally be required to agree to refrain from engaging in any outside employment without the written consent of the employer.

Hiring a Competitor's Employees

Employers often may find themselves in a position to hire a competitor's employees. In these cases, it is worthwhile to take some precautionary steps because state courts may find that a new employer's interference with valid noncompete agreements constitutes "tortious interference" with the former employer's relationship with the employee.

An employer should first determine if the employee is subject to any restrictions. An employer should not be satisfied with a vague answer to a question whether the employee has any sort of restrictive agreement with the former employer. The employer should have the employee sign a statement that the individual is not subject to any noncompete or other agreement. If an employer hires a competitor's employee knowing that the employee is subject to a restrictive covenant, the organization could be sued for interfering with the previous employer's contractual rights, just as employers could sue an organization that hired one of their employees subject to such an agreement.

The key to lawsuits regarding violation of another organization's restrictive covenant is the hiring organization's knowledge of the restriction and its decision to employ the person in spite of this knowledge. This is why the first step in such a case may be the sending of a certified letter by the old employer to the new, putting the new employer "on notice" of the restriction. If, in fact, it can be proven that the nature of an individual's work for the new employer makes it virtually impossible for the individual not to use or disclose the old employer's confidential information, a court may be persuaded to restrain the employee from working for the competition at all.

If an employer learns that a new hire does have a restrictive covenant, the employer should get a copy of it and have legal counsel examine it. It may be that the prohibitive activity does not match the duties of the position to be filled. The agreement may also appear too broad. It may also be that there was no consideration in return for the agreement being signed.

Once an employer knows how enforceable the agreement is, the employer can decide how to proceed. An employer may want to begin negotiations with the other employer in cases where the agreement seems especially strong. The employer should be especially cautious about hiring employees with noncompetition agreements if the organization requires such agreements of its employees. It will be very difficult to enforce agreements, based on what the employer argues is a legitimate reason for having employees sign them, if an employer finds it acceptable to violate another employer's agreements.

Employer Practices

Employers are protected by common law from the misuse of their trade secrets by former employees. To ensure their confidential information is protected, employers must actually treat this information as confidential and restrict access to it, instituting restricted-access procedures, and posting appropriate signs. Employees should be trained in the proper handling of confidential information.

In situations where employers fear that employees may leave and take customers with them or share crucial information with a new employer, employers should carefully draft appropriate restrictive covenants and have their employees sign them. Restrictive covenants must follow reasonable guidelines if there is to be any hope of their being enforced. They must protect a legitimate interest of the employer and they must be as narrow as possible, avoiding broad and lengthy restrictions.

Employers are encouraged to limit disclosure of confidential information in the workplace by:

- Requiring employees to sign reasonable nondisclosure agreements and noncompete agreements where possible.

- Disseminating information on a need-to-know basis.

- Restricting access to file drawers and offices containing proprietary information.

- Developing and maintaining a sensible document retention and destruction policy.

- Conducting systematic inventories of confidential information.

Furthermore, upon the departure of an employee with access to trade secret information, an organization should conduct an exit interview to obtain knowledge about the scope and duties of the employee's new position and to repossess or delete any trade secret information held by the employee (including home files).

Likewise, employers interviewing candidates should also take certain precautions to ensure that new employees do not become the subject of an injunction based on their former positions. Employers should first investigate whether a particular candidate is bound by a noncompete agreement or a nondisclosure agreement. If such an agreement(s) exists, the employer should obtain a written representation from the new employee that the employee complied with all obligations set forth within the agreement(s).

Employers also should be aware of a new employee's prior work product, which may be subject to "work for hire" limitations. As defined by the federal Copyright Act, ***work made for hire*** is, if the parties expressly agree in a written instrument signed by them that the work is considered a work made for hire, either of the following:

- A work prepared by an employee within the scope of their employment.

- A work specially ordered or commissioned for use as a contribution to a collective work or a compilation.

Limitations apply to such work due to the contractual agreements entered by the parties.

Finally, employers should remember to use practical methods to avoid the appearance of impropriety such as creating a new position for employees hired from competitors or documenting new employees' activities in ways that show independent action.

Chapter 12
Wages and Hours

Introduction

The federal Fair Labor Standards Act (FLSA), located at 29 U.S.C. §§ 201 et seq., establishes minimum wage, overtime pay, recordkeeping, and child labor requirements for full-time and part-time employees in the private sector and in federal, state, and local governments. The Davis-Bacon Act, located at 40 U.S.C.A. §§ 3141 – 3148, applies to the rate of wages and hours for laborers and mechanics employed by contractors and subcontractors on public buildings. Employers are also required to abide by hourly regulations where employees are commercial motor vehicle (CMV) drivers or passenger-carrying vehicle drivers.

FLSA

The FLSA applies to those employers engaged in interstate commerce or the production of goods for commerce and that have annual gross sales or business volume of $500,000 or greater. The FLSA also applies to all public agencies, most hospitals and other health care entities, and schools.

Covered Employees

The FLSA covers all individuals employed by a covered employer. However, although an employer is subject to the FLSA, certain employees may be exempt from some or all of the statutory requirements.

Exemptions are typically applied on an individual workweek basis, taking various tests and stringent criteria into consideration when determining exempt status. Employees performing exempt and nonexempt duties in the same workweek are normally not considered exempt in that workweek. In considering the possible exempt status of employees, employers and their attorneys must consider a lengthy list of exemptions. Some exemptions are common to both federal and state statutes (for example, the "white-collar" exemptions for executive, administrative, or professional employees, although definitions may vary), while others may appear in only one statute.

Some individuals who are not employed by a covered employer may be individually protected by the FLSA. The FLSA also covers workers who are engaged in commerce or in the production of goods for commerce. Under individual employee coverage, employees are covered if their work regularly involves them in interstate commerce, the production of goods for commerce, or work in activities that are closely related and directly essential to the production of goods for commerce. For example, a worker assembling components in a factory or a secretary typing letters in an office that will regularly be sent out of state to perform the work are individually covered by the FLSA. In addition, the law normally covers domestic service workers, such as housekeepers, full-time babysitters, and cooks.

Exemptions

The FLSA exempts some employees from both the minimum wage and overtime pay requirements, while other employees are exempt only from the overtime pay requirements.

Minimum Wage and Overtime

The following employees are exempt from **both** the minimum wage and overtime pay requirements:

- Executive, administrative, and professional employees. (*See* **White-Collar Exemptions** section.)
- Outside sales employees.
- Certain skilled computer professionals.
- Employees of certain seasonal amusement or recreational establishments.
- Employees of certain small newspapers.
- Employees engaged in newspaper delivery.
- Switchboard operators of small telephone companies.
- Seamen employed on foreign vessels.
- Employees engaged in fishing operations.
- Agricultural workers employed on small farms.
- Casual babysitters and persons employed as companions to the elderly or infirm.

Overtime

The following employees are **only** exempt from the overtime pay requirements:

- Certain commissioned employees of retail or service establishments.
- Auto, truck, trailer, farm implement, boat, or aircraft salespersons employed by nonmanufacturing establishments primarily engaged in selling these items to ultimate purchasers.
- Auto, truck, or farm implement parts-clerks and mechanics employed by nonmanufacturing establishments primarily engaged in selling these items to ultimate purchasers.
- Railroad and air carrier employees.
- Taxi drivers.
- Certain employees of motor carriers.
- Seamen on American vessels.
- Local delivery employees paid on approved trip rate plans.
- Announcers, news editors, and chief engineers of certain nonmetropolitan broadcasting stations.
- Domestic service workers who reside in their employers' residences.
- Employees of motion picture theaters.
- Farm workers.

The following employees may be **partially exempt** from the overtime pay requirements:

- Employees engaged in certain operations on agricultural commodities.

- Employees of certain bulk petroleum distributors.

- Employees of hospitals and residential care establishments that have agreements with the employees that they will work 14-day periods in lieu of 7-day workweeks (if the employees are paid overtime premium pay within the requirements of the FLSA for all hours worked over 8 in a day or 80 in the 14-day work period — whichever is the greater number of overtime hours).

- Employees who lack a high school diploma or who have not completed the eighth grade, who spend part of their workweeks in remedial reading or training in other basic skills that are not job specific. Employers may require such employees to engage in these activities up to 10 hours in a workweek. Employers must pay normal wages for the hours spent in such training, but need not pay overtime premium pay for training hours.

White-Collar Exemptions

Section 13(a)(1) of the FLSA exempts executive, administrative, and professional employees from the minimum wage and overtime requirements of the FLSA.

In order to establish that employees are exempt under the executive, administrative, and professional employee exemptions, the employer is required to establish the following:

- **Salary Basis Test.** An employee is paid on a salary basis rather than on an hourly basis. To meet this requirement, the employee must receive a full salary for any workweek in which any work is performed without regard to the number of days or hours worked. The salary basis test does not apply to practicing doctors, attorneys, and certain teachers.

- **Salary Level Test.** An employee makes at least the minimum salary level required by the exemption. To meet this requirement, the employee must be compensated on a salary basis at a rate not less than $455 per week ($23,660 annually, based on a 52 week year). Administrative, professional, and computer employees may be paid on a fee basis at a rate that would amount to not less than $455 per week. Computer employees may also be paid an hourly rate of not less than $27.63 per hour.

- **Duties Test.** An employee performs the type of duties required by the particular exemption sought to be relied on by the employer as follows:

  - **Executive Exemption.** To meet the duty requirements for the executive exemption, the following must apply:

    - The employee must be compensated on a salary basis at a rate not less than $455 per week.

    - The employee's primary duty must be managing the enterprise, or managing a customarily recognized department or subdivision of the enterprise.

    - The employee must customarily and regularly direct the work of at least two or more other full-time employees or their equivalent. *Customarily and regularly* means a frequency that must be greater than occasional but may be less than constant. Tasks or work performed customarily and regularly includes tasks normally and recurrently performed every workweek; it does not include isolated or one-time tasks.

    - The employee must have the authority to hire or fire other employees, or the employee's suggestions and recommendations as to the hiring, firing, advancement, promotion, or any other change of status of other employees must be given particular weight.

- **Administrative Exemption.** To meet the duty requirements of the administrative exemption, the following must apply:

  - The employee must be compensated on a salary basis or fee basis at a rate of not less than $455 per week.

  - The employee's primary duty must be the performance of office or nonmanual work directly related to the management or general business operations of the employer or the employer's customers.

  - The employee's primary duty includes the exercise of discretion and independent judgment with respect to matters of significance.

- **Professional Exemption.** To meet the duty requirements of the professional exemption, the following must apply:

  - The employee must be compensated on a salary basis or fee basis at a rate of not less than $455 per week.

  - The employee's primary duty must be the performance of work requiring ***advanced knowledge***, defined as work that is predominantly intellectual in character and which includes work requiring the consistent exercise of discretion and judgment.

  - The advanced knowledge must be customarily acquired by a prolonged course of specialized intellectual instruction.

  - The advanced knowledge must be in a field of science or learning.

    Note: To qualify for the creative professional employee exemption, the employee's primary duty must be the performance of work requiring invention, imagination, originality, or talent in a recognized field of artistic or creative endeavor.

As used for purposes of determining white-collar exemptions, ***primary duty*** means the principal, main, major, or most important duty an employee performs. Determination of an employee's primary duty must be based on all the facts in a particular case, with the major emphasis on the character of the employee's job as a whole.

Salary Basis

As previously described, ***salary basis*** means an employee regularly receives a predetermined amount of compensation each pay period on a weekly, or less frequent, basis.

The predetermined amount cannot be reduced because of variations in the quality or quantity of the employee's work. This is referred to as the ***no-docking rule***. Subject to certain exceptions, an exempt employee must receive the full salary for any week in which the employee performs any work, regardless of the number of days or hours worked. However, exempt employees do not need to be paid for any workweek in which they perform no work. If the employer makes deductions from an employee's predetermined salary (for example, because of the operating requirements of the organization), that employee is not paid on a salary basis. Thus, if the employee is ready, willing, and able to work, deductions may not be made for time when work is not available.

Exceptions to the No-Docking Rule (Permissible Deductions from a Salaried Employee)

Deductions from the salary of an exempt employee are permissible under the following circumstances:

- **Deductions from Salary for Disciplinary Suspensions.** An employer may impose unpaid disciplinary suspensions of a full day or more if:

- The deductions or suspensions are imposed in good faith for infractions of workplace conduct rules. A violation of ***workplace conduct rules*** means serious misconduct such as sexual harassment, workplace violence, or violation of drug or alcohol policies. It does not include rules relating to performance or attendance.

- The deductions or suspensions are imposed pursuant to a generally applicable written policy. The written policy must be sufficient to put employees on notice of the consequences of a violation.

◆ **Deductions for Absences due to Personal Reasons.** Deductions for absences for personal reasons other than sickness or disability are permissible, but only for full-day absences. An employer may deduct a pro rata portion of salary where an employee who regularly works Monday through Friday takes Friday off for a vacation day, assuming no contract or policy requires payment for that day.

◆ **Deductions for Sick or Disability Leave.** Except for leave taken under the Family and Medical Leave Act (FMLA), deductions for absences for sickness or disability are permissible only for full-day absences and only in accordance with a bona fide plan, policy, or practice that provides compensation for salary lost due to illness.

◆ **Deductions during FMLA Leave.** Pursuant to 29 C.F.R. 541.602(b)(7), "An employer is not required to pay the full salary for weeks in which an exempt employee takes unpaid leave under the FMLA," but rather "may pay a proportionate part of the full salary for time actually worked." Employers and employees sometimes have the right under the FMLA to substitute paid leave for FMLA leave. To the extent paid leave is substituted for FMLA leave, no deductions may be made.

◆ **Penalties for Safety Violations.** An employer may offset salary with penalties imposed in good faith for violations of safety rules of major significance.

◆ **First and Last Weeks of Employment.** If an employee does not work a full workweek during the first or last week of employment, an employer is only required to pay a pro rata percentage of the salary for that workweek.

◆ **Deductions for Jury or Witness Fees and for Temporary Military Duty.** An employer may offset salary with jury duty or witness fees and temporary military pay.

Note: According to IRS Revenue Ruling 2009-11 and the Internal Revenue Code § 3401(h), differential wage payments made to an individual on active duty for more than 30 days are subject to income tax withholding, but not to Social Security and Medicare (FICA) or unemployment tax (FUTA). A ***differential wage payment*** is a payment of part or all of the wages the employee would have received if the employee still provided services to the employer. Employers must report the differential wage payments and the amounts withheld on the employee's Form W-2.

◆ **Deductions from Accrued Leave Accounts.** Employers may deduct from a salaried employee's accrued paid leave time an amount of time equal to the duration of the employee's tardiness or absence. For example, if an employer has a vacation or sick leave policy under which an employee accrues paid time off, the employer may deduct from such accrual for **any** absences. *See* WH Admin Op. FLSA 2005-7 (Jan 7, 2005). However, employers should remember that deductions from accrued leave for absences related to sickness or disability may violate the ADA or the FMLA.

Note: An employer is not required to pay the full salary in the initial or terminal week of employment or for weeks in which an exempt employee takes unpaid leave under the FMLA.

Improper Deductions from a Salaried Employee

The employer will lose the exemption if it has an actual practice of making improper deductions from an employee's salary.

If an actual practice is found, the exemption is lost during the time period of the deductions for employees in the same job classification working for the same managers responsible for the improper deductions.

Factors to consider when determining whether an employer has an actual practice of making improper deductions include, but are not limited to, the following:

♦ The number of improper deductions, particularly as compared to the number of employee infractions warranting deductions.

♦ The time period during which the employer made improper deductions. The number and geographic location of the employee(s) whose salary was improperly reduced and the manager(s) responsible.

♦ Whether the employer has a clearly communicated policy permitting or prohibiting improper deductions.

Note: Isolated or inadvertent improper deductions will not result in loss of the exemption if the employer reimburses the employee for the improper deductions.

Safe Harbor

Based upon safe harbor provisions, employers will not lose an exemption if the employer complies as follows:

♦ Has a clearly communicated policy prohibiting improper deductions, which includes a complaint mechanism.

♦ Reimburses employees for any improper deductions.

♦ Makes a good faith commitment to comply in the future.

However, the exemption will be lost if the employer willfully violates the policy by continuing the improper deductions after receiving employee complaints.

Note: The regulations state that the best evidence of a clearly communicated policy is a written policy that was distributed to employees prior to the improper pay deductions; for example, by providing a copy at the time of hire or publishing the policy in an employee handbook.

Fee Basis

Administrative, professional, and computer employees may be paid on a fee basis rather than on a salary basis. A *fee basis* means that an employee is paid an agreed sum for a single job, regardless of the time required for its completion. A fee payment is generally paid for a unique job, rather than for a series of jobs repeated a number of times and for which identical payments repeatedly are made.

To determine whether the fee payment meets the minimum salary level requirement to qualify for the exemption, the test is to consider the time worked on the job and determine whether the payment is at a rate that would amount to at least $455 per week if the employee worked 40 hours. For example, an artist paid $250 for a picture that took 20 hours to complete meets the minimum salary requirement since the rate would yield $500 if 40 hours were worked.

Outside Sales Exemption

To qualify for the outside sales employee exemption, **both** of the following tests must be met:

♦ The employee's primary duty must be making sales (as defined by the FLSA) or obtaining orders or contracts for services or for the use of facilities for which a consideration will be paid by the client or customer.

♦ The employee must be customarily and regularly engaged away from the employer's place(s) of business.

There is no minimum salary requirement for the outside sales exemption.

Promotion Work

Promotion work may or may not be exempt outside sales work, depending upon the circumstances under which it is performed.

Promotion work that is actually performed incidental to and in conjunction with an employee's own outside sales or solicitations is exempt work. However, promotion work that is incidental to sales made or to be made by someone else is not exempt outside sales work.

Drivers Who Sell

Drivers who deliver products and also sell such products may qualify as exempt outside sales employees only if the employee has a primary duty of making sales.

Several factors should be considered in determining whether a driver has a primary duty of making sales, including the following:

♦ A comparison of the driver's duties with those of other employees engaged as drivers and as salespersons.

♦ The presence or absence of customary or contractual arrangements concerning amounts of products to be delivered.

♦ Whether or not the driver has a selling or solicitor's license when required by law.

♦ The description of the employee's occupation in collective-bargaining agreements.

♦ Other factors set forth in the regulation.

Highly Compensated Employees

Highly compensated employees performing office or nonmanual work and paid a total annual compensation of $100,000 or more (which must include at least $455 per week paid on a salary or fee basis) are exempt from the FLSA if they customarily and regularly perform at least one of the duties of an exempt executive, administrative, or professional employee identified in the standard duties test (*see* **White-Collar Exemptions** section). Production line workers or those who primarily perform repetitive duties or physical work do not qualify for this exemption, regardless of their level of compensation.

Commissions and nondiscretionary bonuses are included for purposes of determining whether the $100,000 threshold is met. There are also special rules for prorating the annual compensation if employees work only part of the year, and which allow payment of a single lump-sum, make-up amount to satisfy the required annual amount at the end of the year and similar make-up payments to employees who terminate before the year ends.

Computer Employee Exemption

To qualify for the computer employee exemption, the following tests must be met:

♦ The employee must be compensated either on a salary basis or a fee basis at a rate not less than $455 per week, or, if compensated on an hourly basis, at a rate not less than $27.63 an hour.

♦ The employee must be employed as a computer systems analyst, computer programmer, software engineer, or other similarly skilled worker in the computer field performing the primary duties as following:

  • The application of systems analysis techniques and procedures, including consulting with users, to determine hardware, software, or system functional specifications.

  • The design, development, documentation, analysis, creation, testing, or modification of computer systems or programs, including prototypes, based on and related to user or system design specifications.

  • The design, documentation, testing, creation, or modification of computer programs related to machine operating systems.

  • A combination of the previously mentions duties, the performance of which requires the same level of skills.

Minimum Wage

The FLSA requires employers to pay covered employees, who are not otherwise exempt to the FLSA, a minimum wage of at least $7.25 per hour.

Youth Minimum Wage

Unless prohibited by state or local law, employers may pay a youth subminimum wage of no less than $4.25 per hour to employees under age 20 for the first 90 consecutive calendar days — not working days — of initial employment. However, employers may not discriminate against older workers to take advantage of the youth minimum wage.

Tipped Employees

Tipped employees are those who customarily and regularly receive more than $30 a month in tips. Tips actually received by tipped employees may be counted as wages for purposes of FLSA (known as a tip credit), but the employer must pay not less than $2.13 an hour in direct wages. If the $2.13 plus tips does not equal the current minimum wage, the employer must make up the difference to ensure that each tipped employee makes at least the minimum wage. If an employer elects to use the tip credit, the employer must:

♦ Inform each tipped employee about the tip credit allowance (including amount to be credited) before the credit is utilized.

♦ Be able to show that the employee receives at least the minimum wage when direct wages and the tip credit allowance are combined.

♦ Allow the tipped employee to retain all tips, whether or not the employer elects to take a tip credit for tips received, except to the extent the employee participates in a valid tip pooling arrangement.

Exceptions to Minimum Wage

The FLSA allows the following employees to be paid less than minimum wage under certificates issued by the Department of Labor:

♦ **Student Learners.** Student learners must be at least 16 years old and be students enrolled in cooperative, vocational education programs approved by a state board of education. Learners must be employed on a part-time basis at no less than 75 percent of the employer's regular minimum wage. A special student-learner certificate will be effective for a maximum time period of one school year, unless a longer period is justified by extraordinary circumstances. Importantly, employers must be aware that the Department of Labor regulations distinguish between student-learners and other types of learners, messengers, and apprentices.

♦ **Individuals with a Disability.** After receiving a certificate from the Wage and Hour Division of the Department of Labor, employers may pay special subminimum wages (less than the federal minimum wage) for the job being performed to employees with a disability; for example, an employee whose earning or productive capacity is impaired by a physical or mental disability, including those related to age or injury, may be paid a special subminimum wage.

Disabilities that may affect productive capacity include, but are not limited to, the following:

- Blindness.

- Mental illness.

- Intellectual disability.

- Cerebral palsy.

- Alcoholism.

- Drug addiction.

Special minimum wages must be commensurate wage rates based on the worker's individual productivity in proportion to the wage and productivity of experienced workers — without disabilities — performing essentially the same type, quality, and quantity of work as the employee with a disability. Employers must evaluate the quality and quantity of the productivity of the employee with a disability and review and adjust all special minimum wages at periodic intervals accordingly.

♦ **The Full-Time Student Program.** This program is for full-time students employed in retail or service stores, agriculture, or colleges and universities. An employer that hires students may obtain a certificate from the Department of Labor, which allows the student to be paid not less than 85 percent of the minimum wage. The certificate also limits the hours that the student may work to eight hours in a day and no more than 20 hours a week when school is in session and 40 hours when school is out, and requires the employer to follow all child labor laws. Once students graduate or leave school for good, they must be paid the minimum wage.

Internships

Covered and nonexempt individuals who are "suffered or permitted to work" must be compensated under the FSLA for the services they perform for an employer. Interns in the for-profit private sector who qualify as employees rather than trainees typically must be paid at least the minimum wage and overtime compensation for hours worked over 40 in a workweek. However, there are some circumstances under which individuals who participate in for-profit private sector internships or training programs may do so without compensation.

The Supreme Court has held that the term "suffer or permit to work" cannot be interpreted so as to make a person whose work serves only their own interest an employee of another who provides aid or instruction. This may apply to interns who receive training for their own educational benefit if the training meets certain criteria. The determination of whether an internship or training program meets this exclusion depends upon all of the facts and circumstances of each such program.

The following six criteria must be applied when making this determination:

  ♦ **The internship, even though it includes actual operation of the facilities of the employer, is similar to training which would be given in an educational environment.** The more an internship program is structured around a classroom or academic experience as opposed to the employer's actual operations, the more likely the internship will be viewed as an extension of the individual's educational experience.

  ♦ **The internship experience is for the benefit of the intern.** The more the internship provides the individual with skills that can be used in multiple employment settings, as opposed to skills particular to one employer's operation, the more likely the intern would be viewed as receiving training.

  ♦ **The intern does not displace regular employees, but works under close supervision of existing staff.** If the employer would have hired additional employees or required current employees to work additional hours but for the presence of interns, the internship better resembles an employment relationship. Alternatively, if the employer provides shadowing opportunities where the intern performs no or minimal work, then the scenario more closely resembles an educational experience.

  ♦ **The employer that provides the training derives no immediate advantage from the activities of the intern and on occasion its operations may actually be impeded.** If the intern receives the same level of supervision as the employer's regular workforce, this would suggest an employment relationship, rather than training.

  ♦ **The intern is not necessarily entitled to a job at the conclusion of the internship.** The internship should be for a fixed duration, established prior to the outset of the internship, and not be used as a trial period in which the employer evaluates the intern's work performance for future work.

  ♦ **The employer and the intern understand that the intern is not entitled to wages for the time spent in the internship.**

If all six criteria are met, an employment relationship does not exist under the FLSA. Consequently, the FLSA's minimum wage and overtime provisions do not apply to the intern.

Important: Each situation must be evaluated on a case-by-case basis.

Compensation

For nonexempt employees, compensation is required for the time an employee is suffered or permitted to work, even if not specifically asked to do so. As a general rule, all hours that the employee is required to be at the workplace should be considered to be compensable work time, including short rest breaks that are usually 20 minutes or less.

Preliminary and Postliminary Activities

The Portal to Portal Act prohibits minimum wage or overtime claims for any preliminary or postliminary activity engaged in by an employee unless such activities are made compensable by contract, custom, or practice.

The term principal activities includes all activities that are an integral part of a necessarily required activity. Employers may exclude from hours worked certain travel and walking times and other similar pre- and post-work activities.

Integral Parts of Principal Activities

The following two examples demonstrate an integral part of a principal activity:

♦ Frequently, a lathe operator must necessarily install a new blade or oil, grease, and clean the lathe at the beginning of the workday. Such activities are an integral part of the principal activity and are included within such term.

♦ A garment employee in a textile mill must report 30 minutes before other employees report to begin principal activities. During those 30 minutes, the employee distributes clothing or parts of clothing to the workbenches of other employees and prepares machines for operation by other employees. These activities are among the principal activities of that employee.

Such preparatory activities are regarded as compensable work regardless of contrary custom or contract.

Similarly, if the employee must carry out closely related, indispensable activities to perform a job, these also form an integral part of the principal activity. Perhaps, for example, employees in a chemical plant cannot perform their principal activities without protective clothing. Thus, changing clothes on the employer's premises before and after work is an integral part of the employees' principal activity.

Note: On the other hand, if employees change clothes for convenience rather than necessity, this is a preliminary or post-work activity rather than a principal part.

Two cases decided by the U.S. Supreme Court further illustrate integral activities. In one, employees changed their clothes and took showers in a battery plant where the manufacturing process involved the extensive use of caustic and toxic materials. In another case, butchers in a meatpacking plant sharpened their knives before and after their scheduled workday. In both cases, the Supreme Court held that these activities are an integral and indispensable part of the employees' principal activities.

Donning and Doffing

Alvarez

In *IBP, Inc. v. Alvarez*, 126 S.C. 514 (2005), the U. S. Supreme Court overturned long held assumptions concerning the scope of the compensable workday for employees who are required to wear protective garments or gear to perform their jobs.

The court concluded that the donning of protective gear prior to an employee's shift commences the workday, and that time spent walking to employees' workstations is encompassed within the compensable workday.

The court's holding also addressed the corresponding question of time spent removing protective gear at the end of the workday, concluding such time is compensable and any preceding time spent walking from a workstation to a locker room or other location for removing gear is also compensable. With respect to time spent waiting during the process of donning and doffing protective garments or gear, the court held that time generally is **not** compensable under the FLSA, where the waiting time happens before the donning activity, which signals the beginning of the compensable workday, or follows the correspondingly compensable doffing activity.

In light of the court's opinion, employers should evaluate their timekeeping systems and practices to ensure that all compensable time, as now defined by the court, is captured. Under the court's holding in *Alvarez*, employers are required to include in such an evaluation the actual time employees spend donning and doffing protective gear at the beginning of their shift, before and after unpaid breaks, and at the end of their shift, as well as associated walking time. Such activities will now be encompassed within the compensable workday, **unless** they are, in the aggregate, de minimis.

Wage and Hour Division

According to the U.S. Department of Labor Wage and Hour Division, Administrator's Interpretation No. 2010-2, unionized employers cannot treat time spent donning and doffing certain protective equipment as unpaid time, even if an applicable union contract or practice treats the time as unpaid. According to the Interpretation:

♦ The FLSA does not permit industries to rely upon a union contract or a practice in a unionized setting to exclude time spent donning or doffing protective equipment from an employee's compensable worktime.

♦ Clothes changing covered by the FLSA (at 29 U.S.C. § 203) may be a principal activity. Where that is the case, subsequent activities, including walking and waiting, are compensable.

According to the FLSA, *principal activities* are the activities which an employee is employed to perform. These activities include any work of consequence performed for the employer, no matter where the work is performed. An employee's principal activities also include all activities which are an integral (or essential) part of their principal activities.

Meal and Break Periods

Bona fide meal periods — typically 30 minutes or more — are **not** considered compensable hours. When taking an unpaid 30-minute or longer meal break, the employee must be relieved of all duties, whether active or passive, and must be free to leave the post in order to be considered a true break and thus noncompensable.

When an employer has expressly and unambiguously communicated to employees that authorized breaks may only last for a specific length of time, unauthorized extensions of authorized work breaks are **not** counted as compensable hours.

Other examples of compensable work time are as follows:

♦ Participating in charitable work requested or controlled by the employer.

♦ Participation in fire drills.

♦ Being required to show up before one's shift begins to complete paperwork.

♦ Traveling from one worksite to another.

♦ Time during which an employee is required to be on duty or on an employer's premises or at a prescribed workplace.

♦ Time during which an employee is allowed to be actually working, whether or not required to do so, even though performed away from the employer's premises, away from the jobsite, or at the employee's home. Thus, an employer must compensate its employees for unauthorized work that, even though prohibited, is performed with the knowledge or acquiescence of management.

♦ Time spent in idleness or on call if the employee is "engaged to be waiting" — that is, required to be engaged in these activities as part of the employee's job and is not completely relieved from duty for a period of time long enough to effectively use the time for the employee's own purposes.

♦ Time spent in incidental activities before or after work, such as preparing for work or cleaning up, if the activities are an integral and indispensable part of the employee's principal activities.

♦ Meal periods during which the employee is required to perform duties.

♦ Required attendance at training programs.

♦ Certain travel time (that is not in-town commuting time).

When recording time worked by nonexempt employees, the employer must record, among other things, the total hours worked each workday and workweek. This will include signing/punching out at the end of the workday.

Additionally, all other hours worked, such as for compensable travel time, training time, and time spent doing paperwork, must be recorded.

Note: Employers should consider requiring time records for employees whose exempt status is in question, because time records assist in defending against employee claims for unpaid overtime.

Nursing Mothers in the Workplace

According to the FLSA at 29 U.S.C. § 207(r), an employer must provide both of the following:

- ♦ A reasonable break time for an employee to express breast milk for her nursing child for one year after the child's birth each time she needs to express the milk. This reasonable break time is not required to be compensated by the employer.

- ♦ A place, other than a bathroom, that is shielded from view and free from intrusion from co-workers and the public, which may be used by an employee to express breast milk.

An employer with less than 50 employees is not required to comply with these breastfeeding requirements if such requirements would impose an undue hardship by causing the employer significant difficulty or expense when considered in relation to the size, financial resources, nature, or structure of the employer' business. However, this federal law does not pre-empt a state law that provides greater protections to employees who are nursing mothers than the federally-provided protections.

Travel Time and the Portal-to-Portal Act

According to the Portal to Portal Act, located at 29 U.S.C. § 254(a), and applicable regulations at 29 CFR 785.34, employers are not required to pay minimum wage or overtime compensation for an employee's time spent in walking, riding, or traveling to and from the actual place of performance of the principal activity or activities that such employee is employed to perform under either circumstance:

- ♦ Prior to the time on any particular workday when an employee commences their principal activity or activities.

- ♦ Subsequent to the time on any particular workday when the employee ceases their principal activity or activities.

An employer is required to pay the minimum wage or overtime compensation if the activity is compensable by express contract or by custom or practice not inconsistent with an express contract. Consequently, travel time at the commencement or cessation of the workday which was originally considered as working time under the FLSA (such as underground travel in mines or walking from time clock to work-bench) need not be counted as working time unless it is compensable by contract, custom, or practice. If compensable by express contract or by custom or practice not inconsistent with an express contract, such travel time must be counted in computing hours worked.

However, ordinary travel from home to work need not be counted as hours worked even if the employer agrees to pay for it. According to 29 CFR 785.35, an employee who travels from home before the regular workday and returns home at the end of the workday is engaged in ordinary home to work travel which is a normal incident of employment. This is true whether the employee works at a fixed location or at different job sites. Normal travel from home to work is not work time.

Use of Employer's Vehicle and Employee Commuting Flexibility Act

The Employee Commuting Flexibility Act amended the Portal to Portal Act by adding that the use of an employer's vehicle for travel by an employee and activities performed by an employee which are incidental to the use of such vehicle for commuting are not considered part of the employee's principal activities if both of the following apply:

- ◆ The use of such vehicle for travel is within the normal commuting area for the employer's business or establishment.

- ◆ The use of the employer's vehicle is subject to an agreement on the part of the employer and the employee or representative of such employee.

On-Call Time

Some employers wish to have their employees ready to work in the event of an emergency or other occurrence. This is known as ***on-call time***.

Many employers — for example, ambulance services — have been sued in recent years by employees seeking compensation and overtime compensation for time during which they are subject to being called to work.

Although each case depends on its own particular circumstances, generally employees must be compensated for on-call time **only** if they cannot effectively use the on-call time for their own personal benefit. For instance, an employee who is required to remain on call on the employer's premises should be considered working while on call. However, with exception, an employee who is permitted to be on call at home or who is allowed to leave a message where the employee may be reached is **not** considered working while on call.

Example: If an employee is subject to being called in on the off-shift and is actually called numerous times each day, the employee's on-call time might not be used for personal benefit. In this case, the employee would be entitled to overtime pay for the on-call time.

Technology and Hours Worked

The FLSA requires that employers pay nonexempt employees for all time suffered or permitted to work. Technology allows employees to complete work from home and allows managers to contact employees at any time. Additionally, through the use of technology some supervisors have grown to expect employees to be readily available for questions or respond to email messages, text messages, and phone calls at all hours of the day. A company-provided cellular phone, BlackBerry, computer laptop, pager, and/or a personal digital assistant makes it easy for employers to communicate with employees during nonworking hours and create an impression that the employee is on-call at any time. Consequently, changing workplace technology can form the basis for FLSA lawsuits.

Two high-profile court cases focused on hourly work directly relate to the issue of technology and hours worked: *Agui v. T-Mobile USA* and *Rulli v. CB Richard Ellis Inc.* Each case addresses complaints of hourly paid workers who were required to continue to work after hours on company-issued cell phones, fielding service calls and technical-support issues, without compensation.

In *Agui v. T-Mobile*, No. 1:2009cv02955 (E.D.N.Y., July 10, 2009), the plaintiffs seek to recover wages on behalf of themselves and other retail sales associates and supervisors for time worked for which they received no compensation. Specifically, the plaintiffs allege that they were required to review and respond to T-Mobile emails and text messages at all hours of the day, whether or not they were logged in to T-Mobile's computer-based timecard system. Pursuant to the FLSA, which permits liability against individuals, the case is brought as a putative collective action against T-Mobile and its management; the case is also being brought as a putative class action pursuant to California Wage Law. Those putative plaintiffs who do opt-in to the collective action, pursuant to the FLSA, may hold the individual managers jointly and severally liable for damages.

In *Rulli v. CB Richard Ellis, Inc.*, (E.D. Wisconsin, filed March 15, 2009), maintenance workers who were issued phones or pagers were expected to have them on at all times — day and night. All calls were expected to be returned within 15 minutes, usually to answer questions or provide advice. At times, the workers were also expected to field calls and then perform work at specific locations. The suit raises the issue of how much time every 24 hours the workers should actually receive pay for this constant on-call duty. It asks for hourly pay and overtime pay for all the company's maintenance workers, nationwide, for this off-hour/on-call work.

Companies must make sure that their payroll practices stay on par with all technological changes, and capture all work related activities, whether they occur at work, at home, or via new channels of communication (like a BlackBerry or text messaging). The following may assist employers in minimizing FLSA claims:

- Determination of whether it is necessary that nonexempt employees have remote access through mobile technology.

- Implementation of clear policies requiring employees to report all work time regardless of where and when it occurs.

- Notifying and reminding supervisors that they should not request an employee to work off the clock.

- Imposing a requirement that employees sign an acknowledgment form noting the obligation to report to work at all times if the employer issues a BlackBerry or remote access technology to nonexempt employees.

- If nonexempt employees log in and out of work on their computers, employees may be permitted to manually input time instead of automatic time stamping (which may eliminate claims for lost time due to lengthy start ups or other required steps before accessing software).

Training Time

Generally, attendance at training programs **does not** constitute hours worked if all four of the following conditions are met:

- Attendance is outside normal working hours.

- Attendance is voluntary.

- The training is not directly related to the employee's job.

- The employee performs no work of value for the employer during the training time.

Overtime

Unless employees are subject to a specific exemption from overtime pay eligibility, the FLSA mandates that employees receive one and one-half times their regular hourly rate for working more than 40 hours in a workweek. Because these exemptions deprive employees of a statutory benefit, the courts narrowly construe them. Consequently, it is the employer's obligation to prove that each employee classified as exempt is actually covered by a statutory exemption.

An exemption **does not apply** unless all of the statutory prerequisites have been satisfied. With respect to administrative, professional, supervisory, and outside sales staff, employers must show that the employee in question is paid on a salary basis and primary duties are administrative, professional, or supervisory in nature. Unless both prongs of the exempt status test are satisfied fully, the employee must receive overtime compensation after working more than 40 hours in a workweek.

Computing Overtime Compensation

Overtime must be computed separately for each workweek. If an employee works 30 hours one week and 50 the next, the employer must pay the employee overtime compensation for 10 hours for the second week regardless of the "short" prior week.

An employer is not required to include paid time off (for example, sick days, vacation, or paid holidays) in hours worked for purposes of computing overtime. Thus, if holiday pay, sick pay, or any other type of pay for hours not actually worked is included in the weekly pay, the overtime rate does not have to be paid until the hours actually worked exceed 40 hours.

Rate of Pay

The rate of pay for overtime hours is one and one-half times the employee's regular rate of pay. The regular rate of pay cannot be less than the minimum wage. In determining the employee's regular rate for purposes of computing overtime, an employer must include the hourly wages and any bonus, shift premium incentive, or longevity pay, plus any commissions the employee receives. Even if the employee will not receive a bonus until later (for example, a quarterly production bonus), if the employee has a contractual right to receive that bonus, the payments must be included in the overtime compensation computation. This may require retroactively adjusting the overtime pay computation when the amount of the bonus is determined.

The regular rate for salaried employees may be determined by dividing the salary by the number of hours for which the salary is intended to compensate. Two methods are permissible for determining the regular rate for an employee who works at more than one rate of pay during a single workweek. The usual method is to calculate the regular rate for that week by determining the weighted average of the two rates. The regular rate is determined by dividing the total amount of compensation by the total number of hours worked.

Example: If an employee works 30 hours of production work at $9 per hour and 20 hours of custodial work at $8 per hour, the employee's regular rate would be determined as follows:

Total Compensation	=	(30 hours x $9 per hour) + (20 hours x $8 per hour)
	=	$270 + $160 = $ 430
Total Hours	=	50 Hours
Regular Rate	=	$430 ÷ 50 = $8.60 per hour
Overtime Premium	=	$8.60 ÷ 2 = $4.30 per hour
Overtime Hourly Rate	=	$8.60 + $4.30 = $12.90 per hour
Overtime Premium for Hours Worked Over 40	=	10 hours x $4.30 per hour = $43 (Note: $8.60 regular rate is previously reflected in the total compensation, therefore only the overtime premium must be calculated here)
Regular Rate	=	$430 + $43 = $473

Alternatively, where an employee performs two or more different types of work with different hourly rates, an accord may be reached before overtime hours are accrued. This agreement would determine the terms for the payment of overtime depending upon the specific type of work performed. The established rate of overtime pay (one and one-half times the hourly nonovertime rate) would directly coordinate with the type of work the employee performed during the accumulated overtime hours. This agreement must be in writing and created before the performance of any overtime work.

This method would reduce overtime compensation costs when an employee's overtime hours are typically spent on the lower paying of two job functions, as the custodial work in the previous example. However, extra overtime compensation for any additional pay — for example, bonuses — would still need to be computed and paid.

Unauthorized Overtime

Even when an employee does not have specific permission to work overtime, extra hours will count toward the total hours worked and thus be included in overtime as long as the employer knew or should have known that the employee was working extra hours and permitted the employee to do so. The employer may discipline an employee for working unauthorized overtime; however, the employer may not refuse to count the hours worked for purposes of determining overtime.

Scheduling the Workweek

Employers are free to set the day and hour when the seven-day workweek starts and ends, although it must be a fixed time. A change may be made later, although it must be intended to be permanent. The employer cannot attempt to minimize overtime payments by juggling the workweek to respond to changes in the pattern of hours worked.

Wage Payment

Subject to state law, failure to pay wages promptly may possibly subject the employer to liability for unpaid wages and additional damages. A written contract between the employer and the employee may provide for other methods of payment, or the custom of the industry may prevail.

As there is little guidance about what constitutes a custom justifying variance from the statutory rule on prompt payment, employers are cautioned to consult with counsel regarding this issue.

Deductions from Pay

Deductions made from wages for items such as cash or merchandise shortages, required uniforms, and tools of the trade are illegal if they reduce the wages of employees below minimum wage or reduce the amount of due overtime pay.

Required Deductions

Employers are required to make deductions for contributions and applicable local, state, and federal income taxes, Social Security, and Medicare taxes. The employer must submit the amounts withheld to the appropriate governmental agency. Additionally, employers generally may make deductions to correct errors, such as overpayment.

Employers who make deductions from the wages of exempt-status employees, however, run the risk of losing the exempt status of those employees. Moreover, deductions for shortages, debts to the employers, uniforms, and uniform maintenance generally are found to destroy exempt status.

Savings Bonds and Charitable Donations

Employees may authorize deductions from their paychecks for various reasons, including purchasing savings bonds or making charitable donations. Employers should only make deductions after first having obtained the employee's written authorization for such discretionary deductions.

Unions

Generally, employers are not required to deduct employees' union dues. However, a negotiated collective-bargaining agreement with a dues check off clause may require the employer to deduct dues.

Political Candidates

In accordance with state law, employees may voluntarily request a deduction from an employee's wages for any of the following:

- ♦ Support of political candidates.
- ♦ Political action committees.
- ♦ Political parties.
- ♦ Ballot issues.

An employee must provide an employer with the written authorization of voluntarily designation of wages. The employer either may absorb the administrative costs of the deductions or may deduct the administrative costs from the amount deducted before transmitting the balance to the designated recipient.

Note: While not a federal wage/hour issue, employers should be careful to apply the same policy for all deductions, regardless of the candidate or the issue.

Wares, Tools, or Machinery

Subject to state law, an employee must provide an employer with written authorization for any deductions made from the employee's wages for destroyed or damaged wares, tools, or machinery. However, such deductions may destroy an employee's exempt status.

Wage Garnishment

Wage garnishment occurs when, as the result of a court order or other procedure, an employer withholds a specific percentage of an employee's earnings for the payment of a debt. For example, if an employee's creditor obtains a court judgment against the employee, the creditor may collect the judgment by garnishing the employee's wages. Under this procedure, the creditor obtains a court order directing the employer (the garnishee) to withhold a certain amount from the employee's wages and pay that amount directly to the court. However, garnishment proceedings may not be instituted until the creditor has first given the employee an opportunity to make voluntary payment and the employee has failed to do so.

Regulations governing wage garnishment protects employees by limiting the amount of earnings that may be garnished in any workweek or pay period. In any given workweek or pay period, employers may garnish a maximum of 25 percent of the employee's disposable pay or the amount by which disposable earnings are 30 times greater the federal minimum wage. Disposable pay is the amount of remaining earnings after legally required deductions have been made.

Such legal deductions include, but are not limited to, the following:

- ♦ Federal, state, and local taxes.
- ♦ Social Security.
- ♦ Unemployment insurance.
- ♦ State employee retirement systems.

Example: An employee earns $500 per week after taxes. Twenty-five percent of the employee's disposable earnings is $125. Thirty times the federal minimum wage is $217.50 ($7.25 x 30). The portion of the employee's disposable earnings exceeding 30 times the federal minimum wage is $282.50 ($500 – $217.50). The employer should not withhold more than $125.

Complying with a Garnishment Order

An employer first learns of a garnishment proceeding when it receives a court order with an *Order and Notice of Garnishment and Answer of Employer*, which sets forth an employer's obligations. Along with the payment (via garnished wages), employers must review the form and submit a completed *Interim Report and Answer of Garnishee*, unless the garnishment has been satisfied to the extent required by law, in which case the employer shall submit a completed *Final Report and Answer of Garnishee* to the court. State and federal law limit the amount of money subject to garnishment. A step-by-step procedure for calculating the amount that may be garnished is contained in the report.

If the employee is no longer employed at the time the employer receives the notice, the employer should so indicate on the report and simply return it.

A continuing garnishment order remains in effect until one of the following occurs:

♦ The amount described in the garnishment order is paid in full.

♦ The judgment creditor files notice that the judgment is paid in full or otherwise satisfied.

♦ The court's continuous order is stayed by a bankruptcy court or because a trustee has been appointed.

♦ A garnishment order of higher priority under state or federal law, for example a child support order or a tax levy, is issued to the garnishee from a different judgment creditor with respect to the same debtor.

Note: State law may impose other requirements or limitations.

Employee Discharge Due to Excessive Garnishment

Employers may not discharge an employee whose earnings are subject to one creditor's successful garnishment in a 12-month period. However, unless the employer is otherwise prohibited from discharging the employee, two or more successful garnishments by separate creditors within the same 12-month period are valid grounds for discharge. Employers adopting a policy of discharging employees for multiple garnishments should be careful that such a policy does not have a discriminatory impact on any protected group of employees and does not violate protective state laws.

Violations of the garnishment laws may result in reinstatement of the discharged employee, payment of back wages, and restoration of improperly garnished amounts. Employers who willfully violate the discharge provisions of the law may be prosecuted criminally and fined up to $1,000, imprisoned up to one year, or both.

Child Support Orders

As the result of divorce or support proceedings, courts may order employers to make regular payroll deductions for the collection of child support payments.

Child support payments are given priority over other garnishment or wage-withholding orders and, depending on the employee's circumstances, the garnishment law allows up to 60 percent of an employee's disposable earnings to be garnished for child support. An additional 5 percent may be garnished for support payments more than 12 weeks in arrears. The amount to be deducted is fixed by court order and the employer should treat such a deduction as it would any payroll tax, paying the deducted payments regularly to the proper agency.

An employer may not discipline, discharge, or refuse to hire an individual because of a withholding order for child support. An employer violating these provisions may be liable both for statutory penalties and subject to a civil suit for wrongful discharge.

Equal Pay

The Equal Pay Act (EPA), enacted in 1963 as an amendment to the FLSA, prohibits employers from discriminating in wages between male and female employees. Pursuant to the EPA, an employer cannot pay lower wage rates to employees of one sex than to those of the other when the work that they do requires equal skill, effort, and responsibility and is performed under similar working conditions. However, individuals who perform roughly equivalent work under similar conditions may be paid at different rates when the payment is made under one of the following bona fide conditions:

- A seniority system.

- A merit system.

- A system that measures earnings by quality and quantity of production.

- Any other nondiscriminatory factor, such as job performance or qualifications.

Violations of the EPA subject employers to recovery of damages. Employers are prohibited from discriminating against employees in retaliation for the employees having made a complaint to the employer, the Department of Labor, or a state agency that they have not been paid proper wages.

Recordkeeping and Posting Requirements

The FLSA requires employers to maintain three general categories of records for nonexempt employees for at least three years:

- Payroll records, including the employee's name, Social Security number, address, birth date (if younger than 19), sex, occupation, time and day of week when employee's workweek begins, daily hours worked, total workweek hours, basis of the employee's wages, regular hourly pay rate, total daily or weekly straight-time earnings, total workweek overtime earnings, all additions or deductions from the employee's wages, total wages paid each pay period, date of payment, and the pay period covered by the payment.

- Certificates, agreements, plans, and notices, including collective-bargaining agreements, trusts, and employment contracts.

- Sales and purchase records (total volume).

Additionally, the FLSA requires employers to maintain the following record for at least two years:

- Basic employment and earnings records including time and earning cards or sheets.

- Wage rate tables.

- Work and time schedules.

- Order, shipping, and billing records.

- Records of additions to or deductions from wages paid.

Employers must also maintain summaries of federal and state minimum wage and overtime laws and regulations and post them in a conspicuous and accessible location in the workplace.

Enforcement

The Wage and Hour Division of the Department of Labor administers, investigates, and enforces compliance with the FLSA. Investigators must be allowed to enter any place of business to inspect the books, payrolls, or other records that relate to wages, hours, and conditions of employment and to question employees about whether their employer is complying with the act.

The Secretary of Labor, an individual employee, or group of employees may sue an employer to collect past-due wages. If the FLSA violation is willful, employees may also recover liquidated damages in an amount equal to past-due wages, plus interest and attorneys' fees and costs.

Note: Generally, a two-year statute of limitations applies to the recovery of backpay. In the case of a willful violation, however, the suit may be brought up to three years after the violation occurred.

The Davis-Bacon Act

The Davis-Bacon Act, located at 40 U.S.C.A. §§ 3141 – 3148, applies to the rate of wages and hours for laborers and mechanics employed by contractors and subcontractors on public buildings. The Davis-Bacon Act requires that each contract over $2,000 to which the United States or the District of Columbia is a party for the construction, alteration, or repair of public buildings or public works must contain a clause setting forth the minimum wages to be paid to various classes of laborers and mechanics employed under the contract. Accordingly, contractors or their subcontractors must pay workers employed directly on the worksite no less than the locally prevailing wages and fringe benefits paid on similar projects.

Note: The U.S. Secretary of Labor determines the local prevailing wage rates.

Davis-Bacon Contracts

Every contract covered by the Davis-Bacon Act must contain the following stipulations:

- The contractor or subcontractor must pay all mechanics and laborers employed directly on the worksite as follows:
  - Unconditionally and at least once a week.
  - Without subsequent deduction or rebate on any account.
  - All the full amounts accrued at the time of payment.
  - Computed at wage rates not less than those stated in the advertised specifications, regardless of any contractual relationship that may be alleged to exist between the contractor or subcontractor and the laborers and mechanics.
- The contractor will post the scale of wages to be paid in a prominent and easily accessible place at the worksite.
- There may be withheld from the contractor an amount of accrued payments, as the contracting officer deems necessary, to compensate laborers and mechanics employed by the contractor or any subcontractor on the work the difference between the following, and not refunded to the contractor or subcontractors or their agents:
  - The rates of wages required by the contract to be paid laborers and mechanics on the work.
  - The rates of wages received by the laborers and mechanics.

Every contract must also contain a provision that if the contracting officer finds that any laborer or mechanic employed by the contractor or any subcontractor directly on the worksite covered by the contract has been or is being paid a rate of wages less than the rate of wages required by the contract to be paid, the federal government by written notice to the contractor may terminate the contractor's right to proceed with the work or the part of the work as to which there has been a failure to pay the required wages. The government may have the work completed, by contract or otherwise, and the contractor and the contractor's sureties will be liable to the government for any excess costs the government incurs.

Note: On a weekly basis, each contractor and subcontractor must furnish a statement on the wages paid to each employee during the prior week.

Discharge of Obligation

The obligation of a contractor or subcontractor to make payment in accordance with the prevailing wage determinations of the Secretary of Labor, under the Davis-Bacon Act and other laws incorporating the act, may be discharged by any of the following payments:

- Making payments in cash.

- Making contributions to a trustee or to a third person under a fund, plan, or program.

- Assuming an enforceable commitment in providing benefits to laborers and mechanics and to bear the costs of a plan or program that may be reasonably anticipated, which was communicated in writing to the laborers and mechanics affected.

- Any combination of payment, contribution, and assumption, where the aggregate of the payments, contributions, and costs is no less than the basic hourly rate of pay plus the amount for medical or hospital care, pensions on retirement or death, compensation for injuries or illness resulting from occupational activity, or insurance to provide any of the foregoing, for unemployment benefits, life insurance, disability and sickness insurance, or accident insurance, for vacation and holiday pay, for defraying the costs of apprenticeship or other similar programs, or for other bona fide fringe benefits, but only where the contractor or subcontractor is not required by other federal, state, or local law to provide any of those benefits.

Overtime Pay

Overtime pay to which a laborer or mechanic is entitled under any federal law is calculated using the laborer or mechanic's regular or basic hourly rate of pay (or other alternative rate on which premium rate of overtime compensation is computed). However, where the amount of payments, contributions, or costs incurred with respect to the laborer or mechanic exceeds the applicable prevailing wage, the regular or basic hourly rate of pay (or other alternative rate) is the amount of payments, contributions, or costs actually incurred with respect to the laborer or mechanic minus the greater of the amount of contributions or costs actually incurred with respect to the laborer or mechanic or the amount determined to be owed but not actually paid.

Violations and Enforcement

The U.S. Comptroller General will directly pay to laborers and mechanics, from any accrued payments withheld under the terms of a contract, any wages found to be due to the laborers and mechanics. If the accrued payments withheld under the terms of the contract are insufficient to reimburse all the laborers and mechanics who have not been paid the wages required, the laborers and mechanics may bring a civil action and intervene against the contractor and the contractor's sureties.

During a civil suit, the following are not applicable defenses in regard to the laborers and mechanics actions:

- The acceptance of or agreement to accept less than the required rate of wages.

- A voluntarily made refund.

The Comptroller General will also distribute to all departments of the federal government a list of the names of persons whom the Comptroller General found to have disregarded their obligations to employees and subcontractors. Moreover, no contract will be awarded to persons appearing on the list or to any firm, corporation, partnership, or association in which the persons have an interest until three years have elapsed from the date of publication of the list.

Additional Information

Furloughs and the FLSA

According to 5 U.S.C. § 7551, a *furlough* occurs when an employee is placed in a temporary status without duties and pay because of lack of work or funds or for other nondisciplinary reasons. Most employers seeking to reduce labor costs without layoffs consider the following two alternatives:

♦ Mandatory furloughs.

♦ Reduced work hours.

However, employers that cannot meet the monetary requirements of payroll are still required to pay employees on the regular payday. An employer must pay covered nonexempt employees the full minimum wage and any statutory overtime due on the regularly scheduled payday for the workweek in question. Failure to do so constitutes a violation of the FLSA. When the correct amount of overtime compensation cannot be determined until some time after the regular pay period, however, the requirements of the FLSA will be satisfied if the employer pays the excess overtime compensation as soon after the regular pay period as is practicable.

Reduction in Salary and Hours

Employers may legally reduce the wages and number of hours of an hourly employee. The FLSA requires that all covered, nonexempt employees receive at least the applicable federal minimum wage for all hours worked. In a week in which employees work overtime, they must receive their regular rate of pay and overtime pay at a rate not less than one and one-half times the regular rate of pay for all overtime hours. However, the act does not:

♦ Preclude an employer from lowering an employee's hourly rate, provided the rate paid is at least the minimum wage, or from reducing the number of hours the employee is scheduled to work.

♦ Require employers to pay nonexempt employees for hours they did not work. For example, an employer is not required to pay an hourly employee for a full day of work if the employee was scheduled for a full day but only worked a partial day due to lack of work.

Exempt Employees

The FLSA exempts from minimum wage and overtime pay any employee employed in a bona fide executive, administrative, or professional capacity. An employee qualifies for exemption if the duties and salary tests are met. The FLSA requires payment of at least $455 per week on a salary basis for those employed as exempt executive, administrative, or professional employees. A *salary* is a predetermined amount constituting all or part of the employee's compensation, which is not subject to reduction because of variations in the quality or quantity of the work performed.

An employer must pay an exempt employee the full, predetermined salary amount for any week in which the employee performs any work without regard to the number of days or hours worked. However, there is no requirement that the predetermined salary be paid if the employee performs no work for an entire workweek. Deductions may not be made from the employee's predetermined salary for absences occasioned by the employer or by the operating requirements of the business. If the employee is ready, willing, and able to work, deductions may not be made for time when work is not available. Salary deductions are generally not permissible if the employee works less than a full day. Except for certain limited exceptions, reductions in the predetermined salary of an employee who is exempt will ordinarily cause a loss of the exemption. Such an employee must then be paid the minimum wage and overtime required by the FLSA. However, in some circumstances a prospective reduction in salary may not cause a loss of the exemption. An employer is not prohibited from prospectively reducing the predetermined salary amount to be paid regularly to an exempt employee during a business or economic slowdown, provided the change is both:

- Bona fide.

- Not used as a device to evade the salary basis requirements.

Such a predetermined regular salary reduction, not related to the quantity or quality of work performed, will not result in loss of the exemption, as long as the employee still receives on a salary basis at least $455 per week. Alternatively, deductions from predetermined pay occasioned by day-to-day or week-to-week determinations of the operating requirements of the business constitute impermissible deductions from the predetermined salary and would result in loss of the exemption. The difference is that the first instance involves a prospective reduction in the predetermined pay to reflect the long-term business needs, rather than a short-term, day-to-day, or week-to-week deduction from the fixed salary for absences from scheduled work occasioned by the employer or its business operations.

According to 29 C.F.R. 541.710, and applicable to salaried exempt employees who are public sector employees, deductions from the pay of an employee of a public agency for absences due to a budget-required furlough disqualify the employee from being paid on a salary basis only in the workweek when the furlough occurs and for which the pay is accordingly reduced. Additionally, the application of the FLSA is not affected if the state or local government employee is considered an essential or critical employee for the purposes of a required furlough.

Physicians, lawyers, outside salespersons, or teachers in bona fide educational institutions are not subject to any salary requirements. Deductions from the salary or pay of such employees will not result in loss of the exemption.

Employee Leave

An employer can substitute or reduce an exempt employee's accrued leave (or run a negative leave balance) for the time an employee is absent from work, even if it is less than a full day and even if the absence is directed by the employer because of lack of work, without affecting the salary basis payment, provided that the employee still receives payment equal to the employee's predetermined salary in any week in which any work is performed even if the employee has no leave remaining.

Additionally, if the employer seeks volunteers to take time off due to insufficient work, and the exempt employee volunteers to take the day(s) off for personal reasons other than sickness or disability, salary deductions may be made for one or more full days of missed work. However, the employee's decision must be completely voluntary.

On-Call Time

Whether on-call time is hours worked under the FLSA depends upon the particular circumstances. Generally, the facts may show that the employee was engaged to wait (which is work time) or the facts may show that the employee was waiting to be engaged (which is not work time). Employees who perform part or all of their normal job duties during a furlough day are working while performing such duties.

Enforcement

The following remedies are available to correct violations of the FLSA when employees are not paid on a timely basis:

- The U.S. Secretary of Labor may bring suit for back wages and an equal amount as liquidated damages or for interest on the back wages, or the secretary may bring suit for an injunction against the failure to pay wages when due.

- Employees who have filed complaints or provided information during an investigation are protected under the law. They may not be discriminated against or discharged for filing complaints or providing information; if they are discriminated against or discharged, they may file a suit or the secretary may file a suit on their behalf for relief, including reinstatement to their jobs and payment of wages lost plus monetary damages.

- An employee may file suit to recover back wages, and an equal amount in liquidated damages, plus attorney's fees and court costs.

- Civil money penalties may be assessed for repeat and/or willful violations of the FLSA's minimum wage or overtime requirements.

- Employers willfully violating the law also may face criminal penalties, including fines and imprisonment.

Hours-of-Service for Property Carrying Commercial Motor Vehicle Drivers

Property carrying, commercial motor vehicle (CMV) drivers must comply with the following hours-of-service regulations, located at 49 C.F.R. 395:

- May drive a maximum of 11 hours after 10 consecutive hours off duty.

- May not drive and/or work longer than 14 hours in any one shift, following 10 consecutive hours off duty.

- May not drive more than 60 hours over a seven-day period or 70 hours over an eight-day period. However, a driver may restart a seven or eight consecutive day period after taking 34 or more consecutive hours off duty to recover from cumulative fatigue.

- Drivers using a sleeper berth must take at least eight consecutive hours in the sleeper berth, plus two consecutive hours either in the sleeper berth, off duty, or any combination of the two.

Short-Haul Operators

Drivers of property-carrying CMVs, which do not require a Commercial Driver's License for operation, and who operate within a 150 air-mile radius of their normal work reporting location must comply with the following:

- May drive a maximum of 11 hours after coming on duty following 10 or more consecutive hours off duty.

- Are not required to keep records-of-duty status (RODS).

- May not drive after the 14th hour after coming on duty five days a week or after the 16th hour after coming on duty two days a week.

Employers are required to maintain and retain accurate time records for a period of 6 months demonstrating all of the following:

- The time the duty period began and ended.

- Total hours on duty each day in place of RODS.

Drivers who use the short-haul provision are not eligible to use the 100 air-mile provision (49 C.F.R. 395.1(e)) or the current 16-hour exception (49 C.F.R. 395.1(o)).

Passenger-Carrying Vehicle Drivers

According to 49 C.F.R. 395.5, subject to the exceptions and exemptions, motor carriers must comply with and enforce the following regulations for passenger-carrying vehicle drivers:

♦ Drivers may not work/drive more than 10 hours following eight consecutive hours off duty.

♦ Drivers may not work/drive for any period after having been on duty 15 hours following eight consecutive hours off duty.

Motor carriers may not permit or require a driver of a passenger-carrying commercial motor vehicle to drive, nor may any driver drive a passenger-carrying commercial motor vehicle, regardless of the number of motor carriers using the driver's services, for any period after any of the following occur:

♦ The driver was on duty 60 hours in any seven consecutive days if the employing motor carrier does not operate commercial motor vehicles every day of the week.

♦ The driver was on duty 70 hours in any period of eight consecutive days if the employing motor carrier operates commercial motor vehicles every day of the week.

Frequently Asked Questions

Q **If a salaried exempt employee reports to work late or leaves early, can the salary be reduced because of that lost work time?**

A No. Payment on a salary basis means that the employer has promised to pay at least a fixed amount for a predetermined period of time. Late arrival at work or leaving before the end of the workday cannot result in reductions of the employee's base salary. Of course, appropriate disciplinary action may result from unreliable attendance or other misconduct.

Q **If a salaried exempt employee takes an extended meal break, can the salary be reduced because of that lost work time?**

A No. Similar to arriving late to work or leaving early, missing part of a workday because of extended meal breaks cannot result in reduction in the employee's base salary. While the FLSA does not mandate that meal breaks be provided, various state laws direct that meal breaks be given to certain employees, usually depending upon the number of hours worked in a day.

Q **Can any deduction be made from an employee's salary due to a missed part of a workday?**

A No. When an exempt employee reports to work on a workday, the employee must be paid for the entire day.

Q **If the facility is closed because of a snowstorm or other inclement weather, must the salaried exempt employees be paid for that workday?**

A Yes. Salary cannot be reduced because of the quality or quantity of work performed in any given workweek. Thus, if work is not available because the workplace is closed (for whatever reason), exempt employees must be paid their full salary for that workweek if any work has been performed during that week.

Q **Are there times when an exempt employee's salary is subject to reduction because of lost work time?**

A Yes. Under the following very limited circumstances, the base salary can be reduced:

• An employee is absent for one or more days for personal reasons other than sickness or accident.

• An employee is absent for one or more days for sickness or accident and the deduction is in accordance with a bona fide sickness and accident plan, policy, or practice.

• An employee is absent due to service of jury or military duty (at which time there is an offset for military service or jury duty pay, rather than an actual salary deduction).

• Good-faith penalties for infractions of safety rules of major significance.

• For unpaid disciplinary suspensions of one or more full days imposed in good faith for workplace conduct rule infractions.

- An employee misses an entire week of work.
- Intermittent leaves pursuant to the Family and Medical Leave Act (FMLA). The FMLA specifically provides that deductions for intermittent leaves of less than one day will not violate the salary basis test (but may result in loss of exempt status under state law).

Q   What constitutes an infraction of a safety rule of major significance?

A   Deductions from an exempt employee's base salary for reasons other than full-day absences are so disfavored that any deduction will be examined closely. While deductions are permitted to penalize salaried employees who violate major safety rules, the Department of Labor or a court rarely will recognize misconduct as satisfying this exception to the no-docking rule. Nonetheless, examples of violations of safety rules that may satisfy this standard are set forth in the Wage-Hour Administrator's regulations; for example, smoking cigarettes in an explosives factory or oil refinery. Thus, unless the infraction is of comparable magnitude (which probably will result in termination of employment, rather then a monetary penalty) docking should be avoided as a means of punishing violation of a work or safety rule.

Q   If an exempt employee reports to work and then leaves early because of illness and does not report to work on the following day, can a deduction be made for all the time missed?

A   No. Although it is permissible to make a deduction in an amount of a day or more for sickness or accident, as long as bona fide sick pay plan exists, it is not proper to make such a deduction in an increment of less than a day. Thus, a full day deduction is permitted for the second day of the illness; however, the employee must be paid for the entire day the first day when the employee reported to work and then became ill. However, if the employee is eligible for leave under the FMLA and the employee's health care provider has certified that it is medically necessary for the employee to take intermittent leave, a partial-day deduction may be permissible. Since this practice otherwise would violate the FLSA, any deduction should be made with great care and after an in-depth analysis of these conflicting statutory provisions and state law.

Q   If an employee has used up all paid sick days under the sick pay plan or is not yet eligible to participate in the plan and is absent for two days, can a deduction be made for these full-day absences?

A   Yes. As long as a bona fide sick pay plan exists, the employer is permitted to make deductions for full-day absences.

Q   Can deductions be made from accrued paid time off if a salaried employee is absent for less than a complete workday?

A   Yes. According to the Department of Labor, but not necessarily all courts, use of accrued paid time off to recompense for absences of less than a full day is permissible. The Department of Labor permits an employer who provides bona fide vacation and sick time benefits to substitute or reduce the accrued benefits for the time an employee is absent from work. Additionally, the substitution or reduction is permitted if the absence is less than a full day, without affecting the salary basis of payment, if the employee continues to receive in payment an amount equal to the guaranteed salary. However, where an employee has exhausted these benefits, deductions may be made in increments of full days only for absences for personal reasons or illness. Deductions from the salaries of otherwise exempt employees for partial-day absences after they have exhausted their vacation or sick time benefits have never been permitted under the FLSA regulations. Docking of accrued paid time off when an exempt employee is absent for less than a full workday may expose the organization to loss of exempt status.

Q   If an exempt employee were summoned for jury duty after working part of a workweek, must the employee be paid for that workweek?

A Yes. An employee who works at all during any workweek must be paid the entire week's salary. An offset is permitted to account for any monies received from the court for that jury service.

Q **If an exempt employee is called to perform reserve duty, to serve in the National Guard, or to participate in other military service, must the employee be paid for that time of service?**

A Yes. An exempt employee who works at all during the workweek when military service begins or ends must be paid the entire week's salary. An offset is permitted to account for any monies received for military service.

Q **What is the penalty if improper deductions are made?**

A When an employer improperly docks an exempt employee's pay, courts and the Department of Labor conclude that the employer did not intend to compensate the employee on a salary basis. If the facts show that the employer had an actual practice of making improper deductions, the employer will lose the exemption for the period in which the improper deductions were made for the entire class of employees in the job classification and working for the manager(s) responsible for the improper deductions. The exemption may be retained if any of the following occur:

- The deduction resulted from inadvertence.

- The deduction is corrected promptly after the discovery of the error.

- The employer demonstrates that pay practices have been implemented to avoid repetition of similar errors.

Although the regulations provide for this window of correction, deductions from salary due to partial-day absences are contrary to the intent of the salary basis test and should be avoided. Courts offer no assurances where employers have made improper deductions. An employer's acts to correct wrongful deductions are not guaranteed to fulfill this limited defense to loss of exempt status.

Q **What is the effect of the deductions made pursuant to the FMLA for absences of less than a full workday upon exempt status?**

A An employer may be called upon to grant leave of absence under the FMLA on a partial-day basis, rather than an ongoing basis. The FMLA permits employers to make deductions from an employee's salary for any hours taken as intermittent or reduced FMLA leave within a workweek without affecting the exempt status of the employee. In contrast, if the employee misses part of a workday for a condition not covered by the FMLA and the employer made a deduction from the base salary, loss of exempt status would result.

Q **What liability will result if employees are wrongfully treated as exempt?**

A If employees are classified as exempt, but are nonexempt, liability would include the following:

- Liability for all unpaid overtime compensation.

- Attorneys' fees and costs if litigation is necessary to determine where the liability existed.

- Liquidated damages equaling the amount of backpay due to the employee.

- A fine of $1,000 per violation. Willful violations may be prosecuted criminally and the violator fined up to $10,000.

Contact Information
Department of Labor, Wage and Hour Division

200 Constitution Avenue, NW
Washington, DC 20210

Telephone: 866-4-USWAGE or 866-4-USA-DOL
Internet: *www.dol.gov/whd*

Illinois Law

Minimum Wage and Overtime

The Illinois Minimum Wage Law is located at 820 Ill. Comp. Stat. §§ 105/1 – 105/15 and Ill. Admin. Code tit. 56, pt. 210.100 – 210.1050.

Every employer must pay to all employees age 18 or older in every occupation a minimum wage of at least $8.25 per hour. The minimum wage increases in an amount of 25 cents each year on July 1.

Any employee not exempt under the Illinois minimum wage statute that works for more than 40 hours per week must be paid for overtime at the rate of one and one-half times the regular rate of pay.

Where Illinois law does not address a specific topic, but the Fair Labor Standards Act (FLSA) does, employers should abide by the FLSA. **Moreover, i**n areas where the state and federal governments have concurrent powers under their respective statutes, the stricter of the two laws prevails.

Covered Employers

Illinois' Minimum Wage Law covers any individual, partnership, association, corporation, limited liability company, business trust, governmental or quasi-governmental body, or any person or group of persons acting directly or indirectly in the interest of an employer in relation to an employee for which one or more persons are gainfully employed on some day within a calendar year.

An employer is subject to the law in a calendar year on and after the first day of the calendar year in which the employer employs one or more persons, and for the following calendar year.

Covered Employees

Illinois' Minimum Wage Law covers any individual permitted to work by an employer in an occupation.

Ridesharing Arrangements

Participation by an employee in any kind of ridesharing arrangement will not result in the application of the Minimum Wage Law to the period of time necessary to effectively use such an arrangement.

Minimum Wage and Overtime Exemptions

Exempt employees do not earn an hourly minimum wage and employers are not required to pay exempt employees an overtime wage.

The following employees are **exempt** from the provisions of Illinois' Minimum Wage Law:

- ♦ Individuals working for an employer employing fewer than four employees exclusive of the employer's parent, spouse, or child or other members of the immediately family.

- ♦ Employees employed in agriculture or aquaculture if any of the following apply:

  - The employee is employed by an employer that did not use more than 500 working days of agricultural or aquacultural labor during any calendar quarter during the preceding calendar year.

  - The employee is the parent, spouse, child, or other member of the employer's immediate family.

- The employee is employed as a hand-harvest laborer and is paid on a piece-rate basis in an operation that is customarily and generally recognized as paying on a piece-rate basis in the region of employment, the employee commutes daily from the employee's permanent residence to the farm on which the employee is employed, and the employee has been employed in agriculture fewer than 13 weeks during the preceding calendar year.

- If the employee, not including commuting hand harvest laborers, is the following:

  - Sixteen years of age or under, employed as a hand-harvest laborer, and paid on a piece-rate basis in an operation that is generally recognized as paying on a piece-rate basis in the region of employment.

  - Employed on the same farm with the parent or person standing in the place of the parent.

  - Paid at the same piece rate as employees over 16 years of age and over on the same farm.

- Individuals employed in domestic service in a private home.

- ***Outside salespersons***, defined as employees regularly engaged in making sales or obtaining orders or contracts for services where a major portion of the duties are performed away from the employer's place of business.

- Members of a religious corporation or organization.

- Individuals employed at an accredited Illinois college or university at which the employee is a student who is covered under the provisions of the FLSA.

- Individuals working for a motor carrier whose qualifications and maximum hours of service are regulated by the U.S. Secretary of Transportation or the state of Illinois.

Camp Counselors

Camp counselors who reside on the premises of a nonprofit seasonal camp are not subject to the adult minimum wage if the counselor works 40 or more hours a week and receives a total weekly salary of not less than the adult minimum wage for a 40-hour week. Counselors working fewer than 40 hours per week must be paid the minimum wage for each hour worked. Every employer of a camp counselor is entitled to an allowance for meals and lodging as part of the minimum hourly wage rate, not to exceed 25 percent of the minimum wage rate.

Similarly, a camp counselor employed at a day camp is not subject to the adult minimum wage if the camp counselor is paid a stipend on a one-time or periodic basis. If the camp counselor is a minor, the minor's parent, guardian, or other custodian must provide written consent to the terms of payment before the commencement of the employment. A *day camp* is a seasonal recreation program in operation for no more than 16 weeks intermittently throughout the calendar year, accommodating for profit or under philanthropic or charitable auspices, five or more children under age 18, not including overnight programs. A day camp does not include a day care agency, child care facility or foster family home as licensed by the Illinois Department of Children and Family Services.

Uniform Allowances

According to Ill. Admin. Code tit. 56, pt. 210.140, no allowance for supply, maintenance, or laundering of required uniforms is permitted as part of the minimum wage.

Subminimum Wages

In certain limited cases, individuals that are not exempt may be paid wages lower than Illinois' minimum wage.

Illinois law provides for the payment of subminimum wages in the following circumstances:

- **Employees with Impaired Earning Capacity.** Individuals whose earning capacity is impaired by age or physical or mental deficiency or injury may be employed at subminimum wages and for periods of time fixed in a special license issued by the director. No person who maintains a production level within the limits required of other employees may be paid at less than the minimum wage.

- **Learners.** Learners may be employed at lower than the minimum wage under regulations issued by the Illinois Director of Labor. However, under no circumstances may a learner, age 18 or older, be paid less than 70 percent of the minimum wage. An employee may not be treated as a learner in any occupation for which the required training has been completed. In addition, an employee may not be treated as a learner after six months of required training, unless the director finds that for the particular occupation a minimum of proficiency cannot be acquired in six months.

Unless an employee's wages are reduced as a learner, then in lieu of the minimum wage an employer may pay an employee who is 18 years of age or older during the first 90 consecutive calendar days after the employee is initially employed by the employer, a wage that is not more than 50 cents less than the minimum wage. However, an employer may not pay less than the minimum wage to:

- A day or temporary laborer (as defined in the Day and Temporary Labor Services Act) who is age 18 or older.

- An employee who is age 18 or older and whose employment is occasional or irregular and requires no more than 90 days to complete.

At no time may the wages of an employee under 18 years of age be more than 50 cent less than the wage required to be paid to employees who are at least 18 years of age.

Tipped Employees

Tipped employees must also receive the minimum wage; however, the employer may take credit for the employee's tips in an amount not exceeding 40 percent of the Illinois minimum wage. Currently, the tipped employee rate is $4.95 per hour.

Important: The tipped employee rate is different for youths under 18 years of age. Currently the tipped employee rate for youths under 18 is $4.65 per hour.

The tip credit may be no more than the amount of tips actually received by the employee and not returned to the employer. Tips plus wages must equal or exceed the minimum wage. Tips may only be credited where they are customarily part of the employee's remuneration, and employers must provide substantial evidence of the amounts of tips claimed as a credit.

Discrimination

Under the Minimum Wage Law, an employer may not discriminate between employees on the basis of sex or mental or physical disability, except as otherwise provided in the law by paying wages to employees at a rate less than the rate at which the employer pays wages to employees for the same or substantially similar work on that require equal skill, effort, and responsibility and that are performed under similar working conditions, except where the payment is made pursuant to any of the following:

- A seniority system.

- A merit system.

- A system that measures earnings by quantity or quality of production.

- A differential based on any other factor other than sex or mental or physical disability, except as otherwise provided in the Minimum Wage Law.

Overtime

Except as otherwise provided by law, no employer may employ an employee for a workweek of more than 40 hours unless the employee receives compensation for employment in excess of the 40 hours at a rate not less than one and one-half times the regular rate at which the employee is employed.

Overtime Exemptions

Illinois' overtime law **does not apply** to the following:

♦ Employees working in small businesses with fewer than four employees.

♦ Employees in agriculture or aquaculture.

♦ Domestics.

♦ Outside salespersons.

♦ Members of religious organizations.

♦ Students working for colleges or universities they attend.

♦ Motor carriers.

♦ Any salesperson or mechanic primarily engaged in selling or servicing automobiles, trucks, or farm implements, if the salesperson is employed by a nonmanufacturing establishment primarily engaged in selling vehicles or implements to ultimate purchasers.

♦ Any salesperson primarily engaged in selling trailers, boats, or aircraft, if the salesperson is employed by a nonmanufacturing establishment primarily engaged in selling trailers, boats, or aircraft to ultimate purchasers.

♦ Any employer of agricultural labor, with respect to the agricultural labor.

♦ Any employee of a governmental body excluded from the definition of employee under paragraph (e)(2)(C) of § 3 of the FLSA.

♦ Any employee employed in a bona fide executive, administrative, or professional capacity.

This includes any radio or television announcer, news editor, or chief engineer, as defined by or covered by the FLSA and the rules adopted under that law, as both exist on March 30, 2003, but compensated at the amount of salary specified in subsections (a) and (b) of 29 C.F.R. 541.600 as proposed in the Federal Register on March 31, 2003, or a greater amount of salary as may be adopted by the U.S. Department of Labor.

The Director of the Department of Labor may adopt a weekly wage rate standard by regulation lower than that provided for executive, administrative, and professional employees covered under the FLSA for bona fide executive, administrative, and professional employees of not-for-profit corporations.

♦ Any commissioned employee, as described by the FLSA.

♦ Any employment of an employee working for another under a work time exchange agreement between the employees.

♦ Any employee of a not-for-profit educational or residential child care institution who is directly involved on a daily basis in educating or caring for children (such as orphans, foster children, abused, neglected, or abandoned children or other homeless children) and who resides in the institution's residential facilities. The employee must be compensated at an annual rate of not less than $13,000 or, if the employee resides in the facilities and receives board and lodging from the institution without cost, not less than $10,000.

♦ Any employee employed as a crewmember of any uninspected towing vessel operating in any navigable waters in or along the boundaries of Illinois.

Additionally, an employer **may not** employ any employee for period(s) of more than 10 hours in a workweek over the maximum hours without paying overtime compensation if during the period(s) the employee is receiving remedial education that meets all of the following requirements:

♦ Is provided to employees who lack a high school diploma or educational attainment at the eighth grade level.

♦ Is designed to provide reading and other basic skills at an eighth grade level or below.

♦ Does not include job specific training.

Workweek

An employee's workweek is a fixed and regularly recurring period of 168 hours, seven consecutive 24-hour periods. The workweek need not coincide with the calendar week, but it may begin on any calendar day and at any hour of the day. A *calendar week* is the seven consecutive day period beginning at 12:01 a.m. Sunday morning and ending on the following Saturday night at midnight. Once the beginning time of a workweek is established, it remains fixed, regardless of the schedule of hours worked by the employee. The beginning of the workweek may be changed if the change is intended to be permanent and is not designed to evade the overtime requirements. In the event an employer fails to establish a fixed and regular workweek, the director will consider a calendar week as the applicable workweek.

Employers are not required to pay overtime compensation for any of the following:

♦ Hours in excess of eight per day.

♦ Work on Saturdays, Sundays, holidays, or regular days of rest, unless hours worked exceed 40 per week.

Additionally, employers are not required to include holiday, vacation, sick pay, or other similar causes in the regular rate of the employee. Hours that are paid for, but not worked, will not increase the regular rate. Sums paid as gifts, such as those made at holidays or other amounts that are not measured by or dependent on hours worked may not be credited towards, or used to offset from, overtime compensation due by law.

Regular Rate of Pay and Computation of Overtime

Overtime is computed on the basis of the employee's *regular rate*.

If an employee is employed solely based on a single hourly rate, the hourly rate is the regular rate. For overtime hours, the employees must be paid, in addition to the straight time hourly earning, a sum determined by multiplying one-half the hourly rate by the number of hours worked over the maximum set by statute. However, if an employee is employed solely on a weekly salary basis, the regular hourly rate of pay is computed by dividing the salary by the number of hours which the salary is intended to compensate.

When an employee is employed on a piece-rate basis (so much per piece, dozen, and gross) the regular rate of pay is computed by adding together the total earnings for the workweek from piece rates and all other earnings (such as bonuses) and any sums paid for waiting time or other hours worked. This sum is then divided by the number of hours worked in that week to yield the piece worker's regular rate for that week. For the overtime work the piece worker is entitled to be paid, in addition to the total straight time weekly earnings, one-half this regular rate for each hour over the maximum set by statute.

When computing day rates and job rates an employee may be paid a flat sum for a day's work or for doing a particular job, without regard to the number of hours worked in the day or at the job, and receive no other form of compensation. In such a case, the employee's regular rate is found by totaling all sums received at the day rates or job rates in the workweek and dividing by the total hours actually worked. The employee is then entitled to extra half-time pay at this rate for all hours worked over the maximum set by statute.

Exclusions from Regular Rate

The following payments are **excluded** from the regular rate computation:

- ♦ Sums paid as gifts, such as those made at holidays or other amounts that are not measured by or dependent on hours worked.

- ♦ Payments made for occasional periods when no work is performed due to a vacation, holiday, illness, failure of employer to provide sufficient work, or other similar cause.

- ♦ Sums paid in recognition of services performed, which are:

  - • Determined at the sole discretion of the employer.

  - • Made pursuant to a bona fide thrift or savings plan.

  - • In recognition of a special talent.

- ♦ Contributions irrevocably made by an employer to a trustee or third person pursuant to a bona fide plan for providing old age, retirement, life, accident, or health insurance or similar benefits for employees

- ♦ Extra compensation provided by a premium rate paid for certain hours worked by the employee in any day or workweek because the hours are hours worked in excess of eight a day where the premium rate is not less than one and one-half times the rate established in good faith for like work performed in nonovertime hours on other days.

- ♦ Extra compensation provided by a premium rate paid to employees on Saturdays, Sundays, holidays, or regular days of rest where the premium rate is not less than one and one-half times the rate established in good faith for like work performed in nonovertime hours on other days.

- ♦ Extra compensation provided by a premium rate paid to the employee, in pursuance of an applicable employment contract or collective-bargaining agreement, for work outside of the hours established in good faith by the contract or agreement as the basic workday where the premium rate is not less than one and one-half times the rates established in good faith by the contract or agreement for like work performed during the workday or workweek.

Compensation Time

Private employers are prohibited from using compensation time (comp time) to make up for overtime work by nonexempt employees.

The practice of using comp time is prohibited even if the comp time is provided at the rate of time and a half.

Mandated Overtime Prohibited for Nurses

With exception, the following nurses (who receive an hourly wage and are directly responsible for overseeing or carrying out nursing care) **may not** be required to work mandated overtime:

- ♦ Advanced practice nurses. However, a certified registered nurse anesthetist who is primarily engaged in performing the duties of a nurse anesthetist is not covered by the mandated overtime protections.

- ♦ Registered professional nurses.

- ♦ Licensed practical nurses.

Mandatory overtime is hospital-required work in excess of an agreed-to, predetermined work shift.

Time spent by nurses required to be available as a condition of employment in specialized units, such as surgical nursing services, **does not apply** to any calculation in determining the amount of time worked in the application of the prohibition against mandated overtime.

Nurses are also entitled to a specific amount of off-duty time. When a nurse is mandated to work up to 12 consecutive hours, the nurse must be allowed at least eight consecutive hours of off-duty time immediately following the completion of a shift.

However, nurses may be required to work mandated overtime in cases of unforeseen emergent circumstances when overtime is required only as a last resort. The mandated overtime **may not** exceed four hours beyond an agreed-to, predetermined work shift.

An unforeseen emergent circumstance exists when any of the following occurs:

♦ Any declared national, state, or municipal disaster, other catastrophic event that will substantially affect or increase the need for health care services.

♦ Any implementation of a hospital's disaster plan that will substantially affect or increase the need for health care services.

♦ Any circumstance where a patient's health care situation demands specialized nursing skills through the completion of a procedure.

An unforeseen emergent circumstance **does not** include the failure of a hospital to have enough nursing staff to meet the usual and reasonably predictable nursing needs of the patients.

No hospital may discipline, discharge, or take any other adverse employment action against a nurse solely because the nurse refused to work mandated overtime as prohibited by law. Any nurse may file a complaint with the Illinois Department of Public Health regarding an alleged violation of the mandatory overtime protections.

Any violation must be proved by clear and convincing evidence that a nurse was required to work overtime against the nurse's will. The hospital may defeat the violation claim by presenting clear and convincing evidence that an unforeseen emergent circumstance that required overtime work existed at the time the employee was required or compelled to work.

The complaint must be filed within 45 days following the occurrence of the incident giving rise to the alleged violation. The department must forward notification of the alleged violation to the hospital in question within three business days after the complaint is filed. Upon receiving a complaint of a violation, the department may take any enforcement action authorized under the Hospital Licensing Act, 210 Ill. Comp. Stat. §§ 85/1 – 85/16.

Collective Bargaining

The Minimum Wage Law **does not** limit the right of employees to bargain collectively through representatives of their own choosing to establish wages or other conditions of work in excess of the applicable minimum legal standards.

Posting Requirements

Every employer covered by the Minimum Wage Law must keep an approved summary of the law and copies of applicable regulations or a summary of the regulations posted in a conspicuous and accessible place in the workplace.

Additionally, all employers must conspicuously post and maintain the Illinois Department of Labor *Notice to Employers and Employees* poster covering the payment of wages, child labor law, overtime, the Wage Payment and Collection Act, and the One Day Rest in Seven Act.

Recordkeeping Requirements

According to Ill. Admin. Code tit. 56, pt. 210.700, every employer subject to the Minimum Wage Law must make and keep, for a period of not less than three years, true and accurate records of all the following for each employee:

- ◆ Name and address.
- ◆ Birth date.
- ◆ Social Security number.
- ◆ Sex and occupation in which employed.
- ◆ Time of day and day of week when workweek begins.
- ◆ Basis on which wages are paid.
- ◆ Additions and deductions from wages for each pay period and an explanation of additions and deductions.
- ◆ Type of payment (such as hourly rate, salary, or commission), straight time, and overtime pay and total wages paid each pay period.
- ◆ Dates of payment of each pay period covered by the payment.
- ◆ Any other information and reports required by the director.

Additionally, any employer that provides paid vacation to employees must maintain true and accurate records of the number of vacation days earned for each year and the dates on which the vacation days were taken and paid for no less than three years.

Records must be open for inspection or transcription by the director or an authorized representative at any reasonable time. In addition, every employer must furnish to the director or an authorized representative on demand a sworn statement of the records and information upon forms prescribed or approved by the director.

Learners or Individuals with a Disability

Individuals employed as a learner or individuals with disabilities employed at a subminimum wage must be identified on the payroll as learners or individuals with disabilities, together with their rate of pay and occupation.

Whenever possible, records of learners and individuals with disabilities are to be maintained in a separate file or folder for ready accessibility.

Tipped Employees

With respect to employees whose compensation is derived in part from gratuities, every employer must, in addition to all other required records, also maintain and preserve records containing the following information and data with respect to each employee:

- ◆ An identifying symbol, letter, or number on the payroll record indicating that the employee is a person whose wage is determined in part by gratuities.
- ◆ The report received from the employee setting forth gratuities received during each workday. These reports submitted by the employee must be signed and include the employee's Social Security number.

♦ The amount by which the wage of each employee has increased by gratuities as determined by the employer (not in excess of 40 percent of the applicable statutory minimum wage). The amount per hour that the employer takes as a gratuity credit must be reported to the employee in writing each time it is changed from the amount per hour taken in the preceding pay period.

♦ Hours worked each workday in any occupation in which the employee does not receive gratuities and the total daily or weekly straight-time payment made by the employer for the hours.

♦ Hours worked each workday in an occupation in which the employee received tips or gratuities and total daily or weekly straight-time earnings for the hours.

Farm Employees

Farm labor contractors who pay farm employees on their own behalf or on the behalf of another must keep the following payroll records:

♦ Employees' total earnings for each pay period.

♦ All withholdings from wages.

♦ Net earnings.

Additionally, for farm workers employed on a time basis, the number of units of time employed and the rate per unit of time must be recorded on the payroll records, and for farm workers employed on a piece rate basis, the number of units of work performed and the rate per unit must be recorded on such records.

Homeworkers

Every six months Illinois employers are required to provide the state Department of Labor with a record of the names and addresses of each industrial homeworker employed.

Additional Provisions

Should any part of the records or documents be located in a place other than the business premises of the employer, the records or documents must be made available to the duly authorized representatives of the director for examination.

Should any part be located outside of the geographic boundaries of Illinois, the employer must pay all expenses of examination by the director's representatives, including travel, travel time, meal, and lodging for each representative of the director conducting the examination or investigation.

Enforcement and Penalties

The director or an authorized representative has the authority to:

♦ Investigate and gather data regarding the wages, hours, and other conditions and practices of employment in any industry covered by the Minimum Wage Law.

♦ Enter and inspect places and records and make transcriptions at reasonable times during regular business hours (not including lunchtime at a restaurant), question employees, and investigate facts, conditions, practices, or matters deemed necessary or appropriate to determine whether any person has violated the Minimum Wage Law or to enforce the law.

The director may also require employers to comply with the following:

♦ Submit full and correct statements and reports in writing, including sworn statements of the wages, hours, names, addresses, and other information pertaining to employees as necessary for the enforcement of the Minimum Wage Law.

♦ Require by subpoena, as signed and issued by the director, the attendance and testimony of witnesses and the production of all books, records, and other evidence relative to a matter under investigation or hearing. If a person fails to comply with any subpoena lawfully issued or a witness refuses to produce evidence or testify to any matter regarding which the witness may be lawfully interrogated, the court may, upon application of the Director, compel obedience by proceedings for contempt.

Wage Violations

An employer, an employer's agent, or the officer or agent of any private employer that pays or agrees to pay to any employee wages at a rate less than required by the Minimum Wage Law is guilty of a Class B misdemeanor.

Each week on any day of which the employee is paid less than the applicable wage rate constitutes a separate offense.

Records Violations

An employer, an employer's agent, or the officer or agent of any private employer is guilty of a Class B misdemeanor if the employer, agent, or officer commits any of the following:

♦ Fails to keep the records required under the Minimum Wage Law or to furnish required records or any other required information to the director or an authorized representative upon request.

♦ Fails to make and preserve required records.

♦ Falsifies records.

♦ Refuses to make records available to the director or an authorized representative.

♦ Refuses to furnish a sworn statement of its records or any other information required for the proper enforcement of the Minimum Wage Law.

♦ Fails to post a summary of the Minimum Wage Law or a copy of any applicable regulations.

Each day of the failure to keep the records required under the Minimum Wage Law, to furnish records or information to the director or an authorized representative, or to post required information constitutes a separate offense.

Interference with Enforcement

An employer, an employer's agent, or the officer or agent of any private employer that hinders or delays the director or an authorized representative in the performance of the enforcement duties or refuses to admit the director or an authorized representative to any place of employment is guilty of a Class B misdemeanor.

Each day an employer fails to furnish records or information to the director or an authorized representative constitutes a separate offense.

Discrimination

An employer, an employer's agent, or the officer or agent of any private employer that discharges or in any other manner discriminates against any employee because of any of the following is guilty of a Class B misdemeanor:

◆ The employee has made a complaint to the employer or to the director or an authorized representative that the employee has not been paid wages in accordance with the provisions of the Minimum Wage Law.

◆ The employee has caused to be instituted or is about to cause to be instituted any overtime pay proceeding.

◆ The employee has testified or is about to testify in an overtime pay investigation or proceeding.

Civil Liability

Any employee paid less than the employee is entitled under the Minimum Wage Law may recover the following in a civil action:

◆ The amount of any under payments together with costs and reasonable attorney fees as may be allowed by the court.

◆ Damages of 2 percent of the amount of any under payments for each month following the date of payment during which the under payments remain unpaid.

Any agreement between employer and employee to work for less than the required minimum wage is no defense to a civil action.

At the request of the employee or on motion of the director, the state Department of Labor may make an assignment of a wage claim in trust for the assigning employee and may bring any legal action necessary to collect the claim, and the employer will be required to pay the costs incurred in collecting the claim. The action must be brought within three years from the date of the under payment.

An employer that under paid employees is liable to the department for up to 20 percent of the total employer's under payment where the employer's conduct is proven by a preponderance of the evidence to be willful, repeated, or with reckless disregard of the law. The employer will be additionally liable to the employee for damages in the amount of 2 percent of the amount of any under payments for each month following the date of payment during which the under payments remain unpaid. These penalties and damages may be recovered in a civil action brought by the director in any circuit court and the Attorney General will represent the director.

If an employee collects damages of 2 percent of the amount of under payments as a result of an action brought by the director, the employee may not also collect those damages in any of the following:

◆ A private action brought by the employee for the same violation.

◆ An action brought by the Director of the Department of Labor for the same violation.

If the employee has not collected damages (for the same violation), the director is authorized to supervise the payment of the unpaid minimum wages and the unpaid overtime compensation owing to any employee or employees and may bring any legal action necessary to recover the amount of the unpaid minimum wages and unpaid overtime compensation and an equal additional amount as damages. The employer will also be required to pay the costs incurred in collecting the claim. The employer will be additionally liable to the department for up to 20 percent of the total employer's under payment where the employer's conduct is proven by a preponderance of the evidence to be willful, repeated, or with reckless disregard of the law. The action must be brought within five years from the date of the failure to pay the wages or compensation.

Prevailing Wage Act

The Illinois Prevailing Wage Act, located at 820 Ill. Comp. Stat. §§ 130/1 – 130/12, requires contractors and subcontractors to pay all laborers, workers, and mechanics (workers) employed on public works projects no less than the general prevailing rate of wages for work of a similar character in the locality in which the work is performed.

The ***general prevailing rate of hourly wages*** are the hourly cash wages, plus fringe benefits for approved training and apprenticeship programs, health and welfare, insurance, vacations and pensions paid generally in the locality in which the work is being performed, to employees engaged in work of a similar character on public works.

However, the Prevailing Wage Act **does not** provide either of the following:

♦ A prohibition against the payment of more than the prevailing rate of wages to any laborer, worker, or mechanic employed on any public work

♦ A limitation to the hours of work that may be performed by any person in any particular period of time.

Note: All entities that wish to do business with any agency, board, or commission of the state of Illinois must register for an eligible bidder number through the Illinois Department of Human Rights (IDHR) by filing Form PC-1, *Employer Report Form*, with the IDHR Public Contracts unit. Additionally, all those filing for or renewing an IDHR number will be charged a $75 registration fee and the registration will be valid for five years from the date of issuance.

All potential bidders must file if any one of the following applies:

♦ The business entity employs 15 or more persons at the time of application for a public contract.

♦ The business entity has employed 15 or more persons at any time during the 365-day period prior to the date of applying for a public contract.

♦ The business entity is directed to file by a contracting agency of the state of Illinois, any political subdivision, or a municipal corporation.

Form PC-1 is available on the IDHR's Web site and is deemed filed when it is properly completed, signed, and received at the IDHR Chicago office with the $75 registration fee payable to the Illinois Department of Human Rights in the form of a certified check, cashier's check, or money order. No entity will be issued an IDHR number without a properly completed and signed form, the $75 payment, and declaration of an existing sexual harassment policy.

Covered Employers and Employees

Only the following employees in the execution of any contract or contracts for public works with any public body are deemed employed on public works:

♦ Workers directly employed by contractors or subcontractors in actual construction work on the site of the building or construction job. ***Construction*** is all the work on public works involving laborers, workers, or mechanics. This includes any maintenance, repair, assembly, or disassembly work performed on equipment whether owned, leased, or rented.

♦ Workers engaged in the transportation of materials and equipment to or from the site.

The transportation by the sellers and suppliers or the manufacture or processing of materials or equipment does not qualify for public works prevailing wages.

The act applies to the wages of workers employed in any public works by any public body and to anyone under contracts for public works. This includes any maintenance, repair, assembly, or disassembly work performed on equipment whether owned, leased, or rented.

Public works are all fixed works constructed or demolished by any public body or paid for wholly or in part out of public funds. Public works includes all projects financed in whole or in part with bonds, grants, loans, or other funds made available by or through the state or any of its political subdivisions, including, but not limited to, the following:

♦ Bonds issued under the Industrial Project Revenue Bond Act, the Industrial Building Revenue Bond Act, the Illinois Finance Authority Act, the Illinois Sports Facilities Authority Act, or the Build Illinois Bond Act.

♦ Loans or other funds made available pursuant to the Build Illinois Act.

♦ Funds from the Fund for Illinois' Future.

♦ Funds for school construction and funds authorized under the School Construction Bond Act.

♦ Funds for school infrastructure under the State Finance Act.

♦ Funds for transportation purposes under the General Obligation Bond Act.

♦ Funds from the Department of Commerce and Economic Opportunity under the Illinois Renewable Fuels Development Program Act for which there is no project labor agreement.

♦ At leased facility property used for airport purposes under the Local Government Facility Lease Act.

However, public works does not include:

♦ Work done directly by any public utility company, whether or not done under public supervision or direction, or paid for wholly or in part out of public funds.

♦ Projects undertaken by the owner at an owner-occupied single-family residence or at an owner-occupied unit of a multifamily residence.

A ***public body*** is any of the following:

♦ The state or any officer, board, or commission of the state.

♦ Any political subdivision or department of the state.

♦ Any institution supported in whole or in part by public funds.

Every county, city, town, village, township, school district, irrigation, utility, reclamation improvement or other district and every other political subdivision, district or municipality of the state whether the political subdivision, municipality, or district operates under a special charter or not.

Prevailing Wages and Notice

All workers employed by any public body engaged in the construction or demolition of public works must be compensated as follows:

♦ Not less than the general prevailing rate of hourly wages for work of a similar character on public works in the locality in which the work is performed.

♦ Not less than the general prevailing rate of hourly wages for legal holiday and overtime work.

This includes any maintenance, repair, assembly, or disassembly work performed on equipment whether owned, leased, or rented.

The public body or other entity awarding the contract must insert in the project specifications and the contract a stipulation that no less than the prevailing rate of wages must be paid to all laborer, workers, and mechanics performing under the contract. If the contract is awarded without a public bid, then the required written notice of prevailing wages must be provided on the purchase order or on a separate document, as applicable. The Illinois Department of Labor will penalize the public body or other entity upon failure to provide such notice. However, failure to provide notice does not relieve the contractor of the duty to comply with the prevailing wage rate and requirements or the obligation to pay back wages. Back wages will be limited to the difference between the actual amount paid and the prevailing rate of wages required to be paid for the project.

Contractors awarded a public works contract are required to insert into each subcontract, and into the project specifications for each subcontract, a written stipulation stating that not less than the prevailing rate of wages will be paid to all workers performing work under the contract. Each subcontractor must also insert into each lower tiered subcontract, and into the project specifications for each lower tiered subcontract, a stipulation stating that not less than the prevailing rate of wages will be paid to all workers. A contractor or subcontractor who fails to comply with the stipulation requirement is in violation of this act.

Certified Payroll

On a monthly basis, contractors and each subcontractor must either in person, by mail, or electronically a certified payroll to the public body in charge of the project. The certified payroll must consist of a complete copy of the required records of all workers employed on the project, but may exclude the starting and ending times of work each day. The public body in charge of the project must keep the submitted records for at least three years. Additionally, a statement, signed by the contractor or subcontractor, which asserts the following, must accompany the certified payroll:

- The records are true and accurate

- The hourly rate paid to each worker is not less than the general prevailing rate of hourly wages required by law.

- The contractor or subcontractor is aware that filing a certified payroll known to be false is a Class B misdemeanor.

General contractors may rely on the certification of a lower tier subcontractor, provided the general contractor does not knowingly rely upon a subcontractor's false certification.

Upon seven business days' notice, the contractor and each subcontractor must make the certified payroll records available for inspection to the public body in charge of the project, its officers and agents, and to the Illinois Director of Labor and deputies and agents. Upon seven business days' notice, the contractor and each subcontractor must make such records available at all reasonable hours at a location within the state.

Public Records

Upon submission, the certified payroll records become public records and made available in accordance with the Freedom of Information Act. However, an employee's address, telephone number, and Social Security number are **not** part of the public record.

Retaliation Prohibited

No person may discharge, discipline, or in any other way discriminate against or cause to be discharged, disciplined, or discriminated against any employee or any authorized representative of employees because the employee or representative:

- Filed, instituted, or caused to be filed or instituted any proceeding under the Prevailing Wage Act.

- Testified or is about to testify in any proceeding resulting from the administration or enforcement of the act.

- Offered any evidence of any violation of the act.

Within 30 days after the alleged violation, any employee or a representative of employees who believes they were illegally discharged, disciplined, or otherwise discriminated against may apply to the Illinois Director of Labor for a review of the discharge, discipline, or alleged discrimination.

A copy of the application will be sent to the person who allegedly committed the violation and upon receipt of an application the director will investigate, as necessary.

The investigation will provide an opportunity for a public hearing at the request of any party to the review to enable the parties to present information relating to the alleged violation. The parties will be given written notice of the time and place of the hearing at least five days before the hearing. Upon receiving the report of the investigation, the director will make findings of fact. If the director finds that there was no violation, an order denying the application will be issued.

If the director finds that a violation occurred, a decision incorporating the findings will be issued and the party committing the violation will be required to take such affirmative action to abate the violation, including, but not limited to, the following:

- Rehiring or reinstatement of the employee or representative of employees to the former position.

- Compensating the employee for the period or unemployment.

The party committing the violation will also be liable to the Illinois Department of Labor for a penalty of $5,000 for each violation.

Posting Requirements

Contractors or construction managers awarded a public works contract are required to post the prevailing wage rates for each craft or type of work or mechanic needed to execute the contract, project, or work to be performed. Posting must be made at a location on the project site of the public works that is easily accessible to the workers engaged on the project. In lieu of posting on the project site of the public works, a contractor which has a business location where laborers, workers, and mechanics regularly visit may either:

- Post in a conspicuous location at that business the current prevailing wage rates for each county in which the contractor is performing work.

- Provide such laborer, worker, or mechanic engaged on the public works project a written notice indicating the prevailing wage rates for the public works project.

A failure to post or provide a prevailing wage rate is a violation of the act.

Recordkeeping Requirements

While participating on public works, the contractor and each subcontractor must create and maintain records of all workers employed on the project.

The records must be maintained for at least three years and contain all the following information regarding each worker:

- Name, address, and telephone number, when available.

- Social Security number and classification(s).

- Hourly wages paid in each pay period.

- Number of hours worked each day.

- Starting and ending times of work each day.

Contractors and subcontractors must also include a provision in all of their contracts that not less than the prevailing rate of wages will be paid to all laborers, employees, and mechanics performing work under the contract.

Enforcement and Penalties

The Illinois Department of Labor and Illinois Attorney General administers and enforces the Prevailing Wage Act.

The following are guilty of a Class A misdemeanor:

- Any officer, agent, or representative of any public body who willfully violates or omits to comply with any of the provisions of the Prevailing Wage Act.

- Any contractor or subcontractor doing public work who commits either of the following:

  - Neglects to keep or cause to be kept an accurate record of the names, occupation, and actual wages paid to each worker in connection with the public work.

  - Refuses to allow access to required records at any reasonable hour to any person authorized to inspect the records.

Contractors and subcontractors are also liable as follows:

- Failure to submit a certified payroll or knowingly files a false certified payroll is in violation of the Prevailing Wage Act and guilty of a Class B misdemeanor.

- Failure to post prevailing wage rates as required by law is a violation of the Prevailing Wage Act.

Additionally, a contractor or subcontractor found to have violated the act on two occasions within a five-year period may be barred from public works projects for four years.

Under Payments

Contractors or subcontractors who compensate a worker at less than the stipulated rates for work completed under a public works contract will be liable as follows:

- To the worker for the difference between the amount paid and the rates provided by the contract.

- To the worker for the costs and reasonable attorney's fees allowed by the court.

- To the Illinois Department of Labor for 20 percent of the under payments and to the worker, for punitive damages, in the amount of 2 percent of the under payments, for each month following the date of payment during which the under payments remain unpaid.

Additionally, for a second or subsequent action to recover under payments, the contractor or subcontractor will be liable to the department for 50 percent of the under payments and to the worker in the amount of 5 percent of the under payments for each month following the date of payment during which the under payments remain unpaid.

The department also has a right of action on behalf of any individual who has a right of action under the law. An action brought to recover for the individual will be deemed to be a suit for wages, and any and all judgments entered will have the same force and effect as other judgments for wages.

At the request of any laborer, worker, or mechanic employed by the contractor or by any subcontractor who is compensated at less than the required prevailing wage rate, the Illinois Department of Labor may take an assignment of the wage claim in trust for the assigning laborer, worker, or mechanic.

The department may also bring any legal action necessary to collect the claim, and the contractor or subcontractor will be required to pay the costs incurred in collecting the claim.

One Day Rest in Seven Act

The Illinois One Day Rest in Seven Act, located at 820 Ill. Comp. Stat. §§ 140/1 – 140/9, covers employers who are persons, partnerships, joint stock companies or corporations, that employ any person to work, labor or exercise skill in connection with the operation of any business, industry, vocation or occupation.

Accordingly, every covered employer must allow every covered employee at least 24 consecutive hours of rest in every calendar week, in addition to the regular period of rest allowed at the close of each working day.

However, the requirement for 24 consecutive hours of rest **does not apply** to any of the following:

♦ Part-time employees whose total work hours for one employer during a calendar week do not exceed 20 hours.

♦ Employees needed in case of breakdown of machinery or equipment or other emergency requiring the immediate services of experienced and competent labor to prevent injury to person, damage to property, or suspension of necessary operation.

♦ Employees employed in agriculture or coal mining.

♦ Employees engaged in the occupation of canning and processing perishable agricultural products, if employees are employed by an employer in the occupation on a seasonal basis and for not more than 20 weeks during any calendar year or 12-month period.

♦ Employees employed as security guards.

♦ Employees who are employed in a bona fide executive, administrative, or professional capacity or in the capacity of an outside salesman, as defined by the FLSA, and those employed as supervisors as defined by the National Labor Relations Act (NLRA).

♦ Employees who are employed as crewmembers of any uninspected towing vessel operating in any navigable waters in or along the boundaries of Illinois.

Meal Periods

Employees working 7½ hours per day must be provided with at least a 20-minute meal break, which must begin no later than five hours after the start of the work period. However, the meal period requirement does not apply to the following:

♦ Employees whose meal periods are established in a collective-bargaining agreement.

- Employees who monitor persons having developmental disabilities, mental illness, or both, and who, in the course of those duties, must be on call the entire eight-hour work period. However, these employees must be allowed to eat a meal during the eight-hour work period while continuing to monitoring the individuals.

Hotel Room Attendants

A *hotel room attendant* (attendant) is a person who cleans or puts in order guest rooms in a hotel or other establishment licensed for transient occupancy. Attendants who are employed by hotels and other establishments licensed for transient occupancy that are located in a county with a population greater than 3,000,000 are granted special protections.

Specifically, every attendant of the hotels or other establishments must receive both of the following rest periods during each workday the attendant works at least seven hours:

- A minimum of two 15-minute paid rest breaks.
- One 30-minute meal period.

Employers **may not** require any attendant to work during a break period and must keep a complete and accurate record of the break periods of all attendants.

At all times, an attendant's employer must make a room available on the employer's premises with adequate seating and tables for the purpose of allowing attendants to enjoy break periods in a clean and comfortable environment. The room must also provide clean drinking water without charge to the employees.

Employers who violate the required break periods for attendant's must pay the attendant three times the attendant's regular hourly rate of pay for each workday during which the required breaks were not provided. Additionally, it is unlawful for any employer, employer's agent, or representative to take any action against any person in retaliation for the exercise of rights to the required break periods.

In any civil proceeding, if the plaintiff establishes all of the following then a rebuttable presumption will apply that the employer's action were taken in retaliation for the exercise of rights established by attendant protections:

- The hotel room attendant employment relationship with the employer.
- The attendant did either of the following and was then terminated, demoted, or otherwise penalized by the employer:
  - Exercised rights to required break periods.
  - Alleged in good faith that the employer was not complying with the break period regulations.

To rebut the presumption, the employer must prove that the sole reason for the termination, demotion, or penalty was a legitimate business reason.

In addition to the remedies provided by the One Day Rest in Seven Act, a person claiming violation of the break periods for attendants will be entitled to all of the following:

- All remedies available under law or in equity, including, but not limited to, damages, backpay, reinstatement, or injunctive relief.
- Any person terminated in violation of the law will recover triple the employee's lost normal daily compensation and fringe benefits, together with interest, and any consequential damages suffered by the employee.
- In an enforcement action, the court will also award reasonable attorneys' fees and costs to a prevailing plaintiff.

Related Case Law

The case of *520 South Michigan Ave. Associates, Ltd, dba The Congress Plaza Hotel. v. Shannon* (549 F.3d 1119) was brought by a hotel against the Illinois Director of Labor seeking a judgment that the Hotel Room Attendant Amendment to the One Day Rest in Seven Act was unconstitutional. The Court of Appeals held that the amendment was pre-empted by the NLRA. The court held:

- The amendment was not a law of general application, but rather applied to one occupation, in one industry, in one country, thereby discouraging collective bargaining by encouraging lobbying for targeted legislation.

- The amendment was not a true minimum labor standard, in light of the minimal standard of general application in effect in Illinois at the time and the formidable enforcement mechanism provided by the amendment.

- The amendment further interfered with the NLRA by overriding the dispute resolution mechanisms already in place and by interfering with the pay and quota structure established for room attendants.

According to the NLRA at 29 U.S.C.A. § 151, et seq., the NLRA pre-emption doctrine applied by the court was the *Machinists* pre-emption, which protects against state interference with policies implicated by the structure of the NLRA itself, by pre-empting state law and state causes of action concerning conduct that Congress intended to be unregulated. This pre-emption doctrine governs pre-emption questions that arose concerning activity that was neither arguably protected against employer interference, nor arguably prohibited as an unfair labor practice.

Children at Work

According to 820 Ill. Comp. Stat. § 205/4, no minor under 16 years of age may be employed or permitted to work in any gainful occupations mentioned for more than five continuous hours without an interval of at least 30 minutes for a meal period, and no period of less than 30 minutes is deemed to interrupt a continuous period of work.

Exception

An employer cannot require an employee to work on their designated day of rest. However, the Illinois Director of Labor may grant permits authorizing employment on days of rest.

These permits may not authorize the employment of persons for seven days a week for more than eight weeks in any one year, unless the director finds that the necessity for employment of persons on their designated day of rest cannot be remedied by increasing the number of employees or by adjusting production schedules. In deciding whether to grant a permit, the director will consider business necessity and economic viability.

Posting Requirements

Before the first day of a calendar workweek, the employer must post a work schedule in a conspicuous place that lists the names of employees required to work on Sunday and that designates the day of rest for each of those employees. Additionally, all employers must conspicuously post and maintain the Illinois Department of Labor *Notice to Employers and Employees* poster covering One Day Rest in Seven Act.

Recordkeeping Requirements

Every employer must keep a time book showing the names and addresses of all employees and the hours worked by each of them on each day, and the time book must be open to inspection at all reasonable hours by the director.

Enforcement and Penalties

The director enforces the provisions of and prosecutes all violations of the Illinois' One Day Rest in Seven Act. A violation of the act is a petty offense, and each offense is subject to a fine between $25 and $100.

The Day and Temporary Labor Services Act

The Illinois Day and Temporary Labor Services Act (820 Ill. Comp. Stat. §§ 175/1 et seq.) provides for the regulation of day and temporary labor agencies, establishes worker rights and protections, specifies the duties and responsibilities of day and temporary labor agencies and third party clients, sets forth penalties and enforcement procedures for violations of the act, and requires third party clients that contract with day or temporary labor agencies to verify that they are registered with the Illinois Department of Labor (department) or face monetary penalties.

As used in the act:

♦ *Day or temporary laborer* means a natural person who contracts for employment with a day and temporary labor service agency.

♦ *Day and temporary labor* means work performed by a day or temporary laborer at a third party client, the duration of which may be specific or undefined, pursuant to a contract or understanding between the day and temporary labor service agency and the third party client. Day and temporary labor does not include labor or employment of a professional or clerical nature.

♦ *Day and temporary labor service agency* means any person or entity engaged in the business of employing day or temporary laborers to provide services, for a fee, to or for any third party client pursuant to a contract with the day and temporary labor service agency and the third party client.

♦ *Third party client* means any person that contracts with a day and temporary labor service agency for obtaining day or temporary laborers.

Registration

Day and temporary labor service agencies located in or transacting business in Illinois must register with the department, provide proof of required unemployment insurance contributions and valid workers' compensation insurance and report any lapse in workers' compensation coverage to the department.

Posting Requirement

Every day and temporary labor service agency must post in the public access area of each work location or branch office a notice provided by the department summarizing the provisions of the Illinois Day and Temporary Labor Services Act, along with the toll-free number for reporting violations and complaints. This notice must be in English or any other language generally understood in the locale of the agency. Agencies must also post in public access areas any other state or federally mandated postings.

Required Notices to Employees

Day and temporary labor service agencies must provide workers with an employment notice at the time of dispatch describing the terms and conditions of their employment, including the following:

♦ The nature of work to be performed.

♦ The wages to be paid.

♦ The name, address, and location of where the work will be performed.

- The terms of transportation.

- Whether meals or equipment will be provided, and any costs associated with such meals and equipment.

Day and temporary labor service agencies must also provide each worker with a wage notice at the time of payment that includes:

- The name, address, and telephone number of each third party client for whom work was performed.

- The number of hours worked by the laborer at each third party client each day during the pay period.

- The rate of pay for all hours worked, including any premium or bonus pay.

- Total earnings during the pay period.

- All deductions made for meals, equipment, income tax, and Social Security withholdings and any other deductions.

For workers contracted to work a single day, third party clients must provide workers with a work verification form at the end of the workday that contains the date, worker's name, work location, and hours worked that day.

A worker who is sent by the agency to a third party client, but is then not utilized by that client, must be paid a minimum of four hours of pay at the agreed upon rate by the day and temporary labor agency. However, if that worker is given work during the same shift at another location, the worker must be paid for two hours of pay at the agreed upon rate of pay (in addition to the pay for hours worked during that shift).

A third party client is required to pay the wages and related payroll taxes to a licensed day and temporary labor service agency for the services performed by the day or temporary laborer for the third party client. Such payment must be made in accordance to payment terms outlined on invoices, service agreements, or stated terms provided by the agency. A third party client who fails to comply with these requirements is subject to penalty.

The department will review a complaint filed by an agency. The department will also review the payroll and accounting records of the agency and the third party client for the period in which the violation is alleged to have occurred. The purpose of this review is to determine if wages and payroll taxes have been paid to the agency and whether the day or temporary laborer was paid the wages owed.

Wages and Deductions

The wages paid to day laborers must be in compliance with all state and federal laws, including minimum wage and overtime laws, and the total amount deducted for meals and equipment may not cause a worker's hourly wage to fall below the state or federal minimum wage. Agencies cannot make deductions from a worker's paycheck unless the worker approves the deductions in writing on a form approved by the department, and agencies may not charge workers for cashing paychecks issued by their agency.

Recordkeeping Requirements

Day and temporary labor service agencies must keep and maintain for a period of three years detailed records relating to every day laborer's work, and these records must be open to inspection by the Department of Labor during normal business hours. In addition, records relating to an individual worker and any hours billed to third party clients for that worker's labor must be available for review or copying by the worker within five days following a written request.

Transportation

Day and temporary labor agencies and third party clients (and their contractors or agents) are prohibited from charging workers for transportation between the agency and the designated worksite. Agencies and third party clients (and their contractors or agents) are responsible for the conduct and performance of persons providing transportation, and drivers must have a valid and appropriate motor vehicle license and proof of financial responsibility as well as seats and safety belts for every passenger. Any violations of these requirements discovered by the Department of Labor must be forwarded to appropriate law enforcement or regulatory agencies.

Placement Fee Restrictions

Day and temporary labor agencies cannot restrict the right of a laborer to accept a permanent position with a third party client to whom they have been referred for work. They also cannot restrict the right of third party clients to offer employment to a day and temporary laborer; however, day and temporary labor agencies may charge limited placement fees to third party clients who offer employment to day laborers.

Retaliation

Day and temporary labor agencies and third party clients are prohibited from retaliating against workers for exercising their rights, including making a complaint, testifying, or participating in an investigation under the act. Any retaliation taken against a worker in violation of the act may be subject to civil penalties or a private cause of action. In addition to administrative remedies available through the Department of Labor, a person aggrieved by any violation of the act may file suit in Illinois circuit court.

Recovery

A day and temporary labor service agency (agency) may recover attorney's fees and costs in a civil action brought by the agency against a third-party client for the client's breach of contract in relation to services provided by the agency to the client. However, to obtain such recover the agency must prevail in the lawsuit.

A person aggrieved by a violation of the act by a day and temporary labor service agency or a third party client may file suit in circuit court within either of the following:

- Three years from the final date of employment by the day and temporary labor agency or the third party client.

- Three years from the date of termination of the contract between the day and temporary labor service agency and the third party client.

This limitation period is tolled if a day labor employer has deterred a day and temporary labor service agency or day or temporary laborer's exercise of rights under the act by contacting or threatening to contact law enforcement agencies.

Penalties

A day and temporary labor service agency or third party client that violates any of the provisions of the act is subject to a civil penalty of up to $6,000 for violations found in the first audit by the department.

Following a first audit, a day and temporary labor service agency or third party client is subject to a civil penalty of up to $2,500 for each repeat violation found by the department within three years. Each violation of the act for each day or temporary laborer and for each day the violation continues constitutes a separate and distinct violation.

In determining the amount of a penalty, the director will consider the appropriateness of the penalty to the day and temporary labor service agency or third party client charged, upon the determination of the gravity of the violations. For any violation determined by the department to be willful which is within three years of an earlier violation, the department may revoke the registration of the violator, if the violator is a day and temporary labor service agency.

Nursing Mothers

Nursing Mothers in the Workplace Act

The Illinois Nursing Mothers in the Workplace Act is located at 820 Ill. Comp. Stat. §§ 260/1 – 260/99.

The act applies to any individual, corporation, partnership, labor organization, or unincorporated association, the state, an agency or political subdivision of the state, or any other legal, business, or commercial entity that has more than five employees exclusive of the employer's parent, spouse, or child or other members of the employer's immediate family.

Under the act, an employer must provide reasonable unpaid break time each day to an employee who needs to express breast milk for her infant child. The break time must, if possible, run concurrently with any break time already provided to the employee. An employer is not required to provide break time under this section if to do so would unduly disrupt the employer's operations.

In addition, the employer must make reasonable efforts to provide a room or location, in close proximity to the work area, other than a toilet stall, where a nursing mother employee can express her milk in privacy.

Right to Breastfeed Act

The Illinois Right to Breastfeed Act is located at 740 Ill. Comp. Stat. §§ 137/1 – 137/99. Pursuant to the Act, a nursing mother may breastfeed her baby in any location, public or private, where the mother is otherwise authorized to be, irrespective of whether the nipple of the mother's breast is uncovered during or incidental to the breastfeeding.

Remedies

A woman who has been denied the right to breastfeed by the owner or manager of a public or private location, other than a private residence or place of worship, may bring an action to enjoin future denials of the right to breastfeed. If the woman prevails in her suit, she will be awarded reasonable attorney's fees and reasonable expenses of litigation.

Wage Payment and Collection Act

The Illinois Wage Payment and Collection Act is located at 820 Ill. Comp. Stat. §§ 115/1 – 115/16.

Covered Employers and Employees

The act covers **all** public and private employers.

An *employer* is any individual, partnership, association, corporation, business trust, or any person or group of persons acting — directly or indirectly — in the interest of an employer in relation to an employee, for which one or more persons is gainfully employed.

The act covers ***employees***, who are any individual permitted to work by an employer in an occupation; however, the following individuals are not covered employees under the terms of the act:

- Those who have been and will continue to be free from control and direction over the performance of their work, both under the contract of service with the employer and in fact.

- Those who perform work that is either outside the usual course of business or is performed outside all of the places of business of the employer, unless the employer is in the business of contracting with third parties for the placement of employees.

- Those who are in an independently established trade, occupation, profession, or business.

Form of Payment

Employers must pay wages in cash, by check convertible to cash on demand at full face value, or by direct deposit, unless a collective-bargaining agreement provides otherwise. An employer may not designate a particular financial institution for the exclusive payment or deposit of a check for wages.

Frequency and Timing of Payment

Every employer must pay all wages according to the following:

- At least semimonthly to every employee all wages earned during the semimonthly pay period.

- Wages of executive, administrative, and professional employees may be paid once a month.

- Commissions may be paid once a month.

All wages earned during a semimonthly or biweekly pay period must be paid no later than 13 days after the end of the pay period in which the wages were earned. All wages earned during a weekly pay period must be paid no later than seven days after the end of the pay period in which the wages were earned. All wages paid on a daily basis must be paid on the same day as earned, if possible, but in any event no later than 24 hours after the day on which the wages are earned.

Wages of executive, administrative, and professional employees may be paid on or before 21 days after the period during which they were earned.

Any employee who is absent at the time fixed for payment or who for any other reason is not paid at that time must be paid on demand at any time within a five-day period after the time fixed for payment. After the five days, payment must be made within five days of the employee's demand. If the employee requests it in writing, payment must be made by mail.

Employers must also pay to workers on strike or layoff, no later than the next regular payday, all wages earned up to the time of the strike or layoff.

The frequency and timing of payment regulations **do not apply** if a valid collective-bargaining agreement exists that provides for a different date or for different arrangements for the payment of wages.

Employment/Placement Agency Employees

At the request of a person employed by an employment or labor placement agency that in the ordinary course of business makes daily wage payments to employees, the agency must hold the daily wages and make either weekly or semimonthly payments.

Upon the written request of the employee, the wage must be paid in a single check representing the wages earned during the period — either weekly, biweekly, or semimonthly — designated by the employee. Employment and labor placement agencies that make daily wage payments must provide written notification to all daily-wage payments employees of the right to request weekly or semimonthly checks. The employer may provide this notice by conspicuously posting the notice at the location where the daily-wage employees receive the wages.

Deductions

Deductions by employers from wages or final compensation are prohibited unless such deductions are:

- ♦ Required by law.

- ♦ To the benefit of the employee.

- ♦ In response to a valid wage assignment or wage deduction order.

- ♦ Made with the express written consent of the employee, given freely at the time the deduction is made.

- ♦ Made by a municipality with a population of 500,000 or more, a county with a population of 3,000,000 or more, a community college district in a city with a population of 500,000 or more, a housing authority in a municipality with a population of 500,000 or more, the Chicago Park District, the Metropolitan Transit Authority, the Chicago Board of Education, the Cook County Forest Preserve District, or the Metropolitan Water Reclamation District to pay a debt owed by the employee to a municipality with a population of 500,000 or more, a county with a population of 3,000,000 or more, the Cook County Forest Preserve, the Chicago Park District, the Metropolitan Water Reclamation District, the Chicago Transit Authority, the Chicago Board of Education, or a housing authority of a municipality with a population of 500,000 or more; provided, however, that the amount deducted from any one salary or wage payment must not exceed 25 percent of the net amount of the payment.

- ♦ Made by a housing authority in a municipality with a population of 500,000 or more or a municipality with a population of 500,000 or more to pay a debt owed by the employee to a housing authority in a municipality with a population of 500,000 or more; provided, however, that the amount deducted from any one salary or wage payment must not exceed 25 percent of the net amount of the payment.

Note: In regard to the above, the employee must be afforded an opportunity for a hearing to dispute the debt.

The law mandates that taxes and FICA be deducted. Other deductions, such as payroll savings, insurance and union dues, and charitable contributions may be made at the written request of the employee. A court may require deductions such as garnishments, child support payments, or debtor's judgments.

Where the legitimacy of any deduction from wages is in dispute, the amount in question may be withheld if the employer notifies the Department of Labor on the date the payment is due in writing of the amount that is being withheld and stating the reasons for which the payment is withheld. Upon such notification, the Department of Labor will conduct an investigation and render a judgment as promptly as possible. The employer must pay the wages due upon order of the Department of Labor within 15 calendar days of issuance of a judgment on the dispute.

Benefit Contributions

If an employer is legally committed through a collective-bargaining agreement, or otherwise, to make contributions to an employee benefit, trust, or fund on the basis of a certain amount per hour, day, week, or other period of time, the amount due from the employer is treated as wages subject to the provisions of the wage payment law.

Termination of Employment

Every employer must pay the final compensation of separated employees in full at the time of separation if possible, but in no case later than the employee's next regularly scheduled payday. If the employee requests in writing that the final compensation is paid by check and mailed, the employer must do so.

Vacation Pay

Unless otherwise provided in a collective-bargaining agreement, whenever a contract of employment or employment policy provides for paid vacations, and an employee resigns or is terminated without having taken all vacation time earned, the monetary equivalent of all earned vacation must be paid to the employee as part of the final compensation at the employee's final rate of pay. No employment contract or employment policy may provide for forfeiture of earned vacation time upon separation.

Notice of Wage Payments and Practices

Employers must notify employees, at the time of hiring, of the rate of pay and of the time and place of payment. Whenever possible, the notification must be in writing and must be acknowledged by both parties. Employers must also notify employees of any changes in these arrangements before the time of change.

Wage Statements

Employers must furnish each employee with an itemized statement of deductions made form each pay period's wages. Employers must post one or more notices indicating the regular paydays, the place and time for employee payment, and a copy or summary of the provisions of the wage payment law.

Day and Temporary Labor

Under 820 Ill. Comp. Stat § 175/30, at the time of payment of wages, a day and temporary labor service agency must provide each day or temporary laborer with a detailed itemized statement, on the day or temporary laborer's paycheck stub or on a form approved by the Department of Labor, listing the following:

- ◆ The name, address, and telephone number of each third party client at which the day or temporary laborer worked. If this information is provided on the day or temporary laborer's paycheck stub, a code for each third party client may be used so long as the required information for each coded third party client is made available to the day or temporary laborer.

- ◆ The number of hours worked by the day or temporary laborer at each third party client each day during the pay period.

- ◆ The rate of payment for each hour worked, including any premium rate or bonus.

- ◆ The total pay period earnings.

- ◆ All deductions made from the day or temporary laborer's compensation made either by the third party client or by the day and temporary labor service agency, and the purpose for which deductions were made, including for the day or temporary laborer's transportation, food, equipment, withheld income tax, withheld Social Security payments, and every other deduction.

- ◆ Any additional information required by rules issued by the Department of Labor.

The total amount deducted for meals, equipment, and transportation may not cause a day or temporary laborer's hourly wage to fall below the state or federal minimum wage. However, a day and temporary labor service agency may deduct the actual market value of reusable equipment provided to the day or temporary laborer by the day and temporary labor service agency which the day or temporary laborer fails to return, if the day or temporary laborer provides a written authorization for such deduction at the time the deduction is made.

A day and temporary labor service agency must also provide each worker an annual earnings summary within a reasonable time after the preceding calendar year, but in no case later than February 1.

Posting Requirements

All employers must conspicuously post and maintain the Illinois Department of Labor *Notice to Employers and Employees* poster covering the payment of wages and the Wage Payment and Collection Act.

Enforcement

The Director of the Department of Labor generally enforces Illinois' wage payment law, but the state's attorney of any county may prosecute violations of the law independently and without specific direction of the department.

The director or any other person in the department designated by the director is authorized to assist any employee and act on the employee's behalf in the collection of wages or final compensation.

Employees may also make their own complaints and prosecute their own claims for not timely paid wages, final compensation, or wage supplements due. Complaints must be filed within one year after the wages, final compensation, or wage supplements were due. Applications are reviewed by the department to determine whether there is cause for investigation.

Violations and Penalties

Failure to Pay Wages

Any employee not timely paid wages, final compensation, or a wage supplement by their employer is entitled to recover both of the following:

♦ The amount of any such underpayments.

♦ Damages of 2 percent of the amount of any such underpayments for each month following the date of payment during which such underpayments remain unpaid.

In a civil action, such employee will also recover costs and all reasonable attorneys' fees.

Note: The claim may be filed with either the Department of Labor or in a civil action, but not both.

Additionally, any employer that willfully refuses to pay wages, final compensation, or wage supplements, falsely denies the amount or validity that is due, with intent to secure for themselves or other person any underpayment of indebtedness or with intent to annoy, harass, oppress, hinder, delay, or defraud the person to whom the indebtedness is due, upon conviction, is guilty of the following:

♦ For unpaid wages, final compensation, or wage supplements in the amount of $5,000 or less, a Class B misdemeanor.

♦ For unpaid wages, final compensation, or wage supplements in the amount of more than $5,000, a Class A misdemeanor.

Each day during which any violation of the law continues is a separate and distinct offense. Employers who commit subsequent violations within two years of a prior criminal conviction are guilty, upon conviction, of a Class Four felony.

Failure to Obey Order to Pay

Any employer that has been demanded or ordered by the Department of Labor or the court to pay wages, final compensation, or wage supplements due to an employee will be required to pay a nonwaivable administrative fee of $250 to the department. Any employer who has been so demanded or ordered by the department or ordered by a court to pay such wages, final compensation, or wage supplements and who fails to seek timely review and who fails to comply within 15 calendar days after the demand or within 35 days of an administrative or court order is entered will also be liable to pay both of the following penalties:

- Twenty percent of the amount found owing due to the department.
- One percent of the amount overdue, per calendar day, to an employee for each day of delay in paying wages.

Retaliation

Any employer that discharges or in any other manner discriminates against any employee because of any of the following is guilty of a Class C misdemeanor:

- The employee has made a complaint to the employer or to the Director of Labor or an authorized representative, in a public hearing, or to a community organization that payment was not in accordance with the provisions of Illinois' wage payment law.
- The employee has caused to be instituted any proceeding under or related to Illinois' wage payment law.
- The employee has testified or is about to testify in an investigation or proceeding under Illinois' wage payment law.

Additionally, any employee who has been unlawfully retaliated against is entitled to recover through a claim filed with the department or in a civil action, but not both, all legal and equitable relief as may be appropriate. In a civil action, such employee will also recover costs and all reasonable attorney fees.

Wage Assignments, Garnishments, and Support Orders

An employer may be required to pay part of an employee's wages to an employee's creditor as a result of outstanding debt. The employer's obligation may arise from a voluntary wage assignment, garnishment, or support order. Employers can be held liable for the debt for not complying with a wage assignment or court order to make payments to an employee's creditor.

Wage Assignment

A *wage assignment* is a written document signed by the employee and given to the creditor. The wage assignment authorizes the creditor to claim part of the employee's wages if the employee fails to make timely payments on a debt. Unlike garnishments and support orders, a wage assignment may be enforced without a court order.

Garnishment

A *garnishment* is a court order that directs the employer to pay part of the employee's wages directly to the creditor. To obtain a garnishment, a creditor must first bring a lawsuit against the employee and obtain court approval.

Support Orders

A judgment, court order, or order of a child support enforcement agency compels the employer to withhold child support payments from the wages of the person named in the order or judgment. An employee that owes child support may also request the employer to withhold payments from wages without a child support order.

Judgments

Under Illinois law, the amount of wages, salaries, commissions, and bonuses that may be applied toward a judgment or subjected to collection under a deduction order is limited to the lesser of the following:

- Fifteen percent of gross weekly wages.

- The amount by which disposable earnings for a week exceed the total of 45 times the federal minimum hourly wage or (under a wage deduction summons served on or after January 1, 2006) the Illinois minimum hourly wage — whichever is greater.

Under federal law, the amount of wages that may be applied toward a judgment is limited to the lesser of the following:

- Twenty-five percent of disposable earnings for a week.

- The amount by which disposable earnings for a week exceed 30 times the federal minimum hourly wage.

Interstate Support Orders

The Uniform Interstate Family Support Act is in effect in Illinois and states that an income withholding order issued in another state may be sent to the employer of the person owing support without filing of petition, comparable pleading, or registration with an Illinois tribunal. Upon receiving an income withholding order issued in another state, an employer must immediately provide a copy of the order to the affected employee and must treat the order as if issued by an Illinois tribunal.

Employers must withhold and distribute the funds by complying with the terms of a support order that specify the following:

- The duration and amount of periodic payments of current child support.

- The person or agency and the address of those designated to receive payments.

- Health care coverage, whether in the form of periodic cash payment, stated as a certain sum, or ordering the employee to provide health insurance coverage for the child under a policy available through employment.

- The amount of periodic payments of fees and costs for a support enforcement agency, the issuing tribunal, and the employee's attorney.

- The amount of periodic payment of arrears and interest on arrears.

An employer must comply with the law of the state of the employee's principal place of employment for withholding from income with respect to the following:

- The employer's fee for processing an income withholding order.

- The maximum amount permitted to be withheld from the employee's income.

- The times within which the employer must implement the withholding order and forward the child support payment.

If an employer receives multiple orders to withhold child support from the earnings of the same employee, the employer satisfies the terms of the multiple orders by complying with the law of the state of the employee's principal place of employment. This compliance is to establish the priorities for withholding and allocation of income for multiple child support.

Employers that comply with income withholding orders issued by other states are not subject to civil liability to an individual or agency because the employer withholds child support from the employee's income. Any employer that willfully fails to comply with an income withholding order issued by another state and received for enforcement is subject to the same penalties that may be imposed for noncompliance with an order issued by an Illinois tribunal.

Amount of Payment

The amount the employer should withhold will be specified in the order of withholding; however, the amount should not exceed the federal limits.

Fees

The employer is entitled to receive $5 per month from the income of the employee for support order deductions as an administrative cost.

Medical Support Orders

An employer, upon receiving an order requiring that a minor child be named as a beneficiary under a health insurance plan available through the employer, must immediately enroll the child in the plan designated by the court order.

The employer must withhold any required premiums and pay over any amounts so withheld and any additional amounts the employer pays to the insurance carrier in a timely manner.

Priority

Income withholding is done without regard to any prior or subsequent garnishments, attachments, wage assignments, or other claims of creditors.

Retaliation

It is unlawful for any employer to refuse to hire a prospective employee, to discharge an employee, or to take any other disciplinary action against an employee because of an assignment of wages.

Multiple Support Orders

An employer may combine all amounts withheld for the benefit of a person owed child support or public office into a single payment and transmit the payment with a listing of the employees from whom the withholding is made. If an employer has been served with more than one order for the same employee, the employer must allocate income available for withholding after withholding for all current support obligations. If there is income available after withholding for current support, the employer will allocate the income to past-due support payments ordered in Aid to Families with Dependent Children (AFDC) matters and then to past-due support payments ordered in AFDC matters, both on a proportionate-share basis.

Notification to Employer

The clerk of the court will serve a specially certified copy of the order for withholding on the employer, superintendent, manager, or other agent by regular or certified mail or facsimile. The employer must mail information on the dependent coverage plan to the other parent within 15 days of enrollment or upon request of a notice of the date of coverage, and all forms needed to be reimbursed for covered health expenses. If insurance coverage is terminated or changed for any reason, the employer must notify the other parent within 10 days of the termination or change date, along with a notice of conversion privileges.

Termination of Employment

Whenever an employee is no longer receiving income from an employer, the employer is to return a copy of the order for withholding to the other parent or public office and provide information to help enforce the child support obligation.

Deadlines

The court may require the withholding order to take effect immediately. The employer will deduct the amount designated in the order beginning no later than the next payment of income that is payable to the employee that occurs 14 days following the date the order and any notice of delinquency were mailed by certified mail or placed for personal delivery.

The employer will pay the amount withheld to the other parent or public office redirecting payments within seven calendar days of the date income is paid. Payment is considered made when it has been mailed or the date an electronic funds transfer is initiated.

The employer will mail information on the dependent coverage plan and all forms needed to be reimbursed for covered health expenses to the other parent within 15 days of enrollment or upon request of a notice of the date of coverage. If the insurance coverage is terminated or changed for any reason, the employer will notify the other parent within 10 days of the termination or change along with a notice of conversion privileges.

Violations and Penalties

Income Withholding Violations

If an employer knowingly fails to pay any amount pursuant to a properly served income withholding notice to the other parent or public office, the employer is liable for the total amount it should have deducted and willfully failed to pay.

According to 750 Ill. Comp. Stat. 28/50, any officer or employee of any payor who has the control, supervision, or responsibility for withholding and paying over income pursuant to an income withholding notice properly served on the payor and who willfully fails to withhold or pay over income as required by the income withholding notice is personally liable for a penalty equal to the total amount that was not withheld or paid over by the payor.

Officers or employees of any payor include a partner of a partnership, a manager, or member of a limited liability corporation, and a member of a registered limited liability partnership. However, only where the employer has incurred sums and is unable to pay such amounts may personal liability attach to a responsible officer or employee who has willfully failed to withhold and pay over income as required under the income withholding notice. Additionally, this imposed personal liability will survive the dissolution of a partnership, limited liability company, or corporation.

Retaliation

If an employer willfully discharges, disciplines, refuses to hire, or penalizes an employee as a result of income withholding, the court may order employment or reinstatement of, or restitution to the employee, or both, and a fine not to exceed $200.

Frequently Asked Questions

Q **What is the minimum wage in Illinois?**

A The minimum wage in Illinois is $8.25 per hour. The minimum wage increases in an amount of 25 cents each year on July 1.

Q **What is the minimum wage for tipped employees?**

A Tipped employees must be paid minimum wage, but an employer may take credit for the employee's tips in an amount not to exceed 40 percent of the wage.

Q **When is overtime pay legally due?**

A Employees are entitled to pay at one and one-half times their regular rate of pay if they work over 40 hours in a workweek. However, employers may have different criteria for defining "workweek."

Q **Does an employer have to pay time and one-half or double time for working a legal holiday or a Sunday?**

A Not necessarily. If working the legal holiday or Sunday puts an employee over 40 hours in a workweek, the employer must pay the employee at one and one-half times the employee's regular rate of pay for those hours over 40. However, if the employer's policy allows for payment of time and one-half or double time, then the employer must honor the agreement.

Q **If an employee is paid salary, does the employee still qualify for overtime pay?**

A Maybe. Employees are paid salary if they regularly receive a predetermined amount constituting all or part of their compensation that is not subject to reduction due to variations in the quality or quantity of the work performed on a weekly or less frequent basis. Nonetheless, an employee that is paid on a salary basis is not automatically exempt from receiving overtime pay. The primary duties the employee performs must also be exempt to disqualify an employee from overtime pay.

Q **Can an employee be required to work overtime?**

A Yes, unless the work would violate the One Day Rest in Seven Act.

Q **Is "comp time" legal?**

A No. Compensatory time off, also known as comp time, in place of payment for overtime is not legal in the private sector.

Q **Are employees entitled to holiday pay?**

A No, unless it specified in the employment contract or agreement.

Q **How soon after an employee quits or is terminated does the employee have to be paid?**

A All final compensation, including bonus payments, vacation pay, wages, and commissions must be paid on the next regularly scheduled payday.

Q **Can an employer reduce an employee's rate of pay?**

A Yes, as long as the employee is notified of the change prior to performing the work and the wage does not fall below minimum wage.

Q **Must an employer provide a statement of deductions?**

A Yes. The Illinois law requires that each employee be furnished with an itemized statement of deductions for each pay period.

Q **How often must an employer pay wages?**

A Every employer is required to pay all wages earned at least semimonthly. The wages are to be paid no later than 13 days after the end of the pay period in which the wages were earned. Wages of executive, administrative, and professional employees as defined in the FLSA may be paid once per month.

Q **If an employee quits or is terminated, is the employee entitled to payment for unused accrued vacations time?**

A Yes. A former employee has a claim for the collection of the monetary equivalent of vacation time earned in accordance with the employment contract, agreement, or policy.

Q **Are employees entitled to severance pay, sick pay, or holiday pay upon separation?**

A No, unless provided for in the employment contract or agreement.

Q **Can an employer hold an employee's paycheck until the employee returns a uniform, tools, a pager, etc.?**

A No. An employer cannot withhold or deduct from wages pending the return of uniforms, tools, pagers, or any other employer-owned equipment.

Q **Can an employer take money out of an employee's wages to cover cash register shortages or damages to the employer's equipment/property?**

A No. An employer cannot deduct money from an employee's pay for cash or inventory shortages or damages to the employer's equipment or property, unless the employee has signed an express written agreement allowing the deductions at the time the deduction is made.

Q **Can an employer make an employee pay for a uniform?**

A No, unless the employee signs an express written agreement at the time the deduction is made.

Q **Can an employer require employees to accept their pay by direct deposit?**

A No. An employer must pay each employee wages in a form that the employee may readily convert into cash (without the need of a personal bank account), unless an employee volunteers to be paid by direct deposit in an account at a bank or financial institution of the employee's choice.

Q **Is it legal to pay employees in cash?**

A Yes. Illinois law allows wages or final compensation to be paid in lawful money of the United States or by check, redeemable upon demand and without discount at a bank or other financial institution, or by deposit of funds in an account in a bank or other financial institution designated by the employee.

Q **What is the law regarding breaks and meal periods?**

A An employee who is to work seven and one-half continuous hours or more must be provided an unpaid meal period of at least 20 minutes. The meal period must be given to an employee no later than five hours after beginning work. Illinois has no law regarding breaks.

Q **Can an employer require employees to work seven days in a row?**

A The One Day Rest in Seven Act allows for at least 24 hours of rest in every calendar week. A *calendar week* is defined as seven consecutive 24 hour periods starting at 12:01 a.m. Sunday morning and ending at midnight the following Saturday. Under this act, employers may ask the Illinois Department of Labor for a relaxation of this requirement. If the department grants a relaxation, it requires a statement from the employer demonstrating that all employees who will be working seven days in a row are in fact volunteers.

Contact Information
Illinois Department of Labor

1 West Old State Capitol Plaza, Room 300
Springfield, IL 62701

Telephone: 217-782-6206
Fax: 217-782-0596
Internet: *www.state.il.us/agency/idol*

Chapter 13

Payroll Taxes and Withholding

Introduction

Employers are cautioned not to interpret this chapter as the complete text on payroll taxes and withholding. Tax rates are subject to changes annually. Employers should consult the many Internal Revenue Service (IRS) documents, other available resources, or an applicable legal entity on this topic. For example, the IRS' Circular E, *Employer's Tax Guide*, outlines the rules and regulations for payroll deductions and deposits. Such forms may be obtained by contacting the IRS.

Who Is an Employee

Employees vs. Independent Contractors

Employers must be able to identify their taxable employees. Employers are required to withhold and pay taxes for those workers properly classified as employees. Employers with one employee will most likely be required to withhold federal income tax as well as Social Security tax from that employee's wages. Employers may also be subject to federal unemployment tax. Once a worker is deemed an employee for tax purposes, the fact that the employee works only part time, on a temporary basis, or is a minor ordinarily will not remove the need to withhold and pay taxes on that employee's wages.

Generally, an *employee* is an individual who performs services for an employer under the employer's direct control of when, where, and how the work is done. For payroll tax purposes, the IRS and state tax agencies rely on common-law rules to determine who is an employee. Under the common-law definition, if an employer maintains the legal right to control worker's activities, the workers are deemed employees. Although some workers may have discretion in determining their work performance, they are still legally considered employees. Employers must be aware that the actual employment relationship is most important in determining whether workers are employees. Should an employer-employee relationship exist, the labeling of the relationship has no value. Rather, the substance of the relationship governs the worker's status, not the label.

The status of an individual as an independent contractor or an employee for purposes of the federal tax laws (and state income tax laws) is determined, with few exceptions, under the common-law tests for determining whether an employment relationship exists.

Common-Law Employee Status

The federal employment tax regulations (such as FICA, FUTA, and income tax withholding) provide that an individual is an employee if, under the usual common-law tests, the relationship between the individual and the person for whom an individual performs services is the legal relationship of employer and employee.

Such a relationship generally exists if the person for whom the services are performed has the right to control and direct the services, not only as to the result to be accomplished by the work, but also as to the details and means by which that result is accomplished. Specifically, an employee is subject to the will and control of the employer as to not only what shall be done, but also how it shall be done.

The regulations state that the determination is to be based upon the particular facts in each case and warn that the designation or description of the relationship by the parties will not be determinative when facts prove otherwise.

The IRS has issued guidelines for conducting an independent contractor versus employee analysis, which focuses on evidence gathered in the following three primary categories:

- Behavioral control.

- Financial control.

- Relationship of the parties.

A more detailed discussion of this analysis is provided in the **Independent Contractors** and **Temporary Employees and Contingent Employment** chapters.

Taxes and Family Members

Employing family members may save payroll taxes, although if they are common-law employees they are subject to the same payroll taxes as any employee. In some situations, however, there may be savings in FICA taxes and unemployment taxes if the business is not run through a corporation or partnership (except for husband/wife partnerships).

Some basic rules apply to employing relatives as follows:

- Employers are not required to withhold and pay Social Security and Medicare taxes for their children under age 18 who work for them if the trade or business is a sole proprietorship or a partnership in which each partner is the child's parent. If the children's services are for work other than in the parent's home, taxes are not required to be paid until the child reaches 21.

- Wages paid by a parent to a child under 21 are not subject to FUTA tax. However, the wages of a child may be subject to income tax withholding.

- With exception, the wages for the services of a child or spouse are subject to income tax, Social Security, Medicare, and FUTA taxes when employed by a corporation, partnership, or estate of a parent or spouse.

- Employers must pay income, Social Security, and Medicare taxes — but not FUTA taxes — for spouses they employ in a trade or business. No taxes are paid if the work is for other than a trade or business, such as domestic service in a private home.

- The wages of parents employed by their children are subject to income tax withholding and Social Security and Medicare taxes. Social Security and Medicare taxes do not apply if the service is other than a trade or business unless it is for service caring for a child who lives with a son or daughter and who is under age 18 or that requires adult supervisor for more than four consecutive weeks in a calendar quarter due to a mental or physical condition. Wages paid to a parent who is employed by a child are never subject to FUTA taxes.

Employee Rights and Obligations

Social Security Card

Employees, including resident and nonresident aliens, are required to have Social Security numbers for the purpose of completing Forms W-2. An employee must show an employer the card if it is available. Employees without a Social Security card may obtain one by completing Form SS-5, *Application for a Social Security Card,* available from a Social Security Administration (SSA) office.

Once an employee receives a card, a corrected wage and tax statement (Form W-2c) should be submitted. Employees must ensure that the name is correct on the card.

Employers must record Social Security numbers for resident and nonresident aliens. Aliens who are not eligible for a Social Security card may request an individual taxpayer identification number (ITIN) for tax purposes, however, employers cannot accept an ITIN in place of a Social Security number.

Form W-4

A newly hired employee must complete a Form W-4, notifying the employer how many withholding allowances to use when deducting federal income taxes. The more withholding exemptions an employee claims, the less taxes an employer will have to withhold. Employees may claim fewer exemptions than they are entitled to in an effort to reduce later tax obligations. Employees may also ask employers to take additional money from their wages in anticipation of a larger tax bill. The IRS provides Publication 505, *Tax Withholding and Estimated Tax*, and Publication 919, *How Do I Adjust My Withholding*, to help employees complete the form.

Employees may not claim more exemptions than those of which they are entitled. Employees may claim one for themselves (unless they can be claimed as a dependent by another taxpayer), one for their spouse (if the spouse is not claiming a personal exemption on a Form W-4), and one exemption for each child or other dependent claimed on their tax return.

Some employees may qualify for a no-tax-liability exemption, thus relieving the employer of having to withhold federal income taxes (but not FICA taxes). To qualify for this exemption, the employee must have had no tax liability for the previous year, is not being claimed as a dependent on someone else's tax return, must have under a specified nonwage income and must be under a specified income. In the past, employers routinely had to send the IRS any Form W-4 of an employee making over $200 claiming complete exemption from withholding if $200 or claiming more than 10 allowances. Employers no longer have to submit these Form W-4's to the IRS. However, in certain circumstances, the IRS may direct employers to submit copies of these Form W-4's to the IRS or make the originals available for inspection.

It is the employee's responsibility to identify personal exemptions. Employees who submit a Form W-4 that results in less tax being withheld than properly allowable are subject to a steep monetary fine. Employers are under no obligation to confirm the validity of the exemptions, although if they discover that an employee has improperly claimed an exemption they must inform the IRS, request a new Form W-4 from the employee, and send the IRS a copy of the invalid form. Employers must also send the IRS copies of Form W-4 on which more than 10 exemptions are claimed.

Tips

Employees who make $20 or more in tips in any month are required to report all tips received to their employers. This must be in the form of a written report submitted by the 10th day of the following month. Employees who receive under $20 in tips in any month are not required to submit a report; however, they must include the tips on their tax return. Service charges added to bills are considered wages and not tips. Employers are responsible for withholding taxes on tips employees receive from customers.

Employees report the tips on Form 4070, *Employee's Report of Tips to Employer*, or a similar statement showing their name, address, and Social Security number.

Employers must collect income tax, Social Security tax, and Medicare tax on the tips from either wages or other funds the employee makes available. Employers that operate large food or beverage establishment (more than 10 employees on a typical day and food or beverages consumed on the premises), are required to allocate tips if the total tips reported are less than 8 percent of gross sales. The allocated amount must be reported on the employee's W-2 at the end of the year.

Wages

Employers have a considerably more complex responsibility in the tax process, beginning with exactly what constitutes wages for income tax purposes. Wages subject to federal employment taxes include all pay for services performed. This includes salaries and supplemental pay, such as vacation allowances, bonuses, commissions, and fringe benefits and may be paid in cash or in other forms.

The IRS Publication 15-A, *Employer's Supplemental Tax Guide*, provides information on other forms of compensation that may or may not be taxable, such as the following:

♦ Most awards and gifts are taxable unless clearly unrelated to employee performance (such as a wedding gift).

♦ Christmas gifts or cash are taxable (turkeys are not).

♦ Paid vacation time is considered taxable, as is any form of time-off pay.

♦ Wages in the form of property are taxable and present the special problem of withholding the taxable amount.

Exemptions

Certain types of payments are **exempt** from withholding taxes as follows:

♦ **Business Expense Reimbursement.** Employees who have incurred deductible expenses while performing services as an employee, have accounted to their employers for these expenses, and have been paid for their expenses are not subject to income tax withholding or payment of Social Security, Medicare, and FUTA taxes for the reimbursement — as long as they return any excess payment within a reasonable amount of time. Employees who are not required to account for and substantiate their expenses are subject to Social Security, Medicare, and Unemployment and Income Withholding taxes. Employees who are paid on a per-diem rate are considered to have accounted for their expenses if they have stayed within federal guidelines.

♦ **Noncash Payments.** Noncash payments, otherwise known as "in kind" payments, for household work, agricultural labor, and service not in an employer's trade or business are not subject to Social Security, Medicare, and FUTA taxes. Payment in kind for work done within an employer's trade or business is taxable.

♦ **Moving Expenses.** Reimbursed and employer-paid qualified moving expenses need not be included in an employee's income unless the employer knows the employee previously deducted expenses on a tax return. IRS Publication 521, *Moving Expenses*, explains this further.

- **Meals and Lodging.** The value of meals is not taxable income if the meals are furnished for the employer's convenience and on the employer's premises. This is also true of the value of lodging furnished for the employer's convenience, on the employer's premises, and as a condition of employment.

- **Health Insurance Plans.** Payments to employees' accident or health insurance plans are not taxable as income unless the employee owns more than 2 percent of an S corporation and the S corporation is paying the cost of the insurance.

- **Medical Saving Accounts.** Employer contributions to employees' medical savings accounts are not taxable if there was expectation they would not be included in income. Employee contributions are, however, taxable.

- **Medical Care Reimbursements.** Medical care reimbursements paid for under an employer's self-insured medical reimbursement plan are not taxable. Sick pay remunerated to an employee unable to work because of illness or injury is subject to FICA and FUTA taxes for a period up to six months after the last calendar month the employee worked for the employer. After six months, sick pay is exempt from FICA and FUTA taxes.

- **Fringe Benefits.** Ordinarily, fringe benefits (such as cars, company-provided air travel, service discounts, club memberships, and tickets) are taxable as income. However, services that do not cost the employer anything, minimal value fringes (such as local transportation benefits and parking) and services such as tuition reduction and the use of on-premise athletic facilities are not considered income.

- **Casual Labor.** Employers are not required to withhold federal taxes and most state income taxes or to pay federal and state unemployment taxes for cash payments of less than $50 in a calendar quarter if the employee was engaged in casual labor fewer than 24 different days during the quarter.

Withholding Period

Employers are required to withhold taxes for each payroll period that period of service for which wages are usually paid, even if an employee does not work for the full pay period. Employers without a payroll period should withhold the tax as if wages were paid for a daily or miscellaneous pay period.

For commissions paid on completion of a sale and other wages unrelated to a specific number of days, taxes are calculated based on the number of days back to the last payment or the date employment began (if during the same calendar year) or back to January 1 — whichever was most recent.

Applicable Taxes

Once employers know which workers require the collection and payment of taxes, on what income and how often these taxes must be collected, employers need to know exactly which taxes to collect.

Note: All tax rates are subject to changes annually. Employers should consult with the IRS or other applicable legal entity for current rates and scheduled changes.

Income Tax Withholding

Income tax must be withheld from an employee's wages, as previously defined, for each payroll period. Income tax withholding is based on the Form W-4 filled out by each employee. The IRS Circular E provides valuable information for employers on handling Forms W-4. Basically, however, the amount of income tax withholding is based on an employee's marital status and withholding allowances.

Some employees may claim an exemption from withholding based on having no income tax liability last year and on the expectation of having none for this year. However, this employee's wages are still subject to Social Security and Medicare taxes.

Employers are also required to withhold income tax from the wages of nonresident aliens. However, IRS Publication 515, *Withholding of Tax on Nonresident Aliens and Foreign Corporations*, and IRS Publication 519, *U.S. Tax Guide for Aliens*, present exceptions to this requirement.

Employers must withhold income tax from each pay period. The IRS provides wage-bracket tables to help employers calculate withholding tax. These are easy-to-use tax tables similar to those used to calculate taxes owed on the standard Form 1040. The IRS also supplies percentage-method tables based on the particular pay period an employer uses (such as weekly and biweekly), which are slightly more complicated to use. Employers that wish to use a method other than the wage-bracket or the percentage method should consult a tax specialist. Whatever method is used, employers may not withhold less than the prescribed amount.

Note: Part-time and temporary workers are treated the same as full-time employees for purposes of income tax withholding.

Advanced Earned Income Credit Payment

An employee who is eligible for the earned income credit (EIC) and has a qualifying child is entitled to receive EIC payments with pay during the year. To receive these payments, the employee must submit a completed Form W-5 to the employer.

Employers are required to make advance EIC payment to employees who provide them with a completed and signed Form W-5. Unless revoked by the employee, the Form W-5 remains in effect until the end of the calendar year.

Social Security and Medicare Taxes

The Federal Insurance Contribution Act (FICA) is intended to provide a system of old age, survivor, disability (OASDI), and hospital insurance. The first three of these are financed by the Social Security tax, and the hospital insurance is financed by Medicare tax. The taxes are reported separately.

Both employees and employers are responsible for paying these taxes. Employers withhold and pay the employees' share and pay a matching amount. The amount the employer pays is the same as the employee's tax, with the 2010 Social Security tax restricted to the wage base limit of $106,800. The wage base limit is adjusted annually. Thus in 2010, both employees and employers must pay a tax of 6.2 percent on the first $106,800 of an employee's salary, for a total of 12.4 percent. For Medicare's Hospital Insurance Program (HI), after 1993 there has been no limitation on HI-taxable earnings. Tax rates under the HI program are 1.45 percent for employees and employers, each, and 2.9 percent for self-employed persons.

Part-time employees, temporary employees, and employees with more than one job are all treated the same as full-time employees for purposes of Social Security and Medicare taxes. IRS publication 15-A explains the part-year-employment method of figuring taxes or the same method as used for full-time workers may be used.

Hiring Incentives to Restore Employment Act (HIRE Act)

The Hiring Incentives to Restore Employment Act (HIRE Act) provides two tax benefits to employers hiring workers who were previously unemployed or only working part time. Specifically, employers who hired unemployed workers after February 3, 2010 and before January 1, 2011 may qualify for a 6.2-percent payroll tax incentive, in effect exempting them from their share of Social Security taxes on wages paid to these workers after March 18, 2010. However, this reduced tax withholding will have no effect on the employee's future Social Security benefits, and employers would still need to withhold the employee's 6.2-percent share of Social Security taxes, as well as income taxes. The employer and employee's shares of Medicare taxes would also still apply to these wages.

Additionally, for each worker retained for at least a year, businesses may claim an additional general business tax credit, up to $1,000 per worker, when filing their 2011 income tax returns. The two tax benefits are especially helpful to employers who are adding positions to their payrolls. New hires filling existing positions also qualify, but only if the workers they are replacing left voluntarily or for cause. Family members and other relatives do not qualify.

The HIRE Act also requires that the employer get a statement from each eligible new hire certifying that they were unemployed during the 60 days before beginning work or, alternatively, worked fewer than a total of 40 hours for someone else during the 60-day period. The IRS revised Form W-2 and Form-W-3 to reflect changes under the act and released the Form W-11 affidavit which employees use to confirm that they are qualified employees under the act.

Businesses, agricultural employers, tax-exempt organizations, and public colleges and universities all qualify to claim the payroll tax benefit for eligible newly-hired employees. Household employers cannot claim this new tax benefit.

Employers claim the payroll tax benefit on the federal employment tax return they file, usually quarterly, with the IRS. Eligible employers will be able to claim the new tax incentive on their revised employment tax form for the second quarter of 2010.

Calculate the Benefits with the HIRE Act Estimator

Use the **Hire Act Estimator** (available online within Ceridian's HR Compliance Reference System) to estimate the value of the HIRE Act incentives for each qualified employee hired.

Note: A newer version of Adobe reader may be required to use this estimator effectively. Download the newest version of Adobe Reader free at *www.adobe.com*.

HIRE Act Frequently Asked Questions

Q **How does the HIRE Act impact payroll?**

A The following payroll-related provisions are included in the final version of the HIRE Act:

- Social Security tax exemption for qualified employers at the rate of 6.2 percent (.062) of Social Security wages up to the annual Social Security wage cap for 2010 of $106,800. This amounts to a maximum annual hiring incentive of $6,621.60 per employee ($106,800 x 6.2 percent).

- Qualifying employees must have been hired after February 3, 2010, and before January 1, 2011.

- Qualifying employees cannot have worked more than 40 hours of work over the most recent 60 days (ending on the employee's start date). Employers must get a signed affidavit from each employee as proof of compliance.

- The employer may not take the Social Security tax offset on employees hired to replace involuntarily terminated employees. Employees hired to replace voluntarily terminated employees and those who were terminated for cause will qualify.

- An additional tax credit of 6.2 percent of federal income taxable wages, not to exceed $1,000, for each qualifying employee retained for at least 52 weeks may be taken on the employer's business tax return in 2011.

Q How do employers claim Social Security tax credit on qualified employee wages?

A The Internal Revenue Service (IRS) created a modified 2010 Form 941, *Employer's Quarterly Federal Tax Return*, and the related instructions. The form includes new lines to claim the employer Social Security tax exemption and report the number of qualifying employees.

Q How soon can employers claim the Social Security tax credit?

A Credit for the employer's Social Security tax exemption cannot be taken until the second quarter of 2010. Any earned credit in the first quarter can be carried forward to the second quarter of 2010. This allows the IRS time to update its forms and systems to accommodate the new information.

Q Will there be any changes to Schedule B?

A Only the Schedule B instructions will change. The contents will not change since Schedule B is a record of liabilities (not payments).

Q Is there any W-2 reporting required as part of the HIRE Act?

A The IRS published updated Form W-2 instructions that included the new Box 12 code "cc" to report HIRE Exempt Wages and Tips. Form W-3 was also changed to include HIRE Exempt Wages and Tips in new box 12B.

Q Do employers have to report a list of qualified employees to the IRS?

A Currently there is no requirement to provide a detailed listing of employees to the IRS as part of the quarterly Form 941 filing process. Further IRS guidance is forthcoming.

Q What does an employee affidavit look like?

A The IRS has released Form W-11, *Hiring Incentives to Restore Employment (HIRE) Act Employee Affidavit*, to help employers comply with the affidavit provision of the HIRE Act.

Q Is an electronic signature valid on the employee affidavit?

A Yes. Employers can choose to collect affidavit information, including the employee signature, electronically. Currently, the IRS does not plan to issue an electronic version of Form W-11. Employers should follow the IRS guidelines set forth for electronic signature on the Form W-4 if they choose to develop an electronic affidavit form.

Q If an employer hires a new employee to replace a terminated employee, will the new employee's wages qualify for the credit?

A The law specifies that an employer can claim the credit for new positions, or positions where they are replacing a worker who terminated voluntarily or was terminated for cause.

Q Can part time, seasonal, and summer workers be qualified employees?

A Yes, if an employee meets all of the other criteria to be considered qualified. On a recent call, the IRS clarified that intermittent or seasonal employees who were originally hired and worked for an employer prior to February 3, 2010, only qualify if the prior employment relationship was ended (i.e. the employee was terminated) before beginning work for the new period/season.

Q Can temporary staffing agencies claim the Social Security tax exemption credit for qualified employees?

A Yes, based on when the employee begins employment with the temporary agency, and not based on when the employee begins work at a client business of the temporary agency.

Q Can employees who work in a U.S. territory be qualified employees?

A Yes, if an employee meets all of the other criteria to be considered qualified. The HIRE Act applies to all 50 states, U.S. territories, possessions, and tribal governments. Federal, state, and local governments are not eligible for the tax exemption under the law.

Q Can employees hired to work in the United States under a visa (noncitizens) be qualified employees?

A Yes, if an employee meets all of the other criteria to be considered qualified.

Q If an employer hired a qualified employee after February 3, but before the law went into effect on March 19, are all of the employee's wages eligible for the Social Security tax exemption?

A The 6.2 percent exemption credit is available to employers based on the date the employee was paid. Only wages paid from March 19, 2010, through December 31, 2010, (up to the $106,800 limit) are eligible for the employer's Social Security tax exemption.

Q Does the HIRE Act exemption credit affect the Work Opportunity Tax Credit (WOTC)?

A The IRS has provided guidance on the FAQs 'About Claiming the Payroll Exemption' page of its Web site. The IRS posted additional guidance on May 6.

Q Does the HIRE Act employer Social Security tax exemption affect the employer tip credit?

A An employer that applies the payroll tax exemption with respect to a qualified employee will be entitled to a smaller 45B credit because the employer will pay only Medicare tax (and not Social Security tax) on the employee's wages, including reported tips.

Q Does the HIRE Act employer Social Security tax exemption impact the treatment of severance arrangements?

A The IRS is researching this scenario and will provide guidance in the future.

Q Can an employer claim the Social Security tax exemption credit on Form 941 for wages paid to a qualified employee in a previous quarter?

A Generally, no. The credit must be claimed in the quarter in which the eligible wages were paid. However, on the second quarter Form 941, the IRS will allow an employer to claim the credit for eligible wages paid in both first quarter 2010 and second quarter 2010. The credit on eligible first quarter wages (paid March 19 – 31, 2010) could only be claimed on the second quarter 941.

Q Can an employer claim the Social Security tax exemption credit on wages paid to a new employee who has not yet signed a Form W-11 (affidavit) but is otherwise qualified?

A No. An employer cannot claim the credit for the Social Security tax exemption on wages paid to any employee who has not submitted a signed Form W-11 (or alternate affidavit).

Q If an employer receives a Form W-11 from a qualified employee after the second quarter Form 941 is filed, how does the employer claim the Social Security tax exemption credit on the eligible first/second quarter wages?

A An employer can claim credit on eligible first/second quarter wages by filing an amended Form 941 for second quarter. The same situation applies for third and fourth quarter — the employer must file an amended 941 to claim the credit for eligible wages paid during the specific quarter.

Q Can an employer claim the HIRE Act incentives if the employer hires an employee who began working for that employer through a temporary agency?

A Yes, if the employee had not worked as an employee for any business (including the temporary agency) for more than 40 hours in the 60 days prior to beginning employment with the hiring employer.

Q Are employers required to claim the HIRE Act incentives on all qualified employees?

A No. Employers can choose to claim the exemption on all, some or none of its qualified employees.

Q Can an employer claim a credit on a rehired employee that had been laid-off previously?

A Yes, if the employee meets all of the other criteria to be considered qualified. On a recent call, the IRS clarified that employees who were laid-off only qualify if the prior employment relationship was ended (i.e. the employee was terminated) at the time of the lay-off.

Q Is there a deadline by which the employer must collect the W-11 from the employee?

A Yes, the employer must have the signed affidavit by the time the employer files an employment tax return applying the payroll tax exemption.

Q What happens if an employer incorrectly claims the tax exemption on a nonqualified employee?

A The employer is liable for Social Security tax on the nonqualified employee and must file Form 941-X for each prior quarter for which the exemption was erroneously applied.

Q Is an affidavit (Form W-11) valid if it is signed by an employee who is a minor?

A Yes, minors can legally sign an affidavit.

Q What are employers required to do with the completed Form W-11?

A The IRS requires employers to maintain the Forms W-11 as part of the employees' payroll records. Employers may choose to scan signed forms W-11 and retain the electronic copies as part of the employees' records in lieu of retaining the paper copy.

Federal Unemployment Tax Act

The Federal Unemployment Tax Act (FUTA), with state unemployment systems, provides for payments of unemployment compensation to workers who have lost their jobs.

Most employers pay both a federal and state unemployment tax. A list of state unemployment tax agencies may be found in IRS Publication 926, *Household Employer's Tax Guide*.

Employers with one or more employees — other than farm or household workers or their own children — are subject to FUTA if the wages total $1,500 or more in any calendar quarter in the current or previous tax year or if they employ workers for at least one day in each of 20 calendar weeks, regardless of whether the calendar weeks were consecutive. However, some state laws differ from the federal law and employers should contact their state workforce agencies to learn the exact requirements.

Employers of domestic employees must pay state and federal unemployment taxes if they pay cash wages to household workers totaling $1,000 or more in any calendar quarter of the current or preceding year. A household worker is an employee who performs domestic services in a private home, for example:

- Babysitters and caretakers.

- Cleaning people, drivers, and nannies.

- Health aides, yard workers, and private nurses.

Employers that paid more than $20,000 in cash wages to farm workers during any calendar quarter of the current or previous tax year or who employed 10 or more farm workers during at least part of a day during any 20 or more weeks in either the current or previous tax year are also subject to FUTA. The 20 weeks need not be consecutive weeks, nor must they be the same 10 employees, nor must all employees be working at the same time of the day.

FUTA tax is computed on the first $7,000 of wages paid to every employee each year, with the tax rate varying by state. The federal FUTA tax rate currently is 6.2 percent of the first $7,000. The federal wage base is $7,000. The state wage base may be different, and employers can generally take a credit — up to a maximum of 5.4 percent — against the FUTA tax for amounts they pay to the state unemployment fund.

If an employer is entitled to the maximum 5.4 percent credit, the FUTA tax rate after the credit is 0.8 percent. FUTA tax rates are subject to changes annually. Employers should consult with the IRS or other applicable legal entity for current rates and scheduled changes.

Only the employer pays FUTA, and it is not deducted from an employee's wages.

State Income Taxes

Most states — all but Alaska, Florida, Nevada, New Hampshire, South Dakota, Tennessee, Texas, Washington, and Wyoming — impose a personal income tax. Employers conducting business in those states must withhold that tax along with the federal taxes.

Employers can usually use the same methods to calculate state income taxes that they used to calculate federal ones. Most states have their own equivalent to the federal Form W-4.

In some cities, employers may have to withhold local income taxes in addition to federal and state income taxes. Multistate employers may have to withhold taxes for several states when employees live and work in different states. The services of a tax specialist are highly recommended as these situations become more complex.

Military Spouses Residency Relief Act

The federal Military Spouses Residency Relief Act allows a military spouse who moves out of a state with their service member under military orders to have the option to claim the same state of domicile as their active duty spouse, regardless of where they are stationed. Service members themselves have long had such an option and spouses did not, thereby resulting in split residencies for many families.

The act is effective for tax years after 2008 and amends the Servicemembers Civil Relief Act to prohibit all of the following solely because the person is absent from a state because they are accompanying their spouse who is absent from the state in compliance with military or naval orders:

- Losing a residence or domicile in a state.

- Acquiring a residence or domicile in any other state.

- Becoming a resident in or of any other state.

The act also prohibits both of the following:

♦ A service member's spouse from either losing or acquiring a residence or domicile for purposes of taxation because of being absent or present in any U.S. tax jurisdiction solely to be with the service member in compliance with the service member's military orders if the residence or domicile is the same for the service member and the spouse.

♦ A spouse's income from being considered income earned in a tax jurisdiction if the spouse is not a resident or domiciliary of such jurisdiction when the spouse is in that jurisdiction solely to be with a service member serving under military orders.

State Unemployment Taxes

Most states require employers to pay part of the first $7,000 to a state unemployment fund to provide the benefits for former employees terminated without cause after working for at least 20 weeks. A company's liability is based on the prior year's claims experience. Companies are required to register with the state and file quarterly tax returns. The state unemployment tax rate will be adjusted to ensure that the company maintains a minimum balance relative to its experience rating.

Note: State unemployment tax rates are subject to changes annually. Employers should consult with the IRS or other applicable legal entity for current rates and scheduled changes.

Paying the Taxes

Employers should keep in mind a few of the following important issues to ensure accurate withholding and timely payment of various taxes:

♦ Failure to pay over taxes withheld may subject business owners to an obligation for the tax withheld plus interest and penalties. Individuals responsible for payroll are liable for the taxes withheld portion of payroll taxes due, and bankruptcy does not protect someone from this obligation.

♦ Deposits of less than the required amounts may subject employers to penalties unless the shortage is less than the greater of $100 or 2 percent of the required amount and the shortage was paid or deposited by the by the shortfall makeup dates specified in Circular E.

♦ Failure to deposit income tax and FICA by the due date results in a 2-percent penalty for deposits 1 to 5 days late, a 5-percent late-payment penalty for deposits made 6 to 15 days late, and up to a 15-percent penalty for deposits unpaid more than 10 days after an IRS notification.

♦ Employers must submit federal payroll taxes with the appropriate financial institution at least monthly.

♦ State tax payments must be sent to the administering agency quarterly.

♦ Employers must notify employees of payroll taxes withheld.

Employer Identification Number

To file the various tax returns, employers need a federal Employer Identification Number (EIN). Other than a sole proprietor with no employees, every employer needs an EIN. Employers must use an EIN on all items sent to the IRS and Social Security Administration (SSA). Employers may obtain their EIN by filing Form SS-4, available at most Social Security Administration and IRS offices. Additionally, the number may be obtained by mail, fax, or by phone.

Note: If the organization or ownership of a business changes, an employer may have to apply for a new EIN.

Federal Taxes

Income Tax and FICA Tax

Withheld income taxes, Social Security, and Medicare taxes (less any advance earned income credits) must be deposited by mailing or delivering a check, money order, or cash to an authorized financial institution or Federal Reserve Bank. These deposits are usually made monthly (by the 15th of the following month) or semiweekly (within the next week), as the IRS determines for the individual employer.

The frequency of deposits is based on an employer's total taxes, as reported on Form 941 in a four-quarter look-back period beginning July 1 and ending June 30. Taxes of less than $50,000 are usually deposited monthly. Taxes of over $50,000 are deposited semiweekly.

New employers deposit taxes monthly for their first calendar year, although there is an exception to this — the $100,000 Next-Day Deposit Rule — explained in Circular E. Employers who incur a tax liability of $100,000 or more on any day during a deposit period must deposit the tax by the next banking day, whether they are on a monthly or semiweekly depositing schedule. Taxes of less than $2,500 for a quarter may be paid directly with the quarterly return rather than being deposited.

Note: Income tax and FICA tax rates are subject to changes annually. Employers should consult with the IRS or other applicable legal entity.

FUTA Taxes

Federal unemployment tax is usually deposited quarterly, on the last day of the month that follows the end of each quarter. Thus, payments are due by April 30, July 31, October 31, and January 31. Employers with a FUTA liability of less than $500 are not required to deposit the tax. Rather, such employers may carry the tax forward and add it to the liability of the next quarter to determine whether a deposit must be made. Form 8109, *Federal Tax Deposit Coupon*, which the IRS supplies with the EIN, must accompany deposits of federal payroll taxes. The deposit coupon is how the IRS credits an employer's tax account. The authorized financial institution or Federal Reserve Bank cannot accept payment without a deposit coupon.

Note: FUTA tax rates are subject to changes annually. Employers should consult with the IRS or other applicable legal entity.

Electronic Transfer of Funds

Employers with FUTA tax liability over $500, including any FUTA tax carried forward from an earlier quarter must, deposit the FUTA tax by an electronic funds transfer or in an authorized financial institution using Form 8109, *Federal Tax Deposit Coupon*.

Additionally, employers must electronically deposit all depository taxes (employment tax, excise tax, and corporate income tax) using the Electronic Federal Tax Payment System (EFTPS) if either of the following applies:

♦ The total deposits of such taxes in the previous tax year were more than $200,000.

♦ An employer was previously required to use EFTPS.

Penalties

Employers that are required to use EFTPS and fail to do so are subject to a 10 percent penalty. Employers that are not required to use the system may do so voluntarily.

State Taxes

State income taxes withheld and employer payments for state unemployment taxes must be submitted to the appropriate state agency at least quarterly, although some states, notably California, have special requirements.

Note: State tax rates are subject to changes annually. Employers should consult with the IRS or other applicable legal entity.

Recordkeeping

Employers' tax responsibility **does not** end once the taxes are withheld and deposited. They must also comply with elaborate recordkeeping requirements.

General Employment Tax Records

Employers are required to keep the following employment tax records for at least four years from the due dates of the relevant returns or from the dates the taxes were paid:

- ◆ Amounts and dates of wages paid and tips reported.

- ◆ The fair market value of noncash wages.

- ◆ The names, addresses, Social Security numbers, and job titles of all employees.

- ◆ The dates of all employees' employment.

- ◆ The rate of pay of each employee.

- ◆ Copies of Form W-4 showing each employee's withholding allowances.

- ◆ Duplicate copies of Forms 940 and 941 filed.

- ◆ The dates and amounts of all tax deposits.

- ◆ Periods for which employees and recipients were paid while absent due to sickness or injury and the amount and weekly rate of payments made by the employer or third party.

- ◆ Canceled checks or check stubs for all wages paid and deposits made.

- ◆ Undeliverable Forms W-2.

Note: These records must be kept in such a way as to allow them to be easily accessed by the IRS or by state authorities.

Form 941

All employers, who are not farmers, who pay wages subject to income tax withholding or Social Security or Medicare taxes, must file Form 941, *Employer's Quarterly Federal Income Tax Return.* Agricultural employers file an annual return, Form 943.

Employers with more than one location or division must only file one Form 941 per quarter — January – March, April – June, July – September, and October – December. The form is due by the last day of the month following the end of the quarter. Employers that qualify may file the form by phone or electronically in the cases of reporting agents filing for groups of taxpayers. A final Form 941 is required for employers who go out of business. Form 941 reports the following:

- ♦ Wages paid, including, any tips employees have received.

- ♦ Federal income tax withheld.

- ♦ Social Security and Medicare taxes withheld and the employer's share of Social Security and Medicare taxes.

- ♦ Advance earned income credit payments.

An adjustment line is available to correct the Social Security and Medicare taxes employers were unable to collect on employees' tips or for Social Security and Medicare taxes withheld from employees' sick pay from a third party, such as an insurance company. The income tax withheld is added to the Social Security and Medicare taxes on the form and any advance earned income credit payments are subtracted. The remainder is the amount of employment taxes owed for the quarter. Employers with a tax liability of more than $2,500 must complete a special portion of Form 941 or Schedule B (Form 941).

Employers are required to resolve discrepancies between Form 941 filed with the IRS and the Forms W-2 and W-3 filed with the Social Security Administration. Employers should reconcile all amounts entered on the forms, comparing the Forms W-3 with the quarterly Form 941. Employers must use an adjusted Form 941 to resolve these discrepancies.

Form 940

Employers may also have to file a federal unemployment tax return Form 940 by January 31 of each year if they paid $1,500 or more in wages in any calendar quarter in the current or previous tax year or had at least one employee work for some part of a day in any 20 different weeks the current or previous tax year. This includes regular, temporary, and part-time workers.

Note: As of the 2008 tax period, the IRS is no longer using or accepting Form 940-EZ. Employers who would have filed a 940-EZ form must now use the simplified Form 940.

Agricultural Occupations

Agricultural employers will have to file Form 940 or 940-EZ if they paid cash wages of $20,000 or more to farm workers in the current or previous tax year or employed 10 or more farm workers for at least part of a day during any 20 or more different weeks in the current or previous tax year.

Schedule H

Employers who do not report employment taxes for household employees on Form 941 or 943 must report FUTA taxes for those employees on Schedule H of Form 1040.

Form W-2

Employers required to file a Form 941 must inform their employees how much has been withheld from the employees' wages for federal and state income taxes and FICA taxes. This reporting is done by supplying each employee with a Form W-2, *Wage and Tax Statement*, by January 31 of the month following the reporting year. Copies of Forms W-2 must be filed with the Social Security Administration by the end of February.

Termination

Employees who were terminated before the end of the year may request the Form W-2 earlier, and the form must be furnished within 30 days of the request.

Form 1099-Misc.

Independent contractors who have been paid at least $600 for their services receive a copy of the federal information return form (Form 1099-Misc.) that employers must file with the IRS. The independent contractor must receive the form by January 31, and the IRS must receive the form by February 28.

Caution

The material provided in this chapter is intended solely as an introduction to a very complex topic. Employers are urged to read IRS publications, consult additional publications, and confer with a tax professional to assist with a thorough understanding of this very complicated subject.

Contact Information

Electronic Federal Tax Payment System

Telephone (Toll-Free): 800-555-8778 or 303-967-5916
Internet: *www.eftps.gov*

Internal Revenue Service

Telephone (Toll-Free): 800-829-4933 for business tax questions
Internet: *www.irs.gov*

Social Security Administration Headquarters

6401 Security Boulevard
Baltimore, MD 21235

Telephone (Toll-Free): 800-772-1213
Internet: *www.ssa.gov*

Employer Reporting Service Center

Telephone (Toll-Free): 800-772-6270
Internet: *www.ssa.gov/employer*

Business Services Online

Telephone (Toll-Free): 800-772-6270
Fax: 410-597-0237
Internet: *www.ssa.gov/bso*

Chapter 14

Employment of Minors

Introduction

Federal and state laws closely regulate the employment of minors, imposing special restrictions on the terms and conditions of their employment. These laws also impose additional administrative duties on employers. For instance, an employer may be subject to criminal penalties, civil liability, and a substantial penalty under workers' compensation statutes if a minor is injured while working illegally. Accordingly, employers must fully comply with both federal and state employment-of-minors laws.

This chapter reviews the laws regarding employment of minors, including prohibited employment and limitations on work hours.

Federal Laws

Covered Employees

Child labor laws generally cover all employees under age 18. However, the federal Fair Labor Standards Act (FLSA) sets a 14-year minimum age that applies to **all** employment subject to FLSA's child labor provisions in any occupation other than in agriculture and limits the number of hours worked by minors under age 16. The FLSA also sets an 18-year minimum age for any employment in an occupation found and declared by the Secretary of Labor to be particularly hazardous for the employment of minors or detrimental to the health or well-being of a minor.

The FLSA allows for exceptions to the regulation of minors when the minors are:

♦ Employed in agriculture during nonschool hours for the school district where they live.

♦ Employed by their parents in occupations not prohibited to minors.

♦ Participating in a vocational program approved by a state department of education.

♦ Employed for any of the following:

• Delivering newspapers.

• Mowing residential lawns.

• Shoveling snow on a casual basis.

• Acting or performing in motion pictures or in theatrical, radio, or television productions.

• Wreath making.

• Loading scrap balers or paper box compactors (if certain requirements are met).

Certification and recordkeeping requirements **do not apply** to minors who perform volunteer work for a nonprofit organization.

The FLSA generally permits the employment of children younger than 16 years of age in agricultural work, provided that certain conditions are met. Nevertheless, hazardous agricultural work may not be performed by minors under age 16, except where such minors are enrolled in certain vocational or training programs. The rules governing child labor in agricultural occupations sets a 14-year minimum for a minor to be employed on farms outside of school hours except in occupations designated as hazardous.

Certificates of Age

Employers may obtain a certificate of age to provide protection against unwitting violations of the FLSA's minimum age standards. An unexpired certificate of age validates that the minor is above the oppressive child labor age, and furnishes an employer with proof of the age of a minor employee upon which the employer may rely in determining whether the minor is at least the minimum age for the occupation in which the minor will be employed. Employers should be aware that expired or revoked certificates of age have no force or effect under the FLSA after notice of revocation.

Employers may obtain either a federal or a state certificate of age. A person authorized by the Administrator of the Wage and Hour Division must issue a federal certificate of age. The certificate must demonstrate that the minor is above the oppressive child labor age applicable to the occupation in which the minor is employed. A state certificate, which may be in the form of and known as an age, employment, or working certificate or permit, must be issued by or under the supervision of a state agency.

The FLSA advises employers to always obtain a certificate where the minor claims to be only one or two years above the applicable minimum age for the occupation in which the minor is to be employed. A certificate should also be obtained for every minor claiming to be older than two years above the applicable minimum age if the minor's physical appearance indicates otherwise.

Contents and Retention of Certificate

Certificates of age must contain the following:

- The name and address of minor and the minor's parent(s).
- The place and date of birth of the minor, together with a statement indicating the evidence on which this is based.
- Sex of the minor.
- Signature of the minor and issuing officer.
- Date and place of issuance.

If the minor is less than 18 years old, the certificate must also contain the following:

- The name and address of the employer.
- Industry of employment.
- Occupation of the minor.

The U.S. Department of Labor will send a certificate of age for a minor under age 18 to the minor's prospective employer. The employer must then keep the certificate on file at the minor's place of employment. Additionally, the employer must return the certificate to the minor when the minor terminates employment. The minor may subsequently present the previously issued certificate to future employers as proof of age.

If an employer receives a certificate of age from an employee age 18 or 19, the certificate must be returned to the employee upon termination of employment.

Hours of Employment

Minors Under 16

Minors under 16 **may**:

♦ Only be employed three hours a day and 18 hours a week when school is in session.

♦ Be employed up to eight hours a day and 40 hours a week when school is not in session.

♦ Work until 9 p.m. from June through August.

Minors under 16 **may not**:

♦ Be employed during school hours except as part of certain vocational training programs.

♦ Work more than three hours in a day between the hours of 7 a.m. and 7 p.m. during the school year.

Minors 14 and 15

Minors 14 and 15 years old may be employed as follows:

♦ Outside school hours.

♦ When school is not in session, no more than 40 hours in any one week and no more than 8 hours in any one day.

♦ When school is in session no more than 18 hours in any one week and no more than 3 hours in any one day, including Fridays.

♦ Between 7 a.m. and 7 p.m. in any one day, except during the summer (June 1 through Labor Day) when the evening hour will be 9 p.m.

♦ Those who are enrolled in an approved work-study program may be employed for no more than 18 hours in any one week when school is in session, a portion of which may be during school hours in accordance with the following formula based on a continuous four-week cycle:

 • In three of the four weeks, the participant is permitted to work during school hours on only one day per week, and for no more than for eight hours on that day.

 • During the remaining week of the four-week cycle, such minor is permitted to work during school hours on no more than two days, and for no more than for eight hours on each of those two days.

 • The employment of such minors would still be subject to the time of day and number of hours standards.

 • To the extent that these provisions are inconsistent with the hours of work and conditions of employment permitted, these work-study formula provisions are controlling.

♦ Performing sports-attending services at professional sporting events outside the scope of the time restrictive regulations. For example, minors 14 and 15 **may** be employed where the duties of the sports-attendant occupation consist of the following:

 • Pre- and post-game practice.

- Set up of balls and equipment prior to or during a sporting event.
- Clearing the field or court of debris or moisture during play.
- Providing ice, drinks, or towels to players during play.
- Working in concession stands.
- Selling or promotional activities.

State Regulations

Although the FLSA does not limit the number of hours or times of day for minors 16 years and older, stricter state child labor law may regulate such employment. Because states have enacted child labor laws as well, in situations where both the FLSA child labor provisions and state child labor laws apply, the higher minimum standard must be obeyed.

Wages

The minimum wage laws applicable to adults generally cover minors with a few noted **exceptions** as follows:

- **Student Learners.** Student learners that are at least 16 years old who are enrolled in cooperative, vocational education programs approved by a state board of education may be paid 75 percent of the minimum wage, for as long as the student is enrolled in the vocational education program.

- **Full-Time Students.** Full-time students employed in retail or service stores, agriculture, colleges, or universities may be paid 85 percent of the minimum wage. Full-time students are limited to working only eight hours in a day and no more than 20 hours a week when school is in session and 40 hours when school is out. Employers must abide by all child labor laws and once students graduate or leave school for good, they must be paid the federal minimum wage.

- **Youth Minimum Wage Program.** The FLSA's youth minimum wage program provides for a temporary subminimum wage for youth. The youth minimum wage must be at least $4.25 an hour and applies only to workers under 20 during the first 90 consecutive calendar days after the employee is initially hired. After the 90 consecutive days of employment, or when the worker reaches 20 — whichever occurs first — the worker must receive the federal minimum wage. It is unlawful for an employer to displace a current employee or reduce the employee's work hours or benefits to pay the opportunity wage.

- **The Fair Labor Standards Act (FLSA).** The act exempts employees of organized camps, amusement or recreational establishments, and religious or nonprofit educational conference centers from minimum wage and overtime requirements if the facility does not operate for more than seven months in a calendar year or if its average receipts for any six months of the previous year do not exceed 33⅓ percent of the receipts for the remaining six months of that year. However, private entities providing services or facilities in a national park, forest, or wildlife refuge are not exempt from federal wage requirements unless the services or facilities are related to skiing.

Prohibited/Permitted Occupations
Minors Under 18

The U.S. Department of Labor has adopted detailed regulations prohibiting the employment of any minor in occupations potentially hazardous or detrimental to the minor's health. (Employers should consult state laws and regulations for additional restrictions.)

Minors under 18 **may not** be employed in the following occupations declared hazardous by federal regulations:

♦ Occupations in or about plants or establishments manufacturing or storing explosives or articles containing explosive components, including ammunition, black powder, blasting caps, fireworks, high explosives, primers, and smokeless powder.

♦ Occupations as a motor vehicle driver or helper.

♦ Occupations in connection with mining, including coal mining.

♦ Occupations in logging, sawmill, lath mill, shingle mill, or cooperage mill operations.

♦ Occupations in forest fire fighting and forest fire prevention, in timber tracts, in forestry services, logging, and the operation of any sawmill, lath mill, shingle mill, or cooperage stock mill.

♦ Occupations involved in the operation of power-driven hoisting apparatus (for example, an elevator or crane).

♦ Occupations involving the operation of circular saws, band saws, or guillotine shears.

♦ Occupations involving the operation of power-driven hoisting apparatuses, including operating or assisting to operate certain elevators, cranes, derricks, hoists, riggers, or high-lift trucks.

♦ Occupations involving the operation of power-driven metal forming, punching, or shearing machines.

♦ Occupations involving the operation of power-driven meat processing machines or involving slaughtering, meat packing, processing, or rendering.

♦ Occupations involving the operation of bakery machines.

♦ Occupations involving the operation of power-driven meat processing machines, involving slaughtering, meat packing, processing, or rendering, or handlifting or handcarrying any carcass of beef, pork, horse, deer, or buffalo.

♦ Occupations involving the operation of bakery machines, setting up or adjusting a cookie or cracker machine.

♦ Occupations involving the manufacture of brick, tile, or similar products.

♦ Occupations involving wrecking, demolition, or shipbreaking operations.

♦ Occupations involving exposure to radioactive substances or ionizing radiations.

♦ Occupations in roofing operations and on or about a roof, including all work performed upon or in close proximity to a roof.

♦ Excavation operations.

Motor Vehicle Occupations for Minors Between 16 and 18

With exception, minors between 16 and 18 **may not** be employed as a motor vehicle driver and outside helper on any public road, highway, in or about any mine (including an open pit mine or quarry), place where logging or sawmill operations are in progress, or in any particularly hazardous excavation.

However, a 17-year-old minor may drive automobiles and trucks on public roads in the course of employment if **all** the following conditions are met:

♦ The minor holds a state license valid for the type of driving involved in the job performed and has successfully completed a state-approved driver education course.

♦ The minor has no record of any moving violation at the time of hire.

♦ The automobile or truck is equipped with a seat belt or similar restraining device for the driver and any passengers and the employer has instructed the minor that the seat belts must be used.

- ◆ The minor's driving is restricted to daylight hours and the automobile or truck does not exceed 6,000 pounds of gross vehicle weight.

- ◆ The driving is only occasional and incidental to the minor's employment. The term *occasional and incidental* means no more than one-third of a minor's work time in any workday and no more than 20 percent of a minor's work time a week.

- ◆ The driving **does not** include the following:

  - Towing vehicles.

  - Route deliveries or route sales.

  - Transporting for hire of property, goods, or passengers.

  - Urgent, time-sensitive deliveries. *Urgent, time-sensitive deliveries* are trips, which, because of such factors as customer satisfaction, the rapid deterioration of the quality, or change in temperature of the product are subject to timelines, schedules, and turn-around times that might cause the driver to hurry to complete the delivery. Urgent, time-sensitive deliveries would not depend on the delivery's origin and termination, and includes the delivery of people and things to and from the workplace. Prohibited trips include, but are not limited to, delivery of the following:

    - Pizzas or prepared foods.

    - Materials under a deadline (such as deposits to a bank at closing).

    - Shuttling of passengers to and from transportation departments to meet transport schedules.

  - More than two trips away from the primary place of employment a day to transport passengers (other than employees) or to deliver goods to a customer of the employer (other than urgent, time-sensitive deliveries, which are completely banned).

  - Transporting more than three passengers, including employees of the employer.

  - Driving beyond a 30-mile radius from the minor's place of employment.

Minors under 16 **may not** be employed to drive a motor vehicle in any capacity. However, certain exceptions are available for training programs in agriculture. In addition, minors under 16 **may not**:

- ◆ Deliver goods, merchandise, commodities, papers (except newspapers), or packages from a motor vehicle regardless of the vehicle's size or type.

- ◆ Serve as helpers on motor vehicles.

- ◆ Be employed in occupations that must be performed on any form of transportation.

Minors Between 14 and 16

Student learners may be between the ages of 14 and 16; however, apprentices must be at least 16 years old to participate in apprentice programs.

Student Learners

Student learners must be enrolled in an approved cooperative vocational training program. They must be employed under a written agreement that states all of the following:

- ◆ The student learner's work in the hazardous occupation is incidental to the training.

- ◆ The work must be intermittent, brief, and closely supervised by a qualified, experienced person.

- ◆ Safety instructions must be given by the school and correlated by the employer with on-the-job training.

- ◆ A schedule of organized and progressive work processes to be performed must be prepared.

Additionally, the written agreement must contain the student learner's name and the signatures of the employer and school coordinator or principal. Copies of the agreement must be kept on file by both the school and the employer.

Apprentices

Apprentices **must** be at least 16 and in an approved apprenticeship program of a recognized apprenticeable trade. However, individuals must usually be 18 years old to be an apprentice in hazardous occupations. Apprentice work must be intermittent and for short periods under the direct and close supervision of a journey-level employee.

The apprentice must be registered by the Bureau of Apprenticeship and Training of the Department of Labor or by a state apprenticeship agency as employed in accordance with the bureau's standards or be employed under a written apprenticeship agreement and conditions that the Secretary of Labor finds to conform with such standards.

Minors Between 14 and 15

Minors between 14 and 15 **may not** be employed to work in the following occupations as prohibited by federal regulations:

- ◆ Manufacturing, mining, or processing, including duties of any kind in workplaces where goods are manufactured, mined, or processed.

- ◆ Occupations that the Secretary of Labor may find and declare to be hazardous for the employment of minors between age 16 and 18 or detrimental to their health or well-being.

- ◆ Operating or tending to a hoisting apparatus or any power-driven machinery other than office machines.

- ◆ Work performed in or about boiler or engine rooms or in connection with the maintenance or repair of the establishment, machines, or equipment.

- ◆ Occupations that involve operating, tending, setting up, adjusting, cleaning, oiling, or repairing any power driven machinery, included but not limited to, lawn mowers, golf carts, all-terrain vehicles, trimmers, cutters, weed-eaters, edgers, food slicers, food grinders, food choppers, food processors, food cutters, and food mixers. However, minors age 14 and 15 may operate office equipment, vacuum cleaners, and floor waxers.

- ◆ Operating motor vehicles or serving as helpers on motor vehicles and the riding on a motor vehicle, inside or outside of an enclosed passenger compartment.

- ◆ Outside window washing that involves working from window sills, and all work requiring the use of ladders, scaffolds, or their substitutes.

- ◆ All baking and cooking activities, with exception.

- ◆ Work in freezers and meat coolers and all work in the preparation of meats for sale. However, the employment of minors age 14 and 15 is not prohibited if their duties require them to occasionally enter freezers only momentarily to retrieve items.

- ◆ Youth peddling (the selling of goods at locations other than the workplace). For example, door-to-door sales and street sales. This ban does not cover charitable or fundraising efforts such as selling Girl Scout cookies.

- ◆ Loading and unloading of goods or property onto or from motor vehicles, railroad cars, or conveyors, except the loading and unloading of personal nonpower-driven hand tools, personal protective equipment, and personal items to and from motor vehicles.

- ◆ Catching and cooping of poultry in preparation for transportation or for market.

- Public messenger services.

- Transporting persons or property by rail, highway, air, water, pipeline, or other means.

- Warehousing and storage.

- Communications and public utilities.

- Construction, including demolition and repair.

Note: Minors 14 and 15 **may** work in the previously listed industries in the occupations generally permitted to them only if their duties are not performed on any media of transportation or at the actual site of construction.

Food Service, Retail, and Gasoline Service

Prohibited Occupations

Minors between 14 and 15 **may not** be employed in the following occupations in retail, food service, and gasoline service establishments as provided in federal regulations:

- Work performed in or about boiler or engine rooms.

- Work in connection with the maintenance or repair of the establishment, machines, or equipment.

- Work requiring the use of ladders, scaffolds, or their substitutes, including outside window washing that involves working from sills.

- Baking and cooking such as, but not limited to, cooking with rotisseries, broilers, pressurized equipment, fryolators, and cooking devices that operate at extremely high temperatures. However, cooking is permitted with electric or gas grills that do not involve cooking over an open flame. Additionally, cooking is permitted with deep fryers that are equipped with and utilize a device that automatically lowers the baskets into the hot oil or grease and automatically raises the basket from the hot oil or grease.

- Work that involves operating, setting up, adjusting, cleaning, oiling, or repairing power-driven food slicers and grinders, food choppers, cutters, or bakery-type mixers.

- Work in freezers and meat coolers or in preparing meat for sale. Wrapping, sealing, labeling, weighing, pricing, and stocking goods are permitted only if performed in areas physically separate from freezers and meat coolers.

- Loading or unloading goods on and off trucks, railroad cars, or conveyors.

- Occupations in warehouses, except office and clerical work.

Permitted Occupations

Minors between 14 and 15 **may** be employed in the following occupations and types of work in retail, food service, and gasoline service establishments as provided in federal regulations:

- Office and clerical work.

- Work of an intellectual or artistically creative nature such as, but not limited to, computer programming, the writing of software, teaching or performing as a tutor, serving as a peer counselor or teacher's assistant, singing, the playing of a musical instrument, and drawing, as long as such employment complies with all the other applicable requirements. Artistically creative work is limited to work in a recognized field of artistic or creative endeavor.

- Cooking with an electric or gas grill which does not involve cooking with an open flame. Cooking is also permitted with deep fryers that are equipped with and utilize a device which automatically lowers the baskets into the hot oil or grease and automatically raises the baskets from the hot oil or grease.

- Cashiering, selling, modeling, artistic work, work in advertising departments, window trimming, and comparative shopping.

- Price marking and tagging by hand or by machine, assembling orders, packing, and shelving.

- Bagging and carrying out customers' orders.

- Errand and delivery work by foot, bicycle, or public transportation.

- Clean up work, including the use of vacuum cleaners and floor waxers, and maintenance of grounds (not including the use of power-driven motors, cutters, trimmers, edgers, or similar equipment).

- Cleaning kitchen equipment (not otherwise prohibited), removing oil or grease filters, pouring oil or grease through filters, and moving receptacles containing hot grease or hot oil, but only when the equipment, surfaces, containers, and liquids do not exceed 100 degrees Fahrenheit. Minors may also occasionally enter freezers momentarily to retrieve items in conjunction with restocking or food preparation.

- Kitchen work and other work involved in preparing and serving food and beverages, including the operation of machines and devices used in the performance of work, such as, but not limited to, dishwashers, toasters, dumbwaiters, popcorn poppers, milk shake blenders, coffee grinders, automatic coffee machines, devices used to maintain the temperature of prepared foods (such as warmers, steam tables, and heat lamps), and microwave ovens that are used only to warm prepared food without the capacity to warm above 140 degrees Fahrenheit.

- Loading onto and unloading from motor vehicles light-weight, nonpower-driven hand tools and personally protective equipment that the minor will use as part of their employment at the worksite.

- Lifeguard, but only for minors age 15 and older.

- Work in connection with cars and trucks (if confined to dispensing gasoline and oil), courtesy service, and car cleaning.

- Cleaning vegetables and fruits.

- Work inside or outside business where machinery is used to process wood so long as the minor is exempt by statute or judicial order from compulsory school attendance beyond 8th grade, supervised by an adult relative (or adult member of the same religious sect or division as the minor), does not operate or assist in the operation of power-driven woodworking machines, is protected from wood particles or other debris by appropriate barriers, and is required to use personal protective equipment.

Agricultural

Prohibited Occupations

Minors between 14 and 15 **may not** be employed in any of the following agricultural occupations declared hazardous by federal regulations:

- Operating a tractor of more than 20 PTO horsepower or connecting or disconnecting an implement or any of its parts to and from such a tractor.

- Operating or helping operate (including starting, stopping, adjusting, feeding, and any activities involving physical contact with the operations) any of the following machines:

  - Corn pickers, cotton pickers, grain combines, hay mowers, forage harvesters, hay balers, potato diggers, or mobile pea viners.

- Feed grinder, crop dryer, forage blower, auger conveyor, or the unloading mechanism of a nongravity-type self-unloading wagon or trailer.

- Power post-hole diggers, power post-drivers, or nonwalking-type rotary tillers.

- Trenchers or earthmoving equipment.

- Forklifts.

- Potato combines.

- Power-driven circular, band, or chain saws.

♦ Working on a farm in a yard, pen, or stall occupied by any of the following:

- Bull, boar, or stud horse maintained for breeding purposes.

- Sow with suckling pigs or cow with newborn calf (with umbilical cord present).

♦ Felling, bucking, skidding, loading, or unloading timber with butt diameter of more than 6 inches.

♦ Working from a ladder or scaffold (including painting, repairing, or building structures; pruning trees; and picking fruit) from a height of more than 20 feet.

♦ Driving a bus, truck, or automobile when transporting passengers or riding on a tractor as a passenger or helper.

♦ Working inside any of the following:

- A fruit, forage, or grain storage designed to retain an oxygen-deficient or toxic atmosphere.

- An upright silo within two weeks after silage has been added or when a top-unloading device is in operating position.

- A horizontal silo while operating a tractor for packing purposes.

- A manure pit.

♦ Handling or applying (including cleaning or decontaminating equipment, disposing or returning empty containers, or serving as a flagman for aircraft) agricultural chemicals classified under the Federal Insecticide, Fungicide, and Rodenticide Act as Category I of toxicity, identified by the word "poison" and the skull and crossbones on the label, or Category II of toxicity, identified by the word "warning" on the label.

♦ Handling or using a blasting agent, including dynamite black powder, sensitized ammonium nitrate, blasting caps, and primer cord.

♦ Transporting, transferring, or applying anhydrous ammonia.

Note: The terms describing machinery, equipment, or facilities in these agricultural occupations are defined in the current edition of *Agricultural Engineering*, a dictionary and handbook published by Interstate Printers and Publishers, Danville, Illinois. Copies are available for examination in the regional offices of the U.S. Department of Labor's Wage and Hour Division.

Exception: Parents and guardians have a special exemption when employing their children in agricultural occupations.

Minors Under 14

Employers **may not** employ children under 14 unless they are specifically permitted, as detailed in **Covered Employees** at the beginning of this chapter.

Recordkeeping and Postings

In addition to compliance with recordkeeping and posting obligations imposed by the FLSA (*see* the **Wages and Hours** chapter), employers should consult with legal counsel to confirm compliance with state law obligations regarding the employment of minors, if applicable.

Filing a Complaint

Complaints regarding federal child labor standards and federal wage and hour standards may be filed with the Wage and Hour Division of the U.S. Department of Labor.

Punishment for Violations

A violation of federal regulations concerning prohibited employment of minors and recordkeeping requirements subjects an employer to substantial monetary penalties, such as the following:

♦ $11,000, for each employee who was the subject of a violation.

♦ $50,000 with regard to each such violation that causes the death or serious injury of any employee under age 18, which may be doubled where the violation is repeated or willful.

The appropriateness of the penalty and the gravity of the violation are considered in determining an employer's penalty amount.

Note: Additional sanctions may also be imposed under state law for violation of state restrictions.

Child Labor Enhanced Penalty Program

The U.S. Department of Labor, Wage and Hour Division, created the Child Labor Enhanced Penalty Program (CLEPP) to incorporate the applicable provisions of the Genetic Information Nondiscrimination Act (GINA) into its existing child labor civil money penalty (CL CMP) assessment process. Specifically, for each child labor violation occurring after May 20, 2008 that causes the death of a minor employee, the division will generally assess a CL CMP of $50,000 because the miscellaneous provisions in GINA impose a civil penalty of up to $50,000 for each child labor violation that causes the death or serious injury of an employee under the age of 18.

Although the division may allot a penalty reduction based on the size of the business or any other relevant factor, this reduction is inappropriate where a violation resulted in a youth's death. Rather, the division will consider the facts of each individual case before making such a penalty deduction determination. Because the CLEPP statutory provisions provide for a CL CMP assessment of up to $50,000 for each violation "that causes the death . . . of *any* employee under 18," the maximum CL CMP can be assessed for a death even if the minor employed in violation was not the minor employee that suffered the death, provided that the violation actually caused the death. The initial assessment amount may be doubled, up to $100,000 per violation, if the violations are determined to be willful or repeated.

CLEPP Injuries

According to 29 U.S.C. § 216, a *CLEPP serious injury* is an injury that occurred after May 20, 2008 that was caused by a child labor violation and involves any of the following:

♦ A permanent loss or substantial impairment of one of the senses (sight, hearing, taste, smell, tactile sensation).

♦ A permanent loss or substantial impairment of the function of a bodily member, organ, or mental faculty, including the loss of all or part of an arm, leg, foot, hand, or other body part.

♦ A permanent paralysis or substantial impairment that causes loss of movement or mobility of an arm, leg, foot, hand, or other body part.

To be *caused by a child labor violation* requires a relationship between the violation that occurred and the serious injury or death of the minor employee.

A *non-CLEPP serious injury* is any injury which does not meet the definition of CLEPP serious injury because it meets one of the following stipulations:

- Occurred before May 20, 2008.
- Did not fall within one of the three categories of serious injuries defined by CLEPP.
- Failed to meet the level of causation required by CLEPP, but which requires treatment more extensive than first aid or curtails normal activities.

Specifically, a non-CLEPP serious injury is an injury that requires the care of a medical practitioner beyond the initial treatment or curtails the youth's normal activities (school, work, sports) for at least five days. Serious injuries include situations where a minor is required to return to a medical practitioner after an accident to have stitches removed or for an evaluation of the healing process.

Additional CLEPP Penalty Amounts

A civil penalty of $15,000, $25,000, or $40,000 will generally be assessed for each child labor violation that causes a CLEPP serious injury of a minor employee other than death. The fine depends on the severity and permanency of the injury considering the totality of the circumstances. For example, a $40,000 penalty would generally be assessed for each child labor violation that caused a CLEPP serious injury resulting in a total body impairment of 35 percent or more. These penalties can be doubled, up to $100,000, for willful or repeated violations.

A civil penalty of $6,000, $8,000, or $10,000 will generally be assessed for child labor violations resulting in a non-CLEPP serious injury of a minor employee. As with CLEPP serious injuries, these fines will also depend on the on the severity and permanency of the injury considering the totality of the circumstances. These penalties can be increased to up to $11,000 per violation if the child labor violations are willful or repeated. A maximum civil penalty of $11,000 can be assessed against an employer for a minor employee who suffers a nonserious injury.

Some of these civil penalties may be reduced by 30 to 50 percent based on the size of the employer's business for employers whose gross business is less than $1,000,000 and who employ fewer than 100 employees. However, reductions are not available if:

- The violation resulted in the death of a minor employee.
- The original assessment was $40,000 or more.
- Multiple child labor violations were involved.
- The violations were willful or repeated.
- The employer falsified or concealed child labor violations.

Contact Information

Department of Labor
Wage and Hour Division

Frances Perkins Building
200 Constitution Avenue, NW
Washington, DC 20210

Telephone: 866-4-USWAGE or 866-4-USA-DOL
Internet: *www.dol.gov/whd*

Illinois Law

Illinois' child labor law is located at 820 Ill. Comp. Stat. §§ 205/1 – 205/22. Corresponding regulations are located in the Illinois Administrative Code, located at Ill. Admin. Code tit. 56, pt. 250.100 – 250.860.

Generally, Illinois employers may employ minors in nonhazardous occupations, as long as applicable hour restrictions are observed and the required permit is obtained.

Coverage

According to Ill. Admin. Code tit. 56, pt. 250.200, an employer becomes subject to the state's child labor law if any of the following apply:

♦ A minor performs work on the employer's premises.

♦ A minor is included on the payroll.

♦ A minor receives or has a reasonable expectation of receiving compensation from the employer. However, compensation does not have to be monetary and does not include provision of food, clothing, and shelter by a parent or legal guardian.

Prohibited Employment
Minors Under 16

Minors under 16 are **prohibited** from selling any cigar, cigarette, smokeless tobacco, or tobacco in any of its forms at a retail establishment selling tobacco products. However, a sales clerk in a family-owned business that can prove that the sales clerk is in fact a son or daughter of the owner is **not** regulated by this tobacco provision.

Minors under 16, **except** for minors 14 or 15 participating in federally funded career education programs under the direction of the State Board of Education, **may not** be employed at any gainful occupation in connection with any of the following:

♦ A theater, concert hall, or place of amusement.

♦ A mercantile institution, including stores, offices, hotels, laundries, manufacturing establishments, mills, canneries, factories or workshops, restaurants, lunch rooms, beauty parlors, barber shops, bakeries, and coal, brick, or lumberyards.

♦ Any type of construction work in Illinois.

Minors between 14 and 16 **may** work outside school hours and during school vacations, but not in hazardous factory work or in occupations otherwise prohibited by law.

Minors under 12, **except** members of a farmer's family who live with the farmer at the farmer's main place of residence, **may not** work in a gainful occupation in connection with agriculture, except that minors 10 and over **may** be permitted to work in connection with agriculture during school vacations or outside school hours.

Alcoholic Beverages

All minors are prohibited from being employed in establishments that involve serving alcoholic beverages, including, but not limited to, establishments where there are bands, rock groups, and other types of nontheatrical entertainment, except as a bus boy or in kitchen employment not otherwise prohibited when in connection with serving meals at any private club, fraternal organization, or veteran's organization. However, such regulations do not apply to employment performed on property owned or operated by a park district if law does not otherwise prohibit the employment.

Hazardous Occupations

Generally, minors **may not** work in any of the following hazardous occupations:

- In a car wash that uses power-driven machinery or moving motor vehicles in its operation, except in office and nonhazardous work around a carwash.

- In or about an airfield, including storage areas, hangers, baggage areas, runways, taxi strips, and fueling areas, but not including areas such as gift shops, restaurants, or other rental establishments in the terminal that do not expose the minors to power-driven machinery or alcoholic beverages sold for consumption on the premises.

- In an outdoor or drive-in movie theater, except for work in the indoor part of those theaters. Employment in an indoor movie theater is not a hazardous occupation.

Minors under 16 **may not** work in any of the following hazardous occupations:

- In or in connection with a public messenger or delivery service.

- In or in connection with a bowling alley, poolroom, skating rink, exhibition park, or other place of amusement, not including ice skating rinks owned and operated by a school or unit of local government.

- In any garage.

- As a bellhop in a hotel or rooming house.

- About or in connection with power-driven machinery.

- In oiling, cleaning, or wiping machinery or shafting.

- In or about a mine or quarry, except for office and messenger work and other nonhazardous employment.

- In stone cutting or polishing.

- In or about any hazardous factory work.

- In or about a plant that manufactures, uses, or transports explosives or articles with explosive components, except for office and messenger work and other nonhazardous employment.

- In or about an iron or steel manufacturing plant, ore reduction works, smelters, foundries, forging shops, hot rolling mills, or other places that heat or melt metals, except for office and messenger work and other nonhazardous employment.

- In operating machinery used in cold-rolling heavy metal stock or operating power-driven punching, shearing, stamping, or metal plate-bending machines.

- In or about sawmills or lath, shingle, or cooperage-stock mills, except for office and messenger work and other nonhazardous employment.

- In operating power-driven woodworking machines or off-bearing from circular saws.

- In operating freight elevators or hoisting machines and cranes.

- In spray painting or in occupations involving exposure to lead or its compounds or to dangerous dyes and chemicals.

- In oil refineries, gasoline blending plants, or pumping stations on oil transmission lines.

- In operating laundry, dry cleaning, or dyeing machinery.

- In occupations involving exposure to radioactive substances.

- In or about any filling station or service station.

- In construction work, including demolition and repair.

- In roofing operations.

- In excavating operations.

- In logging operations.

- In public and private utilities and related services.

- In operations in or in connection with slaughtering, meatpacking, poultry processing, and fish and seafood processing.

- In operations that involve working on elevated surfaces with or without use of equipment, including ladders and scaffolds.

- In security positions or in occupations that require using or carrying a firearm or other weapon.

- In occupations that involve handling or storing human blood, human blood products, human body fluids, or human body tissues.

- In occupations in connection with the carnival, midway, and mechanical ride parts of any of the following:

  - State, county, or local fairs.

  - Park districts.

  - Permanently constructed entertainment centers.

- In places where intoxicating alcoholic liquors are served, sold for consumption on the premises, or where liquors are manufactured and bottled, except as a bus boy and kitchen employment, not otherwise prohibited, when in connection with serving meals at any private club, fraternal organization, or veteran's organization. However, such regulations do not apply to employment performed on property owned or operated by a park district if law does not otherwise prohibit the employment.

Exceptions to Prohibited Employment

Illinois' child labor laws **do not apply** to any of the following:

- The employment of minors in agriculture, except for people restricted from working in a gainful occupation in connection with agriculture in § 205/1.

- The sale and distribution of magazines and newspapers at hours when school is not in session.

- The employment of minors outside school hours in or about a home at work usual to the employer's home, as long as the work is not in connection with the employer's business, trade, or profession.

♦ The employment of a minor age 13 or older in caddying at a golf course.

♦ The employment of a minor between the ages of 12 and 13 in officiating youth sport activities for a not-for-profit youth club, park district, or municipal parks and recreation department if each of the following restrictions is met:

  • The minor's guardian, parent, or an adult designated by the parent or guardian is present at the sporting event being officiated by the minor. Failure of the parent, guardian, or designated adult to be present may result in the revocation of the employment certificate.

  • The employer obtains the proper certification.

  • The participants in the sports activity are at least three years younger than the officiating minor, or an adult must be officiating the same youth sports activity. For the purposes of this restriction, an adult is an individual age 16 or older.

  • Employment does not exceed a maximum of four hours per nonschool day (three hours on school days), not to exceed 10 hours a week, and does not continue any later than 9 p.m.

♦ A minor age 14 or 15, from May 1 through September 30, in an occupational, vocational, or educational program funded by the Job Training Partnership Act.

Permitted Employment

Minors **may** be employed in all of the following occupations:

♦ In offices using power-driven equipment, including, but not limited to, the following:

  • Typewriters.

  • Adding machines.

  • Copying machines.

♦ In occupations using a power-driven dishwasher if all of the following apply:

  • The dishwasher is enclosed on all sides.

  • The dishwasher is self-sealing.

  • The dishwasher can be fastened completely shut.

  • The dishwasher has no moving parts that are exposed or otherwise hazardous.

♦ In nonhazardous messenger employment.

♦ In occupations using machines to dispense frozen custards and similar types of soft ice cream, milkshake machines, and other soda fountain machinery without sharp edges, blades, or other hazardous open, moving parts.

♦ In establishments that sell packaged liquors if no liquor is actually manufactured or bottled on the premises, if no containers are opened, and if the alcoholic beverages are not sold or served for consumption on the premises.

♦ In occupations at any of the following, except in connection with carnivals, midways, and mechanical rides:

  • State, county, or local fairs.

  • Park districts.

  • Permanently constructed entertainment centers.

Models or Performers

Subject to reasonable conditions imposed by the Illinois Department of Labor, minors under 16 **may** be employed as models or performers as follows:

- ♦ On live or pre-recorded radio or television.

- ♦ In motion pictures.

- ♦ In other entertainment-related performances.

This provision **does not apply** to the employment of minors under age 16 appearing in theatrical productions.

Additionally, minors under 14 may be employed as models but must be accompanied by a parent, guardian, or an adult designated in writing by the parent or guardian. For a minor under 10, the employer may not be the designated adult, unless the employer is the parent

Hours of Employment

Minors Under 16

With exception, minors under 16 **may not** work in any gainful occupation for **more** than any of the following time periods:

- ♦ Six consecutive days in a week.

- ♦ Eight hours a day.

- ♦ Forty-eight hours a week.

Additionally, minors under 16 **may not** work during either of the following hours

- ♦ Between 7 p.m. and 7 a.m. from Labor Day until June 1.

- ♦ Between 9 p.m. and 7 a.m. from June 1 until Labor Day.

Minors under age 16 who are employed outside of school hours **may not** work more than any of the following time periods:

- ♦ More than three hours a day on days when school is in session

- ♦ The combined hours of work outside and in school may not exceed a total of eight hours per day.

However, minors under age 16 **may** work both Saturday and Sunday for no more than eight hours each day if both of the following conditions are met:

- ♦ The minor does not work outside school more than six consecutive days in any one week.

- ♦ The number of hours worked by the minor outside school in any week does not exceed 24.

Minors 14 and Older

Minors age 14 or older who are employed in a recreational or educational activity by a park district, not-for-profit youth club, or municipal parks and recreation department while school is in session may work up to three hours per school day twice a week no later than 9 p.m. However, the number of hours worked by the minor outside school in any week may not exceed 24 or as follows:

- ♦ Between 10 p.m. and 7 a.m. during that school district's summer vacation.

- ♦ If the school district operates on a 12-month basis, the period during which school is not in session for the minor.

Entertainment Industry Hours

Employers who employ minors under 16 in a television, motion picture, or related entertainment production may apply to the state Director of the Department of Labor (or the director's representative) for a special waiver from the regulations that prohibit the employment of a minor under 16 to work the following hours:

- Between 7 p.m. and 7 a.m. from Labor Day to June 1.

- Between 9 p.m. and 7 a.m. from June 1 until Labor Day.

The waiver will be issued if, after investigation, it is found that the following are true:

- The employment will not be detrimental to the minor's health or welfare.

- The minor will be supervised adequately.

- The minor's education will not be neglected.

The waiver must also contain signatures showing the consent of the minor's parent or legal guardian, the employer, and an authorized representative of a collective-bargaining unit if a union represents the minor upon employment.

The department will provide an official application form for a work-hours-waiver. Employers are required to provide answers to all questions on the form, including, but not limited to, the following:

- Minor's name, address, and date of birth.

- Specific work hours during a particular date for which the employer requests the waiver.

- Name, address, and telephone number of the person the employer assigned to supervise the minor during the work hours covered by the waiver application.

- Specific description of the minor's performance, including information about the plot of the movie or television series and, if a commercial or music video, the essential lyrics.

- Description and address of the exact places where the minor will work during the hours covered by the waiver application, including information about the physical set or physical environment.

The employer must attach a copy of the minor's valid work permit to the application. The application must be signed and dated by all of the following:

- The minor's parent or legal guardian.

- The employer.

- An authorized representative of a collective-bargaining unit if a union represents the minor upon employment.

The employer must submit an application for the waiver as soon as possible, but no later than 12 p.m. for any hours requested to be worked between 7 and 9 p.m. on that day and 7 a.m. the following calendar day.

The department will investigate the statements made on the employer's application and issue a certificate for a work hours waiver for the employer to employ the minor for the hours, under the conditions specified by the application, when it is satisfied that the minor's health, welfare, and education will not be jeopardized by the work. An employer applying for a work hour's waiver may not consider its request granted until it receives a certificate for a waiver from the department, signed by the director or the director's representative.

When the waiver expires, employers may re-apply for a new waiver for a date and time certain in the future. Employers are subject to the same terms and conditions as required for an original application.

Modeling Hours

Minors **may not** be employed as models during the hours school is in session. Minors under 8 years of age **may not** be employed as models for more than two hours a day or more than 10 hours a week.

Additionally, minors between 8 and 13 **may not** be employed as models beyond the following:

♦ More than three hours a day when school is in session.

♦ More than four hours a day when school is not in session.

♦ More than 18 hours a week when school is in session for three or more days.

♦ More than 20 hours during a week when school is not in session for at least three days.

Meal and Rest Periods

Minors under 16 **may not** be employed for more than five continuous hours without an interval of at least 30 minutes for a meal period. A period of less than 30 minutes is not considered to interrupt a continuous period of work.

Employment Certificates

Minors under 16 may not be employed in any gainful occupation, unless the employer obtains and keeps on file an employment certificate. Employment certificates allow minors to work during school vacation and outside of school hours. The original employment certificate, issued by the superintendent or applicable agent, will be mailed to the minor's employer and is valid for one year.

The minor's parent, legal guardian, or school principal may ask to revoke the certificate by petitioning the Illinois Department of Labor in writing, stating the reasons it appears the employment is interfering with the minor's best physical, intellectual, or moral development. The department will then revoke the certificate in a written notice to the employer.

Employer Duties

As part of the application process for an employment certificate the prospective employer or duly authorized representative must sign a statement of intention to employ that demonstrates all of the following:

♦ The specific nature of the occupation in which the employer intends to employ the minor.

♦ The specific hours of each day, the number of hours per day, and the specific days per week the minor would be employed.

During the period of employment of a minor under age 16, every employer must keep on file at the place of employment an employment certificate issued for such minor. Any employer, upon termination of the employment of a minor, must immediately return the certificate issued to the issuing officer. An employment certificate will be valid only for the employer for whom issued, and a new certificate **may not** be issued for the employment of a minor under age 16 except on the presentation of a new statement of intention to employ.

The failure of any employer to produce for inspection an employment certificate for each minor in the workplace will be *prima facie* evidence that the minor is employed without a certificate.

Nonresident Minor Certificates

Out-of-state minors seeking employment in Illinois must obtain an employment certificate under the same guidelines established for minors who are residents of Illinois. Dissimilar to minors who are residents and for any employment during a school vacation, out-of-state minors are required to obtain a letter from their out-of-state principals verifying that they are on vacation and that school is not in session for the specified period of time.

Additionally, for out-of-state minors seeking to obtain an Illinois employment certificate, the Department of Labor will work with a City or Regional Superintendent of Schools, or the State Superintendent of Education to issue the certificate. The superintendent may waive the requirement that a minor submit their application in person, if the minor resides in another state.

Child Model Certificates

Employment certificates for child models are required and obtained through the same means as for any other minor seeking employment in Illinois. Issuing officers issue employment certificates to minors enrolled in school, and the City or Regional Superintendent of Schools issues employment certificates to minors under school age. If the minor applying for the certificate is over age 10, the minor's consent to employment must be obtained in writing on the certificate.

The certificate for a child model expires one year after the date of issuance. A minor and/or the minor's parent or guardian may re-apply following the standard procedures for a minor employment certificate renewal.

A copy of the employment certificate for the child model must accompany the minor at each work location where the minor is employed, used, or exhibited as a model.

Theatrical Certificates

The City or County Superintendent of Schools or their duly authorized agents may issue theatrical employment certificates for minors under age 16. A theatrical employment certificate allows minors to appear in plays or musical comedies, as long as the following conditions are met:

- The appearance is with a professional traveling theatrical production or on the stage of a duly licensed theater.

- No more than two performances are given a day.

- No more than eight performances are given a week or nine per a week when a holiday occurs during the week.

The theatrical employment certificate also allows minors to participate in music recitals and concerts.

Theatrical certificates also require the following:

- Minors must be accompanied by their parents or guardians or by a person the parents or guardians have put in charge of caring for the minor.

- A person put in charge of a minor must have limited connections with the performance or with theater operations and the individual's duties must be limited to caring for the minor.

- Minors must not appear on stage in a music recital or concert, attend rehearsals, or be present in connection with such appearances or rehearsals in the theater where the play or musical comedy is produced or in the place where the concert is given for more than six hours a day, more than six days a week, more than 24 hours a week, or after 11 p.m. Additionally, minors will not be excused from attending school except as authorized by the Illinois School Code.

Application for the certificates must be made to the City or County Superintendent of Schools or the superintendent's agent at least 14 days before the appearance. The application may be made by any of the following:

- The manager of the theater.
- The person in the district responsible for the concert.
- The minor's parent or guardian.

The superintendent or agent may issue a certificate if satisfied that adequate provision has been made for all of the following:

- The minor's educational instruction.
- Safeguarding the minor's health.
- The minor's proper moral supervision.
- The theater will provide proper rest and dressing room facilities.

The City or Regional Superintendent of Schools or duly recognized agent is also authorized to issue an employment certificate for minors under 16 that permits the appearance of a minor as a model or in a motion picture, radio, or television production.

Certificates of Age

On request, the officer issuing an employment certificate will issue a certificate of age to anyone between ages 16 and 20 when presented with the same proof of age as required for Illinois employment certificates.

Reporting Requirements

If an employer is required to file a report with the Illinois Workers' Compensation Commission under the state's workers' compensation law or occupational diseases law, the report relates to the work-related death, injury, or illness of a minor, the employer must file a copy of the report with the Department of Labor.

Posting Requirements

All employers covered by the state's child labor laws must post in a conspicuous place where minors under 16 are employed a printed abstract of the law and a list of the occupations prohibited to those minors. The department will supply the abstract and list of prohibited occupations. In addition, employers must post a printed notice, on a form provided by the department, stating the following:

- The hours of starting and stopping work.
- The hours when the time allowed for meals begins and ends.
- The department's toll-free telephone number.

Recordkeeping Requirements

Employers that employ minors under age 16 must retain the following records for each minor:

- Name, age, and place of residence.
- Starting and ending dates of employment.
- Starting and ending dates of each workday.
- Starting and ending time of each meal break.
- Number of hours worked daily and weekly.

These records must be retained for three years.

Employment Certificates

While a minor under 16 is employed, employers must keep on file at the place of employment an employment certificate issued for the minor. The department and truant officers and other school officials authorized by the Board of Education may inspect employment certificates on file. Employers must also keep copies of work hour's waivers at the exact places where the minors are working during the hours covered by the waiver. Employers must maintain the waiver for each minor employee for at least three years, whether or not the minor has been terminated. Employers must make all waivers available for inspection and transcription by a duly authorized agent of the department.

Register of Minors

Every employer of minors between ages 14 and 16 must keep a register upon the premises where the work is being done that records the name, age, and place of residence of each minor.

Time Records

Employers must keep the required time records, or copies of the records, at the place of employment where the minor is currently employed and must retain time records there for at least three years, whether or not the employee has been terminated and for at least six months after an employee is terminated. A duly authorized agent of the department must make the records available for inspection and transcription during the employer's regular business hours.

Time records must include the following information for each minor:

- Name, address, and date of birth.
- The starting and ending dates of employment.
- The starting and ending times of each workday.
- The starting and ending time of each meal break.
- The number of hours worked daily and weekly.

Work Hour Waivers

Employers must keep a copy of the certificate for a work hour's waiver at the place(s) and address(es) where the minor is working during the hours covered by the waiver. The certificate for a work hour waiver must be retained for three years, irrespective of whether the employee has been terminated. An employer must make all certificates for a work hour's waiver available for inspection and transcription by a duly authorized agent of the state Department of Labor.

Enforcement and Penalties

The Illinois Department of Labor enforces the state's child labor laws. The department may visit and inspect all places covered by the child labor laws at all reasonable times and as often as possible. Truant officers, school directors, and other school officials authorized by the Board of Education may also enter any place where minors are, or are believed to be, employed and may inspect the employment certificates on file.

The department, deputies, and inspectors may suspend any certificate as an emergency action imperatively required for the public health, safety, and welfare of minors if they judge it was improperly issued or if the minor is illegally employed.

If a certificate is suspended, the employer and all interested parties will be notified of the suspension in writing. The minor may not work until the department issues a final order after a hearing that either reinstates or revokes the certificate. The hearing must begin within 21 days of the date of any suspension.

If the certificate is revoked, the minor may not work until a new certificate for the minor's employment has been obtained.

When the department using evidence from an investigation finds that an employer has violated the child labor law or department regulations, the department may hold an informal investigative conference to obtain evidence, identifying the issues in the dispute, and exploring the possibility of a negotiated settlement.

Notice of the conference must be given to the employer at least 10 days before and must identify the individuals requested to attend, along with any books or documents the employer must produce at the conference. The department will consider the matter resolved if a settlement has been reached before the conference date. If the informal conference is held but does not resolve the dispute, a final determination on the amount of civil penalties will be made in an administrative hearing.

The department will conduct hearings upon written complaint by a department investigator, by a truant officer or other school official, or by any interested person of a violation of the law or to revoke any certificate under the law. The director or the director's representative may compel by subpoena the attendance and testimony of witnesses and the production of books, payrolls, records, papers, and other evidence in any investigation or hearing.

After the hearing, if supported by evidence, the department may do any of the following:

♦ Issue an order to cease and desist from violation of the law.

♦ Take further action as deemed reasonable to eliminate the effect of the violation.

♦ Revoke any certificate.

♦ Determine the amount of any civil penalty allowed by law.

Criminal Penalties

All of the following actions are illegal and punishable as a Class A misdemeanor:

♦ Any person or entity that willfully employs, permits, or allows any minor to be employed or to work in violation of the law.

♦ Any person or entity that obstructs the department, inspectors or deputies, or any other person legally authorized to inspect places of employment.

♦ Any person or entity that willfully fails to comply with the legal provisions requiring the posting of hours and maintaining a time record.

♦ Any person or entity having under their control or custody any minor that willfully permits or allows a minor to be employed or to work in violation of the law.

Each day during which any such violation continues will constitute a separate and distinct offense, and the employment of any minor in violation of the law will, with respect to each minor so employed, constitute a separate and distinct offense.

Civil Penalties

Employers that violate any of the provisions of the state's child labor law are subject to a civil penalty of up to $5,000 for each violation. In determining the amount of the penalty, the size of the business and the gravity of the violation will be considered. When determined, the amount of the penalty may be recovered in a civil action brought by the director in any circuit court or ordered by the court, to be paid to the director.

A determination of civil penalties made in an administrative hearing is final.

Prohibition of Goods from Child Labor

The State Prohibition of Goods from Child Labor Act is located at 30 Ill. Comp. Stat. §§ 584/1 – 584/99.

Pursuant to the act, every contract entered into by any state agency for the procurement of equipment, materials, or supplies, other than procurement related to a public works contract, must specify that no foreign-made equipment, materials, or supplies furnished to the state under the contract may be produced in whole or in part by the labor of any child under the age of 12. The contractor must agree to comply with this provision of the contract.

Any contractor contracting with the state who knew that the foreign-made equipment, materials, or supplies furnished to the state were produced in whole or part by the labor of any child under age 12 when entering into a contract as described previously may have any or all of the following sanctions imposed:

- The contract under which the prohibited equipment, materials, or supplies were provided may be voided at the option of the state agency to which the equipment, materials, or supplies were provided.

- The contractor may be assessed a penalty which must be the greater of $1,000 or an amount equaling 20 percent of the value of the equipment, materials, or supplies that the state agency demonstrates were produced in whole or in part by child labor and that were supplied to the state agency under the contract.

- The contractor may be suspended from bidding on a state contract for a period not to exceed 360 days.

When imposing the sanctions the contracting agency must notify the contractor of the right to a hearing if requested within 15 days after the date of the notice. The hearing must be before an administrative law judge according to the Illinois Administrative Procedure Act. The administrative law judge must consider any measures the contractor has taken to ensure compliance with this section and may waive any or all of the sanctions if it is determined that the contractor has acted in good faith. The agency must be assessed the cost of the administrative hearing, unless the agency has prevailed in the hearing, in which case the contractor will be assessed the cost of the hearing.

Contact Information

Illinois Department of Labor

1 West Old State Capitol Plaza, Room 300
Springfield, IL 62701

Telephone: 217-782-6206
Fax: 217-782-0596
Internet: *www.state.il.us/agency/idol*

Chapter 15

Discrimination in Employment

Introduction

According to federal and state antidiscrimination laws, employers may not base adverse employment decisions on the protected status or protected conduct of employees or applicants. This chapter details the various types of prohibited discrimination and protected conduct, outlines the penalties associated with losing discrimination claims, considers possible employer defenses against discrimination claims, and suggests methods so as to avoid discrimination in employment decisions.

Federal Law

Although this section is titled **Federal Law** and emphasizes federal statutes against various forms of discrimination, it should be noted that state antidiscrimination laws generally agree with the federal law. Additionally, some local laws provide even further protections than either federal or state regulations.

Protected Areas/Protected Status

Federal and state laws **prohibit** discrimination based on the following:

- ◆ Race/skin color.

- ◆ National origin and citizenship.

- ◆ Religion.

- ◆ Sex.

- ◆ Pregnancy.

- ◆ Sexual orientation.

- ◆ Age (40 years of age or older).

- ◆ Disability.

- ◆ Genetic information.

- ◆ Military status.

The U.S. government does not discriminate in employment on the basis of race, color, religion, sex, national origin, political affiliation, sexual orientation, gender identity, marital status, disability, age, membership in an employee organization, or other nonmerit factor.

Typical Discrimination Situations

Discrimination claims most frequently arise out of the following situations:

- The recruitment process.

- The application and interview process.

- Failing to hire an applicant.

- Preselecting an employee for a position or promotion.

- Failing to promote an employee.

- Challenges to job qualifications or requirements.

- Terminations or reductions in workforce.

- Sexual harassment.

- Racial harassment.

- Working conditions so difficult, uncomfortable, or unpleasant that an employee is forced to resign (also known as constructive discharge).

- Performance evaluation and disciplinary measures.

Protected Conduct and Retaliation

In addition to the protected areas or status as previously listed, the law prohibits employers from retaliating against employees for engaging in protected conduct. ***Protected conduct*** occurs when an individual exercises their legally guaranteed rights.

The following are examples of protected conduct:

- Filing a charge of discrimination with the Equal Employment Opportunity Commission (EEOC) or with the state civil rights agency.

- Testifying on behalf of another employee in connection with a charge of discrimination.

- Requesting a reasonable accommodation for a disability.

- Requesting leave under the Family and Medical Leave Act (FMLA).

- Filing an internal sexual harassment complaint against another employee in good faith.

Moreover, employers are barred from retaliating against an employee for either of the following:

- Participating in an investigation or proceeding involving a claim of discrimination.

- Opposing an unlawful discriminatory practice.

Title VII and Antiretaliation Provisions

Burlington

The U.S. Supreme Court ruled in *Burlington Northern & Santa Fe Railway Co. v. White*, 126 S.Ct. 2405, 2409 (2006), that a retaliation claim under Title VII could arise out of any employer action that would cause a reasonable employee to refrain from making or supporting a charge of discrimination.

In *Burlington*, Sheila White was a railroad forklift operator and incurred sexual harassment from her immediate supervisor. After she complained, her immediate supervisor was disciplined for sexual harassment, but she was removed from forklift duty to standard track laborer tasks. She filed a complaint with the EEOC, claiming that the reassignment was unlawful gender discrimination and retaliation for her sexual harassment complaint. Subsequently, she was suspended without pay for insubordination.

The Railway Company later found that White had not been insubordinate, reinstated her, and awarded her backpay for the 37 days she was suspended. The suspension led to another EEOC retaliation charge. After exhausting her administrative remedies, White filed an action against Burlington in federal court claiming that Burlington's actions in changing her job responsibilities and suspending her for 37 days amounted to unlawful retaliation under Title VII.

A jury awarded White compensatory damages. In affirming, the Sixth Circuit applied the same standard for retaliation that it applies to a substantive discrimination offense, holding that a retaliation plaintiff must show an adverse employment action, defined as a materially adverse change in the terms and conditions of employment.

The circuits have come to different conclusions about whether the challenged action has to be employment or workplace related and about how harmful that action must be to constitute retaliation.

After granting certiorari, the Supreme Court restated that Title VII forbids employment discrimination and contains a separate section of the act, the antiretaliation provision.

The antiretaliation provision forbids an employer from discriminating against an employee or job applicant because that individual completed any of the following:

♦ Opposed any practice made unlawful by Title VII.

♦ Made a charge, testified, assisted, or participated in a Title VII proceeding or investigation.

The Supreme Court concluded that the antiretaliation provision does not confine the actions and harms it forbids to those that are related to employment or occur at the workplace. The antiretaliation provision covers those, and only those, employer actions that would have been materially adverse to a reasonable employee or job applicant. The employer's actions must be harmful to the point that they could dissuade a reasonable worker from making or supporting a charge of discrimination.

In relation to *Burlington*, the Supreme Court held that many reasonable employees would find a month without a paycheck to be a serious hardship and an indefinite suspension without pay could act as a deterrent to filing a claim, even if the suspended employee eventually received backpay.

A reasonable employee with the choice between retaining a job (and paycheck) and filing a discrimination complaint might choose to retain the employment and compensation rather than file the complaint. Such actions are the exact motivations in the design of Title VII antiretaliation provisions, to protect against an employee not choosing to file a complaint. Consequently, the antiretaliation provision of Title VII provides broader protection than the antidiscrimination provisions because the antidiscrimination provisions require a showing that an employee suffered an adverse employer action that affects employment or alters the conditions of the workplace.

Crawford

The Supreme Court unanimously ruled in *Crawford v. Metropolitan Government of Nashville and Davidson County, Tennessee*, 129 S. Ct. 846 (2009), that the protection against retaliation provided by Title VII extends to an employee who speaks out about discrimination not on her own initiative, but in answering questions during an employer's internal investigation. In *Crawford*, in response to questions from an official of respondent local government (Metro) during an internal investigation into rumors of sexual harassment by the Metro School District employee relations director (Hughes), petitioner Crawford reported that she had been sexually harassed by Hughes. Metro took no action against Hughes, but soon fired Crawford, alleging embezzlement.

Crawford filed suit under Title VII, claiming that Metro was retaliating for her report of Hughes's behavior in violation of the Title VII antiretaliation provision, 42 U.S.C. §2000e–3(a), which makes it unlawful for an employer to discriminate against any employee who either has:

♦ Opposed any practice made unlawful by Title VII (opposition clause).

♦ Made a charge, testified, assisted, or participated in a Title VII proceeding or investigation (participation clause).

The U.S. District Court granted Metro a summary judgment, and the U.S. Court of Appeals for the Sixth Circuit affirmed, holding that Crawford could not satisfy the opposition clause of Title VII because she had not instigated or initiated any complaint, but had merely answered questions by investigators in an already-pending internal investigation, initiated by someone else. In its decision, the Sixth Circuit continued that the opposition clause demands active, consistent opposing activities to warrant protection against retaliation, whereas Crawford did not claim to have instigated or initiated any complaint prior to her participation in the investigation, nor did she take any further action following the investigation and prior to her firing. The Supreme Court rejected the Sixth Circuit decision.

The Supreme Court held that because "oppose" is undefined by statute, it carries its ordinary dictionary meaning of resisting or contending against. Thus, Crawford's statement was covered by the Title VII opposition clause, as an ostensibly disapproving account of Hughes's sexually obnoxious behavior toward her. The Supreme Court continued that to "oppose" goes beyond "active, consistent" behavior in ordinary discourse, and may be used to speak of someone who has taken no action at all to advance a position beyond disclosing it. Thus, a person can "oppose" by responding to someone else's questions just as surely as by provoking the discussion. Nothing in Title VII requires a rule protecting an employee who reports discrimination on her own initiative but not one who reports the same discrimination in the same words when asked a question.

Metro argued for the Sixth Circuit's "active, consistent opposition rule" claiming that the lower the bar for retaliation claims, the less likely it is that employers will look into what may be happening outside the executive suite. As they see it, if retaliation is an easy charge when things go bad for an employee who responded to inquiries, employers will avoid the headache by refusing to raise questions about possible discrimination. However, the Supreme Court found such argument unconvincing because it underestimates the strong inducement employers have to ferret out and put a stop to discriminatory activity in their operations because of *Burlington Industries, Inc. v. Ellerth* and *Faragher v. Boca Raton*. *Ellerth* and *Faragher* held that an employer is subject to vicarious liability to a victimized employee for an actionable hostile environment created by a supervisor with authority over the employee.

The Supreme Court argued that the Sixth Circuit's rule could undermine the Ellerth-Faragher scheme, along with the statute's primary objective of avoiding harm to employees, because if an employee reporting discrimination in answer to an employer's questions could be penalized with no remedy, prudent employees would have a good reason to keep quiet about Title VII offenses.

Consequently, the Supreme Court concluded that Crawford's conduct is covered by the opposition clause and that the protection against retaliation provided by Title VII extends to an employee who speaks out about discrimination not on their own initiative, but in answering questions during an employer's internal investigation.

Additional Retaliation Concerns

On May 27, 2008, the Supreme Court issued two decisions allowing employees to bring retaliation claims against their employers under antidiscrimination statutes, even though the statutes contained no antiretaliation provisions.

In *CBOCS West, Inc. v. Humphries*, 128 S. Ct. 1951 (2008), the Supreme Court held that an employee could bring a race retaliation claim against the employee's employer under 42 U.S.C. § 1981, despite the fact that nowhere in § 1981 is the word retaliation ever mentioned. This ruling is significant because § 1981 has a longer statute of limitations than Title VII and, unlike Title VII, contains no limitations on the amount of punitive and pain and suffering damages available to a plaintiff. In addition, a plaintiff must file a charge of discrimination with the EEOC prior to suing in federal court under Title VII within 300 days of the alleged discriminatory act. In contrast, under § 1981, a plaintiff may file a lawsuit immediately, and has four years in which to do so.

Similarly, in *Gómez-Pérez v. Potter*, 553 F.3d 19 (2008), the court held that federal employees who complain about age discrimination are protected from retaliation by their employers under the Age Discrimination in Employment Act (ADEA), even though the ADEA contains no antiretaliation provisions in regards to public employees.

After examining these two cases, employers should adopt the conclusion that the Supreme Court has basically established a general presumption that federal civil right statutes prohibit retaliation whether it is explicitly stated or not.

Types of Discrimination Prohibited

All employment decisions should only be based on job-related merit factors. Consequently, the law forbids two types of discrimination — discriminatory treatment and discriminatory impact — in the workplace.

Discriminatory Treatment

Discriminatory treatment occurs when an individual is treated differently, from other applicants or employees who are similarly situated, because of that individual's protected status. For example, replacing a 45-year-old employee with an equally qualified 25-year-old would be discriminatory if no legitimate business reason can be shown for the action.

Discriminatory Impact

Discriminatory (or *disparate*) *impact* occurs when an employment policy or practice adversely affects a protected group and no legitimate business reason can be shown for the policy or practice. For example, it would be discriminatory for an employer to maintain a minimum height requirement that is not necessary for job performance if it tends to exclude women and members of certain ethnic groups from employment.

Any job requirement not necessary for effective performance that has a significant and adverse impact on a protected group is unlawful (for example, a high school diploma for custodians).

Laws Prohibiting Discrimination

The following are the major federal antidiscrimination laws:

♦ **Title VII of the Civil Rights Act of 1964 (Title VII).** Title VII governs the employment practices of most public and private employers. Title VII prohibits employment discrimination based on race, color, religion, sex, pregnancy, and national origin.

Title VII applies to private employers and governmental agencies with 15 or more employees for all workdays in each of 20 or more calendar weeks in the current or preceding calendar year. Individual supervisors and managers are not considered liable under Title VII and cannot be held personally liable for their own discriminatory acts. However, they may be liable under state law.

♦ **The Civil Rights Act of 1991.** The Civil Rights Act of 1991 amended several sections of Title VII and added a new section, 42 U.S.C. § 1981. Section 1981 requires equal treatment for all persons without regard to race or color and prohibits intentional employment discrimination.

Intentional discrimination is discrimination practiced with malice or reckless indifference to the federally protected rights of an individual. In some cases, § 1981 has been held to prohibit discrimination based on ethnicity, ancestry, or citizenship. It does not apply to discrimination based on sex, religion, age, or disability.

Note: Section 1981 has generally been interpreted to be consistent with the requirements of Title VII, but there are some differences between the two laws as follows:

- Unlike Title VII, § 1981 does not require a charge to be filed with and investigated by the EEOC before a lawsuit can be filed. Employees can immediately pursue their claims against the employer under this statute in federal court.

- Cases under § 1981 are not restricted by the short statute of limitations contained in Title VII. Federal courts have held that state law determines the statute of limitations for cases under § 1981.

- Section 1981 allows compensatory and punitive damages to be recovered where intentional discrimination is demonstrated. Any party to the lawsuit may demand a jury trial.

- Compensatory damages under § 1981 do not include backpay, interest on backpay, or any other type of relief authorized by § 706(g) of the 1964 Civil Rights Act. However, § 1981 damages are available in additional to any relief authorized under § 706(g). Nonetheless, the amount of recoverable compensable damages under § 1981 depends upon the number of employees that were employed by the discriminatory employer. Additionally, § 1981 damages are only authorized in cases of intentional discrimination rather than where the charge alleges that neutral employment practices have an adverse impact.

- Unlike Title VII, which applies only to employers of 15 or more employees, § 1981 applies to **all** employers.

- **Americans with Disabilities Act (ADA).** The ADA is a federal law prohibiting employment discrimination against qualified individuals on the basis of disability who are able to perform a job with or without reasonable accommodation. The ADA applies to all private employers, state and local governments, and education institutions with 15 or more employees.

♦ **Rehabilitation Act of 1973.** The Rehabilitation Act of 1973 is similar to the ADA. It applies to all federal agencies and employers conducting business under certain federal contracts.

- **Age Discrimination in Employment Act (ADEA).** The ADEA prohibits employment discrimination against people 40 years of age or older. The act prohibits discrimination against those over 40 in favor of younger people and prohibits discrimination within the over-40 age group. The ADEA applies to private employers with 20 or more employees for each working day in 20 or more consecutive calendar weeks in the current or preceding calendar year. The ADEA applies to all private employers, state and local governments (including school districts), employment agencies, and labor organizations.

- **Older Workers' Benefit Protection Act (OWBPA).** The OWBPA amends the ADEA. The OWBPA grants older workers protection with respect to waiver and releases of ADEA rights. The OWBPA sets standards for evaluating the validity of employee waivers under the ADEA because some seniors were effectively signing away ADEA rights as a condition for taking an employer-offered incentive for retirement. Moreover, the OWBPA amended the ADEA to specifically prohibit employers from denying benefits to older employees. An employer may reduce benefits based on age only if the cost of providing the reduced benefits to older workers is the same as the cost of providing benefits to younger workers.

- **Equal Pay Act (EPA).** The EPA is an amendment to the federal Fair Labor Standards Act (FLSA) that prohibits paying different wages to employees of different sexes who perform equal work under similar conditions. Virtually all employers are subject to the provisions of this act.

- **Uniformed Services Employment and Re-Employment Rights Act (USERRA).** USERRA protects the job rights of individuals who voluntarily or involuntarily leave employment positions to undertake military service. USERRA also prohibits employers from discriminating against past and present members of the uniformed services, and applicants to the uniformed services. Additionally, employers may not retaliate against anyone assisting in the enforcement of USERRA rights, including testifying or making a statement in connection with a proceeding under USERRA, even if that person has no service connection.

USERRA covers almost all employees, including part-time and probationary employees, and all U.S. employers regardless of size. USERRA provides for health benefit continuation for people who are absent from work to service in the military, even when COBRA does not cover the employer. With exception, USERRA requires that all employer-sponsored health care plans provide COBRA-type coverage for up to 24 months after the employee's absence begins due to military service or for the period of uniformed service.

The maximum period of coverage for such an employee and their dependents is the lesser of 24 months beginning on the date the employee's absence began or the day after the date on which the employee failed to apply for or return to a position of employment. Additionally, employees or dependents who elect this coverage may be required to pay a premium similar to COBRA (no more than 102 percent of the full premium under the plan). However, a person who performs military service for less than 31 days may not be required to pay more than the employee share, if any, for coverage.

Employers are also required to provide employees with posted notice of the USERRA rights, benefits, and obligations. The preservice employer must re-employ service members returning from a period of service in the uniformed services if those service members meet five criteria as follows:

- The person must have held a civilian job.

- The person must have given notice to the employer that they were leaving the job for service in the uniformed services, unless giving notice was precluded by military necessity or otherwise impossible or unreasonable.

- The cumulative period of service must not have exceeded five years.

- The person must not have been released from service under dishonorable or other punitive conditions.

- The person must have reported back to the civilian job in a timely manner or have submitted a timely application for re-employment.

Usually an employee returning from active military service must be restored to the position the employee would have attained had the employment relationship continued without interruption. Restoration includes the appropriate seniority, status, and pay unless, business conditions have so changed as to make the employee's restoration to the former position impossible. Employers are prohibited from discharging certain re-employed veterans, in the absence of just cause, for up to one year. Additionally, employers are required to provide and continue health coverage to individuals (and their dependents) who are absent from employment due to their position with the armed forces. Per USERRA and upon re-employment, an employee maintains the right to be reinstated in the employer's health plan who did not elect to continue coverage during their military service. Generally, such reinstatement is permitted without any waiting period or exclusions, except for service-connected illnesses or injuries.

USERRA obligates employers to credit employees with years of service while on uniformed service leave and to fund both defined benefit and defined contribution plans for those years. Contributions to defined contribution plans are based upon the rate of pay that employees would have received for that period or for the employees' average compensation during the 12 months preceding the period of service. However, employees are not entitled to earnings or forfeitures that would have been added to their accounts during the leave. Employees must also be allowed to make up elective deferrals and required employee contributions. In addition, the employer must make any matching contributions required by the plan. Employees have three times the length of their leave (a maximum of five years) to make these contributions.

Additionally, according to the Veterans' Benefits Improvement Act of 2008, there is no limit on the period for filing a complaint or claim under USERRA.

♦ **USERRA and the Pension Protection Act of 2006 (PPA).** The Pension Protection Act of 2006 provides that, for individuals called to active military duty for at least 179 days, early withdrawals from a 401(k) plan, 403(b) plan, or similar arrangement can be made without paying the 10 percent excise tax on early distributions.

The PPA also permits individuals who received "qualified reservist distributions" to make an after-tax contribution to a qualified retirement plan up to the amount of the qualified reservist distribution that had been received. The contribution may be made for up to two years after the end of active duty, but it is not deductible. This provision applies to all individuals called to active duty after September 11, 2001, and before December 31, 2007.

♦ **The Vietnam Era Veterans' Readjustment Assistance Act (VEVRAA).** The VEVRAA prohibits discrimination against specified categories of veterans protected by the act and requires affirmative action in the employment of such veterans. Effective December 1, 2003, the Jobs for Veterans Act (JFA) amended VEVRAA's federal contracting provisions regarding coverage, protected groups, and mandatory job listing requirements for all federal contracts entered into on or after December 1, 2003. Federal contracts entered into before this date are subject to the VEVRAA requirements as they stood before enactment of JVA.

Applications

This section offers greater insight in regard to some of the laws previously outlined, as they apply to specific discriminatory practices.

Racial Discrimination

Discriminatory Treatment

Title VII forbids discrimination on the basis of race and unalterable characteristics — such as skin color — associated with race. Treating an employee less favorably than other employees solely based on the employee's race is illegal. For example, it would be discriminatory and disparate race-based treatment should an employer discipline an African-American employee differently than a Caucasian employee for the same rule violation.

Courts also have found disparate treatment under Title VII when an employer discriminates against an individual for their interracial marriage/dating, racially oriented expression of attitudes and beliefs, and/or membership in racially oriented groups.

Racial Harassment

Employers are prohibited from engaging in racially motivated harassment or from tolerating a racially hostile work environment.

Hostile environment harassment occurs when unwelcome, severe, and repeated racial comments or acts unreasonably interfere with an individual's job performance or create an intimidating, hostile, or offensive working environment. A racially hostile environment may be created when a group of employees tells racial jokes and refers to employees of other racial groups in racially derogatory terms.

In such situations, the following few key points should be noted:

♦ The intent of the harasser does not matter. The test for harassment is from the viewpoint of a reasonable person.

♦ Employers will generally be liable for the acts of their employees if the employers knew or should have known that such acts occurred.

♦ Hostile environment harassment must be severe and pervasive. One incident is unlikely to create liability.

Segregation and Classification of Employees

Employers are in violation of Title VII where minority employees are segregated by physically isolating them from other employees or from customer contact. Additionally, employers are prohibited from assigning primarily minorities to predominately minority establishments or geographic areas. It is also illegal to exclude minorities from certain positions or to group or categorize employees or jobs so that minorities generally hold certain jobs.

Coding applications/résumés to designate an applicant's race, by either an employer or employment agency, constitutes evidence of discrimination where minorities are excluded from employment or from certain positions.

Disparate Impact

Certain employment practices can have a disparate impact on minority applicants and employees and lead to disparate-impact discrimination claims.

The following are examples of such practices:

♦ Rejecting applicants on the basis of arrest records rather than conviction records. An arrest does not prove an individual committed a crime.

♦ Using aptitude or intelligence tests unrelated to job skills.

♦ Requiring a high school diploma when a high school education is not necessary to perform the tasks of the job.

National Origin Discrimination

Employers are prohibited from discriminating against an individual due to birthplace, ancestry, culture, or linguistic characteristics common to a specific ethnic group. Title VII also prohibits employer actions that have the purpose or effect of discriminating against persons because of their national origin.

For example, a rule requiring that employees speak only English on the job may violate Title VII unless an employer shows that the requirement is necessary for conducting business.

Furthermore, Title VII prohibits discrimination against a person because of an association with an individual of a particular national origin. This prohibition includes discrimination against an individual because of marriage to a person of a particular national origin or because of participation in organizations identified with a particular origin.

Section 1981 of the Civil Rights Act of 1991

In addition to claims brought under Title VII, victims of national origin discrimination may also bring claims under § 1981 of the Civil Rights Act of 1991.

Although § 1981 does not explicitly prohibit national origin discrimination, the Supreme Court has held that the law prohibits discrimination based on ancestry or ethnic characteristics.

Citizenship

Discrimination based on citizenship violates Title VII if it has the purpose or effect of discriminating on the basis of national origin. For example, a citizenship requirement would be unlawful if it is a pretext for national origin discrimination or if it is part of a wider scheme of national origin discrimination.

In addition to national origin claims under Title VII, individuals who are not U.S. citizens may have claims under the following federal statutes:

♦ **Immigration Reform and Control Act of 1986 (IRCA).** The IRCA prohibits employers with four or more employees from discriminating because of citizenship status against U.S. citizens and foreign nationals authorized to work in the Unites States with respect to hiring, referral, or discharge. Such employers are also prohibited from committing document abuse. Document abuse occurs when an employer requests that an employee or applicant produce a specific document, as well as requesting additional or different documents than are required, to establish employment eligibility or rejects valid documents that reasonably appear genuine on their face. Employers may not retaliate against an employee or individual who files a complaint against the employer, cooperates in an investigation, or testifies at a hearing.

  Note: Small employers, those with 4 to 14 employees, are also prohibited by the IRCA from engaging in national origin discrimination.

♦ **Fair Labor Standards Act (FLSA).** The FLSA requires, among other things, that covered workers, including nonresidents, be paid no less than the federal minimum wage.

♦ **Special Visa Programs.** Employment of foreign nationals under special visa programs, such as H-1B and H-2A visas, may also be subject to certain requirements related to wages, working conditions, or other aspects of employment.

English-Only Rules

The EEOC has held that English-only rules are presumed to violate Title VII when they require that English be spoken at all times in the workplace.

Employers who require that their employees be able to speak English must show that fluency in English is a bona fide occupational qualification or a business necessity for the position in question. However, an employer's rule that requires employees to speak English at all times, including during their work break and lunch time, is an example of an employment practice that discriminates against persons whose primary language is not English.

The following are some situations in which a business necessity could justify an English-only rule:

◆ For communications with customers, co-workers, or supervisors who only speak English.

◆ In emergencies or situations when workers must speak a common language to promote safety.

◆ For cooperative work assignments in which the English-only rule is needed to promote efficiency.

◆ To enable a supervisor who only speaks English to monitor the performance of an employee whose job duties require communication with co-workers.

Employers should ensure that affected employees are notified about an English-only rule and the consequences for a violation of the rule. The employer may provide notice by any reasonable means under the circumstances, such as a meeting, email, or posting.

Note: In some cases, it may be necessary for an employer to provide notice in both English and the other native languages spoken by the employees.

Harassment

Harassment on the basis of national origin is a violation of Title VII. An employer has a duty to maintain a working environment free of harassment on the basis of national origin. Additionally, employers may be open to charges of discrimination if they allow their employees to direct ethnic slurs at other employees and fail to take disciplinary action against those who are making the ethnic comments, thus creating a hostile work environment.

Ethnic slurs and other verbal or physical conduct relating to an individual's national origin constitute harassment when this conduct produces any of the following:

◆ Has the purpose or effect of creating or intimidating hostile or offensive working environment.

◆ Has the purpose or effect of unreasonably interfering with an individual's work performance.

◆ Otherwise adversely affects an individual's employment opportunities.

Religious Discrimination

It is illegal for employers to discriminate against applicants or employees because of their religion. For purposes of this law, *religion* includes religious observance and practice as well as belief. It also includes individual moral and ethical beliefs sincerely held with the strength of traditional religious views.

Employers must make reasonable accommodations for the religious beliefs of their employees unless an accommodation would cause undue hardship on the employer. Factors such as the size of the company, the nature of the employee's job, the feasibility of transferring job duties or changing work schedules, and the amount of employee cooperation affect the reasonableness of an accommodation.

Employers could claim undue hardship when accommodating an employee's religious practices if allowing such practices requires more than ordinary administrative costs. Undue hardship may also be shown if changing a bona fide seniority system to accommodate one employee's religious practices denies another employee the job or shift preference guaranteed by the seniority system.

Some reasonable accommodations and limits on accommodations might be the following:

- ♦ Whenever possible, an employer should try to accommodate an employee's request to take time off for religious holidays. This could be done by allowing the employee to use vacation time, a day off without pay, using floating holidays, or allowing employees to trade shifts.

- ♦ An employer should try to accommodate an employee's scheduling needs for certain days or shifts to accommodate the employee's religious practices or beliefs. This could be done by having a flexible work schedule or by allowing employees to swap shifts. However, employers are not required to accommodate a scheduling request if the change would conflict with a seniority system established in a collective-bargaining agreement. An employer also is not required to make accommodations that would involve more than minimal cost, such as by hiring another employee or paying premium wages to other employees as substitutes.

- ♦ An employer should try to accommodate an employee's religious practices with respect to the way the employee dresses. However, the employer need not do this if the particular mode of dress would create a safety hazard. For example, an employer could ban loose clothing around machinery or require employees to be clean-shaven if their job requires the use of a respirator. An employer may also enforce dress and grooming policies for employees whose jobs require extensive contact with the public.

Employers are not required to accommodate religious beliefs until employees have requested such accommodation. Additionally, employees have no right to a particular type of accommodation, and employers may offer different reasonable accommodations than the employee suggested.

Federal Health Care Conscience Protection Statutes

The federal health care conscience protection statutory provisions, located at 45 C.F.R. 88 – 88.6, protects the rights of health care entities, both individuals and institutions, to refuse to perform health care services and research activities to which they may object for religious, moral, ethical, or other reasons.

The nondiscrimination protections of the statutes apply to institutional health care providers as well as to individual employees working for recipients of certain funds from the DHHS. Additionally, recipients of specified DHHS funds must certify their compliance with the health care conscience protections.

Sex Discrimination

Employers are prohibited from discriminating against applicants and employees on the basis of sex — male or female — or sexual orientation. For example, for disciplinary purposes both female and male employees must be treated the same.

Title VII prohibitions against sex discrimination specifically cover the following:

- ♦ **Sexual Harassment.** Practices ranging from direct requests for sexual favors to workplace conditions that create a hostile environment for persons of either gender, including same sex harassment.

- ♦ **Pregnancy Based Discrimination.** Pregnancy, childbirth, and related medical conditions must be treated in the same way as other temporary illnesses or conditions.

Sexual Orientation Discrimination

Although Title VII and the EEOC do not provide or enforce the protections that prohibit discrimination and harassment based on sexual orientation, other federal agencies and many states and municipalities do.

The Civil Service Reform Act of 1978 (CSRA) has been interpreted to prohibit federal employees who have authority to take, direct others to take, recommend, or approve any personnel action from discriminating against applicants and employees on the basis of race, color, sex, sexual orientation, religion, national origin, age, disability, marital status, or political affiliation.

Executive Order 13087 was signed on May 28, 1998 to provide a uniform policy for the federal government to prohibit discrimination based on sexual orientation. Additionally, some federal agencies have developed parallel Equal Employment Opportunity (EEO) complaint procedures allowing federal employees to file EEO complaints based on sexual orientation within their agencies.

Related Information

Federal Benefits and Nondiscrimination

On June 17, 2009, President Barack Obama signed a Presidential Memorandum on Federal Benefits and Nondiscrimination. The memorandum follows a review by the U.S. Director of the Office of Personnel Management (OPM) and the U.S. Secretary of State regarding what benefits may be extended to the same-sex partners of federal employees in the civil service and the foreign service within the confines of existing federal laws and statutes.

For civil service employees:

♦ Domestic partners of federal employees can be added to the long-term care insurance program.

♦ Supervisors can also be required to allow employees to use their sick leave to take care of domestic partners and nonbiological, nonadopted children.

For foreign service employees, a number of benefits were identified, including, but not limited to, the following:

♦ The use of medical facilities at posts abroad.

♦ Medical evacuation from posts abroad.

♦ Inclusion in family size for housing allocations.

The Presidential Memorandum requested that the Director of the OPM and the Secretary of State act to extend to same-sex partners of federal employees the aforementioned benefits. The memorandum also requested the heads of all other executive branch departments and agencies to conduct internal reviews to determine whether other benefits they administer might be similarly extended, and to report the results of those reviews to the Director of the OPM.

The memorandum also directed the OPM to issue guidance within 90 days to all executive departments and agencies regarding compliance with, and implementation of, the civil service laws, which make it unlawful to discriminate against federal employees or applicants for federal employment on the basis of factors not related to job performance.

Sexual Harassment

Definition of Sexual Harassment

Sexual harassment is a form of sex discrimination that violates Title VII.

The Equal Employment Opportunity Commission (EEOC) defines *sexual harassment* in employment as unwelcome sexual conduct when submission to such conduct is made either explicitly or implicitly a term or condition of an individual's employment. The victim does not have to be the person harassed, it could be anyone affected by the offensive conduct.

Sexual harassment can occur in a variety of circumstances and examples/elements of harassment include the following:

♦ The harasser's conduct must be unwelcome.

♦ Offering an employee a benefit, such as a job, promotion, pay increase, or trip out of town, for agreeing to sexual demands.

♦ Punishing an employee for not agreeing to a sexual advance by discharging or refusing to hire the employee, assigning the employee to disagreeable tasks, not promoting the employee, or not granting a salary increase.

♦ Unlawful sexual harassment may occur without economic injury to or discharge of the victim.

The EEOC Guidelines define two types of sexual harassment as follows:

♦ **Quid Pro Quo Sexual Harassment.** When submission to or rejection of unwelcome sexual conduct by an individual is used as the basis for employment decisions affecting such individual.

♦ **Hostile or Offensive Work Environment Sexual Harassment.** The unwelcome sexual conduct has the purpose or effect of unreasonably interfering with an individual's work performance or creating an intimidating, hostile, or offensive working environment. No employment benefits need be lost or gained, and this type of harassment may be engaged in by not only management or supervisors, but also by co-workers or nonemployees.

Employees may also claim that harassing conduct constitutes unlawful misconduct under state law, such as intentional infliction of emotional distress.

Potential Liability

Potential remedies under Title VII include reinstatement, backpay, attorneys' fees, injunctive orders, and compensatory and punitive damages. Because Title VII caps available compensatory and punitive damages at $300,000 or less, depending on the size of the employer, a plaintiff who brings a successful state law claim may obtain a higher recovery than a federal law claim.

Who Can Commit Harassment

The harasser can be the victim's supervisor, an agent of the employer, a supervisor in another area, a co-worker, or a nonemployee. Nonemployees include vendors, contractors, and customers. The victim as well as the harasser may be a man or a woman. Additionally, the victim does not have to be of the opposite sex.

Same Sex Harassment

Title VII prohibits sexual harassment by members of the same sex, that is, males sexually harassing males or females sexually harassing females. The relevant issue is whether one individual is harassing another individual because of that person's gender.

The following are examples of same sex harassment:

♦ Female employee who was subjected to name-calling and accused of promiscuity by her female co-workers may file a complaint due to a hostile work environment.

♦ A male employee who subjected to sexual harassment by his male supervisor will be able to make a claim under Title VII if he demonstrates that female employees were not similarly harassed, thereby demonstrating the harassment was due to his gender.

When an Employer Is Liable for Sexual Harassment

Vicarious Liability for Sexual Harassment by Supervisors

Employers are subject to vicarious liability for unlawful harassment by supervisors. Liability is enforced because employers are responsible for the act of their supervisors and employers should be encouraged to prevent harassment.

The following **liabilities** apply to supervisors:

♦ **Automatic Liability for Adverse Employment Action.** Employers are automatically liable if the harassing supervisor takes a tangible employment action, such as a discharge, demotion, or undesirable transfer, against the complaining employee.

♦ **Affirmative Defense Available if no Adverse Employment Action.** If the supervisor's harassment does not result in a tangible employment action against the complaining employee, then employers may avoid liability if both of the following are proven to be true:

• That the employer exercised reasonable care to prevent and promptly correct any harassing behavior.

• That the employee unreasonably failed to take advantage of any preventive or corrective opportunities provided by the employer or to avoid harm otherwise.

Prevention is the best tool to avoid harassment in the workplace. Courts have held that having an antiharassment policy with complaint procedures is an important consideration in determining whether the employer has satisfied the first step of the affirmative defense.

Liability for Sexual Harassment by Nonsupervisor

An employer is responsible for such conduct only if the employer knew or should have known of the conduct and failed to take appropriate corrective action.

Personal Liability for Sexual Harassment by Supervisors

Most courts have held that supervisors may not be held personally liable under Title VII for sexual harassment. However, supervisors may be named as individual defendants in state law claims brought with the Title VII suit.

Knowing if Sexual Harassment Has Occurred

Not all sexual conduct is sexual harassment. In order for conduct to constitute sexual harassment, it must be unwelcome. Consensual flirtation, dirty jokes, or even sexual relations will not be considered harassment unless they are unwelcome. Nonetheless, mere acquiescence or passiveness to sexual advances does not necessarily mean that such conduct is welcome.

Unwelcome Sexual Conduct

Unwelcome sexual conduct must be unwelcome in the sense that the individual did not solicit or incite it, and in the sense that the individual regarded the conduct as undesirable or offensive. Unwelcome sexual conduct becomes harassment when it creates a working environment that is unreasonably intimidating or offensive. The standard is both objective and subjective. That is, a work environment is not considered hostile unless a reasonable person would find it offensive and the complaining employee actually perceived it as offensive. When determining the issue of welcomeness, the EEOC evaluates each discrimination claim on a case-by-case basis, appraises the employer's record as a whole, and considers the totality of the circumstances.

Hostile Work Environment

To constitute hostile work environment harassment, the conduct must substantially affect the work environment. A hostile environment claim usually requires a pattern of conduct with a repetitive and debilitating effect.

Some of the factors to consider in determining whether the work environment is so hostile or offensive as to constitute harassment are as follows:

- Whether the conduct is verbal, physical, or both.

- How frequently the acts are repeated.

- Whether the conduct is hostile and patently offensive.

- Whether a co-worker or supervisor perpetuates the conduct.

- Whether other people joined in the activity.

- Whether the conduct was directed at an individual or a group.

Although hostile environment cases usually involve a pattern of conduct, a single instance of extremely severe sexual conduct, as for example, the touching of intimate body areas, may suffice to create a claim.

Adopting a Zero Tolerance Policy

Many employers have concluded that the only practical way to avoid liability for a hostile environment is to adopt workplace policies banning all sexually oriented jokes, comments, and behavior from the workplace. The reasoning behind such principles is that it is inefficient to discipline some employees but not others for sexually oriented behavior or to initiate discipline policies for the second or third but not the first, sexually oriented joke. While zero tolerance policies go beyond the requirements articulated by the courts or the EEOC, they have the virtue of being simple to understand and enforce.

Sexual Harassment Outside of Work

Conduct that would otherwise constitute sexual harassment when performed before or after work or off the employer's premises constitutes sexual harassment if it is job related.

For example, claims of sexual harassment may arise from conduct at informal after work get-togethers, company parties, and out-of-town business trips.

The Employer's Obligation to Correct Problems

An employer is automatically liable if a harassing supervisor actually takes an employment action against the complaining employee. The only way to avoid liability for this type of harassment is to make sure that the problem does not occur. Employers should carefully monitor supervisory actions with respect to discipline, discharge, evaluation, salary increase, promotions, and assignments to ensure that the supervisor's actions are unrelated to gender.

In the case of hostile environment harassment or situations where supervisors threaten to but do not actually condition employment consequences on an employee's response to unwelcome sexual advances, liability is usually imposed only as a result of an employer's failure to have a policy prohibiting harassment or to adequately follow-up and investigate claims of sexual harassment. Employers have a duty to reasonably respond to, investigate, and resolve claims of sexual harassment. The employer should promptly, adequately, and completely respond to a problem or complaint no matter how it learns of the problem, documenting its investigation along the way. The responsive action should be appropriate in light of the evidence uncovered. For example, if the victim quits due to the harassing environment, the employer may be required to offer reinstatement to the victim.

When Enough Has Been Done

The courts evaluate the employer's response by looking at the following:

- Whether the employer had a policy against sexual harassment.

- Whether that policy was adequately publicized to employees.

- Whether the policy had an adequate complaint procedure.

- The promptness and adequacy of the employer's responses to employee complaints.

Note: The employer's response must be prompt. Tacit approval of the harassment by delay may be as damaging to the employer as the conduct itself.

The employer may also be held liable for improper or inadequate responses. Employers have been held liable in the following situations:

- When a verbal reprimand proved ineffective and the employer took no further action when informed of the harasser's persistence.

- Where co-workers harassed the victim for over four years. When informed of the problem by numerous complaints, the supervisor took no action other than occasionally reminding employees of the company policy against the conduct. No investigation or action occurred until the EEOC charge was filed.

- Where a victim's first level supervisor responsible for correcting the problem was also the harasser.

Prevention

Employers have an affirmative duty to prevent sexual harassment and to make a reasonably diligent inquiry into situations that might constitute sexual harassment. The employer cannot wait for the problem to come to them.

Some of the preventive actions the employer should adopt include the following:

- Affirmatively raising the subject with all employees to emphasize opposition to such conduct and to make employees aware of the problem.

- Expressing strong disapproval of the misconduct.

- Informing employees of their rights and the consequences of violating the employer's policy, federal law, and state law when applicable against harassment.

The most important action the employer can take to prevent harassment and to minimize liability is to develop and effectively implement an explicit policy against sexual harassment, and to communicate this policy clearly and regularly. Furthermore, employers must have and communicate a policy against harassment and discrimination in order to limit an employer's potential liability for punitive damages.

What to Include in a Policy

The written policy should include the following:

- A provision stating that sexual harassment will result in discipline up to and including discharge.

- A prohibition against sexual harassment as defined by the EEOC, as well as the applicable state law. The policy must be explicitly clear in regard to the illegality of sexual harassment. The policy should give illustrations detailing types of prohibited conduct and specify that the policy applies to all employees. The policy should include an enforceable statement that such conduct is forbidden under state and federal law.

- The following assurances:

- That the complaining employee will not be retaliated against for bringing complaints in good faith.

- That the complaint will be kept confidential to the extent consistent with the employer's need to investigate.

♦ A guarantee within the employer's procedure that employee complaints of sexual harassment will be addressed promptly. The procedure should give employees a limited choice of company officials to complain to in order to ensure that the employee is not required to bring the complaint to the alleged harasser.

♦ The employee should be made aware of the legal remedies and complaint process available through both state and federal administrative agencies.

The policy should be routinely distributed to all current employees, on a periodic basis, and to all new employees, at the time of hire, to ensure that all employees know and understand the policy.

Investigating a Claim

Alleged harassers may bring a claim against an employer who performs a careless investigation, including claims for wrongful termination, grievances, or claims for defamation or discrimination. Employers must fully investigate a harassment claim without disclosing specific information about the matter, except to those with a need to know.

During an investigation, the employer should fully inform the complainant of their rights under any company sexual harassment policy and any other relevant policy, such as one relating to internal grievances.

All complaints of sexual harassment must be promptly and thoroughly investigated. It is insufficient to simply elicit a denial by the alleged harasser. The employer should obtain all potentially relevant information, including the accounts of witnesses and other parties. Relevant information may include eyewitness accounts, statements from individuals with whom the complainant discussed the incident, statements from co-workers who may have observed the alleged victim's demeanor either before or after the claimed incident, and statements from other employees who may have been harassed by the alleged harasser. Both the accused and the accuser should be given the opportunity to offer any evidence or identify any witnesses who can support their version of events.

Again, the employer's primary duty is to investigate claims thoroughly. However, the investigation should protect the privacy of the accuser, the accused, and any witnesses. In most instances, fairness will require that the accused be apprised of the identity of the person who made the sexual harassment accusation in order to allow the accused a genuine opportunity to respond to the claims.

To preserve the confidentiality of the investigation, witnesses should be questioned in private. Unless disclosure is necessary to obtain information from the witness, witnesses should not be asked leading questions or told the exact allegations. Rather, the witnesses should be provided with an opportunity to tell their own, uninfluenced, and truthful version of the facts. The witnesses should be asked to keep their conversations with the investigator confidential.

The investigation of hostile environment claims should determine the nature, frequency, context, and intended target of the complained-of conduct. Some of the issues the employer might want to explore include the following:

♦ Did the alleged harasser single out the victim?

♦ Did the victim willingly and voluntarily participate?

♦ What was the relationship between the victim and the alleged harasser?

♦ Were any remarks hostile and derogatory?

Each step of the investigation should be thoroughly documented. The resulting determination should be communicated to the complaining employee and the alleged harasser. Should sexual harassment be found, a prompt and effective remedy must be provided to the complaining employee and disciplinary action must be taken against the harasser. The employer should ensure that no further harassment or retaliation would occur against the complaining party and the witnesses.

An investigation can result in three conclusions, sexual harassment has occurred, the employer cannot make a determination based on the evidence, or the allegation was unfounded.

Sexual Harassment Has Occurred

If the allegations are found to be true, the employer's duty is to take appropriate corrective action. What that action should be depends upon the individual circumstances of each case, including the severity of the misconduct.

Appropriate corrective action may include the following:

- Discharge.

- Reprimand.

- Suspension or probation of the harasser.

- Reinstatement with backpay of the victim.

- Transfer with equal pay and equal duties for the victim.

- Transfer or demotion of the harasser.

- Discipline of supervisors or co-workers who failed to report the harassment.

The employer should also perform follow-up inquiries. This includes investigating to ensure that there are no other victims and, in the case of a hostile environment, that the hostile environment has been completely cured.

The employer should develop a checklist of remedial actions to ensure that all necessary steps to deal with the complaint have been taken.

A sample checklist might include the following:

- Was the complaint investigated promptly and thoroughly?

- Were the offenders appropriately dealt with (such as reprimand or discharge)?

- Was the victim made whole, including the restoration of benefits and lost opportunities?

- Has any hostile environment been eradicated?

- Have steps been taken to avoid future problems?

The Allegation Was Unfounded

When the employer finds the allegation to be unfounded, it should thoroughly document the investigation and clearly state the reasons for concluding that the allegation was unfounded. In such cases, it may be in the best interests of both the accused and the accuser to physically separate their locations in the workplace.

Importantly, although an employee made an accusation determined to be unfounded, Title VII protects employees who have opposed discriminatory employment practices from retaliation even if their claims of discrimination are unfounded. Even if the person is wrong, an employee who has made a good faith allegation of sexual harassment cannot be disciplined.

On the other hand, there may be instances where an employee knowingly lies in an attempt to cause the discharge of a fellow employee with whom they have a dispute or to protect themselves from a negative employment action by supervisors. Where an employee has knowingly made a false allegation, the employee may be disciplined or even terminated. In order to defend any subsequent charge of retaliation, there must be strong evidence that the employee knowingly misrepresented the facts.

Based on the Evidence, the Employer Cannot Make a Determination

In these instances, the employer should document the investigation and clearly state why the employer cannot make a determination. The employer should advise the accused individual of the results of the investigation, remind the accused of the employer's policy against harassment, and inform the accused that any proven incidents of harassment in the future will subject the person to disciplinary action. The employer should also advise the complainant of the results of the investigation and encourage the individual to bring forward any further evidence or to notify the employer of any future complaints. It may also be appropriate for the employer to separate the accused party and the complainant. Such separation may not always be possible, particularly if it would result in a less favorable job for the alleged victim.

Practical Pointers

An employer **should** take the following precautions:

- Maintain a written policy that is communicated to all employees defining and strictly prohibiting sexual harassment and informing employees to whom harassment complaints are brought.

- Ensure that all supervisors and employees sign a form acknowledging their responsibility to read and learn the terms of the written policy.

- Train employees that sexual harassment is prohibited and will result in discipline.

- Ensure that supervisors are trained to recognize sexually harassing behavior and know to report the conduct and/or discipline the employee(s) who engage in the behavior.

- Promptly and thoroughly investigate any complaints of sexual harassment and take appropriate remedial action sufficient to stop the harassment if the investigation concludes harassment has occurred.

- Investigate claims of same gender harassment in the same manner as claims of opposite gender harassment.

- Refuse to disclose any specific information about a sexual harassment complaint or the actions taken with respect to the complaint, except to those with a need to know.

- Discipline an employee who has committed sexual harassment before/after work or outside the workplace, if the conduct was job related.

- Follow up with employees who previously complained of harassment to ensure that the harassment has been stopped.

- Develop institutional checks on the authority of lower-level supervisors and managers, such as requiring that at least two management persons be responsible for all significant employment decisions.

- Apply and enforce the policy consistently.

An employer **should not** allow or tolerate any of the following:

- Put off investigating or neglect to thoroughly investigate a complaint of sexual harassment.

- ◆ Tolerate inappropriate and unwelcome sexual harassment on the theory that "boys will be boys."

- ◆ Repeatedly warn employees to stop engaging in sexual harassment, where the warnings do not stop the conduct and more severe discipline is required.

- ◆ Discipline an employee who makes a good faith allegation of sexual harassment if the employer's investigation determined no harassment occurred.

- ◆ Transfer a victim of sexual harassment to a lesser position to end the harassment.

- ◆ Refuse to seriously consider and investigate harassment claims made by men.

- ◆ Decide against investigating a harassment claim because the complaining employee asked that the matter be kept confidential.

- ◆ Assume no responsibility for harassment committed by contract employees or vendors.

- ◆ Permit lewd conversation and publication of sexually explicit jokes, photos, or cartoons.

- ◆ Allow employees to forward sexually offensive emails around the office.

State Tort Law

A victim may also have one or more causes of action in common law tort against individual co-workers for sexually harassing conduct. These are claims based not on a statute, such as Title VII, but on common law developed through case law of each state individually. The requirements of such claims are subject to the individual state's judicial decisions and precedent.

Behavior that satisfies statutory definitions of "sexual harassment" may also satisfy the common law standards for, among other things, battery, assault, intentional infliction of mental distress, false imprisonment, defamation, and wrongful discharge. For example, a male worker who constantly fondles a female co-worker against her will may be liable for damages derived from the sexually harassing conduct.

Such behavior also satisfies the common law tort requirements of a battery — which is the intentional infliction of a harmful or offensive bodily contact. Similarly, harassing behavior may put the victim in apprehension of offensive or harmful conduct — the common law standard for assault — or be sufficiently outrageous thereby amounting to the intentional infliction of emotional distress. In each of these cases of common law tort, the defendant's liability is individual or personal. Significantly, in cases of such intentional torts punitive damages are also available.

There are two major obstacles to recovery in tort for sexual harassment. First, the harassing conduct may not necessarily satisfy the requirements of any judicially or statutorily established tort. For example, frequent unwelcome solicitations for sex by a co-worker or supervisor constitute harassment, but probably do not rise to the level of extreme outrageousness generally required to make out a claim for the intentional infliction of mental distress, and because such solicitations do not involve offensive touching or imminent threats of such touching, they do not state a claim in battery of assault.

Second, some courts have interpreted provisions of state antidiscrimination statutes as providing the sole remedy for sexually harassing behavior. In other words, state statutes pre-empt common law tort remedies.

Many of these courts do create exceptions to the pre-emption doctrine where the facts underlying the common law claims are not identical to those constituting sexual harassment claims under the state statute. However, a tort claim may be pursued where there are additional, independent elements necessary for the tort claim. For example, a male employee who, motivated by the victim's gender, punched a female co-worker could be sued in tort for battery. The harmful conduct would be found to have gone beyond what would be necessary to support a state antidiscrimination or harassment claim and the resulting tort would therefore not be pre-empted by state statute.

Employers may be personally liable on the theory of negligence for the sexual-harassment-related torts of their employees. At common law, an employer may be liable for the failure to take due care in the hiring, training, or supervising of employees.

For example, an employer who knew or should have known that an individual the employer hired as a night watchman had a history of assault and rape would be liable on a theory of negligence if that employee assaulted a female employee. Where an employee has engaged in sexually harassing behavior that also amounts to an intentional tort, the employer may be personally liable to the victim if it can be shown that, under all the circumstances, the employer failed to take reasonable steps to prevent the harasser's misconduct.

Courts have made clear, however, that such employer liability for negligence cannot be based on employee conduct that does nothing more than violate state antidiscrimination or antiharassment statutes. If the employee's harassing conduct does not amount to an independent tort, holding the employer personally liable for the employee's action would amount to an end-run around state statutes that have been held to exclude personal liability for sexual harassment. Finally, whether or not a plaintiff's common law tort actions have merit, the litigation costs of defending against a sexual harassment claim can be devastating.

Pregnancy Discrimination

The Pregnancy Discrimination Act of 1978 (PDA), an amendment to Title VII, prohibits discrimination because of pregnancy, childbirth, or related medical conditions.

For the most part, women incapacitated by pregnancy, childbirth, or medical conditions related to pregnancy or childbirth must be treated the same as individuals incapacitated by other disabilities, including receiving benefits and being allowed to perform "light-duty" work.

Employer policies and benefits, including general leave policies, must be applied the same way to pregnant employees as they are to other employees requiring leave because of a temporary disability. Requiring an employee to be employed for at least six months before becoming eligible for leave, if applied equally to all employees, has been found not to discriminate against pregnant women. The FMLA, however, may require granting a leave.

An employer cannot refuse to hire a woman because of her pregnancy-related condition as long as she is able to perform the major functions of her job. An employer cannot refuse to hire her because of the employer's prejudices against pregnant workers or the prejudices of co-workers, clients, or customers. Furthermore, pregnant employees must be allowed to work until they are medically unable to do so. Employers who pressure pregnant employees to begin leave before leave is medically necessary are liable for unlawful discrimination.

Any health insurance provided by an employer must cover expenses for pregnancy related conditions on the same basis as costs for other medical conditions. Pregnancy related expenses should be reimbursed exactly as those incurred for other medical conditions, whether payment is on a fixed basis or a percentage of reasonable and customary charge basis.

Employers may not use pregnancy or maternity leave as an excuse for terminating employment. However, an employer may lawfully discharge a pregnant employee if the discharge was due to a legitimate business necessity. For example, an employer who experienced a dramatic business downturn, which in turn caused the position of a pregnant woman or of a woman on maternity leave to be eliminated may be justified in discharging the woman or refusing to reinstate her at the end of her leave. Conversely, discrimination may be found where an employer has been tolerating poor performance or poor attitude from an employee and then fires her when she takes pregnancy leave. If the employer would have continued to accept the poor performance or poor attitude and would not have fired the employee had she not taken leave, then the pregnancy leave was the impermissible factor leading to the discharge.

Age Discrimination

The ADEA broadly bans age discrimination and the Older Workers Benefit Protection Act (OWBPA) amended the ADEA.

The ADEA applies to employers with 20 or more employees, including state and local governments, employment agencies, labor organizations, and the federal government. The ADEA protects individuals who are 40 years of age or older from employment discrimination based on age. The ADEA's protections apply to both employees and job applicants.

Under the ADEA, employers are prohibited from discriminating against any person due to their age with respect to any term, condition, or privilege of employment. These protections include, but are not limited to, the employment areas of hiring, firing, promotion, layoff, compensation, benefits, job assignments, and training. Importantly, the U.S. Supreme Court has held that the ADEA's text, structure, purpose, history, and relationship to other federal statutes show that the act does not mean to stop an employer from favoring an older employee over a younger one.

Hiring

Employers may not include age preferences, limitations, or specifications in job notices or advertisements. Although employers are not prohibited from asking an applicant's age or date of birth, such requests will be closely scrutinized to make sure that the inquiry was made for a lawful purpose.

Advertising

The ADEA also prohibits the use of employment advertising that in any way discriminates against older individuals or indicates a preference based on age. This prohibition does not only apply to advertisements that state an age below 40 for potential candidates but to any indication of a preference for one age group over the group protected by the act.

Examples of prohibited phrasings include the following:

♦ "Recent college graduates" should be simply "college graduates."

♦ "Young professional" must be avoided.

♦ "Age 50 or over" discriminates against those 40 to 49 in the protected group.

Disparity in Ages

Although the ADEA protects individuals age 40 and over from being treated differently, an important consideration in determining if age discrimination exists is the actual disparity in ages. For instance, if a 40-year-old employee replaces a 55-year-old employee, discrimination may well be found. On the other hand, if an employee who is 55 replaces a 60-year-old employee, there is less likely to be a finding of discrimination.

The ADEA prohibits limiting or classifying employees over 40 in any way that might deprive them of employment opportunities or affect their employment status.

Exceptions: In some circumstances as follows, employers are allowed to consider age:

♦ In situations where age preference is necessary in the operation of a business, employers may claim a bona fide occupational qualification (BFOQ).

♦ Job requirements that may affect employees over 40 may be set as long as they are based on some factor other than age, such as a physical requirement for doing a job.

Mandatory or Involuntary Retirement

The ADEA **does not** prohibit compulsory retirement of any of the following employees:

♦ Who have been in an executive or high policy-making position for at least two years before retirement.

♦ Who are at least 65 years old at the time of retirement.

♦ Who are entitled to an immediate, nonforfeitable annual retirement income of $44,000.

Benefits

Employers may not use age as a basis for discontinuing contribution or accrual of retirement benefits or for reducing the rate of contribution or, accrual under a retirement plan. However, a plan is lawful if it limits the total contribution or benefits or number of years of service, provided those limits are not based upon age.

A retirement plan may require participation for a certain amount of years for benefit eligibility, yet cannot exclude participation because an employee is too old.

Under the OWBPA, employees eligible for early retirement incentive plans must be provided with complete and accurate information concerning what benefits are available under the plan.

Note: Employers should be careful to avoid early retirement programs presented in such a way as to imply that employees will be discharged should they fail to accept the offer. OWBPA regulations also require that the actual amount of benefits paid or costs incurred by the employer for benefits to older workers may not be less than that paid or incurred on behalf of younger workers.

Disparate Impact Claims

In a decision of great significance, the U. S. Supreme Court in *Smith v. City of Jackson*, 2005 WL 711605 (U.S.), ruled that an individual protected by the Age Discrimination in Employment Act (ADEA) can sue an employer if a policy, practice, or other employment action has had a disparate impact because of that individual's age. In a split decision, the court determined that the ADEA authorizes recovery of damages resulting from the adverse impact of an employer's actions upon an age-protected individual or group of individuals.

The case decided by the court involved a change in the pay plan for the city of Jackson, Mississippi's police officers and police dispatchers. The city attempted to bring the starting salaries for such positions up to the regional average by raising the pay of existing officers according to their years of service. Officers with less than five years of service were given proportionately larger raises than officers with more seniority. Those with more seniority also tended to be age 40 or over.

The plaintiffs, 30 police officers over age 40, sued the city under the ADEA claiming they were adversely affected by the plan because of their age. They were unsuccessful in their claims at the federal district and federal appeals courts. In affirming the lower court's grant of summary judgment for the city, the U.S. Court of Appeals for the Fifth Circuit ruled that disparate impact claims are categorically unavailable under the ADEA, even though the same facts brought under Title VII of the Civil Rights Act of 1964 would have entitled them to relief.

Affirming the result of the Fifth Circuit's reasoning, the U.S. Supreme Court found the older workers did not have a valid claim under a theory of disparate impact. However, in a significant development in the law of discrimination based on age, the court found that the language of the ADEA and Title VII is identical in its broad prohibition on discriminatory actions based on a protected characteristic. As such, the ADEA supports a disparate impact claim that is comparable to a disparate impact claim under the legal standards under Title VII.

The court explained there are important textual differences between the ADEA and Title VII: the ADEA permits any "otherwise prohibited" action "where the differentiation is based on reasonable factors other than age." The result is that the ADEA's protection against the adverse effects of an employer's action because of age is narrower in scope. If reasonable factors other than age account for the disparate impact, the action will not be found unlawful. This limitation is grounded in the fact that age may often be relevant to an individual's capacity to engage in certain types of employment.

In this case, the U.S. Supreme Court held that the older workers had not established a valid claim for age discrimination based on the adverse effects of the city's pay raise plan. The older workers did not identify any specific test, requirement, or practice within the plan that adversely impacted the older workers, beyond pointing out that the plan was less generous to them. The court also held that the city's stated reasons for the pay plan, including the need to bring the junior officers' salaries into line with comparable positions in the labor market, were reasonable. As such, the court found no basis to support the older workers' claims of disparate impact resulting from the city's actions.

Employers should, among other things, review their current compensation, benefit, and other employee policies to evaluate their impact upon older workers and address any unintended consequences in light of this decision, which authorizes courts to look beyond disparate treatment (where the adverse treatment based upon age is clearly deliberate) to disparate impact (where the adverse impact on older workers is disproportionate even if not deliberate).

Waiver of Rights

Under certain circumstances, laid down by the OWBPA, older workers may waive their rights under the ADEA if they do so knowingly and voluntarily.

Minimum standards for such a waiver are the following:

- The agreement must be in writing and understandable to the average person.

- The agreement must specifically refer to ADEA rights or claims arising under the ADEA.

- The employee will not waive future rights or claims.

- The employee must be given a benefit, such as a sum of money, which would otherwise not be made available to the employee in return for the employee's waiver of ADEA rights.

- The employee must be given 21 days to consider the agreement before signing (45 days in cases of group termination).

- The employee must be advised in writing to seek attorney counsel before signing the agreement.

- The agreement must provide for a seven-day period after signing during which the employee may revoke the agreement.

- Information regarding selection criteria and employees affected must be provided to those who are discharged in a group termination.

Disability Discrimination

The ADA prohibits employers from discriminating against qualified individuals on the basis of disability in job application procedures, hiring, firing, advancement, compensation, job training, and other terms, conditions, and privileges of employment. The ADA **covers all public employers and private employers with 15 or more employees**. A private employer is subject to ADA regulations if it employs 15 or more individuals on each working day in each of 20 or more calendar weeks in the current or preceding calendar year. The ADA covers labor organizations, employment agencies, and joint labor-management committees regardless of the number of employees.

Disability and Impairment

According to the ADA, the term *disability* means, with respect to an individual, any of the following:

- A physical or mental impairment that substantially limits one or more major life activities of the individual.

- A record of an impairment.

- Begin regarded as having an impairment.

Additionally, an individual who has a relationship or association with someone with a known disability is protected by the ADA.

An ***impairment*** is an abnormal physical or mental condition, such as blindness, schizophrenia, or disfigurement or a chronic debilitating illness, such as cancer, AIDS, arthritis, or acquired conditions such as the following:

- Substance addiction, eating disorders, or emotional illness.

- The long-term or permanent effects of accidents and illnesses.

An impairment **does not** include any of the following:

- Illegal drug use (although drug addiction could be considered an impairment), criminal behavior, or compulsive gambling.

- Temporary impairments regardless of severity (a broken leg that mends without complications) or impairments that are fully corrected with medication or other mitigating measures (nearsightedness where eyesight is fully correctable with eyeglasses).

- Conditions that fall within normal ranges of differences between individuals in the general population, including any of, but not limited to, the following:

  - Height or weight.

  - Hair or eye color.

  - Age-related intelligence.

  - Physical fitness differences (not results of actual impairments) or athletic ability.

  - Financial condition, creativity, or self-discipline.

  - Cosmetic disfigurement, such as missing teeth.

  - Temperament, aggressiveness, or work ethics.

Substantial Limits

Generally, whether an individual is substantially limited is a case-by-case determination. However, and according the ADAAA (ADA Amendments Act of 2008):

- An impairment that substantially limits one major life activity need not limit other major life activities in order to be considered a disability.

- An impairment that is episodic or in remission is a disability if it would substantially limit a major life activity when active.

- The determination of whether an impairment substantially limits a major life activity must be made without regard to the ameliorative effects of mitigating measures such as any of the following:

  - Medication, medical supplies, equipment, or appliances, low-vision devices (which do not include ordinary eyeglasses or contact lenses), prosthetics including limbs and devices, hearing aids and cochlear implants or other implantable hearing devices, mobility devices, or oxygen therapy equipment and supplies.

- Use of assistive technology.
- Reasonable accommodations or auxiliary aids or services. An auxiliary aid and services include all of the following:
  - Qualified interpreters or other effective methods of making aurally delivered materials available to individual with hearing impairments.
  - Qualified readers, taped texts, or other effective methods of making visually delivered materials available to individuals with visual impairments.
  - Acquisition of modification of equipment or devices.
  - Other similar services and actions.

♦ Learned behavioral or adaptive neurological modifications.

However, the ameliorative effects of the mitigating measures of ordinary eyeglasses or contact lenses may be considered in determining whether an impairment substantially limits a major life activity.

The ADA does not apply to impairments that are relatively insignificant or are common to a majority of persons at one time or another. For example, a severe cold or broken leg would not qualify as an ADA impairment.

An individual with epilepsy, paralysis, HIV infections, AIDS, a substantial hearing or visual impairment, mental disabilities, or a specific learning disability is inherently covered by the ADA.

The following factors are considered in determining whether an individual is substantially limited by an impairment:

♦ The nature and severity of the impairment.

♦ The duration or expected duration of the impairment.

♦ The permanent or long-term impact of the impairment.

An individual is not substantially limited in a major life activity if the limitation, when viewed in light of the factors previously noted, does not amount to a significant restriction when compared with the abilities of the average person.

Major Life Activities

Major life activities include, but are not limited to, all of the following:

♦ Caring for one's self, performing manual tasks, or working.

♦ Walking, sleeping or standing.

♦ Seeing, hearing, eating, or breathing.

♦ Speaking, lifting, or bending.

♦ Learning, reading, concentrating, thinking, and communicating.

A major life activity also includes the operation of a major bodily function, including but not limited to, all of the following:

♦ Functions of the immune system and normal cell growth.

♦ Digestive, bowel, and bladder functions.

- Neurological, brain, and respiratory functions.
- Circulatory, endocrine, and reproductive functions.

Except for the major life activity of working, other major life activities are considered as self-defined. However, the major life activity of working is defined by two factors:

- The jobs for which the individual can qualify as a result of training, abilities, and experience.
- The general availability of jobs within the geographical area that are reasonably accessible.

An individual who due to an impairment is unable to perform one particular job, but can perform many other common jobs, may **not** be considered substantially limited in the performance of working. On the contrary, an individual is substantially limited in working if the individual is significantly restricted in the ability to perform a class of jobs or a broad range of jobs in various classes, when compared with the ability of the average person with comparable qualifications to perform these same jobs.

Record of Impairment or Regarded as Having an Impairment

Employers are prohibited from discriminating on the basis of a prior record or history of disability. Additionally, disability protections apply to an individual being regarded as having a physical or mental impairment if the individual establishes that they have been subjected to an action prohibited under the ADA because of an actual or perceived physical or mental impairment whether or not the impairment limits or is perceived to limit a major life activity. Three different ways an individual may be regarded as having an impairment are as follows:

- An impairment exists that does not substantially limit a major life activity but is perceived by the employer as constituting a substantially limiting impairment.
- An impairment exists that substantially limits a major life activity only because of the attitudes of others toward the impairment.
- No impairment exists but the employer views the individual as having a substantially limiting impairment.

However, the protections against discrimination for being regarded as having an impairment do not apply to impairments that are transitory and minor. A ***transitory impairment*** is an impairment with an actual or expected duration of 6 months or less.

The important factor in determining disability discrimination is whether an employer perceived the individual as having a disability, whether or not the impairment limits or is perceived to limit a major life activity. An individual rejected from a job because of the myths, fears, and stereotypes associated with disabilities would be covered under the ADA, whether or not the employer's perception was shared by others in the field and whether or not the individual's actual physical or mental condition would be considered a disability.

Relationship with an Individual with a Disability

The ADA also prohibits discrimination based on the relationship an individual may have with a person with a disability. Protection is not limited to those who have a familial relationship with an individual with a disability.

This provision applies where an employer declines to hire an individual because of **any** of the following:

- The individual is related to or works with individuals with a disability.
- The employer fears it may be responsible for medical care costs through the dependency provisions of its insurance plan.

♦ The employer fears that the individual may be absent from work on a frequent basis.

♦ The employer fears that the individual may become infected with a serious disease.

Specific Conditions Under the ADA

Drug and Alcohol Use

Illegal use of drugs — whether controlled substances or prescription drugs — is not protected by the ADA regardless of whether employees are addicts or occasional users. Persons who are addicted to illegal drugs are protected if they are not current users. However, employers need not accommodate or tolerate either of the following:

♦ In-plant or in-office drug traffickers.

♦ Employees who currently engage in the illegal use of drugs or are under the influence of drugs at work.

Alternatively, current alcohol use may be protected by the ADA as alcohol addiction. Nevertheless, employers may require that employees not be under the influence of alcohol while at work and may discipline employees for poor work performance caused by alcohol use. Without a competent diagnosis of alcoholism, the disability laws do not prevent discipline based on use of alcohol, particularly when the alcohol use occurs during work hours or causes an impairment of work performance. A person's status as a drug addict or alcoholic should not be presumed merely from the fact that the person has used drugs or became intoxicated.

Other Conditions

The following conditions may or may not be protected by the ADA:

♦ **Obesity.** Weight within normal ranges is not a disability. Where morbid obesity results from physiological or psychological impairment, however, it may be symptomatic of a disability.

♦ **Pregnancy.** Pregnancy itself is not a disability, but an impairment that affects the ability of a woman to conceive or give birth may be a disability. The Supreme Court has stated that the ability to reproduce is a major life activity.

♦ **Mental Disorders.** If a condition is substantially limiting, severe, not temporary, and expected to create a long-term impact, then the condition is protected under the ADA.

♦ **Carpal Tunnel Syndrome.** Carpal tunnel syndrome, as well as all other musculo-skeletal conditions, such as lower back disorders, elbow joint pain, and shoulder and finger pain, require a competent diagnosis to be regarded as impairments subject to the disability laws. Whether carpal tunnel syndrome is a disability will also depend on the severity, expected duration, and extent of any permanent restrictions as compared with the individual's training, experience, and abilities for job opportunities.

When an Applicant or Employee Is Qualified

To be protected from discrimination under the ADA, an applicant or employee with a disability must be qualified to perform the essential functions or duties of the position, with or without reasonable accommodation.

Essential Functions of the Job

A qualified job applicant with a disability who can perform the essential functions of a job — with or without a reasonable accommodation — may not be denied the job based upon a disability. An applicant's inability to perform marginal job functions cannot be used to disqualify the applicant. In determining what functions are essential, an employer should consider whether current employees in the job perform those functions and whether the job would be fundamentally transformed if employees did not perform those functions.

A function is essential if **any** of the following apply:

- The job exists to accomplish the function.

- Only a limited number of employees can perform the function.

- The function is highly specialized and an employee is hired for their expertise in the area.

Before advertising or posting a job opening, an employer should determine the essential functions of the job. The ADA does not require an employer to develop written job descriptions. However, where provided, written job descriptions should be prepared before the job opening is advertised or posted. Moreover, the job descriptions should focus on the results or outcome of the essential functions of the job, rather than the usual methods of achieving those results and should be updated regularly.

Note: Apart from physical and intellectual essential functions, the ability to attend work on a regular basis, to adhere to safety rules and other reasonable regulations pertaining to the job, the ability to refrain from violence or excessive irascibility, and the ability to work in cooperation with other workers may be considered essential functions.

Employment Actions Affected by the ADA

Interviews, Applications, and Accessibility

The ADA protects job applicants from disability-related questions that could be used to screen out qualified individuals with disabilities and ensures that the application process is accessible to persons with disabilities.

An employer may not screen out individuals with a disability from the interview and application process by making those procedures inaccessible. Reasonable accommodations may be required to enable applicants with a disability to participate in pre-employment procedures.

Prohibited Questions

An employer is prohibited from inquiring about the disability of a prospective employee on application forms or during interviews.

Prohibited questions include those touching upon **any** of the following:

- Actual or perceived disabilities and the nature or severity of the disability of an applicant.

- Past medical history, workers' compensation history or hospitalization history

- Treatment for drug or alcohol addiction and treatment for psychiatric problems.

- The applicant's need for leave for treatment.

- The applicant's physical characteristics.

- Disabilities that may affect the applicant's ability to do the job or disabilities of the applicant's family members.

Permitted Questions

An employer is allowed to determine an applicant's ability to perform a job, including the ability to attend work on a regular basis.

Permitted questions include the following:

♦ Whether the applicant is able to perform the essential functions of the job and how such functions will be accomplished.

♦ Whether the applicant is able to perform each of a position's listed essential functions.

♦ Whether the applicant can meet described attendance requirements.

♦ Inquiries into the applicant's previous attendance history, as long as the questions do not refer to disabilities or illnesses.

Employers are prohibited from refusing to hire an applicant who cannot perform marginal job functions. Employers are not prohibited from discussing marginal job functions.

Selection Criteria

Job applicants with a disability and employees with a disability may not be segregated or classified in any manner that their job opportunities are adversely affected. An employer may not use tests or other criteria that tend to screen out the persons with a disability.

Tests must be job related and consistent with business necessity. An employer may not give tests to applicants with impaired sensory, manual, or speaking skills in a format requiring the use of those skills, unless the test is intended to measure such skills. Additionally, employers may not use qualification standards, employment tests, or other selection criteria based on a individual's uncorrected vision unless the standard, test, or other selection criteria, as used by the employer, is shown to be job-related for the position in question and consistent with business necessity.

An employer may not refuse to hire an applicant because the applicant is related to or associated with someone with a disability. This is true even if the employer believes that the applicant would often be absent to care for the person with a disability. If the applicant states that they can meet the employer's attendance requirements, then the employer cannot refuse to hire the applicant based on its beliefs to the contrary. However, an employer is not required to provide reasonable accommodations to those associated with someone with a disability. The ADA mandates reasonable accommodations only for individuals with a disability.

Medical Examinations

Under the ADA, an employer's ability to require medical examinations depends upon the phase of the employment relationship. An employer may not require a medical examination of an applicant before making a job offer. Once a job offer is extended, the offer may be made conditional upon the results of a medical examination if all employees in same job category have to undergo a medical examination. Information received during medical examinations should be treated as confidential, including keeping the records separate from employees' personnel files.

Exceptions to the confidentiality requirement exist under the ADA. For example, supervisors may be told of necessary restrictions and/or accommodations. First aid/safety personnel may be told if the individual with a disability may need treatment. Additionally, government officials investigating the employer's compliance with the ADA may have access to employees' medical information.

If a medical examination reveals a disability, a job offer cannot be withdrawn unless the following occurs:

♦ The reason is job related, consistent with business necessity, and no reasonable accommodation can be made.

♦ The disability would result in a direct threat, meaning a significant risk of substantial harm to the health and safety of other employees. A threat to one's own health (the applicant's) does not constitute a direct threat under the ADA.

An employer may not require current employees to undergo a medical examination or ask them if they have a disability, unless the examination is related to the business and consistent with a business need. An employer is not prohibited from conducting voluntary medical examinations as part of a health program. Additionally, if an employee initially provides insufficient information to substantiate that they have an ADA disability, an employer may require an employee to go to an appropriate health care professional of the employer's choice. If the employer exercises this option, the employer must pay for the examination costs.

Health and Safety Issues

The ADA does not prohibit an employer from enforcing health and safety standards in the workplace. An employer is not required to hire individuals who are unable to comply with legitimate health and safety standards or who pose direct threats to the health and safety of those in the workplace.

To determine whether an individual would pose a direct threat, employers must consider the following:

♦ The duration of the risk.

♦ The nature and severity of the risk.

♦ The likelihood that potential harm will occur.

♦ The imminence of the potential harm to others.

Therefore, an employer may not refuse to hire or discharge an employee with a disability because of a speculative, or even slightly increased, risk of harm to other employees. An employer's conclusion that an employee with a disability would pose a direct threat must be based upon objective, factual information. Moreover, the employer must be sure that a reasonable accommodation would not eliminate the risk or reduce it to an acceptable level.

During the Employment Relationship

An employer may not discriminate against employees with a disability in terms of insurance, advancement, performance appraisals, and the following:

♦ **Fringe benefits and training programs**. The same benefits and training program opportunities must be provided to employees with a disability as provided to other employees.

♦ **Leave policies.** However, leave granted outside the scope of the uniformed policy may be considered a reasonable accommodation.

♦ **Contractual relations.** Contractors who perform services for the company must comply with the ADA.

♦ **Discipline and discharge.** Employees with a disability are subject to the same standards for discipline and discharge.

Reasonable Accommodation

Employer Obligations

An employer must provide reasonable accommodation to known physical and mental limitations of qualified applicants and employees with disabilities, unless the accommodation would impose an undue hardship on the employer's business.

Employers are not expected to accommodate disabilities of which it is unaware. The employer must engage in an interactive process with the employee or applicant to determine what accommodation is necessary. However, an employer need not accommodate an applicant who is not otherwise qualified for the position. If an applicant does not meet the educational or skill requirements for the job then the employer is not required to reasonably accommodate. Additionally, the employer is not required to provide the exact accommodation requested by the employee because any accommodation that will effectively enable the employee to perform the job is sufficient.

A *reasonable accommodation* is a modification to a job, employment practice, or work environment that makes it possible for an applicant or employee with a disability to perform the functions of a job.

Examples include, but are not limited to, the following:

♦ Making facilities readily accessible to and usable by an individual with a disability.

♦ Restructuring a job by reallocating or redistributing marginal job functions.

♦ Altering when or how an essential job function is performed.

♦ Modifying work schedules.

♦ Allowing an employee to provide equipment or devices that an employer is not required to provide.

Employee Obligations

Generally, it is the responsibility of the individual with a disability to inform the employer when an accommodation is needed.

An applicant or employee with a disability who wants to be reasonably accommodated must:

♦ Make the need for an accommodation known to the employer, unless the need is obvious or the employer has good reason to know that accommodation may be required.

♦ Provide the employer with sufficient information about a disability and corresponding limitations to allow the employer to make a reasoned decision about whether an accommodation is necessary and/or helpful.

♦ Cooperate with the employer in determining the type of accommodation that is necessary and/or helpful.

Undue Hardship

An employer is not required to make an accommodation that would impose an undue hardship on the employer's business or other employees.

Undue hardship is an action that presents significant difficulty, disruption, or expense in relation to the size of the employer, its resources, and the nature of its operations or that would require violation of safety/health laws and regulations.

In determining whether an accommodation would impose an undue hardship on an employer, the following factors may be considered:

♦ Nature and net cost of the needed accommodation in relation to employer's type of operation, including the composition, structure, and functions of the workforce.

♦ Overall financial resources of the facility or facilities involved in the provision of the reasonable accommodation, the number of persons employed at such facility, and the effect on expenses and resources.

♦ Overall financial resources of the employer, overall size of the employer's business with respect to the number of employees, and the number, type, and location of the facilities.

♦ Impact of the accommodation upon the operation of the facility, including the impact on the ability of other employees to perform their duties and the impact on the facility's ability to conduct business.

Light-Duty and Temporary Positions

Many employers use light-duty and other temporary positions to bridge employees who are recovering from an occupational injury until they are released to full duty. However, employers are not required to create new light-duty positions as an accommodation. The employer may be required to offer such a position as a reasonable accommodation if light-duty positions exist or are created for occupationally injured employees.

The employer may designate light-duty positions for employees with a temporary disability temporarily and limit the length of time an employee may serve in the position. The employee may be removed from a light-duty position and placed on disability leave if the employee is unable to return to their original position after a designated amount of time. However, if employees with a permanent disability are removed from light-duty positions, the employer must be prepared to prove that the light-duty position was truly a temporary placement.

ADA Interaction with State Laws in Defining Disability

Employers are required to comply with the ADA, state, and local laws that provide similar or even greater protection to individuals with disabilities.

State laws may provide more or less extensive rights than the ADA in a number of respects, one of which is the scope of coverage.

Employers should become familiar with the disability discrimination laws in all states where they have operations, because state laws that provide more extensive protections than the ADA remain enforceable.

Workplace Violence

Employer concerns about workplace violence intersect with employee protections under the ADA when the violence results from a mental impairment. An employer that fails to take effective action to prevent such violence may be liable for resulting injuries. Additionally, failure to accommodate employees with mental disabilities may violate the ADA.

The ADA provides a way to resolve this conflict, but it is sometimes difficult to apply in practice. The ADA provides that an employer's obligation to reasonably accommodate employee disabilities does not require actions that pose a direct threat to the health and safety of others. Determinations of direct threat must be individualized and based on current medical and other objective evidence.

When an employee becomes violent in the workplace or engages in misconduct that suggests a significant risk of violence, the employer may take appropriate preventative action, including discharging the employee, despite the existence of a disability. An employer may discipline an employee with a disability for engaging in misconduct if it would impose the same discipline on an employee without a disability.

Waivers of Discrimination Claims in Employee Severance Agreements

Employee reductions and terminations have been an unfortunate result of the current economic downturn. An employer's decision to terminate or lay off certain employees, while retaining others, may lead discharged workers to believe that they were discriminated against based on their age, race, sex, national origin, religion, or disability. To minimize the risk of potential litigation, many employers offer departing employees money or benefits in exchange for a release (or waiver) of liability for all claims connected with the employment relationship, including discrimination claims under the civil rights laws enforced by the Equal Employment Opportunity Commission (EEOC), such as the Age Discrimination in Employment Act (ADEA), Title VII, the Americans with Disabilities Act (ADA), and the Equal Pay Act

(EPA). The EEOC has published significant guidance to assist employers in understanding waivers of discrimination claims in employee severance agreements.

Although most signed waivers are enforceable if they meet certain contract principles and statutory requirements, an employer **cannot** lawfully:

♦ Limit an employee's right to testify, assist, or participate in an investigation, hearing, or proceeding conducted by the EEOC.

♦ Prevent an employee from filing a charge of discrimination with the agency.

♦ Require an employee to return the money or benefits provided to the employee in exchange for waving their rights if the employee chooses to file a charge.

Severance Agreements and Release of Claims

A *severance agreement* is a contract, or legal agreement, between an employer and an employee that specifies the terms of an employment termination, such as a layoff. Sometimes this agreement is called a "separation agreement," "termination agreement," or "separation agreement general release and covenant not to sue." Like any contract, a severance agreement must be supported by consideration. *Consideration* is something of value to which a person is not already entitled that is given in exchange for an agreement to do, or refrain from doing, something.

The consideration offered for the waiver of the right to sue cannot simply be a pension benefit or payment for earned vacation or sick leave to which the employee is already entitled but, rather, must be something of value in addition to any of the employee's existing entitlements. An example of consideration would be a lump sum payment of a percentage of the employee's annual salary or periodic payments of the employee's salary for a specified period of time after termination. The employee's signature and retention of the consideration generally indicates acceptance of the terms of the agreement.

Recognizing the Severance Agreement

A severance agreement often is written like a contract or letter and generally includes a list of numbered paragraphs setting forth specific terms regarding the date of termination, severance payments, benefits, references, return of company property, and release of claims against the employer. Agreements that specifically cover the release of age claims must also include additional information intended to comply with OWBPA requirements.

Validity of Waivers

Most employees who sign waivers in severance agreements never attempt to challenge them. However, some discharged employees may feel that they have no choice but to sign the waiver, even though they suspect discrimination, or they may learn something after signing the waiver that leads them to believe they were discriminated against during employment or wrongfully terminated.

If an employee who signed a waiver later files a lawsuit alleging discrimination, the employer will argue that the court should dismiss the case because the employee waived the right to sue, and the employee will respond that the waiver should not be binding because it is legally invalid. However, before looking at the employee's discrimination claim, a court first will decide whether the waiver is valid. If a court concludes that the waiver is invalid, then the court will decide the employee's discrimination claim, but courts will dismiss a claim if the waiver is found to be valid.

A waiver in a severance agreement is generally valid when an employee knowingly and voluntarily consents to the waiver. The rules regarding whether a waiver is knowing and voluntary depend on the statute under which suit has been, or may be, brought. The rules for waivers under the ADEA are defined by statute — the OWBPA. Under other laws, such as Title VII, the rules are derived from case law.

In addition to being knowingly and voluntarily signed, a valid agreement also must:

♦ Offer some sort of consideration, such as additional compensation, in exchange for the employee's waiver of the right to sue.

♦ Not require the employee to waive future rights.

♦ Comply with applicable state and federal laws.

Knowing and Voluntary

To determine whether an employee knowingly and voluntarily waived their discrimination claims, some courts rely on traditional contract principles and focus primarily on whether the language in the waiver is clear. However, most courts look beyond the contract language and consider all relevant factors — or the totality of the circumstances — to determine whether the employee knowingly and voluntarily waived the right to sue. For example, when looking beyond the contract language courts will examine the following circumstances and conditions, under which the waiver was signed, to determine whether the employee knowingly and voluntarily waived the right to sue:

♦ Whether the waiver was written in a manner that was clear and specific enough for the employee to understand based on education and business experience.

♦ Whether the waiver was induced by fraud, duress, undue influence, or other improper conduct by the employer.

♦ Whether the employee had enough time to read and think about the advantages and disadvantages of the agreement before signing.

♦ Whether the employee consulted with an attorney or was encouraged or discouraged by the employer from doing so.

♦ Whether the employee had any input in negotiating the terms of the agreement.

♦ Whether the employer offered the employee consideration (for instance, severance pay or additional benefits) that exceeded what the employee already was entitled to by law or contract and the employee accepted the offered consideration.

Regardless of a signed waiver releasing an employer from all claims, employees may still file a charge with the EEOC if they believe they have been discriminated against based on age, race, sex, or disability. Although the severance agreement may use broad language to describe the claims that an employee is releasing, an employee may still file a charge with the EEOC if they believe they were discriminated against during employment or wrongfully terminated. Additionally, no agreement between an employee and an employer can limit an employee's right to testify, assist, or participate in an investigation, hearing, or proceeding conducted by the EEOC under the ADEA, Title VII, the ADA, or the EPA. Any provision in a waiver that attempts to waive these rights is invalid and unenforceable.

Filing Charges and Returning Severance Pay

Employees that file charges with the EEOC after signing a waiver are not required to return severance pay. Provisions in severance agreements that attempt to prevent employees from filing a charge with the EEOC or participating in an EEOC investigation, hearing, or proceeding are unenforceable, therefore employees are not required to return severance pay, or other consideration, before filing a charge. Moreover, according to the ADEA, an employee is not required to return severance pay, or other consideration received for signing the waiver before bringing an age discrimination claim. Under Title VII, the ADA, or the EPA, however, the law is less clear. Some courts conclude that the validity of the waiver cannot be challenged unless the employee returns the consideration, while other courts apply the

ADEA's "no tender back" rule to claims brought under Title VII and other discrimination statutes and allow employees to proceed with their claims without first returning the consideration.

Even if a court does not require an employee to return the consideration before proceeding with a lawsuit, the court may reduce the amount of any money an employee is awarded if the suit is successful by the amount of consideration the employee received for signing the waiver.

Waivers of ADEA Claims

General Requirements for Employees Age 40 and Over

In 1990, Congress amended the ADEA by adding the Older Workers Benefit Protection Act (OWBPA) to clarify the prohibitions against discrimination on the basis of age. The OWBPA establishes specific requirements for a knowing and voluntary release of ADEA claims to guarantee that an employee has every opportunity to make an informed choice whether or not to sign the waiver. There are additional disclosure requirements under the statute when waivers are requested from a group or class of employees.

Knowing and Voluntary

The OWBPA lists the following seven factors that **must** be satisfied for a waiver of age discrimination claims to be considered knowing and voluntary:

♦ **A waiver must be written in a manner that can be clearly understood.** EEOC regulations emphasize that waivers must be drafted in plain language that is geared to the level of comprehension and education of the average individual(s) eligible to participate. Usually this requires the elimination of technical jargon and long, complex sentences. In addition, the waiver must not have the effect of misleading, misinforming, or failing to inform participants and must present any advantages or disadvantages without either exaggerating the benefits or minimizing the limitations.

♦ **A waiver must specifically refer to rights or claims arising under the ADEA.** EEOC regulations specifically state that an OWBPA waiver must expressly spell out the ADEA by name.

♦ **A waiver must advise the employee in writing to consult an attorney before accepting the agreement.**

♦ **A waiver must provide the employee with at least 21 days to consider the offer.** The regulations clarify that the 21-day consideration period runs from the date of the employer's final offer. If material changes to the final offer are made, the 21-day period starts over.

♦ **A waiver must give employees seven days to revoke their signature.** The seven-day revocation period cannot be changed or waived by either party for any reason.

♦ **A waiver must not include rights and claims that may arise after the date on which the waiver is executed.** This provision bars waiving rights regarding new acts of discrimination that occur after the date of signing, such as a claim that an employer retaliated against a former employee who filed a charge with the EEOC by giving an unfavorable reference to a prospective employer.

♦ **A waiver must be supported by consideration in addition to that to which the employee already is entitled.**

If a waiver of age claims fails to meet any of these seven requirements, it is invalid and unenforceable. In addition, an employer cannot attempt to "cure" a defective waiver by issuing a subsequent letter containing OWBPA-required information that was omitted from the original agreement.

Additional Factors

Invalidating a Waiver of Age Claims. Even when a waiver complies with OWBPA's requirements, a waiver of age claims, like waivers of Title VII and other discrimination claims, will be invalid and unenforceable if an employer used fraud, undue influence, or other improper conduct to coerce the employee to sign, or if the waiver contains a material mistake, omission, or misstatement.

Compensation Issues. Although severance packages often are structured differently for different employees depending on position and tenure, an employer is not required to give employees who are age 40 or older a greater amount of consideration than is given to a person under the age of 40 solely because they are protected by the ADEA. Additionally, an employer may offset money paid to an employee in exchange for a waiver of age claim if the employee successfully challenges the waiver, proves age discrimination, and obtains a monetary award against the employer. However, the employer's recovery may not exceed the amount paid for the waiver or the amount of the employee's award if it is less.

Abrogation of Duties. According to EEOC regulations, an employer cannot abrogate its duties under an ADEA wavier, even if the employee challenges the waiver in court. Under OWBPA, employees are entitled to have a court determine a waiver's validity and it is unlawful for an employer to stop making promised severance payments or withhold any other benefits the employer agreed to provide.

Additional Requirements for Group Layoffs of Employees Age 40 and Over

When employers decide to reduce their workforce by laying off or terminating a group of employees, they usually do so pursuant to the following two types of programs:

♦ Exit incentive programs. An *exit incentive program* is a voluntary program where an employer offers two or more employees, such as older employees or those in specific organizational units or job functions, additional consideration to persuade them to voluntarily resign and sign a waiver.

♦ Other employment termination programs. *Other employment termination programs* generally refer to programs where two or more employees are involuntarily terminated and are offered additional consideration in return for their decision to sign a waiver.

Whether a program exists depends on the facts and circumstances of each case. However, the general rule is that a program exists if an employer offers additional consideration — or, an incentive to leave — in exchange for signing a waiver to more than one employee. By contrast, if a large employer terminated five employees in different units for cause (for instance, poor performance) over the course of several days or months, it is unlikely that a program exists. In both exit incentive and other termination programs, the employer determines the terms of the severance agreement, which typically are non-negotiable.

Additionally, when a waiver is offered to employees in connection with one of these types of programs, an employer must provide enough information about the factors it used in making selections to allow employees who were laid off to determine whether older employees were terminated while younger ones were retained.

Program and Additional Notification

Employers that lay off a group of employees (and ask those employees to sign a waiver of age claim) are required to provide all employees who are being terminated with written notice of the layoff and at least 45 days to consider the waiver before signing. Specifically, the employer must provide written notification regarding all of the following:

♦ The decisional unit. The *decisional unit* is the class, unit, or group of employees from which the employer chose the employees who were and who were not selected for the program. The particular circumstances of each termination program determine whether the decisional unit is the entire company, a division, a department, employees reporting to a particular manager, or workers in a specific job classification.

- Eligibility factors for the program.

- Time limits applicable to the program.

- Job titles and ages of all individuals who are eligible or who were selected for the program (the use of age bands broader than one year, such as "age 40-50," does not satisfy this requirement) and the ages of all individuals in the same job classifications or organizational unit who are not eligible or who were not selected.

Additionally, the wavier must meet the minimum OWBPA knowing and voluntary requirements.

Genetic Information Nondiscrimination Act

According to the Genetic Information Nondiscrimination Act (GINA), deciphering the sequence of the human genome and other advances in genetics opens major new opportunities for medical progress. However, these advances give rise to the potential misuse of genetic information to discriminate in health insurance and employment. For example:

- Congress was informed of examples of genetic discrimination in the workplace and therefore had a compelling public interest in relieving the fear of discrimination and in prohibiting its actual practice in employment and health insurance.

- Federal law addressing genetic discrimination in health insurance and employment is incomplete in both the scope and depth of its protections.

- Many states have enacted some type of genetic nondiscrimination law; however, these laws vary widely with respect to their approach, application, and level of protection.

- Congress has collected substantial evidence that the American public and the medical community find the existing patchwork of state and federal laws to be confusing and inadequate to protect them from discrimination.

Consequently, federal legislation establishing a national and uniform basic standard was necessary to fully protect the public from discrimination and allay their concerns about the potential for discrimination, thereby allowing individuals to take advantage of genetic testing, technologies, research, and new therapies.

GINA Coverage

Title I of GINA, which amends portions of the Employee Retirement Income Security Act (ERISA), the Public Health Service Act, and the Internal Revenue Code, addresses the use of genetic information in health insurance. Title I of GINA applies to group health plans sponsored by private employers, unions, and state and local government employers; issuers in the group and individual health insurance markets; and issuers of Medicare supplemental (Medigap) insurance.

Title I generally:

- Prohibits discrimination in group premiums or contribution amounts for any employer, or any group of similarly situated individuals under the plan, on the basis of genetic information and the use of genetic information as a basis for determining eligibility or setting premiums in the individual and Medigap insurance markets.

- Places limitations on genetic testing and the collection of genetic information in group health plan coverage, the individual insurance market, and the Medigap insurance market.

- Provides a clarification with respect to the treatment of genetic information under privacy regulations promulgated pursuant to the Health Insurance Portability and Accountability Act of 1996 (HIPAA).

Title II applies to private employers and state and local government employers with 15 or more employees, employment agencies, labor unions, and joint labor-management training programs. It also covers Congress and federal executive branch agencies. Title II of GINA:

- Prohibits use of genetic information in the employment context.

- Prohibits the intentional acquisition of genetic information about applicants and employees by employers and other entities covered by Title II.

- Strictly limits such entities from disclosing genetic information.

Genetic Nondiscrimination in Health Insurance

The genetic nondiscrimination in health insurance regulations are in connection with the following federal regulations:

- Employee Retirement Income Security Act (ERISA).

- HIPAA, in relation to the application of privacy and confidentiality of personal health information requirements.

- Internal Revenue Code (IRC).

- Public Health Service Act (PHSVC Act).

- Social Security Act (SSA).

Genetic information is, with respect to any individual, information about:

- An individual's genetic tests. A *genetic test* is an analysis of human DNA, RNA, chromosomes, proteins, or metabolites, which detects genotypes, mutation, or chromosomal changes. However, a genetic test **is not** an analysis of proteins or metabolites that is directly related to a manifested disease, disorder, or pathological condition. For instance, an HIV test, complete blood count, cholesterol test, liver function test, or test for the presence of alcohol or drugs is not a genetic test.

  A *manifestation* or *to be manifested* means, with respect to a disease, disorder, or pathological condition, that an individual has been or could reasonably be diagnosed with the disease, disorder, or pathological condition by a health care professional with appropriate training and expertise in the field of medicine involved. For instance, a disease, disorder, or pathological condition is not manifested if a diagnosis is based principally on genetic information.

- The genetic tests of family members of an individual. A *family member* is, with respect to any individual:

  - A dependent of the individual.

  - Any other individual who is a first-degree, second-degree, third-degree, or fourth-degree relative of the individual or of the individual's dependent. Relatives by affinity (such as by marriage or adoption) are treated the same as relatives by consanguinity (relatives who share a common biological ancestor). In determining the degree of the relationship, relatives by less than full consanguinity (such as half-siblings who share only one parent) are treated the same as relatives by full consanguinity (such as siblings who share both parents). Additionally, the following rules apply:

    - First-degree relatives include parents, spouses, siblings, and children.

    - Second-degree relatives include grandparents, grandchildren, aunts, uncles, nephews, and nieces.

    - Third-degree relatives include great-grandparents, great-grandchildren, great aunts, great uncles, and first cousins.

- Fourth-degree relatives include great-great grandparents, great-great grandchildren, and children of first cousins.

♦ The manifestation of a disease or disorder in family members of an individual.

♦ Any request for, or receipt of, genetic services or participation in clinical research, which includes genetic services by the individual or any family member of the individual. *Genetic services* are genetic tests, genetic counseling (including obtaining, interpreting, or assessing genetic information), or genetic education.

Any reference to genetic information concerning an individual or family member of an individual also:

♦ With respect to such an individual or family member of an individual who is a pregnant woman, includes genetic information of any fetus carried by such pregnant woman.

♦ With respect to an individual or family member utilizing an assisted reproductive technology, includes genetic information of any embryo legally held by the individual or family member.

Genetic information does **not** include information about the sex or age of any individual.

A group health plan, and a health insurance issuer offering group health insurance coverage in connection with a group health plan (hereafter generally referred to as a group health plan), may not adjust premium or contribution amounts for the group covered under the plan on the basis of genetic information.

However, a health insurance issuer offering health insurance coverage in connection with a group health plan is not limited in its ability to increase the premium for an employer based on the manifestation of a disease or disorder of an individual who is enrolled in the plan. In such case, the manifestation of a disease or disorder in one individual cannot also be used as genetic information about other group members and to further increase the premium for the employer.

Limits on Genetic Testing

A group health plan may not request or require an individual or a family member of such individual to undergo a genetic test. However, this limitation on genetic testing does **not**:

♦ Limit the authority of a health care professional who is providing health care services to an individual to request that such individual undergo a genetic test.

♦ Preclude a group health plan from obtaining and using the results of a genetic test in making a determination regarding payment. A group health plan may request only the minimum amount of information necessary to make a determination regarding payment.

Research Exception

A group health plan may request, but may not require, that a participant or beneficiary undergo a genetic test if all of the following conditions are met:

♦ The request is made, in writing, pursuant to research that complies with federal regulations, or equivalent federal regulations, and any applicable state or local law or regulations for the protection of human subjects in genetic research. *Inclusion of genetic services and participation in genetic research* includes, with respect to any individual, any request for, or receipt of, genetic services, or participation in clinical research which includes genetic services, by such individual or any family member of such individual.

♦ The plan or issuer clearly indicates to each participant or beneficiary (or in the case of a minor child, to the legal guardian of such beneficiary) to whom the request is made that compliance with the request is voluntary; and noncompliance will have no effect on enrollment status, premium amounts, or contribution amounts.

♦ No genetic information collected or acquired is used for underwriting purposes. *For underwriting purposes* means, with respect to any group health plan:

287

- Rules for, or determination of, eligibility (including enrollment and continued eligibility) for benefits under the plan or coverage (including changes in deductibles or other cost-sharing mechanisms in return for activities such as completing a health risk assessment or participating in a wellness program).

- The computation of premium or contribution amounts under the plan or coverage (including discounts, rebates, payments in kind, or other premium differential mechanisms in return for activities such as completing a health risk assessment or participating in a wellness program).

- The application of any pre-existing condition exclusion under the plan or coverage.

- Other activities related to the creation, renewal, or replacement of a contract of health insurance or health benefits.

If an individual seeks a benefit under a group health plan, the plan may limit or exclude the benefit based on whether the benefit is medically appropriate, and the determination of whether the benefit is medically appropriate is not within the meaning of underwriting purposes. Accordingly, if an individual seeks a benefit under the plan and the plan conditions the benefit based on its medical appropriateness and the medical appropriateness of the benefit depends on genetic information of the individual, then the plan is permitted to condition the benefit on the genetic information. A plan is permitted to request only the minimum amount of genetic information necessary to determine medical appropriateness. The plan may deny the benefit if the patient does not provide the genetic information required to determine medical appropriateness. If an individual is not seeking a benefit, the medical appropriateness exception to the definition of underwriting purposes does not apply.

- The plan or issuer notifies the U.S. Secretary of Health and Human Services in writing that the plan or issuer is conducting activities pursuant to the research exception, including a description of the activities conducted.

- The plan or issuer complies with such other conditions as the secretary may require for activities conducted under the research exception.

Collection of Genetic Information

A group health plan may not request, require, or purchase genetic information as follows:

- For underwriting purposes.

- With respect to any individual prior to the individual's enrollment under the plan or coverage in connection with enrollment. Whether or not an individual's information is collected prior to the effective date of coverage is determined at the time of collection.

However, if a group health plan obtains genetic information incidental to the requesting, requiring, or purchasing of other information concerning any individual, such request, requirement, or purchase is not a violation of the prohibition on the collection of genetic information prior to enrollment if the request, requirement, or purchase is also not for underwriting purposes. However, this incidental collection exception does not apply in connection with any collection where it is reasonable to anticipate that health information will be received, unless the collection explicitly states that genetic information should not be provided.

Penalties and Enforcement

The secretary may impose a penalty against any plan sponsor of a group health plan for any failure by such sponsor or issuer to meet the requirements of GINA with respect to genetic information in connection with the plan. The penalty for noncompliance is $100 for each day in the noncompliance period with respect to each participant or beneficiary to whom such failure relates.

A *noncompliance period* is, with respect to any failure, the period:

♦ Beginning on the date such failure first occurs.

♦ Ending on the date the failure is corrected.

In the case of one or more compliance failures with respect to a participant or beneficiary, that are not corrected before the date on which the plan receives a notice from the secretary of such violation and which occurred or continued during the period involved, the penalty will be at least $2,500 for each participant or beneficiary. Where a failure to comply continues for a year or more, the minimum penalty amount is $15,000 for each participant or beneficiary.

Limitations and Waiver

No penalty is imposed for any compliance failure during any period where it is established to the satisfaction of the secretary that the person otherwise liable for the penalty did not know, and exercising reasonable diligence would not have known, that such failure existed. Additionally, no penalty will be imposed on any failure if:

♦ Such failure was due to reasonable cause and not to willful neglect.

♦ Such failure is corrected during the 30-day period beginning on the first date the person otherwise liable for the penalty knew, or exercising reasonable diligence would have known, that such failure existed.

In the case of a failure to comply that is due to reasonable cause and not to willful neglect, the maximum penalty imposed for the failure is the lesser of the following:

♦ Ten percent of the aggregate amount paid or incurred by the plan sponsor (or predecessor plan sponsor) during the preceding taxable year for group health plans.

♦ $500,000.

Additionally, in the case of a failure to comply that is due to reasonable cause and not to willful neglect, the secretary may waive part or the entire penalty amount imposed to the extent that the payment of such penalty would be excessive relative to the failure involved.

HIPAA – Privacy and Confidentiality

According to 42 U.S.C.A. § 1320d-9, genetic information must be treated as protected health information per HIPAA.

Any of the following covered entities' use or disclosure of protected health information that is genetic information about an individual for underwriting purposes is not a permitted use or disclosure:

♦ Group health plan.

♦ Health insurance issuer that issues health insurance coverage.

♦ Issuer of a Medicare supplemental policy.

Employment Discrimination on the Basis of Genetic Information

According to Title II of GINA, the following are unlawful employment practices:

♦ Where an employer:

• Fails to hire, refuses to hire, or discharges any employee (or otherwise discriminates against any employee) with respect to the compensation, terms, conditions, or privileges of employment because of genetic information with respect to the employee.

- Limits, segregates, or classifies employees in any way that would deprive or tend to deprive any employee of employment opportunities or otherwise adversely affect the status of the employee as an employee because of genetic information with respect to the employee.

♦ Where an employment agency:

- Fails or refuses to refer for employment or otherwise discriminates against any individual because of genetic information with respect to the individual.

- Limits, segregates, or classifies individuals or fails or refuses to refer for employment any individual in any way that would deprive or tend to deprive any individual of employment opportunities or otherwise adversely affect the status of the individual as an employee because of genetic information with respect to the individual.

- Causes or attempts to cause an employer to discriminate against an individual in violation of GINA protections.

♦ Where a labor organization:

- Excludes or expels from the organization's membership or otherwise discriminates against any member because of genetic information with respect to the member.

- Limits, segregates, or classifies the members of the organization, or fails or refuses to refer for employment any member, in any way that would deprive or tend to deprive any member of employment opportunities, or otherwise adversely affects the status of the member as an employee, because of genetic information with respect to the member.

- Causes or attempts to cause an employer to discriminate against a member in violation of GINA protections.

♦ Where an employer, labor organization, joint labor-management committee controlling apprenticeship, or other training or retraining, including on-the-job programs:

- Discriminates against any individual because of genetic information with respect to the individual in admission to, or employment in, any program established to provide apprenticeship or other training or retraining.

- Limits, segregates, or classifies the applicants for or participants in an apprenticeship or other training or retraining, or fails or refuses to refer for employment any individual, in any way that would deprive or tend to deprive any individual of employment opportunities, or otherwise adversely affects the status of the individual as an employee, because of genetic information with respect to the individual.

- Causes or attempts to cause an employer to discriminate against an applicant for or a participant in an apprenticeship or other training or retraining in violation of GINA protections.

Exceptions

It is an unlawful employment practice for an employer, employment agency, labor organization, or joint labor-management committee (all of which are hereby referred to as an employment entity) to request, require, or purchase genetic information with respect to an individual or a family member of the individual, **except**:

♦ Where an employment entity inadvertently requests or requires family medical history of the individual or family member of the individual.

♦ Where the following occur:

- Health or genetic services are offered by the employment entity, including such services offered as part of a wellness program.

- The individual provides prior, knowing, voluntary, and written authorization.

- Only the individual (or family member if the family member is receiving genetic services) and the licensed health care professional or board certified genetic counselor involved in providing such services receive individually identifiable information concerning the results of such services.

- Any individually identifiable genetic information (provided to the individual and the licensed health care professional or board certified genetic counselor involved in providing such services in connection with health or genetic services offered by the employment entity) is only available for purposes of such services and may not be disclosed to the employment entity except in aggregate terms that do not disclose the identity of specific individuals.

♦ Where an employment entity requests or requires family medical history from the individual to comply with the certification provisions of the Family and Medical Leave Act (FMLA) or such requirements under state family and medical leave laws.

♦ Where an employment entity purchases documents that are commercially and publicly available (including newspapers, magazines, periodicals, and books, but not including medical databases or court records) that include family medical history.

♦ Where the information involved is to be used for genetic monitoring of the biological effects of toxic substances in the workplace, but only if:

- The employment entity provides written notice of the genetic monitoring to the individual.

- The individual provides prior, knowing, voluntary, and written authorization.

- The genetic monitoring is required by federal or state law.

- The individual is informed of individual monitoring results.

- The monitoring is in compliance with any federal genetic monitoring regulations, including any such regulations that may be promulgated by the Secretary of Labor pursuant to the Occupational Safety and Health Act (OSH Act), the federal Mine Safety and Health Act, the Atomic Energy Act, or state genetic monitoring regulations.

- The employment entity, excluding any licensed health care professional or board certified genetic counselor that is involved in the genetic monitoring program, receives the results of the monitoring only in aggregate terms that do not disclose the identity of specific individuals.

Confidentiality of Genetic Information

If an employment entity possesses genetic information about an employee or member, such information must be maintained on separate forms and in separate medical files and be treated as a confidential medical record of the employee or member.

An employment entity is considered to be in compliance with the maintenance of information requirements with respect to genetic information that is maintained with and treated as a confidential medical record under § 102(d)(3)(B) of the Americans with Disabilities Act (ADA) (42 U.S.C.A. § 12112(d)(3)(B)).

Disclosure Exceptions

An employment entity **may not** disclose genetic information concerning an employee or member, **except**:

♦ To the employee or member of a labor organization (or family member if the family member is receiving the genetic services) at the written request of such employee or member.

♦ To an occupational or other health researcher if the research is conducted in compliance with the regulations and protections provided for under 45 C.F.R. 46 (Protection of Human Research Subjects).

♦ In response to an order of a court, except that:

• The employment entity may disclose only the genetic information expressly authorized by such order.

• If the court order was secured without the knowledge of the employee or member to whom the information refers, the employment entity must inform the employee or member of the court order and any genetic information that was disclosed pursuant to such order.

♦ To government officials who are investigating compliance with GINA if the information is relevant to the investigation.

♦ To the extent that such disclosure is made in connection with the employee's compliance with the certification provisions of the FMLA or such requirements under state family and medical leave laws.

♦ To a federal, state, or local public health agency only with regard to specific information and that concerns a contagious disease that presents an imminent hazard of death or life threatening illness, and that the employee whose family member or family members is or are the subject of a disclosure is notified of such disclosure.

Note: With respect to the privacy and confidentiality regulations promulgated by the Secretary of Health and Human Services under the SSA and HIPAA, GINA does not prohibit a covered entity from any use or disclosure of health information that is authorized for the covered entity.

Prohibition Against Retaliation

No person may discriminate against any individual because:

♦ The individual opposed any act or practice made unlawful by GINA.

♦ The individual made a charge, testified, assisted, or participated in any manner in an investigation, proceeding, or hearing under GINA.

Note: The remedies and procedures otherwise provided for are available to aggrieved individuals with respect to violations of the prohibition against retaliation.

Additional Provisions

Disparate Impact

Disparate impact on the basis of genetic information does not establish a cause of action under GINA.

Medical Information that Is Not Genetic Information

An employment entity is not in violation of GINA based on the use, acquisition, or disclosure of medical information that is not genetic information about a manifested disease, disorder, or pathological condition of an employee or member, including a manifested disease, disorder, or pathological condition that has or may have a genetic basis.

Stipulations

GINA **does not**:

♦ Limit the rights or protections of an individual under any other federal or state statute that provides equal or greater protection to an individual than the rights or protections provided for under GINA, including the protections of an individual under the ADA or under the Rehabilitation Act of 1973.

♦ Limit the rights or protections of an individual to bring an action under GINA against an employment entity for a violation of GINA or provide for enforcement of, or penalties for violation of, any requirement or prohibition applicable to any employment entity subject to enforcement for a violation under:

  • The amendments made by Title I of GINA.

  • Applicable sections of ERISA, the PHSVC Act, and the Internal Revenue Code (IRC) with respect to genetic information and genetic information as a health status-related factor.

♦ Apply to the Armed Forces Repository of Specimen Samples for the Identification of Remains.

♦ Limit or expand the protections, rights, or obligations of employees or employers under applicable workers' compensation laws.

♦ Limit the authority of a federal department or agency to conduct or sponsor occupational or other health research that is conducted in compliance with the regulations contained in 45 C.F.R. 46 (or any corresponding or similar regulation or rule).

♦ Limit the statutory or regulatory authority of the Occupational Safety and Health Administration (OSHA) or the Mine Safety and Health Administration to promulgate or enforce workplace safety and health laws and regulations.

♦ Require any specific benefit for an employee, member, or a family member of an employee or member under any group health plan or health insurance issuer offering group health insurance coverage in connection with a group health plan.

GINA Frequently Asked Questions

Q Who must comply with Title II of GINA?

A Title II applies to private and state and local government employers with 15 or more employees, employment agencies, labor unions, and joint labor-management training programs. It also covers Congress and federal executive branch agencies. A *covered entity* refers collectively to all entities subject to Title II of GINA.

Q When are entities subject to Title II of GINA required to comply with the law?

A Title II of GINA became effective on November 21, 2009.

Q Why is GINA needed?

A GINA was enacted, in large part, in recognition of developments in the field of genetics, the decoding of the human genome, and advances in the field of genomic medicine. Genetic tests now exist that can inform individuals whether they may be at risk for developing a specific disease or disorder. However, just as the number of genetic tests increase, so do the concerns of the general public about whether they may be at risk of losing access to health coverage or employment if insurers or employers have their genetic information.

Congress enacted GINA to address these concerns by prohibiting discrimination based on genetic information and restricting acquisition and disclosure of such information, so that the general public would not fear adverse employment- or health coverage-related consequences for having a genetic test or participating in research studies that examine genetic information.

Q   What is genetic information?

A   The statute and the NPRM include a detailed description of what constitutes genetic information. For example, genetic information includes information about an individual's genetic tests, genetic tests of a family member, and family medical history. Genetic information does not include information about the sex or age of an individual or the individual's family members, or information that an individual currently has a disease or disorder. Genetic information also does not include tests for alcohol or drug use. The EEOC specifically invites public comment on other kinds of tests that covered entities may conduct and whether they should be considered genetic tests.

Q   What practices are prohibited by GINA Title II?

A   Title II of GINA prohibits use of genetic information in making decisions related to any terms, conditions, or privileges of employment, prohibits covered entities from intentionally acquiring genetic information, requires confidentiality with respect to genetic information (with limited exceptions), and prohibits retaliation.

Q   Are there any exceptions to the prohibition on use of genetic information?

A   No. This prohibition is absolute. Covered entities may not use genetic information in making employment decisions under any circumstances.

Q   Are there any exceptions to the general rule against acquisition of genetic information?

A   Yes. Although the general rule is that covered entities may not request, require, or purchase genetic information with respect to an employee/applicant or family member of an employee/applicant, there are exceptions.

One exception, sometimes referred to as the "water cooler" exception, applies to inadvertent acquisition of genetic information. This may occur, for example, where a supervisor overhears a conversation between co-workers in which genetic information is discussed or receives genetic information in response to a question about the general health of an employee or employee's family member, or where an employer receives genetic information as part of documentation an employee submits in support of a request for reasonable accommodation under the ADA or other similar law. Other exceptions are described in the statute and the NPRM.

Q   What are GINA's rules on confidentiality?

A   Covered entities in possession of genetic information about applicants or employees must treat it the same way they treat medical information generally. They must keep the information confidential and, if the information is in writing, must keep it apart from other personnel information in separate medical files. A covered entity may keep genetic information in the same file as medical information subject to the ADA.

There are limited exceptions to GINA's prohibition on disclosure of genetic information, which are described in detail in the statute and NPRM.

Q   Are disparate impact claims permitted under Title II of GINA?

A   No. However, GINA directs that a commission be formed six years after enactment to report on the possibility of allowing disparate impact claims.

Q Does Title II of GINA prohibit harassment?

A Title II of GINA does not directly address the issue of harassment claims. However, in describing the prohibited practices under Title II, Congress adopted language similar to that used in Title VII of the Civil Rights Act of 1964 and other equal employment opportunity statutes, evincing its intent to prohibit discrimination with respect to a wide range of practices, including harassment.

Q Does Title II of GINA apply to employment decisions based on health benefits?

A To some extent, yes. However, Title II of GINA includes a "firewall" provision intended to eliminate "double liability" by preventing claims under Title II from being asserted regarding matters subject to enforcement under Title I of GINA or the other genetics provisions for group coverage in ERISA, the Public Health Service Act, and the Internal Revenue Code. The firewall seeks to ensure that health plan or issuer requirements or prohibitions are addressed and remedied through ERISA, the Public Health Service Act, or the Internal Revenue Code and not through Title II and other employment discrimination procedures.

The firewall does not provide immunity to covered entities from liability for decisions and actions taken that violate Title II, including employment decisions based on health benefits, because such benefits are within the definition of compensation, terms, conditions, or privileges of employment. For example, an employer that fires an employee because of anticipated high health claims based on genetic information remains subject to liability under Title II.

Alternatively, acts or omissions relating to health plan eligibility, benefits, or premiums, or a health plan's request for or collection of genetic information remain subject to enforcement under Title I of GINA exclusively.

Q What effect does Title II of GINA have on other laws addressing genetic discrimination in employment?

A Title II of GINA does not preempt any state or local law that provides equal or greater protections from employment discrimination on the basis of genetic information or improper access or disclosure of genetic information. Additionally, Title II of GINA does not limit the rights or protections under federal, state, local, or tribal laws that provide greater privacy protection to genetic information, and does not affect an individual's rights under the ADA, the Rehabilitation Act, or state or local laws that prohibit discrimination on the basis of disability.

However, Title II of GINA does limit an employer's ability to obtain genetic information after making a job offer. Although the ADA currently permits a covered entity to obtain family medical history or conduct genetic tests of job applicants once an offer of employment has been made, provided this is done for all entering employees in the same job category, such action will be prohibited upon the effective date of GINA.

Q What are the remedies for a violation of GINA Title II?

A The same remedies available under Title VII are available under Title II of GINA. An aggrieved individual may seek reinstatement, hiring, promotion, backpay, injunctive relief, pecuniary and nonpecuniary damages (including compensatory and punitive damages), and attorneys' fees and costs. Title VII's cap on combined compensatory and punitive damages also applies to actions under Title II of GINA. The cap on combined compensatory and punitive damages (excluding past monetary losses) ranges from $50,000 for employers with 15-100 employees to $300,000 for employers with more than 500 employees. Punitive damages are not available against federal, state, or local government employers.

Enforcement

The EEOC enforces federal antidiscrimination laws. Before instituting any action, the EEOC will attempt to eliminate the discriminatory or alleged discriminatory practices, and to effect voluntary compliance with legal requirements through informal methods of conciliation, conference, and persuasion.

Charges may be filed in person, by mail, or by telephone by contacting the nearest EEOC office.

Discrimination Complaint Procedure

Title VII of the Civil Rights Act

Charges brought under Title VII must be filed with the EEOC within 180 days of the alleged discriminatory act. However, in states or localities with antidiscrimination regulations, a charge must be presented to the appropriate state or local agency. In such jurisdictions, charges may be filed with the EEOC within 300 days of the discriminatory act or 30 days after receiving notice that the corresponding agency has stopped processing the charge — whichever is earlier.

Note: It is best to promptly contact the EEOC when discrimination is suspected, to avoid missing required deadlines.

The Lilly Ledbetter Fair Pay Act

Under the recently passed Lilly Ledbetter Fair Pay Act of 2009 (LLFPA), an unlawful employment practice occurs, with respect to discrimination in compensation, when any of the following occurs:

- ◆ A discriminatory compensation decision or other practice is adopted.

- ◆ A person becomes subject to a discriminatory compensation decision or other practice.

- ◆ A person is affected by application of a discriminatory compensation decision or other practice, including each time wages, benefits, or other compensation is paid, resulting in whole or in part from such a decision or other practice.

In addition, the LLFPA establishes a "paycheck accrual" rule specifying that discriminatory pay decisions or other discriminatory practices that start the 180-day time period (or 300-day period if applicable) for filing a charge of discrimination with the EEOC occur each time a discriminatory paycheck is issued. As long as employees file their charges within 180 days of a discriminatory paycheck, their charges would be considered timely. Therefore, once an employee files a charge, they need not file new charges with each new paycheck.

Americans with Disabilities Act

The time requirements for filing a charge under the Americans with Disabilities Act (ADA) are the same as those for Title VII charges.

Age Discrimination in Employment Act

As with the ADA, the ADEA time requirements for filing a charge are the same as those for Title VII charges.

Equal Pay Act

Individuals are not required to file an Equal Pay Act (EPA) charge with the EEOC before filing a private lawsuit. Charges may be filed with the EEOC and some cases of wage discrimination may also be violations of Title VII.

The procedure for filing an EPA charge with the EEOC is the same as for charges brought under Title VII. Importantly, as soon as an individual becomes aware that the EPA may have been violated, charges should be filed because the time limits for filing in court are different under the EPA.

EEOC Investigations

After its investigation, the EEOC determines whether there is probable cause to support the charge of discrimination.

The following are the possible results of an EEOC investigation:

- ◆ The EEOC may find probable cause. In this case, the EEOC will attempt to conciliate the charge and reach a voluntary agreement with the employer to remedy the discrimination. If conciliation is unsuccessful, the EEOC must either sue in federal court or issue a right-to-sue letter allowing the individual to sue the employer in federal court.

- ◆ The EEOC may seek to settle a charge at any stage of the investigation if the charging party and the employer express an interest in conciliation.

  Note: The investigation continues if settlement efforts are unsuccessful.

- ◆ If the EEOC finds no probable cause, it will dismiss the charge and issue a right-to-sue letter allowing the employee to sue the employer in court.

- ◆ Although the EEOC may not have completed the investigation, under Title VII and the ADA an employee may request a right-to-sue letter 180 days after the charge was first filed. The employee may then bring suit within 90 days after receiving this notice.

- ◆ Under the ADEA, a suit may be filed 60 days after filing a charge with the EEOC, but no later than 90 days after the EEOC gives notice that it has completed action on the charge.

- ◆ Under the EPA, a lawsuit must be filed within two years (three years for willful violations) of the discriminatory act.

After receiving a right-to-sue letter, the employee has 90 days in which to file a lawsuit. In some instances, the employee may request a jury trial thereby creating more liability risk for employers.

Remedies

Employees who win their discrimination suits are entitled to various remedies, including the following:

- ◆ Compensatory and punitive damages.
- ◆ Backpay and benefits.
- ◆ Being hired, reinstated, promoted, or upgraded.
- ◆ Front pay (in cases where the employee is not reinstated).
- ◆ Liquidated damages if the discrimination was intentional (under the EPA or the ADEA).
- ◆ Reasonable accommodation.
- ◆ Interest on back wages.
- ◆ Attorneys' fees and costs.
- ◆ Court costs.
- ◆ Cease and desist orders.
- ◆ Affirmative action by the employer to correct discriminatory practices.
- ◆ Posting of compliance notices.

Damage Caps

Compensatory and punitive damages available under the Civil Rights Act are limited by the size of the employer, as follows:

- ♦ $50,000 for employers with between 15 and 100 employees.

- ♦ $100,000 for employers with between 101 and 200 employees.

- ♦ $200,000 for employers with between 201 and 500 employees.

- ♦ $300,000 for employers with more than 500 employees.

Damage caps are applied to each aggrieved individual. For example, where the EEOC files suit on behalf of 10 complaining parties, against an employer who has 1,000 employees, each complaining party may receive (to the extent appropriate) up to $300,000. Thus, the respondent's total liability for all 10 complaining parties may be up to $3,000,000.

Employer Defenses Against Discrimination Charges

The best defense employers have against discrimination claims is to show that there is a legitimate business reason for taking the disputed employment action. In fact, in some cases a legitimate business reason defense is valid even when there has been intentional discriminatory treatment of a protected group or when employment practices had an adverse impact on members of a protected group.

Examples of valid defenses of this type include the following:

- ♦ **Bona Fide Occupational Qualifications (BFOQs).** BFOQs are a defense against charges of disparate treatment in selection cases by showing that the selection criteria are BFOQs. Employers are not liable for intentional discrimination on the basis of sex, religion, national origin, or age if the discrimination is the result of a BFOQ. A BFOQ is a specific job requirement for a particular position reasonably necessary to the normal operation of the business. For example, sex-based BFOQs may be recognized for some attendant jobs in prisons or mental institutions. Yet, sex-based BFOQs have been rejected as a hiring basis for nursing home aides.

- ♦ **Business Necessity.** Employers may defend against disparate-impact claims on the basis that the practice that led to the discriminatory impact was job related and consistent with business necessity. This protection will not work, however, if an employer knows of but does not use a different available practice that would accomplish the same result without being discriminatory. Importantly, the business necessity defense is not valid where discrimination is based on race or the discrimination is intentional.

- ♦ **Bona Fide Seniority or Merit Systems.** Title VII permits employment practices based upon a legitimate seniority or merit system even if the practice adversely affects members of a protected group. The purpose of the practice must be to reward employees for such things as longevity or merit, not to discriminate. For example, a seniority system that protects senior employees in the event of layoffs at the expense of employees from protected groups may be a bona fide seniority system. However, the system cannot be designed to evade the effects of antidiscrimination laws.

In all cases, defenses against discrimination claims must be supported by appropriate documentation. Documentation may demonstrate that an employment action, on which a claim of discriminatory or disparate treatment was based, was taken for a legitimate business reason and not a pretext for discrimination.

In discriminatory impact cases, the employee must demonstrate that race, color, religion, sex, age, or national origin was a motivating factor for the challenged employment practice. In disparate impact claims, it need not be proven that the discrimination was intentional, just that it occurred. In such claims, the employee must prove disparate impact by producing relevant evidence showing the challenged employment practice causes a disparate impact.

Defenses Against Sexual Harassment Claims

Because of the serious implications of sexual harassment claims, employers would be wise to follow the EEOC's suggested procedures for avoiding sexual harassment in the workplace.

The following suggestions will help an employer comply with EEOC guidelines for avoiding charges of sexual harassment and will also help an employer avoid charges of any form of harassment in the workplace:

- Develop, implement, publicize, and distribute an antiharassment policy. This policy should do the following:

  - Prohibit any form of harassment in the workplace, especially sexual harassment.

  - Encourage employees to report any unwelcome sexual conduct or other forms of sexual harassment or other harassment.

  - Specify clear ways for employees to voice complaints — ideally to someone other than their immediate supervisors — about possible harassment.

  - Assure employees of a prompt and effective investigation.

  - Assure employees that retaliation for voicing a complaint will not be tolerated.

- Educate and sensitize the workforce about the following sexual harassment issues:

  - Remind employees about the antiharassment policy.

  - Advise employees that those who violate the antiharassment policy will be subject to corrective action.

  - Warn employees that certain kinds of conduct (such as jokes or touching) may be viewed as harassment.

  - Train supervisors to recognize and respond to observed problems and to handle harassment complaints properly.

- Develop and implement a fair and effective procedure for thoroughly investigating all complaints of harassment. Assign responsibility for investigating harassment complaints to individuals who are trained to be objective, thorough, and sensitive to the concerns of the victim, the alleged harasser, and the witnesses.

- Prompt and adequate investigations are critical in preventing or minimizing liability for harassment. Various interests must be considered as follows:

  - The interest of the complainant in not having to endure unwelcome conduct at work.

  - The interest of the alleged harasser in not losing a job or reputation on the basis of an accusation that turns out to be mistaken, false, or trivial.

  - The interest of other employees who may have witnessed harassment or may be exposed to harassment in the future.

- Follow these guidelines for investigating a harassment complaint:

  - **Interview the Complainant.** After reassuring the complainant of protection for reporting the harassment, the company's commitment to take appropriate action, and the company's intention to maintain confidentiality as much as possible, the investigator should obtain from the complainant the following information:

- A complete description of all offensive conduct.

- A list of all potential witnesses.

- A detailed chronology of incidents.

- Any allegations of retaliatory conduct by the alleged harasser.

- **Interview the Alleged Harasser.** Employers should inform the alleged harasser of the company's duty to investigate and the alleged harasser's corresponding duty to cooperate fully and truthfully with the investigation. The alleged harasser should be warned against retaliation. The alleged harasser may also be entitled to have a co-worker present during the interview if a proper request is made, and the employee has reason to believe that the investigative interview may result in discipline. The investigation should obtain the following:

  - A detailed response to each charge.

  - Information on whether the complainant may have had a motive to fabricate or exaggerate charges.

- **Interview the Witnesses.** Employers should question potential witnesses without identifying the complainant or the alleged harasser except to the extent necessary to frame an understandable inquiry. The witnesses should be reminded of the need to keep the investigation confidential.

- **Conclude the Investigation.** When the investigation is complete, the employer should reach one of the following three conclusions:

  - **Misconduct Occurred.** In these cases, employers must ensure that any discipline imposed is severe enough to satisfy the legal duty to take effective remedial action. The employer must also consider the harasser's rights under any employment contract, employment discrimination statute, or common law principles that protect privacy and reputations. It is often possible to conclude that the company's antiharassment policy has been violated and that discipline is appropriate without concluding that unlawful harassment has occurred. Many companies forbid, for example, even isolated or ambiguous conduct that may give the appearance of unlawful harassment.

  - **Misconduct Did Not Occur.** In cases where the investigator concludes that no harassment occurred — because the alleged incident did not occur, the allegedly unwelcome incidents were actually welcome, or the incidents were actually harmless and could not reasonably be interpreted as harassment — the parties should still be informed of the results of the investigation. The complainant and the alleged harasser should be reminded of the importance of keeping the investigation confidential and about the company's policy against retaliation for reporting harassment.

  - **Results are Inconclusive.** There is insufficient evidence to reach a conclusion. In such cases, both parties should be told of the results, why no conclusion could be reached, and be reminded of the company's no-retaliation policy.

  In all cases, the employer should reinforce the prohibition of harassment with all involved.

- Take the following prompt remedial action when necessary:

  - Determine what corrective action is necessary, if any, to end the harassing conduct.

  - Discipline the harasser as appropriate.

- Report results of the investigation to the complainant, including steps taken to prevent further harassment, if applicable.

- Assure the complainant that no retaliation for making the complaint will be tolerated.

♦ Follow up on the investigation to prevent retaliation.

♦ Document all steps taken in response to the complaint.

Recordkeeping Requirements

Employers covered by federal antidiscrimination laws must keep for at least one year from the date they were made, personnel and employment records concerning the following:

♦ Hiring.

♦ Promotions.

♦ Demotions.

♦ Transfers.

♦ Layoffs.

♦ Terminations.

♦ Rates of pay.

♦ Selections for training and apprenticeship programs.

Covered employers are generally advised to keep such records for six years or more.

If an employee is involuntarily terminated, the personnel records must be retained for one year from the date of termination.

Age Discrimination in Employment Act

Under the Age Discrimination in Employment Act (ADEA) recordkeeping requirements, employers must keep all payroll records for a minimum of three years.

Additionally, employers must keep on file any employee benefit plan (such as pension and insurance plans) and any written seniority or merit system for the full period that the plan or system is in effect and for at least one year after its termination.

Fair Labor Standards Act

Under the Fair Labor Standards Act (FLSA) recordkeeping requirements applicable to the EPA, employers must keep payroll records for at least three years.

In addition, employers must keep for a minimum of two years all records (including, but not limited to, wage rates, job evaluations, seniority and merit systems, and collective-bargaining agreements) that explain the basis for paying different wages to employees of opposite sexes in the same establishment.

Federal Antidiscrimination Laws

Regardless of whether a charge has been filed against an employer, these requirements apply to all employers covered by federal antidiscrimination laws.

When a charge has been filed, employers have additional recordkeeping obligations. Further recordkeeping requirements are listed in the **Posting and Recordkeeping Requirements** chapter.

Note: Discrimination and retaliation issues arising under other than EEO statutes are addressed in chapters dealing with those laws.

Reporting Requirements
EEO-1

The EEOC requires all employers with 100 or more employees, private employers with fewer than 100 employees who are owned by or affiliated with another company to make up an enterprise totaling 100 or more employees, and all federal contractors with 50 or more employees that have federal contracts totaling at least $50,000 to annually file an *Employer Information Report* known as the EEO-1. This report must include statistical information about the number of minority-group employees in the total workforce.

Employers must keep the latest copy of the report and make it available to an EEOC representative upon request.

Method of Filing

The preferred method for completing the EEO-1 reports is the Web-based filing system. Online filing requires the employer to log into their company's database with a login ID and password. All companies should have received EEO-1 filing materials by mail no later than mid-August 2010. Employers that cannot locate their login ID and/or password may contact the EEO-1 Joint Reporting Committee at e1.techassistance@eeoc.gov.

The EEOC offers the following additional information regarding online filing:

- **No Installation:** The online form is totally Web based. There is no software to download or install.

- **Data Reuse:** As much as possible, information is pre-filled from the previous year to speed up data entry.

- **Secure:** Data is transferred over the Internet using encryption, assuring privacy.

- **Historical Access:** Employers can access up to 10 years worth of EEO-1 data for their establishments.

Note: The EEOC also offers EEO-1 online filing procedures for Type 6 and Type 8 Records.

EEO-4, EEO-5, and EEO-6

Public employers with more than 15 employees must file an EEO-4 annually. Public school systems or districts must file an EEO-5 biannually. All public or private institutions of higher learning must file an EEO-6 biannually. Lastly, the requirements for the EEO-4, EEO-5, and EEO-6 are similar to those for EEO-1.

EEO-1 Frequently Asked Questions

Q **What is the EEO-1 report?**

A The EEO-1 report (*Employer Information Report*) is a government form requiring many employers to provide a count of their employees by job category and then by ethnicity, race, and gender. The EEO-1 report is submitted to both the EEOC and the Department of Labor, Office of Federal Contract Compliance Programs (OFCCP).

Q **Who is required to file the EEO-1 report?**

A All employers with 100 or more employees, or all federal government contractors and first-tier subcontractors with 50 or more employees and a contract amounting to $50,000 or more.

Q **When must the EEO-1 report be filed?**

A   The EEO-1 report must be filed annually with the EEOC by September 30. It must use employment numbers from any pay period in July through September of that year.

Q   **How can a login ID and password be confirmed?**

A   Employers that cannot locate their login ID and password may contact the EEO-1 Joint Reporting Committee by calling 866-286-6440, sending a fax to 202-663-7185, or by email to e1.techassistance@eeoc.gov.

Q   **Where should copies of the completed EEO-1 report be sent?**

A   If an employer files online, there is no need to send anything to the EEOC. If an employer uses paper forms (by request only), then the company must mail the signed, original report to the EEO-1 Joint Reporting Committee. Employers should retain a copy of the EEO-1 report for their files.

Q   **What is a company's EEO-1 identification number?**

A   The number printed on the 'Company Name and Address' sheet or the EEO-1 form as CO=XXXXXXX is the unique identification number assigned to the company. The number indicated in a company's database located in the EEO-1 Online Filing System or printed on an EEO-1 form as U=XXXXXXX is the unique identification number for a company establishment. The Unit Number never changes for an establishment. Company Number and Unit Number are used together to identify an establishment within a company.

Q   **If a company merged with another entity, then how should the EEO-1 report be completed?**

A   The EEO-1 Joint Reporting Committee should be contacted and provided with the name and address of the new parent company.

Q   **Does the EEO-1 report require data about job applicants?**

A   No. The EEO-1 report only requires data by race/ethnicity, gender, and job categories of employees.

Q   **For the paper EEO-1 form and EEO-1 data file, what general quick check can be made for accuracy of reported employment?**

A   For single-establishment companies: The sum on Line 10, Column A, Section D – Employment Data, must equal the sum of Line 10 for Columns B-K.

Multi-establishment companies: The total sums indicated on the Headquarters Report, Establishment Report(s), and/or Establishment List (locations employing fewer than 50 employees) must equal the employment sums indicated on the Consolidated Report or EEOC Form 352B.

Q   **Are first-level supervisors, such as supervisors of typing pools, maintenance crews, or others, classified as 'Officials and Managers'?**

A   No. First level supervisors who regularly join employees under their supervision to do the work itself, must be classified along with those employees they supervise.

Q   **How can EEOC-approved specifications for EEO-1 alternate reporting format (such as a data file), a sample copy of the EEO-1 form, instructions, and the *EEO-1 Job Classification Guide* be obtained?**

A Each of these documents may be printed from the following Web site: *www.eeoc.gov/eeo1survey.*

Q **May employment data from any payroll period during the current survey year be used?**

A No. Employment data must be used from one payroll period during the third quarter (July, August, or September) of the current survey year.

Q **How do employers file EEO-1 reports?**

A The EEOC strongly recommends that EEO-1 reports be submitted through the EEO-1 Online Filing System or as an electronically transmitted data file. Paper EEO-1 forms will be generated on request only and only in extreme cases where Internet access is not available to the employer. Instructions on how to file are available on the EEOC's Web site at *www.eeoc.gov/eeo1survey/howtofile.html.*

Q **Is EEO-1 data confidential?**

A Yes. The EEOC is required by law to keep individual employer EEO-1 reports strictly confidential (42 U.S.C. 2000e-8(e)).

Q **What do the EEOC and the Office of Federal Contract Compliance Programs (OFCCP) do with the EEO-1 survey data?**

A Both the EEOC and OFCCP have used the EEO-1 since 1966.

The EEOC uses the data to support civil rights enforcement. The EEOC also uses the data to analyze employment patterns, such as the representation of female and minority workers within companies, industries, or regions.

The OFCCP uses EEO-1 data to determine which employer facilities to select for compliance evaluations. The OFCCP's system uses statistical assessment of EEO-1 data to select facilities where the likelihood of systematic discrimination is the greatest.

Q **Where can employers find more information about the EEO-1?**

A General information about the EEO-1 can be found at the EEOC's Web site at *www.eeoc.gov/eeo1survey/index.html.*

Contact Information

Equal Employment Opportunity Commission

131 M Street, NE
Washington, DC 20507

Telephone: 202-663-4900
Toll-Free: 800-669-4000
Internet: *www.eeoc.gov*

EEOC Publications Distribution Center

P.O. Box 12546
Cincinnati, OH 45212

Telephone (Toll-Free): 800-669-3362
Fax: 513-489-8692

Illinois Law

The Illinois Human Rights Act

The Illinois Human Rights Act is located at 775 Ill. Comp. Stat. §§ 5/1-101 et seq. The goal of the Human Rights Act is as follows:

♦ To secure for all individuals within Illinois the freedom from discrimination against any individual because of the individual's race, color, religion, sex, national origin, ancestry, age, order of protection status, marital status, physical or mental disability, military status, sexual orientation, or unfavorable discharge from military service in connection with employment, real estate transactions, access to financial credit, and the availability of public accommodations.

♦ To prevent sexual harassment in employment and sexual harassment in higher education.

♦ To prevent discrimination based on citizenship status in employment.

♦ To prevent discrimination based on familial status in real estate transactions.

♦ To promote public health, welfare, and safety by protecting the interest of all people in Illinois in maintaining personal dignity, in realizing their full productive capacities, and in furthering their interests, rights, and privileges as citizens of the state.

♦ To secure and guarantee the rights established by the Illinois Constitution.

♦ To establish equal opportunity and affirmative action as the policies of Illinois in all of its decisions, programs, and activities, and to assure that all state departments, boards, commissions, and instrumentalities rigorously take affirmative action to provide equality of opportunity and eliminate the effects of past discrimination in the internal affairs of state government and in their relations with the public.

♦ To protect citizens of Illinois against unfounded charges of unlawful discrimination, sexual harassment in employment, sexual harassment in higher education, and discrimination based on citizenship status in employment.

Covered Employers

The Illinois Human Rights Act covers the following:

♦ Persons employing 15 or more employees within Illinois during 20 or more calendar weeks within the current or preceding calendar year.

♦ Persons employing one or more employees when a complaint alleges unlawful discrimination based upon physical or mental disability unrelated to ability or sexual harassment.

♦ The state and any political subdivision, municipal corporation, or other governmental unit or agency, without regard to the number of employees.

♦ Parties to a public contract without regard to the number of employees.

♦ Joint apprenticeship or training committees without regard to the number of employees.

The act **does not** cover any of the following that rely upon treatment by prayer through spiritual means in accordance with the tenets of a recognized church or religious denomination for the employment of individuals of a particular religion to perform its work activities:

♦ Religious corporation.

♦ Association.

♦ Educational institution.

♦ Society.

♦ Nonprofit nursing institution.

Covered Employees

The Illinois Human Rights Act protects the following:

♦ Any individual performing services for remuneration within Illinois for an employer.

♦ An apprentice.

♦ An applicant for any apprenticeship.

However, the act **does not** cover any of the following:

♦ Domestic servants in private homes.

♦ Individuals employed by persons who are not covered employers as previously listed.

♦ Elected public officials or the members of their immediate personal staffs.

♦ Principal administrative officers of the state or of any political subdivision, municipal corporation, or other governmental unit or agency.

♦ A person in a vocational rehabilitation facility certified under federal law who has been designated as an evaluee, trainee, or work activity client.

Definitions

As used in the provisions related to employment in the Human Rights Act:

♦ *Citizenship status* means the status of being:

- A born U.S. citizen.

- A naturalized U.S. citizen.

- A U.S. national.

- A person born outside the United States and not a U.S. citizen who is not an unauthorized alien and who is protected from discrimination under 8 U.S.C. § 1324b.

♦ *Disability* means a determinable physical or mental characteristic of a person, including, but not limited to:

- A determinable physical characteristic which necessitates the person's use of a guide, hearing, or support dog.

- The history of such characteristic.

- The perception of such characteristic by the person complained against, which may result from disease, injury, congenital condition of birth or functional disorder.

♦ *Military status* means a person's status:

- On active duty in the U.S. Armed Forces.

- As a veteran of the U.S. Armed Forces.

- As a current member or veteran of any reserve component of the U.S. Armed Forces.

♦ *National origin* means the place in which a person or one of the person's ancestors was born.

♦ ***Order of protection status*** means a person's status as being a person protected under an order of protection issued pursuant to the Illinois Domestic Violence Act of 1986 or an order of protection issued by a court of another state.

♦ ***Religion*** includes all aspects of religious observance and practice, as well as belief, unless an employer demonstrates that the employer is unable to reasonably accommodate an employee's or prospective employee's religious observance or practice without undue hardship on the conduct of the employer's business.

♦ ***Sexual harassment*** means any unwelcome sexual advances or request for sexual favors or any conduct of a sexual nature when:

  • Submission to such conduct is made either explicitly or implicitly as a term or condition for an individual's employment.

  • Submission to or rejection of such conduct by an individual is used as the basis for employment decisions affecting such individual.

  • Such conduct has the purpose or effect of substantially interfering with an individual's work performance or creating an intimidating, hostile, or offensive work environment.

♦ ***Sexual orientation*** means the actual or perceived heterosexuality, homosexuality, bisexuality, or gender-related identity, whether or not traditionally associated with the person's designated sex at birth.

Unlawful Discriminatory Practices

Pursuant to the Illinois Human Rights Act, the following are designated as unlawful discriminatory practices:

♦ For an employer to refuse to hire, to segregate, or to act with respect to recruitment, hiring, promotion, renewal of employment, selection for training or apprenticeship, discharge, discipline, tenure, or terms, privileges, or conditions of employment on the basis of unlawful discrimination or citizenship status.

♦ For an employer to impose a restriction that has the effect of prohibiting a language from being spoken by an employee in communications that are unrelated to the employee's duties. The term *language* means a person's native tongue, such as Polish, Spanish, or Chinese. It does not include such things as slang, jargon, profanity, or vulgarity.

♦ For an employment agency to fail or refuse to classify properly, accept applications, and register for employment referral or apprenticeship referral, refer for employment, or refer for apprenticeship on the basis of unlawful discrimination or citizenship status or to accept from a person a job order, requisition, or request for referral of applicants for employment or apprenticeship that makes or has the effect of making unlawful discrimination or discrimination on the basis of citizenship status a condition of referral.

♦ For a labor organization to limit, segregate, or classify its membership or to limit employment opportunities, selection, and training for apprenticeship in a trade or craft, or otherwise to take or fail to take an action that adversely affects a person's status as an employee, as an applicant for employment, as an apprentice, or as an applicant for apprenticeships, or wages, tenure, hours of employment or apprenticeship conditions on the basis of unlawful discrimination or citizenship status.

♦ For an employer, employee, agent of an employer, employment agency, or labor organization to engage in sexual harassment. Additionally, an employer will be responsible for sexual harassment of employees by nonemployees or nonmanagerial and nonsupervisory employees if the employer becomes aware of the conduct and fails to take reasonable corrective measures.

- For a public employer to refuse to permit a public employee under its jurisdiction to take time off from work in order to practice religious beliefs and to engage in work during hours other than the employee's regular working hours, consistent with operational needs of the employer and in order to compensate for work time lost for religious reasons. An employee who elects deferred work must be compensated at the wage rate earned during the originally scheduled work period. The employer may require that an employee who plans to take time off from work in order to practice religious beliefs provide the employer with a notice of the intention to be absent from work at least five days before the date of absence.

- For an employer, employment agency, or labor organization to discriminate against a person on the basis of age in the selection, referral for, or conduct of apprenticeship or training programs.

- In immigration related practices, for an employer to request for purposes of satisfying the requirements of 8 U.S.C. § 1324a more or different documents than are required under the law or to refuse to honor documents tendered that on their face reasonably appear to be genuine; or for an employer participating in the Basic Pilot Program, as authorized by 8 U.S.C. § 1324a, to refuse to hire, to segregate, or to act with respect to recruitment, hiring, promotion, renewal of employment, selection for training or apprenticeship, discharge, discipline, tenure or terms, privileges or conditions of employment without following the procedures under the Basic Pilot Program. It is not a civil rights violation for an employer to take any action that is required by 8 U.S.C. § 1324a, as now or after amended.

- For a public employer to refuse to temporarily transfer a pregnant female peace officer or pregnant female fire fighter to a less strenuous or hazardous position for the duration of her pregnancy if she so requests, with the advice of her physician, where that transfer can be reasonably accommodated.

- For an employer, employment agency, or labor organization to inquire into or to use the fact of an arrest or criminal history record information ordered expunged, sealed, or impounded as a basis to refuse to hire, to segregate, or to act with respect to recruitment, hiring, promotion, renewal of employment, selection for training or apprenticeship, discharge, discipline, tenure or terms, privileges, or conditions of employment. This does not prohibit a state agency, unit of local government, school district, or private organization from utilizing conviction information obtained from the Department of State Police in evaluating the qualifications and character of an employee or a prospective employee.

  The prohibition against the use of the fact of an arrest must not be construed to prohibit an employer, employment agency, or labor organization from obtaining or using other information that indicates that a person actually engaged in the conduct for which the person was arrested.

- For a public contractor or eligible bidder to do the following:

  - Practice unlawful discrimination and discrimination based on citizenship status in employment.

  - Fail to comply with the public contractor's or eligible bidder's duties of affirmative action. A minimum of 60 days to comply with the requirements of the Human Rights Act must be afforded to the public contractor or eligible bidder before the department may issue formal notice of noncompliance.

- To consider the color, race, sex, nationality, religion, or religious affiliation of an applicant seeking employment either as a superintendent, principal, teacher, or otherwise in the public elementary or high schools as either a qualification or disqualification for employment. Color, race, sex, nationality, religion, or religious affiliation may not be considered in assigning a person to an office or position or to a school in the school system.

Additionally, according to the Illinois School Student Records Act, no school employee may be subjected to adverse employment action, the threat of adverse employment action, or any manner of discrimination because the employee is acting or has acted to protect communications as privileged or confidential pursuant to applicable provisions of state or federal law or rule or regulation.

♦ To discriminate on the basis of age, religion, ancestry, marital status, physical or mental disability, military status, sexual orientation, unfavorable discharge from military service, sex, race, color, arrest record, citizenship status, or national origin.

♦ To retaliate against employees because they have done any of the following:

• Opposed an unlawful discrimination practice or sexual harassment.

• Filed a complaint or made a charge of discrimination.

• Testified, assisted, or participated in an investigation, proceeding, or hearing under the act.

Note: It is not a civil rights violation for an employer to take any action that is required by § 1324a, as now or after amended.

Exclusions

The following are **not** considered discriminatory practices under the Illinois Human Rights Act:

♦ Hiring or selecting between persons for bona fide occupational qualifications or any reason except the civil-rights violations specifically identified by Illinois discrimination law.

♦ Giving preferential treatment to veterans and their relatives as required by the laws or regulations of the United States, the state of Illinois, or a unit of local government.

♦ Using unfavorable discharge from military service as a valid employment criterion when authorized by federal law or regulation or when a position of employment involves the exercise of fiduciary responsibilities as defined by rules and regulations that the Department of Human Rights must adopt.

♦ Giving or acting upon the results of a professionally developed ability test, if the test, its administration, or action upon the results is not used as a subterfuge for or does not have the effect of unlawful discrimination.

♦ Applying different standards of compensation, terms, conditions, or privileges of employment related to a merit or retirement system if the system or its administration is not used as a subterfuge for or does not have the effect of unlawful discrimination.

♦ Compulsory retirement of an employee who has attained 65 years of age and who, for the two-year period immediately preceding retirement, is employed in a bona fide executive or a high policymaking position if the employee is entitled to an immediate nonforfeitable annual retirement benefit from a pension, profit-sharing, savings, or deferred compensation plan or a combination of plans that equals in total at least $44,000. The retirement benefit must be in a form other than a straight life annuity (with no ancillary benefits) under a plan to which employees do not contribute and no rollover contributions are made.

♦ Establishing an educational requirement as a prerequisite to selection for a training or apprenticeship program if the requirement does not operate to discriminate on the basis of a prohibited classification except age.

♦ Imposing a mandatory retirement age for firefighters, paramedics, or law enforcement officers and discharging or retiring the individuals according to the mandatory retirement age if the action is taken according to a bona fide retirement plan and the law enforcement officer, firefighter, or paramedic has attained the age of retirement in effect under applicable state or local law on March 3, 1983, or if the applicable state or local law was enacted after the date of enactment of the federal Age Discrimination in Employment Act (ADEA) Amendments of 1996.

♦ Failing or refusing to hire an individual because of the individual's age if the action is taken with respect to the employment of an individual as a firefighter, paramedic, or a law enforcement officer and the individual has attained either of the following:

- The age of hiring or appointment in effect under applicable state or local law on March 3, 1983.

- The age of hiring in effect on the date of the failure or refusal to hire under applicable state or local law enacted after the date of enactment of the ADEA Amendments of 1996.

♦ Making legitimate distinctions based on citizenship status if specifically authorized or required by state or federal law.

Additional Provision

According to 775 Ill. Comp. Stat. § 5/5-102.1, it is not a civil rights violation for a medical, dental, or other health care professional or a private professional service provider such as a lawyer, accountant, or insurance agent to refer or refuse to treat or provide services to an individual in a protected class for any nondiscriminatory reason if, in the normal course of operations or business, the professional would for the same reason refer or refuse to treat or provide services to an individual who is not in the protected class of the individual who seeks or requires the same or similar treatment or services.

Ability Tests

Employers may give or act upon the results of any professionally developed ability test provided that the test, its administration, or action upon the results is not used as a subterfuge for unlawful discrimination.

Drugs and Alcohol

Under the Illinois Human Rights Act, an employer may perform any of the following:

♦ Prohibit the illegal use of drugs and the use of alcohol at the workplace by all employees.

♦ Require that employees shall not be under the influence of alcohol or be engaging in the illegal use of drugs at the workplace.

♦ Require that employees behave in conformance with the requirements established under the Drug-Free Workplace Act and the federal Drug-Free Workplace Act of 1988 (11 U.S.C. §§ 701 et seq.).

♦ Hold an employee who engages in the illegal use of drugs or who is an alcoholic to the same qualification standards for employment or job performance and behavior that the employer holds other employees, even if any unsatisfactory performance or behavior is related to the drug use or alcoholism of the employee.

♦ With respect to federal regulations regarding alcohol and the illegal use of drugs, require the following:

- Employees comply with the standards established in the regulations of the U.S. Department of Defense if the employees of the employer are employed in an industry subject to the regulations, including complying with regulations (if any) that apply to employment in sensitive positions in such an industry, in the case of employees who are employed in such positions (as defined in the regulations of the department).

- Employees comply with the standards established in the regulations of the Nuclear Regulatory Commission if the employees of the employer are employed in an industry subject to the regulations, including complying with regulations (if any) that apply to employment in sensitive positions in such an industry, in the case of employees who are employed in such positions (as defined in the regulations of the commission).

- Employees comply with the standards established in such regulations of the U.S. Department of Transportation if the employees of the employer are employed in a transportation industry subject to the regulations, including complying with the regulations (if any) that apply to employment in sensitive positions in such an industry, in the case of employees who are employed in such positions (as defined in the regulations of the department).

For purposes of the Illinois Human Rights Act, a test to determine the illegal use of drugs will **not** be considered a medical examination. Furthermore, nothing in the act should be construed to encourage, prohibit, or authorize the conducting of drug testing for the illegal use of drugs by job applicants or employees or making employment decisions based on test results.

Public Contractors

The Illinois Human Rights Act requires every party to a public contract and every eligible bidder to:

♦ Refrain from unlawful discrimination and discrimination based on citizenship status in employment and undertake affirmative action to assure equality of employment opportunity and eliminate the effects of past discrimination.

♦ Comply with the procedures and requirements of the Department of Human Rights regulations concerning equal employment opportunities and affirmative action.

♦ Provide such information, with respect to its employees and applicants for employment, and assistance as the Department of Human Rights may reasonably request.

♦ Have written sexual harassment policies that include, at a minimum, the following information:

  - The illegality of sexual harassment.

  - The definition of sexual harassment under state law.

  - A description of sexual harassment, utilizing examples.

  - The vendor's internal complaint process, including penalties.

  - The legal recourse and investigative and complaint process available through the Department of Human Rights and the Human Rights Commission.

  - Directions on how to contact the Department or Human Rights and the Human Rights Commission.

  - Protection against retaliation as provided by the Human Rights Act. A copy of the policies will be provided to the department upon request.

It is a civil rights violation for any public contractor or eligible bidder to fail to comply with either of the following:

♦ The public contractor's or eligible bidder's duty to refrain from unlawful discrimination and discrimination based on citizenship status in employment.

♦ The public contractor's or eligible bidder's duties of affirmative action, provided however, that the department has notified the public contractor or eligible bidder in writing by certified mail that the public contractor or eligible bidder may not be in compliance with affirmative action requirements. A minimum of 60 days to comply with the requirements will be afforded to the public contractor or eligible bidder before the department may issue formal notice of noncompliance.

State Agencies

Every state executive department, state agency, board, commission, and instrumentality must:

- ◆ Comply with the procedures and requirements of the department's regulations concerning equal employment opportunities and affirmative action.

- ◆ Provide such information and assistance as the department may request.

- ◆ Establish, maintain, and carry out a continuing affirmative action plan consistent with this act and the regulations of the department designed to promote equal opportunity for all state residents in every aspect of agency personnel policy and practice. For purposes of these affirmative action plans, the race and national origin categories to be included in the plans are African American, Hispanic or Latino, Native American, Asian, and any other category as required by department rule. This plan must provide a current detailed status report including the following information:

  - • Indication of — by each position in state service — the number, percentage, and average salary of individuals employed by race, national origin, sex and disability, and any other category that the department may require by rule.

  - • Identification of all positions in which the percentage of the people employed by race, national origin, sex, and disability, and any other category that the department may require by rule is less than four-fifths of the percentage of each of those components in the state workforce.

  - • Specification of the goals and methods for increasing the percentage by race, national origin, sex, and disability and any other category that the department may require by rule in state positions.

  - • Indication of progress and problems toward meeting equal employment opportunity goals, including, if applicable, but not limited to, Department of Central Management Services recruitment efforts, publicity, promotions, and use of options designating positions by linguistic abilities.

  - • Establishment of a numerical hiring goal for the employment of qualified persons with disabilities in the agency as a whole to be based on the proportion of people with work disabilities in the Illinois labor force as reflected in the most recent decennial census.

- ◆ If the agency has 1,000 or more employees, appoint a full-time equal employment opportunity officer — subject to the department's approval — whose duties will include the following:

  - • Advising the head of the particular state agency with respect to the preparation of equal employment opportunity programs, procedures, regulations, reports, and the agency's affirmative action plan.

  - • Evaluating in writing each fiscal year the sufficiency of the total agency program for equal employment opportunity and reporting thereon to the head of the agency with recommendations as to any improvement or correction in recruiting, hiring, or promotion needed, including remedial or disciplinary action with respect to managerial or supervisory employees who have failed to cooperate fully or who are in violation of the program.

  - • Making changes in recruitment, training, and promotion programs and in hiring and promotion procedures designed to eliminate discriminatory practices when authorized.

  - • Evaluating tests, employment policies, practices, and qualifications and reporting to the head of the agency and to the department any policies, practices, and qualifications that have unequal impact by race, national origin as required by department rule, sex, or disability or any other category that the department may require by rule, and to assist in the recruitment of people in underrepresented classifications. This function will be performed in cooperation with the state Department of Central Management Services.

- Making any aggrieved employee or applicant for employment aware of the remedies under the act.

♦ Establish, maintain, and carry out a continuing sexual harassment program that must include the following:

- Develop a written sexual harassment policy that includes at a minimum the following information:

  ▪ The illegality of sexual harassment.

  ▪ The definition of sexual harassment under state law.

  ▪ A description of sexual harassment, utilizing examples.

  ▪ The agency's internal complaint process including penalties.

  ▪ The legal recourse, investigative and complaint process available through the department and the commission.

  ▪ Directions on how to contact the department and commission.

  ▪ Protection against retaliation as provided by § 6-101 of this act. The policy must be reviewed annually.

- Post in a prominent and accessible location and distribute in a manner to assure notice to all agency employees without exception the agency's sexual harassment policy. Such documents may meet, but may not exceed, the sixth grade literacy level. Distribution must be effectuated within 90 days of the effective date of this amendatory act of 1992 and must occur annually thereafter.

- Provide training on sexual harassment prevention and the agency's sexual harassment policy as a component of all ongoing or new employee training programs.

♦ Notify the department 30 days before effecting any layoff. Once notice is given, the following must occur:

- No layoff may be effective earlier than 10 working days after notice to the department, unless an emergency layoff situation exists.

- The state executive department, state agency, board, commission, or instrumentality in which the layoffs are to occur must notify each employee targeted for layoff, the employee's union representative (if applicable), and the state Dislocated Worker Unit at the Department of Commerce and Economic Opportunity.

- The state executive department, state agency, board, commission, or instrumentality in which the layoffs are to occur must conform to applicable collective-bargaining agreements.

- The state executive department, state agency, board, commission, or instrumentality in which the layoffs are to occur should notify each employee targeted for layoff that transitional assistance may be available to the employee under the Economic Dislocation and Worker Adjustment Assistance Act administered by the Department of Commerce and Economic Opportunity. Failure to give notice will not invalidate the layoff or postpone its effective date.

State Employee Protections

In any meeting, investigation, negotiation, conference, or other proceeding between a state employee and an equal employment opportunity officer, a state employee who is not covered by a collective-bargaining agreement and who is the complaining party or the subject of the proceeding may be accompanied, advised, and represented by either of the following:

♦ An Illinois licensed attorney.

♦ A representative of an employee organization whose membership is composed of employees of the state and of which the employee is a member (representative).

A representative, other than an attorney, may observe but may not actively participate or advise the state employee during the course of such meeting, investigation, negotiation, conference, or other proceeding. Any representative who is present with the consent of the employee may not — during or after termination of the relationship with the state employee — use or reveal any of the following:

♦ Information obtained during the course of the meeting, investigation, negotiation, conference, or other proceeding without the consent of the complaining party and any state employee who is the subject of the proceeding.

♦ Information obtained during the course of the meeting, investigation, negotiation, conference, or other proceeding pursuant to rules and regulations governing confidentiality of such information as promulgated by the appropriate state agency.

Intentional or reckless disclosure of information in violation of the confidentiality requirements constitutes a Class B misdemeanor.

Note: The law does not permit any person who is not licensed to practice law in Illinois to deliver any legal services or otherwise engage in any activities that would constitute the unauthorized practice of law.

Recordkeeping Requirements

Employers subject to the Illinois Human Rights Act must retain the following records:

♦ For one year from the date of application, employers must retain applications, résumés, interview forms, tests, personal history and background information, medical histories, physical exam results, and other documents pertaining to each applicant.

♦ For one year from the date of termination or separation from employment, employers must retain employee personnel files, including performance evaluations, attendance/tardiness records, suspension, layoff, termination, or resignation records.

♦ Job descriptions, production standards, and other records of required job duties, qualifications, and performance criteria, must be retained for a period of one year following the date such descriptions and information ceases to be effective.

Note: When an employer is served with a charge (of violating the Human Rights Act), the employer must preserve all records and other evidence pertaining to the charge until the matter has been finally adjudicated.

Remedy

Charges

Within 180 days after the date that a civil rights violation allegedly has been committed, a charge in writing under oath or affirmation may be filed with the Illinois Department of Human Rights by an aggrieved party or issued by the department itself under the signature of the director.

The charge must be in detail as to substantially apprise a party properly concerned as to the time, place, and facts surrounding the alleged civil rights violation.

EEOC Charges

A charge filed with the Equal Employment Opportunity Commission (EEOC) within 180 days after the date of the alleged civil rights violation is deemed as filed with the department on the date filed with the EEOC.

Upon receipt of a charge filed with the EEOC, the department will notify the complainant that they may proceed with the department. The complainant must then provide written notification of their decision to the department within 35 days of receipt of the department's notice.

The department will also close the case if the complainant does provide notice of the complainant's decision. If the complainant proceeds with the department, the department will take no action until the EEOC makes a determination on the charge.

Upon receipt of the EEOC's determination, the department will cause the charge to be filed under oath or affirmation and in such detail as to substantially apprise any party properly concerned as to the time, place, and facts surrounding the alleged civil rights violation. At the department's discretion, the department will either adopt the EEOC's determination or process the charge pursuant to the Illinois Human Rights Act.

Note: Adoption of the EEOC's determination is a determination by the department for all purposes under the act.

Notice, Response, and Review of Charge

Within 10 days of the date that the charge was filed, the department must serve a copy of the charge on the respondent. The department will require the respondent to file a verified response to the allegations contained in the charge within 60 days of receipt of the notice of the charge. All allegations contained in the charge not timely denied by the respondent will be deemed admitted, unless the respondent states that it is without sufficient information to form a belief with respect to an allegation.

Mediation and Investigation

The complainant and respondent may agree to voluntarily submit the charge to mediation without waiving rights otherwise available to either party and without incurring an obligation to accept the result of the mediation process. Nothing occurring in mediation may be disclosed by the department or is admissible in evidence in a subsequent proceeding, unless the complainant and the respondent agree in writing that a disclosure is made.

After the respondent has been notified, the department must conduct a full investigation of the allegations set forth in the charge. The director has the authority to request any member of the commission to issue subpoenas to compel the attendance of a witness or the production for examination of any books, records, or documents. If any witness whose testimony is required for any investigation resides outside the state, or through illness or any other good cause as determined by the director is unable to be interviewed by the investigator or appear at a fact finding conference, the witness's testimony or deposition may be taken, within or without the state, in the same manner as is provided for in the taking of depositions in civil cases in circuit courts.

Upon reasonable notice to the complainant and the respondent, the department will conduct a fact finding conference prior to 365 days after the date on which the charge was filed, unless the director has determined whether there is substantial evidence that the alleged civil rights violation has been committed or the charge has been dismissed for lack of jurisdiction. If the parties agree in writing, the fact finding conference may be held at a time after the 365 day limit. Any party's failure to attend the conference without good cause will result in dismissal or default. A notice of dismissal or default will be issued by the director.

A notice of default issued by the director will notify the respondent that a request for review may be filed in writing with the commission within 30 days of the receipt of notice. A notice of dismissal issued by the director provides the complainant notice of the right to seek review of the dismissal before the Human Rights Commission or commence a civil action in the appropriate circuit court. If the complainant chooses to have the Human Rights Commission review the dismissal order, a request for review with the commission must be submitted within 90 days after receipt of the director's notice. A civil action in a circuit court may not be commenced if the complainant chooses to file a request for review with the commission. If the complainant chooses to commence a civil action in a circuit court, it must commence within 90 days after receipt of the director's notice.

Report and Substantial Evidence

Each charge will be the subject of a report to the director. The report will be a confidential document subject to review by the director, authorized department employees, the parties, and, where indicated by law, members of the commission or their designated hearing officers.

Upon review of the report, the director will determine whether there is substantial evidence that the alleged civil rights violation has been committed. The determination of substantial evidence is limited to determining the need for further consideration of the charge and includes, but is not limited to, findings of fact and conclusions, as well as the reasons for the determinations on all material issues.

Substantial evidence is evidence which a reasonable mind accepts as sufficient to support a particular conclusion and which consists of more than a mere amount but may be somewhat less than a preponderance.

If the director determines that there is no substantial evidence, the charge will be dismissed by order of the director and the director will give the complainant notice of their right to seek review of the dismissal order before the Human Rights Commission or commence a civil action in the appropriate circuit court. If the complainant chooses to have the commission review the dismissal order, they must file a request for review with the commission within 90 days after receipt of the director's notice. If the complainant chooses to file a request for review with the commission, they may not later commence a civil action in a circuit court. If the complainant chooses to commence a civil action in a circuit court, they must do so within 90 days after receipt of the director's notice.

If the director determines that there is substantial evidence, the director will notify the complainant and respondent of that determination. The director will also notify the parties that the complainant has the right to either commence a civil action in the appropriate circuit court or request that the Department of Human Rights file a complaint with the Human Rights Commission on their behalf. Any such complaint must be filed within 90 days after receipt of the director's notice. If the complainant chooses to have the department file a complaint with the Human Rights Commission on their behalf, the complainant must, within 30 days after receipt of the director's notice, request in writing that the department file the complaint. If the complainant timely requests that the department file the complaint, the department will file the complaint on their behalf. If the complainant fails to timely request that the department file the complaint, the complainant may file the complaint with the commission or commence a civil action in the appropriate circuit court. If the complainant files a complaint with the Human Rights Commission, the complainant must give notice to the department of such commission filing.

Conciliation

If there is substantial evidence, the director must designate a department employee who is an attorney licensed to practice in Illinois to endeavor to eliminate the effect of the alleged civil rights violation and to prevent its repetition by means of conference and conciliation.

Complaint and Time Limit

When the complainant requests that the department file a compliant with the commission on the complainant's behalf, the department must prepare a written complaint, under oath or affirmation, stating the nature of the civil rights violation as alleged in the charge previously filed and the relief sought on behalf of the aggrieved party. The complaint must be filed with the Human Rights Commission.

When a charge of a civil rights violation has been properly filed, the department, within 365 days or within any extension of that period agreed to in writing by all parties, will issue its report. Any such report must be duly served upon both the complainant and the respondent.

If the department has not issued its report within 365 days after the charge is filed, or any such longer period agreed to in writing by all the parties, the complainant has 90 days to either file their own complaint with the Human Rights Commission or commence a civil action in the appropriate circuit court.

The aggrieved party must notify the department that a complaint has been filed and must serve a copy of the complaint on the department on the same date that the complaint is filed with the commission or in circuit court. If the complainant files a complaint with the commission, they may not later commence a civil action in circuit court.

If an aggrieved party files a complaint with the Human Rights Commission or commences a civil action in circuit court, or if the time period for filing a complaint has expired, the department will immediately cease its investigation and dismiss the charge of civil rights violation. Any final order entered by the commission is appealable. Failure to immediately cease an investigation and dismiss the charge of civil rights violation constitutes grounds for entry of an order by the circuit court permanently enjoining the investigation. The department may also be liable for any costs and other damages incurred by the respondent as a result of the action of the department.

The department will suspend any administrative proceedings after the filing of a civil action by or on behalf of the aggrieved party under any federal or state law seeking relief with respect to the alleged civil rights violation.

Penalties

Upon finding a civil rights violation, a hearing officer may recommend and the commission or a three-member panel may provide for relief or penalty — separately or in combination — by entering an order directing the respondent to do the following:

- Cease and desist from the violation.
- Pay actual damages, as reasonably determined by the commission, for injury or loss suffered by the complainant.
- Hire, reinstate, or upgrade the complainant with or without backpay or provide fringe benefits that the complainant may have been denied.
- Admit or restore the complainant to labor organization membership, to a guidance program, apprenticeship-training program, on the job training program, or other occupational training or retraining program.
- Admit the complainant to a public accommodation.
- Extend to the complainant the full and equal enjoyment of the goods, services, facilities, privileges, advantages, or accommodations of the respondent.

♦ Pay to the complainant all or a portion of the costs of maintaining the action, including reasonable attorneys' fees and expert witness fees incurred in maintaining the action before the department, the commission, and in judicial review and judicial enforcement proceedings.

♦ Report as to the manner of compliance.

♦ Take action as may be necessary to make the individual complainant whole, including awards of interest on the complainant's actual damages and backpay from the date of the civil rights violation.

Civil Suit

Within two years after the violation, an aggrieved party may bring a civil lawsuit against a unit of state, county, or local government that excluded the individual from participation in, denied an individual the benefits of, or subjected the individual to discrimination under a program or activity on the grounds of the individual's race, color, national origin, or gender.

Governmental entities are also in violation if the entity utilizes criteria or methods of administration that have the effect of subjecting individuals to discrimination based on race, color, national origin, or gender.

After bringing suit, if the court finds that a violation of participation occurred, the court may award actual and punitive damages. If the court finds that a violation of criteria or methodology occurred, the court may award actual damages.

Additionally, the court may grant any of the following:

♦ Permanent or preliminary injunction.

♦ Temporary restraining order.

♦ Any other order including an order enjoining the entity from engaging in the continued violation or mandating affirmative action.

Moreover, the prevailing party will be awarded reasonable attorneys' fees and costs.

Appeals

A complainant or respondent may apply for and obtain judicial review of a final order by filing a petition for review in the Appellate Court within 35 days from the date that a copy of the decisions sought to be reviewed was served upon the affected party.

Related Provision

Recognition of Domestic Partnership

According to an Executive Order from the Treasurer of Illinois and effective June 13, 2010, within the State Treasurer's Office (office), all policies, benefits, and rights that are afforded and available to spouses are likewise extended to domestic partners. Therefore, for the purposes of all office policies, including but not limited to sick leave, bereavement leave, FMLA, maternity/paternity leave, the Victim's Economic Security and Safety Act (VESSA), employment of relatives, and Executive Order 07-01, the term *spouse* will be interpreted to include domestic partners even if not required by state and/or federal law.

Similarly, any references to children and step-children will be understood to refer to the children of a domestic partnership, regardless of biological or adoptive status. References to in-laws will be understood to refer to the family of an employee's domestic partner.

The Equal Wage Act

Under the Illinois Equal Wage Act (820 Ill Comp. Stat. §§ 110/1 – 110/3), any employer with six or more employees engaged in the manufacture of any article, who pays any employee engaged in such manufacture an unequal wage for equal work — by time or piece work — than is being paid to any other employee in such manufacture, may be charged with a petty offense punishable by a fine of up to $100.

The law does not prohibit a variation in rates of pay based upon either difference in seniority, experience, training, skill, or ability, or difference in duties or services performed (whether regularly or occasionally), or difference in availability for other operations, or any other reasonable classification, excepting difference in sex. In addition, the law does not prohibit such variation where the same is authorized by a contract between an employer and a recognized bargaining agent.

Note: Any action based upon or arising under the Equal Wage Act must be instituted within six months after the date of the alleged violation.

The Equal Pay Act of 2003

The Illinois Equal Pay Act of 2003 is located at 820 Ill. Comp. Stat. §§ 112/1 et seq.

Covered Employers

The Illinois act applies to all of the following with four or more employees gainfully employed in Illinois:

- ◆ Individuals and partnerships.
- ◆ Corporations, associations, and businesses.
- ◆ Trusts or entities.

The act also applies to the following without regard to the number of employees:

- ◆ State of Illinois
- ◆ Any state officer.
- ◆ State department or state agency.
- ◆ Any unit of local government and any school district.

Under the act, employers **may not** discriminate between employees on the basis of sex by paying wages to an employee at a lesser rate than that which the employer pays to another employee of the opposite sex for the same or substantially similar work where performance requires equal skill, effort, and responsibility, under similar working conditions.

Exceptions to the act occur where payment is made under **any** of the following systems:

- ◆ A seniority system.
- ◆ A merit system.
- ◆ A system that measures earning by quantity or quality of production.
- ◆ A differential based on any other factor other than sex or one that would constitute unlawful discrimination.

Employers paying wages that violate these standards **may not** reduce the wages of any other employee in an attempt to comply with the act.

Additionally, employers **may not**:

♦ Interfere with, restrain, or deny the exercise of or the attempt to exercise any right provided under the act.

♦ Discharge or in any manner discriminate against any individual for inquiring about, disclosing, comparing, or otherwise discussing the employee's wages or the wages of any other employee, or for encouraging any person to exercise their rights under the act.

Employers **may not** discharge or in any other manner discriminate against any individual for any of the following reasons:

♦ The individual filed a charge or instituted or caused to be instituted any proceeding under the act.

♦ The individual gave or is about to give information in connection with an inquiry or proceeding relating to any right provided under the act.

♦ The individual testified or is about to testify in an inquiry or proceeding relating to any right provided under the act.

Remedy

An employee or former employee may file a complaint with the Illinois Department of Labor alleging a violation of the act by submitting a signed, completed complaint form. All complaints must be filed with the department within one year from the date of the underpayment. The ***date of underpayment*** is each time wages are underpaid.

In an action, the employee may recover from the employer the entire amount of any underpayment together with interest and reasonable attorneys' fees. An employee may also request the department make an assignment of the wage claim, in trust for the employee. The department may bring any legal action necessary to collect the claim thereby requiring the employer to pay the costs incurred in collecting the claim.

Employers in violation of the act are subject to a penalty up to $2,500 for each violation for each employee affected.

Any employer demanded by the Illinois Director of Labor or ordered by the court to pay wages due an employee, and who fails to do so within 15 days after such demand or order is entered, is liable to pay a penalty. The penalty will be 1 percent per calendar day to the employee for each day of delay in paying such wages to the employee, up to an amount equal to twice the sum of unpaid wages due the employee.

Posting and Recordkeeping Requirements

Employers must make records, to be preserved for at least five years, that document the name, address, occupation, and wages paid to each employee. Employers must make reports from these records as prescribed by rule or order of the director, unless the records relate to an ongoing investigation or enforcement action under the act, in which case the records must be maintained until their destruction is authorized by the department or by court order.

All employers must conspicuously post and maintain the Equal Employment Opportunity (EEO) poster entitled, *Equal Employment Opportunity is the Law*, as well as the Illinois Department of Labor provided poster entitled, *Equal Pay Act of 2003*. This poster provides notice about the prohibition from paying unequal wages to men and women for performing the same or substantially similar work, requiring equal skill, effort, and responsibility under similar working conditions for the same employer.

Posters must be continuously posted in conspicuous places on the employers' premises.

Rights of Persons with a Disability

Pursuant to 775 Ill. Comp. Stat. § 30/3, persons with physical disabilities must be employed in all of the following on the same terms and conditions as those who do not have a disability, unless it is shown that the particular disability prevents the performance of the work involved:

- State service and service of political subdivisions.

- Public schools.

- All other employment supported in whole or in part by public funds.

Service Animals

Under 775 Ill. Comp. Stat. § 30/3 and 720 Ill. Comp. Stat. § 630/1, every totally or partially blind, hearing impaired, person who is subject to epilepsy or other seizure disorders, or otherwise with a physical disability or a trainer of support dogs, guide dogs, seizure-alert dogs, seizure-response dogs, or hearing dogs has the right to be accompanied by a support dog or guide dog especially trained for the purpose, or a dog that is being trained to be a support dog, guide dog, seizure-alert dog, seizure-response dog, or hearing dog, in any place to which the general public is invited.

The person is not to be required to pay an extra charge for the animal, as long as the dog is wearing a harness and the person presents credentials for inspection issued by a school for training guide, leader, seizure-alert, or seizure-response dogs. However, the individual is liable for any damage caused by the dog.

Penalty

Any person, firm, or corporation who denies or interferes with admittance to or enjoyment of any public accommodation is guilty of a Class A misdemeanor.

The Emergency Evacuation Plan for People with Disabilities Act

The Emergency Evacuation Plan for People with Disabilities Act is located at 430 Ill. Comp. Stat. §§ 130/10 – 130/25. As of January 1, 2004, every high-rise building owner was required to establish and maintain an emergency evacuation plan for occupants of the building who have a disability who have notified the owner of their need for assistance. Importantly, the evacuation plan must be established even if an occupant with a disability of the building has not notified the owner of a need for evacuation assistance.

As used in this law, *high-rise building* means any building 80 feet or more in height. The owner is responsible for maintaining and updating the plan as necessary to ensure that the plan continues to comply with this law.

Exceptions

This law **does not apply** within a municipality with a population of over 1,000,000 that, before July 19, 2002, has adopted an ordinance establishing emergency procedures for high-rise buildings.

Plan Requirements

The following plan requirements apply under the act:

- The plan must establish procedures for evacuating persons with disabilities from the building in the event of an emergency when those persons have notified the owner of their need for assistance.

♦ The plan must provide for a list to be maintained of persons who have notified the owner that they have a disability and would require special assistance in the event of an emergency. The list must include the unit, office, or room number location that the person with a disability occupies in the building. The lists may not be used or disseminated for any other purpose.

♦ The plan must provide for a means to notify occupants of the building that a list identifying persons with a disability in need of emergency evacuation assistance is maintained by the owner and the method by which occupants can place their name on the list.

♦ The plan must identify the location and type of any evacuation assistance devices or assistive technologies that are available in the building. If the plan provides for areas of rescue assistance, the plan must provide that these areas are to be identified by signs that state "Area of Rescue Assistance" and display the international symbol of accessibility. Lettering must be permanent and must comply with Americans with Disabilities Act (ADA) Accessibility Guidelines.

♦ The plan must include recommended procedures to be followed by building employees, tenants, or guests to assist persons with disabilities in need of emergency evacuation assistance.

♦ In hotels and motels, each plan must provide an opportunity for guests to identify themselves as a person with a disability in need of emergency evacuation assistance.

♦ A copy of the plan must be maintained at all times in a place that is easily accessible by law enforcement or fire safety personnel, such as in the management office of the high rise building, at the security desk, or in the vicinity of the fireman's elevator recall key, the life safety panel, or the fire pump room.

♦ The plan must be made available to local law enforcement and fire safety personnel upon request. The plan must provide the names of and contact information regarding any building personnel to be contacted by law enforcement or fire safety personnel in the event of an emergency requiring implementation of the plan.

♦ The plan must provide for dissemination or availability of the appropriate evacuation procedures portions of the plan to building employees, tenants, or guests.

♦ The plan must identify the roles and responsibilities of building personnel in carrying out the evacuation plan. The plan must provide for appropriate training for building personnel regarding their roles and responsibilities.

♦ The plan must provide for drills regarding evacuation procedures not less than once per year. A written record of the date of the drill must be kept with the evacuation plan.

Penalties

Failure to comply with the Emergency Evacuation Plan for People with Disabilities Act is a petty offense punishable by a $500 fine.

Genetic Information Privacy Act

The Illinois Genetic Information Privacy Act (act) is located at 410 Ill. Comp. Stat. §§ 513/10 – 513/50 and applies to all employers. According to 410 Ill. Comp. Stat. § 513/15, genetic testing and information derived from genetic testing is confidential, privileged, and may only be released to the following:

♦ The individual who was tested.

♦ Persons specifically authorized, in writing, by the individual who was tested to receive the information.

Genetic testing and ***genetic tests*** are a test or analysis of human genes, gene products, DNA, RNA, or chromosomes, proteins, or metabolites that detect genotypes, mutations, chromosomal changes, abnormalities, or deficiencies, including carrier status, that:

♦ Are linked to physical or mental disorders or impairments.

♦ Indicate a susceptibility to illness, disease, impairment, or other disorders, whether physical or mental, or demonstrate genetic or chromosomal damage due to environmental factors.

Genetic testing and genetic tests do not include any of the following:

♦ Routine physical measurements.

♦ Chemical, blood, and urine analyses that are widely accepted and in use in clinical practice.

♦ Tests for use of drugs.

♦ Tests for the presence of the human immunodeficiency virus.

♦ Analyses of proteins or metabolites that do not detect genotypes, mutations, chromosomal changes, abnormalities, or deficiencies.

♦ Analyses of proteins or metabolites that are directly related to a manifested disease, disorder, or pathological condition that could reasonably be detected by a health care professional with appropriate training and expertise in the field of medicine involved.

Genetic information is, with respect to any individual, information about:

♦ The individual's genetic tests.

♦ The genetic tests of a family member of the individual. A ***family member*** is, with respect to an individual, any of the following:

  • The spouse of the individual.

  • A dependent child of the individual, including a child who is born to or placed for adoption with the individual.

  • Any other person qualifying as a covered dependent under a managed care plan.

  • All other individuals related by blood or law to the individual or their spouse or child.

♦ The manifestation or possible manifestation of a disease or disorder in a family member of the individual.

Genetic information does not include information about the sex or age of any individual.

Genetic testing and information derived from such testing is not admissible as evidence, nor discoverable in any action of any kind in any court, or before any tribunal, board, agency, or person. However, results of genetic testing that indicate that the individual tested is at the time of the test afflicted with a disease, whether or not currently symptomatic, are not subject to the confidentiality requirements of the act.

Note: No liability will attach to any hospital, physician, or other health care provider for compliance with the genetic nondiscrimination provisions including a specific written release by the individual.

Exceptions

Genetic testing and genetic information derived from genetic testing is admissible as evidence and discoverable, subject to a protective order, in any of the following legal actions:

♦ Alleging a violation of the act.

♦ Seeking to enforce the act through the Illinois Insurance Code.

♦ Alleging discriminatory genetic testing or use of genetic information under the Illinois Human Rights Act or the Illinois Civil Rights Act of 2003.

♦ Requesting a workers' compensation claim under the Workers' Compensation Act.

Use of Genetic Information by Employers

An employer, employment agency, labor organization, and licensing agency must treat genetic testing and genetic information in such a manner that is consistent with the requirements of federal law, including but not limited to all of the following:

♦ The Genetic Information Nondiscrimination Act of 2008.

♦ The Americans with Disabilities Act.

♦ Title VII of the Civil Rights Act of 1964.

♦ The Family and Medical Leave Act of 1993.

♦ The Occupational Safety and Health Act of 1970.

♦ The Federal Mine Safety and Health Act of 1977.

♦ The Atomic Energy Act of 1954.

An employer may only release genetic testing information as permitted by the act. Additionally, an agreement between a person and an employer, prospective employer, employment agency, labor organization, or licensing agency, or its employees, agents, or members offering the person employment, labor organization membership, licensure, or any pay or benefit in return for taking a genetic test is prohibited.

Employer Restrictions

An employer, employment agency, labor organization, and licensing agency must not directly or indirectly do any of the following:

♦ Solicit, request, require or purchase genetic testing or genetic information of a person or a family member of the person, or administer a genetic test to a person or a family member of the person as a condition of employment, pre-employment application, labor organization membership, or licensure.

♦ Affect the terms, conditions, or privileges of employment, pre-employment application, labor organization membership, or licensure, or terminate the employment, labor organization membership, or licensure of any person because of genetic testing or genetic information with respect to the employee or family member, or information about a request for or the receipt of genetic testing by such employee or family member of such employee.

♦ Limit, segregate, or classify employees in any way that would deprive or tend to deprive any employee of employment opportunities or otherwise adversely affect the status of the employee as an employee because of genetic testing or genetic information with respect to the employee or a family member, or information about a request for or the receipt of genetic testing or genetic information by such employee or family member of such employee.

♦ Retaliate through discharge or in any other manner against any person alleging a violation of the act or participating in any manner in a proceeding under the act.

An employer must not use genetic information or genetic testing in furtherance of a workplace wellness program benefiting employees unless all of the following apply:

♦ Health or genetic services are offered by the employer.

♦ The employee provides written and informed consent.

♦ Only the employee, or family member if the family member is receiving genetic services, and the licensed health care professional or licensed genetic counselor involved in providing such services receive individually identifiable information concerning the results of such services.

♦ Any individually identifiable information is only available for purposes of such services and must not be disclosed to the employer except in aggregate terms that do not disclose the identity of specific employees.

Additional Provisions

However, the act does not prohibit:

♦ Genetic testing of an employee who requests a genetic test, and who provides written and informed consent, from taking a genetic test for the purpose of initiating a workers' compensation claim under the Workers' Compensation Act.

♦ An employer that conducts DNA analysis for law enforcement purposes as a forensic laboratory and that includes such analysis in the Combined DNA Index System pursuant to the federal Violent Crime Control and Law Enforcement Act of 1994 from requesting or requiring genetic testing or genetic information of such employer's employees, but only to the extent that such genetic testing or genetic information is used for analysis of DNA identification markers for quality control to detect sample contamination.

♦ An employer from requesting or requiring genetic information to be used for genetic monitoring of the biological effects of toxic substances in the workplace, but only if all of the following apply:

  • The employer provides written notice of the genetic monitoring to the employee.

  • The employee provides written and informed consent or the genetic monitoring is required by federal or state law.

  • The employee is informed of individual monitoring results.

  • The monitoring is in compliance with any federal genetic monitoring regulations or state genetic monitoring regulations under the authority of the federal Occupational Safety and Health Act of 1970.

  • The employer, excluding any licensed health care professional or licensed genetic counselor that is involved in the genetic monitoring program, receives the results of the monitoring only in aggregate terms that do not disclose the identity of specific employees.

A purchase of commercially and publicly available documents, including newspapers, magazines, periodicals, and books but not including medical databases or court records or inadvertently requesting family medical history by an employer, employment agency, labor organization, and licensing agency does not violate the act.

Despite any lawful acquisition of genetic testing or genetic information, an employer, employment agency, labor organization, and licensing agency still may not use or disclose the genetic test or genetic information in violation of the act.

Additionally, a person must not knowingly sell to or interpret for an employer, employment agency, labor organization, or licensing agency, or its employees, agents, or members, a genetic test of an employee, labor organization member, or license holder, or of a prospective employee, member, or license holder.

Enforcement and Penalties

Any person aggrieved by a violation of the act has a right of action in a state circuit court or as a supplemental claim in a federal district court against an offending party. A prevailing party may recover for each violation:

♦ Against any party who negligently violates a provision of the act, liquidated damages of $2,500 or actual damages, whichever is greater.

♦ Against any party who intentionally or recklessly violates a provision of the act, liquidated damages of $15,000 or actual damages, whichever is greater.

♦ Reasonable attorney's fees and costs, including expert witness fees and other litigation expenses.

♦ Such other relief, including an injunction, as the state or federal court may deem appropriate.

Additionally, any person alleging a violation of the genetic testing privacy protections has a right of action in a state circuit court or a supplemental claim in a federal district court to seek a preliminary injunction preventing the release or disclosure of genetic testing or genetic information pending the final resolution of any action under the act.

Health Care Right of Conscience Act

According to 745 Ill. Comp. Stat. §§ 70/5, 70/7, and 70/12, it is unlawful for any person, public or private institution, or public official to discriminate against any person in any manner, including but not limited to, licensing, hiring, promotion, transfer, staff appointment, hospital, managed care entity, or any other privileges, because of such person's conscientious refusal to receive, obtain, accept, perform, assist, counsel, suggest, recommend, refer or participate in any way in any particular form of health care services contrary to the person's conscience.

It is also unlawful for any public or private employer, entity, agency, institution, official or person, including but not limited to, a medical, nursing or other medical training institution, to deny admission because of, to place any reference in its application form concerning, to orally question about, to impose any burdens in terms or conditions of employment on, or to otherwise discriminate against, any applicant, in terms of employment, admission to or participation in any programs for which the applicant is eligible, or to discriminate in relation thereto, in any other manner, on account of the applicant's refusal to receive, obtain, accept, perform, counsel, suggest, recommend, refer, assist or participate in any way in any forms of health care services contrary to the applicant's conscience.

Penalties

Any person, association, corporation, entity, or health care facility injured by any public or private person, association, agency, entity, or corporation by reason of any of the aforementioned prohibited discriminatory actions may commence a lawsuit, and will recover threefold the actual damages, including all of the following:

♦ Pain and suffering, sustained by such person, association, corporation, entity, or health care facility.

♦ The costs of the suit.

♦ Reasonable attorney's fees.

However, in no case will recovery be less than $2,500 for each violation in addition to costs of the suit and reasonable attorney's fees. These damage remedies are cumulative, and not exclusive of other remedies afforded under any other state or federal law.

Nursing Mothers in the Workplace

Pursuant to 820 Ill. Comp. Stat. § 260/10, all employers having more than five employees (excluding members of the employer's immediate family) are required to provide reasonable unpaid break time each day to an employee who needs to express milk for her infant child, unless to do so would unduly disrupt the employer's operations. The break time must, if possible, run concurrently with any break time already provided to the employee.

An employer shall also make reasonable efforts to provide a room near the employee's workstation, other than a toilet stall, where the employee may express her milk in privacy.

Contact Information

Illinois Department of Human Rights

222 South College, Floor 1
Springfield, IL 62704

Telephone: 217-785-5100
Fax: 217-785-5106
Internet: *www.state.il.us/dhr*

Illinois Human Rights Commission

William G. Stratton Office Building
Room 404
Springfield, IL 62706

Telephone: 217-785-4350
Fax: 217-524-4877
Internet: *www.state.il.us/ihrc*

Chapter 16

Drug and Alcohol Testing in the Workplace

Introduction

According to the 2006 National Survey on Drug Use and Health, 74.9 percent of all adult illicit drug users are employed full or part time and most binge; heavy alcohol users are also employed full or part time. An increasing number of businesses across the country are instituting drug-free workplace policies that include workplace drug-testing programs, for a host of reasons. Some institute the policies to comply with federal regulations, customer or contract requirements, or insurance carrier requirements. Others wish to improve safety, minimize the chance of hiring employees who may be users or abusers, deter "recreational" drug use that could lead to addiction, identify current users and abusers and refer them for assistance, or reduce the costs of alcohol and other drug abuse in the workplace. Drug testing is one way to protect the workplace from the negative effects of alcohol and other drug abuse. A drug- and alcohol-testing program can deter employees from coming to work unfit for duty.

According to the U.S. Department of Health and Human Services Substance Abuse and Mental Health Services Administration (SAMHSA), substance abusing employees often do not make good employees. Studies show that, compared with nonsubstance abusers, they are more likely to:

- Change jobs frequently.

- Be late to or absent from work.

- Be less productive employees.

- Be involved in a workplace accident.

- File a workers' compensation claim.

Workplace substance abuse can also have a serious effect on people other than the abuser. For example, some studies suggest that working alongside a substance abuser can reduce nonabusers' morale and productivity. It also is quite common for substance abusing workers who are involved in workplace accidents to injure other people (rather than themselves), especially if they work in safety-sensitive industries, such as the transportation or construction industry.

SAMHSA also stated that employers who have implemented drug-free workplace programs have important experiences to share:

- Employers with successful drug-free workplace programs report improvements in morale and productivity and decreases in absenteeism, accidents, downtime, turnover, and theft.

- Employers with longstanding programs report better health status among, and decreased use of medical benefits by, many employees and family members.

- ◆ Some organizations with drug-free workplace programs qualify for incentives, such as decreased costs for workers' compensation and other kinds of insurance.

- ◆ Employers find that employees, employee representatives, and unions often welcome drug-free workplace programs. If an employer does not have a program, employees may wonder why.

This chapter discusses drug and alcohol testing limitations, discipline and discharge for substance use, related federal laws, and considerations when implementing a drug- and alcohol-testing program.

Testing Limits

Within reason, all employees **may** be tested. However, testing is limited for certain classes of employees. Such limits depend upon the nature of the employment relationship, as well as federal, state, and local laws.

Private At-Will Employees

At-will employees have brought invasion-of-privacy claims when employers have engaged in random testing, and defamation claims when reports of false positive results have been circulated to others. At-will employees also have sued for breach of contract based upon information about drug testing in an employee handbook.

Union Employees

Courts, interpreting the National Labor Relations Act (NLRA), mandate that employers bargain collectively with unions about substance abuse testing programs.

This prevents an employer from unilaterally implementing drug testing for union employees unless there has been a clear and unmistakable waiver by the union of its right to bargain over these issues.

The National Labor Relations Board (NLRB) generally disfavors such a waiver. The NLRB **does not** require employers to bargain over pre-employment testing programs, except in situations such as hiring halls where the union has become a participant in the hiring process.

Nonunion Contract Employees

A drug-testing program need not necessarily be contained within an employment contract in order for it to be valid. However, to avoid breach-of-contract lawsuits, employees should agree, in writing, to comply with all personnel policies implemented by management before or during employment and should agree specifically to abide by the employer's substance abuse testing program.

Public Sector Employees

Federal, state, and local government employees have Fourth Amendment constitutional protection generally not enjoyed by their private sector counterparts. Drug tests initiated by public employers are subject to prohibitions against unreasonable search and seizure.

Random testing should be limited to employees who work in safety-sensitive positions.

Job Applicants

Applicants have fewer privacy rights than employees. Employers often make offers of regular employment conditioned upon successful completion of a drug test. The Americans with Disabilities Act (ADA) regulations do not hold such a pre-employment test for illegal drugs to be an unlawful pre-employment medical examination. However, no such exclusion is provided for pre-employment alcohol tests. In fact, pre-employment alcohol tests are often regarded as being of questionable value, since applicants may easily abstain from drinking for the short period of time needed to obtain a negative test result.

Administering drug tests before an offer of employment is extended may prove problematical because information gathered from a drug test about a person's medical condition or history **may not** be considered before a job offer proposal. Consequently, employers should delay drug tests until they have extended a conditional offer of employment. Thus, the employer does not have pre-offer knowledge of real or apparent disabilities revealed by test results and cannot be accused of basing a decision not to hire on the actual or perceived disability of an applicant.

Discipline and Discharge for Substance Abuse in a Union Setting

Employer attempts to enforce a drug and alcohol policy within a union workforce will most likely result in challenges through the grievance and arbitration process.

Arbitrators have varying attitudes about the circumstances under which alcoholism or drunkenness is cause for discharge. Some arbitrators will sustain discipline based solely upon employee performance without regard to any explanations for shortcomings. Others consider alcoholic employees to be victims of a disorder who should be offered an opportunity to recover, complete with leaves of absence and appropriate treatment.

While arbitrators tend to view alcoholism as a treatable disorder, there is considerable resistance to the concept of rehabilitating an employee with a drug-related problem. Most drug offenses carry a taint of criminality. Therefore, arbitrators are more inclined to look with disfavor on drug users.

Generally, arbitrators regard an employee's activity during personal time and off the employer's premises as being of no concern to the employer **unless** the employer can demonstrate that the off-duty activity caused any of the following:

♦ Damaged the organization's reputation or product.

♦ Interfered with the employee's work attendance or performance.

♦ Resulted in a peer's reasonable refusal, reluctance, or inability to work with the employee.

Arbitrators tend to uphold the discharge and discipline of employees who test positive for drugs or alcohol when the employer has performed the following:

♦ Defined a drug-testing policy that clarifies possible consequences.

♦ Applied its policy reasonably and consistently.

Americans with Disabilities Act

According to 42 U.S.C.A. § 12114, the Americans with Disabilities Act (ADA) **does not** prohibit discrimination against an individual based on that individual's current use of illegal drugs.

According to the ADA, the term "qualified individual with a disability" does not include any employee or applicant who is currently engaging in the illegal use of drugs, when the covered entity acts on the basis of such use.

Current use of illegal drugs means the illegal use of drugs that occurred recently enough to justify a reasonable belief that a person's drug use is current or that continuing use is a real and ongoing problem. Current users need not be accommodated and may be discharged (or not hired) for testing positive.

A covered entity is not prohibited from adopting or administering reasonable policies or procedures including, but not limited to, drug testing — designed to ensure that an individual who formerly engaged in illegal drug use is not engaging in current illegal use of drugs.

The ADA does, however, protect former drug users who have successfully completed treatment or who are participating in treatment and persons erroneously regarded as illegal drug users.

According to 42 U.S.C.A. § 12114, a covered entity **may not** discriminate on the basis of illegal drug use against an individual who is not engaging in current illegal use and who fulfills one of the following:

♦ Successfully completed a supervised drug rehabilitation program or has otherwise been rehabilitated successfully.

♦ Is participating in a supervised rehabilitation program.

♦ Is erroneously regarded as engaging in such use, but is not engaging in such use.

Additionally, individuals who are using a drug taken under supervision by a licensed health care professional or other legal uses are protected against discrimination.

Under the ADA, alcoholism is treated differently in comparison to illegal drug use. According to the EEOC Enforcement Guidance on Disability-Related Inquiries and Medical Examinations of Employees, tests for alcohol use are classified as "medical examinations." Whereas, tests to determine the current illegal use of drugs are generally **not** considered to be medical examinations. Accordingly, employers may neither require a medical examination nor make inquiries of an employee as to whether the employee is an individual with a disability or as to the nature and severity of the disability.

Alcohol tests must be job related and consistent with business necessity and, if given to applicants, may be administered only after conditional offers of employment are extended. As a practical matter, such pre-employment alcohol tests are of questionable value. Importantly, the ADA **does specifically allow** employers to prohibit the on-the-job use of alcohol and to prohibit employees from being under the influence of alcohol while in the workplace.

Importantly, according to 42 U.S.C.A. § 12114, an employer may also hold an employee who engages in illegal drug use or who is an alcoholic to the same qualification standards for employment or job performance and behavior that such entity holds other employees, even if any unsatisfactory performance or behavior is related to the drug use or alcoholism of the employee.

Individuals who are using a drug taken under supervision by a licensed health care professional or other legal uses are also protected against discrimination. Tests to determine whether employees or applicants are using prescribed drugs must be job related and consistent with business necessity. Under the ADA, employees who receive positive results on fitness for duty tests may be entitled to reasonable accommodation.

Since the ADA increases the legal risks involved in testing for such drugs as pain relievers and tranquilizers, the risks of testing for legal drugs probably outweigh the benefits except in safety-critical jobs or cases where a substance abuse professional has authorized follow-up testing after an employee has returned to work from treatment for drug abuse. Given the distinction between legal and illegal drug use under the ADA, employers should use a physician as a medical review officer to verify test results and separate illegal drug users from persons lawfully taking prescribed medications.

The ADA permits employers to perform any testing required by Department of Transportation (DOT), Department of Defense (DOD), or Department of Energy regulations. It also allows employers to prohibit employees from using or being under the influence of illegal drugs in the workplace and from violating the Drug-Free Workplace Act.

Transportation Employee Drug and Alcohol Testing

Federal law regulated by the Department of Transportation (DOT) requires various forms of drug and alcohol testing by employers in the following transportation industries:

- Motor carrier.
- Railroad.
- Aviation.
- Maritime.
- Mass transit.
- Pipeline.

Employers in these industries are required by the DOT to implement highly specific drug-testing programs conforming to detailed regulations.

Under the DOT regulations, all employees who need a commercial driver's license (CDL) to perform their work are subject to drug testing. The regulations apply to any employer with a single CDL employee. Additionally, all employers should regard the DOT rules as a benchmark for their testing programs.

DOT Drug Testing

The following is a general summary of the existing DOT drug-testing regulations for transportation employees. As the regulations vary between each transportation agency, guidelines should be obtained from each agency with jurisdiction over an employer and legal counsel should be consulted.

DOT-Required Drug Tests

49 C.F.R. 40

49 C.F.R. 40 (Part 40) is a DOT-wide regulation that states how to conduct testing and how to return employees to safety-sensitive duties after they violate a DOT drug and alcohol regulation. Part 40 applies to all DOT-required testing, regardless of what DOT agency-specific rule applies to an employer. For example, whether the employer is an airline covered by FAA rules or a trucking company covered by FMCSA rules, Part 40 procedures for collecting and testing specimens and reporting of test results apply.

Each DOT agency-specific regulation details which employees are subject to testing, when and in what situations for a particular transportation industry.

Pre-Employment Testing

Applicants for employment in covered positions must successfully complete a drug test before performing a safety-sensitive function.

Random Testing

According to 49 C.F.R. 655.45, DOT employers in the motor carrier and mass transit industries must conduct a number of random drug tests each year equal to 50 percent of covered employees. (Different random testing rates may apply to employers in the DOT-covered industries.) Such tests must be spread throughout the year.

Employees **may not** receive any advance warning of the random tests and must have an equal chance of being tested during each period of selection time. Employers may wish to join consortiums or to contract with third-party administrators to reduce some of the administrative problems involved in scheduling random tests.

Post-Accident Testing

Testing is required within a specific number of hours after serious accidents or rule violations. Employees who may have contributed to the accident must be drug tested after receiving any necessary medical attention. According to 49 C.F.R. 382.303, commercial motor vehicle drivers must be tested after reportable accidents if they receive a citation for a moving violation arising out of the accident or if someone dies as a result of the accident.

Reasonable Suspicion Testing

An employer **may** conduct drug and alcohol testing when the employer has reasonable suspicion to believe that the employee has used a prohibited drug or engaged in alcohol misuse. Tests for reasonable suspicion must be based on specific, contemporaneous, articulable observations by a trained supervisor(s) concerning the employee's appearance, behavior, body odors, or speech.

Return-to-Duty Testing and Follow-Up Testing

Employees who violate DOT drug-testing regulations must undergo a return-to-duty test with a verified negative result before performing a safety-sensitive function.

Employees who violate DOT drug-testing regulations and have a drug problem, as diagnosed by a substance abuse professional, are subject to random follow-up testing for up to five years after returning to duty.

Direct Observation

Employers must direct an immediate collection under direct observation with no advance notice to the employee, if:

- ♦ The laboratory reported to the medical review officer (MRO) that a specimen is invalid, and the MRO reported to the employer that there was not an adequate medical explanation for the result.

- ♦ The MRO reported to the employer that the original positive, adulterated, or substituted result had to be cancelled because the test of the split specimen could not be performed.

- ♦ The laboratory reported to the MRO that the specimen was negative-dilute with a creatinine concentration greater than or equal to 2 mg/dL but less than or equal to 5 mg/dL, and the MRO reported the specimen to the employer as negative-dilute and that a second collection must take place under direct observation.

Employers must also direct a collection under direct observation of an employee if the drug test is a return-to-duty test or a follow-up test. Employers must explain to the employee the reason for a directly observed collection. Employees may decline to be directly observed, however, such declination constitutes a refusal to test.

Consequences for Violation of DOT Drug-Testing Regulations

Employees who receive verified positive test results or otherwise violate the regulations must be immediately removed from safety-sensitive positions. Such employees **may not** return to duty until after they undergo evaluation and treatment or pass medical tests. The employees are then subject to random follow-up tests.

Employees who refuse to be tested or engage in conduct that clearly obstructs the testing process are subject to the same consequences as employees who test positive.

DOT regulations neither mandate nor forbid the imposition of additional discipline (such as discharge) by an employer for violating DOT rules. Employers are free to impose additional consequences on their own authority, subject to the legal obligations and limitations previously discussed.

Additional DOT Drug-Testing Requirements

The DOT regulations also require and authorize the following:

♦ Testing only for marijuana, cocaine, opiates, codeine, morphine, 6-acteylmorphine, amphetamines, methamphetamines, MDMA, MDA, MDEA, and phencyclidine (PCP).

♦ Testing only by labs certified by the U.S. Department of Health and Human Services.

♦ An MRO must assess test results. The MRO must determine whether there was a legitimate explanation for positive tests and whether lab the results were scientifically reliable.

♦ Employers must use the split-sample method of urine testing. Under this method, the urine sample provided at the testing site is divided into a primary sample and a split sample. Employees and applicants who receive verified positive results or verified adulterated or substituted results on the primary sample may request that the split-sample be sent to another certified lab for testing.

DOT Alcohol Testing

All employers covered by the DOT drug-testing regulations are also required to have an alcohol-testing program complying with DOT standards.

The alcohol rules provide for breath testing using trained technicians and evidential breath-testing devices. The breath-testing devices must be federally approved. The regulations allow the option of using saliva tests or nonevidential breath-testing devices for screening tests only.

Note: Confirmation tests must be conducted with evidential breath-testing devices.

Consequences for Violation of DOT Alcohol-Testing Regulations

Employees with a confirmation test result indicating a blood alcohol concentration (BAC) of 0.04 or greater or who otherwise violate the DOT alcohol regulations must be immediately removed from performing safety-sensitive duties.

They **may not** return to such duties until they are evaluated by a substance abuse professional and undergo a successful return-to-duty test. Such employees are also subject to follow-up testing and must successfully complete any prescribed treatment program.

Employees who refuse to be tested or obstruct testing are subject to the same consequences as employees testing 0.04 BAC or above. As with DOT drug testing, employers may impose additional discipline subject to the other legal obligations and limitations previously discussed.

Employees with a BAC between 0.02 and 0.39 are **not** deemed to be in violation of the regulations, but must be temporarily removed from safety-sensitive duty for 24 hours.

DOT-Required Alcohol Tests

The DOT regulations generally require covered employers to conduct the following types of alcohol tests:

♦ Post-accident.

- ◆ Reasonable suspicion.
- ◆ Return to duty.
- ◆ Follow-up.
- ◆ Random.

The DOT regulations require that random testing be conducted annually and, according to 49 C.F.R. 655.45, DOT employers in the motor carrier and mass transit industries must conduct a number of random alcohol tests each year equal to 10 percent of covered employees.

DOT Policy Requirement

Employers are required to prepare and distribute a policy explaining the requirements of DOT regulations to all covered employees. Each employee must sign a statement certifying receipt of the policy.

Drug-Free Workplace Act

According to the U.S. Department of Labor, millions of Americans use illicit drugs and nearly 75 percent of these users are employed.

Companies that have implemented drug-free workplace programs achieve dramatic benefits such as decreased absenteeism, a declining number of accidents, and increased productivity.

Covered Employers

All direct recipients of federal grants and most federal contractors holding a single contract under the federal acquisition regulations that exceeds $100,000, not for the acquisition of commercial goods, and performed in part (or in whole) in the United States must comply with the federal Drug-Free Workplace Act.

The act applies to employees and facilities engaged in directly performing work under such contracts and grants. It does not apply to subcontractors or second-tier recipients of pass-through grants, nor does it apply to companies that hold multiple small contracts totaling more than $100,000.

A company would be subject to the act only if the value of a single contract is more than $100,000. A company that has several contracts which, when combined, total more than $100,000, is not subject to the act.

Policy

Covered employers are required to retain a drug-free workplace accompanied by both a policy and a drug-free awareness program. The policy must notify employees performing work under the contract or grant of the following prohibitions and the penalties for convictions:

- ◆ Employee may not manufacture, distribute, possess, or use controlled substances in the workplace.
- ◆ Employees must report any criminal convictions for manufacturing, distributing, dispensing, possessing, or using controlled substances in the workplace to the employer within five days.

With respect to employees who report such convictions, employers have 30 days to take appropriate disciplinary action, up to and including discharge, or to require satisfactory participation in an assistance/rehabilitation program.

The act gives contractors and grantees discretion to decide what action to take. Contractors must also report any employee convictions for workplace drug crimes of which they have been notified to the contracting agency within 10 days.

The act also requires contractors and grantees to establish drug-free awareness programs informing employees of the employer's drug-free workplace policy, the adverse effects of drug abuse, the penalties that will be imposed for workplace drug violations, and any available drug counseling, rehabilitation, or assistance programs. However, the act does not require that a particular rehabilitation program be provided.

Under the act, drug testing, employee assistance programs, and supervisor training are optional. Such options and the ways unionized employers choose to exercise their discretion under the act are subject to collective bargaining. Thus, such employers may have to bargain over whether treatment will be offered and whether employees will be reassigned to jobs that do not involve the performance of federal contract work instead of being fired.

Grantees and contractors should maintain a current list of the facilities and departments performing federal contract work and have operable programs within 30 days of receiving contracts or grants.

Any government audits may include a review of Drug-Free Workplace Act compliance programs.

Department of Defense Regulations

Certain Department of Defense (DOD) contracts involving classified information and national security contain a drug-free workforce clause. DOD contracts should be reviewed individually to see whether they contain such a clause. Ordinarily, contracts to deliver commercial products and contracts to be performed outside the United States are not covered.

The clause requires prime contractors to institute and maintain a drug-free workforce program. Such programs must include the following:

- An employee assistance program (EAP) emphasizing high-level direction, education, counseling, rehabilitation, and coordination with available community resources.

- Supervisory training to identify and address illegal drug use by employees.

- Provisions for self-referrals and supervisory referrals to treatment, with maximum respect for confidentiality consistent with safety and security.

- A means of identifying illegal drug users, including drug testing employees in sensitive positions.

- The removal of identified drug users from sensitive positions. Contractors who are subject to the clause may not allow employees who use drugs illegally to remain on duty or perform in a sensitive position until the contractor determines that they may properly perform in the position.

Sensitive positions are positions involving access to classified information, national security, health or safety, or requiring a high degree of trust and confidence.

The rule provides that the criteria for testing shall be determined by the contractor based on such factors as the nature of the contract, the employee's job duties, and the risks to health, safety, or national security that could result from an employee's failure to perform the job adequately.

Testing is limited to the following:

- Marijuana.

- Cocaine.

- Opiates.

- ◆ PCP.
- ◆ Amphetamines.

In addition, contractors **may** test for the following reasons:

- ◆ When there is reasonable suspicion of use.
- ◆ When an employee is involved in an accident or unsafe practice.
- ◆ As part of treatment or follow-up to rehabilitation.
- ◆ As part of a voluntary testing program.
- ◆ As a part of a random testing program imposed without suspicion that a specific individual is using illegal drugs.

Contractors **may** also test applicants. Contractors who are subject to the clause **may not** allow employees who use drugs illegally to remain on duty or perform in a sensitive position until the contractor determines that they may properly perform in the position. Contractors must also adopt appropriate personnel procedures to deal with employees who use drugs illegally.

Considerations When Implementing a Drug- and Alcohol-Testing Program

Employers must consider a variety of factors when implementing a drug- and alcohol-testing program. The employer should determine the following:

- ◆ Why the program is being implemented.
- ◆ Who will be tested.
- ◆ What types of tests will be given.
- ◆ What substances will be tested.
- ◆ Who will give the tests.
- ◆ The consequences of a positive test.

Reasons to Implement Testing Programs

Testing programs **may** be implemented for the following reasons:

- ◆ To comply with federal requirements. These include requirements for certain Department of Defense (DOD) contractors, employers subject to the Nuclear Regulatory Commission, and employers subject to Department of Transportation (DOT) testing programs.
- ◆ To save money. Studies have shown that annually employers lose billions of dollars due to drug abuse among employees. These costs result from lost productivity, increased absenteeism, drug-related accidents, medical claims, and theft.
- ◆ To control insurance costs.
- ◆ To reduce workers' compensation premiums.
- ◆ For employee safety.

♦ To discourage drug-users from applying for employment. When an employer has a pre-employment drug-testing program, potential applicants who are drug users are less likely to apply for employment.

♦ To avoid negligent hiring and retention claims. An employer with a drug- and alcohol-testing program may be able to avoid claims of negligence for hiring or retaining employees who the employer knew or should have known had a substance abuse problem.

Employees to Be Tested

Employers must decide which employees will be tested. The options are to test applicants only, all employees, or merely those employees in safety-sensitive or security-sensitive positions. Employers may also decide to test only those employees they reasonably suspect are under the influence of alcohol or are using illegal drugs.

Types of Tests

The types of drug or alcohol tests that can be given include the following:

♦ **Pre-Employment.** Testing is given before employment to determine if the applicant is using illegal drugs. Most employers do not give pre-employment alcohol tests.

♦ **Reasonable Suspicion.** An employee may be tested if the employer has a reasonable basis to suspect an employee is using drugs or is at work under the influence of alcohol.

♦ **Post-Accident.** Testing is given after an employee is involved in an accident. Such testing is generally given if it is provided for in the employer's policy, placing the employee on notice of post-accident testing, and either personal injury is involved or damage to property is estimated at a minimal level.

♦ **Random.** Testing is given on an unannounced basis and employees are selected for testing on a random basis.

♦ **Follow-Up.** Testing is given on a scheduled or random basis when an employee returns to work after completing rehabilitation or counseling for substance abuse.

♦ **Periodic.** Testing is given at specified times. This may be used for employees who have returned to the workforce after testing positive or employees who are in safety- or security-sensitive positions. For example, commercial motor vehicle drivers may be required to submit to an annual test in addition to being subjected to random testing.

Testing for Substance Type

Employers **may** test for the following types of substances:

♦ Alcohol.

♦ The five-drug panel required for DOT testing — cocaine, opiates, amphetamines, PCP, and marijuana.

♦ An eight-drug panel or as many substances as a laboratory is capable of accurately testing.

♦ Abused prescription drugs.

The common drugs of abuse are those contained in the five-drug panel required for DOT testing. Employers that test beyond those drugs likely incur an unnecessary expense.

Testing Laboratory

Care should be taken in the selection of a laboratory to analyze the tests.

Employers required to test employees under federal drug-testing programs must use laboratories certified for those programs. Even when not required by law, it is preferable to have a laboratory that is certified to perform drug testing in federal programs.

It is important to have a reputable laboratory, experienced and knowledgeable in the proper methods of handling and analyzing urine samples and breath alcohol tests. A good chain of custody is essential to ensure unadulterated samples have been analyzed and that there may be no question as to which sample has been analyzed.

The laboratory should have the highest quality-control standards. A screening test should be used for samples with a confirming test for positive results. The most reliable confirming test is considered to be gas chromatography/mass spectrometry. Laboratory personnel must be willing to defend results and testify in arbitration or court hearings.

Employees should be given notice of test results and an opportunity to establish a legitimate explanation for positive drug-test results to a medical review officer (MRO). Positive drug test results should be verified by the MRO before being reported to the employer.

Consequences of a Positive Test Result

Any drug- and alcohol-policy must have a clear statement as to the consequences of a positive result or for the refusal by an employee to take a required test.

The consequences for refusing to be tested should be similar to the penalties for failing a test thereby offering employees an incentive to be cooperative. If an employee assistance program is part of the policy, one element should include referral to the EAP.

During policy development, employers must consider the following questions in determining a response to positive test results:

- Will there be an opportunity for rehabilitation?
- Is the program to be a one-, two-, or three-strike program?
- Will an employee be terminated upon their first positive test result?
- Will the employee be required to complete or merely enroll in a rehabilitation program before being permitted to return to work?
- Will the employee be required to enter into a last-chance agreement?
- Will there be a disciplinary suspension or a suspension until the employee is drug free?
- If the employee is in a safety-sensitive or security-sensitive position, will there be a transfer or demotion after a positive test?
- Will the transfer or demotion be for a specified period of time or indefinitely?

Other Features of a Good Testing Policy

A good testing policy will provide the following:

- Clearly describe the prohibited conduct and the consequences for such conduct.
- Consider whether to create an EAP.
- Effectively communicate the policy and program to employees and supervisors. Employees should be required to separately sign the policy even if they are already required to sign a general acknowledgment of receipt of a policy handbook.
- Ensure adequate training for supervisors and education for employees.

- ◆ Require consent forms for all tests and make clear that refusal to comply will be considered a violation of the policy.

- ◆ Ensure an employee's privacy is protected in the testing process and dissemination of test results.

- ◆ Document all performance inadequacies.

State Law Considerations Concerning a Drug- and Alcohol-Testing Program

Employers who are not covered by federal laws or regulations must consider whether state or local laws or regulations concerning drug and alcohol testing apply. Most states allow an employer to deny or reduce workers' compensation payments if alcohol or drugs are found to be the proximate cause of the employee's injury. Recently, however, states have taken action to promote drug-free workplace programs by offering a premium reduction for all employers who comply with the regulations. The regulations typically require companies to have a written substance abuse policy that is distributed to all employees, conduct drug and alcohol testing, and provide EAPs for those testing positive. Today 11 states including Florida, Hawaii, and Washington offer such insurance reductions.

Some states have implemented drug-free workplace programs for state contractors. These laws require any individual or company receiving a grant from the state to have a drug-free workplace program. Only seven states have enacted such legislation — California, Florida, Georgia, Illinois, Oregon, South Carolina, and Tennessee. Although only a handful of states have implemented drug-free workplace programs for state contractors, 20 states regulate drug-testing procedures to ensure that employees' rights are not violated. Some states like Alaska, Mississippi, and Utah have taken this a step further by providing legal protection to employers who establish drug- and alcohol-testing programs.

Employee Drug Use

Drug and Alcohol Abuse — Performance Indicators

Changes in job performance and in behavior on the job may be indicators that an employee has a problem with drugs or alcohol.

It is vital for employers to objectively and carefully document such changes.

Some performance indicators that may indicate an employee has a drug or alcohol problem are the following:

- ◆ Frequent tardiness or absences for implausible reasons.

- ◆ Unreasonably long lunch, coffee, or bathroom breaks.

- ◆ Frequently missed deadlines.

- ◆ Disruption of fellow employees.

- ◆ Withdrawal from interaction with fellow employees.

- ◆ Overreaction to constructive criticism.

- ◆ Frequent mistakes related to poor judgment.

- ◆ Decreased productivity.

♦ Great variations in productivity from day to day.

♦ Inability to concentrate on work.

Guidelines for Supervisors When Confronting a Troubled Employee

The following are actions an employer **should** take if an employee is suspected of drug or alcohol abuse on the job:

♦ **Do** establish expected levels of work performance.

♦ **Do** document any and all significant facts and information.

♦ **Do** be consistent in dealing with the employee.

♦ **Do** be firm with expectations of the employee and consequences should expectations fail to be met.

♦ **Do** be prepared to deal with the employee's resistance, denial, defensiveness, and hostility.

♦ **Do** base confrontation on job performance and/or on specific, observed behavior including, for example:

  • Slurred speech.

  • Stumbling gait.

  • Bloodshot eyes.

  • The smell of alcohol on breath.

♦ **Do** be direct with the employee.

♦ **Do** provide the information and make appropriate referral according to company policy.

♦ **Do** take the responsibility to intervene.

♦ **Do** continue to monitor and document.

♦ **Do** provide an environment where the employee may be honest and open with perceived troubles.

The following are actions an employer **should not** take if an employee is suspected of drug or alcohol abuse on the job:

♦ **Do not** be a diagnostician or counselor.

♦ **Do not** make value judgments or moralize.

♦ **Do not** allow the employee to pit a supervisor against higher management or the union.

♦ **Do not** make idle disciplinary threats.

♦ **Do not** discuss drinking of alcohol unless it occurs on the job.

♦ **Do not** treat employees differently.

♦ **Do not** ignore the problem.

Contact Information

Department of Health and Human Services

200 Independence Avenue, SW
Washington, DC 20201

Telephone: 202-619-0257
Toll-Free: 877-696-6775
Internet: *www.hhs.gov*

Drug Enforcement Administration

Mailstop: AES
8701 Morrissette Drive
Springfield, VA 22152

Telephone: 202-307-1000
Internet: *www.justice.gov/dea/index.htm*

Employee Assistance Professionals Association

4350 North Fairfax Drive
Suite 410
Arlington, VA 22203

Telephone: 703-387-1000
Fax: 703-522-4585
Internet: *www.eapassn.org*

Substance Abuse and Mental Health Services Administration

1 Choke Cherry Road
Rockville, MD 20857

Telephone: 240-276-2130
Fax: 240-276-2135
Internet: *www.samhsa.gov*

Working Partners for an Alcohol- and Drug-Free Workplace

200 Constitution Avenue, Room S-2312
Washington, DC 20210

Telephone: 202-693-5919
Fax: 202-693-5961
Internet: *www.dol.gov/workingpartners*

Illinois Law

The Illinois Drug-Free Workplace Act

The Illinois Drug-Free Workplace Act, located at 30 Ill. Comp. Stat. §§ 580/1 – 580/11, requires that grantees and contractors provide a drug-free workplace. A *drug-free workplace* is a site where work is completed in connection with a specific grant or contract and the employees of the site are prohibited from engaging in the unlawful manufacture, distribution, possession, or use of a controlled substance (as defined by the Illinois Controlled Substance Act and Cannabis Control Act).

Any actions undertaken by a contractor or grantee in compliance with the Illinois Drug-Free Workplace Act and in establishing a drug-free workplace will create a rebuttable presumption of good faith compliance with the act and will **not** be considered a violation of the Illinois Human Rights Act.

Covered Employers

The act applies to the following grantees and contractors as follows:

♦ Corporations, partnerships, or other entities with 25 or more employees at the time of issuing the grant or at the time of letting the contract.

♦ Departments, divisions, or other units directly responsible for the specific performance under a grant or contract of $5,000 or more from Illinois.

However, grantees and contractors **do not** include corporations, partnerships, or other entities that receive public funds in connection with any of the following:

♦ The WIC Vendor Management Act.

♦ Medical assistance reimbursements to pharmacies for prescribed drugs and reimbursements for durable medical supplies covered under Article V of the Illinois Public Aid Code.

♦ The vendor's discount for collection of use and occupation taxes pursuant to the Use Tax Act.

♦ The Service Use Tax Act.

♦ The Service Occupation Tax Act.

♦ The Retailers' Occupation Tax Act.

♦ The Superfund program contained in the Illinois Environmental Protection Act.

♦ The lease or rental of real property.

♦ Grants or loans made for the purpose of solid waste management or reduction.

♦ The subcontractor of a grantee or a railroad subject to a federally mandated drug-testing program.

Contracts and Grants

Before receiving a grant or being awarded a property or service contract from Illinois, the contractor or grantee must certify the providing of a drug-free workplace by completing the following:

♦ Publishing a statement containing the following:

• Notice to employees that the unlawful manufacture, distribution, dispensation, possession, or use of a controlled substance (including cannabis) is prohibited in the workplace.

- Specification of the actions taken against employees for violations of the prohibition.

- Notice to employees that as a condition of employment under the contract or grant, the employee must abide by the terms of the drug-free workplace statement and notify the employer of any criminal drug statute conviction for a violation occurring in the workplace no later than five days after the conviction.

♦ Establishing a drug-free awareness program to inform employees about the following:

- The dangers of drug abuse in the workplace.

- The grantee's or contractor's policy of maintaining a drug-free workplace.

- Any available drug counseling, rehabilitation, and employee assistance programs (EAPs).

- The penalties that may be imposed on employees for drug violations.

♦ Giving copies of the drug-free workplace statement to each employee involved in the performance of the contract or grant and posting the statement in a prominent place in the workplace.

♦ Notifying the contracting or granting agency within 10 days after receiving notice of a criminal drug statute conviction.

♦ Imposing sanctions on any convicted employee or requiring the employee to participate in a drug abuse assistance or rehabilitation program.

♦ Assisting employees select a course of action when drug counseling, treatment, and rehabilitation are required and indicating that a trained referral team is in place.

♦ Making a good faith effort to continue to maintain a drug-free workplace through implementation of the requirements.

Rebuttable Presumption of Good-Faith Compliance

Any actions undertaken by a contractor or grantee in compliance with this act and in establishing a drug-free workplace will create a rebuttable presumption of good-faith compliance with this act and will not be considered a violation of the Illinois Human Rights Act.

Requirements for Individuals

Illinois may not enter into a contract for more than $5,000 or make a grant of more than $5,000 with any individual unless the contract or grant includes a certification by the individual that the individual will not engage in the unlawful manufacture, distribution, dispensation, possession, or use of a controlled substance in the performance of the contract.

Enforcement

Employee Sanctions and Remedies

Within 30 days after receiving notice from an employee of a conviction of a violation of a criminal drug statute occurring in the workplace, a grantee or contractor must complete the following:

♦ Take appropriate personnel action against the employee up to, and including, termination.

♦ Require the employee to satisfactorily participate in a drug-abuse assistance or rehabilitation program approved by a federal, state, or local health, law enforcement, or other appropriate agency.

Contractor or Grantee Suspension, Termination, or Debarment

Each contract or grant awarded by Illinois is subject to suspension of payments, termination, or both.

The contractor, grantee, individual entering the contract, and recipient of the grant are subject to suspension or debarment if the head of the agency determines any of the following:

◆ The contractor, grantee, individual, or recipient made a false certification.

◆ The contractor or grantee violates the certification by failing to carry out the requirements.

◆ The contractor or grantee fails to take appropriate remedial action against employees convicted on drug offenses.

◆ The number of employees convicted of criminal drug statute violations, which occurred in the workplace demonstrates that the contractor or grant recipient failed to make a good-faith effort to provide the required drug-free workplace.

For a period of one to five years, a debarred contractor, grantee, or individual will be ineligible for the award of any contract or grant by the state.

Waiver

The head of an agency may waive any termination, suspension of payments, suspension, or debarment under the Illinois Drug-Free Workplace Act. However, the head of the agency must determine that suspension or debarment of the contractor, grantee, or individual would severely disrupt the agency's operation to the detriment of the general public or would not be in the public interest.

Substance Abuse Prevention on Public Works Projects Act

The Illinois Substance Abuse Prevention on Public Works Projects Act, located at 820 Ill. Comp. Stat. §§ 265/1 – 265/99, applies to a contract to perform work on a public works project for which bids are opened on or after January 1, 2008, or, if bids are not solicited for the contract, to a contract to perform such work entered into on or after January 1, 2008. Employers covered by the act are contractors or subcontractors performing a public works project. Employees covered by the act are laborers, mechanics, or other workers employed in any public works by anyone under a contract for public works.

According to the act:

◆ No employee may use, possess, distribute, deliver, or be under the influence of a drug, or use or be under the influence of alcohol, while performing work on a public works project. A *drug* is a controlled substance as defined in the Illinois Controlled Substances Act or cannabis as defined in the Cannabis Control Act for which testing is required by an employer under its substance abuse prevention program under the act. A drug also includes prescribed medications not used in accordance with a valid prescription.

◆ An employee is considered to be under the influence of alcohol for purposes of the act if the alcohol concentration in the employee's blood or breath at the time alleged, as shown by analysis of the their blood or breath, is at or above 0.02. *Alcohol* is any substance containing any form of alcohol including, but not limited to, ethanol, methanol, propanol, and isopropanol. *Alcohol concentration* is either the number of grams of alcohol per 210 liters of breath or the number of grams of alcohol per 100 milliliters of blood.

Note: The provisions of the act apply only to the extent there is no collective-bargaining agreement in effect dealing with substance abuse prevention on public works projects.

Prevention Programs

Before an employer commences work on a public works project, the employer must have in place a written program which meets or exceeds the program requirements in the act, to be filed with the public body engaged in the construction of the public works and made available to the general public, for the prevention of substance abuse among its employees. The testing must be performed by a laboratory that is certified for Federal Workplace Drug Testing Programs by the Substance Abuse and Mental Health Service Administration of the U.S. Department of Health and Human Services.

At a minimum, the program must include all of the following:

♦ A minimum requirement of a 9 panel urine drug test plus a test for alcohol. Testing an employee's blood may only be used for post-accident testing; however, blood testing is not mandatory for the employer where a urine test is sufficient.

♦ A prohibition against substance abuse or conditions thereof.

♦ A requirement that employees performing the work on a public works project submit to prehire, random, reasonable suspicion, and post-accident drug and alcohol testing. Testing of an employee before commencing work on a public works project is not required if the employee has been participating in a random testing program during the 90 days preceding the date on which the employee commenced work on the public works project.

♦ A procedure for notifying an employee who violates the prohibition against substance abuse, who tests positive for the presence of a drug in their system, or who refuses to submit to drug or alcohol testing as required under the program that the employee may not perform work on a public works project until the employee meets certain conditions.

Reasonable Suspicion Testing

An employee whose supervisor has reasonable suspicion to believe the employee is under the influence of alcohol or a drug is subject to discipline up to and including suspension, and must be required to undergo an alcohol or drug test. *Reasonable suspicion* is a belief, based on behavioral observations or other evidence, sufficient to lead a prudent or reasonable person to suspect an employee is under the influence and exhibits slurred speech, erratic behavior, decreased motor skills, or other such traits. Circumstances, both physical and psychological, are given consideration in determining reasonable suspicion.

Whenever possible before an employee is required to submit to testing based on reasonable suspicion, the employee must be observed by more than one supervisory or managerial employee. Observation of such an employee should be performed by a supervisory or managerial employee who has successfully completed a certified training program to recognize drug and alcohol abuse.

The employer who is requiring an employee to be tested based upon reasonable suspicion must provide transportation for the employee to the testing facility and may send a representative to accompany the employee to the testing facility. Under no circumstances may an employee thought to be under the influence of alcohol or a drug be allowed to operate a vehicle or other equipment for any purpose. The employee will be removed from the jobsite and placed on inactive status pending the employer's receipt of notice of the test results.

The employee has the right to request a representative or designee to be present at the time they are directed to provide a specimen for testing based upon reasonable suspicion. If the test result is positive for drugs or alcohol, the employee is subject to termination. If the test result is negative, the employee is placed on active status and put back to work by the employer. The employee must be paid for all lost time to include all time needed to complete the drug or alcohol test and any and all overtime according to the employee's contract.

Costs

Employers must pay all costs related to reasonable suspicion testing. Additionally, employers are responsible for the cost of developing, implementing, and enforcing a substance abuse prevention program, including the cost of drug and alcohol testing of its employees under the program, except when these costs are covered under provisions in a collective-bargaining agreement. The contracting agency is not responsible for that cost, for the cost of any medical review of a test result, or for any rehabilitation provided to an employee.

Employee Access

An employer may not permit an employee who violates the substance abuse prohibitions, who tests positive for the presence of a drug in their system, or who refuses to submit to drug or alcohol testing as required under the employer's substance abuse prevention program to perform work on a public works project until the employee meets certain conditions.

An employer must immediately remove an employee from work on a public works project if any of the following occurs:

- ♦ The employee violates the substance abuse prohibitions, tests positive for the presence of a drug in their system, or refuses to submit to drug or alcohol testing as required under the employer's substance abuse prevention program.

- ♦ An officer or employee of the contracting agency, preferably one trained to recognize drug and alcohol abuse, has a reasonable suspicion that the employee is in violation of the substance abuse prohibitions and requests the employer to immediately remove the employee from work on the public works project for reasonable suspicion testing.

Certain Conditions

An employee who is barred or removed from work on a public works project may commence or return to work on the public works project upon their employer providing to the contracting agency documentation showing all of the following:

- ♦ That the employee has tested negative for the presence of drugs in their system and is not under the influence of alcohol.

- ♦ That the employee has been approved to commence or return to work on the public works project in accordance with the employer's substance abuse prevention program.

- ♦ Testing for the presence of drugs or alcohol in an employee's system and the handling of test specimens was conducted in accordance with guidelines for laboratory testing procedures and chain-of-custody procedures established by the Substance Abuse and Mental Health Service Administration of the U.S. Department of Health and Human Services.

Additionally, upon successfully completing a rehabilitation program, an employee will be reinstated to their former employment status if work for which the employee is qualified exists.

The Illinois Human Rights Act

The Illinois Human Rights Act, located at 775 Ill. Comp. Stat. §§ 5/1-101 – 5/10-104, covers **all** public and private employers as follows:

- ♦ Employing 15 or more employees during 20 or more calendar weeks within the calendar year of or preceding an alleged violation.

- Employing one or more employees when a complaint alleges civil rights violations due to unlawful discrimination based on an employees physical or mental disability unrelated to ability.

- Employing one or more employees when a complaint alleges civil rights violations due to unlawful discrimination based on sexual harassment.

- Public employers, parties to a public contract, joint apprenticeship, or training committee without regard to the number of employees.

Disability

According to the Illinois Human Right Act, an employee or applicant will not be legally classified as with a disability where the individual is currently engaged in the illegal use of drugs when an employer acts on the basis of such use.

However, the disability classification exclusion **does not apply** under the following circumstances:

- The employee or applicant successfully completed a supervised drug rehabilitation program, or has been otherwise rehabilitated, and no longer engages in the illegal use of drugs.

- The employee or applicant is participating in a supervised rehabilitation program and is no longer engaging in illegal drug use.

- The employee or applicant was wrongly regarded as engaging in illegal drug use, but is not engaging in such use.

Employers may adopt or administer reasonable policies or procedures, including drug testing, designed to ensure that a rehabilitated individual is no longer engaging in illegal drug use.

Policies

Employers may implement and enforce all of the following policies:

- Prohibit the illegal use of drugs and the use of alcohol by all employees at the workplace.

- Require that employees not be under the influence of alcohol or engage in the illegal use of drugs at the workplace.

- Require employees to comply with the requirements of the federal Drug-Free Workplace Act and the Illinois Drug-Free Workplace Act.

- Hold employees engaging in illegal drug use or alcoholic employees to the same qualification standards for employment, job performance, and behavior as other employees, even if unsatisfactory performance or behavior is related to the drug use or alcoholism.

- Require the following compliance from employees, with respect to federal regulations regarding alcohol and the illegal use of drugs:

  • Compliance with the standards of the U.S. Department of Defense regulations, if the employees are in an industry subject to the regulations.

  • Compliance with the standards of the Nuclear Regulatory Commission regulations, if the employees are in an industry subject to the regulations.

  • Compliance with the standards of the U.S. Department of Transportation regulations, if the employees are in a transportation industry subject to the regulations.

Additional Provisions

Medical Exams

A test to determine the illegal use of drugs will not be considered a medical examination. However, the Illinois Human Rights Act regulations do not encourage, prohibit, or authorize the conduction of drug testing for the illegal use of drugs by job applicants or employees or making employment decisions based on test results.

High-Risk and Safety-Sensitive Jobs

Employers subject to the jurisdiction of the U.S. Department of Transportation are not encouraged, prohibited, restricted, or authorized by the Illinois Human Rights Act to:

♦ Test employees of, and applicants for, safety-sensitive positions for the illegal use of drugs and for on-duty alcohol impairment.

♦ Remove employees and applicants who test positive for illegal drug use and on-duty alcohol impairment from safety-sensitive duties.

Contact Information

Illinois Department of Human Rights

222 South College, Floor 1
Springfield, IL 62704

Telephone: 217-785-5100
Fax: 217-785-5106
Internet: *www.state.il.us/dhr*

Chapter 17

Employee Performance Evaluations

Introduction

The most stressful decisions made by managers often involve employee performance evaluations. Performed correctly, an evaluation facilitates communication between the employer and the employee and provides helpful data for salary increases, bonuses, promotions, demotions, or terminations. Conversely, poorly planned evaluations can result in unnecessary legal complications, such as wrongful termination. The following are the two most important aspects of a successful evaluation system:

- ◆ Communication — including accurate communication of expectations, honesty, effective presentation techniques, open interaction with employees, and confidentiality.
- ◆ Procedure — including consistency, content, documentation, and the use of self-evaluations.

This chapter examines these factors and attempts to provide a legal and commonsense approach to conducting successful evaluations.

Communication

Communication, an important aspect of a successful evaluation process, includes the accurate disclosure of expectations, honesty, presentation techniques, interaction with employees, and confidentiality.

Expectations

Essentially, there are two components to clear communication of expectations. The first is a properly constructed job description that can serve as the basis of the evaluation. The second is a compilation of employer and employee goals for the upcoming evaluation period. After the initial evaluation, the goals can be monitored to chart an employee's progress.

Job Description

The initial step of any successful performance evaluation process must be to establish the legitimate expectations of the employer. The best method for accomplishing this task is to incorporate an accurate job description into the evaluation process. Properly designed job descriptions focus employees on the essential purpose and functions of their jobs, preventing them from becoming sidetracked by inconsequential tasks. A current and well-prepared job description can also be critical in defending a wrongful termination or other lawsuit, since it ensures that the employee knew in advance what was expected and how performance would be measured.

351

Goals

The performance evaluation should also include a description of an employee's goals for the coming year. This should include goals established by the employer as well as goals set by the employee. Goals may include working on specific projects, improving character traits, or meeting certain quota requirements.

Example: ABC Corporation requires managers to evaluate employees once a year and to meet with employees to discuss their performance. Mary, an employee, received an evaluation encouraging her to keep up the good work. However, the manager never specifically explained to Mary what he liked about her work or what she might improve upon. Mary enjoyed the positive reinforcement but would have benefited from a discussion with her employer regarding shared goals for the coming year.

Honesty

The largest problem encountered by employers using formalized evaluations is the reluctance of the evaluator to be candid with the employee. Fear of hurting feelings or creating an uncomfortable work environment results in inaccurate and problematic evaluations. Although some managers have been known to be unduly harsh, the problem usually is misguided praise.

An employer's failure to include justifiable criticism in an employee's evaluation may have legal repercussions. A poorly or marginally performing employee who is terminated may rely on positive evaluations as evidence of adequate performance. For example, if an employee who received perpetual good or even glowing evaluations were terminated, the logical inference would be that the employer terminated the employee for a reason other than performance and that the employer's stated reason for the dismissal was unlawful. In addition, noncritical performance evaluations may result in an employee's eligibility for undeserved pay increases or job promotions.

Example: Due to his constant absenteeism, John, an ABC employee, should receive an "inadequate" rating for productivity but instead receives a "satisfactory." Mary, a good employee who unfortunately was temporarily disabled during the winter, also receives a "satisfactory." John is terminated six weeks later because of poor productivity. John, relying on his evaluations, thought his productivity was acceptable and took no steps to improve. John files a sex discrimination suit against ABC alleging female employees with similar absenteeism records were not discharged. As evidence for John's suit, he compares his productivity evaluation with Mary's.

Presentation

Managers and supervisors must be aware that an evaluation is a very stressful event for the employee. Employees listen very carefully to the manner and content of the employer's message. Care must be taken to avoid any miscommunication or misperceptions. Employers should be particularly careful not to use inflammatory words. Informing an employee that the employer is not satisfied is never easy, but careful wording can reduce stress for both the employer and the employee without reducing the effectiveness of the message.

Employers must avoid using tactless language during an evaluation. For example, an employer can say an employee "lacks interpersonal skills"; however, the employer should not say that the employee "needs a course in charm school." Juries are seldom amused by such comments.

Bear in mind that the language used in one employee's evaluation can lead to a legal claim by another employee. For example, an employer refers to a new vice-president as providing "new blood"; an older employee who did not receive the vice-president position could use this choice of words in a subsequent age discrimination claim. Although the comments were not meant to intentionally harm another employee, such statements can create legal problems for the employer.

Example: John is an older branch manager with ABC. The manager evaluates John's performance by stating that one "can't teach an old dog new tricks." John is ultimately replaced with a younger employee. The employer's inconsiderate and stereotypical comment is used as evidence in John's subsequent age discrimination claim.

Interaction

Efficient communication requires collaborative interaction between the involved parties. Employers should not consider an evaluation as an opportunity to preach to the employee. Rather, the employee should have the opportunity to comment on the evaluation and be encouraged to provide written comments on the evaluation form.

Where feedback is permitted, the evaluation process gains enhanced validity because employees feel that they are a component of the evaluation system. Even when an employee disagrees with the substance of the evaluation, providing the employee an opportunity to speak may lessen the employee's potential hostility or resentment.

Allowing the employee to provide an oral or written response to an evaluation is beneficial to the employee and the employer. Perceptive employers can learn a great deal from employee-provided feedback. Consistent employee dissatisfaction within the same section or department may indicate that a manager or supervisor is unduly harsh or perhaps discriminatory. Similarly, a pattern of unjustified complaints by a particular employee should warn the employer of a potential problem.

Example: An employer receives several comments from female employees stating that their evaluations from a particular supervisor are undeservedly low and overly harsh. This should cause the perceptive employer to look closely at the supervisor for possible discriminatory conduct. The employee comments bring the supervisor's actions into question, where without employee comments the supervisor's potential abuse of the evaluation process may have been overlooked.

Confidentiality

All employee evaluations are confidential, and access to an employee's evaluations should be strictly limited. Access may only be provided to persons with a legitimate reason to know the evaluation's contents. However, qualified immunity provides employers with reasonable protection from defamation and other causes of action stemming from an evaluation. For example, distributing the evaluation information only to persons involved in the evaluation process (such as managers and human resource personnel) would be an act protected by qualified immunity, while sharing the information with others outside of the process would not be protected and could be a source of liability.

In addition, going beyond statements of opinions about an employee's work performance in an evaluation report and making specific statements of fact (statements capable of objective proof) about what an employee did or did not do, if erroneous, may be a basis for a defamation claim where state law permits. For example, specific statements of fact would be stating that a hospital worker changed the strength of radiation doses prescribed by a physician or misplaced radiation sources to endanger other employees and lied in an effort to cover up these errors.

Example: A manager at ABC made the mistake of telling Mary, a recent nonsupervisory hire and good friend, about his demoralizing evaluation of John. The manager told Mary how John's drinking problem was preventing him from performing adequately. Mary repeats the confidential information to her friends at lunch. This could lead to potential claims of discrimination, defamation, or intentional infliction of emotional distress. It was improper for Mary's manager to discuss John's evaluation with her since Mary had no reason to learn the content of the evaluation.

Procedure

Procedure, another important aspect of the evaluation process, includes the consistency, content, and documentation of employee evaluations, as well as the use of employee self-evaluations to further involve employees in the process.

Consistency

A process should be in place to evaluate all employees on a regular basis at a minimum of once a year. The evaluation procedure should indicate which manager or supervisor is responsible for each employee's evaluation. Issues of inconsistency occur when an employer's evaluation process is not formalized. For example, the evaluation system should include firm dates for which evaluations must be completed. Failure to give an employee a timely evaluation can serve as possible evidence of discriminatory conduct.

Example: ABC is a growing organization with no formal evaluation procedure. Jane is a foreman at ABC who is performing below expectations. ABC decides that in order to create a paper trail Jane will be evaluated next week. Even though the evaluation will be truthful when it states that she is a poor performer, Jane might use the inconsistent timing of the evaluation in subsequent litigation.

Content

An evaluation form is only beneficial if it evaluates the correct information. Too often evaluation forms contain little useful information. For instance, neither the employee nor the employer will gain significant insight from a purely numerical system of evaluation. Words capture a sense of employee performance better than raw numbers. Thus, if an employer chooses to use a numeric scale, it is important to assign a cogent explanation for each potential choice so that the numbers will be meaningful and there is consistency across evaluations.

Although avoiding liability is important, the main goal of the evaluation process is to create an accurate and current record of the employee's overall performance. Specificity is important, particularly when dealing with generalized character traits, such as leadership or knowledge.

Additionally, evaluators should be encouraged to use the entire spectrum of the evaluation and avoid the temptation to group employees together in the middle range. While it is certainly easier to distinguish higher-performing employees from lower-performing employees, it is just as important to draw finer distinctions among employees performing between those extremes. In drawing these distinctions, employers should consider what actually distinguishes each performance level from the other.

Example: A successful evaluation occurs when employees are informed about their employer's expectations. An evaluation form is helpful if it has a legend similar to the following:

Rating		Description
Unsatisfactory	=	Consistently below expectations
Needs Work	=	Sometimes below expectations
Satisfactory	=	Consistently meets expectations
Excellent	=	Sometimes exceeds expectations
Outstanding	=	Consistently exceeds expectations

Importantly, ratings should be accompanied by comments of the evaluator addressing particular elements of the employee's work.

Documentation

An evaluation is of little use if it is not properly documented. In addition to providing a record of the substance of an employee's evaluation, the evaluation form should also indicate the time and date of the evaluation, as well as any comments, complaints, or suggestions made by the employee during the course of the evaluation. Particular attention should be paid when the manager performing the evaluation may not be the employee's immediate supervisor.

A standardized evaluation form is helpful in ensuring that all relevant information is discussed and also provides a level of consistency among various evaluators. A sample of a **Performance Evaluation Checklist** is included at the end of this chapter to help employers ensure a successful evaluation.

Example: A manager at ABC Corporation completes an evaluation form and meets with an employee, Tom Jones, to discuss Tom's employment performance. During the meeting, Tom tells the manager that he is interested in transferring to another department because he is unable to get along with his immediate supervisor. The manager should ask the reasons for the conflict, consider how they might affect the evaluation, and document the discussion in a comments section after the evaluation is complete.

Employee Signature

The employee should sign the evaluation form after the completion of the evaluation. The signature block should clearly explain that the employee's signature is only an indication the employee has reviewed and understood the rating received. It should not suggest that the employee agrees with the substance of the evaluation.

Self-Evaluation

Employers may want to include employee self-evaluations as part of the evaluation process. Employees should complete self-evaluations on the same form used by the employer and should submit the self-evaluation in time for the employer to include it with the supervisor's evaluation. Self-evaluations provide a way to gain employee participation in the evaluation process.

The Post-Evaluation Meeting

After completion of the evaluation, it is important that the employer conveys the content of the evaluation clearly during a post-evaluation meeting in accordance with the following procedures:

- Conduct the post-evaluation meeting in private.
- Conduct the meeting in a professional manner.
- Be specific.
- Do not threaten.
- Explain any consequences thoroughly.
- Encourage dialogue.
- Listen carefully.
- Document the meeting by adding a written summary to the file.

Alternative Methods of Evaluation

Much like the ever-changing business environment, new and purportedly improved methods of evaluations are constantly appearing.

Computer Assistance

Computer software is available to lead managers through the evaluation process while looking out for the use of dangerous vocabulary on the evaluation.

These programs are especially designed to make the evaluation process more consistent among employees and to help employers avoid unintentional legal problems.

Multi-Rater Feedback Systems

Multi-rater feedback systems, also known as *360-degree evaluations*, widen the evaluation base to provide as much information as possible. This method relies on information collected from an employee's direct reports, peers, and supervisors.

Some employers widen the evaluation process even further and include feedback from customer and clients. This is referred to as a *540-degree system*.

For employers to successfully use a multi-rater feedback system, they must be conscientious of the following:

- ◆ Ensure that people provide honest feedback.

- ◆ Ensure that the data remains confidential.

- ◆ Ensure that subjects can use the data to improve their performance.

- ◆ Verify that the data provided is accurate.

- ◆ Understand how the system will affect the overall organization and make any necessary adjustments.

There are some drawbacks to the 360-degree system. For instance, because there is a possibility that peers may falsify input to the detriment of their co-workers for their own benefit, employers should not use peer evaluations as a basis for bonuses or other compensation programs. Further, some managers may find it difficult to share the evaluation process with other employees or to be evaluated by their subordinates.

Example: Jane Smith receives an evaluation from her supervisor yet disregards it because she believes the supervisor does not like her. A year later ABC Corporation implements a 360-degree system. Jane once again gets similar reviews from peers. She places more credibility in the peer review and improves in targeted areas.

Performance Evaluation Checklist (Sample)

❑ Maintain a current and accurate job description for each position that will be evaluated.

❑ Ensure that employees have access to the job description for their positions, so they are aware of the essential job duties and performance objectives for their jobs, as well as the means by which their performance will be measured and evaluated.

❑ Understand that the job of conducting a proper and effective performance evaluation is difficult, and only choose persons who will have the honesty, clarity of judgment, personal fortitude, and interpersonal skills necessary to conduct a proper and effective evaluation.

❑ Ensure that persons selected to serve as evaluators are properly trained. Evaluators must thoroughly understand the job that they are evaluating, as well as the importance of a timely, honest, fair, and confidential performance evaluation.

❑ Evaluators should be provided with clear instructions regarding the manner in which the company would like all performance evaluations to be conducted so there is consistency in the procedures and rating of employees.

❑ After an evaluation has been completed, review its form and content with representatives of the human resource department and/or upper management before sharing it with the employee. Problems can be remedied before they create difficulties — legal or otherwise — and consistency can be maintained in the application of company evaluation procedures.

❑ Ensure that employees are formally reviewed on a regular basis, but no less than once a year. This should be done in a face-to-face evaluation conference.

❑ After the employer shares feedback, allow the employee to state their reaction to the content of the evaluation verbally and in writing.

❑ Require every employee to sign their performance evaluation acknowledging that they have seen the evaluation. Note that this signature should not suggest the employee agrees with the contents of the evaluation, only that the employee has knowledge of the information contained in the evaluation.

❑ Maintain the confidentiality of every employee performance evaluation to the maximum extent possible.

❑ Regularly review and assess the effectiveness of the current evaluation system including evaluation forms, evaluation procedures, evaluator training, and evaluator neutrality. Make any changes that are necessary.

Note: This is a generic sample policy and does not necessarily reflect the employment laws in any or all of the 50 U.S. states. Review the applicable state laws or seek guidance from legal counsel before establishing any company policy.

Chapter 18

Personnel Files

Introduction

Scenario 1

It is 4:30 on a Friday afternoon. As Mr. Smith collects his things to leave, he receives a call from an Office of Federal Contract Compliance Programs (OFCCP) Officer. The officer informs Mr. Smith that a complaint has been filed with his office and an on-site review/investigation will be conducted first thing Monday morning. As part of his investigation, the officer wishes to examine the personnel records of all employees employed within the past two years. He says "good-bye." Mr. Smith's plans for a relaxing weekend on the beach have suddenly transformed into a stress-filled three days of preparation.

Scenario 2

A disgruntled employee has filed a charge with the Equal Employment Opportunity Commission (EEOC) alleging employer discrimination in promotion opportunities. The EEOC investigator calls and informs the employer that she would like to conduct an on-site visit to review the personnel file of the former employee and other relevant persons. The on-site visit is in four days.

Preparation

Scenarios 1 and 2 are not regular incidents, but in the event of their occurrence, employers must be prepared, as follows:

- ♦ All records in personnel files must be accurately and properly maintained.

- ♦ All employment activities.

Failure to maintain accurate personnel files subjects organizations and employers to liability. For example, personnel files should not contain any potentially damaging information, such as interview notes containing insensitive, inappropriate comments. Employers must be confident that all documents in the personnel files could adequately defend all employment decisions. Current and accurate personnel files assist the employer in tracking the workforce, organizing hiring and retention, and protecting the organization from liability. Failure to properly maintain the personnel file can subject the organization to unnecessary litigation.

This chapter will provide helpful tools and practical guidelines to assist with the proper maintenance of personnel files throughout the employment relationship. Additionally, the chapter will examine those documents that should **never** be included in the personnel file, as well as policy considerations regarding access to personnel files and the benefits of periodic file review.

Documenting the Employment Relationship

Ensuring proper maintenance of the personnel file begins with effective documentation, such as preparing accurate and complete personnel records.

The keys to effective documentation include the following four crucial principles:

♦ **Maintain a legal perspective.** In preparing documents, employers should always question what type of impressions or assumptions a judge or jury would draw from the documents. Years after creation, many of the documents contained in an employee's personnel file can potentially be subject to the scrutiny of both a judge and a jury.

♦ **Ensure that documents maintain a degree of objectivity.** A document commenting on a comparison between an employee's performance against established goals is often less likely to reflect supervisory bias than a document containing a subjective comment that the employee "has an attitude." Employers should always focus on specific job-related deficiencies of the employee, as these can be objectively measured.

♦ **Statements must be fact-driven, rather than conclusory.** Factual statements are more legitimate and persuasive than conclusory statements. This is particularly true in cases of performance evaluations and the imposition of discipline. It is more persuasive to state that an employee "was over 20 minutes late to work twice this week, on Tuesday and Thursday (listing specific dates) in violation of our tardiness and attendance policy," versus stating, an employee is "often late to work." By properly recording the facts, the employer makes a position clear, eliminating the need to later scramble to provide a basis for its employment decision(s).

♦ **Ensure that documents are accurate.** Mistakes in documentation can be costly. For example, improperly filling out an EEO-1 report can result in an affirmative action audit by the federal government. Additionally, management's failure to obtain an employee's signature verifying receipt of the employer's sexual harassment policy can have disastrous liability consequences in a future lawsuit.

Additionally, every document produced and created should contain the following:

♦ Date on which the document was created and/or amended.

♦ Name and signature of the document's author.

♦ Page numbers (such as page 1 of 3).

♦ Names and signatures of any witnesses (if applicable).

Documenting Pre-Employment Hiring
Pre-Employment Documentation

The relationship between employer and employee usually begins with pre-employment activities, such as completion and submission of an application, background checks, and the interview. All pre-employment activities generate numerous documents, which must be retained. Retention of pre-employment documents for nonselected candidates is imperative; retaining some of these documents in a newly hired employees personnel file is a matter of policy. However, retaining the background investigation and interview notes in the personnel file of a new employee may be poor decision.

Placing these documents in a newly hired employee's personnel file serves no real purpose, as they are not related to the employment relationship and creates a disorderly file. Rather, such information should be retained in a separate file that documents the entire interview process. In retaining accurate and thorough documentation of the interview process, employers may be protected from liability when a disgruntled applicant fails to obtain an interview or the position. Such thorough files may provide evidence that the employer's selection process is focused, fair, and the person selected was the most qualified applicant.

Hiring Documentation

The employment relationship begins during the pre-employment phase and the creation of the personnel file begins on the date of hire. The first day on any job usually involves an employee spending a good portion of the day completing paperwork, from benefit information to a Form I-9. The issue is whether all such documents should be filed in the new hire's personnel file. Importantly the documents retained in an employee's personnel file should create a paper trail, detailing the steps taken by management in orienting a new employee to the organization.

For example, upon hiring the employee the following documents should be placed in an employee's personnel file:

- Job description for the employment position.
- Offer of employment.
- Job application.
- Employee's résumé (if provided).
- Form W-4.
- Signed Acknowledgement of Receipt of an employee handbook.
- Forms relating to employee benefits.
- Forms providing next of kin and emergency contacts.
- Document acknowledging receipt and review of the Employer's Code of Conduct.

Employers may also include a checklist of the items presented to the employee at orientation. This checklist should be reviewed and signed by the employee and placed in their personnel file. The signed checklist prevents an employee from later claiming, in the midst of litigation, that the employee failed to receive a harassment policy or other crucial documentation.

New employees are also required to complete a Form I-9, which verifies the employee is eligible to work in the United States. However, this document should not be retained in the personnel file. Many government agencies are authorized to inspect Form I-9 when visiting a workplace and if the Form I-9 is maintained in the employee's personnel file, the government is given the opportunity to search entire personnel files. As such, an employer's files would be subject to much broader governmental scrutiny. Anything found in the files may be inspected and may raise additional issues or questions. By keeping a separate I-9 file, employers have the ability to furnish an inspecting agency one file containing all Forms I-9. Thus, an employer maintains control of all records and substantially limits the scope of the inquiry.

Documentation During Employment

The bulk of the paperwork generated in an employment relationship is during an employee's tenure. Proper maintenance of employee documents can be helpful in the event of a lawsuit. Improper maintenance, however, can be extremely harmful.

Compensation Records

Proper maintenance for employee compensation records is essential. The federal Fair Labor Standards Act (FLSA) requires an employer to make, keep, and preserve payroll records.

The following chart lists the record retention requirements under the FLSA and the Equal Pay Act:

Records to Be Retained	Statute	Period of Retention	Form of Retention
Wage and hour records, summary payroll records (for example, the number of hours each employee works, pay rates, total wages, total deductions, date of payment, and the pay period covered by the payment)	FLSA	3 years after the last date of entry	No particular form is specified
Basic time and earnings cards, work time schedules, records of additions to or deductions from wages, overtime earnings, records explaining any wage differentials between employees of the opposite sex (for example, job descriptions, job evaluations, merit, incentive, and seniority systems), and wage rate tables	FLSA	3 years after the last date of entry	No particular form is specified
	Equal Pay Act	2 years	No particular form is specified

An employer's failure to retain and properly maintain these records subjects the employer to costly penalties and lawsuits.

Similar to those documents retained during the hiring process, compensation documents should detail an employee's compensation history. Salary increases and/or decreases as well as denials of raises should be well documented.

The following compensation documents, as well as other additional documents, should be included in the personnel file:

- Form W-4.
- Attendance records.
- Pay advance request records.
- Garnishment orders.
- Compensation history record.
- Compensation recommendations.
- Authorization to release payroll information.
- Notification of wage and/or salary increases and/or decreases.

It may also be beneficial to maintain certain compensation documents in a separate folder, such as the following:

♦ Documents detailing the actual pay rate of an employee.

♦ Daily/weekly timecards and/or time sheets.

♦ Amounts and dates of payment.

Retaining such documents in a separate folder reduces the amount of paper in the file and eliminates possible investigations arising from a governmental agencies inspection of personnel files. Regardless of where these documents are kept, it is essential that all compensation records adhere to the four principles previously discussed.

Performance Evaluations

Performance evaluations are important weapons an employer has when defending a wrongful termination suit. Proper documentation and retention of evaluations can mean the difference between ending a lawsuit at summary judgment and a forced court action where the employer must defend the organization before a jury.

Evaluations must be conducted in a timely fashion. For example, evaluations may be completed yearly, every 30 days, or every 90 days. Regardless of the schedule time frame, the schedule must be followed consistently and universally throughout the organization. Employers should also document when these reviews will be conducted, require the employee's signature on an acknowledgement form, and place the form in the personnel file. If a follow-up session is scheduled after a 90- or 30-day review, an agenda for the session should be prepared detailing those items/goals previously discussed. Any resolutions or decision reached during these sessions should similarly be documented, signed by both the reviewing supervisor and the employee, and placed in the personnel file.

When preparing an evaluation, it is imperative the evaluation be clear and concise, utilizing the four principles previously mentioned (legal perspective, objectivity, fact-driven, and accuracy). Additionally, the evaluation should provide the following:

♦ Identify the standard of behavior or performance by which the employee is judged.

♦ Make clear that the employee was aware of the standard.

♦ Specify any failures(s) to meet the standard.

♦ Afford the employee the opportunity to correct behavior or improve performance to conform to the appropriate standard.

♦ Specify what action will be taken if the employee fails to meet the established standard.

The evaluation should also be fair. For example, the performance rating must mirror the actual performance. The recipient of an outstanding performance rating must meet the standard required for such rating. Otherwise, inaccurate evaluations may later be used against an employer. For example, a multimillion dollar judgment was entered against an employer in a sex discrimination suit after the employer consistently overrated an employee, giving her outstanding and above average ratings. The employer overrated the employee in an effort to appease the employee, but failed to accept the employee's applications for promotion despite the high ratings. The employee's evaluations failed to reflect the true nature of the employee's abilities and thus left the employer open to claims of discrimination where an allegedly outstanding employee was repeatedly denied promotional opportunities.

Upon completion of an evaluation, an employee should review the performance evaluation and be permitted to make any comments, whether positive or negative, about the evaluation. The evaluation should be signed and dated by the employee, acknowledging receipt and review, and placed in the personnel file. Oral evaluations, whether positive or negative, should also be documented and placed in the file, again employing the principles previously stated.

Employee Discipline

Similar to performance evaluations, documents used in disciplining an employee — whether oral or written — can protect an employer against lawsuits filed by a disgruntled employee alleging that a termination was motivated by discrimination or retaliation.

The disciplinary action, whether oral or written, must be properly documented at the time of the infraction. Postponing a discussion with an employee regarding disciplinary matters until the performance review increases an employee's chances of successfully arguing that the discipline was a pretext for either retaliation or discrimination. Additionally, properly documenting the disciplinary problem at the time of the occurrence eliminates any temptation to later rectify documentation deficiencies — a practice frowned upon by courts.

Disciplinary warnings should also be reviewed by the employee and signed, acknowledging that they have reviewed the notice/warning, and then placed in the employee's personnel file. However, documents relating to internal confidential investigations, such as sexual harassment investigations should be maintained in a separate file. Employers may be protected from an employee's, or another whose conduct is discussed in the course of the investigation, invasion-of-privacy claims by retaining these documents in a separate and confidential file.

In addition to those documents previously detailed, the following documents, if applicable, should also be included in the personnel file:

♦ **Training documents,** such as the following:

  • Training history records.

  • Training program applications/requests.

  • Skills inventory questionnaire.

  • Training evaluation forms.

  • In-house training notification letters.

  • Training expense reimbursement records.

♦ **Benefits documents,** such as the following:

  • Life insurance application.

  • Vacation accrual/taken form.

  • Request for leave of absences.

  • Retirement application.

  • Payroll deduction authorization.

  • Hazardous substance notification and/or reports.

  • Tuition reimbursement application and/or payment records.

  • Annual benefits statement acknowledgement.

  • Safety training/meeting attendance/summary forms.

- ♦ **Employee relations documents,** such as the following:
  - Report of coaching/counseling session.
  - Employee Assistance Program (EAP) consent form.
  - Commendations.
  - Completed employee suggestion forms.
  - Suggestion status reports.

Documenting the End of the Employment Relationship

The end of an employment relationship can either be amicable or contentious. How the relationship ends will determine what documentation needs to be placed in the employee's personnel file.

In a typical employee separation, such as resignation, the documents placed in the personnel file should include the following:

- ♦ Exit interview form.
- ♦ Final employee performance appraisal.
- ♦ Exit interviewer's comment form.
- ♦ Record of documents given with final paycheck.
- ♦ COBRA documents.

Again, these documents, as others in the personnel file, should follow the four principles.

An employer's decision to terminate an employment relationship, while including the previously mentioned items, must be supported by proper documentation. The personnel file should contain convincing proof of a violation of a rule or policy for which the employee is being terminated. If the documents in the file cannot alone support a termination, termination may not be the appropriate action. In the case of a reduction in force, any business decision supporting the reduction needs to be adequately documented so those employees selected for layoff will not later use the lack of documentary support as favorable evidence in a discrimination suit. Failure to properly document the reduction in force may result in the organization explaining its employment decision before a jury.

Note: The aforementioned information is not exhaustive and serves to only provide a cursory overview for determining which documents should be included in a personnel file.

Document Maintenance and Access

Self Auditing

The employment relationship and required documentation is governed by many different governmental regulatory agencies, each maintaining different priorities and compliance requirements. Many laws, covering such topics as discrimination, safety, and immigration, charge governmental regulatory agencies with specific objectives and require certain documents when regulating an employer's compliance with these laws. Consequently, an effective plan for limiting an employer's exposure to liability can protect employers from potentially devastating consequences resulting from either a governmental audit or the document request of a plaintiff's attorney.

Periodic self-audits are an important tool in avoiding legal disputes. While numerous laws make a self-audit increasingly complicated, the potential benefit of identifying and proactively addressing potential claims cannot be understated. Employers who fail to conduct periodic evaluations of their policies, procedures, and practices may find themselves with a multitude of legal liability. When conducting a self-audit of personnel files, an employer should ask the following questions:

- Does the file reflect all of the employee's raises, promotions, and commendations?

- Does the file contain every written evaluation of the employee?

- Does the file show every warning or other disciplinary action taken against the employee?

- If company policies provide that written warnings or other records of discipline will be removed from an employee's file after a certain period, have they been removed?

- If the employee was on a performance improvement plan, a probationary or training period, or other temporary status, has it ended? Has the file been updated to reflect the employee's current status?

- If the employee handbook has been updated since the employee started working for the organization, does the file contain a receipt or acknowledgement for the most recent version?

- Does the file contain current versions of every contract or other agreement between the employer and the employee?

In performing a self-audit, through asking the previous questions, an employer can be confident that personnel files will be the best defensive weapon against a discrimination claim.

Documents Not to Be Included in a Personnel File

Employers should carefully consider how to file each and every personnel document maintained. The law requires that employers keep a separate file for medical records, but a solid defensive strategy would also include separate files for other types of employee information.

Employment Eligibility Documents

As previously mentioned, employers should keep Forms I-9 in a separate file. While an employer is permitted to photocopy the documents offered by an employee as proof of work eligibility, such practice is not required. Employers who choose to photocopy and retain these documents should not retain the information in a personnel file. Such a practice can generate a resource of information for a plaintiff or regulatory agency seeking to investigate discriminatory employment practices.

Medical Records

Medical information, such as pre-employment physicals, medical surveillance information, injury reports, medical questionnaires, workers' compensation reports, and drug-testing results, should be maintained separately from the employee personnel file. Employers must limit access to medical information due to privacy and confidentiality concerns and regulations. In fact, a great deal of governmental regulations exists for employers to consider in regard to the maintenance and retention of medical records.

The Americans with Disabilities Act

The Americans with Disabilities Act (ADA) enforces specific guidelines in regard to the gathering and maintenance of employee medical information. For example, prior to an employment offer, all disability related inquiries made by an employer must be job related. The ADA has a narrow exception to the prohibition of pre-employment medical inquiries.

An employer may condition an offer of employment on the results of a medical examination as long as the following criteria are met:

♦ The examination is given to all entering employees.

♦ The results are kept confidential.

♦ The examination is not used to discriminate against individuals with disabilities; however, results may prove that the individual is unqualified for the particular job.

Additionally, the ADA imposes very strict rules for handling medical information obtained during employment. The ADA prevents employers from practicing the following:

♦ Requiring a medical examination before making a job offer.

♦ Inquiring as to whether an employee has a disability.

♦ Inquiring as to the nature or severity of any disability unless the inquiry or examination is job related and consistent with business necessity.

The results of any medical examination must be kept confidential, and segregated from the personnel file. However, the ADA recognizes that employers may have a legitimate need to disseminate the results of medical tests or other medical information, and allows confidential medical information to be shared with the following persons:

♦ Supervisors who need to arrange necessary work restrictions and make necessary reasonable accommodations.

♦ First-aid and safety personnel, should emergency treatment be required.

♦ Government officials investigating compliance.

Employee medical information must be disseminated under the appropriate conditions. Moreover, it is important for employers to strictly limit the amount of information shared to only the amount of information required to answer an inquiry.

The Health Insurance Portability and Accountability Act

The Health Insurance Portability and Accountability Act (HIPAA) was enacted to improve health insurance coverage in the group and individual markets; to combat waste, fraud, and abuse in health insurance and health care delivery; to simplify the administration of health insurance; and for other purposes. Under HIPAA, covered entities **may not** use or disclose an individual's protected health information without the authorization of the individual unless specifically required or allowed by the privacy regulation.

While employers are **not** covered entities, they are affected by the privacy rules based on their sponsorship of health plans and procedures for dealing with the health information of 50 or more participants. If an employer does not have 50 participants in the company health plan, they generally need not be concerned with HIPAA restrictions. Effective April 14, 2004, HIPAA's privacy rules became effective for sponsor small health plans. A *small health plan* is one that paid premiums or claims of $5 million or less in their most recent plan year.

For employers subject to the privacy provisions of HIPAA, the requirements are more stringent for self-funded plans than they are for fully insured plans. Self-funded plan requirements are more stringent because HIPAA assumes that if an employer has a fully insured plan, the employer generally does not have access to protected health information (PHI). In self-funded plans, employers who make initial or final claims determinations need PHI to make claims decisions. This protected health information is protected under HIPAA.

The Family and Medical Leave Act

The release of confidential medical information is also regulated under the federal Family and Medical Leave Act (FMLA), particularly if an employer requests medical certification or requires an employee to take a fitness-for-duty examination when returning from FMLA leave. It is crucial for employers to maintain any tests or results from a medical certification in a separate medical file, apart from the general personnel file.

Background Investigation Records

Every employer's ultimate goal is to hire and retain hard working and productive employees. However, employers may have difficulty in effectively evaluating an individual's capabilities based on an application form and one or two interviews. Employers may choose to further investigate an applicant through a background report. Background reports are sensitive and confidential by their very nature, and by law they must be restricted to those individuals who are directly involved in the hiring process. A thorough reference and background investigation may be able determine if the applicant will become a welcome addition to the team or a threat to the employer, employees, or customers. Additionally, courts may determine that an employer has a duty to conduct a background investigation, especially under circumstances where the failure to conduct a background check creates a liability for negligent hiring or retention.

Under the Fair Credit Reporting Act (FCRA), employers must comply as follows:

♦ Clearly disclose to the applicant, in a separate document, that a background check is being prepared by a third party.

♦ Acquire a signed release from the applicant before checking records such as criminal convictions, pending criminal cases, driving records, credit reports, or educational credentials.

♦ Provide the applicant with a copy of the report and a notice of legal rights if the employer intends to deny employment based on the information contained in the report.

The FCRA is designed to balance an employer's interest in assessing a potential employee with the employee's right of accuracy and privacy regarding their credentials.

Safety Records

The Occupational Safety and Health Administration (OSHA) regulates and monitors workplace safety. Employers should maintain all safety-related records in a separate file for the same reason all Forms I-9 should be maintained in a separate file, to allow an OSHA auditor to see only OSHA-related records during an OSHA audit. This safety record file might also contain documentation relating to an employee's participation or involvement in an OSHA claim or investigation — limiting access to such documentation would make it easier to keep the information from influencing possible adverse decisions against the employee that could in turn result in retaliation claims under OSHA.

Access to Records

Approximately half of all states regulate the maintenance of and access to personnel records. For example, some states have placed restrictions upon the use and release of personnel information with regard to child care employees, sworn police officers, and employees of the state's public and university school systems. Additionally, some state laws require employers to allow employees to inspect and /or to obtain a copy of their files. Access to personnel records is usually subject to some restrictions, for example, inspection only in the presence of management or a prohibition against removal of information.

Most public sector employees have the right under state laws to examine their personnel file. Some states permit public employees to have access at a reasonable time. Public employers should have a policy in place (or defer to an official department policy) that defines the parameters of a reasonable time so employees may enjoy their right of access, without unduly interfering with the employer's mission.

The reasons for limiting employee access to their individual files are not so much legal as they are practical. In certain instances, management may not want an employee to view various types of test results or criticisms of performance. In other cases, a disgruntled or unhappy employee may request to see the file, and proceed to scrutinize the entire record for the purpose of finding a basis for a lawsuit against the employer. This is especially true of former employees. For this reason, granting access to former employees is **not** recommended unless legally required. In the event an employee asks a specific question about what is in a file, management should consider providing an answer or document relating to that specific question or read a document to the employee, rather than turn over the entire file.

Review of an employee's personnel file by third parties should also be carefully controlled. Employees who feel damaged by improper disclosure or referral practices have filed defamation lawsuits. Thus, many employers have adopted strict nondisclosure rules or a policy of providing only "neutral references," and thereby only releasing the former employee's name, position, and dates of employment.

In light of the growing number of defamation lawsuits based on disclosure of personnel file information, some states have legislation providing that an employer will be immune from liability based on providing job performance information to a former employee's prospective employer. However, an employer may incur liability if proven that the employer produced information that was knowingly false, provided with malicious purpose, or violated a civil right of the former employee under state law. Notwithstanding such laws, ample room remains for lawsuits based on employer-provided references. For employers who have a policy of providing references to other employers, it would be wise to obtain a waiver from a current employee prior to their departure from employment. Generally, however, a strict nondisclosure rule may still be the safest option. Often, human resources managers will receive a subpoena from a party in a lawsuit, requesting the production of documents (including personnel files) regarding a former employee. Because the subpoena requires compliance under authority of the court, producing the requested documents in this compelled manner will generally not subject the employer to defamation liability. In such a case, the other party in the lawsuit has the burden to object to an improper request.

Federal law requires that records be maintained for job applicants, current employees, and former workers for certain prescribed lengths of time, so that government agencies will have material to review during investigations. A table outlining the primary federal recordkeeping requirements with regard to what information must be kept and for how long is included at the end of this chapter.

In addition to personnel information normally retained in the course of business, the Equal Employment Opportunity Commission (EEOC), state and local EEO agencies, and other agencies require that once a complaint of an unlawful employment practice has been received, the employer must preserve all personnel records, production records and other evidence which may pertain to the complaint until the matter has been resolved. Similarly, the breadth of an investigation into a complaint may extend beyond records relating to the charging party, and include records regarding all employees holding positions similar to the one held or sought by the charging party.

Federal Recordkeeping Requirements

Documentation	Retention Requirements
Personnel records including application forms and records concerning hiring, promotion, demotion, transfer, layoffs, terminations, and terms of compensation.	1 year from date of personnel action taken with respect to the particular record or date record was made — whichever is later (29 C.F.R. 1602.14).
Records relevant to complaint of unlawful employment practice.	Until final disposition of charge (29 C.F.R. 1602.14).
Employers with 100 or more employees: Copy of EEO-1 Report.	Copy of most recent report filed for each reporting unit must always be retained at unit or company/division headquarters (29 C.F.R. 1602.7).
Federal contractors, subcontractors: Affirmative Action Plans.	No period specified (2 years recommended).
Form I-9.	1 year from date of termination or 3 years after creation — whichever is later.
Written employee benefit plans; merit or seniority systems.	While plan is in effect, plus 4 years after termination of plan (29 C.F.R. 1627.3).
Payroll or other records containing each employee's name, address, date of birth, occupation, rate of pay, and compensation earned per week.	3 years from date of creation (29 C.F.R. 1627.3).
Supplemental basic records, including wage rate tables, time schedules, and order and shipping records.	2 years from date of creation (29 C.F.R. 1620.32).
Records pertaining to certification of leave as qualifying under the Family and Medical Leave Act (FMLA) and any disputes regarding such certification.	3 years from date of creation.

Illinois Law

Personnel Record Review Act

The Illinois' Personnel Record Review Act is located at 820 Ill. Comp. Stat. §§ 40/0.01 et seq. and does not diminish a right of access to records already otherwise provided by law.

Covered Employees and Employers

The act applies to employees who are persons currently employed or subject to recall after layoff or leave of absence with a right to return at a position with an employer or a former employee who has terminated service within the preceding year.

The act applies to employers that are an individual, corporation, partnership, labor organization, unincorporated association, the state, an agency or a political subdivision of the state, or any other legal, business, or commercial entity that has five employees or more than five employees exclusive of the employer's parent, spouse, or child or other members of immediate family and includes an agent of the employer.

Open Records and Inspection

According to the act, every employer must, upon an employee's request (which the employer may require be in writing on a form supplied by the employer), permit the employee to inspect any personnel documents that have been or are intended for use in determining the employee's qualifications for any of the following:

- ◆ Employment.
- ◆ Promotion.
- ◆ Transfer.
- ◆ Additional compensation.
- ◆ Discharge.
- ◆ Other disciplinary action.

With exception, employees may request all or any part of their records. Additionally, an employee's right to inspect personnel files includes personnel documents in the possession of a person, corporation, partnership, or other association having a contractual agreement to keep or supply a personnel record.

Employers must grant at least two inspection requests by an employee in a calendar year when requests are made at reasonable intervals, unless otherwise provided for in a collective-bargaining agreement. The employer must provide an employee with an opportunity to inspect the records within seven working days after the employee makes the request. If the employer can reasonably show that the deadline cannot be met, the employer will be permitted an additional seven days to comply with the employee's request.

Inspections must take place at a location reasonably near the employee's place of employment and during normal working hours. The employer may allow the inspection to take place at a time other than working hours or at a place other than where the records are maintained if that time or place would be more convenient for the employee.

Employees have the right to obtain a copy of the information contained in their files; however, they are not permitted to remove any part of the files from the employer's premises. Employees that demonstrate their inability to review their personnel records at the employing unit must, upon written request, be mailed a copy of the requested records by the employer. Each employer retains the right to protect records from loss, damage, or alteration to insure their integrity.

After the review time provided by law, an employee may obtain a copy of the information or part of the information contained in the employee's personnel record. An employer may charge a fee for providing a copy of such information. However, the fee is limited to the actual cost of duplicating the information.

Inspection by Representative

An employee who is involved in a current grievance against the employer may designate in writing a representative of the employee's union or collective-bargaining unit or other representative to inspect the employee's personnel record that may have a bearing on the resolution of the grievance. The employer will allow the designated representative to inspect that employee's personnel record in the same manner as the employee is entitled.

Contested Information

If an employee disagrees with any information contained in the personnel record, a removal or correction of that information may be mutually agreed upon by the employer and the employee. If an agreement cannot be reached, the employee may submit a written statement explaining the employee's position. The employer must attach the employee's statement to the disputed portion of the personnel record. The employee's statement must also be included whenever that disputed portion of the personnel record is released to a third party, as long as the disputed information is part of the file. The inclusion of any written statement attached in the record without further comment or action by the employer, does not imply or create any presumption of employer agreement with its contents.

If either the employer or the employee knowingly places false information in the personnel record, the other party will have remedy through legal action to have the information expunged.

Employer Restrictions

Nonemployment Activity Records

Employers are prohibited from gathering or keeping a record of an employee's associations, political activities, publications, communications, or nonemployment activities, unless the employee submits the information in writing or authorizes the employer in writing to keep or gather the information. However, this prohibition **does not apply** to the activities that occur on the employer's premises or during the employee's working hours that interfere with the performance of the employee's duties or the duties of other employees or activities that constitute criminal conduct or may be expected to harm the employer's property, operations, or business or that could cause the employer financial liability.

Note: A nonemployment activity record that is kept by the employer, as permitted by law, will be part of the personnel record.

Employee Subject to Children and Family Services Department Investigation Records

An employer may not gather or keep a record identifying an employee as the subject of an investigation by the Illinois Department of Children and Family Services if the investigation by the Department resulted in an unfounded report as specified in the Abused and Neglected Child Reporting Act. An employee, upon receiving written notification from the Department of Children and Family Services that an investigation has resulted in an unfounded report will take the written notification to their employer and have any record of the investigation expunged from their employee record.

Employee Restrictions

The right of employees or their designated representatives to inspect their personnel records **does not apply** to the following:

♦ Letters of reference for employees or external peer review documents for academic employees of institutions of higher education.

♦ Test documents, except that employees may see a cumulative total test score for either a section of or the entire test.

♦ Staff planning materials, such as matters relating to business development, expansion, closing, or operational goals where the materials relate to or affect more than one employee. However, this restriction does not apply if the materials are, have been, or are intended to be used by the employer in determining an individual employee's qualifications for employment, promotion, transfer, or additional compensation or in determining an employee's discharge or discipline.

♦ Personal information about a person other than the employee, if disclosure would constitute a clearly unwarranted invasion of the other person's privacy.

♦ Employers that do not maintain personnel records.

♦ Records relevant to any other pending claim between the employer and employee that may be discovered in a judicial proceeding.

♦ Investigatory or security records maintained by an employer to investigate criminal conduct by an employee or other activity by the employee that could reasonably be expected to harm the employer's property, operations, or business or could cause the employer financial liability, unless and until the employer takes adverse personnel action based on information in the records.

Employee Protections

Employers or former employers cannot divulge a disciplinary report, letter of reprimand, or other disciplinary action to a third party, to a party who is not a part of the employer's organization, or to a party who is not a part of a labor organization representing the employee without first sending written notice by first-class mail to the employee the day before or the day the information is divulged.

Written notice to the employee must be made by first-class mail to the employee's last known address.

This provision **does not apply** under any of the following conditions:

♦ The employee has specifically waived written notice as part of a written, signed employment application with another employer.

♦ The disclosure is ordered to a party in a legal action or arbitration.

♦ Information is requested by a government agency as a result of a claim or complaint by the employee or as a result of a criminal investigation by such an agency.

An employer who receives a request for records of a disciplinary report, letter of reprimand, or other disciplinary action in relation to an employee under the Freedom of Information Act may provide notification to the employee in written form or through electronic mail, if available.

However, employers must review a personnel record before releasing information to a third party and, except when the release is ordered to a party in a legal action or arbitration, delete disciplinary reports, letters of reprimand, or other records of disciplinary action which are more than four years old.

Enforcement

The Director of the Illinois Department of Labor or an authorized representative has the power to administer and enforce the provisions of the Illinois' Personnel Record Review Act. If an employee alleges that their rights have been denied under the law, the employee may file a complaint with the department. The department will investigate the complaint and has the authority to request the issuance of a search warrant or subpoena to inspect the files of the employer, if necessary. The department will attempt to resolve the complaint by conference, conciliation, or persuasion.

If the complaint is not resolved and the department finds the employer has violated the law, the department may commence an action in the circuit court to enforce the provisions of the law, including an action to compel compliance. The circuit court for the county in which the complainant resides, in which the complainant is employed, or in which the personnel record is maintained will have jurisdiction in such actions. If an employer violates the act, an employee may commence an action in the circuit court to enforce the provisions of the act in situations where the department has not commenced an action in circuit court to redress the violations.

Judicial or Quasi-Judicial Proceeding

Personnel record information that was not included in the personnel record, but should have been included as required by the act, **may not** be used by an employer in a judicial or quasi-judicial proceeding. However, personnel record information which, in the opinion of the judge in a judicial proceeding or the hearing officer in a quasi-judicial proceeding, was not intentionally excluded from the personnel record may be used by the employer in the proceeding if the employee agrees or has been given a reasonable time to review the information. Material that should have been included in the personnel record will be used at the request of the employee.

Penalties

Violations of the act are penalized as follows:

- An employer or agent of an employer that violates the provisions of the act is guilty of a petty offense.

- Any employer, agent, office, or agent of a private employer that discharges or in any manner discriminates against an employee based on the following is guilty of a petty offense:

  - The employee has complained to the employer, the director, or the director's authorized representative.

  - The employee has instituted or caused to be instituted any proceeding under or related to the act.

  - The employee has testified or is about to testify in an investigation or proceeding.

- An employer that fails to comply with an order of the court may be punished as in contempt of court and the court will award the following:

  - Actual damages, plus court costs.

  - For a willful and knowing violation of the law, $200, plus costs, reasonable attorneys' fees, and actual damages.

Contact Information

Illinois Department of Labor

1 West Old State Capitol Plaza, Room 300
Springfield, IL 62701

Telephone: 217-782-6206
Fax: 217-782-0596
Internet: *www.state.il.us/agency/idol*

Chapter 19

Discipline

General Principles

Discipline of employees often gives rise to employment litigation. The following general guidelines for managing employees with disciplinary problems may help employers avoid litigation. Employers must have clear disciplinary standards and evidence that employees were given notice of the standards. In implementation, the standards must be applied uniformly. Additionally, the organization should retain the right to determine the amount and/or type of discipline that will be imposed in each individual situation. Employers must create a discipline policy that will not limit their right to enforce appropriate disciplinary measures.

A disciplinary procedure should follow these four rules:

♦ The employee must know the nature of the problem.

♦ The employee must know what to do to fix the problem.

♦ The employee must have a reasonable period of time in which to fix the problem.

♦ The employee must understand the consequences of inaction.

Progressive Discipline

Companies should consider using a progressive discipline system. The progressive discipline system generally begins with the recruitment process and continues through orientation, training, performance evaluations, and daily supervision.

A progressive discipline system consists of the following:

♦ Verbal warning.

♦ Written warning.

♦ Suspension.

♦ Termination.

Elements of Due Process

In most cases, private sector employers do not have a legally mandated due process obligation in the employment relationship, although this obligation may be imposed by state law or by an employer's policy or practice. However, it is often in the employer's best interest to attempt to rehabilitate problematic employees. Progressive discipline is a form of due process, and its use demonstrates the affirmative steps taken by an employer to correct an employee's behavioral and performance-based problems. For example:

- **Knowledge.** For an employer's discipline program to be effective, employees must know the employer's expectations and the consequences should an employee fail to meet those expectations.

- **Consistency.** Discipline should be applied consistently and an employer's responses to rule violations should be predictable. Violations must not be corrected on an ad hoc basis, because the employer will be perceived as arbitrary, unreasonable, and discriminatory.

- **Appropriateness.** The discipline chosen for a particular problem must be appropriate. Occasional poor performance, tardiness, and absenteeism are certainly actionable, but probably not cause for termination. An employee's performance record and previous disciplinary record should be taken into account.

- **Opportunity.** An employer must allow an employee to respond to allegations of misconduct before administering discipline. In a system structured for rehabilitation, failure to allow an employee a chance to offer a defense or alternate position will likely create employee relations problems and may be a catalyst for litigation.

- **Reasonableness.** To be effective, progressive discipline must allow employees a reasonable period of time to improve their performance.

Investigating Employees and Liability

When employers investigate employee misconduct in the workplace, they are often caught in a "catch-22." For example, on one hand, employers must conduct inquiries into employee performance and allegations of rules violations or misconduct because the Supreme Court has held that failure to promptly and thoroughly investigate reported employee misconduct may disqualify an employer from an "affirmative defense" against liability for workplace discrimination and subject the employer to punitive damages. (See *Burlington Indus., Inc. v. Ellerth*, 524 U.S. 742 (1998) and *Faragher v. City of Boca Raton*, 524 U.S. 775 and 789 (1998).)

On the other hand, investigating employee misconduct creates the possibility of exposure to legal liability. For example, employers conducting workplace investigations often are subject to requirements of the Fair Credit Reporting Act (FCRA), which since 1999 had been interpreted to govern such an investigatory process if third parties were used. (See *Federal Trade Commission Staff Opinion Letter* Vail, April 5, 1999 at *www.ftc.gov/os/statutes/fcra/vail.htm.*)

Under that interpretation, the Federal Trade Commission (FTC) required employers using third-party investigators to notify employees suspected of misconduct before conducting an investigation, to obtain the employee's prior consent before commencing the investigation, and to fully disclose investigative reports before taking any adverse action against an employee. Such stringent requirements made workplace investigations extremely difficult while increasing the risk of liability, especially the vulnerability to claims of retaliation actions.

As one can see, applying the requirements of the FCRA to an investigation of a typical case leads to an absurd result. If an impartial third party is used to conduct an investigation, the employer would have to comply with the act's requirements as follows:

- Have the alleged harasser's written consent before the third party could begin the investigation.

- Provide the alleged harasser with a copy of the resulting investigative report before taking any adverse action.

- Disclose to the alleged harasser the name of the alleged victim, the investigator's identity, and the names of all persons interviewed during the investigation.

With the cloak of anonymity absent, victims and witnesses were less likely to provide the most accurate accounts of incidents, and employers were left in uncertainty.

With the enactment of the Fair and Accurate Credit Transactions Act (FACT Act), on March 31, 2004, employers have enjoyed relief from the FCRA's stringent investigation requirements. Although the FACT Act reincorporates the majority of the FCRA's provisions, it lessens the investigative burdens on employers by countering the 1999 FTC opinion letter. Specifically, the FACT Act eliminates the need for prior consent before third parties conduct workplace investigations and removes the pre-adverse action disclosure to the employee being investigated for the alleged misconduct if communication of the third-party investigator's report is limited to the employer or an agent of the employer. As a practical matter, the report should not be disclosed to the complaining party; doing so may bring it within the scope of an investigative "consumer report" otherwise triggering the disclosure requirements.

In the event adverse action is taken against the employee based on the results of the third-party investigation, the FACT Act still requires the employer to provide the employee a summary of the third-party investigative report. Employers using third parties to conduct internal investigations must therefore remember to provide this summary whenever an adverse action is taken, even if a mere written warning results. The summary, however, does not need to identify the individuals interviewed or identify other sources of information. If employers follow the FACT Act's requirements regarding third-party investigations, they will eliminate the "catch-22" created by the FCRA under the FTC's interpretation.

Creating and Implementing a Disciplinary System

An effective disciplinary policy consists of several interrelated components, such as the following:

- Establishing a fair system of work rules and expected standards of behavior and performance.
- Ensuring the consistent application of discipline.
- Requiring detailed documentation.

Consistency and documentation are the foundation of an effective disciplinary policy. Regardless of the quality of an organization's policies, without consistent application the policies will lead to disputes in labor and management relations. A disciplinary policy must provide for adequate documentation. For example, in any type of legal action, an employer that is forced to defend its disciplinary decisions may use the documentation as proof of its fair, consistent, and nondiscriminatory discipline system. Importantly, each component of the disciplinary system must be designed with the individual organization's needs and capabilities in mind.

Establishing the Rules

A disciplinary system must notify employees of what actions or inactions will constitute grounds for discipline. Although disciplinary policies are varied due to the many differences among employers and their operations, a few general rules may be gleaned from these divergent approaches.

Drafting of an effective disciplinary policy requires the knowledge of business operations. Disciplinary rules should not be adopted from another employer because a borrowed policy will not reflect the needs of all employers, but rather the employer for which the policy was designed. Additionally, an adopted policy may cause unnecessary problems and require constant amendment. A disciplinary policy should be suited to a specific operation. For example, employers should seek input from each level of supervisory personnel, and then draft a policy that addresses the particular concerns.

Employers with nonunion workforces should exercise caution to ensure their disciplinary policy does not contain language that may be construed as a promise altering the employment-at-will relationship. Qualifying language that is prominently displayed in the disciplinary policy may reduce the risk of inadvertently altering the at-will relationship.

For example, a disciplinary policy may incorporate the following qualifying language:

- All employment is employment-at-will. Nothing contained in this disciplinary policy is intended to create a contract of employment or change the at-will nature of this employment.

- Nothing in this disciplinary policy restricts the employer from terminating employees for reasons unrelated to discipline, providing the reason is not contrary to law.

- The following list of offenses is not all-inclusive. This list is only intended to provide an example of offenses warranting discipline or discharge. The employer fully reserves the right to discipline employees for misconduct that is not specifically referenced in this list, up to and including discharge.

Establishing Effective Policies

Disciplinary procedures may be established through an employee handbook or personnel policy. The following issues should be evaluated in considering whether to implement an employee handbook or personnel policy:

- Employers should retain discretion to address each situation on a case-by-case basis.

- Handbooks should have a disclaimer stating that the handbook is not an employment contract. The disclaimer should be prominently displayed on the first page of the handbook.

- At least once a year employers should review all written policies to ensure they are current and comply with all applicable laws.

- Employees should be required to sign an acknowledgement form stating that they have received a copy of the handbook. The form should contain a disclaimer stating that the employee recognizes that the handbook is not an employment contract and that employment is at-will. These forms should be maintained in the employee's personnel file.

An annual evaluation process should be established. The advantages of a well-developed evaluation process are as follows:

- Both the employee and supervisor are aware of performance deficiencies.

- A specific record of performance is created that documents the issues of a problem employee and others with whom the problem employee's performance could be compared.

- Management is forced to establish legitimate performance goals.

The elements of an effective evaluation process include the following:

- Written evaluations, based on documented criteria, which are distributed to all managers.

- Regularly scheduled evaluations.

- Honest and candid appraisals of performance.

- Multiple levels of management review the evaluation.

♦ Communication of the evaluation to the employee.

♦ An opportunity for the employee to raise any objections to or comments on the evaluation.

Enforcing the Rules

Once the rules are determined, a process must be established for initiating disciplinary action whenever there is a rule violation.

For example, the process may include the following three steps:

♦ Investigation.

♦ Decision, explanation, and imposition of discipline.

♦ Appeal process.

Investigation

Once an employer becomes aware that a possible infraction of the rules has occurred, an appropriate management official should immediately conduct a preliminary investigation. An ***appropriate official*** may be a supervisor, a human resources department professional, or someone in authority who is completely removed from the incident. The only essential requirement is that the person conducting the investigation must be capable of objectively evaluating the facts and the persons involved. A related consideration is whether the person conducting the investigation will be perceived by the employees involved as someone who is fair and objective. If employees do not have confidence in the objectivity of the person conducting the investigation, the result of the investigation will not provide the finality necessary for the resolution of the problem.

The official investigating an incident should determine the following:

♦ Whether misconduct occurred.

♦ Which employees were involved in the misconduct.

♦ Who witnessed the misconduct.

♦ What was the specific misconduct.

♦ The consequences of the misconduct, such as the following:

• Whether anyone was injured.

• Whether production was hindered.

Immediately after the event, an interview should be conducted with the employee suspected of the misconduct. The employee's supervisor or another appropriate representative of management should conduct the interview in private, away from other employees. If the misconduct is serious, the interviewer should consider having another management representative present should a witness be needed to verify what occurred during the interview.

The employee should have the opportunity to explain what happened and why it happened. The employee should be encouraged to identify any other employees who may have knowledge of the incident. At the conclusion of the interview, the employee should be told that they will be contacted upon completion of the investigation. If serious misconduct is involved, the employer may suspend the employee — with or without pay — during the course of the investigation. The interviewer must keep detailed and accurate notes of the interview.

Interviews should be conducted with all witnesses as soon as possible after the incident. Interviews with witnesses should be conducted separately and detailed notes should be taken. If the misconduct involved is serious, the interviewer should get signed statements from each witness. In some cases, such as those involving alleged harassment, it may be preferable to interview other witnesses identified by a complainant before conducting an interview with the suspected perpetrator.

Decision, Explanation, and Imposition of Discipline

The personnel department or management staff should review the information obtained from the investigation. At least one person in the decision-making process should be familiar with past disciplinary actions taken relevant to the group of employees involved. The personnel file of the employee should be reviewed to identify circumstances that would either increase or reduce the discipline imposed.

An employee's supervisor must complete a written disciplinary form upon the decision that an employee should be disciplined for misconduct. The employee's name, job classification, department, and supervisor should be identified on the form. In describing the nature of the misconduct, the following information should be provided:

- The date and time of the offense.

- A brief description of the events surrounding the incident.

- All of the rules or policies violated by the misconduct.

- The effective date and nature of the discipline to be administered. If the discipline is a final warning, it should be clearly stated that future offenses will result in discharge.

Employers may develop a standardized *Disciplinary Action Form*. In addition to the *Disciplinary Action Form*, in cases of serious misconduct a complete factual account of the incident should be maintained in the employee's personnel file. Importantly, because fair employment practice agency charges and complaints constitute only allegations, they should be maintained separately from personnel files.

When the offense and corresponding disciplinary action are clearly explained the employee should be allowed to review the *Disciplinary Action Form*. The employee must understand exactly what action the organization will take if another violation of company rules occurs. The employee should also be asked to sign the *Disciplinary Action Form*, which demonstrates the employee's notice of and understanding of the situation. If the employee refuses to sign, an attempt should be made to have the employee sign a notation on the document stating, "Employee refused to sign." If the employee still refuses, the supervisor should indicate on the document that the employee refused to sign, and, if possible, have a management witness verify this fact.

At all meetings it is essential that detailed notes are made and witnesses are present. The management official must retain composure at all times and the employer should not argue with the employee but should be willing to listen to the employee.

Appeal Process

Another part of the disciplinary procedure is the appeal process, particularly in instances of serious misconduct. The appeal should be made to a high-level management official who was not involved in the original disciplinary process. The appeal process may be initiated verbally; however, the issues and outcome of the appeal should be reduced to writing. The person considering the appeal should review the detailed notes of the investigation and compare the disciplinary action with discipline imposed in previous cases. The reviewing official must make certain that the discipline is fair and consistent with past practice. The appeal process should be timely, requiring no longer than a week to complete. Alternative dispute resolution (ADR), such as peer review, mediation, or arbitration may also be used in these circumstances.

Note: Under some union contracts, an employee's time to grieve discipline resulting from misconduct may be expressly limited. If the employee or union does not exercise this right to appeal in a timely manner, the matter may be deemed settled.

Documentation

The best-designed disciplinary policy may be rendered useless by the failure to maintain adequate documentation. Upholding any disciplinary action will require the employer to show the action is consistent with the employer's normal disciplinary policy. Without proper documentation, an employer will have difficulty ensuring consistent disciplinary actions and assuring a third party of that consistency.

If possible, a separate file should be maintained for each company rule or policy. Any time an employee is disciplined for violating a company rule or policy, a copy of the *Disciplinary Action Form* should be placed in the corresponding "offense file." For example, all discipline imposed on employees for insubordination would be in one file for easy reference and comparison. If more than one company rule or policy is violated by an employee's misconduct, one copy of the *Disciplinary Action Form* should be placed in each corresponding offense file.

Employers should also keep a record of policy or rule violations where no disciplinary action is taken. For example, an employee breaks a company rule, but the investigation reveals reason to support a reduced discipline. In such circumstances, a memorandum should be placed in the offense file indicating that a violation of the rule or policy was excused for a particular reason. This filing system should not replace the organization's personnel filing system; it is an additional system designed to help supervisors administer consistent discipline.

Warnings

The typical progressive discipline formula begins with a verbal warning and progresses to a written and then a final written warning before termination. Usually the impetus that moves the process from one stage to the next is a repeated violation of the same rule or type of rule (for example, repeated tardiness or unexcused absences). Disciplinary actions include the following verbal and written warnings, suspension, and discharge.

Verbal Warnings

When giving a verbal warning, the employer should speak privately with the employee. Verbal warnings are proper for infractions of a relatively minor degree. The supervisor should inform the employee at all times that the employee is receiving a verbal warning and that the employee is being given an opportunity to correct the behavior.

It is important the employee be notified of the following:

♦ The number of days the warning will continue.

♦ That failure to correct the behavior will result in more severe disciplinary measures.

A written record of the verbal warning should be completed and placed in the employee's personnel file.

Written Warnings

If the employee continues to disregard the verbal warning or if the infraction is severe, the supervisor should issue a written warning. The supervisor should give a detailed description of the infraction in the warning and sign the written notice of infraction. An employer should take the following steps when issuing a written warning:

- ◆ Discuss the warning with the employee.

- ◆ Confirm that the employee understands the reasons for the disciplinary action.

- ◆ Inform the employee of the number of days the warning will operate.

- ◆ Provide the employee with a copy of the warning at the time of the discussion.

- ◆ Obtain the employee's signature, with the current date, on the warning copy acknowledging the employee's receipt.

- ◆ Place the original warning in the employee's personnel file.

Example:

Date: _____

Employee Name: _____

Any further violations (more absences, tardiness).

Within the next _____ (days, months).

Will result in _____ (next step in disciplinary process).

Employee Signature: _____

Supervisor Signature: _____

Suspension

Suspension is the most severe form of discipline — short of termination — given by a supervisor. Supervisors should reserve suspension for severe infractions of a rule, standards, or for excessive violations. Usually, the employee has already received a written warning and has made little or no effort to improve performance or behavior. Suspension should be utilized only after a thorough evaluation by the supervisor.

Employers should follow these steps when imposing a suspension:

- ◆ Present all the facts that initiated the reason for the disciplinary suspension and the duration of the suspension.

- ◆ Inform the employee of the reasons for the disciplinary action and give the employee an opportunity to respond before the suspension is imposed.

- ◆ The original notice of suspension should be placed in the employee's personnel file.

After the employee returns from a period of disciplinary suspension, the supervisor should make certain that the employee may return to the workplace without injury to the employee's dignity or self-worth.

Note: Many employers believe employee suspensions only increase absenteeism and therefore use final written warnings rather than suspensions.

Discharge

If the employee fails to improve after the supervisor has issued a suspension, the last option available to the employer is termination. When the supervisor is unsure whether termination is proper, the "last chance" letter should be considered. This last chance letter alerts the employee that they should be terminated; however, the employer is willing to offer the employee one more chance to rectify the actions that may lead to termination. However, any future form of misconduct will result in an immediate discharge.

Summary Discharge

Progressive discipline is an employee benefit. However, employers are not required to offer progressive discipline to someone whose actions are illegal or intolerable in the workplace. If an employee engages in illegal activity or other egregious conduct (such as gross insubordination, gross negligence, or drug use on company premises), employers may be justified in the prompt termination of the individual.

Note: Immediate discharge actions should be avoided in most cases in order to allow adequate time for appropriate review of these serious decisions. Alternatively, an employer may suspend an employee "pending further review and final decision regarding discharge"

Employers need to remember that discipline must be administered consistently. Where appropriate, the application of discipline should logically and sequentially follow upon previous disciplinary actions documented in the employee's file.

Rehabilitation

The purpose of progressive discipline systems is to rehabilitate, and employers must try to assist employees in solving their problems.

Employers should document their efforts by performing the following procedures when disciplinary action occurs:

♦ Clearly state in writing the nature of the problem and how the employee's performance or conduct damaged the organization.

♦ Provide a clear and unequivocal warning that the employee's failure to improve will result in discipline, up to and including termination.

♦ Prove through progressive disciplinary actions that the employee's poor performance continued despite repeated warnings.

♦ Demonstrate that discipline was dispensed in a fair and consistent manner, so as to notify any future employee that termination under similar circumstances may be reasonably expected.

Protected-Class Employees

Employers must be especially careful about documentation when dealing with protected-class persons. Special attention should be paid to the following when dealing with protected-class employees:

♦ Uniformity.

♦ Absence of evidence of discriminatory intent.

♦ Use of "last chance" technique (*see* **Warnings: Discharge** section).

Absenteeism

Absenteeism tends to be a prevalent disciplinary problem. Absenteeism results in inefficiency and decreased productivity as employers reassign workers and rearrange schedules to substitute for absent employees.

Employers pay a heavy price when employees consistently fail to report to work.

Establish an Attendance Policy

The first step in combating absenteeism is to establish an attendance policy that encourages and rewards attendance while discouraging absenteeism. A formalized plan provides an objective goal for the employee and a framework for uniform implementation that ensures equal and just treatment for all employees.

Incentive Plans

Reward and Penalty Type Plan

A comprehensive attendance policy should have elements of both reward and penalty. For example, an employee may receive a reward for exemplary attendance. Many employers offer additional time off for employees who do not use sick days; for instance, for every six-month period during which an employee has not used a sick day, the employee earns a personal day.

There is no requirement that the incentive take the form of extra days. Some employers offer cash incentives, awards, prizes, or dinners to employees who achieve exemplary attendance. An effective incentive program offers a reward worth achieving within a reasonable time frame. Quarterly incentives are often more effective than yearly incentives, which may often seem unreachable to an employee. However, the Occupational Safety and Health Administration (OSHA) has criticized incentive plans that discourage employees from fully reporting occupational injuries and illnesses, such as those which offer rewards based on having the fewest lost work time accidents.

The penalty component of the attendance plan may be as varied as the reward portion. Such a policy may take the form of a traditional plan distinguishing between excused and unexcused absences or it may be a no-fault plan. Both types contain progressively severe penalties for increased absenteeism. Traditional plans usually share several features. Importantly, plans provide absent employees with an option, distinguishing between excused and unexcused absences. In addition, such plans typically allow employers to take special circumstances into account and provide for progressive discipline. The result is a plan in which supervisory personnel exercise significant discretion.

No-Fault Plan

No-fault plans diminish supervisory discretion by eliminating the excused and unexcused distinction while informing employees that a certain number of absences will result in a definite disciplinary action. Typically, such a plan also seeks to foster consistent attendance by maintaining a rolling tally where points drop off with the passage of time, or by returning the absenteeism tally to a zero after a certain period of perfect attendance. However, despite having a no-fault policy, some arbitrators still require an employer to take into account all relevant factors in determining whether to discharge an employee. Furthermore, in large organizations, prompt enforcement of such plans may prove difficult, since there often will be a day between the time the employee incurs a triggering absence and the time the human resources officials calculate the running total and direct disciplinary action. This could give rise to the appearance of inconsistent treatment.

Family and Medical Leave Act

In developing a no-fault plan, the employer must assess any Family and Medical Leave Act (FMLA) absences and not count them against the employee. Additionally, government investigators looking into allegations of unlawful retaliation for the exercise of protected rights under various labor and employment laws may view with skepticism an employer's reliance on a lock-stop policy to explain a suspect termination, especially where it is not enforced with a high degree of consistency.

In particular, employers should be mindful of the requirements of the FMLA, the Americans with Disabilities Act (ADA), and similar state and local laws in applying any policies or practices discussed in this chapter.

Chronic Absenteeism
Physician Certificates

An important component of any successful attendance policy provides for verification and reintegration of absent employees returning to work. Employees absent for more than a few days due to a medical issue should be required to provide medical verification of their condition. The number of days used to trigger this requirement should range between three to five workdays. Accordingly, an employee who calls in sick for more than five days should be required to provide a physician's note verifying the existence of an injury or illness and, if applicable, releasing the employee to return safely to the workforce.

A physician verification policy protects the following:

- The employee who may try to return to work too soon after a serious illness.

- Other employees who may be subjected to an infectious illness.

- The employer against employees using sick leave for unauthorized purposes.

A policy may also be developed that requires a physician's note if a sick day is taken in conjunction with other forms of leave or in conjunction with weekends. A proficient policy will allow the employer to request a physician's note whenever the employee is suspected of abusing sick leave.

Return-to-Work Physicals

A comprehensive attendance policy should also allow the employer to require an employee returning to work after a long illness or injury to undergo a physical examination.

The purpose of the physical examination is to ensure that the employee is fit to return to the workplace. This examination must be limited to verifying that the employee is able to meet the legitimate physical requirements for the employment position (subject to any appropriate accommodation).

Absenteeism Without Violation of Policy

Regardless of the type of attendance plan used, an organization may still be concerned about the following:

- A chronically absent employee.

- An employee who does not technically violate the basic attendance policy.

- An employee who negatively affects productivity.

Regular attendance is a basic requirement and an employer cannot maintain efficiency and productivity without consistent attendance from employees. Arbitrators recognize the rights of employers to ensure that their operations do not experience productivity declines and inefficiency resulting from chronic absenteeism, even if the absenteeism results from illness or other legitimate reasons.

In cases of chronic absenteeism, the employee may be disciplined and discharged, although the employee has not directly violated the absenteeism policy. The key in such cases is to first determine what constitutes excessive chronic absenteeism, and then to develop a method for disciplining such an employee that meets a just-cause standard.

Calculating Absenteeism

Often a statistical approach is used to determine what constitutes excessive absenteeism. For example, to obtain a simple percentage the number of days missed are divided into the number of days scheduled. This percent may then be compared to the absentee rates throughout the employer's facility.

Employers should also consider the gross number of absences and the frequency of absence. For example, an employee who is out for a single 36-day period for surgery or other medical problem may cause less disruption than an employee who randomly misses work an average of three times per month, although both employees have a yearly absenteeism rate of 13.8 percent.

With proper employee-provided notice, employers may prepare for a single 36-day absence and arrange for a suitable, temporary replacement. However, employers will have more difficultly in the efficient replacement of an employee who is randomly absent due to the unpredictable nature of the absence.

Discipline

Employers should construct a system for disciplining the chronically absent employee that takes into account the following factors:

- Has the employee been notified of attendance requirements?

- How frequently has the employee been absent?

- Of what duration were the absences and over what period of time?

- What are the reasons for the absences or tardiness?

- Did the employee provide timely notice and required documentation?

- Has progressive discipline or other corrective action been taken?

- How does the employee's record compare to other employees' records?

- Have employees in similar situations been treated the same way?

Note: Particular attention must be paid to special leaves of absence. Leaves of absence protected by the FMLA may not be counted against an employee's attendance record. In addition, the Equal Employment Opportunity Commission (EEOC) has taken the position that an extension of leave beyond that authorized by company policy may constitute a reasonable accommodation under the ADA.

Categories for Discipline

Situations that necessitate discipline fall into the following three broad categories and require different approaches, for example:

- ◆ **Misconduct.** Employees are doing something they should not be doing.
- ◆ **Poor Performance.** Employees are not doing something they should be doing.
- ◆ **Attendance Policy Violations.** Employees are unreasonably or excessively absent from the workplace or tardy to the workplace.

Caution: Managers or supervisors should never use a confrontational, blaming approach with an employee who is not performing up to standard.

Misconduct

Examples of misconduct include the following:

- ◆ Violation of work rules.
- ◆ Sexual harassment.
- ◆ Intoxication at the workplace.
- ◆ Sleeping on the job.
- ◆ Smoking on the job or jobsite.
- ◆ Conducting personal business on the job.

Of course, extreme examples include criminal behavior, such as drug dealing, rape, and murder. In every case, the supervisor must act — rather than react — with as much control as possible. However, when someone or something is in danger, a quick reaction is necessary.

Some forms of conduct for which discipline may be necessary include the following:

- ◆ Illegal conduct.
- ◆ Intentionally false representations on a job application.
- ◆ Insubordination.
- ◆ Poor interactions with subordinates and/or co-workers.
- ◆ Failure to meet new policy standards.

Poor Performance

Poor performance should always be handled with a combination of coaching and progressive discipline. Initially, employees who are not correctly performing their duties should be presumed to be in need of coaching or counseling. Should this approach be ineffective, the employer may begin the progressive discipline. If the employee does not or cannot make the changes necessary for proper performance, the employee may be terminated. The important elements are as follows:

- ◆ Treating everyone fairly and consistently.
- ◆ Documenting any warnings given.
- ◆ Documenting any failure to improve performance.

Absenteeism and Tardiness

A widespread discipline problem for employers is absenteeism and tardiness. Some employers have established programs designed to minimize absenteeism and tardiness. Effective programs must be communicated to employees. Employees must know what the attendance policies are and what attendance records will merit incentives or discipline.

Small employers may find a combination of approaches to be most effective.

Incentives

In some work environments, an attendance policy that rewards good attendance may be a good addition to a penalty system for poor attendance.

The following suggested incentives might improve attendance and punctuality in the workplace:

- ◆ Departmental competitions that award a small bonus to the department with the best attendance record for a month or quarter.

- ◆ Using an employee's attendance record as a factor in granting salary increases.

- ◆ Offering attendance awards in the form of cash, extra leave, or recognition at a special lunch for employees who meet certain attendance standards.

- ◆ Paying for unused sick leave time at the year's end or upon termination.

- ◆ Allowing employees to annually carry over unused sick leave or convert the unused leave to vacation or personal days.

Additionally, some employers use the concept of "personal days." Each employee receives a number of personal days, rather than sick days, each year. Employees may take personal days at any time, for any reason (with proper notice where possible). This practice may greatly improve employee morale, as the employees are granted more freedom in their workplace decisions.

Discipline

Establishing clear standards for attendance may involve designating steps for discipline, such as the following:

- ◆ An employee who is absent or tardy for _____ days within a _____ day period will get a verbal warning.

- ◆ An employee who is absent or tardy for _____ days within a _____ day period, after the verbal warning, will receive a written warning.

- ◆ An employee who is absent or tardy for _____ days within a _____ day period, after the written warning, will be suspended without pay.

- ◆ An employee who is absent or tardy for _____ days within a _____ day period after suspension will be terminated.

Note: Employers should carefully monitor their attendance policy. Adherence to a strict attendance policy may be unlawful if giving an employee time off would be a reasonable accommodation for an employee's disability under the Americans with Disabilities Act (ADA).

Types of Work Rules

The following is a list of the areas in which many employers have developed work rules. However, every employer should not have rules on all of the listed topics.

Most small employers have written rules on only a few areas that are either important to the organization or chronic problems in the particular workplace, industry, locale, or labor pool from which the employer hires.

Employers should consider creating work rules on the following topics:

- Attendance.
- Punctuality.
- Telephone usage costs.
- Confidential information.
- Visitor rules.
- Access to premises.
- Smoking.
- Moonlighting.
- Off-the-job conduct.
- Personal appearance and dress.
- Employee records.
- Gifts and gratuities.
- Ethical business conduct.
- Customer service.
- Insubordination.
- Poor interactions with subordinates or co-workers.
- Intentional false misrepresentations on a job application or about reasons for absences.
- Sexual harassment.
- Substance abuse.
- Personal use of company equipment.
- Personal phone calls.
- Email policy.
- Privacy policy.
- Reference policy.
- Personal demeanor.
- Safety and health.
- Solicitations and distribution of literature.
- Use of company bulletin boards.
- Theft and fraud.
- Unauthorized overtime.
- Sleeping on the job.

♦ Fighting.

♦ Poor job performance.

♦ Failure to meet new policy standards.

When an employer lists any violations that may lead to discipline or termination, the employer should also add a disclaimer similar to the following:

> Listed are some of our work rules. The list includes types of behavior and conduct that the organization considers inappropriate and which could lead to disciplinary action up to and including termination of employment without prior warning. This list should not be viewed as being all-inclusive. Additionally, management reserves the right to impose discipline up to and including termination for other inappropriate or dangerous actions or misconduct.

Violations

An employer should reserve the right to list what actions are in violation of company policy and the appropriate discipline, if any. The following statement should precede the list of violations incurring actions, "Violations of any of the following performance standards may result in disciplinary action or immediate discharge."

A typical list of actionable violations contains the following:

♦ Failure or refusal to follow the written or verbal instructions of a supervisor or manager.

♦ Insubordination.

♦ Neglecting job duties and responsibilities.

♦ Engaging in unauthorized personal business during work hours.

♦ Falsifying or misrepresenting company or employment records.

♦ Discourtesy or rudeness in dealing with employees, representatives of clients, or prospects.

♦ Failure to give proper notice when unable to report for or continue work as scheduled.

♦ Unexcused or excessive absenteeism.

♦ Abuse of sick leave privileges.

♦ Theft, abuse, or misuse of company property, materials, or supplies.

♦ Unauthorized use of company property and equipment, including telephones, copy machines, and mail service.

♦ Threatening, harassing, or inflicting bodily harm to fellow employees.

♦ Making false and malicious statements concerning employees or the organization.

♦ Intentionally discriminating against employees in violation of applicable laws and engaging in harassment of any employee.

♦ Possession, use, purchase, consumption, transfer, or sale of alcoholic beverages, controlled substances, or illegal drugs at any time during working hours, on company premises, while representing the organization, or reporting to work under the influence of alcohol, controlled substances, or illegal drugs.

♦ Violating any company policies, rules, regulations, or practices.

Off-Duty Time

A conflict may develop between an employee's freedom to spend off-duty time free from employer restrictions and the employer's ability to discipline an employee based on off-duty conduct. Generally, the employer may not regulate an employee's conduct or actions outside the scope of the workplace.

An employee that is terminated or disciplined for off-duty conduct may successfully assert an invasion of privacy claim based on a theory of unreasonable intrusion into private affairs. To limit exposure to possible liability, employers may consider discipline only when the employee's off-duty conduct directly interferes with the employer's business operations and interests and only in the context of consistent and careful application of its rules and policies.

Preventive Measures

All employers will have situations involving employees with poor attitudes, poor work habits, poor job performance, and absenteeism or tardiness. It is essential that an employer appropriately respond to a problematic employee by helping to correct behavior or by engaging in disciplinary procedures.

Supervisors should review employee performance regularly. Whenever problems develop, the supervisor should discuss the problem with the employee as soon as possible and suggest ways of correcting the problem. Discussions should be documented and placed in an employee's file. Verbal and written warnings should be given to the employee whenever specific problems occur. A progressive discipline procedure should be followed in all cases except serious misconduct.

If unacceptable behavior continues, the supervisor should contact the personnel or human resources department and provide a detailed explanation of the problem. A specific meeting between human resources personnel and the employee should be arranged. At that time the precise aspects of work behavior that are unacceptable should be explained to the employee and the employee should be specifically told, in writing, what action or activity must be corrected. The employee also should be told that failure to comply with these requirements will result in discharge.

Checklist

An employer should customarily follow a basic checklist whenever disciplining or terminating an employee.

Employers should never discipline an employee unless they can answer in the affirmative to all of the following:

- ♦ Has the following analysis been applied:
  - The employee knew of the rule or performance standard.
  - The rule or standard is reasonable and that its enforcement would be reasonable under all the circumstances.
  - Review of all relevant materials including employee handbooks, contracts, policy statements, the employee's disciplinary history, evaluations, and attendance records.
  - All employees or third parties who may know of or were involved in the misconduct have been interviewed.

- Accurate notes have been taken from all interviews and investigations about who, what, where, when, and why.

- The employee was confronted about the misconduct.

- The employee was given a fair opportunity to explain or deny the misconduct.

- Based upon the interviews, records, and the investigation process the employer has confidence that all the necessary facts (who, what, where, when, why, and how) have been revealed.

- The proposed disciplinary action has been reviewed to ensure accuracy, consistency, and completeness.

- The disciplinary action is consistent with how other employees have been disciplined for the same or similar conduct.

- The disciplinary action is the proper corrective measure under applicable policies and the employee's disciplinary history.

- The discipline memo or provided notice is accurate and complete and states the following:

  - Date of violation.

  - Specific rule violated.

  - Number of prior warnings.

  - Detailed description of misconduct.

  - Corrective action and penalty.

  - Date and signature of supervisor.

- Personnel have approved the proposed disciplinary action.

- Arrangements for the presence of a reliable management witness if an employer is concerned about how the employee may react.

- During a private conference with the supervisor and employee, has the following been completed:

  - Review of the disciplinary notice/memorandum with the employee.

  - Review of the facts with the employee.

  - Explanation of the following:

    - The employee's misconduct and why the misconduct is unacceptable.

    - The penalty given.

    - The penalty that will result if the misconduct is repeated.

    - How to improve performance/conduct.

  - If the employee is to be discharged, the supervisor must provide the employee written notice (a copy of which should be kept in the employee's personnel file) of the effective time and date of the discharge.

- After the disciplinary conference, the supervisor must immediately make the necessary entries in the personnel file and other applicable records.

Note: Although an employer has the right to regulate and monitor workplace conduct, employers should seek an attorney when considering disciplining employees for conduct or social behavior that occurs off the premises and during nonwork time. This is advisable no matter how serious the conduct may be (for instance, arrest, or conviction for sexual offenses or drug possession).

Limitations on Right to Terminate

Employers using disciplinary policies that list cardinal offenses that result in termination may limit their right to terminate for offenses not listed. A 2000 Ninth Circuit Court of Appeals decision also discusses when termination for just cause might not be permitted when an employer uses the list procedure.

In this case, the employer was subject to a collective-bargaining agreement prohibiting termination without a written warning within the previous nine months for the same type of offense. The agreement also listed seven cardinal offenses which allowed immediate termination without first receiving a warning. The employee was terminated for conduct not in the agreement. After an arbitrator ruled for the employer, the Ninth Circuit reversed, holding that if an employee has not committed a cardinal offense and has not received the required warning notice, the employer may not terminate the employee even for just cause. Although in the present case, the cardinal offenses policy was in a collective-bargaining agreement, the same conclusion could be reached based on the same policy in an employee handbook.

Employee Right to Co-Worker or Union Presence During Investigatory

If an employee who is represented by a union reasonably believes that an investigatory interview with the employer might result in disciplinary action, it is unlawful for an employer to deny the employee's request for a union representative's presence at the interview. This right of representation during investigatory interviews in a unionized workplace is referred to as the employee's *Weingarten* rights. Seeking the assistance of a union representative in a confrontation with an employer is a legitimate exercise of the employee's right to engage in concerted activity for mutual aid or protection and denying this right, threatening or retaliating against an employee for asserting this right is a violation of the National Labor Relations Act (NLRA).

Once an employee who is represented by a union asserts the right to union representation during an investigatory interview, the employer may either:

♦ Grant the request and delay the interview until the union representative arrives and has a chance to speak with the employee

♦ Deny the request and end the interview immediately.

♦ Offer the employee the choice of continuing the interview without a union representative or ending the interview.

The employee may not insist on the presence of a fellow employee, who is not a union steward or representative.

The employer must honor an employee's or union's request for a particular union representative during the investigative meeting, as long as that representative is reasonably available.

In *IBM Corp*, 341 NLRB No. 148 (2004), the NLRB declined to extend *Weingarten* to nonunion employees, reversing a 2000 decision in which it held that employers were required to allow nonunion employees to have another employee present during an investigatory interview. Employers are not required to inform employees of this new right. However, employers should review personnel policies, grievance procedures and work rules to confirm they do not interfere with these employee rights. Employers should train all supervisors and managers to ensure they are prepared and able to process employee requests for representation.

Chapter 20

Negligent Retention and Supervision

Introduction

The recommendations discussed in the **Recruiting and Hiring** chapter relate primarily to the pre-employment process. Employers should also pay close attention to behavior and information gained about employees after the hiring decision has been made. In particular, given the frequency of negligent retention claims involving allegations of sexual harassment, employers should document and respond decisively to any indication that an employee has engaged in harassing conduct or potentially violent behavior.

This chapter looks at problems — grouped under the categories of negligent retention and negligent supervision — associated with employers' failure to monitor their employees closely.

Negligent Retention

The negligent retention theory arose out of fellow servant law, which imposed a duty on employers to select employees who would not endanger their fellow employees by their presence on the job. The theory evolved from one designed to protect employees to one designed to protect employees and the general public. Thus, the doctrine of negligent retention involves the employer's continued employment of an unfit individual.

Elements of Negligent Retention

To establish a claim for negligent retention, an individual must generally meet the following requirements similar to those found in the negligent hiring context:

- ◆ The employer retains an employee who is incompetent or unfit for the job.

- ◆ The employer knew, or should have known, that an employee presents an unreasonable risk of harm to others.

- ◆ The employee commits an intentional or negligent act, which results in injury to a third party.

- ◆ The third party's injuries are proximately caused by the employer's retention of the incompetent or unfit employee.

The Basis for Claims of Negligent Retention

Negligent retention claims may arise even when the employer has conducted an extensive investigation into an employee's background at the time of hire. During the course of employment, the employer may become aware of problems with an employee that indicate unfitness.

A claim of negligent retention will arise when an employer becomes aware of problems with a particular employee but fails to take further action such as investigating, disciplining, discharging, or reassigning the employee. In such cases, the employer has a duty to take appropriate action to protect other employees and the public. This duty is not limited to actions occurring on the employer's premises.

The Employer Knew or Should Have Known

Negligent retention claims often focus on whether the employer knew or should have known of the employee's unfitness for duty.

This question is often very fact-specific, but the courts have identified a number of factors that may be relevant to such a determination, as follows:

- The employee's overall work record.

- Whether the employer had received any complaints about the employee.

- The degree to which the employee's negative activities were related to the job.

- Whether any managers or supervisors witnessed the alleged negative activities.

Appropriate Employer Action

A second and related issue that often arises in the negligent retention context concerns the nature of appropriate employer action. Even if an employer learns of an employee's negative activities, the employer will only be held liable for negligent retention if the employer fails to take appropriate action to address the activities.

Appropriate action may include the following:

- Disciplining the employee.

- Removing the employee from a position in which the person could harm other employees or members of the public.

- Exercising closer supervision over the employee.

- Terminating the employee.

Negligent Supervision

Another claim recognized in the employment context is negligent supervision.

To establish a claim of negligent supervision, an individual generally must demonstrate the following elements:

- The employer knows, or should have known, that an employee is engaging in wrongful conduct.

- The employee's wrongful conduct is substantially certain to cause injury to a third party.

- The employee's conduct, through intentional or negligent action, results in injury to a third party.

- The injury was a reasonably foreseeable consequence of the employer's lack of supervision.

Negligent supervision claims are brought most often in the context of sexual harassment lawsuits. An employee may allege that poor supervision by the employer of another employee allowed the harassing conduct to continue.

In these circumstances, the success of the negligent supervision claim may depend on the following circumstances:

- Whether the employee/victim reported the harassment to the employer.

- Whether the employer otherwise knew or should have known about the harassment.

- Whether the employer took prompt action to prevent further harassment.

Negligent supervision claims also arise when injuries occur to nonemployees through the conduct of an employee. For an employer to be found liable, courts generally require that the harmful conduct must have occurred on the employer's property or with something belonging to the employer (for example, an automobile). Courts sometimes examine whether the conduct occurred while the employee was working or on duty.

Thus, a negligent supervision claim might be successful if the employee's conduct occurred while subject to the supervision or control of the employer. Even then, employers generally must have had some reason to anticipate the harmful conduct by the employee before they may be held liable for failing to prevent the harm through properly supervising the employee.

Claims for negligent supervision are still fairly new in most states, but the number of such claims is likely to grow. A claim that an employer failed to take proper care in supervising its employees fills the gap between a claim for negligent hiring and a negligent retention claim. The best way for an employer to avoid negligent supervision claims is to pay close attention to the conduct of employees after they are hired, to take prompt action if observation indicates that a particular employee may be behaving inappropriately, and to clearly document such actions and observations as they occur.

The success of a claim for negligent supervision or negligent retention may also depend on whether the employee or injured individual has brought claims under the state antidiscrimination laws. Taking advantage of such state law remedies may nullify the employee's claims for negligence.

Negligent Training

Employees may also raise claims of negligent training arising out of facts similar to their claims of negligent supervision and negligent retention.

Many state courts have not yet addressed the issue of negligent training, but the trend to recognize such claims is growing.

Chapter 21
Termination

Introduction

Termination is when an employee is fired, laid off, suspended for an unreasonably long period, or constructively discharged.

Most employment-related lawsuits follow an employee's termination. Employers can reduce their exposure to wrongful-termination lawsuits and damage awards by deciding carefully whether, when, and how to terminate an employee and by implementing and following effective strategies and procedures for hiring, evaluating, and disciplining employees, as discussed in previous chapters.

This chapter reviews proper versus improper termination, looks closely at types of wrongful discharge, and considers some ways to avoid liability for improper termination.

Proper Termination

Employment-at-Will Employees

When an employee is hired under an employment-at-will relationship, the employee may be terminated at any time with or without a reason, and the employer need not follow any particular procedure in discharging the employee. Therefore, an employer is at liberty to discharge an at-will employee unless the termination violates a statute, is constitutionally impermissible, or breaches an express limitation in a contract of employment. The precise contours of the at-will doctrine vary from state to state. Employers should consult with an employment law attorney prior to terminating the employment of an employee presumed to be at-will.

Exceptions to the Employment-at-Will Doctrine

Public-Policy Exception

Under the public-policy exception to the employment-at-will doctrine, an employee is wrongfully discharged when the termination is against an explicit, well-established public policy of the state.

For example, in most states, an employer cannot terminate an employee for filing a workers' compensation claim after being injured on the job or for refusing to break the law at the request of the employer. The majority view among states is that public policy may be found in a state constitution, statute, or administrative rule; however, some states have either restricted or expanded the doctrine beyond this bound. The public-policy exception is the most widely accepted exception, recognized in 43 states.

Implied-Contract Exception

Another exception to the employment-at-will doctrine is applied when an implied contract is formed between an employer and employee, even though no express, written instrument regarding the employment relationship exists. Although employment is typically not governed by contract, an employer may make oral or written representations to the employee regarding job security or procedures that will be followed when adverse employment actions are taken. If so, these representations may create a contract for employment. This exception is recognized in 38 states.

Covenant-of-Good-Faith Exception

Recognized in only 11 states, the covenant-of-good faith exception reads a covenant of good faith and fair dealing into every employment relationship. It has been interpreted to mean either of the following:

♦ Employer personnel decisions are subject to a just cause standard.

♦ Terminations made in bad faith or motivated by malice are prohibited.

Contractual Employees

Employees who are not hired under an employment-at-will relationship are promised some type of job security. Employees working under a union contract, for example, can usually only be fired for just cause. In addition, employees hired for a definite period of time often may be terminated only for just cause. *Just cause* may include, but is not limited to, the following:

♦ Misconduct, including the following:

- Theft.

- Workplace violence.

- Intoxication on the job.

- Bringing firearms to work.

- Engaging in serious racial or sexual harassment.

- Insubordination.

♦ Unsatisfactory performance, including the following:

- Excessive absenteeism.

- Poor quality of work.

- Failure to meet numerical production standards.

Serious misconduct often subjects an employee to immediate dismissal even under a union contract. However, unsatisfactory job performance often may not result in discharge for cause until the employee has received a series of warnings and has failed to improve.

Progressive Discipline

An effective discharge procedure is generally based on progressive discipline. Although there are situations that require varying from progressive procedures, a progressive approach is based upon a presumption that employees, by nature, do not wish to engage in misconduct and if allowed will correct their behavior. Such a system recognizes discharge generally as a last resort.

Retain Employees When Possible

Obviously, retaining employees precludes the possibility of wrongful-discharge problems. Whenever possible, employers should try to retain their employees.

Consider the following **before** discharging an employee:

♦ Establish fair and reasonable work rules, related to valid business interests, and apply them uniformly to all employees. Fair and reasonable rules foster good employee morale since employees know what is expected of them.

♦ Always investigate thoroughly before disciplining an employee.

♦ Respond to inappropriate employee behavior or performance with appropriate disciplinary or corrective procedures. The degree of the penalty should relate to the seriousness of the offense. Factors to be considered in this determination include the need for corrective action, the employee's past record, the employee's length of service, whether the employee knew the conduct would result in discipline, and whether management contributed to the misconduct.

♦ Progressive discipline systems generally involve a three- or four-step approach before an employee is discharged. For example, an employee may initially be given a verbal warning for an offense, followed by a written warning for the same offense, and then a short suspension from one to five days for a third offense. The fourth offense may result in discharge.

  Note: Progressive discipline systems vary from employer to employer. Consult with an employment law attorney prior to adopting any specific procedure.

♦ While rules must be enforced consistently, a disciplinary system should maintain some degree of flexibility in both procedure and substance.

Handle Discharges Correctly

Sometimes discharge is unavoidable. On occasion, discipline or performance problems are so severe that discharge is the only viable option.

However, employers will minimize their liability and help maintain the dignity of their employees if they take the following steps:

♦ Termination should be done in person. Have two managers or a manager and a human resources representative present at firings.

♦ Do not discharge someone before birthdays, holidays, or the like.

♦ Make certain the individuals communicating the termination are prepared to be calm, concise, and factual as to the reason for the employer's action.

♦ Do not encourage the employee to feel the termination is the end of a career.

♦ Maintain control over the situation. Be compassionate yet firm. Employees should not feel they control the outcome.

♦ Consider providing job counseling for terminated employees.

♦ Collect keys and other security-sensitive property.

♦ Make any severance package consistent with what other employees have been offered.

♦ Consider a general release of all claims and/or prospective claims in appropriate cases.

- ♦ Ensure that the final decision to discharge is made by the executive in charge, based on recommendations of lower management and human resource executives.

- ♦ Conduct an exit interview even though the termination is involuntary. Assess the employee's attitude about the employer and cover pay, benefit matters, final checks, and insurance options.

- ♦ Consult with an employment law counsel.

Improper Termination

Wrongful Discharge

Terminating employment-at-will employees for an illegal reason or terminating contractual employees without following proper procedures or without just cause may be examples of wrongful discharge.

Restrictions on Employment-at-Will

Notwithstanding the general exceptions to the employment-at-will doctrine, the most commonly recognized restrictions on employment-at-will are the specific rights provided by federal and state laws and regulations. These laws and regulations state that employers may not fire at-will employees because they are members of a statutorily protected group.

These classifications include, but are not limited to, the following:

- ♦ Race.
- ♦ Creed.
- ♦ Color.
- ♦ Sex/gender.
- ♦ National origin.
- ♦ Religion.
- ♦ Age.
- ♦ Marital status.
- ♦ Disability.
- ♦ Union activity.
- ♦ Sexual orientation.
- ♦ Parental status.
- ♦ Military status.
- ♦ Whistleblower activity.
- ♦ Serving on a jury.
- ♦ Filing a workers' compensation claim.
- ♦ Assisting in a government investigation.

Employees fired for any of these reasons may sue for wrongful discharge. Many federal and state statutes exist to protect employees from being terminated for discriminatory reasons, greatly restricting employment-at-will. In addition, many statutes prohibit employers from retaliating against employees who have exercised their rights under the law.

States (and some localities) have their own statutes prohibiting discrimination in employment and otherwise prohibiting employment actions based on certain grounds. For example, many states' laws prohibit disciplining or discharging employees for engaging in whistleblowing activity, filing workers' compensation claims, or serving on jury duty.

Federal Statutes Limiting Employment-at-Will

Federal statutes that limit employment-at-will include the following:

- **Age Discrimination in Employment Act (ADEA)** (29 U.S.C.A. § 621). Prohibits employment discrimination against workers 40 years old or older and bars retaliation against people exercising their ADEA rights.

- **Americans with Disabilities Act (ADA)** (42 U.S.C.A. § 12101). Prohibits employment discrimination against qualified individuals on the basis of disability and bars retaliation against those exercising the ADA rights.

- **Bankruptcy Code** (11 U.S.C.A. § 525). Prohibits employers from discriminating against or terminating an employee solely because the person has filed for bankruptcy.

- **Civil Service Reform Act of 1978** (5 U.S.C.A. § 7513a). Permits removing federal civil service employees only for efficiency-related reasons.

- **Civil Rights Act of 1964, Title VII** (42 U.S.C.A. §§ 2000e-2 and 2000e-3a). Prohibits discharge based on race, color, religion, sex, or national origin, and prohibits reprisal for exercising rights under the act.

- **Clean Air Act** (42 U.S.C.A. § 7622). Prohibits terminating employees for assisting in any proceeding under the act.

- **Consumer Credit Protection Act** (15 U.S.C.A. § 1674a). Prohibits firing employees because of garnishment of wages for any one indebtedness.

- **Employee Retirement Income Security Act of 1974 (ERISA)** (29 U.S.C.A. §§ 1140 and 1141). Prohibits terminating employees to prevent them from obtaining vested pension rights.

- **Energy Reorganization Act of 1974** (42 U.S.C.A. § 5851). Prohibits firing employees who assist in any proceedings under the act.

- **Fair Labor Standards Act (FLSA)** (29 U.S.C.A. §§ 215(a)(3) and 216b). Prohibits discharge for exercising FLSA rights.

- **Family and Medical Leave Act of 1993 (FMLA)** (29 U.S.C. §§ 250 et seq.). Prohibits discharge for exercising rights under the act; bars retaliation against those exercising FMLA rights.

- **Federal Water Pollution Control Act** (33 U.S.C.A. § 1367). Prohibits firing employees who assist in any proceeding under the act.

- **Immigration Reform and Control Act of 1968 (IRCA)** (8 U.S.C.A. § 1324b). Prohibits employment discrimination against individuals, except unauthorized aliens, because of national origin and against U.S. citizens or aliens eligible for citizenship because of citizenship status.

♦ **Judiciary and Judicial Procedure Act** (28 U.S.C.A. § 1875). Prohibits firing employees for service on grand or petit juries.

♦ **National Labor Relations Act (NLRA)** (29 U.S.C.A. §§ 158(a)(1), 158(a)(3), and 158(a)(4)). Prohibits termination for union activity, protected concerted activity, or filing charges or giving testimony under the act.

♦ **Occupational Safety and Health Act of 1970 (OSH Act)** (29 U.S.C.A. §§ 651 et seq.). Prohibits firing employees for exercising OSHA rights.

♦ **Rehabilitation Act of 1973** (29 U.S.C.A. §§ 793 and 794). Prohibits federal contractors or any program or activity receiving federal funds from discriminating against persons with disabilities.

♦ **Uniformed Services Employment and Re-Employment Rights Act (USERRA)** (38 U.S.C. §§ 4301 – 4333). Requires reinstatement of and protects returning veterans for a limited time against discharge without just cause.

Constructive Discharge

Sometimes employees quit, but they do not do so voluntarily. When employees are forced or coerced into quitting, it may be considered a ***constructive discharge***. For example, an employee who is victimized by her supervisor's constant sexual harassment may feel compelled to quit. The employee's leaving might be considered a constructive discharge.

Generally, a discharge is considered constructive if the following apply:

♦ The employer deliberately created or condoned working conditions for the employee that a reasonable person in the employee's position would find intolerable.

♦ Any reasonable employee would quit rather than endure the situation.

Employees may be constructively discharged for a number of reasons including, but not limited to, the following:

♦ Discrimination.

♦ Dangerous duties.

♦ Hazardous situations.

♦ Harassment.

♦ Demeaning or malicious assignments.

♦ An employer's failure to give the employee any work to do.

Avoiding Constructive Discharge Claims

When an employee quits after complaining of intolerable work conditions, the employer should immediately investigate to verify the employee's claim and, if appropriate, remedy the situation. The employer may wish to consider offering the employee unconditional and immediate reinstatement. The employer should assure the employee that the intolerable conditions have been corrected.

This approach can reduce potential liability and severely undercut an employee's claim of constructive discharge. If an employee who raised a complaint of discrimination or similar violation of law is reinstated, however, great care must be taken in dealing with the employee to avoid claims of retaliation.

Claims Brought After Termination

This section reviews the sorts of claims terminated employees might bring against employers. This section also outlines some procedures to help employers protect themselves from liability resulting from these claims.

Breach of Contract

In the most common wrongful termination lawsuits, plaintiffs claim that their discharge breached a contract — whether formal or informal, express or implied — not to terminate employment except for good cause. Consequently, employers must structure employment documents and policies carefully and precisely in case a terminated employee later sues for alleged breach of contract. If possible, seek the advice of an employment law counsel prior to executing an employment contract. Doing so may help avoid future litigation or provide a successful defense of a future breach of contract claim.

Express written and oral contracts and implied contracts, such as employee handbooks and disciplinary procedures (as discussed in the **Employee Handbooks** and **Discipline** chapters), are enforceable in many states. Juries have often treated informal oral statements such as those made by a supervisor to an employee, a series of positive performance evaluations, or offer letters as binding contracts.

Interference with Contractual Relationships

This type of claim alleges that individual supervisors or managers interfered with the contractual relationship between an employee and an employer. An example of such a claim is where a supervisor knowingly communicates false information about an employee to higher management and that information results in the employee's termination. These claims are normally brought against supervisors or managers who are acting maliciously outside the scope of their employment.

Constructive Discharge Claims

Employees who are forced to quit as a result of constructive discharge may claim that their resignation was not voluntary but rather the result of an employer's actions or the employer's failure to correct an intolerable working environment. In such situations, the employees may sue for wrongful discharge.

Discharges in Violation of Public Policy

In certain states, a separate public-policy exception to employment-at-will exists if the reason for terminating an employee is contrary to clearly established public policy. This is known as ***wrongful discharge in violation of public policy***.

While the elements of such a claim vary by state and statute, the discharged employee must usually prove that the individual was discharged under circumstances that would jeopardize public policy and for reasons motivated by conduct damaging to public policy rather than for overriding legitimate business reasons.

Examples of conduct that may be protected include, but are not limited to, the following:

♦ Whistleblowing — reporting unlawful activities by an employer to law-enforcement officials. This may also be something as simple as complaining to another employee or to the media.

♦ Filing a workers' compensation claim.

♦ Refusing to perform illegal, unethical, or unsafe activities on behalf of an employer.

- Fulfilling a legal duty, such as serving on a jury or attending court when subpoenaed as a witness, or for taking time off to vote.

- Cooperating in a governmental investigation involving the employer.

Many statutes also prohibit employers from taking retaliatory action against an employee who engages in such activities.

Under some whistleblowing laws, employees must first report the alleged unlawful activities to the employer who has a certain time period to correct or initiate a reasonable good faith effort to correct the unlawful activities. If the employer makes no reasonable effort to correct the problem, the employee may report the conduct to the prosecuting authority of the county, a peace officer, an appropriate inspector general, or other appropriate officials or agencies. Employers may take no retaliatory action against employees who follow this procedure.

Employers must be aware of public policy discharge cases because they are often treated like personal injury cases; that is, plaintiffs may actually recover compensation for mental anguish and punitive damages as well. Punitive damages "punish" the defendants by awarding damage amounts that are often much greater than the actual economic damages of lost wages and benefits.

Under the federal False Claims Act, employees may file suit against their employers for suspected fraud against the government. This law entitles employees to recover a percentage of any amounts recovered by the government. Employers doing business with the government need to be aware that disgruntled employees have this option open to them. The act prohibits retaliation against an employee who files an action, testifies, or otherwise helps the government in an investigation under the act.

Good Faith and Fair Dealing

Many state courts have held that contractual employment relationships contain an implied promise or covenant of good faith and fair dealing. In theory, one party to the contract must not act in bad faith and deprive the other party of the benefits of the agreement.

Such cases may involve the following:

- Terminating an employee to avoid paying a sales commission.

- Retaliating against an employee who refuses to become romantically involved with a manager or supervisor.

- Retaliating against an employee who publicizes a wrongdoing on the part of the employer.

Intentional Infliction of Emotional Distress

Intentional infliction of emotional distress is defined as the actions of one party, who by extreme and outrageous conduct, intentionally or recklessly causes severe emotional distress to another party. The law in this area varies from state to state.

Under some circumstances, at-will employees may accuse former employers of intentionally inflicting emotional distress during the termination of employment. This type of claim may include allegations of intentional and extremely abusive discharge of the employee. The employee also may claim the discharge was conducted in a degrading and humiliating manner. Furthermore, allegations of sexual harassment may amount to intentional infliction of emotional distress.

To win in this claim, the employee must show that the following occurred:

♦ The employer intended to cause severe emotional distress or the employer knew or should have known that the actions taken would result in severe emotional distress by an employee.

♦ The employer's conduct was extreme or outrageous.

   Note: In many states, this requires the plaintiff to show that the alleged outrageous conduct so transcends the bounds of decency as to be regarded as atrocious and intolerable in a civilized society.

♦ The employer's actions proximately caused the employee's severe emotional distress.

♦ The mental anguish the employee suffered was serious.

If the employee is successful in the claim, the employer may be liable for the emotional distress as well as for any bodily harm — if any — that results from it.

Reducing Liability for Emotional Distress Claims

Employers are not liable for any resulting emotional distress when they have merely exercised their legal rights to terminate an employee. However, the mere fact that an employee's termination was done lawfully will not necessarily preclude a claim for intentional infliction of emotional distress.

To reduce the chances of liability for causing emotional distress, employers should do the following:

♦ Avoid anger in administering discipline.

♦ Require review of any contemplated disciplinary decisions by another supervisor or manager who has no personal bias against the employee.

♦ Use common sense and avoid embarrassing the employee in front of others.

♦ Document, sign, and date every critical incident.

Since the type and degree of behavior that amounts to outrageous conduct varies by state, employers should consult with an employment law counsel when faced with such a claim or potential claim.

Fraud and Negligent Misrepresentation

A terminated employee may also bring a fraud claim against an employer, alleging that the employer made false assurances of job security or benefits either in writing or orally. It may be that the employee has discovered that the job is not all it appeared to be during the pre-employment interviews.

The job duties may be different, the bonuses may be difficult to earn, or the boss is more difficult to work with than expected. Under these circumstances, the employee may claim to have accepted the job offer because the employer made statements that seemed sincere but were actually statements the employer knew or should have known were not true. This is especially likely to happen when the discharged employee was in a highly compensated job. In addition, an employee may claim that during the hiring process the employer knowingly made false representations about the future to induce the employee to join the employer.

To succeed in a fraud claim, the employee generally must show the following:

♦ The employer made a representation.

♦ The representation was significant to the transaction.

♦ The representation was made falsely.

♦ The representation was made with the intent to mislead.

♦ The employee relied on the misrepresentation.

- The employee's reliance on the misrepresentation was justified.

- The representation proximately caused an injury to the employee.

Employees who can demonstrate the existence of these elements can recover damages for their losses and possibly receive punitive damages for the employer's conduct.

Defamation Suits

Defamation claims are often linked to wrongful termination. An employee or former employee may sue a current or former employer based upon alleged false or defamatory statements of fact communicated to another person that purportedly injured the employee's reputation.

Statements by an employer that an employee was guilty of or had any of the following could lead to potential defamation claims:

- Gross misconduct, theft, embezzlement, or falsifying records.

- Using or abusing drugs.

- Professional incompetence.

- Criminal convictions or arrests.

- A communicable or venereal disease.

Defamation claims may be based on oral or written statements communicated to individuals inside or outside the organization. Any derogatory or negative statements can be the basis for a defamation action. In some states, comments made by a terminated employee have been considered compelled self-defamation.

Employers have a right to make truthful statements about employees, even if they are viewed as negative or derogatory. Additionally, employers have a *qualified privilege* right to communicate derogatory statements about employees to others who share a common interest in the information. When there is a legal requirement to make the derogatory statements — as in judicial or quasi-judicial proceedings — this is known as *absolute privilege* and no defamation exists.

Reducing Liability for Defamation Claims

Employers can avoid defamation claims by acquiring and applying a basic understanding of the law in this sensitive area and by following a few simple precautions:

- Discuss an employee's alleged misconduct, poor performance, or termination only with those who need to know. Caution those with whom the information is shared to be discreet.

- Investigate and document incidents of employee misconduct before imposing discipline.

- Keep medical data, especially drug-test results, strictly confidential.

- Respond to reference requests only by providing objective facts, such as dates of employment and position held.

- Obtain a signed release from employees before releasing any employment data.

- Provide adverse information only if it is factually based and verified as true.

- Balance discussion of weaknesses with discussion of strengths.

- Distinguish opinion from assertions of fact and denominate it as such.

Truth is a complete defense to a defamation suit since it defeats an essential element of the suit — the claim that a false statement was made. True statements, even if damaging to an employee's reputation, may not give rise to a legal claim.

Consent is another defense against defamation claims. An employee's agreement to the publication or communication of the alleged defamation serves as a complete defense recognized by the courts.

The ***statute of limitations*** can provide another complete defense to a defamation claim. If the employee does not bring a claim within the statutorily defined period (which often is short, such as one year), the claim is lost and cannot be initiated.

Invasion of Privacy

Employees also have raised invasion-of-privacy claims in employment litigation. Invasion-of-privacy claims often accompany defamation suits.

These claims may be based on one of the following theories:

- ♦ Unreasonable intrusion into an individual's personal affairs.

- ♦ Publication of an individual's private affairs, including embarrassing and private facts, which the public has no right to know.

- ♦ Publishing facts that are literally true but give a false and negative impression of an individual.

Invasion-of-privacy claims are most likely to come out of such employment-related situations as the following:

- ♦ Checking references.

- ♦ Testing for drug use.

- ♦ Disclosing employee records.

- ♦ Disclosing reports on discipline or misconduct.

- ♦ Searching employees' persons or belongings.

- ♦ Transmitting data electronically.

Since the viability and elements of invasion-of-privacy claims vary significantly from state to state, employers should consult with employment law counsel when faced with such a claim or potential claim.

Avoiding Liability for Invasion of Privacy Claims

Employers can avoid liability for invasion-of-privacy claims by simply removing the expectations of privacy if doing so is permitted under the law. Employers can establish, distribute, and post policies stating that personal items, lockers, purses, and automobiles are subject to search and that drug testing may be required under certain circumstances during employment.

Employers may consider the following after consulting with an employment law counsel:

- ♦ Inform employees with email access that email is not private and may be read by anyone having access to the system, including the employer.

- ♦ Obtain consent to provide employment references, search employee person and property, or perform drug testing.

- ◆ Protect the confidentiality of employee performance evaluations, medical records, and disciplinary records.

- ◆ Limit undercover investigations to workplace surveillance.

General Techniques for Avoiding Liability for Wrongful Termination

Employers can limit liability arising from certain wrongful termination claims by explicitly stating in employee handbooks, policy manuals, offer letters, and application forms the following:

- ◆ The employment offered, if accepted, is employment-at-will.

- ◆ No contract or other enforceable obligation is intended.

- ◆ Only a few specified managers or administrators can alter the at-will employment relationship.

Employers can minimize termination claims by reviewing all aspects of the employment relationship and using appropriate techniques throughout the relationship, such as the following:

- ◆ **Perfect Hiring Techniques,** including the following:

  - • Review all writings, offer letters, contracts, and employment applications to ensure they specify employment-at-will.

  - • Provide training to interviewers and recruiters so they make no statements that will cause problems for the employer.

  - • Adopt a checklist of what interviewers should cover and what they should avoid.

- ◆ **Review the Personnel Policy Manual or Employee Handbook,** as follows:

  - • Should it deal with termination at all?

  - • To whom should it be addressed?

  - • Should there be more than one version?

  - • Should there be a disclaimer?

  - • Has the employer reserved the right to terminate at will?

  - • Has the employer reserved the right to change the manual at any time?

  - • Should there be training periods rather than probationary periods?

  - • Is the manual current with changes in law or circumstances?

- ◆ **Review Personnel Policies and Procedures,** as follows:

  - • Remove references to job security, just cause, or good cause or other promises to employees.

  - • Maintain documentation.

  - • Base documentation on fact, not opinion.

  - • Review documentation with employees.

  - • Give employees a chance to respond in writing.

  - • Be consistent in application.

  - • Delete policies not being followed or enforced.

- Develop a procedure for deleting outdated materials in personnel files that is consistent with record retention laws and litigation requirements.

- Put performance appraisals, criticisms, and warnings about the employee in writing.

- Ensure that performance appraisals reflect warnings given to an employee to avoid inconsistency.

If an employer considers evaluations during termination decisions, the employer must verify the quality of the evaluation. Evaluations must be done right or not at all. If employee evaluations were considered, the employer should make sure they were based on actual performance as indicated by the job title, job description, and the actual duties the employee performed. Additionally, the employer should ensure that the evaluations were done when required by company policy, provided information about significant performance or behavioral problems, and provided a plan or mechanism for correction.

♦ **Follow Progressive Discipline,** as follows:

- Make the discipline appropriate.

- Treat employees fairly and provide them with due process.

- Let employees know what is expected of them.

- Give employees warnings of the consequences of their actions.

- Give employees time to correct or lessen their deficiencies.

- Be uniform and consistent in applying discipline.

♦ **Adopt Specific Discharge Procedures,** such as the following:

- The discharge procedure should include progressive discipline, with room left for exceptions.

- The procedure may include a list of capital offenses. Any list should contain language such as "or similar offenses" to indicate that the list is not exhaustive.

- A grievance procedure may be included in the discharge procedure (an employment law counsel should be consulted on establishing any alternative dispute resolution procedure).

- Care should be taken not to create inconsistencies with the general employment-at-will rule.

♦ **Communicate the Final Decision Correctly.** Communicating the termination decision is an important part of the process. The employee should understand the organization's reasons for the decision to discharge. Some techniques for effectively communicating the termination are the following:

- Try to lessen the severity by making the news not unexpected. In many situations, for example, the employee will be on probation or possibly expecting termination.

- Make the termination notice brief and candid. Do not apologize.

- Treat the employee with dignity and respect.

- If the employee is to leave the premises immediately, carry out the discharge at the end of the day, after co-workers have left.

♦ **Give the Employee Appropriate Termination Benefits.** A terminated employee is entitled to the following:

- The payment of all wages actually earned. Such payment is to be made on or before the next regularly occurring payday. State laws often regulate such payment and may impose penalties for nonpayment or late payment of final pay.

- Vacation pay if such vacation is earned and vested in accordance with the employer's policies about unused vacations. State laws vary regarding the handling of vacation time.

- Severance pay as provided in the employer's policies, by practice, by contract, or by plan.

- Group health insurance at the employee's expense, according to the requirements of COBRA.

- Sixty days' advance notice of termination, if such termination results from plant closings or mass layoffs according to the requirements of the WARN Act. Employees are entitled to full pay and benefits during these 60 days.

- Such additional benefits as may specifically be required by an employee's employment contract, company policy, or a collective-bargaining agreement.

♦ **Consider Separation Agreements.** Especially in cases where employers have reason to believe discharged employees may file lawsuits, employers and employees may enter into separation agreements that may include additional severance benefits for the employee in exchange for the employee's general waiver of all claims and prospective claims against the employer. A noncoerced, written waiver or release of claims (also known as "a covenant not to sue") may effectively prevent an employee from later filing a suit against an employer for wrongful termination or discrimination.

If the waiver includes a waiver of age discrimination claims under the Age Discrimination in Employment Act (ADEA), the statute requires, among other things, that the following criteria are met:

- The release must be written in ordinary language the employee can understand.

- The release must specifically refer to employee rights and claims under the ADEA.

- There can be no waiver of claims arising after the date the release is executed.

- There must be additional consideration of value given for the release, such as paid benefits or cash. Such consideration must be in addition to that the employee would have received had there been no separation agreement.

- The employer must advise the employee to consult an attorney.

- The employer must give the employee at least 21 days to consider the release. An employee must be given 45 days if the waiver is part of group termination procedure.

- The employee must have at least seven days to revoke the release after signing it.

- Additional statistical information must be given to employees terminated as part of a group termination program.

According to recent rulings by the U.S. Supreme Court, if a separation agreement does not meet these requirements the release is ineffective and the employee may still sue the employer under the ADEA, while still keeping the benefits paid by the employer. Employers must be certain the release identifies specifically what claims the employee is agreeing not to pursue and must specify the employer's rights if the employee fails to follow the agreement.

Employers should always consult with an employment law attorney prior to entering into a severance agreement and/or general release of claims with a former employee.

♦ **Consider Arbitration Agreements.** Employers may substantially reduce the costs and risks of employment litigation by directing formal disputes to final and binding arbitration.

Termination Checklist

A central authority should review individual terminations to confirm that all procedures have been followed and that the discharge is consistent with prior treatment of other employees. Before any final decision is made to discharge an employee, the personnel department or human resources department should become involved.

The human resources manager should review the termination decision. It is not sufficient for a department head to review a supervisor's decision. The human resources department should check for oversights, ensuring uniform and consistent treatment of all employees.

An employer should develop a checklist of things to be reviewed for each proposed termination, using questions such as the following:

♦ **Termination for Poor Performance,** such as the following:

- Is the termination consistent with the employee's performance appraisals?

- Were performance standards and expectations communicated to the employee? Was the employee told how to improve and when needed to meet expectations?

- Is the deficiency capable of objective assessment (for example, "bad attitude" vs. "employee refused to assist customer")?

- Is the action consistent with prior incidents of a similar nature?

- Was the employee given a notice of poor performance? If there has been a sudden drop in the employee's performance, can it be justified?

- Was the employee given an opportunity to improve?

- Is the articulated reason for discharge the real reason?

- Was the employee ever told that the failure to improve could result in termination?

♦ **Termination for Misconduct,** including the following:

- Was the rule the employee violated published? Can the employer document where and when it was published?

- Did the employee receive a written copy of the work rules? The employer should distribute employee handbooks upon hiring and have all employees sign an acknowledgement of receipt specifying they have read and understood the content of the document.

- Was the event triggering disciplinary action thoroughly investigated?

- Did the employee have an opportunity to explain the actions?

- Are the witnesses credible?

- Did the employee receive warnings and an opportunity to correct the behavior?

- Was the employee notified of the possible results of such conduct?

- Was progressive discipline tried?

- Have rules been applied consistently? Have other employees been terminated for the same or similar conduct?

- Are there previous documented violations of the same rule or standard of conduct?

- Does the degree of discipline imposed on the employee reflect the seriousness of the offense?

- Is there proper documentation of the misconduct, including names of witnesses?

- Has the employer considered the extent, if any, that the organization contributed to the problem?

- Was the information regarding the infraction obtained lawfully (for example, drug or alcohol test, private investigator, or body search)?

- **Procedural,** including the following:

  - Has the supervisor complied with all provisions of personnel policies or the employee handbook?

  - Would this termination be consistent with the organization's actions in the past?

  - If they exist, were contractual procedures followed?

  - Have alternatives to termination — for example, last-chance agreements, demotion, option to resign, settlement agreements — been considered?

  - Has the employer considered the employee's length of employment?

  - Has human resources checked to see that all relevant requirements have been met?

  - Will the interview be conducted in private with a witness?

  - Has the employer made every effort to make the termination as humane as possible?

  - Has a checklist been prepared of what the employee needs to return to the employer?

  - Have appropriate steps been taken to ensure confidentiality?

  - Has the final paycheck and other pay, such as accrued vacation, been taken care of?

  - Have COBRA benefits, notifications, and paperwork been prepared?

- **Legal,** including the following:

  - Taken as a whole, does this case appear to be an example of fairness, honesty, and good faith?

  - Are there potential legal problems? Do the circumstances suggest discrimination, unjust discharge, or violation of any other laws?

  - Is there evidence this employee has been singled out and treated differently?

  - If the employee is a member of any protected group, has that employee been treated the same as members of other groups?

Terminating employees who may claim discrimination — for example, pregnant employees, older employees, minority employees, or employees with a disability — is especially sensitive. With these types of employees, the potential problem of a subsequent claim or lawsuit is obvious. An employer should take special care with these employees during termination procedures not to make any reference to anything that could be considered discriminatory. The termination interview should never contain any references to sex, age, race, religion, national origin, or disability.

- Has the employee filed any kind of claim against the organization — workers' compensation, benefits pay claim, etc. — or filed a discrimination charge? Could the termination be seen as reprisal and therefore be open to a retaliatory discharge claim?

- Has the employee complained about company policies or activities the employee considered illegal or immoral? Could the termination be seen as reprisal for whistleblowing?

- Has the employer consulted with an employment law counsel?

Additional Information

Unemployment Compensation

Employers should handle unemployment compensation claims carefully and meticulously. Often an employee will state a different reason for termination than that given by the employer.

An unemployment compensation hearing provides a useful opportunity to learn the former employee's position. An unemployment compensation decision favoring the employer may help persuade the employee not to pursue matters further.

It may also help convince the Equal Employment Opportunity Commission (EEOC) or a court that any claim an employee may make is not valid.

Replacing Terminated Employees

Employers should replace terminated employees carefully. Obviously, an employer should seek the most qualified employees.

Contact Information

Department of Labor

Frances Perkins Building
200 Constitution Avenue, NW
Washington, DC 20210

Telephone: 866-4-USWAGE or 866-4-USA-DOL
Internet: *www.dol.gov* and *www.dol.gov/compliance/topics/termination-issues.htm*

Illinois Law

Employment-at-Will

In Illinois, in the absence of an express agreement of duration of employment, the employment relationship is presumed to be one of employment-at-will. Under the employment-at-will doctrine, the employment relationship is terminable by either party for any reason or for no reason at all (as long as the termination does not violate state or federal discrimination laws).

In addition, Illinois courts **recognize** the following exceptions to the employment-at-will doctrine:

♦ **Public-Policy Exception.** Under the public-policy exception, an employer may be liable for wrongful discharge if an employee is terminated in light of an explicit, well-established public policy prohibiting such conduct. Protected public policy is usually found in the areas of crime prevention and public safety. In some circumstances policies associated with social and economic regulation have been recognized. The greatest protection is found in the area of whistle blowing. A public policy is most clearly mandated if the activity is protected by statute or arises from a statute. For example, it would be unlawful for an employer to terminate an employee for filing a workers' compensation claim or reporting a violation of federal or state health and safety law.

♦ **Implied-Contract Exception.** Under the implied-contract exception, oral or written representations made to an employee may be viewed by the courts as an implied contract, making the employer liable under a breach of contract theory for any representations that were not honored. For example, statements in an employee handbook may modify the employment status of an employee under the theory that the handbooks is, in essence, a "contract" between the employer and employee. *Duldulao v. St. Mary of Nazareth*, 115 Ill.2d 482,505 N.E. 2d 314, 106 Ill. Dec. 8 (Ill. 1987).

Job Reference Liability

Under Illinois' Employment Record Disclosure Act, located at 745 Ill. Comp. Stat. §§ 46/1 – 46/99, any employer or authorized employee or agent acting on behalf of an employer who, upon inquiry by a prospective employer, provides truthful written or verbal information or information believed in good faith to be truthful about a current or former employee's job performance is presumed to be acting in good faith and is immune from civil liability for the disclosure and the consequences of the disclosure.

The presumption of good faith may be rebutted by a preponderance of evidence that the information disclosed was known to be false or in violation of a civil right of the employee or former employee.

Frequently Asked Questions

Q Can an employer terminate an employee without advance notice or without giving a reason for the termination?

A Yes. Illinois is an *employment-at-will state*, which means that an employer or employee may terminate the relationship at any time, without any reason or cause. However, an employer may not discriminate based on race, color, religion, sex, national origin, ancestry, citizenship status, age, marital status, physical or mental disability, military service, or unfavorable military discharge.

Q **Is an employee required to give two weeks' notice before quitting?**

A No. Because Illinois is an employment-at-will state, an employee may terminate the working relationship without notice or reason. Additionally, notice is not required by either party based on the employment-at-will doctrine.

Q **How soon after an employee is terminated must the employee be paid?**

A All final compensation, including bonus payments, vacation pay, wages, and commissions, must be paid by the next regularly scheduled payday.

Q **Can an employer hold part of an employee's paycheck until the employee returns a uniform or other employer-owned property?**

A No. An employer cannot withhold or deduct any part of an employee's salary pending the return of uniforms, tolls, pagers, or any other employer-owned property.

Q **Can an employee obtain the employee's personnel records from the employer?**

A An employee may choose to review the employee's personnel records up to one year after leaving employment. Although certain documents are exempt, an employee must be provided an opportunity to inspect the employee's personnel records. Additionally, a current employee may request their personnel records from an employer two times per year. If the employer refuses a former or current employee's request to review personnel documents, the employee may file a complaint with Illinois Department of Labor. Under the Personnel Records Review Act, an employee may obtain a copy of the information or part of the information contained in the employee's records. However, an employer is allowed to charge the employee a fee equal to the actual cost of duplicating the material.

Contact Information

Illinois Department of Labor

1 West Old State Capitol Plaza, Room 300
Springfield, IL 62701

Telephone: 217-782-6206
Fax: 217-782-0596
Internet: *www.state.il.us/agency/idol*

Chapter 22

Plant Closings and Workforce Reduction

Introduction

The federal Worker Adjustment and Retraining Notification Act (WARN Act) provides protection to employees, their families, and communities by requiring employers to provide notification in advance of plant closings and mass layoffs. Advance notice to employees and their families provides some transition time to adjust to the prospective loss of employment, to seek and obtain alternative jobs, and to enter skill-training classes that will allow employees to successfully compete in the job market.

The WARN Act regulations establish basic definitions and rules for giving notice and implementing the provisions of the act. However, notice is still encouraged where not required.

An employer who is not required to comply with the WARN Act notice requirements should, to the extent possible, provide notice to its employees about a proposal to close a plant or permanently reduce its workforce. Although the WARN Act requirements only offer a minimum notice requirement, employers are encouraged to voluntarily provide longer periods of advance notice.

This chapter reviews federal law relating to workforce reduction, defines relevant terms, and summarizes the provisions and requirements of the WARN Act. The WARN Act is located at 29 U.S.C.A. § 2101 – 2109 and the regulations are located at 20 C.F.R. 639.1 – 639.10.

The WARN Act

The WARN Act requires employers to provide notification in advance of plant closing and mass layoffs. A *plant closing* is the permanent or temporary shutdown of a single site of employment or one or more facilities or operating units within a single site of employment if the shutdown results in an employment loss during any 30-day period at the single site of employment for 50 or more employees, excluding any part-time employees.

An *employment loss* is all of the following:

- ♦ An employment termination, other than a discharge for cause, voluntary departure, or retirement.
- ♦ A layoff exceeding six months.
- ♦ A reduction in hours of work of individual employees of more than 50 percent during each month of any six-month period.

Where a termination or a layoff is involved, an employment loss does not occur when an employee is reassigned or transferred to employer-sponsored programs, such as retraining or job search activities, as long as the reassignment does not constitute a constructive discharge or other involuntary termination.

An employee is **not** considered to have experienced an employment loss if the closing or layoff is the result of the relocation or consolidation of part or all of the employer's business and, prior to the closing or layoff, the employer offers either of the following transfers:

♦ To transfer the employee to a different site of employment within a reasonable commuting distance with no more than a six-month break in employment.

♦ To transfer the employee to any other site of employment regardless of distance with no more than a six-month break in employment, and the employee accepts within 30 days of the offer or of the closing or layoff — whichever is later.

A *relocation or consolidation* of part or all of an employer's business is that some definable business — whether customer orders, product lines, or operations — is transferred to a different site of employment and that transfer results in a plant closing or mass layoff.

A *shutdown* is an employment action that results in the effective cessation of production or the work performed by a unit, even if a few employees remain. A *temporary shutdown* triggers the notice requirement only if there are a sufficient number of terminations, layoffs exceeding six months, or reductions in hours of work.

A *mass layoff* is a reduction in force that is not the result of a plant closing and results in an employment loss at the single site of employment during any 30-day period for all of the following:

♦ At least 33 percent of the active employees, excluding part-time employees.

♦ At least 50 employees, excluding part-time employees.

Where 500 or more employees (excluding part-time employees) are affected, the 33 percent requirement does not apply, and notice is required if the other criteria are met. Plant closings involve employment loss that results from the shutdown of one or more distinct units within a single site or the entire site. A mass layoff involves employment loss, regardless of whether one or more units are shut down at the site. Additionally, employees, other than part-time employees, who are exempt from WARN notice requirements are nonetheless counted as employees for purposes of determining coverage as an employer. For example, if an employer closes a temporary project on which 10 permanent and 40 temporary employees are employed, a covered plant closing has occurred although only 10 employees are entitled to notice.

A *single site of employment* refers to either a single location or a group of contiguous locations. A single site of employment may also apply to truly unusual organizational situations where the aforementioned criteria do not reasonably apply. The application of this definition with the intent to evade the purpose of the act to provide notice is not acceptable.

Foreign sites of employment are not covered under the WARN Act. However, U.S. workers at foreign sites of employment are counted to determine whether an employer is covered as an employer by the act.

Covered Employers

The WARN Act covers employers that either:

♦ Employ 100 or more employees, excluding part-time employees.

♦ Employ 100 or more employees who work at least a combined 4,000 hours per week, including part-time employees but excluding overtime hours.

Employers also include all of the following:

♦ Nonprofit organizations of the requisite size.

- Public and quasi-public entities that engage in business, are separately organized from the regular government, have their own governing bodies, and have independent authority to manage their own personnel and assets.

- Employers with one or more sites of employment under common ownership or control. For example, a major automaker has dozens of automobile plants throughout the country; each plan is a site of employment but the automaker is the only employer.

Regular federal, state, local, and federally recognized Indian tribal governments are not covered by the act.

Covered Employees

The WARN Act covers all affected employees and supervisors.

Affected employees are those who may reasonably be expected to experience an employment loss as a consequence of a proposed plant closing or mass layoff by their employer. This includes individually identifiable employees who will likely lose their jobs because of bumping rights or other factors, to the extent that such individual employees reasonably can be identified at the time notice is required to be given. Affected employees include managerial and supervisory employees, but not business partners.

Bumping rights exist in a seniority system, where the rights of workers with greater seniority whose jobs are abolished then replace (bump) workers with less seniority so that the worker who ultimately loses their job is not the worker whose job was abolished.

Consultant or contract employees who have a separate employment relationship with another employer and are paid by that other employer or who are self-employed are not affected employees of the business to which they are assigned. In addition, for purposes of determining whether coverage thresholds are met, either incumbent workers in jobs being eliminated or, if known 60 days in advance, the actual employees who suffer an employment loss may be counted.

Employees on temporary layoff or on a leave of absence who have a reasonable expectation of recall are also counted as employees for purposes of the WARN Act. An employee has a *reasonable expectation of recall* upon the understanding that, through notification or through industry practice, their employment has been temporarily interrupted and that they will be recalled to the same or to a similar job.

Part-time employees are employees who are employed for an average of fewer than 20 hours per week or who were employed for fewer than 6 of the 12 months preceding the date on which notice is required, including employees who work full time. The period used for calculating whether an employee has worked an average of fewer than 20 hours per week is the shorter of the actual time the employee has been employed or the most recent 90 days. Additionally, part-time employees include seasonal employees.

Notice Required

Notice must be given at least 60 calendar days prior to any planned plant closing or mass layoff. When all employees are not terminated on the same date, the date of the first individual termination within the statutory 30-day or 90-day period triggers the 60-day notice requirement. An employee's last day of employment is considered the date of that employee's layoff. The first and each subsequent group of terminees are entitled to a full 60 days' notice.

Aggregation

In order for an employer to decide whether issuing notice is required, the employer should examine both of the following time periods:

- Look ahead 30 days and behind 30 days to determine whether employment actions both taken and planned will, in the aggregate for any 30-day period, reach the minimum numbers for a plant closing or a mass layoff and thus trigger the notice requirement.

- Look ahead 90 days and behind 90 days to determine whether employment actions both taken and planned, each of which separately is not of sufficient size to trigger WARN coverage, will, in the aggregate for any 90-day period, reach the minimum numbers for a plant closing or a mass layoff and thus trigger the notice requirement. However, an employer is not required to give notice if the employer demonstrates that the separate employment losses are the result of separate and distinct actions and causes, and are not an attempt to evade the requirements of the WARN Act.

Service of Notice

Employers must not order a plant closing or mass layoff until the end of a 60-day period after the employer serves written notice of such an order to the following:

- Each representative of the affected employees as of the time of the notice or, if there is no such representative at that time, to each affected employee.

- The state or entity designated by the state to carry out rapid response activities and the chief elected official of the unit of local government within which such closing or layoff is to occur. *Rapid response activities* encompass the activities necessary to plan and deliver services to enable dislocated workers to transition to new employment as quickly as possible, following either a permanent closure or mass layoff, or a natural or other disaster resulting in a mass job dislocation.

If there is more than one such unit, the unit of local government that the employer must notify is the unit of local government to which the employer pays the highest taxes for the year preceding the year for which the determination is made.

Notice may be served by any reasonable method of delivery to the required parties. Such service must be designed to ensure receipt of notice of at least 60 days before separation is acceptable (for example, first-class mail or personal delivery with optional signed receipt). In the case of notification directly to affected employees, insertion of notice into pay envelopes is another viable option. However, a ticketed notice does not meet the requirements of the WARN Act. A *ticketed notice* is a preprinted notice regularly included in each employee's paycheck or pay envelope.

Reduction of Notification Period

An employer may order a plant closing or mass layoff before the conclusion of the 60-day period if either of the following applies:

- The closing or mass layoff is caused by business circumstances that were not reasonably foreseeable as of the time that notice would have been required.

- As of the time that notice would have been required the employer was actively seeking capital or business, which, if obtained, would have enabled the employer to avoid or postpone the shutdown and the employer reasonably and in good faith believed that giving the notice required would have precluded the employer from obtaining the needed capital or business.

Extension of Layoff Period

A layoff of more than six months, which, at its outset, was announced to be a layoff of six months or less, must be treated as an employment loss unless either of the following applies:

- The extension beyond six months is caused by business circumstances (including unforeseeable changes in price or cost) not reasonably foreseeable at the time of the initial layoff.

- Notice is given at the time it becomes reasonably foreseeable that the extension beyond six months will be required.

Additional Notice Due to Postponement

Additional notice is required when the date or schedule of dates of a planned plant closing or mass layoff is extended beyond the date or the ending date of any 14-day period announced in the original notice as follows:

- If the postponement is for less than 60 days, the additional notice should be given as soon as possible to the affected employees and should include reference to the earlier notice, the date (or 14-day period) to which the planned action is postponed, and the reasons for the postponement. The notice should be given in a manner that will provide the information to all affected employees.

- If the postponement is for 60 days or more, the additional notice should be treated as new notice subject to the applicable WARN Act provisions.

Rolling notice, in the sense of routine periodic notice, given whether or not a plant closing or mass layoff is impending, and with the intent to evade the purpose of the act rather than give specific notice as required by the WARN Act, is **not** acceptable.

Contents of a WARN Act Notice

All notice must be specific. The information provided in a WARN Act notice must be based on the best information available to the employer at the time the notice is served. When referenced, the term *date* refers to a specific date or to a 14-day period during which a separation(s) is expected to occur. If separations are planned according to a schedule, the schedule should indicate the specific dates on which, or the beginning date of each 14-day period during which, any separation(s) is expected to occur. Where a 14-day period is used, notice must be given at least 60 days in advance of the first day of the period.

The required elements of notice differ according to whether the notice is for the affected employees, employee representatives, or representatives of state and local governments. However, all notices may include additional information useful to the employees such as information on available dislocated worker assistance and, if the planned action is expected to be temporary, the estimated duration if known.

Notice for Affected Employees

The notice to each affected employee who does not have a representative must be written in language that is understandable to the employee and must contain the following:

- A statement as to whether the planned action is permanent or temporary and whether the entire plant will be closed.

- The expected date when the plant closing or mass layoff will commence and the expected date when the individual employee will be separated.

- An indication of whether or not bumping rights exist.

- The name and phone number of the company official to contact for further information.

Notice for Employee Representatives

The notice to each representative of affected employees must contain the following:

- The name and address of the employment site where the plant closing or mass layoff will occur, and the name and telephone number of a company official to contact for further information.

- A statement as to whether the planned action is permanent or temporary.
- A statement as to whether the entire plant will be closed.
- The expected date of the first separation and the anticipated schedule for separations.
- The job titles of positions to be affected and the names of employees currently holding affected jobs.

The notice may include additional information useful to the employees, such as information on available dislocated worker assistance and, if the action is expected to be temporary, the estimated duration if known.

Notice for State and Local Governments

The notices separately provided to the state dislocated worker unit and to the chief elected official of the unit of local government must contain all of the following:

- The name and address of the employment site where the plant closing or mass layoff will occur, and the name and telephone number of the company official to contact for information.
- A statement whether the action is temporary or permanent, and whether the entire plant will close.
- The expected date of first separation, and the anticipated schedule for making separations.
- The job titles of positions to be affected, and the number of affected employees in each job classification.
- An indication as to whether bumping rights exist.
- The name of each union representing affected employees, and the name and address of the chief elected office of each union.

Alternatively, this notice may be abbreviated as long as more specific information is maintained on site and made available to governmental representatives upon request. If this information is not available when requested, it will be deemed a failure to give required notice.

Additional Provisions

Where voluntary notice has been given more than 60 days in advance, but does not contain all of the required elements, the employer must ensure that all of the information required is provided in writing to the applicable parties at least 60 days in advance of a covered employment action.

Notice may be given conditional upon the occurrence or nonoccurrence of an event, such as the renewal of a major contract, only when the event is definite and the consequences of the event's occurrence or nonoccurrence will necessarily, in the normal course of business, lead to a covered plant closing or mass layoff less than 60 days after the event. For example, if the nonrenewal of a major contract will lead to the closing of the plant that produces the articles supplied under the contract 30 days after the contract expires, the employer may give notice at least 60 days in advance of the projected closing date, which states that if the contract is not renewed, the plant closing will occur on the projected date. The notice must contain each of the required elements.

Exceptions

The WARN Act **does not apply** to a plant closing or mass layoff if either of the following applies:

- The closing is of a temporary facility or the closing or layoff is the result of the completion of a particular project or undertaking, and the affected employees were hired with the understanding that their employment was limited to the duration of the facility or the project or undertaking.
- The closing or layoff constitutes a strike or constitutes a lockout not intended to evade the WARN Act requirements.

A *lockout* is when, for tactical or defensive reasons during the course of collective bargaining or during a labor dispute, an employer lawfully refuses to utilize some or all of its employees for the performance of available work. A lockout not related to collective bargaining that is intended as a subterfuge to evade the act does not qualify for an exemption. A plant closing or mass layoff at a site of employment where a strike or lockout is taking place, which occurs for reasons unrelated to a strike or lockout, is not covered by the notification exceptions.

Employers are not required to give notice when permanently replacing a person who is an economic striker under the National Labor Relations Act (NLRA). However, nonstriking employees at the same single site of employment who experience a covered employment loss as a result of a strike are entitled to notice. Situations in which a strike or lockout affects nonstriking employees at the same plant may constitute an unforeseeable business circumstance and reduced notice may apply. Similarly, the faltering company exception may apply in strike situations.

Where a union that is on strike represents more than one bargaining unit at the single site, nonstrikers includes the nonstriking bargaining unit(s). Notice also is due to those employees who are not a part of the bargaining unit(s) that is involved in the labor negotiations that led to the lockout. Employees at other plants which have not been struck, but at which covered plant closings or mass layoffs occur as a direct or indirect result of a strike or lockout, are not covered by the strike/lockout exemption. The unforeseeable business circumstances exception to 60 days' notice also may apply to these closings or layoffs at other plants.

Faltering Company

The faltering company exception applies to plant closings but not to mass layoffs, and should be narrowly construed. To qualify for reduced notice of less than 60 days under the faltering company exception all of the following must apply:

♦ An employer must have been actively seeking capital or business at the time that 60-day notice would have been required.

The employer must have been seeking financing or refinancing through the arrangement of loans, the issuance of stocks, bonds, or other methods of internally generated financing; or the employer must have been seeking additional money, credit, or business through any other commercially reasonable method. The employer must be able to identify specific actions taken to obtain capital or business.

♦ There must have been a realistic opportunity to obtain the financing or business sought.

♦ The financing or business sought must have been sufficient, if obtained, to have enabled the employer to avoid or postpone the shutdown. The employer must be able to objectively demonstrate that the amount of capital or the volume of new business sought would have enabled the employer to keep the facility, operating unit, or site open for a reasonable period of time.

♦ The employer reasonably and in good faith believed that giving the required notice would have precluded the employer from obtaining the needed capital or business.

The employer must be able to objectively demonstrate that it reasonably thought that a potential customer or source of financing would have been unwilling to provide the new business or capital if notice were given; that is, if the employees, customers, or the public were aware that the facility, operating unit, or site might have to close.

This condition may be satisfied if the employer can show that the financing or business source would not choose to do business with a troubled company or with a company whose workforce would be looking for other jobs.

The actions of an employer relying on the faltering company exception will be viewed in a company-wide context. Thus, a company with access to capital markets or with cash reserves may not avail itself of this exception by looking solely at the financial condition of the facility, operating unit, or site to be closed.

Unforeseeable Business Circumstances

The unforeseeable business circumstances exception to WARN Act notification requirements applies to plant closings and mass layoffs caused by business circumstances that were not reasonably foreseeable at the time that 60-day notice would have been required.

An important indicator of a business circumstance that is not reasonably foreseeable is that the circumstance is caused by some sudden, dramatic, and unexpected action or condition outside the employer's control. Each of the following might be considered a business circumstance that is not reasonably foreseeable:

- A principal client's sudden and unexpected termination of a major contract with the employer.
- A strike at a major supplier of the employer.
- An unanticipated and dramatic major economic downturn.
- A government ordered closing of an employment site that occurs without prior notice.

The test for determining when business circumstances are not reasonably foreseeable focuses on an employer's business judgment. The employer must exercise such commercially reasonable business judgment as would a similarly situated employer in predicting the demands of its particular market. However, the employer is not required to accurately predict general economic conditions that may also affect demand for its products or services.

Natural Disaster

No WARN Act notice is required if the plant closing or mass layoff is due to any form of natural disaster. To qualify for the natural disaster exception, an employer must be able to demonstrate that a plant closing or mass layoff is a direct result of a natural disaster. A *natural disaster* is any of, but not limited to, the following:

- Floods.
- Earthquakes.
- Droughts.
- Storms.
- Tidal waves.
- Tsunamis.
- Similar disastrous effects of nature.

While a disaster may preclude full or any advance notice, such notice as is practicable, containing as much of the required information as is available in the circumstances of the disaster still must be given — whether in advance or after the fact of an employment loss caused by a natural disaster.

Where a plant closing or mass layoff occurs as an indirect result of a natural disaster, the natural disaster exception does not apply; however, the unforeseeable business circumstance exception, as previously discussed, may be applicable.

Enforcement and Penalties

The U.S. District Courts enforce the WARN Act. Any employer who orders a plant closing or mass layoff in violation of the WARN Act notice requirements is liable to each aggrieved employee who suffers an employment loss as a result of the closing or layoff for all of the following:

- Backpay for each day of violation at a rate of compensation not less than the higher of the average regular rate received by an employee during the last three years of employment or the final regular rate received by the employee.

- Benefits under an employee benefit plan, including the cost of medical expenses incurred during the employment loss that would have been covered under an employee benefit plan if the employment loss had not occurred.

An *aggrieved employee* is an employee who has worked for the employer ordering the plant closing or mass layoff and who, as a result of the failure by the employer to comply with the WARN Act notice requirements, did not receive timely notice either directly or through their representative.

Liability is calculated for the period of the violation, up to a maximum of 60 days, but in no event for more than one-half the number of days the employee was employed by the employer.

The amount for which an employer is liable is reduced by any of the following:

- Wages paid to the employee for the period of the violation.

- Voluntary and unconditional payment by the employer to the employee that is not required by any legal obligation.

- Payment by the employer to a third party or trustee (such as premiums for health benefits or payments to a defined contribution pension plan) on behalf of and attributable to the employee for the period of the violation.

In addition, any liability incurred with respect to a defined benefit pension plan may be reduced by crediting the employee with service for all purposes under such a plan for the period of the violation.

Any employer who violates the WARN Act notice requirements with respect to a unit of local government is subject to a civil penalty of up to $500 for each day of a violation. However, the penalty **does not apply** if the employer pays to each aggrieved employee the amount for which the employer is liable to that employee within three weeks from the date the employer orders the shutdown or layoff.

If an employer who has violated the WARN Act proves, to the satisfaction of the court, that the violating act or omission was done in good faith and that the employer had reasonable grounds for believing that the act or omission was not a violation of the WARN Act, the court may, in its discretion, reduce the amount of the liability or penalty.

In any such suit, the court, in its discretion, may allow the prevailing party a reasonable attorney's fee as part of the costs. The remedies provided by the WARN Act are the exclusive remedies for any violation of the act. Additionally, a federal court does not have authority to enjoin a plant closing or mass layoff.

Note: It is not a violation of the WARN notice requirements where errors in the notice's information are caused by either a subsequent change in events or the errors are minor and inadvertent.

Contact Information

Department of Labor, Employment and Training Administration
Office of National Response, Division of Worker Dislocation and Special Response

200 Constitution Avenue, NW
Room N-5422
Washington, DC 20210

Telephone: 202-693-3519
Toll-Free: 877-US2-JOBS (877-872-5627)
Internet: *www.doleta.gov/layoff/warn.cfm*

Illinois Law

The Illinois Worker Adjustment and Retraining Notification Act

The Illinois Worker Adjustment and Retraining Notification Act (WARN Act), located at 820 Ill. Comp. Stat. §§ 65/1 – 65/99, applies to plant closings or relocations occurring in Illinois since January 1, 2005.

Whenever possible, the act will be interpreted in a manner consistent with the federal Worker Adjustment and Retraining Notification Act (WARN Act) (*see* 29 U.S.C. §§ 2101 et seq.) and the federal regulations and court decisions interpreting that act to the extent that the provisions of federal and state law are the same.

Definitions

The following definitions apply within the Illinois WARN Act:

♦ *Affected employees* are employees who may reasonably be expected to experience an employment loss as a consequence of a proposed plant closing or mass layoff by their employer.

♦ *Employment loss* is any of the following:

- An employment termination, other than a discharge for cause, voluntary departure, or retirement.

- A layoff exceeding six months.

- A reduction in hours of work of more than 50 percent during each month of any six-month period.

Employment loss does not include instances when the plant closing or layoff is the result of the relocation or consolidation of part or all of the employer's business and, before the closing or layoff, the employer offers to transfer the employee to a different site of employment within a reasonable commuting distance with no more than a six-month break in employment, or the employer offers to transfer the employee to any other site of employment, regardless of distance, with no more than a six-month break in employment, and the employee accepts within 30 days of the offer or of the closing or layoff — whichever is later.

♦ *Employers* are any business enterprises that employ the following:

- 75 or more employees, excluding part-time employees.

- 75 or more employees who in the aggregate work at least 4,000 hours per week (exclusive of hours of overtime).

♦ A *mass layoff* is a reduction in force that is not the result of a plant closing and results in an employment loss at the single site of employment during any 30-day period for either of the following:

- At least 33 percent of the employees (excluding any part-time employees) and at least 25 employees (excluding any part-time employees).

- At least 250 employees (excluding any part-time employees).

◆ ***Part-time employees*** are employees who are employed for an average of fewer than 20 hours per week or who have been employed for fewer than 6 of the 12 months preceding the date on which notice is required.

◆ A ***plant closing*** is the permanent or temporary shutdown of a single site of employment or one or more facilities or operating units within a single site of employment, if the shutdown results in an employment loss at the single site of employment during any 30-day period for 50 or more employees (excluding any part-time employees).

◆ A ***representative*** is the exclusive representative of employees within the meaning of the National Labor Relations Act (NLRA) or the Railway Labor Act, as applicable.

Notice

An employer must provide notice prior to a mass layoff, relocation, or employment loss. The notice must be provided, in writing, 60 days before the order takes effect and provided to both of the following:

◆ Affected employees and representatives of affected employees.

◆ The Illinois Department of Commerce and Economic Opportunity and the chief elected official of each municipal and county government within which the employment loss, relocation, or mass layoff occurs.

Employers that are required by state law to provide notice of any mass layoff, relocation, or employment loss must also include within the notice the elements required by the federal WARN Act.

Mailing the notice to an employee's last known address or inclusion of notice in the employee's paycheck are acceptable methods for fulfillment of the employer's obligation to give notice to each affected employee under the act.

Where an employer sells part or all of the business, the seller must abide by the general notice requirements for any plant closing or mass layoff, up to and including the effective date of the sale. After the effective date of the sale, the responsibility of providing notice shifts to the purchaser. The purchaser must provide the required notice for any plant closing or mass layoff after the date of sale. Sellers must provide notice to all affected employees and their representatives. Additionally, any person who is an employee of the seller (other than a part-time employee) as of the effective date of the sale will be considered an employee of the purchaser immediately after the effective date of the sale.

Employers that are not required to comply with the notice requirements of the Illinois WARN Act should, to the extent possible, provide notice to their employees about a proposal to close a plant or permanently reduce their workforce.

Note: An employer that is receiving state or local economic development incentives for doing or continuing to do business in Illinois may be required to provide additional notice pursuant to the Business Economic Support Act.

Exceptions

Employers are not required to provide notice if a mass layoff, relocation, or employment loss is necessitated by a physical calamity or an act of terrorism or war. Additionally, an employer is **not** required to comply with the notice requirements if any of the following apply:

◆ The plant closing is of a temporary facility or the plant closing or layoff is the result of the completion of a particular project or undertaking, and the affected employees were hired with the understanding that their employment was limited to the duration of the facility or the project or undertaking.

- The closing or layoff constitutes a strike or constitutes a lockout not intended to evade the requirements of Illinois WARN Act.

- When an employer is permanently replacing a person who is an economic striker under the NLRA.

The Illinois WARN Act does not validate or invalidate any judicial or administrative ruling relating to the hiring of permanent replacements for economic strikers under the NLRA.

In the case of a plant closing, an employer is not required to comply with the notice requirements if the Illinois Department of Labor determines the following:

- At the time that notice would have been required, the employer was actively seeking capital or business and the capital or business sought, if obtained, would have enabled the employer to avoid or postpone the relocation or termination; and the employer reasonably and in good faith believed that giving the required notice would have precluded the employer from obtaining the needed capital or business.

- The need for a notice was not reasonably foreseeable at the time the notice would have been required.

To determine whether the employer was actively seeking capital or business or that the need for notice was not reasonably foreseeable the employer must provide both of the following to the Illinois Department of Labor:

- A written record consisting of documents relevant to the determination of whether the employer was actively seeking capital or business or that the need for notice was not reasonably foreseeable.

- An affidavit verifying the contents of the documents contained in the record.

Employers relying on the exceptions to notice requirements must provide as much notice as is practicable and at that time the employer must also provide a brief statement of the basis for reducing the notification period.

Notice to Employers

Before September 30 of each year, the state Department of Commerce and Economic Opportunity, with the cooperation of the Department of Employment Security, must issue a written notice to each employer that reported to the Department of Employment Security that the employer paid wages to 75 or more individuals with respect to any quarter in the immediately preceding calendar year. The notice must provide the following information:

- Indicate that the employer may be subject to the Illinois WARN Act.

- Generally advise the employer about the requirements of the WARN Act and the remedies provided for violations of the act.

Extension of Layoff Period

A layoff of more than six months that, at its outset, was announced to be a layoff of six months or less must be treated as an employment loss under the Illinois WARN Act, unless both of the following apply:

- The extension beyond six months is caused by business circumstances (including unforeseeable changes in price or cost) not reasonably foreseeable at the time of the initial layoff.

- Notice is given at the time it becomes reasonably foreseeable that the extension beyond six months will be required.

Determination With Respect to Employment Loss

Unless the employer demonstrates that the employment losses are the result of separate and distinct actions and causes, and are not an attempt by the employer to evade the requirements of the Illinois WARN Act, the following elements, taken collectively, constitute a plant closing or mass layoff:

♦ Employment losses for two or more groups at a single site of employment.

♦ Each loss is less than the minimum number of employees required by the Illinois WARN Act.

♦ Each loss, in the aggregate, exceeds the minimum number of employees required by the Illinois WARN Act.

♦ Each loss occurred within any 90-day period.

Enforcement

The Illinois Director of Labor regulates, investigates, and conducts proceedings to enforce the Illinois WARN Act. The director also has the authority to examine the books and records of an employer, but only to the extent to determine whether an Illinois WARN Act violation has occurred.

Confidentiality

All information obtained from any employer subject to the Illinois act regarding the books, records, or wages paid to workers during the administration of the act are confidential and may **not** be used as follows:

♦ Published or open to public inspection.

♦ In any court in any pending action or proceeding.

♦ As admissible in evidence in any action or proceeding, other than one arising out of the act.

No finding, determination, decision, ruling, or order (including any finding of fact, statement, or conclusion made therein) issued pursuant to the Illinois act may:

♦ Be admissible or used in evidence in any action other than one arising out of the act.

♦ Be binding or conclusive, except as provided in the act.

♦ Constitute *res judicata* (an adjudicated issue that cannot be relitigated) regardless of whether the actions were between the same or related parties or involved the same facts.

Penalties

Confidentiality Violations

Any officer or employer of Illinois, any officer or employee of any entity authorized to obtain information pursuant to the Illinois WARN Act, and any agent of Illinois or of such entity who, except with the authority of the director, discloses information is guilty of a Class B misdemeanor and is disqualified from holding any appointment or employment by the state. The director has the authority to determine any liabilities or civil penalties.

Employer Violations

An employer who fails to give notice as required before ordering a mass layoff, relocation, or employment loss is liable to each employee entitled to notice who lost employment for the following:

- Backpay at the average regular rate of compensation received by the employee during the last three years of employment, or the employee's final rate of compensation — whichever is higher.

- The value of the cost of any benefits to which the employee would have been entitled had the employee's employment not been lost, including the cost of any medical expenses incurred by the employee that would have been covered under an employee benefit plan.

However, the following may reduce the amount of an employer's liability:

- Any wages, except vacation moneys accrued before the period of the employer's violation, paid by the employer to the employee during the period of the employer's violation.

- Any voluntary and unconditional payments made by the employer to the employee that were not required to satisfy any legal obligation.

- Any payments by the employer to a third party or trustee, such as premiums for health benefits or payments to a defined contribution pension plan, on behalf of and attributable to the employee for the period of the violation.

- Any liability paid by the employer under federal law.

An employer's liability is calculated for the period of the employer's violation, up to a maximum of 60 days, or one-half the number of days that the employee was employed — whichever period is smaller.

Liability incurred by an employer with respect to a defined benefit pension plan may be reduced by crediting the employee with service for all purposes under the plan for the period of the violation. Additionally, if the employer proves to the satisfaction of the director that the act or omission that violated the Illinois WARN Act was in good faith and that the employer had reasonable grounds for believing that the act or omission was not a violation, the amount of liability may be reduced at the director's discretion.

Civil Penalties

An employer who fails to give notice as required is subject to a civil penalty of no more than $500 for each day of the employer's violation. The employer is not subject to a civil penalty if the employer pays to all applicable employees the amounts for which the employer is liable by law (for example, backpay and the value of the cost of any benefits) within three weeks from the date the employer orders the mass layoff, relocation, or employment loss.

The total amount of civil penalties for which an employer may be liable will not exceed the maximum amount of penalties for which the employer may be liable under federal law for the same violation. Additionally, any penalty amount paid by the employer under federal law will be considered a payment made under the Illinois act. Similar to an employer's liability to an employee, the amount of civil penalties may be reduced, at the director's discretion, where the employer proves the violating act or omission was in good faith and the employer had reasonable grounds for believing the act or omission was not a violation.

The Illinois Business Economic Support Act

The Illinois Business Economic Support Act (BESA), located at 30 Ill. Comp. Stat. §§ 760/1 – 760/15, requires that any business or industry required to provide notice under the Illinois WARN Act and receiving state or local economic development incentives for doing or continuing to conduct business in the state, in addition to the notice required under the act, must also provide at the same time a copy of that notice to all of the following:

- Governor.

- Speaker and Minority Leader of the House of Representatives.

◆ President and Minority Leader of the Senate.

◆ Mayor of each municipality where the private entity has locations in the state.

If a private entity receiving state or local economic development incentives does not give the required notice required, then all of the following transpires:

◆ All or part of the state or local economic development incentives may be terminated.

◆ The due date of all or part of any indebtedness to the state or unit of local government may be accelerated by notice to the private entity.

At the time a private entity begins to receive state or local economic development incentives, the entity will be advised in writing of the BESA requirements by the state or local government unit. No private entity will be penalized by the failure of the state or local government unit to provide timely notice.

The Illinois Human Rights Act

Pursuant to the Illinois Human Rights Act (775 Ill. Comp. Stat. §§ 5/1-101 et seq.) every state executive department, state agency, board, commission, and instrumentality must notify the Department of Human Rights 30 days before effecting any layoff. Once notice is given, the following must occur:

◆ No layoff may be effective earlier than 10 working days after notice to the department, unless an emergency layoff situation exists.

◆ The state executive department, state agency, board, commission, or instrumentality in which the layoffs are to occur must notify each employee targeted for layoff, the employee's union representative (if applicable), and the State Dislocated Worker Unit at the Department of Commerce and Community Affairs.

◆ The state executive department, state agency, board, commission, or instrumentality in which the layoffs are to occur must conform to applicable collective-bargaining agreements.

Additionally, the state executive department, state agency, board, commission, or instrumentality in which the layoffs are to occur should notify each employee targeted for layoff that transitional assistance may be available under the Economic Dislocation and Worker Adjustment Assistance Act administered by the Department of Commerce and Community Affairs. Failure to give such notice will not invalidate the layoff or postpone its effective date.

For more information on the Illinois Human Rights Act, please refer to the chapter entitled **Discrimination in Employment.**

The Illinois State Facilities Closure Act

Under the State Facilities Closure Act (30 Ill. Comp. Stat. §§ 608/5-1 – 608/99-995), before a state facility may be closed, the state executive branch officer with jurisdiction over the facility must file notice of the proposed closure with the Commission on Government Forecasting and Accountability. The notice must be filed within two days after the first public announcement of any planned or proposed closure. Within 10 days after it receives notice of the proposed closure, the commission, in its discretion, may require the state executive branch officer with jurisdiction over the facility to file a recommendation for the closure of the facility with the commission.

The commission must require the executive branch officers to file a recommendation for closure in the case of a proposed closure of:

◆ A prison, youth center, work camp, or work release center operated by the Department of Corrections.

- A school, mental health center, or center for the developmentally disabled operated by the Department of Human Services.

- A residential facility operated by the Department of Veterans' Affairs.

The recommendation must be filed within 30 days after the commission delivers the request for recommendation to the state executive branch officer.

The recommendation must include, but is not limited to, the following information:

- The location and identity of the state facility proposed to be closed.

- The number of employees for which the state facility is the primary stationary work location and the effect of the closure of the facility on those employees.

- The location or locations to which the functions and employees of the state facility would be moved.

- The availability and condition of land and facilities at both the existing location and any potential locations.

- The ability to accommodate the functions and employees at the existing and at any potential locations.

- The cost of operations of the state facility and at any potential locations and any other related budgetary impacts.

- The economic impact on existing communities in the vicinity of the state facility and any potential facility.

- The ability of the existing and any potential community's infrastructure to support the functions and employees.

- The impact on state services delivered at the existing location, in direct relation to the state services expected to be delivered at any potential locations.

- The environmental impact, including the impact of costs related to potential environmental restoration, waste management, and environmental compliance activities.

If a recommendation is required by the commission, a 30-day public comment period must follow the filing of the recommendation. The commission, in its discretion, may conduct one or more public hearings on the recommendation. The commission must conduct one or more public hearings on the recommendation if the recommendation calls for the proposed closure of:

- A prison, youth center, work camp, or work release center operated by the Department of Corrections.

- A school, mental health center, or center for the developmentally disabled operated by the Department of Human Services.

- A residential facility operated by the Department of Veterans' Affairs.

Public hearings conducted by the commission must be conducted no later than 35 days after the filing of the recommendation. At least one of the public hearings on the recommendation must be held at a convenient location within 25 miles of the facility for which closure is recommended. The commission must provide reasonable notice of the comment period and of any public hearings to the public and to units of local government and school districts that are located within 25 miles of the facility.

Within 50 days after the state executive branch officer files the required recommendation, the commission must issue an advisory opinion on that recommendation. The commission must file the advisory opinion with the appropriate state executive branch officer, the Governor, the General Assembly, and the Index Department of the Office of the Secretary of State and must make copies of the advisory opinion available to the public upon request.

No action may be taken to implement the recommendation for closure of a state facility until 50 days after the filing of any required recommendation.

The requirements of this section do not apply if all of the functions and employees of a state facility are relocated to another state facility that is within 10 miles of the closed facility.

The Illinois Public Utilities Act

Pursuant to 220 Ill. Comp. Stat. § 5/7-213, found in the Illinois Public Utilities Act, in the event of a sale, purchase, or any other transfer of ownership, including, without limitation, the acquisition by eminent domain, of a water system operated by a privately held public water utility, the water utility's contract or agreements with the acquiring entity (or, in the case of an eminent domain action, the court order) must require that the acquiring entity hire a sufficient number of nonsupervisory employees to operate and maintain the water system by initially making offers of employment to the nonsupervisory workforce of the water system at no less than the wage rates, and substantially equivalent fringe benefits and terms and conditions of employment that are in effect at the time of transfer of ownership of the water system.

The wage rates and substantially equivalent fringe benefits and terms and conditions of employment must continue for at least 30 months after the time of the transfer of ownership unless the parties mutually agree to different terms and conditions of employment within that 30-month period.

The privately held public water utility must offer a transition plan to those employees who are not offered jobs by the acquiring entity because that entity has a need for fewer workers. The transition plan must mitigate employee job losses to the extent practical through such means as offers of voluntary severance, retraining, early retirement, outplacement, or related benefits.

Before any reduction in the workforce during a water system transaction, the privately held public water utility must present to the employees, or their representatives, a transition plan outlining the means by which the utility intends to mitigate the impact of the workforce reduction of its employees.

Illinois Department of Commerce and Economic Opportunity
Bureau of Workforce Development

500 East Monroe, 9th Floor
Springfield, IL 62701-1643

Telephone: 217-785-6006
Internet: *www.illinoisbiz.biz/dceo/Bureaus/Workforce_Development/WARN*

Illinois Department of Labor

1 West Old State Capitol Plaza, Room 300
Springfield, IL 62701

Telephone: 217-782-6206
Fax: 217-782-0596
Internet: *www.state.il.us/agency/idol*

Chapter 23

Health Care Plans and COBRA

Introduction

Health insurance is one of the most important benefits that employers can provide for their employees. Employers that sponsor group health plans enable employees and their families to take care of their essential medical needs, ensuring that employees are free to devote their energies to productive work. Because of the critical importance of good health, employer-sponsored group health insurance programs benefit employees, employers, and society as a whole.

Health Care Reform

On March 23, 2010, President Obama signed into law the Patient Protection and Affordable Care Act (referred to as health care reform). The following summary of the new law, and changes made to the law by subsequent legislation, focuses on provisions of the law that affect employers. Employers should note that the new law is complex and subject to clarification from forthcoming regulations.

Overview

The main purpose of health care reform law is to ensure that all individuals are covered by an employer-provided health plan or individual health insurance policy that provides minimum essential coverage. To achieve this end, the law:

♦ Expands existing federal health care programs (Medicare, Medicaid, and CHIP).

♦ Creates new state health care exchanges.

♦ Provides incentives and sanctions for employers to either provide health coverage for their employees or subsidize their coverage through an exchange.

Affected Health Plans and Insurance Requirements

The health care reform law applies to both fully-insured and self-insured health plans. It distinguishes between grandfathered group health plans (those in existence as of March 23, 2010) and new group health plans. The law also applies to self-insured group health plans and multi-employer welfare arrangements unless otherwise exempted.

Grandfather Provisions

The health care reform law exempts "grandfathered plans" from certain requirements applicable to health plans in the group and individual markets. ***Grandfathered plans*** include any group health plan or individual plan that was in existence on March 23, 2010, the date of enactment. The law provides that family members are permitted to join the grandfathered coverage if the terms of the plan in effect on the date of enactment would allow such enrollment. New employees (and their families) may enroll in a grandfathered group health plan. Grandfathered group health plans provided by employers are deemed to meet the "minimum essential coverage" for purposes of the individual mandate to have insurance.

Employer Health Plan Requirements

The following requirements are generally applicable to employer group health plans for plan years beginning on or after September 23, 2010 (subject in some cases to grandfather rules and other limitations):

- ◆ **Prohibition on Lifetime Limits.** Insurers will be prohibited from establishing lifetime limits on the dollar value of benefits.

- ◆ **Restriction on Annual Limits.** Insurers will be subject to restrictions on annual limits developed by the Secretary of Health and Human Services.

- ◆ **Prohibition on Rescissions.** Insurers will be prohibited from rescinding coverage except in cases of fraud or misrepresentation.

- ◆ **Prohibition on Denial of Coverage to Children with Pre-Existing Conditions.** Insurers will be prohibited from denying coverage to children with pre-existing conditions.

- ◆ **Requirement to Offer Coverage to Dependants Under Age 26.** Insurers that offer dependant coverage must make coverage available to adult children until age 26. Until 2014, insurers will not have to offer this coverage if the adult child is eligible to enroll in a new employer-sponsored health plan.

- ◆ **Requirement to Cover Preventive Health Services.** Insurers must provide coverage for preventative health services, such as certain vaccinations, and cannot impose cost-sharing for these services. This coverage is expanded to all health plans in 2018.

- ◆ **Prohibition of Discrimination Based on Salary.** New group insurers will be prohibited from promulgating rules that discriminate in favor of higher-wage employees.

The following requirements are generally applicable to employer group health plans for plan years beginning on or after January 1, 2014:

- ◆ **Prohibition on Annual Limits.** Annual limits will be prohibited.

- ◆ **Prohibition on the Denial of Coverage Based on Pre-Existing Conditions.** Insurers will be prohibited from denying coverage to children and adults based on pre-existing conditions.

- ◆ **Requirement that All Plans in the Small Group and Individual Market Include an "Essential Heath Benefits Package."** The Secretary of Health and Human Services will define an "essential health benefits package," which will be designed to include benefits "equal to the scope of benefits provided under a typical employer plan" (such as hospitalization and maternity care). The package will also mandate restrictions on cost-sharing (these restrictions will also apply to group plans), and, in the case of small group plans, establish dollar limits for deductibles. All plans will also be required to have an actuarial value of at least 60 percent.

- ◆ **Prohibition of Discrimination Based on Health Status.** Insurers will be prohibited from establishing eligibility requirements linked to health status-related factors, such as medical condition, claims experience, genetic information, or disability.

♦ **Prohibition on Discriminatory Premium Rates.** Individual and small group insurers will be prohibited from charging disparate premiums to enrollees with the same plan, unless the premium difference is due to individual versus family coverage, the enrollee's geographic area within a state, the enrollee's age (within limits) or the enrollee's tobacco use (within limits).

♦ **Guaranteed Acceptance by Insurers.** Insurers offering insurance in a state will be required to accept every employer and individual in the state that applies for such coverage.

♦ **Prohibition of Waiting Periods Exceeding 90 Days.** Group insurers will be prohibited from applying waiting periods that exceed 90 days.

Temporary Reinsurance Program

By June 21, 2010, the Secretary of Human Services is required to establish a temporary reinsurance program for employers providing group health coverage to retirees over age 55 who are not eligible for Medicare (and their eligible spouses, surviving spouses, and dependents). The program will reimburse eligible employers for 80 percent of a participant's claims between $15,000 and $90,000. The reimbursement must be used to lower costs for the plan, for example, to reduce premium contributions, co-payments, deductibles, co-insurance, or other out-of-pocket costs for plan participants. The temporary program expires on January 1, 2014.

Voluntary Assisted Living Insurance

Included in the health care reform law is the Community Living Assistance and Supports Program (CLASS). CLASS is a voluntary insurance program that pays benefits of an average of $50 per day to individuals with functional limitations to purchase nonmedical services. It is intended to provide the support necessary to enable individuals to continue living in a residential setting. This is relevant to employers because they are required to automatically enroll employees in a system of voluntary payroll deductions. Employees must opt-out of the program. It is effective January 1, 2011, but requires a five year vesting period before benefits are provided.

Health Insurance Exchanges

Starting in 2014, states will begin to operate health insurance exchanges for both the individual and the small group market, referred to as the Small Business Health Options Program (SHOP) Exchange. Exchanges are intended to facilitate the purchase of health care insurance for the individual and small group markets. The exchanges are meant to serve as portals for consumers and will provide consumer-oriented information to enrollees and prospective enrollees. Exchanges will also certify that insurance offered through them complies with new federal standards for "essential health benefits."

States may combine the individual and SHOP exchanges. For the purposes of SHOP, a small employer is defined as having between one and 100 employees. However, until 2016, states can limit the small group market to employers with 50 or fewer employees. Beginning in 2017, states may allow large companies — those with more than 100 employees — to participate in the exchanges.

New Requirements for Employers
Pay or Play

Beginning January 1, 2014, large employers who do not offer health insurance to full-time employees will be subject to a penalty in the event that at least one employee receives a federal subsidy to enroll in a health insurance plan through an exchange.

The fines are as follows:

- Employers with more than 50 employees that do not offer health care coverage and have at least one full-time employee (FTE) who receives a premium tax credit from the federal government will be fined $2,000 per FTE per year. In calculating the number of FTEs, the first 30 FTEs are exempted.

- Employers with more than 50 employees that do offer health care coverage and have at least one FTE who receives a premium tax credit from the federal government will be fined the lesser of $3,000 for each employee receiving a credit or $2,000 for each FTE.

Employers who are part of a controlled group must count all employees in the controlled group to determine whether the employer is subject to the fines.

An FTE is one employed at least 30 hours per week on average (part-time employees are converted into full-time equivalents by dividing their average monthly hours by 120); for example, a business with 51 full-time employees that does not offer coverage must pay a monthly penalty of 21 times the per employee penalty amount (assuming at least one employee satisfies the tax credit requirement).

Free Choice Vouchers

Beginning January 1, 2014, employers with 50 or more employees that offer health insurance coverage to their employees must offer "free choice vouchers" to eligible employees who do not participate in the employer-offered health plan. This free choice voucher represents the monthly portion of the cost of coverage that the employer would have otherwise paid if the employee was covered under the employer's plan. An employee can use the free choice voucher to purchase alternative coverage through health care exchanges. The employer must pay the amount of the voucher directly to the exchange and, if the amount of the voucher exceeds the cost of the exchange coverage, the excess is to be paid to the employee. The amount of the free choice voucher is deductible by the employer.

To be eligible for a free choice voucher, the employee must:

- Be required to contribute between 8 percent and 9.5 percent of his or her household income to receive coverage under the employer-sponsored plan.

- Have a household income not more than 400 percent of the federal poverty level.

- Choose to enroll in a plan in the exchange.

Automatic Enrollment

Beginning January 1, 2014, employers with more than 200 FTEs that offer health insurance are required to automatically enroll new full-time employees in a group health plan if a plan is offered by that employer. Employees must be given reasonable advance notice and the opportunity to elect to enroll in a different level of coverage, if available, or to opt-out altogether.

Employee Notice

Employers must provide a summary of benefits to each employee that meets all of the following criteria:

- Is not more than four pages in length.

- Is written in a culturally and linguistically appropriate manner.

- Contains certain content related to covered benefits, exclusions, cost sharing, and continuation coverage.

The Department of Health and Human Services has 12 months from the date of enactment to provide guidance regarding the uniform explanation of coverage, and employers have 24 months from the date of enactment to provide such explanation to employees. In addition, the explanation must be updated for material modifications to coverage not less than 60 days in advance of effective date of the change. Failure to comply may result in a $1,000 penalty for each failure.

In addition, beginning on March 13, 2013, employers must provide written notice to current employees, and new employees as they are hired, of the existence of a health insurance exchange and how the employee may contact the exchange to request assistance. If the employer's share of the total costs of benefits is less than 60 percent of the costs (actuarial value), the employer must inform each employee that he or she may be eligible for a premium tax credit if the employee purchases insurance through the exchange, but that the employee will lose the employer contribution (if any) made with respect to health coverage. Under these circumstances, the employer would not be subject to any fines.

Reporting Requirements

The health care reform law has several new reporting and disclosure requirements. Beginning January 1, 2011, employers are required to report on their Form W-2 the cost of any employer-sponsored plan coverage.

The health care reform law has several new reporting and disclosure requirements. Beginning January 1, 2011, employers are required to report on their Form W-2 the cost of any employer-sponsored plan coverage. However, the IRS released Notice 2010-69 providing interim relief to employers with respect to reporting the cost of coverage under an employer-sponsored group health plan on Form W-2. Specifically, the notice provided that reporting the cost of such coverage will not be mandatory for Forms W-2 issued for 2011. The Treasury Department and the IRS have determined that this relief is appropriate to provide employers with additional time to make any necessary changes to their payroll systems or procedures in preparation for compliance with the reporting requirement.

If an employer does decide to report the aggregate cost of employer coverage on the Form W-2, the IRS also released a draft Form W-2 that includes the codes that employers may use to report the cost of coverage under an employer-sponsored group health plan.

In addition, beginning January 1, 2014, employers with more than 50 FTEs must certify to the IRS all of the following:

- ◆ Whether they offer employees minimum essential coverage.
- ◆ The length of any waiting period.
- ◆ The amount of monthly premiums.
- ◆ The employer's share of the total costs of benefits.
- ◆ The number of FTEs per month.
- ◆ Any identifying employee information, including whether the employee was covered under any benefit plan.

The IRS may by regulation require additional information. Employers must also provide employees with notice of the information provided to the IRS.

Tax Changes

Flexible Spending Accounts

Beginning on January 1, 2013, contributions to a flexible spending account for medical expenses are limited to $2,500 per year, increased annually by a cost of living adjustment.

Medicare Tax

Beginning on January 1, 2013, the employee-side Medicare Part A tax rate is increased from 1.45 percent to 2.35 percent on individuals earning more than $200,000 (indexed) and married couples filing jointly earning more than $250,000 (indexed). There is no corresponding increase in the employer-side payroll taxes. The law also imposes a 3.8 percent tax on unearned income for higher-income taxpayers, for which the thresholds are not indexed.

Also effective January 1, 2013, the law eliminates the deduction for the portion of the cost of an employer's retiree prescription drug coverage that is offset by the government subsidy (provided to the employer because the employer's prescription drug coverage is at least as valuable as Medicare Part D coverage).

Note: While this takes effect in 2013, the loss of the deduction may require disclosure on public company financial statements in 2010. Employers are encouraged to consult their accountants about this provision.

Cadillac Health Plans

Beginning on January 1, 2018, an excise tax will be imposed on employer-sponsored group health plans (both self-funded and fully-insured) whose annual premiums exceed $10,200 for an individual and $27,500 for family. The law indexes the threshold premium to the consumer price index for urban consumers (CPI-U) beginning in 2020. In addition, threshold amounts will be increased for retirees age 55 and older who are not eligible for Medicare and for employees in high-risk professions. The tax is equal to 40 percent of the value of the plan that exceeds the threshold amounts.

Small Employer Tax Credit

The new health care reform law gives a tax credit to certain small employers that provide health care coverage to their employees, effective with tax years beginning in 2010. To qualify for this tax credit:

♦ An employer must have less than 25 full-time equivalent employees for the tax year.

♦ The average annual wages of employees for the year must be less than $50,000 per FTE.

♦ The employer must pay the premiums under a qualifying arrangement.

For tax years 2010 through 2013, the law provides a tax credit of up to 35 percent of the employer's contribution toward the employee's health insurance premium if the employer contributes at least 50 percent of the total premium cost or 50 percent of a benchmark premium. The full credit will be available to employers with 10 or fewer employees and average annual wages of less than $25,000. The credit phases out as firm size and average wage increases. Tax-exempt small businesses meeting these requirements are eligible for tax credits of up to 25 percent of the employer's contribution toward the employee's health insurance premium.

For tax years 2014 and later, for eligible small businesses that purchase coverage through the state exchange, provide a tax credit of up to 50 percent of the employer's contribution toward the employee's health insurance premium if the employer contributes at least 50 percent of the total premium cost. The credit will be available for two years. The full credit will be available to employers with 10 or fewer employees and average annual wages of less than $25,000. The credit phases out as firm size and average wage increases. Tax-exempt small businesses meeting these requirements are eligible for tax credits of up to 35 percent of the employer's contribution toward the employee's health insurance premium.

Calculating the Credit

Only premiums paid by the employer under a qualifying arrangement are counted in calculating the credit. Under a *qualifying arrangement*, the employer pays premiums for each employee enrolled in health care coverage offered by the employer in an amount equal to a uniform percentage (not less than 50 percent) of the total premium cost of the coverage. If an employer pays only a portion of the premiums, only the portion paid by the employer is counted in calculating the credit. For purposes of the credit (including the 50-percent requirement), any premium paid pursuant to a salary reduction arrangement under a § 125 cafeteria plan is not treated as paid by the employer. The IRS has stated that premiums paid by the employer in 2010, but before the new health reform legislation was enacted (March 23, 2010), may be counted in calculating the credit.

The amount of an employer's premium payments that counts when calculating the credit may not exceed the average premium for the small group market in the particular state (or an area within the state) in which the employer offers coverage for the same arrangement. The average premium for the small group market in a state (or an area within the state) will be determined by the Department of Health and Human Services (HHS) and published by the IRS.

Maximum Credit Amounts

As stated previously, for tax years beginning in 2010 through 2013, the maximum credit is 35 percent of the employer's premium expenses that count towards the credit. Over that same time period, the maximum credit for a tax-exempt qualified employer is 25 percent of the employer's premium expenses that count towards the credit. However, the amount of the credit cannot exceed the total amount of income and Medicare (i.e., Hospital Insurance) tax the employer is required to withhold from employees' wages for the year and the employer share of Medicare tax on employees' wages.

Reducing the Credit

If the number of FTEs exceeds 10 or if average annual wages exceed $25,000, the amount of the credit is reduced. If the number of FTEs exceeds 10, the reduction is determined by multiplying the otherwise applicable credit amount by a fraction, the numerator of which is the number of FTEs in excess of 10 and the denominator of which is 15. If average annual wages exceed $25,000, the reduction is determined by multiplying the otherwise applicable credit amount by a fraction, the numerator of which is the amount by which average annual wages exceed $25,000 and the denominator of which is $25,000. In both cases, the result of the calculation is subtracted from the otherwise applicable credit to determine the credit to which the employer is entitled. For an employer with both more than 10 FTEs and average annual wages exceeding $25,000, the reduction is the sum of the amount of the two reductions. This sum may reduce the credit to zero for some employers with fewer than 25 FTEs and average annual wages of less than $50,000.

Counting Full-Time Employees

The number of an employer's FTEs is determined by dividing the total hours for which the employer pays wages to employees during the year (but not more than 2,080 hours for any employee) by 2,080.

$$\frac{\text{Total hours employer paid wages to employees during the year}}{2{,}080} = \text{FTEs}$$

If the result is not a whole number, then the result is rounded to the next lowest whole number. Because the limitation on the number of employees is based on FTEs, an employer with 25 or more employees could qualify for the credit if some of its employees work part time.

Computing Average Annual Wages

The amount of average annual wages is determined by first dividing the total wages paid by the employer to employees during the employer's tax year by the number of the employer's FTEs for the year.

$$\frac{\text{Total wages paid by employer to employees during the year}}{\text{FTEs}} = \text{Average Annual Wages}$$

The result is then rounded down to the nearest $1,000. For this purpose, *wages* means wages as defined for FICA purposes (without regard to the wage base limitation).

Seasonal Workers

Seasonal workers are disregarded in determining FTEs and average annual wages unless the seasonal worker works for the employer on more than 120 days during the tax year. A sole proprietor, a partner in a partnership, a shareholder owning more than two percent of an S corporation, and any owner of more than five percent of other businesses are not considered employees for purposes of the credit. Thus, the wages or hours of these business owners and partners are not counted in determining either the number of FTEs or the amount of average annual wages, and premiums paid on their behalf are not counted in determining the amount of the credit. A family member of any of the business owners or partners member of such a business owner's or partner's household, is also not considered an employee for purposes of the credit.

For this purpose, a *family member* is defined as the following:

♦ A child (or descendant of a child).

♦ A sibling or stepsibling.

♦ A parent (or ancestor of a parent).

♦ A stepparent.

♦ A niece or nephew.

♦ An aunt or uncle.

♦ A son-in-law, daughter- in-law, father-in-law, mother-in-law, brother-in-law, or sister-in-law.

Controlled Groups

Members of a controlled group (for example, businesses with the same owners) or an affiliated service group (for example, related businesses of which one performs services for the other) are treated as a single employer for purposes of the credit. Thus, for example, all employees of the controlled group or affiliated service group, and all wages paid to employees by the controlled group or affiliated service group, are counted in determining whether any member of the controlled group or affiliated service group is a qualified employer.

How to Claim the Credit

Employers will claim the credit on their annual income tax return. The IRS will provide further guidance on how tax exempt organizations are to claim the credit. As a general business credit, an unused credit amount can generally be carried back one year and carried forward 20 years. Because an unused credit amount cannot be carried back to a year before the effective date of the credit, an unused credit amount for 2010 can only be carried forward. The IRS states that the credit can be reflected in determining estimated tax payments for the year to which the credit applies in accordance with regular estimated tax rules. For a tax-exempt employer, the credit is a refundable credit, so that even if the employer has no taxable income, the employer may receive a refund so long as it does not exceed the income tax withholding and Medicare tax liability.

Deductions from Health Insurance Premiums

In determining the employer's deduction for health insurance premiums, the amount of premiums that can be deducted is reduced by the amount of the credit.

Frequently Asked Questions

Q   Which employers are eligible for the small employer health care tax credit?

A Small employers that provide health care coverage to their employees and that meet certain requirements (qualified employers) generally are eligible for a federal income tax credit for health insurance premiums they pay for certain employees. In order to be a *qualified employer*, all of the following conditions must be met:

- The employer must have fewer than 25 full-time equivalent employees (FTEs) for the tax year.
- The average annual wages of all employees for the year must be less than $50,000 per FTE.
- The employer must pay the premiums under a qualifying arrangement.

Q Can a tax-exempt organization be a qualified employer?

A Yes. The same definition of qualified employer applies to an organization described in I.R.C. § 501(c) that is exempt from tax under I.R.C. § 501(a). However, special rules apply in calculating the credit for a tax-exempt qualified employer.

Q What expenses are counted in calculating the credit?

A Only premiums paid by the employer under an arrangement meeting certain requirements (a qualifying arrangement) are counted in calculating the credit. Under a qualifying arrangement, the employer pays premiums for each employee enrolled in health care coverage offered by the employer in an amount equal to a uniform percentage (not less than 50 percent) of the premium cost of the coverage.

If an employer pays only a portion of the premiums for the coverage provided to employees under the arrangement (with employees paying the rest), the amount of premiums counted in calculating the credit is only the portion paid by the employer. For example, if an employer pays 80 percent of the premiums for employees' coverage (with employees paying the other 20 percent), the 80 percent premium amount paid by the employer counts in calculating the credit. For purposes of the credit (including the 50-percent requirement), any premium paid pursuant to a salary reduction arrangement under a § 125 cafeteria plan is not treated as paid by the employer.

In addition, the amount of an employer's premium payments that counts for purposes of the credit is capped by the premium payments the employer would have made under the same arrangement if the average premium for the small group market in the state (or an area within the state) in which the employer offers coverage were substituted for the actual premium. If the employer pays only a portion of the premium for the coverage provided to employees (for example, under the terms of the plan the employer pays 80 percent of the premiums and the employees pay the other 20 percent), the premium amount that counts for purposes of the credit is the same portion (80 percent in the example) of the premiums that would have been paid for the coverage if the average premium for the small group market in the state were substituted for the actual premium.

Q What is the average premium for the small group market in a state (or an area within the state)?

A The average premium for the small group market in a state (or an area within the state) will be determined by the Department of Health and Human Services (HHS) and published by the IRS. Publication of the average premium for the small group market on a state-by-state basis is expected to be posted on the IRS Web site by the end of April.

Q What is the maximum credit for a qualified employer (other than a tax-exempt employer)?

A For tax years beginning in 2010 through 2013, the maximum credit is 35 percent of the employer's premium expenses that count towards the credit.

Example: For the 2010 tax year, a qualified employer has nine FTEs with average annual wages of $23,000 per FTE. The employer pays $72,000 in health care premiums for those employees (which does not exceed the average premium for the small group market in the employer's state) and otherwise meets the requirements for the credit. The credit for 2010 equals $25,200 (35% x $72,000).

Q What is the maximum credit for a tax-exempt qualified employer?

A For tax years beginning in 2010 through 2013, the maximum credit for a tax-exempt qualified employer is 25 percent of the employer's premium expenses that count towards the credit. However, the amount of the credit cannot exceed the total amount of income and Medicare (i.e., Hospital Insurance) tax the employer is required to withhold from employees' wages for the year and the employer share of Medicare tax on employees' wages.

Example: For the 2010 tax year, a qualified tax-exempt employer has 10 FTEs with average annual wages of $21,000 per FTE. The employer pays $80,000 in health care premiums for those employees (which does not exceed the average premium for the small group market in the employer's state) and otherwise meets the requirements for the credit. The total amount of the employer's income tax and Medicare tax withholding plus the employer's share of the Medicare tax equals $30,000 in 2010.

The credit is calculated as follows:

1) Initial amount of credit determined before any reduction: (25% x $80,000) = $20,000.

2) Employer's withholding and Medicare taxes: $30,000.

3) Total 2010 tax credit is $20,000 (the lesser of $20,000 and $30,000).

Q How is the credit reduced if the number of FTEs exceeds 10 or average annual wages exceed $25,000?

A If the number of FTEs exceeds 10 or if average annual wages exceed $25,000, the amount of the credit is reduced as follows (but not below zero). If the number of FTEs exceeds 10, the reduction is determined by multiplying the otherwise applicable credit amount by a fraction, the numerator of which is the number of FTEs in excess of 10 and the denominator of which is 15. If average annual wages exceed $25,000, the reduction is determined by multiplying the otherwise applicable credit amount by a fraction, the numerator of which is the amount by which average annual wages exceed $25,000 and the denominator of which is $25,000. In both cases, the result of the calculation is subtracted from the otherwise applicable credit to determine the credit to which the employer is entitled. For an employer with both more than 10 FTEs and average annual wages exceeding $25,000, the reduction is the sum of the amount of the two reductions. This sum may reduce the credit to zero for some employers with fewer than 25 FTEs and average annual wages of less than $50,000.

Example: For the 2010 tax year, a qualified employer has 12 FTEs and average annual wages of $30,000. The employer pays $96,000 in health care premiums for those employees (which does not exceed the average premium for the small group market in the employer's state) and otherwise meets the requirements for the credit.

The credit is calculated as follows:

1) Initial amount of credit determined before any reduction: (35% x $96,000) = $33,600.

2) Credit reduction for FTEs in excess of 10: ($33,600 x 2/15) = $4,480.

3) Credit reduction for average annual wages in excess of $25,000: ($33,600 x $5,000/$25,000) = $6,720.

4) Total credit reduction: ($4,480 + $6,720) = $11,200.

5) Total 2010 tax credit: ($33,600 – $11,200) = $22,400.

Q Can premiums paid by the employer in 2010, but before the new health reform legislation was enacted, be counted in calculating the credit?

A   Yes. In computing the credit for a tax year beginning in 2010, employers may count all premiums described in the previous answer for that tax year.

Q   **How is the number of FTEs determined for purposes of the credit?**

A   The number of an employer's FTEs is determined by dividing (1) the total hours for which the employer pays wages to employees during the year (but not more than 2,080 hours for any employee) by (2) 2,080. The result, if not a whole number, is then rounded to the next lowest whole number.

Example: For the 2010 tax year, an employer pays five employees wages for 2,080 hours each, three employees wages for 1,040 hours each, and one employee wages for 2,300 hours. The employer's FTEs would be calculated as follows:

   1) Total hours not exceeding 2,080 per employee is the sum of:

   a. 10,400 hours for the five employees paid for 2,080 hours each (5 x 2,080).

   b. 3,120 hours for the three employees paid for 1,040 hours each (3 x 1,040).

   c. 2,080 hours for the one employee paid for 2,300 hours (lesser of 2,300 and 2,080).

   These add up to 15,600 hours.

   2) FTEs: 7 (15,600 divided by 2,080 = 7.5, rounded to the next lowest whole number).

Q   **How is the amount of average annual wages determined?**

A   The amount of average annual wages is determined by first dividing (1) the total wages paid by the employer to employees during the employer's tax year by (2) the number of the employer's FTEs for the year. The result is then rounded down to the nearest $1,000 (if not otherwise a multiple of $1,000). For this purpose, wages means wages as defined for FICA purposes (without regard to the wage base limitation).

Example: For the 2010 tax year, an employer pays $224,000 in wages and has 10 FTEs. The employer's average annual wages would be $22,000 ($224,000 divided by 10 = $22,400, rounded down to the nearest $1,000).

Q   **Can an employer with 25 or more employees qualify for the credit if some employees work part time?**

A   Yes. Because the limitation on the number of employees is based on FTEs, an employer with 25 or more employees could qualify for the credit if some of its employees work part time. For example, an employer with 46 half-time employees (meaning they are paid wages for 1,040 hours) has 23 FTEs and therefore may qualify for the credit.

Q   **Are seasonal workers counted in determining the number of FTEs and the amount of average annual wages?**

A   Generally, no. Seasonal workers are disregarded in determining FTEs and average annual wages unless the seasonal worker works for the employer on more than 120 days during the tax year.

Q   **If an owner of a business also provides services to it, does the owner count as an employee?**

A   Generally, no. A sole proprietor, a partner in a partnership, a shareholder owning more than 2 percent of an S corporation, and any owner of more than 5 percent of other businesses are not considered employees for purposes of the credit. Thus, the wages or hours of these business owners and partners are not counted in determining either the number of FTEs or the amount of average annual wages, and premiums paid on their behalf are not counted in determining the amount of the credit.

Q Do family members of a business owner who work for the business count as employees?

A Generally, no. A family member of any of the business owners or partners, or a member of such a business owner's or partner's household, is not considered an employee for purposes of the credit. Thus, neither their wages nor their hours are counted in determining the number of FTEs or the amount of average annual wages, and premiums paid on their behalf are not counted in determining the amount of the credit. For this purpose, a *family member* is defined as any of the following:

- A child (or descendant of a child).
- A sibling or stepsibling.
- A parent (or ancestor of a parent).
- A stepparent.
- A niece or nephew.
- An aunt or uncle.
- A son-in-law, daughter- in-law, father-in-law, mother-in-law, brother-in-law, or sister-in-law.

Q How is eligibility for the credit determined if the employer is a member of a controlled group or an affiliated service group?

A Members of a controlled group (such as businesses with the same owners) or an affiliated service group (related businesses of which one performs services for the other) are treated as a single employer for purposes of the credit. Thus, for example, all employees of the controlled group or affiliated service group, and all wages paid to employees by the controlled group or affiliated service group, are counted in determining whether any member of the controlled group or affiliated service group is a qualified employer.

Q How does an employer claim the credit?

A The credit is claimed on the employer's annual income tax return. For a tax-exempt employer, the IRS will provide further information on how to claim the credit.

Q Can an employer (other than a tax-exempt employer) claim the credit if it has no taxable income for the year?

A Generally, no. Except in the case of a tax-exempt employer, the credit for a year offsets only an employer's actual income tax liability (or alternative minimum tax liability) for the year. However, as a general business credit, an unused credit amount can generally be carried back one year and carried forward 20 years. Because an unused credit amount cannot be carried back to a year before the effective date of the credit, though, an unused credit amount for 2010 can only be carried forward.

Q Can a tax-exempt employer claim the credit if the employer has no taxable income for the year?

A Yes. For a tax-exempt employer, the credit is a refundable credit, so that even if the employer has no taxable income, the employer may receive a refund (so long as it does not exceed the income tax withholding and Medicare tax liability).

Q Can the credit be reflected in determining estimated tax payments for a year?

A   Yes. The credit can be reflected in determining estimated tax payments for the year to which the credit applies in accordance with regular estimated tax rules.

Q   **Does taking the credit affect an employer's deduction for health insurance premiums?**

A   Yes. In determining the employer's deduction for health insurance premiums, the amount of premiums that can be deducted is reduced by the amount of the credit.

Q   **May an employer reduce employment tax payments (withheld income tax, Social Security tax, and Medicare tax) during the year in anticipation of the credit?**

A   No. The credit applies against income tax, not employment taxes.

COBRA

The Consolidated Omnibus Budget Reconciliation Act (COBRA) amends the Employee Retirement Income Security Act (ERISA), the Internal Revenue Code (IRC), and the Public Health Service Act to provide continuation of health care coverage that might otherwise be terminated.

COBRA gives workers and their families who lose their health benefits the right to choose to continue group health benefits provided by their group health plan for limited periods of time under certain circumstances, such as any of the following:

- Voluntary or involuntary job loss.
- Reduction in the hours worked.
- Transition between jobs.
- Death.
- Divorce.
- Other life events.

Qualified individuals may be required to pay the entire premium for coverage up to 102 percent of the cost to the plan.

COBRA generally requires that group health plans sponsored by employers with 20 or more employees in the prior year offer employees and their families the opportunity for a temporary extension of health coverage (continuation coverage) in certain instances where coverage under the plan would otherwise end.

COBRA outlines how employees and family members may elect continuation coverage and requires employers and plans to provide respective notice.

Overview

COBRA requires employers of 20 or more full- or part-time employees to offer a continuation of group insurance coverage to qualified beneficiaries who might otherwise lose that coverage after any of the following:

- An employee leaves a company (ceases employment).
- A family member becomes ineligible for coverage under the employer's plan.
- Because of another qualifying event.

The cost of the continued coverage is generally paid by the employee or dependent at or near the employer's group rate.

Coverage

The following types of group health care plans are covered under COBRA:

- Medical insurance.

- Dental insurance.

- Prescription drug plans.

- Vision insurance.

- Employee assistance programs (EAPs) that provide direct counseling services.

- On-site health care facilities.

Note: Life insurance is **not** covered under COBRA.

Eligibility

A *qualified beneficiary* is a covered employee, spouse, or dependent enrolled in an employer-sponsored care plan the day before a qualifying event.

A *qualifying event* is an occurrence that results in the loss of a beneficiary's coverage under an employer-sponsored care plan. Qualifying events can happen to the employee directly or to a dependent or family member covered under the employee's plan. Length of coverage under COBRA is determined by the type of qualifying event. Depending on the reason for COBRA coverage, the employee or dependent will have access to coverage for 18, 29, or 36 months.

Eighteen-Month Events

Eighteen-month events apply to employees and may be characterized by the following:

- Any voluntary or involuntary termination other than for gross misconduct.

- Reduction in hours to below the minimum required to participate in the employer's plan.

- Labor strike.

- Leave of absence.

- Military leave.

Twenty-Nine-Month Events

Twenty-nine-month events apply to disabled employees, covered spouses, and dependents and may be characterized by the following:

- Any qualified beneficiary who is considered disabled according to Social Security guidelines.

- Individuals must be considered disabled by Social Security at the time of the event, not when COBRA is initiated. However, employers may make exceptions to this rule, as applications for Social Security disability insurance are often initiated after the qualifying event to be retroactive to the qualifying event.

Thirty-Six-Month Events

Thirty-six-month events apply to covered spouses and dependents and may be characterized by the following:

- Employee's death.

- Employee's entitlement to or activation of Medicare, resulting in the family's exclusion from the employer's plan.

- ◆ Divorce or legal separation from a covered employee.

- ◆ Family member no longer considered a dependent under the employer's plan (for example, a child who is no longer a full-time college student or who is above the employer's coverage age for dependents).

If a 36-month event occurs during an 18-month event, COBRA benefits may be extended to the 36th month from the original event date for dependents and spouses only.

Notification Requirement

An initial notice must be furnished to covered employees and spouses at the time coverage under the plan commences, informing them of their rights under COBRA and describing provisions of the act. COBRA information is also required to be contained in the plan's summary plan description (SPD). When the plan administrator is notified that a qualifying event has occurred, it must in turn notify each qualified beneficiary of the right to choose continuation coverage. COBRA allows at least 60 days from the date the election notice is provided to inform the plan administrator that the qualified beneficiary wants to elect continuation coverage.

Under COBRA, the covered employee or a family member has the responsibility to inform the plan administrator of a divorce, legal separation, disability, or a child losing dependent status. Employers have a responsibility to notify the plan administrator of the employee's death, termination of employment, reduction in hours, or Medicare entitlement. If covered individuals change their marital status or their spouses have changed addresses, they should notify the plan administrator.

Rights of COBRA Participants

COBRA participants have the same rights and access to coverage as active employees and their beneficiaries. If employees are allowed to add new spouses or dependents or are offered an opportunity to change coverage plans, then COBRA participants must have the same opportunity to make changes. If coverage changes are made to the plan for employees, those changes apply to COBRA participants as well, even if the new coverage is not as good as the original coverage.

Costs for COBRA Coverage

The rate for coverage due to 18- and 36-month events **may not** exceed the employer's direct costs for coverage, plus 2 percent for administrative costs. The rate for coverage due to 29-month events (coverage between months 19 and 29), may be up to 150 percent of the applicable employer's premium.

COBRA and the Family and Medical Leave Act

During a leave of absence covered by the federal Family and Medical Leave Act (FMLA), the employer and employee must maintain the employee's health benefits, with both parties contributing to the plan in the same manner as prior to the leave.

However, if health benefits are canceled during the FMLA leave because the employee did not pay the premium within a 30-day grace period, the employee is **not** considered eligible for COBRA benefits.

COBRA coverage begins at the end of the FMLA leave or when the employer is made aware of the employee's intention not to return from leave.

COBRA and Medical Benefit Conversion from Group Plan to Individual Plan

COBRA participants must be notified if an insurer offers a conversion policy allowing the COBRA participants to change from a group health insurance plan to an individual insurance plan.

This notice must be sent by either the insurance company or the employer during the last 180 days of the COBRA coverage period.

Detailed Summary

Group Health Plans

A covered employer must offer continuation coverage (COBRA coverage) under a group health plan to any qualified beneficiary covered by that group health plan when coverage under the group health plan is lost due to a qualifying event. A group health plan includes any of the following:

♦ Medical coverage.

♦ Dental coverage.

♦ Vision coverage.

♦ Health spending accounts or flexible spending accounts (FSAs).

♦ Employee assistance plans (EAPs).

The following plans are **not** generally subject to COBRA:

♦ Group term life insurance.

♦ Disability insurance.

♦ Accidental death and dismemberment coverage.

♦ Long-term care plans.

An arrangement to provide medical services on the company's business premises will generally be treated as a group health plan.

However, COBRA requirements **do not apply** to the following:

♦ An on-site facility that primarily provides first aid to current employees at no charge during working hours.

♦ Facilities and programs, such as spas, swimming pools, or fitness centers, which simply further general good health.

♦ Employer-sponsored plans providing long-term care services.

♦ Amounts contributed by an employer to a medical savings account.

COBRA requirements **do apply** to the following:

♦ High-deductible health insurance that an employer provides in connection with a medical savings account.

♦ An employer maintained drug- or alcohol-treatment program, a health clinic, or any other facility or program that is intended to relieve or alleviate a physical condition or health problem. The facility or program is considered to be the provision of health care and so is considered a group health plan.

In the case of cafeteria plans or FSAs, the following apply:

♦ COBRA coverage requirements apply only to the health care benefits an employee has actually chosen to receive.

♦ Health FSAs are generally subject to COBRA; however, COBRA coverage may be limited.

Group Health Plans Subject to COBRA

COBRA generally applies to all private-sector group health plans maintained by employers that have at least 20 employees on more than 50 percent of its typical business days in the previous calendar year. COBRA also applies to plans sponsored by state and local governments.

The act **does not apply**, however, to plans sponsored by the federal government or by churches and certain church-related organizations.

Small Employer Exemption

COBRA continuation coverage **does not apply** to any employer-sponsored group health plan if the employer normally employed less than 20 common law employees on a typical business day during the preceding calendar year.

This requirement is met **only** if the employer had less than 20 common law employees on at least 50 percent of its typical business days during that calendar year.

Both full- and part-time employees are counted to determine whether a plan is subject to COBRA. However, each part-time employee counts as a fraction of a full-time employee, with the fraction equal to the number of hours that the part-time employee worked divided by the hours an employee must work to be considered full time.

Even though self-employed individuals, independent contractors and their employees, and directors are treated as employees for all other purposes, they are not counted as employees for purposes of calculating the number of employees in making the small employer plan determination.

Note: A health care plan that was not a small-employer plan for a given period remains liable for COBRA coverage that was triggered during that period regardless of whether the health care plan later becomes a small-employer plan.

Daily or Pay Period Basis

An employer may determine the number of employees on a daily basis or a pay period basis. Regardless, in both cases, each full-time employee is treated as one employee and each part-time employee is counted as a fraction of an employee.

If an employer makes the determination on a daily basis, the fraction is computed by dividing the number of hours a part-time employee works on a typical business day by the number of hours a full-time employee works on a typical business day in order to be considered full time.

For a pay period basis determination, the fraction is determined by dividing the number of hours a part-time employee works in a pay period by the number of hours a full-time employee works during the pay period in order to be considered full time.

The number of hours to be considered full time is based on the employer's employment practices; however, the hours required **may not** exceed 8 hours for any day or 40 hours for a week.

For example, an employer making a determination on a daily basis, with 10 employees working part time 4 hours a day and 10 employees working full time 8 hours a day, would be considered to have 15 employees for that business day.

For an employer making a determination on a pay period basis that pays weekly, with 10 employees working part time 20 hours a week and 10 employees working full time 40 hours a week, the employer would be considered to have 15 employees for that pay period.

The basis used by the employer must be used with respect to all employees and must be used for the entire year.

Covered Employees and Beneficiaries

Covered Employees

A covered employee under COBRA includes anyone who is covered under a group health plan by virtue of an employment relationship with the employer. For example, retirees or former employees might be covered by the plan because of their former employment with the employer. Although self-employed individuals, independent contractors, and directors do not have to be counted as employees under the small-business category, they are eligible for COBRA if their relationship to the employer makes them eligible to be covered by the employer's health insurance plan. However, employees that are eligible for the plan are not considered covered employees unless they are enrolled in the plan.

Under COBRA, a *qualified beneficiary* is defined as the following:

♦ An employee, spouse of an employee, or dependent child of an employee who is covered under the employer's health care plan on the day before certain qualifying events occur and who would lose coverage under the plan because of the event.

♦ A child born to or placed for adoption with a covered employee during the period of COBRA coverage.

♦ In the case of a qualifying event that is the bankruptcy of the employer, a covered employee who had retired on or before the date of substantial elimination of group health plan coverage is also a qualified beneficiary, as is any spouse, surviving spouse, or dependent child of a covered employee if, on the day before the bankruptcy qualifying event, the spouse, surviving spouse, or dependent child is a beneficiary under the plan.

Exclusions

In general, an individual (other than a child who is born to or placed for adoption with a covered employee during a period of COBRA continuation coverage) who is not covered under a plan on the day before the qualifying event cannot be a qualified beneficiary with respect to that qualifying event, and the reason for the individual's lack of actual coverage (such as the individual's having declined participation in the plan or failed to satisfy the plan's conditions for participation) is irrelevant.

In contrast to a child who is born to or placed for adoption with a covered employee during a period of COBRA continuation coverage, an individual who marries any qualified beneficiary on or after the date of the qualifying event and a newborn or adopted child (other than one born to or placed for adoption with a covered employee) are not qualified beneficiaries by virtue of the following:

♦ Marriage.

♦ Birth.

♦ Placement for adoption.

♦ Individual's status as the spouse of the qualified beneficiary.

♦ Child's status as a dependent of the qualified beneficiary.

These new family members do not themselves become qualified beneficiaries even if they become covered under the plan.

An individual is not a qualified beneficiary if, on the day before a qualifying event, the individual is covered under the group health plan by reason of another individual's election of COBRA continuation coverage and is not already a qualified beneficiary by reason of a prior qualifying event.

A qualified beneficiary who does not elect COBRA continuation coverage in connection with a qualifying event ceases to be a qualified beneficiary at the end of the election period. For example, if a former qualified beneficiary is later added to a covered employee's coverage (such as during an open enrollment period) and then another qualifying event occurs with respect to the covered employee, the former qualified beneficiary does not become a qualified beneficiary by reason of the second qualifying event. If a covered employee who is a qualified beneficiary does not elect COBRA continuation coverage during the election period, then any child born to or placed for adoption with the covered employee on or after the date of the qualifying event is not a qualified beneficiary.

These rules are illustrated by the following examples:

Example 1: B is a single employee who voluntarily terminates employment and elects COBRA continuation coverage under a group health plan. The plan permits a covered employee who marries to have their spouse covered under the plan. One month after electing COBRA continuation coverage, B marries and chooses to have B's spouse covered under the plan.

B's spouse is not a qualified beneficiary. Thus, if B dies during the period of COBRA continuation coverage, the plan does not have to offer B's surviving spouse an opportunity to elect COBRA continuation coverage.

Example 2: C is a married employee who terminates employment. C elects COBRA continuation coverage for C but not C's spouse, and C's spouse declines to elect such coverage. C's spouse thus ceases to be a qualified beneficiary. At the next open enrollment period, C adds the spouse as a beneficiary under the plan.

The addition of the spouse during the open enrollment period does not make the spouse a qualified beneficiary. The plan thus will not have to offer the spouse an opportunity to elect COBRA continuation coverage upon a later divorce from or death of C.

Example 3: Under the terms of a group health plan, a covered employee's child, upon attaining age 19, ceases to be a dependent eligible for coverage.

At that time, the child must be offered an opportunity to elect COBRA continuation coverage. If the child elects COBRA continuation coverage, the child marries during the period of the COBRA continuation coverage, and the child's spouse becomes covered under the group health plan, the child's spouse is not a qualified beneficiary.

Loss of Coverage and Qualifying Events

Qualifying events are those events that result in a loss of coverage under the group health plan. Qualifying events may be different, depending on who is the qualified beneficiary.

Loss of Coverage

A *loss of coverage* is to cease to be covered under the same terms and conditions in effect immediately before the qualifying event.

A loss of coverage need not occur immediately after the event, so long as the loss of coverage occurs before the end of the maximum coverage period. However, if neither the covered employee nor the spouse or a dependent child of the covered employee loses coverage before the end of what would be the maximum coverage period, the event does not constitute a loss of coverage.

If coverage is reduced or eliminated in anticipation of an event (for example, an employer eliminating an employee's coverage in anticipation of the termination of the employee, or an employee eliminating the coverage of their spouse in anticipation of a divorce or legal separation), the reduction or elimination is disregarded in determining whether the event causes a loss of coverage.

Qualifying Events

Qualifying events for covered employees include the following:

- Termination of employment (for any reason other than gross misconduct).
- Reduction in hours of employment.
- An employer filing for bankruptcy (certain retirees and dependents only).

Qualifying events for a covered spouse or dependent child include the following:

- A covered employee's termination of employment (for any reason other than gross misconduct) or reduction in hours of employment.
- A covered employee's death.
- A spouse's divorce or legal separation from a covered employee.
- A covered employee's entitlement to Medicare.
- A dependent child's loss of coverage due to no longer meeting the definition of a dependent under the benefit plan.
- An employer filing for bankruptcy.

Termination

Apart from facts constituting gross misconduct, the facts surrounding the termination or reduction of hours are irrelevant in determining whether a qualifying event has occurred. Thus, it is irrelevant whether the employee voluntarily terminated or was discharged. For example, a strike or a lockout is a termination or reduction of hours that constitutes a qualifying event if the strike or lockout results in a loss of coverage. Similarly, a layoff that results in a loss of coverage is a qualifying event.

Reduction in Hours

A reduction in hours occurs when there is a decrease in the number of hours a covered employee is required to work or actually works, without immediate termination. A switch from full time to part time would thus trigger COBRA coverage if the employee loses health benefits because of the change. An absence due to a disability or a temporary layoff is also considered a reduction in hours, albeit the employee's hours are reduced to zero.

If a plan measures eligibility for coverage by the number of hours worked in a given period, such as the preceding month or quarter, an employee who fails to work the required hours has experienced a reduction in hours resulting in a loss of coverage.

Termination for Gross Misconduct

If an employee is terminated for gross misconduct, any loss of coverage is **not** a qualifying event.

Applicable statutes and regulations do not define gross misconduct. Courts have defined gross misconduct for a manager as the substantial deviation from the high standards and obligations of a managerial employee, which would indicate that the employee could not be entrusted with management duties without danger to the employer. Courts have also relied on state unemployment compensation statutes to define gross misconduct. For example, one court said that in order for an employee's dismissal to be considered on account of gross misconduct, the conduct must have included the following:

- Deliberate violations of the employer's standards of conduct for employees.
- Carelessness or negligence of such a degree or recurrence as to manifest equal culpability, wrongful intent, or evil design aimed at causing injury to the employer or the employee's fellow workers.

Gross misconduct would not include the following:

♦ Mere inefficiency.

♦ Unsatisfactory conduct.

♦ Failure in good performance due to inability.

♦ Inadvertencies or ordinary negligence in isolated instances.

♦ Good faith errors in judgment or discretion.

Effect on a Spouse and Dependents

The U.S. Department of Labor takes the position that a covered spouse and dependent children lose their COBRA rights if a covered employee is discharged for gross misconduct. However, a federal court has ruled that an employee's discharge for gross misconduct had no bearing on the employee's spouse and dependent. The court found that the spouse and dependent still experienced a qualifying event that entitled them to COBRA coverage.

Risks to the Employer

If an employer denies COBRA coverage on the grounds of gross misconduct and the denial is unjustified, the employer may risk any of the following:

♦ Liability for the denied medical coverage.

♦ An excise tax.

♦ Civil penalties.

♦ Attorney's fees.

♦ Costs.

To reduce its potential liability, an employer should:

♦ Have legal counsel draft a policy statement defining gross misconduct that is consistent with local law and federal court decisions.

♦ Furnish all employees with a copy of the policy.

♦ Meticulously document the employee's conduct that gave rise to the dismissal.

♦ Retain the responsibility to decide questions of gross misconduct; COBRA administrators should not be permitted to decide if a particular termination was for gross misconduct.

These rules are illustrated by the following examples:

Example 1: An employee who is covered by a group health plan terminates employment (other than by reason of the employee's gross misconduct) and, beginning with the day after the last day of employment, is given three months of employer-paid coverage under the same terms and conditions as before that date. At the end of the three months, the coverage terminates.

The loss of coverage at the end of the three months results from the termination of employment. Thus, the termination of employment is a qualifying event.

Example 2: An employee who is covered by a group health plan retires (which is a termination of employment other than by reason of the employee's gross misconduct) and, upon retirement, is required to pay an increased amount for the same group health coverage that the employee had before retirement.

The increase in the premium or contribution required for coverage is a loss of coverage. Thus, the retirement is a qualifying event.

Example 3: An employee and the employee's spouse are covered under an employer's group health plan. The employee retires and is given identical coverage for life. However, the plan provides that the spousal coverage will not be continued beyond six months unless a higher premium for the spouse is paid to the plan.

The requirement for the spouse to pay a higher premium at the end of the six months is a loss of coverage. Thus, the retirement is a qualifying event and the spouse must be given an opportunity to elect COBRA continuation coverage.

Termination of Coverage in Anticipation of a Qualifying Event

If an employee discontinues the coverage of a spouse or dependent in anticipation of an event, such as a divorce or legal separation, a plan is required to make COBRA coverage available as of the date of divorce or legal separation, but not for any prior period. The qualified beneficiary will generally be entitled to the coverage that the qualified beneficiary had before the qualifying event. However, if between the date of the elimination or reduction in coverage and the date of the qualifying event the coverage is modified for similarly situated non-COBRA beneficiaries, the modified coverage must be made available to the qualified beneficiary.

Military Leave

If an employee is called to active military duty, and the health plan under which the employee is covered is subject to COBRA and the employer does not voluntarily maintain continuation coverage for employees, then the employee will experience a qualifying event. The plan administrator must then offer the employee and the employee's covered dependents the right to elect COBRA coverage. Qualified beneficiaries must receive a notice of their COBRA rights. Employers that voluntarily maintain coverage under their health plans for employees on military duty are not required to offer COBRA.

The Uniformed Services Employment and Re-Employment Rights Act of 1994 (USERRA) provides for health benefit continuation for people who are absent from work to serve in the military, even when COBRA does not cover the employer. Under USERRA, all employer-sponsored health care plans are required to provide COBRA-type coverage for up to 24 months after the employee's absence begins due to military service or for the period of uniformed service. Specifically, the maximum period of coverage for an employee and their dependents is the lesser of 24 months beginning on the date the employee's absence began or the day after the date on which the employee failed to apply for or return to a position of employment. Additionally, employees or dependents that elect this coverage may be required to pay a premium similar to COBRA (no more than 10 percent of the full premium under the plan). However, a person who performs military service for less than 31 days may not be required to pay more than the employee share, if any, for coverage.

Benefits Under Continuation Coverage

COBRA continuation coverage must be identical to the coverage that is currently available under the plan to similarly situated individuals who are covered under the plan and not receiving continuation coverage. Generally, this is the same coverage that the qualified beneficiary had immediately before the qualifying event. A qualified beneficiary receiving continuation coverage must receive the same benefits, choices, and services that a similarly situated participant or beneficiary is currently receiving under the plan, such as the right during an open enrollment season to choose among available coverage options. The qualified beneficiary is also subject to the same plan rules and limits that would apply to a similarly situated participant or beneficiary, such as co-payment requirements, deductibles, and coverage limits. The plan's rules for filing benefit claims and appealing any claims denials also apply.

Any changes made to the plan's terms that apply to similarly situated active employees and their families will also apply to qualified beneficiaries receiving COBRA continuation coverage. If a child is born to or adopted by a covered employee during a period of continuation coverage, the child is automatically considered to be a qualified beneficiary receiving continuation coverage. The plan must allow the child to be added to the continuation coverage.

Health Flexible Spending Accounts

Health flexible spending accounts (FSAs) must generally be offered under COBRA.

The applicable premium includes any employer subsidy and is computed based on the total cost of coverage, regardless of whether paid by the employer or employee. In addition, the spouse or dependent child experiencing a qualifying event is entitled to continue coverage under the FSA to the same extent they would after an employee's termination of employment if health care expenses incurred for a spouse or dependent child of an active employee can be reimbursed under a health FSA, but were it not for COBRA continuation coverage, would not be reimbursed after any of the following:

♦ The death of the employee.

♦ Divorce from the employee.

♦ Ineligibility of the dependent child.

The following two exceptions apply for health FSAs:

♦ COBRA does not need to be offered in the year in which a qualifying event occurs to qualified beneficiaries who have over spent their accounts as of the qualifying event date.

♦ COBRA must be offered to those qualified beneficiaries who have under spent their accounts, but need not be offered after the end of the year in which the qualifying event occurs.

Alternatives to COBRA Continuation Coverage

Those entitled to elect COBRA continuation coverage may have alternative options to COBRA coverage. One option may be special enrollment in other group health coverage.

Under the Health Insurance Portability and Accountability Act (HIPAA) and upon certain events, group health plans and health insurance issuers are required to provide a special enrollment period during which individuals who previously declined coverage for themselves and their dependents and who are otherwise eligible may be allowed to enroll without having to wait until the next open enrollment period. One event that triggers special enrollment is an employee or dependent of an employee losing eligibility for other health coverage. For example, an employee who loses group health coverage may be able to special enroll in a spouse's health plan. The employee or dependent must request special enrollment within 30 days of the loss of coverage.

If an employee or dependent chooses to elect COBRA instead of special enrollment upon a loss of group health coverage, the employee or dependent will have another opportunity to request special enrollment once COBRA has been exhausted. In order to exhaust COBRA coverage, the individual must receive the maximum period of COBRA coverage available without early termination. To special enroll after exhausting COBRA, an individual must request enrollment within 30 days of the loss of COBRA coverage.

In addition, individuals in a family may be eligible for health insurance coverage through various state programs.

Employee Moves

A COBRA beneficiary who moves outside the area served by an employer's region-specific plan — for example, a health maintenance organization (HMO) — must be provided an opportunity under special rules to elect alternative coverage available to any other active employee of the employer that can be extended to the place of relocation.

However, employers are not required to incur extraordinary costs to extend coverage to qualified beneficiaries in areas with no active employees. Additionally, there is no requirement to offer coverage where all coverage is region-specific and cannot be extended to the place of relocation.

Length of COBRA Coverage

Generally, the COBRA coverage period is 18 months. However, a covered spouse or dependent may be entitled to COBRA coverage for 36 months if the spouse or dependent loses coverage due to any of the following:

♦ The employee's death.

♦ Divorce or legal separation from the employee.

♦ The employee becomes entitled to Medicare.

Additionally, a covered child is entitled to 36 months of COBRA coverage if the child's loss of coverage is due to the child no longer being eligible for coverage as a dependent under the health plan.

Note: The COBRA period begins to run as of the date of the qualifying event, not the date coverage would be lost due to such event. For example, if an employer gratuitously extends medical coverage until the end of the month following termination of employment, the COBRA period would still begin to run as of the employee's termination date.

Disability Extensions

If one of the qualified beneficiaries in a family is disabled and meets certain requirements, all of the qualified beneficiaries in that family are entitled to an 11-month extension of the maximum period of continuation coverage (for a total maximum period of 29 months of continuation coverage). The plan can charge qualified beneficiaries an increased premium, up to 150 percent of the cost of coverage, during the 11-month disability extension.

For a disability extension, the following requirements must be met:

♦ The disabled qualified beneficiary must be determined by the Social Security Administration (SSA) to be disabled at some point during the first 60 days of continuation coverage.

♦ The disability must continue during the rest of the initial 18-month period of continuation coverage.

The disabled qualified beneficiary (or another person on the beneficiary's behalf) must also notify the plan of the SSA determination. The plan can set a time limit for providing this notice of disability; however, the time limit cannot be shorter than 60 days, starting from the latest of the following:

♦ The date on which the SSA issues the disability determination.

♦ The date on which the qualifying event occurs.

♦ The date on which the qualified beneficiary receives the COBRA general notice.

The right to a disability extension may be terminated if the SSA determines that the qualified beneficiary is no longer disabled, and the plan can require disabled qualified beneficiaries to provide notice when such a determination is made. The plan must give the qualified beneficiaries at least 30 days after the SSA determination in which to provide notice.

The rules for how to give a disability notice and a notice of no longer being disabled should be described in the plan's SPD (and in the election notice for any offer of an 18-month period of continuation coverage).

Second Qualifying Event Extensions

An 18-month extension may be available to qualified beneficiaries receiving an 18-month maximum period of continuation coverage (giving a total maximum period of 36 months of continuation coverage) if a qualified beneficiary experiences a second qualifying event that is any of the following:

♦ Death of the covered employee.

♦ Divorce or legal separation of the covered employee and spouse.

♦ Medicare entitlement.

♦ Loss of dependent child status under the plan.

The second event can be a second qualifying event only if it would have caused the qualified beneficiary to lose coverage under the plan in the absence of the first qualifying event. The plan should have rules for how a notice of second qualifying event should be provided, and these rules should be described in the plan's SPD (and in the election notice for any offer of an 18-month period of continuation coverage).

Conversion Plans

Although COBRA specifies certain periods of time that continued health coverage must be offered to qualified beneficiaries, COBRA does not prohibit plans from offering continuation health coverage that goes beyond the COBRA periods.

Some plans allow participants and beneficiaries to convert group health coverage to an individual policy. If this option is available from the plan, participants and beneficiaries have the right to exercise this option under COBRA when their COBRA continuation coverage ends. The option must be given to enroll in a conversion health plan within 180 days before COBRA coverage ends. The premium for a conversion policy may be more expensive than the premium of a group plan, and the conversion policy may provide a lower level of coverage. However, the conversion option is **not** available if the beneficiary ends COBRA coverage before reaching the end of the maximum period of COBRA coverage.

The right to enroll in a conversion plan at the end of the COBRA period must be offered to a qualified beneficiary if the right is available to active employees under the plan. Open enrollment periods must be allowed for continuants on the same basis as for active employees. Continuants must be offered a conversion privilege at the end of the 18- or 36-month period. Additionally, employers must allow existing COBRA continuants to continue coverage as long as they meet the eligibility requirements, even if the employee group size falls below 20 full-time and/or part-time employees. If a conversion option is not generally available, it need not be offered to a qualified beneficiary.

Termination of COBRA Coverage

Once COBRA coverage has been elected, it can be terminated before the end of the maximum coverage period for any of the following reasons:

♦ The failure of the qualified beneficiary to pay the required premium. There is a minimum 30-day grace period for payment of premiums.

♦ The beneficiary becomes entitled to benefits under Medicare (either Part A or B) after the date COBRA coverage is elected.

♦ The employer stops offering any group health plan to any employee.

♦ The beneficiary becomes covered by another group health plan, but only if the following apply:

- The beneficiary becomes covered under the other group health plan after COBRA coverage is elected.

- The other plan does not contain any exclusion or limitation with respect to a pre-existing condition of the qualified beneficiary (or the exclusion is waived under the HIPAA creditable service rules).

Example 1: Employer X maintains a group health plan subject to COBRA. C is an employee covered under the plan. C is also covered under a group health plan maintained by Employer Y, the employer of C's spouse. C terminates employment (for reasons other than gross misconduct), and the termination of employment causes C to lose coverage under X's plan (and, thus, is a qualifying event). C elects to receive COBRA continuation coverage under X's plan.

Under these facts, X's plan cannot terminate C's COBRA continuation coverage on the basis of C's coverage under Y's plan.

Example 2: Employer W maintains a group health plan subject to COBRA. D is an employee covered under the plan. D terminates employment (for reasons other than gross misconduct), and the termination of employment causes D to lose coverage under W's plan (and, thus, is a qualifying event). D elects to receive COBRA continuation coverage under W's plan. Later D becomes employed by Employer V and is covered under V's group health plan. D's coverage under V's plan is not subject to any exclusion or limitation with respect to any pre-existing condition of D.

Under these facts, W can terminate D's COBRA continuation coverage on the date D becomes covered under V's plan.

Example 3: The facts are the same as in Example 2, except that D becomes employed by V and becomes covered under V's group health plan before D elects COBRA continuation coverage under W's plan.

Because the termination of employment is a qualifying event, D must be offered COBRA continuation coverage under W's plan, and W is not permitted to terminate D's COBRA continuation coverage on account of D's coverage under V's plan because D first became covered under V's plan before COBRA continuation coverage was elected for D.

Beneficiaries

An employer can terminate a beneficiary's coverage for cause on the same basis that it would terminate the coverage of a non-COBRA beneficiary. For example, if a plan terminates the coverage of active employees who submit fraudulent claims, a qualified beneficiary's coverage can also be terminated for submission of a fraudulent claim.

Beneficiaries that become covered by another group health plan or by Medicare before the COBRA coverage would otherwise end usually lose the right to COBRA coverage. However, beneficiaries will not lose the right to COBRA coverage if the new group health plan does not cover illnesses or conditions due to their pre-existence before the beneficiary became covered under the new plan.

If an individual who is not a qualified beneficiary has coverage only because of the relationship to a qualified beneficiary, that individual's coverage can be terminated whenever the qualified beneficiary's coverage ceases.

COBRA Notice and Election Procedures

COBRA requires that group health plans provide covered employees and their families with specific notices explaining their COBRA rights. Additionally, covered employees and their families must also be provided the rules for how COBRA coverage is offered, how qualified beneficiaries may elect continuation coverage, and when coverage may be terminated.

Notice Procedures

Summary Plan Description

The COBRA rights provided under the plan, like other important plan information, must be described in the plan's summary plan description (SPD). The SPD is a written document that provides important information about the plan, including the following:

- The benefits available under the plan.

- The rights of participants and beneficiaries under the plan.

- How the plan works.

ERISA requires that group health plans provide an SPD to each participant within 90 days after the individual first becomes a participant in a plan (or within 120 days after the plan is first subject to the reporting and disclosure provisions of ERISA). In addition, if there are material changes to the plan, the plan must give participants a summary of material modifications (SMM) no later than 210 days after the end of the plan year in which the changes become effective.

If the change is a material reduction in covered services or benefits, the SMM must be furnished no later than 60 days after the reduction is adopted. A participant or beneficiary covered under the plan may request a copy of the SPD and any SMMs (as well as any other plan documents), which must be provided within 30 days of a written request.

COBRA General Notice

Group health plans must give each employee and each spouse of an employee who becomes covered under the plan a general notice describing COBRA rights. The general notice must be provided within the first 90 days of coverage. Group health plans can satisfy this requirement by including the general notice in the plan's SPD and giving the SPD to the employee and to the spouse within this time limit.

The general notice must include the following:

- The name of the plan and the name, address, and telephone number of an individual to contact for more information on COBRA and the plan.

- A general description of the continuation coverage provided under the plan.

- An explanation of what qualified beneficiaries must do to notify the plan of qualifying events or disabilities.

- An explanation of the importance of keeping the plan administrator informed of addresses of the participants and beneficiaries.

- A statement that the general notice does not fully describe COBRA or the plan and that more complete information is available from the plan administrator and in the SPD.

The U.S. Department of Labor has developed a model general notice that single-employer group health plans may use to satisfy the general notice requirement. It is available at the Employee Benefits Security Administration (EBSA) Web site located at *www.dol.gov/ebsa*. In order to use this model general notice properly, the plan administrator must fill in the blanks with the appropriate plan information. Use of the model general notice, appropriately completed, will be considered by the department to be good faith compliance with the general notice content requirements of COBRA.

COBRA Qualifying Event Notice

Before a group health plan must offer continuation coverage, a qualifying event must occur. The group health plan is not required to act until receipt of an appropriate notice of a qualifying event.

The employer is required to notify the plan if the qualifying event is one of the following:

- Termination or reduction in hours of employment of the covered employee.
- Death of the covered employee.
- Covered employee becoming entitled to Medicare.

The employer has 30 days after the event occurs to provide notice to the plan.

The covered employee or one of the qualified beneficiaries is responsible for notifying the plan if the qualifying event is one of the following:

- Divorce.
- Legal separation.
- A child's loss of dependent status under the plan.

Group health plans are required to have procedures for how the covered employee or one of the qualified beneficiaries can provide notice of these types of qualifying events. The procedures must give covered employees and qualified beneficiaries at least 60 days after the qualifying event occurs to give notice. Additionally, the procedures must describe the following:

- How and to whom notice should be given.
- What information must be included in the qualifying event notice.

If one person gives notice of a qualifying event, the notice covers all qualified beneficiaries affected by that event.

If a group health plan does not have reasonable procedures for how to provide these notices, qualified beneficiaries are permitted to give notice (either written or oral) to the person or unit at the workplace that handles the employees' benefits matters. If the plan is a multi-employer plan, notice can also be given to the joint board of trustees. If the plan is administered by an insurance company (or the benefits are provided through insurance), notice can be given to the insurance company.

COBRA Election Notice

After receiving a notice of a qualifying event, the plan must provide the qualified beneficiaries with an election notice. An election notice describes qualified beneficiaries rights to continuation coverage and how to make an election for continuation coverage. The election notice must be provided to the qualified beneficiaries within 14 days after the plan administrator receives the notice of a qualifying event.

The election notice must include the following:

- The name of the plan and the name, address, and telephone number of the plan's COBRA administrator.
- Identification of the qualifying event.
- Identification of the qualified beneficiaries (by name or by status).
- An explanation of the qualified beneficiaries' right to elect continuation coverage.
- The date coverage will terminate (or has terminated) if continuation coverage is not elected.
- How to elect continuation coverage.
- What will happen if continuation coverage is not elected or is waived.
- What continuation coverage is available, for how long, and (if it is for less than 36 months) how it can be extended for disability or second qualifying events.

- How continuation coverage might terminate early.

- Premium payment requirements, including due dates and grace periods.

- A statement of the importance of keeping the plan administrator informed of the addresses of qualified beneficiaries.

- A statement that the election notice does not fully describe COBRA or the plan and that more information is available from the plan administrator and in the SPD.

The U.S. Department of Labor has developed a model election notice that plans may use to satisfy their obligation to provide the election notice. In order to use this model election notice properly, the plan administrator must fill in the blanks with the appropriate plan information. Use of the model election notice, appropriately completed, will be considered by the department to be good faith compliance with the election notice content requirements of COBRA.

COBRA Notice of Unavailability of Continuation Coverage

Group health plans may sometimes deny a request for continuation coverage or for an extension of continuation coverage when the plan determines the requester is not entitled to receive such coverage or extension. When a group health plan decides to deny a request for continuation coverage from an individual, the plan must give the individual a notice of unavailability of continuation coverage. The notice must be provided within 14 days after the request is received, and the notice must explain the reason for denying the request.

COBRA Notice of Early Termination of Continuation Coverage

Continuation coverage must generally be made available for a maximum period (18, 29, or 36 months). However, the group health plan may terminate continuation coverage early for several reasons. (*See* **Length of COBRA Coverage** section.) When a group health plan decides to terminate continuation coverage early for any of the aforementioned reasons, the plan must give the qualified beneficiary a notice of early termination. The notice must be given as soon as practicable after the decision is made and must describe the following:

- The date coverage will terminate.

- The reason for termination.

- Any rights the qualified beneficiary may have under the plan or applicable law to elect alternative group or individual coverage, such as a right to convert to an individual policy.

Special Rules for Multi-Employer Plans

Multi-employer plans are allowed to adopt some special rules for COBRA notices. First, a multi-employer plan may adopt its own uniform time limits for the qualifying event notice or the election notice. A multi-employer plan may also choose not to require employers to provide qualifying event notices, and instead to have the plan administrator determine when a qualifying event has occurred. Any special multi-employer plan rules must be set out in the plan's documents and SPD.

Electing COBRA Coverage

Election Procedures

COBRA requires that group health plans provide qualified beneficiaries an election period during which they may decide whether to elect continuation coverage. Additionally, COBRA provides qualified beneficiaries specific election of coverage rights. At a minimum, each qualified beneficiary must be given at least 60 days to choose whether or not to elect COBRA coverage, beginning from the later of the following:

♦ The date the election notice is provided.

♦ The date on which the qualified beneficiary would otherwise lose coverage under the group health plan due to the qualifying event.

Each qualified beneficiary must be given an independent right to elect continuation coverage. Accordingly, when several individuals (such as an employee, the employee's spouse, and their dependent children) become qualified beneficiaries due to the same qualifying event, each individual is entitled to their own, separate election choice. However, the plan must allow the covered employee or the covered employee's spouse to elect continuation coverage on behalf of all of the other qualified beneficiaries for the same qualifying event. A parent or legal guardian of a qualified beneficiary must also be allowed to elect on behalf of a minor child.

If a qualified beneficiary waives continuation coverage during the election period, the individual must be permitted to later revoke the waiver of coverage and elect continuation coverage, as long as the revocation is done before the end of the election period. However, if a waiver is later revoked, the plan is permitted to make continuation coverage begin on the date the waiver was revoked.

Example 1: An unmarried employee without children who is receiving employer-paid coverage under a group health plan voluntarily terminates employment on June 1, 2009. The employee is not disabled at the time of the termination of employment or at any time thereafter, and the plan does not provide for the extension of the required periods.

Case 1: If the plan provides that the employer-paid coverage ends immediately upon the termination of employment, the election period must begin not later than June 1, 2009, and must not end earlier than July 31, 2009. If notice of the right to elect COBRA continuation coverage is not provided to the employee until June 15, 2009, the election period must not end earlier than August 14, 2009.

Case 2: If the plan provides that the employer-paid coverage does not end until six months after the termination of employment, the employee does not lose coverage until December 1, 2009. The election period can therefore begin as late as December 1, 2009, and must not end before January 30, 2010.

If employer-paid coverage for six months after the termination of employment is offered only to those qualified beneficiaries who waive COBRA continuation coverage, the employee loses coverage on June 1, 2009, so the election period is the same as in example one. The difference between case one and two is that in the first case the employee can receive six months of employer-paid coverage and then elect to pay for up to an additional 12 months of COBRA continuation coverage, while in the second case, the employee must choose between six months of employer-paid coverage and paying for up to 18 months of COBRA continuation coverage. In both cases, COBRA continuation coverage need not be provided for more than 18 months after the termination of employment.

If a covered employee or spouse of a covered employee makes a COBRA election that does not specify whether the election is for self-only coverage, the election covers all beneficiaries who lost coverage because of the same qualifying event. However, a beneficiary cannot decline coverage on behalf of another beneficiary.

Example 2: Employee H and H's spouse are covered under a group health plan immediately before H's termination of employment (for reasons other than gross misconduct). Coverage under the plan will end as a result of the termination of employment.

Upon H's termination of employment, both H and H's spouse are qualified beneficiaries and each must be allowed to elect COBRA continuation coverage. Therefore, H might elect COBRA continuation coverage while the spouse declines to elect such coverage or H might elect COBRA continuation coverage for both of them. In contrast, H cannot decline COBRA continuation coverage on behalf of H's spouse. Thus, if H does not elect COBRA continuation coverage on behalf of the spouse, the spouse must still be allowed to elect COBRA continuation coverage.

Special Second Chance to Elect COBRA for Trade-Dislocated Workers

Under the Trade Adjustment Assistance Reform Act of 2002 (TAA Reform Act), certain individuals who lose their job-based health coverage because of the impact of imports on their employers have a limited second chance to elect COBRA.

Such individuals qualify for the second COBRA election period if they meet any of the following criteria:

♦ Receive federal trade adjustment assistance benefits (or would be eligible to receive benefits except for the requirement that the person first exhaust unemployment benefits).

♦ Lost health coverage due to a termination of employment resulting in the person becoming eligible for trade adjustment assistance benefits.

♦ Did not elect COBRA coverage during the regular COBRA election period.

However, election of COBRA coverage under this second period must be made no later than six months after the date a person lost coverage as a result of separation from employment that resulted in the individual becoming eligible for benefits under the trade-adjustment legislation. Additionally, coverage elected during the second COBRA election period is retroactive only to the beginning of that election period rather than to the date of the initial loss of coverage.

Notice of a Qualifying Event

Generally, the employer or plan administrator must determine when a qualifying event has occurred. However, each covered employee or qualified beneficiary is responsible for notifying the plan administrator of the occurrence of a qualifying event that is either a dependent child's ceasing to be a dependent child under the generally applicable requirements of the plan, or a divorce or legal separation of a covered employee.

The group health plan is not required to offer the qualified beneficiary an opportunity to elect COBRA continuation coverage if the notice is not provided to the plan administrator within 60 days after the later of the following:

♦ The date of the qualifying event.

♦ The date the qualified beneficiary would lose coverage on account of the qualifying event.

If more than one qualified beneficiary would lose coverage on account of a divorce or legal separation of a covered employee, a timely notice of the divorce or legal separation that is provided by the covered employee or any one of those qualified beneficiaries will be sufficient to preserve the election rights of all of the qualified beneficiaries.

Coverage During the Election Period

Each qualified beneficiary must decide whether to elect COBRA continuation coverage within 60 days after the later of the following:

♦ The date the qualifying event would cause the individual to lose coverage.

♦ The date notice is provided to the qualified beneficiary of the individual's right to elect COBRA continuation coverage.

If the election is made during that 60-day period, coverage must be provided from the date that coverage would otherwise have been lost.

In the case of an indemnity or reimbursement arrangement, the employer or employee organization can provide for plan coverage during the election period or, if the plan allows retroactive reinstatement, the employer or employee organization can terminate the coverage of the qualified beneficiary and reinstate the individual when the election (and, if applicable, payment for the coverage) is made.

Claims incurred by a qualified beneficiary during the election period are not required to be paid before the election (and, if applicable, payment for the coverage) is made.

If a provider of health care (such as a physician, hospital, or pharmacy) contacts the plan to confirm coverage of a qualified beneficiary during the election period, the plan must give a complete response to the health care provider about the qualified beneficiary's COBRA continuation coverage rights during the election period.

For example, if the plan provides coverage during the election period but cancels coverage retroactively if COBRA continuation coverage is not elected, then the plan must inform a provider that a qualified beneficiary for whom coverage has not been elected is covered but that the coverage is subject to retroactive termination.

Similarly, if the plan cancels coverage but then retroactively reinstates it once COBRA continuation coverage is elected, then the plan must inform the provider that the qualified beneficiary currently does not have coverage but will have coverage retroactively to the date coverage was lost if COBRA continuation coverage is elected.

In the case of a group health plan that provides health services (such as an HMO or a walk-in clinic), the plan can require — with respect to a qualified beneficiary who has not elected and paid for COBRA continuation coverage — that the qualified beneficiary choose between the following:

- Electing and paying for the coverage.

- Paying the reasonable and customary charge for the plan's services, but only if a qualified beneficiary who chooses to pay for the services will be reimbursed for that payment within 30 days after the election of COBRA continuation coverage (and, if applicable, the payment of any balance due for the coverage).

In the alternative, the plan can provide continued coverage and treat the qualified beneficiary's use of the facility as a constructive election. In such a case, the qualified beneficiary is obligated to pay any applicable charge for the coverage, but only if the qualified beneficiary is informed that use of the facility will be a constructive election before using the facility.

Employee Revocation or Reinstatement

During the election period, if a qualified beneficiary waives COBRA continuation coverage, the waiver can be revoked at any time before the end of the election period.

Revocation of the waiver is an election of COBRA continuation coverage. However, if a waiver of COBRA continuation coverage is later revoked, coverage need not be provided retroactively (that is, from the date of the loss of coverage until the waiver is revoked).

Waivers and revocations of waivers are considered made on the date they are sent to the employer, employee organization, or plan administrator, as applicable.

Withholding Money or Benefits

An employer or employee organization may not withhold money or other benefits owed to a qualified beneficiary until the qualified beneficiary either waives COBRA continuation coverage, elects and pays for coverage, or allows the election period to expire.

An employer must not withhold money or other benefits to which a qualified beneficiary is otherwise entitled (by operation of law or other agreement) in order to compel payment for COBRA continuation coverage or to coerce the qualified beneficiary to give up rights to COBRA continuation coverage (including the right to use the full election period to decide whether to elect coverage). Such a withholding constitutes a failure to comply with the COBRA continuation coverage requirements. Furthermore, any purported waiver obtained by means of such a withholding is invalid.

Paying for Continuation Coverage

Payment During the Election Period

Some plans, such as HMOs or walk-in clinics, provide health services directly. A beneficiary who seeks services before electing COBRA may either pay for COBRA coverage or pay the reasonable and customary charge for the services.

If the beneficiary pays for the services, the person must be reimbursed within 30 days after the COBRA election is made and full payment for coverage is received. Alternatively, with notice to the beneficiary, COBRA may treat the use of the services as a constructive (implicit) COBRA election. In that case, the beneficiary must pay the COBRA premium.

Regular Payment for COBRA Coverage

Group health plans can require qualified beneficiaries to pay for COBRA continuation coverage, although plans can choose to provide continuation coverage at a reduced cost or no cost.

The maximum amount charged to qualified beneficiaries cannot exceed 100 percent of the cost to the plan for similarly situated individuals covered under the plan who have not incurred a qualifying event. In calculating premiums for continuation coverage, a plan can include the costs paid by both the employee and the employer, plus an additional 2 percent for administrative costs. All of the necessary information about COBRA premiums, when they are due, and the consequences of payment and nonpayment should be described in the COBRA election notice. For disabled qualified beneficiaries receiving the 11-month disability extension of continuation coverage, the premium for those additional months may be increased to 150 percent of the plan's total cost of coverage.

COBRA charges to qualified beneficiaries may be increased if the cost to the plan increases; however, they generally must be fixed in advance of each 12-month premium cycle. The plan must allow qualified beneficiaries to pay the required premiums on a monthly basis if so requested and may allow payments at other intervals (for example, weekly or quarterly).

Qualified beneficiaries cannot be required to pay a premium in connection with making the COBRA election. Plans must provide at least 45 days after the election (that is, the date the qualified beneficiary mails the election form if using first-class mail) for making an initial premium payment. If a qualified beneficiary fails to make any payment before the end of the initial 45-day period, the plan can terminate the qualified beneficiary's COBRA rights. The plan should establish due dates for any premiums for subsequent periods of coverage, but must provide a minimum 30-day grace period for each payment.

Nonpayment or Late Payment

A plan may cancel coverage for the failure to pay for coverage on time. However, the regulations state that a payment is timely if it is made within 30 days of the payment due date, and a longer grace period may be allowed depending on the plan terms that apply to similarly situated non-COBRA beneficiaries. Once the payment is received, the coverage must be retroactively reinstated to the beginning of the period of coverage.

Partial Payment

Payment for coverage must be made on time and in full. However, if the amount of the payment made to the plan is made in error but is not significantly less than the amount due, the plan is required to notify the beneficiary of the deficiency and grant a reasonable period (approximately 30 days) to pay the difference. Regulations provide that an underpayment is not significant if the underpayment does not exceed $50 or 10 percent of the amount due — whichever is less. The plan is not obligated to send monthly premium notices to beneficiaries.

Federal Income Tax Credit

Certain individuals may be eligible for a federal income tax credit that can alleviate the financial burden of monthly COBRA premium payments. The TAA Reform Act created the Health Coverage Tax Credit (HCTC), an advanceable, refundable tax credit for up to 65 percent of the premiums paid for specified types of health insurance coverage (including COBRA continuation coverage). The HCTC is available to certain workers who lose their jobs due to the effects of international trade and who qualify for TAA Reform Act protections, as well as certain individuals who are receiving pension payments from the Pension Benefit Guaranty Corporation (PBGC). Individuals who are eligible for the HCTC may choose to have the amount of the credit paid on a monthly basis to their health coverage provider as it becomes due or may claim the tax credit on their income tax returns at the end of the year.

Coordination with Other Benefit Laws

FMLA

The FMLA requires an employer to maintain coverage under any group health plan for an employee on FMLA leave under the same conditions coverage would have been provided if the employee had continued working. Group health coverage that is provided under the FMLA during a family or medical leave is **not** COBRA continuation coverage and taking FMLA leave is **not** a qualifying event under COBRA. However, a COBRA-qualifying event may occur when an employer's obligation to maintain health benefits under the FMLA ceases, such as when an employee taking FMLA leave decides not to return to work and notifies an employer of the employee's intent to not return to work.

HIPAA

HIPAA requires that a group health plan or health insurance issuer automatically provide a certificate of health coverage to individuals entitled to elect COBRA continuation coverage at a time no later than when a notice is required to be provided for a qualifying event under COBRA, and to individuals who elected COBRA coverage during the following times:

- ◆ Within a reasonable time after learning that the COBRA coverage has ceased.

- ◆ Within a reasonable time after the end of the grace period for payment of COBRA premiums.

Under HIPAA, upon certain events, group health plans and health insurance issuers are required to provide a special enrollment period during which an individual who previously declined coverage for themselves and/or their dependents may be allowed to enroll without having to wait until the next open enrollment period, regardless of whether the plan has open enrollment or when the next open enrollment period begins.

When an employee or dependent of an employee loses eligibility for other health coverage, a special enrollment right may be triggered. If the other health coverage was COBRA, special enrollment can be requested only after COBRA is exhausted.

Finally, under HIPAA any pre-existing condition exclusion period that would apply under a group health plan or group health insurance coverage generally is reduced by an individual's number of days of creditable coverage that occurred without a break in coverage of 63 days or more. For this purpose, most health coverage, including COBRA coverage, is creditable coverage.

TAA Reform Act

As previously mentioned, the TAA Reform Act amended COBRA to provide certain workers who lose their jobs due to the effects of international trade and who qualify for TAA Reform Act protections with a second opportunity to elect COBRA continuation coverage.

For more information about the operation and scope of the second COBRA election opportunity created by the TAA Reform Act, an employer can call the HCTC Customer Contact Center at 866-628-HCTC (4282) (TDD/TTY: 866-626-HCTC (4282)) or visit the HCTC Web site online at *www.irs.gov* by entering the keyword: "HCTC."

Expansion of COBRA Law in the American Recovery and Reinvestment Act of 2009

Responding to increasing unemployment from the dramatic downturn affecting all sectors of the economy, the U.S. Congress expanded the premium and notice obligations of employers under COBRA.

Provisions in the American Recovery and Reinvestment Act of 2009 (ARRA) created a federal COBRA premium subsidy for *assistance-eligible individuals* — covered employees and their dependents who were involuntarily terminated from their jobs from September 1, 2008 to May 31, 2010, and who were otherwise eligible for COBRA during this period.

These assistance-eligible individuals are only required to pay 35 percent of their COBRA premiums for a maximum of 15 months. The remaining 65 percent of the premium is paid by the employer, which is reimbursed through a reduction in federal payroll tax obligations. The COBRA subsidy is nontaxable to the assistance-eligible individual.

The new provisions also included the following:

- ♦ Second chance COBRA elections.

- ♦ New election options.

- ♦ Revised COBRA notices.

- ♦ Modified COBRA invoices.

- ♦ Interactions with payroll tax deposit mechanisms to fund the 65 percent subsidy.

- ♦ New reporting to the Secretary of the Treasury and assistance-eligible individuals.

- ♦ Adverse individual income tax consequences for assistance-eligible individuals who earn too much income in 2009 or 2010.

Subsidy Details
Amount of Subsidy

Under normal circumstances, an employer can charge qualified beneficiaries who have elected COBRA continuation coverage 102 percent of the total cost of coverage. However, for qualified beneficiaries covered by the ARRA an employer can charge the qualified beneficiary only 35 percent of the total COBRA premium. The employer must pay the remaining 65 percent of the cost and is reimbursed through a payroll tax credit.

Calculation of Premium Reduction

The premium used to determine the 35 percent share that must be paid by (or on behalf of) an assistance-eligible individual is the cost that would be charged to the assistance-eligible individual for COBRA continuation coverage if the individual were not an assistance-eligible individual.

If, without regard to the subsidy, the assistance-eligible individual is required to pay 102 percent of the applicable premium for continuation coverage, generally the maximum permitted under the federal COBRA rules, the assistance-eligible individual is required to pay only 35 percent of the 102 percent of the applicable premium.

However, if the premium that would be charged to the assistance-eligible individual is less than the maximum COBRA premium (for example, if the employer subsidizes the coverage by paying all or part of the cost), the amount actually charged to the assistance-eligible individual is used to determine the assistance-eligible individual's 35 percent share.

Coverage Eligible for Premium Reduction

The premium reduction is available for COBRA continuation coverage of any group health plan, except a flexible spending arrangement (FSA) under I.R.C. § 106(c) offered under a § 125 cafeteria plan. This includes vision-only or dental-only plans and "mini-med plans," whether or not the employer pays for a portion of the costs for active employees. However, the premium reduction is not available for continuation coverage offered by employers for nonhealth benefits that are not subject to COBRA continuation coverage, such as group life insurance.

Note: The premium reduction is available for COBRA continuation coverage under a health reimbursement arrangement (HRA). While an HRA may qualify as an FSA under § 106(c), the exclusion of FSAs from the premium reduction is limited to FSAs provided through a § 125 cafeteria plan, which would not include an HRA.

Note: The COBRA subsidy was extended twice. For further information see **COBRA Subsidy Extensions**.

Effective Date

The subsidy was available for any period of coverage beginning on or after February 17, 2009. In other words, if COBRA coverage was provided based on the first of each month, the subsidy was available beginning March 1, 2009.

Duration

If an individual is eligible for the COBRA subsidy, that eligibility will continue until the earliest of:

- ♦ Fifteen months following the date the individual is first eligible for the subsidy.

- ♦ The date that the eligible individual becomes eligible for Medicare benefits or health coverage under another group health plan (including, for example, a group health plan maintained by a new employer of the individual or a plan maintained by the employer of the individual's spouse).

  It is important to note that the subsidy ends on mere eligibility, whereas COBRA coverage ends when the individual is actually covered. However, the individual will remain eligible for the subsidy if the other group health plan provides only dental, vision, counseling, or referral services (or a combination of the foregoing), is a health flexible spending account or health reimbursement arrangement, or is coverage for treatment that is furnished in an on-site medical facility maintained by the employer and that consists primarily of first-aid services, prevention and wellness care, or similar care (or a combination of such care).

♦ The date the maximum continuation coverage period under COBRA expires. (The ARRA does not extend the maximum COBRA continuation coverage periods.).

♦ The assistance-eligible individual fails to pay the required 35 percent share of the COBRA premium.

Eligibility Requirements
Assistance-Eligible Individual

An individual must be an assistance-eligible individual to be eligible for the premium reduction.

Under ARRA, an assistance-eligible individual is generally an individual who:

♦ Is a qualified beneficiary as the result of an involuntary termination during the period from September 1, 2008 to May 31, 2010.

♦ Is eligible for COBRA continuation coverage related to a qualifying event.

♦ Elects the coverage.

In order to be a qualified beneficiary, the individual must be covered under the group health plan on the day before the involuntary termination.

For purposes of federal COBRA, an individual who loses group health coverage in connection with the termination of a covered employee's employment by reason of the employee's gross misconduct is not a qualified beneficiary and thus cannot be an assistance-eligible individual.

Involuntary Termination

An essential requirement for subsidy eligibility is that individuals must have been involuntarily terminated (other than for gross misconduct) from September 1, 2008 to May 31, 2010. Individuals who have COBRA-qualifying events other than involuntary termination, such as divorce or voluntary termination, are ineligible for the subsidy. The new law, however, failed to define "involuntary termination."

IRS Notice 2009-27 provided clarification on several issues regarding the COBRA subsidy, including the definition of involuntary termination. The notice broadly defines involuntary termination as being "a severance from employment due to the independent exercise of the unilateral authority of the employer to terminate the employment." Although the guidance focuses on employer action, it also recognizes certain employee-initiated terminations as being involuntary if the employee was terminated for good reason based on "employer action that causes a material negative change in the employment relationship."

The IRS further indicates that whether a termination is involuntary is based on all the facts and circumstances. For example, if a termination is designated as voluntary or as a resignation, but the facts and circumstances indicate that, absent such voluntary termination, the employer would have terminated the employee's services, and that the employee had knowledge that the employee would be terminated, the termination is involuntary.

More specifically, the notice sets forth the following situations which are likely to constitute an involuntary termination:

♦ The employer's failure to renew a contract at the time the contract expires, if the employee was willing and able to execute a new contract providing terms and conditions similar to those in the expiring contract and to continue providing the services.

- An employee-initiated termination from employment, if the termination from employment constitutes a termination for good reason due to employer action that causes a material negative change in the employment relationship for the employee.

- An involuntary reduction to zero hours, such as a lay-off, furlough, or other suspension of employment, resulting in a loss of health coverage.

- An employee's voluntary termination in response to an employer-imposed reduction in hours, if the reduction in hours is a material negative change in the employment relationship for the employee.

- A lockout initiated by the employer.

- An employer's action to end an individual's employment while the individual is absent from work due to illness or disability (although mere absence from work due to illness or disability before the employer has taken action to end the individual's employment status is not an involuntary termination).

- Retirement, if the facts and circumstances indicate that, absent retirement, the employer would have terminated the employee's services, and the employee had knowledge that the employee would be terminated.

- A termination for cause.

- Resignation as the result of a material change in the geographic location of employment for the employee.

- A termination elected by the employee in return for a severance package (a "buy-out") where the employer indicates that after the offer period for the severance package, a certain number of remaining employees in the employee's group will be terminated.

An involuntary termination generally does not include:

- A work stoppage as the result of a strike initiated by employees or their representatives (however, a lockout initiated by the employer is an involuntary termination).

- Qualifying events such as divorce or a dependent child ceasing to be a dependent child under the generally applicable requirements of the plan (such as loss of dependent status due to aging out of eligibility).

- Death of an employee or absence from work due to illness or disability.

Dependent Coverage

The 65 percent subsidy also applies to any family members who independently elect COBRA due to an involuntary termination of employment of an assistance-eligible individual.

State Law Continuation Coverage

Individuals are eligible for the COBRA premium subsidy if they are entitled to continued health coverage under a comparable state law, even when they are not entitled to federal COBRA (due to, for example, the small employer exception to federal COBRA).

Comparable continuation coverage under state law does not include every state law right to continue health coverage, such as a right to continue coverage with no rules that limit the maximum premium that can be charged with respect to such coverage. To be comparable, the right generally must be to continue substantially similar coverage as was provided under the group health plan (or substantially similar coverage as is provided to similarly situated beneficiaries) at a monthly cost that is based on a specified percentage of the group health plan's cost of providing such coverage.

A different period of continuation coverage under state continuation coverage programs does not disqualify the state program from being comparable. For example, the fact that a state continuation coverage program only provides for six months of continuation coverage (instead of 18 months) would not result in the state program failing to be comparable. Similarly, state programs providing for different qualifying events, different qualified beneficiaries, or different maximum premiums generally do not fail to be comparable solely for those reasons.

Domestic Partner

The subsidy apparently does not apply to the cost of any COBRA-like coverage offered to domestic partners, civil union partners, or same-sex spouses unless they are dependents under the modified terms of IRC § 152.

Income Limitations

An assistance-eligible individual will be entitled to the subsidy, if during the year in which the subsidy would be received, the individual has adjusted gross income that exceeds $145,000 (or $290,000 if filing a joint return); however, there are income tax implications for taking the subsidy. For an individual with adjusted gross income between $125,000 and $145,000 ($250,000 to $290,000 for joint filers), the amount of the individual income tax liability is reduced.

The ARRA applies the income limitation by requiring that the assistance-eligible individual repay the subsidy on the individual's federal income tax return. Thus, it is not necessary for the employer or other plan sponsor providing COBRA coverage to determine whether the assistance-eligible individual's adjusted gross income exceeds the income limitation.

A plan cannot refuse to provide the premium reduction to an individual because of the individual's income. Even if an assistance-eligible individual's income is high enough that the recapture of the premium reduction would apply, COBRA continuation coverage must be provided upon payment of 35 percent of the premium unless the individual has notified the plan that the individual has elected the permanent waiver of the premium reduction, or the period for the premium reduction has ended.

An assistance-eligible individual who wants to make a permanent election to waive the right to the premium reduction makes the election by providing a signed and dated notification (including a reference to "permanent waiver") to the person who is reimbursed for the premium reduction. There is no separate additional notification to any government agency.

If an assistance-eligible individual makes the permanent election to waive the right to the premium reduction, the individual may not later reverse the election and may not receive the premium reduction for any future period of COBRA continuation coverage in 2009 or 2010, regardless of modified adjusted gross income in those years.

Special Election Period

Congress recognized that many individuals who were terminated may have declined to elect COBRA continuation coverage because of its cost. Accordingly, the act includes a special election opportunity for assistance-eligible individuals who were eligible to elect COBRA coverage when they were terminated from employment, but did not so elect. These individuals are entitled to an extended election period.

Important: This extended election period does not change the fact that the individual's termination from employment remains the qualifying event for purposes of COBRA.

The ARRA requires employers to attempt to locate former employees who previously declined COBRA and provide notice of the right to COBRA coverage with the government subsidy.

If an eligible individual elects COBRA continuation coverage during the special extended election period, COBRA coverage will commence with the first period of coverage beginning on or after the enactment of the ARRA, and is not retroactive to the original date that benefits terminated under the plan.

However, for purposes of determining the maximum COBRA coverage period, the date of the individual's involuntary termination of employment (or the date of the loss of coverage resulting from such termination, if applicable) will continue to be treated as the qualifying event. This means that the COBRA continuation coverage period available to an individual who makes an election during the extended election period will be determined based on the date of the qualifying event as previously described.

Effect on Pre-Existing Condition and Creditable Coverage Limitations

Under the Health Insurance Portability and Accountability Act (HIPAA) creditable coverage and pre-existing condition limitations rules, a plan may refuse to cover pre-existing conditions for a certain period of time for an individual who has a 63-day break in coverage. In the case of individuals who are able to take advantage of the second chance special election and who elect COBRA coverage during this new election period, the period of time beginning with the qualifying event and ending on the effective date of the newly elected COBRA coverage will not be counted as a break in coverage for purposes of this 63-day rule.

Option to Change Coverage

Under COBRA, a qualified beneficiary generally is entitled only to elect continuation of the same coverage option the individual was receiving on the day before the date of the qualifying event. However, the ARRA permits employers to be flexible, but does not require them to do so. Assuming different coverage options are available, an assistance-eligible individual may enroll in coverage under a plan that is different than the coverage in which the individual was enrolled at the time the qualifying event occurred. To make this change, the assistance-eligible individual must make an election change within 90 days after the notice is provided. Such election must be permitted by the employer if the employer has chosen to offer the option.

The premium for such coverage must not exceed the premium for the coverage in which the individual was enrolled prior to termination of employment.

In addition, the different coverage also must be offered to active employees at the time the election is made, and the different coverage may not be coverage providing only dental, vision, counseling, referral services (or a combination of these), or coverage under a flexible spending arrangement or coverage that provides services at certain on-site medical facilities.

Mechanism for Subsidy and Reimbursement
Payroll Tax Offsets

The stimulus plan contains a unique process for funding the 65 percent subsidy. Assistance-eligible individuals will only pay 35 percent of the ordinary COBRA premium directly to the employer, COBRA administrator, multi-employer plan, insurer, or government employer. After receipt of the subsidized payment, the recipient is directed to reduce its payroll tax deposits by an amount equal to the remaining 65 percent of the COBRA premium. For this purpose, payroll tax deposits represent federal income tax wage withholdings and the employer and employee share of FICA tax withholding. The employer (or other recipient of the 65 percent subsidy) will be treated as if it had paid payroll taxes to the Secretary of the Treasury in an amount equal to the subsidy.

For entities that offer COBRA coverage but do not collect payroll taxes, these entities (such as multi-employer plans) will receive a credit or refund check directly from the Secretary of the Treasury in an amount equal to the 65 percent subsidy.

Payment of the subsidy to an employer or another entity is not treated as income, but rather as an employee contribution to a group health care plan.

Reporting Requirements

Under the ARRA, a health plan or employer entitled to reimbursement for the subsidy must submit these reports to the Secretary of the Treasury:

♦ An attestation of involuntary termination of employment for each assistance-eligible individual for whom a reimbursement is claimed.

♦ A report of the amount of payroll taxes offset for the reporting period and estimated offsets of such taxes for the subsequent reporting period.

♦ A report containing the tax identification numbers of all assistance-eligible individuals, the amount of subsidy reimbursed with respect to each assistance-eligible individual, and a designation with respect to each assistance-eligible individual as to whether the subsidy reimbursement is for coverage of one individual or two or more individuals.

The act requires the Secretary of the Treasury to issue regulations or other guidance to assist employers and plans with reporting such information.

COBRA Subsidy Extensions

The COBRA subsidy first provided by the American Reinvestment and Recovery Act of 2009 was extended on December 21, 2009, and again on March 2, 2010 and April 15, 2010. The extensions were authorized by a provision in the 2010 Defense Appropriations Act (2010 DOD Act), the Temporary Extension Act of 2010 (TEA), and the Continuing Extension Act of 2010 (CEA). Employers should become familiar with these extensions and coordinate with their service providers to ensure appropriate steps are taken to implement the changes.

First Extension – 2010 DOD Act

On December 19, 2009, President Obama signed into law an extension and expansion of COBRA premium subsidy law that was due to expire on December 31, 2009. The law extended the following COBRA subsidy provisions:

♦ The subsidy eligibility period was expanded from December 31, 2009 to February 28, 2010. COBRA coverage was not required to begin by the end of the period (February 28). Instead, the person was an assistance eligible individual as long as the COBRA qualifying event (involuntary termination of employment) occurred by February 28, 2010 and the individual was entitled to COBRA coverage as a result of that event.

♦ The duration of subsidy coverage was increased from 9 months to 15 months.

The amendments also provided the following:

♦ A transition period for any assistance eligible individual for whom the premium subsidy applies due to the extension. The *transition period* consists of any period of coverage that begins before the extension's enactment date. Any period during which the applicable premium had been paid is to be treated as a period of coverage, irrespective of any failure to timely pay the applicable premium for such period.

♦ In the case of any premium for a period of coverage during an assistance eligible individual's transition period, the individual will be treated for purposes of any COBRA provision as having timely paid the premium amount if the individual both:

- Was covered under the COBRA coverage to which such premium relates for the period of coverage immediately preceding the transition period.

- Pays, not later than 60 days after the extension enactment date (or, if later, 30 days after the new notices are provided), the amount of the subsidized premium.

♦ In the case of an assistance eligible individual who, during their transition period, paid the full premium amount for such coverage without regard to the subsidy amount, ARRA's rules allowing for that individual to be reimbursed for the excess premiums apply.

Second and Third Extension – Temporary Extension Act of 2010 and Continuing Extension Act of 2010

On March 2, 2010, President Obama signed the TEA, which extended the 65 percent premium COBRA subsidy (due to expire February 28, 2010) through March 31, 2010. On April 15, 2010 the President signed the CEA, which extended the 65 percent premium COBRA subsidy through May 31, 2010. As combined, these extensions provided for all of the following:

♦ A person is an assistance eligible individual so long as the COBRA qualifying event (involuntary termination of employment) occurred during the period that began September 1, 2008 and ends on May 31, 2010.

♦ An involuntary termination that occurred on or after March 2, 2010 but by May 31, 2010 and followed a qualifying event that was a reduction of hours and that reduction in hours occurred at any time from September 1, 2008 through May 31, 2010 is also a qualifying event for purposes of the ARRA.

♦ The premium reduction continues to apply to periods of health coverage that began on or after February 17, 2009 and lasts for up to 15 months.

Note: All COBRA 65 percent assistance payment notices should be revised to reflect the most recent extension date.

Reduction in Hours

The act also overturns prior IRS interpretations by extending the COBRA 65 percent assistance payment provisions to an individual whose COBRA began with a reduction in hours on or after September 1, 2008, and who then suffers an involuntary termination of employment on or after March 2 and by May 31, 2010. For example, an individual who became eligible for and elected COBRA due to a reduction in hours occurring in September 2008, but who subsequently suffered an involuntary termination of employment on March 12, 2010, will be able to receive the COBRA 65 percent assistance payment beginning with the next period of coverage.

Continued Second Chance

The act extends the right of individuals to receive the COBRA 65 percent assistance payment even if they did not make (or made and discontinued) a COBRA election as a result of an initial reduction in hours occurring on or after September 1, 2008, if those individuals experienced an involuntary termination of employment on or after March 2 (and on or before May 31, 2010). Employers must identify these individuals and resolicit them for prospective COBRA benefits for the remainder of their original 18 months of COBRA.

Notices

Notices for individuals who were involuntarily terminated after experiencing a qualifying event of a reduction of hours must be provided by the administrator of the group health plan (or other entity) during the 60-day period beginning on the date of the involuntary termination of employment.

Right of Action and Penalty

The act created new rights for the appropriate secretary or an affected individual to bring a civil action (and obtain appropriate relief) to enforce a determination that an individual is entitled to the COBRA 65 percent assistance payment. The act also created a new $110 per day penalty, imposed by the appropriate secretary, upon employers or insurers that do not comply with a determination of the secretary that an individual is entitled to the COBRA 65 percent assistance payment.

Notices

The ARRA, as amended by the Continuing Extension Act of 2010 (CEA), mandates that plans notify certain current and former participants and beneficiaries about the COBRA premium reduction.

The department created model notices to help plans and employers comply with these requirements. Each model notice is designed for a particular group of qualified beneficiaries and contains information to help satisfy the ARRA's notice provisions, including those amended by the CEA.

Updated General Notice

Plans subject to the federal COBRA provisions must provide the updated *General Notice* to all qualified beneficiaries (not just covered employees) who experienced a qualifying event at any time from September 1, 2008 through May 31, 2010, regardless of the type of qualifying event, and who have not yet been provided an election notice. This model notice includes updated information on the premium reduction, as well as information required in a COBRA election notice.

Note: Individuals who experienced a qualifying event that was a termination of employment from April 1, 2010 through April 14, 2010 may not have been provided proper notice. Those individuals who have not been provided any notice must get the updated *General Notice* and receive the full 60 days from the date the updated notice is provided to make a COBRA election. Those individuals who have been provided a notice that did not include information related to the most recent extension must also be provided this updated information. Depending on the specific circumstances, either the *Supplemental Information Notice* or the *Notice of Extended Election Period* may be used.

Notice of New Election Period

Plans subject to continuation coverage provisions under federal or state law should provide, within 60 days of the date of the termination of employment, a *Notice of New Election Period* to all individuals who meet all of the following conditions:

♦ Experienced a qualifying event that was a reduction in hours at any time from September 1, 2008 through May 31, 2010.

♦ Subsequently experienced a termination of employment at any point from March 2, 2010 through May 31, 2010.

♦ Either did not elect continuation coverage when it was first offered or elected but subsequently discontinued the coverage.

Generally, individuals who experienced a qualifying event that consists of a reduction of hours and who, from March 2, 2010 through May 31, 2010, experienced an involuntary termination of employment must be provided this notice within 60 days of the event. Additionally, the CEA provides that for the April 1, 2010 through April 14, 2010 period, the notice requirement attaches to any termination of employment. The department strongly recommends that notice be provided to individuals who experienced any termination of employment because employers may be subject to civil penalties if it is later determined that the termination was involuntary and notice was not provided.

Supplemental Information Notice

Plans that are subject to continuation coverage provisions under federal or state law should provide the *Supplemental Information Notice* to all individuals who elected and maintained continuation coverage based on either of the following qualifying events:

♦ All qualifying events related to a termination of employment that occurred from March 1, 2010 through April 14, 2010 for which notice of the availability of the premium reduction available under ARRA was not given.

Plans must provide this notice to all individuals with a qualifying event related to any termination of employment if they have not already been provided notice of their rights under ARRA. This notice must be provided before the end of the required time period for providing a COBRA election notice.

♦ Reductions of hours that occurred during the period from September 1, 2008 through May 31, 2010 which were followed by a termination of the employee's employment that occurred on or after March 2, 2010 and by May 31, 2010.

Generally, individuals who experience an involuntary termination of employment from March 2, 2010 through May 31, 2010 after experiencing a qualifying event that consists of a reduction of hours must be provided this notice within 60 days of the termination of employment. However, as previously noted, the CEA requires plans to provide notices to all individuals with qualifying events related to any termination of employment that occurred from April 1, 2010 through April 14, 2010. In those cases, this notice must be provided before the end of the required time period for providing a COBRA election notice. Because employers may be subject to civil penalties if it is later determined that the termination was involuntary, the department strongly recommends that notice be provided to individuals who experienced any termination of employment.

Notice of Extended Election Period

Plans that are subject to continuation coverage provisions under federal or state law must provide, before the end of the required time period for providing a COBRA election notice, the *Notice of Extended Election Period* to all individuals who meet all of the following:

♦ Experienced a qualifying event that was a termination of employment at some time from April 1, 2010 through April 14, 2010.

♦ Were provided notice that did not inform them of their rights under ARRA, as amended by the CEA.

♦ Either chose not to elect COBRA continuation coverage at that time or elected COBRA but subsequently discontinued that coverage.

Updated Alternative Notice

Insurance issuers that offer group health insurance coverage that is subject to comparable continuation coverage requirements imposed by state law must provide the *Alternative Notice* to all qualified beneficiaries, not just covered employees, who have experienced a qualifying event through May 31, 2010. However, because continuation coverage requirements vary among states it should be further modified to reflect the requirements of the applicable state law. Issuers of group health insurance coverage subject to this notice requirement should feel free to use the model *Alternative Notice*, the model *Notice of New Election Period*, the model *Supplemental Information Notice*, the model *Notice of Extended Election Period*, or the model *General Notice* (as appropriate).

Additional Guidance

The Department of Labor has released the following information to assist employers in their obligations under the ARRA, as amended.

Frequently Asked Questions

Q What is COBRA?

A COBRA gives workers and their families who lose their health benefits the right to purchase group health coverage provided by the plan under certain circumstances. If the employer continues to offer a group health plan, the employee and his or her family can retain their group health coverage for up to 18 months by paying group rates. The COBRA premium may be higher than what the individual was paying while employed, but generally the cost is lower than that for private, individual health insurance coverage. The plan administrator must notify affected employees of their right to elect COBRA. The employee and the employee's family each have 60 days to elect the COBRA coverage; otherwise, all rights to COBRA benefits will be lost. COBRA generally does not apply to plans sponsored by employers with fewer than 20 employees. Many states have similar requirements for insurance companies that provide coverage to small employers. The premium reduction is available for insurers covered by these state laws.

Q What is the COBRA premium reduction?

A The American Recovery and Reinvestment Act of 2009 (ARRA), temporarily reduced the premium for COBRA or comparable State continuation coverage for eligible individuals. The Department of Defense Appropriations Act, 2010 (2010 DOD Act) amended ARRA to extend the period to qualify for the COBRA premium reduction, as well as extended the maximum period for receiving the subsidy an additional six months (from nine to 15 months). The Temporary Extension Act of 2010 (TEA) amended ARRA to further extend the period to qualify for the COBRA premium reduction, as well as added that an involuntary termination of employment is a qualifying event for purposes of ARRA if it was preceded by a qualifying event that was a reduction of hours. The Continuing Extension Act of 2010 (CEA) amended ARRA to further extend the period to qualify for the COBRA premium reduction until May 31, 2010. Additionally, under CEA an involuntary termination of employment that occurred on or after March 2, 2010 but by May 31, 2010 is a qualifying event for purposes of ARRA if it was preceded by a qualifying event that was a reduction of hours occurring at any time from September 1, 2008 through May 31, 2010.

Individuals who are eligible for COBRA coverage because of their own or a family member's involuntary termination from employment that occurred during the period from September 1, 2008 through May 31, 2010 and who elect COBRA may be eligible to pay a reduced premium. Eligible individuals pay only 35 percent of the premium for COBRA coverage under their plans for up to 15 months. This premium reduction is generally available for continuation coverage under the federal COBRA provisions, as well as for group health insurance coverage under comparable state continuation coverage laws.

Q How is eligibility determined for the premium reduction?

A ARRA makes the premium reduction available for *assistance eligible individuals*. To be considered an assistance eligible individual and receive reduced premiums, the individual must meet all of the following conditions:

- Must have a continuation coverage election opportunity ("qualifying event") related to an involuntary termination of employment that occurred at any time from September 1, 2008 through May 31, 2010.

- Must elect the coverage (within the appropriate timeframes).

- Must not be eligible for Medicare.

- Must not be eligible for coverage under any other group health plan, such as a plan sponsored by a successor employer or a spouse's employer.

Individuals who lost coverage because of a qualifying event that was a reduction of hours that occurred any time from September 1, 2008 through May 31, 2010 may be eligible for the premium reduction if the employee is then involuntarily terminated on or after March 2, 2010 and no later than May 31, 2010. There is also a new election opportunity for these individuals if they did not elect (or elected and discontinued) COBRA.

Note: A reduction of hours is a qualifying event when the employee and their family lose coverage because the employee, though still employed, is no longer working enough hours to satisfy the group health plan's eligibility requirements.

Q   What are the notice requirements?

A   The ARRA, as amended, mandates that plans notify certain current and former participants and beneficiaries about the premium reduction. The Department of Labor provides model notices to help plans and individuals comply with these requirements. Each model notice will be designed for a particular group of individuals and will contain information to help satisfy ARRA's notice provisions, including those added by amendments.

Plan administrators must provide, as part of the COBRA election notice materials, a *General Notice* to all qualified beneficiaries, not just covered employees, who experienced a qualifying event at any time from September 1, 2008 through March 31, 2010, regardless of the type of qualifying event. Certain individuals who were provided a COBRA election notice package that did not include information that was updated to reflect the changes made to ARRA by the 2010 DOD Act must also be provided notice of these changes.

Individuals who were assistance eligible individuals as of October 31, 2009 (unless they are in a transition period) and individuals who experienced a termination of employment on or after October 31, 2009 and lost health coverage (unless they were already provided a timely, updated *General Notice*) must have been provided notice of the changes made to the premium reduction provisions of ARRA by the 2010 DOD Act by February 17, 2010.

Individuals who are in a transition period must be provided notice of the changes made to the premium reduction provisions of ARRA by the 2010 DOD Act within 60 days of the first day of the transition period. The transition period begins immediately after the end of the nine months of premium reduction in effect under ARRA before the amendments made by the 2010 DOD Act, as long as the premium reduction provisions of the 2010 DOD Act would apply due to the extension from 9 to 15 months.

Q   May individuals request an expedited review of denials of premium reduction?

A   Yes. Individuals who are denied treatment as assistance eligible individuals and thus are denied eligibility for the premium reduction (whether by their plan, employer, or insurer) may request an expedited review of the denial by the U.S. Department of Labor. The department must make a determination within 15 business days of receipt of a completed request for review.

Q   May an assistance eligible individual switch benefit options?

A   Yes. If an employer offers additional coverage options to active employees, the employer may (but is not required to) allow assistance eligible individuals to switch the coverage options they had when they became eligible for COBRA. To retain eligibility for the ARRA premium reduction, the different coverage must have the same or lower premiums as the individual's original coverage. The different coverage cannot be coverage that provides only dental, vision, a health flexible spending account, or coverage for treatment that is furnished in an on-site facility maintained by the employer.

Q   Are there income limits in relation to the premium reduction?

A   Yes. If an individual's modified adjusted gross income for the tax year in which the premium assistance is received exceeds $145,000 (or $290,000 for joint filers), then the amount of the premium reduction during the tax year must be repaid. For taxpayers with adjusted gross income between $125,000 and $145,000 (or $250,000 and $290,000 for joint filers), the amount of the premium reduction that must be repaid is reduced proportionately. Individuals may permanently waive the right to premium reduction but may not later obtain the premium reduction if their adjusted gross incomes end up below the limits.

Q   What is the new penalty provision?

A The TEA provided that the appropriate secretary may assess a penalty against a plan sponsor or health insurance issuer of up to $110 per day for each failure to comply with such secretary's determination 10 days after the date of the plan sponsor's or issuer's receipt of the determination.

HITECH Breach Notification

The U.S. Department of Health and Human Services (HHS) issued regulations requiring health care providers, health plans, and other entities covered by the Health Insurance Portability and Accountability Act (HIPAA) to notify individuals when their health information is breached. These breach notification regulations implement provisions of the Health Information Technology for Economic and Clinical Health Act (HITECH), passed as part of American Recovery and Reinvestment Act of 2009 (ARRA).

The regulations require health care providers and other HIPAA covered entities to promptly notify affected individuals of a breach, as well as the HHS Secretary and the media in cases where a breach affects more than 500 individuals. Breaches affecting fewer than 500 individuals will be reported to the HHS Secretary on an annual basis. The regulations also require business associates of covered entities to notify the covered entity of breaches at or by the business associate.

The regulations were developed after considering public comment received in response to an April 2009 request for information and after close consultation with the Federal Trade Commission (FTC), which has issued companion breach notification regulations that apply to vendors of personal health records and certain others not covered by HIPAA.

To determine when information is unsecured and notification is required by the HHS and FTC rules, the HHS also issued, in the same document as the regulations, an update to its guidance specifying encryption and destruction as the technologies and methodologies that render protected health information unusable, unreadable, or indecipherable to unauthorized individuals. Entities subject to the HHS and FTC regulations that secure health information as specified by the guidance through encryption or destruction are relieved from having to notify in the event of a breach of such information.

The Children's Health Insurance Program Reauthorization Act of 2009

The Children's Health Insurance Program Reauthorization Act of 2009 provides states with the option to subsidize premiums for qualified employer-sponsored health coverage of targeted low-income children (and their families) that are eligible for Medicaid or the Children's Health Insurance Program (CHIP). The child (or the child's parent) must voluntary elect to receive the subsidy and employers may opt out of receiving the subsidy directly, in which case the state would pay the employee.

Qualified employer-sponsored coverage must include an employer premium contribution of at least 40 percent. Health flexible spending arrangements and high-deductible health plans are excluded. Additionally, states are required to provide supplemental coverage to qualifying children who are enrolled in employer-sponsored coverage. The supplemental coverage consists of items or services that are not covered, or are only partially covered, under the employer-sponsored coverage.

The act also imposes on employers the following notice and disclosure requirements:

♦ **Notice to employees.** Employers sponsoring group health plans in states that provide such subsidies must furnish each employee with a written notice informing the employee of potential opportunities for premium assistance available in the state in which the employee resides. Employers must provide initial annual notices to employees beginning with the first plan year after the date on which the initial model notices are first issued. Employers may provide the notice at the same time they furnish materials regarding health plan eligibility or open enrollment, or concurrently with the furnishing of summary plan descriptions.

♦ **Disclosure to the state.** Upon request of the state, the plan administrator of a group health plan must disclose information about the benefits available under the plan, so that the state can determine the cost-effectiveness of providing premium assistance and provide supplemental benefits.

Failure to provide these required notices or disclosures may result in a civil penalty of up to $100 per day per employee or participant/beneficiary.

Model Notice

The U.S. Department of Labor provides a model CHIP notice on their Web site at *www.dol.gov/ebsa/chipmodelnotice.doc*. The model notice must be tailored to each particular plan(s) and must be distributed by the later of the first day of the first plan year beginning after February 4, 2010 or May 1, 2010 (January 1, 2011 for calendar year plans).

The Affordable Care Act and COBRA

The Affordable Care Act requires plans and issuers that offer coverage to children on their parents' plan to make the coverage available until the adult child reaches the age of 26. Key elements to the regulations that enforce the act include all of the following:

♦ **Coverage Extended to More Children.** The goal of the new policy is to cover as many young adults under the age of 26 as possible with the least burden. Plans and issuers that offer dependent coverage must offer coverage to enrollees' adult children until age 26, even if the young adult no longer lives with his or her parents, is not a dependent on a parent's tax return, or is no longer a student. There is a transition for certain existing group plans that generally do not have to provide dependent coverage until 2014 if the adult child has another offer of employer-based coverage aside from coverage through the parent. The new policy providing access for young adults applies to both married and unmarried children, although their own spouses and children do not qualify.

♦ **Effective for Plan or Policy Years Beginning On or After September 23, 2010.** Leading insurance companies have been asked to begin covering young adults voluntarily before the implementation date required by the Affordable Care Act (which is plan or policy years beginning on or after September 23rd). Early implementation would avoid gaps in coverage for new college graduates and other young adults and save on insurance company administrative costs of disenrolling and re-enrolling them between May 2010 and September 23, 2010. Over 65 companies have responded to this call saying they will voluntarily continue coverage for young adults who graduate or age off their parents' insurance before the implementation deadline.

♦ **All Eligible Young Adults Will Have a Special Enrollment Opportunity.** For plan or policy years beginning on or after September 23, 2010, plans and issuers must give children who qualify an opportunity to enroll that continues for at least 30 days regardless of whether the plan or coverage offers an open enrollment period. This enrollment opportunity and a written notice must be provided not later than the first day of the first plan or policy year beginning on or after September 23, 2010. The new policy does not otherwise change the enrollment period or start of the plan or policy year.

♦ **Same Benefits/Same Price.** Any qualified young adult must be offered all of the benefit packages available to similarly situated individuals who did not lose coverage because of cessation of dependent status. The qualified individual cannot be required to pay more for coverage than those similarly situated individuals. The new policy applies only to health insurance plans that offer dependent coverage in the first place; while most insurers and employer-sponsored plans offer dependent coverage, there is no requirement to do so.

Tax Benefits

Under a new tax provision in the Affordable Care Act, and an April 27, 2010 U.S. Treasury guidance, the value of any employer-provided health coverage for an employee's child is excluded from the employee's income through the end of the taxable year in which the child turns 26. This tax benefit applies regardless of whether the plan is required by law to extend health care coverage to the adult child or the plan voluntarily extends the coverage.

Key elements to the new tax provision include all of the following:

♦ **Tax Benefit Continues Beyond Extended Coverage Requirement.** While the Affordable Care Act requires health care plans to cover enrollees' children up to age 26, some employers may decide to continue coverage beyond the child's 26th birthday. In such a case, the act provides that the value of the employer-provided health coverage is excluded from the employee's income for the entire taxable year in which the child turns 26. Thus, if a child turns 26 in March but stays on the plan through December 31st (the end of most people's taxable year), all health benefits provided that year are excluded for income tax purposes.

♦ **Immediate Availability.** The tax benefits are effective March 30, 2010. The exclusion applies to any coverage that is provided to an adult child from that date through the end of the taxable year in which the child turns 26.

♦ **Broad Eligibility.** The expanded health care tax benefit applies to various workplace and retiree health plans. It also applies to self-employed individuals who qualify for the self-employed health insurance deduction on their federal income tax return.

♦ **Both Employer and Employee Shares of Health Premium Are Excluded from Income.** In addition to the exclusion from income of any employer contribution towards qualifying adult child coverage, employees can receive the same tax benefit if they contribute toward the cost of coverage through a cafeteria plan. This benefit is available immediately, even if the cafeteria plan document has not yet been amended to reflect the change. To reduce the burden on employers, they have until the end of 2010 to amend their cafeteria plan documents to incorporate this change.

The Federal Government and COBRA Enforcement

Continuation coverage laws are administered by several agencies. The U.S. Public Health Service administers the continuation coverage law as it affects public-sector health plans. The U.S. Departments of Labor and Treasury have jurisdiction over private health plans. However, the Department of Labor's interpretative and regulatory responsibility is limited to the disclosure and notification requirements. Both Departments of Labor and Treasury share jurisdiction for enforcement. The Internal Revenue Service (IRS) is responsible for publishing regulations on COBRA provisions relating to eligibility and premiums.

Employees who need further information on election or notification of rights with a private-sector plan should contact the nearest office of the Employee Benefits Security Administration (EBSA).

Contact Information

Department of Health and Human Services

200 Independence Avenue, SW
Washington, DC 20201

Telephone: 202-619-0257
Toll-Free: 877-696-6775
Internet: *www.hhs.gov*

Employee Benefits Security Administration

Frances Perkins Building
200 Constitution Avenue NW, Suite N-5619
Washington, DC 20210

Telephone (Employee and Employer Hotline): 866-444-EBSA (3272)
Internet: *www.dol.gov/ebsa*

National Association of Insurance Commissioners

2301 McGee Street, Suite 800
Kansas City, MO 64108

Telephone: 816-842-3600
Fax: 816-783-8175
Internet: *www.naic.org*

Illinois Law

Illinois' insurance regulations are located at 215 Ill. Comp. Stat. §§ 5/1 – 5/5, 5/352 – 5/370t (Illinois Insurance Code), 215 Ill. Comp. Stat. §§ 125/1-1 – 125/6-19 (Health Maintenance Organization Act), and 215 Ill. Comp. Stat. §§ 97/1 – 97/99 (Illinois Health Insurance Portability and Accountability Act).

Illinois does not require employers to provide health insurance for employees. However, employers that do provide insurance must be aware of specific coverage required to be included in health insurance policies and contracts.

General Coverage
Ambulance Services

No contract or evidence of coverage for basic health care services delivered, issued for delivery, renewed, or amended by a health maintenance organizations (HMO) may exclude coverage for emergency transportation by ambulance.

Amino Acid-Based Elemental Formulas

According to 215 Ill. Comp. Stat. § 5/356z.9, a group or individual major medical accident and health insurance policy or managed care plan amended, delivered, issued, or renewed after August 28, 2007 must provide coverage and reimbursement for amino acid-based elemental formulas. This coverage must be provided regardless of delivery method and must be for the diagnosis and treatment of eosinophilic disorders and short bowel syndrome when the prescribing physician has issued a written order stating that the amino acid-based elemental formula is medically necessary.

Blood Processing

No group hospital policy covering miscellaneous hospital expenses issued or delivered in Illinois may contain any exception or exclusion from coverage that would preclude the payment of expenses incurred for the processing and administration of blood and its components.

Bone Mass Measurement for Osteoporosis

According to 215 Ill. Comp. Stat. § 5/356z.6, group or individual policies of accident and health insurance amended, delivered, issued, or renewed on or after January 1, 2005 must provide coverage for medically necessary bone mass measurement and for the diagnosis and treatment of osteoporosis on the same terms and conditions that are generally applicable to coverage for other medical conditions.

Breast Cancer Pain Medication and Therapy

According to 215 Ill. Comp. Stat. § 5/356g.5-1, a group or individual policy of accident and health insurance or managed care plan that is amended, delivered, issued, or renewed on or after March 27, 2009 must provide coverage for all medically necessary pain medication and pain therapy related to the treatment of breast cancer on the same terms and conditions that are generally applicable to coverage for other conditions. *Pain therapy* is treatment that is medically based and includes reasonably defined goals, including, but not limited to, stabilizing or reducing pain, with periodic evaluations of the efficacy of the pain therapy against these goals.

These required pain medication and therapy coverage requirements do not apply to short-term travel, accident-only, limited, or specified-disease policies, or to policies or contracts designed for issuance to persons eligible for coverage under Medicare, or any other similar coverage under state or federal governmental plans.

Breast Implant Removal

According to 215 Ill. Comp. Stat. § 5/356p, no contract offered by HMOs nor any individual or group policy of accident and health insurance may deny coverage for the removal of breast implants when the removal of the implants is medically necessary treatment for a sickness or injury. Required coverage does not apply to surgery performed for removal of breast implants that were implanted solely for cosmetic reasons, but does apply to cosmetic surgery performed as reconstruction resulting from sickness or injury.

Clinical Breast Exams

According to 215 Ill. Comp. Stat. § 5/356g.5, clinical breast examinations are a critical tool in the early detection of breast cancer, while the disease is in its earlier and potentially more treatable stages. Insurer reimbursement of clinical breast examinations is essential to the effort to reduce breast cancer deaths in Illinois.

Consequently, every insurer must provide, in each group or individual policy, contract, or certificate of accident or health insurance issued or renewed for persons who are residents of Illinois, coverage for complete and thorough clinical breast examinations as indicated by guidelines of practice, performed by any of the following:

- A physician licensed to practice medicine in all branches.
- An advanced practice nurse who has a collaborative agreement with a collaborating physician that authorizes breast examinations.
- A physician assistant who has been delegated authority to provide breast examinations.

The breast exam must check for lumps and other changes for the purpose of early detection and prevention of breast cancer as follows:

- At least every three years for women at least age 20 but less than age 40.
- Annually for women 40 years of age or older.

Upon approval of a nationally recognized separate and distinct clinical breast exam code that is compliant with all state and federal laws, rules, and regulations, public and private insurance plans must take action to cover clinical breast exams on a separate and distinct basis.

Colorectal Cancer Screenings

According to 215 Ill. Comp. Stat. § 5/356x, an individual or group policy of accident and health insurance or a managed care plan that provides coverage to an Illinois resident must provide benefits or coverage for all colorectal cancer examinations and laboratory tests for colorectal cancer as prescribed by a physician.

The tests and examinations must be in accordance with the published American Cancer Society guidelines on colorectal cancer screening or other such existing guidelines issued by a nationally recognized professional medical society or federal governmental agency, including the National Cancer Institute, the Centers for Disease Control and Prevention, and the American College of Gastroenterology.

Additionally, coverage may not impose any deductive, co-insurance, waiting period, or other cost-sharing limitation that is greater than that required for other coverage under the policy.

Diabetes

According to 215 Ill. Comp. Stat. § 5/356w, a group policy of accident and health insurance delivered, amended, issued, or renewed in Illinois must provide coverage for outpatient self-management training and education, equipment, and supplies for the treatment of Type 1 and Type 2 diabetes and gestational diabetes mellitus.

Diabetes self-management training is instruction in an outpatient setting which enables a diabetic patient to understand the diabetic management process and daily management of diabetic therapy as a means of avoiding frequent hospitalization and complications. Diabetes self-management training includes the content areas listed in the National Standards for Diabetes Self-Management Education Programs as published by the American Diabetes Association, including medical nutrition therapy.

Coverage must be provided for regular foot care exams by a physician or by a physician to whom a physician has referred the patient. HMOs are also subject to these requirements.

Diethylstilbestrol

No accident or health insurance policy or any renewal may be denied or canceled by the insurer nor may the policy contain any exception or exclusion of benefits solely because the mother of the insured has taken diethylstilbestrol (DES).

Fibrocystic Conditions

According to 215 Ill. Comp. Stat. § 5/356h, the following are prohibited where solely based on the insured's diagnosis as having a fibrocystic breast condition:

- The insurer's denial of or renewal of a group or individual policy of accident or health insurance.

- A policy containing any exception or exclusion of benefits.

However, exceptions apply where the condition was diagnosed by a breast biopsy that demonstrates an increased disposition to the development of breast cancer or the insured's medical history confirms a chronic, relapsing, symptomatic breast condition.

Human Papillomavirus Vaccine

According to 215 Ill. Comp. Stat. § 5/356z.9, a group or individual policy of accident and health insurance or managed care plan amended, delivered, issued, or renewed after August 24, 2007 must provide coverage for a human papillomavirus vaccine (HPV) that is approved for marketing by the federal Food and Drug Administration (FDA).

Infertility

According to 215 Ill. Comp. Stat. § 5/356m, ***infertility*** is the inability to conceive after one year of unprotected sexual intercourse or the inability to sustain a successful pregnancy.

No group policy of accident and health insurance providing coverage for more than 25 employees that provides pregnancy-related benefits may be issued, amended, delivered, or renewed in Illinois unless the policy contains coverage for the diagnosis and treatment of infertility, including, but not limited to, all of the following:

- In vitro fertilization.

- Uterine embryo lavage.

- Embryo transfer.

- Artificial insemination.

- Gamete intrafallopian tube transfer and zygote intrafallopian tube transfer.

- Low tubal ovum transfer.

Coverage for infertility is subject to the following conditions:

- ◆ Coverage for procedures for in vitro fertilization, gamete intrafallopian tube transfer, or zygote intrafallopian tube transfer is required only in the following circumstances:

  - • The covered individual has been unable to attain or sustain a successful pregnancy through reasonable, less costly medically appropriate infertility treatments for which coverage is available under the policy, plan, or contract.

  - • The covered individual has not yet undergone four complete oocyte retrievals, except that if a live birth follows a completed oocyte retrieval, then two more completed oocyte retrievals must be covered.

  - • The procedures are performed at medical facilities that conform to the American College of Obstetrics and Gynecology guidelines for in vitro fertilization clinics or to the American Fertility Society minimal standards for programs of in vitro fertilization.

- ◆ The procedures required to be covered are not required to be contained in any policy or plan issued to a religious institution or organization or to an entity sponsored by a religious institution or organization that finds such procedures in violation of its religious and moral teachings and beliefs.

Intoxication and Narcotics

According to 215 Ill. Comp. Stat. § 367k, a group or individual major medical policy of accident or health insurance or managed care plan amended, delivered, issued, or renewed after January 1, 2008 may not, solely on the basis of the insured being intoxicated or under the influence of a narcotic, exclude coverage for any emergency or other medical, hospital, or surgical expenses incurred by an insured as a result of and related to an injury acquired while the insured is intoxicated or under the influence of any narcotic, regardless of whether the intoxicant or narcotic is administered on the advice of a health care practitioner.

This required coverage may be subject to all of the following:

- ◆ Deductibles, co-payments, and co-insurance.

- ◆ Annual or maximum payment limits that are consistent with deductibles, co-payments, and co-insurance.

- ◆ Annual or maximum payment limits applicable to other similar coverage under the plan.

Mammograms and Mastectomies

According to 215 Ill. Comp. Stat. § 5/356g, every contract or evidence of coverage issued by a health maintenance organization for individuals who are residents of Illinois and every group and individual insurance policy, contract, or certificate issued or renewed for Illinois residents must contain coverage for screening by low-dose mammography for all women 35 years of age or older for the presence of occult breast cancer.

A *low-dose mammography* is the X-ray examination of the breast using equipment dedicated specifically for mammography, including the X-ray tube, filter, compression device, and image receptor, with radiation exposure delivery of less than 1 rad per breast for two views of an average size breast. A low-dose mammography also includes digital mammography.

The coverage must be as follows:

- ◆ A baseline mammogram for any woman 35 to 39 years old.

- ◆ A mammogram every year for any woman 40 years or older.

♦ A mammogram at the age and intervals considered medically necessary by the woman's health care provider for women under age 40 years old with a family history of breast cancer, prior personal history of breast cancer, positive genetic testing, or other risk factors.

♦ A comprehensive ultrasound screening of an entire breast or breasts if a mammogram demonstrates heterogeneous or dense breast tissue, when medically necessary as determined by a physician licensed to practice medicine in all of its branches.

The mammography coverage must be provided at no cost to the insured and may not be applied to an annual or lifetime maximum benefit. However, the 'no cost' provision does not apply when health care services are available through contracted providers and a person does not comply with plan provisions specific to the use of contracted providers. When a person does not comply with plan provisions specific to the use of contracted providers, plan provisions specific to the use of noncontracted providers must be applied without distinction for required mammography coverage and must be at least as favorable as for other radiological examinations covered by the policy or contract.

No policy of accident or health insurance that provides for the surgical procedure known as a mastectomy may be issued, amended, delivered, or renewed in Illinois, unless coverage is also offered for prosthetic devices or reconstructive surgery incident to a mastectomy.

Coverage for breast reconstruction in connection with a mastectomy must include all of the following:

♦ Reconstruction of the breast upon which the mastectomy was performed.

♦ Surgery and reconstruction of the other breast to produce a symmetrical appearance.

♦ Prostheses and treatment for physical complications at all stages of mastectomy, including lymphedemas.

The coverage for prosthetic devices and reconstructive surgery is subject to the deductible and co-insurance conditions applied to the mastectomy and to all other terms and conditions applied to other benefits. When a mastectomy is performed and there is no evidence of malignancy, the offered coverage may be limited to the provision of prosthetic devices and reconstructive surgery within two years after the mastectomy.

An individual or group policy of accident and health insurance or managed care plan that provides surgical coverage must also provide inpatient coverage following a mastectomy. The inpatient coverage must be provided for a specified amount of time, as determined by the attending physician, to be medically necessary and in accordance with protocols and guidelines based on sound scientific evidence.

The duration of inpatient coverage must also be based upon the following:

♦ An evaluation of the patient.

♦ The coverage for and availability of either a post-discharge physician office visit or in-home nurse visit to verify the condition of the patient in the first 48 hours after discharge.

Required Notice

Written notice of the availability of coverage for mammograms and mastectomies must be delivered to the insured both upon enrollment and annually. An insurer may not deny to an insured eligibility or continued eligibility to enroll or to renew coverage under the terms of the plan solely to avoid required coverage.

Additionally, an insurer may not penalize, reduce, or limit the reimbursement of an attending provider or provide incentives (monetary or otherwise) to an attending provider to induce the provider to provide care to an insured in a manner inconsistent with the law.

Maternity Benefits and Newborn Care

According to 215 Ill. Comp. Stat. § 5/356s, a group policy of accident and health insurance that provides maternity coverage must provide coverage for the following:

♦ A minimum of 48 hours of inpatient care for the mother and her newborn following a normal vaginal delivery.

♦ A minimum of 96 hours of inpatient care for the mother and newborn following a delivery by Cesarean section.

A shorter hospital stay may be agreed upon between the mother and the attending physician if the mother and newborn meet the appropriate guidelines under the protocols developed by the American College of Obstetricians and Gynecologists and the American Academy of Pediatrics. The availability, within 48 hours, of a post-discharge physician's office visit or an in-home nurse visit to verify the condition of the infant is part of the decision for early departure from inpatient care.

A shorter length of hospital inpatient stay for services related to maternity and newborn care may be provided if the attending physician licensed to practice medicine in all of its branches determines (in accordance with the protocols and guidelines developed by the American College of Obstetricians and Gynecologists or the American Academy of Pediatrics) that the mother and the newborn meet the appropriate guidelines for that length of stay based upon **both** of the following:

♦ An evaluation of the mother and newborn.

♦ The coverage and availability of a post-discharge physician office visit or in-home nurse visit to verify the condition of the infant in the first 48 hours after discharge.

Prenatal HIV testing

A group policy of accident and health insurance that provides maternity coverage must provide coverage for prenatal HIV testing ordered by an attending physician licensed to practice medicine in all its branches, or by a physician assistant or advanced practice registered nurse who has a written collaborative agreement with a collaborating physician that authorizes these services. HMOs must also provide this coverage.

Multiple Sclerosis Preventative Physical Therapy

Under 215 Ill. Comp. Stat. § 125/5-3, a group policy of accident and health insurance or managed care plan amended, delivered, issued, or renewed after December 29, 2006, must provide coverage for medically necessary preventative physical therapy for insureds diagnosed with multiple sclerosis.

For the purposes of this section, *preventative physical therapy* means physical therapy that is prescribed by a physician licensed to practice medicine in all of its branches for the purpose of treating parts of the body affected by multiple sclerosis, but only where the physical therapy includes reasonably defined goals, including, but not limited to, sustaining the level of function the person has achieved, with periodic evaluation of the efficacy of the physical therapy against those goals.

The coverage required under this section is subject to the same deductible, co-insurance, waiting period, cost sharing limitation, treatment limitation, calendar year maximum, or other limitations as provided for other physical or rehabilitative therapy benefits covered by the policy. HMOs must also provide this coverage.

New Cancer Therapies

An insurer that issues, delivers, amends, or renews a group policy of accident and health insurance in Illinois must offer coverage for routine patient care of insureds, when medically appropriate and the insured has a terminal condition related to cancer that, according to the diagnosis of the treating physician, is considered life threatening, to participate in an approved cancer research trial, and must provide coverage for the patient care provided as part of investigational cancer treatments.

HMOs must also provide this coverage.

Organ Transplants

According to 215 Ill. Comp. Stat. § 5/356k, no contract or evidence of coverage issued by an HMO that provides coverage for health care services may deny reimbursement for an otherwise covered expense incurred for any organ transplantation procedure solely on the basis that the procedure is deemed experimental or investigational, unless either of the following applies:

♦ The theory that the procedure is either experimental or investigational is supported by the Office of Health Care Technology Assessment within the Agency for Health Care Policy and Research of the Department of Health and Human Services determination.

♦ There is insufficient data or experience to determine whether an organ transplantation procedure is clinically acceptable.

This also applies to accident and health insurers providing coverage for hospital or medical expenses.

Pap Tests and Prostate-Specific Antigen Tests

Under 215 Ill. Comp. Stat. § 5/536u, group insurers must provide coverage for all of the following:

♦ An annual cervical smear or Pap smear test for female insureds.

♦ An annual digital rectal exam and prostate-specific antigen test, for male insureds upon the recommendation of a physician licensed to practice medicine in all its branches for:

• Asymptomatic men age 50 and over.

• African-American men age 40 and over.

• Men age 40 and over with a family history of prostate cancer.

♦ Surveillance tests for ovarian cancer for female insureds who are at risk for ovarian cancer.

Prosthetic and Customized Orthotic Devices

According to 215 Ill. Comp. Stat. § 356z.18, a group or individual major medical policy of accident or health insurance or managed care plan or medical, health, or hospital service corporation contract that provides coverage for prosthetic or custom orthotic care must provide coverage for prosthetic and orthotic devices. Benefits must also be provided to any person for expenses incurred in obtaining a prosthetic or custom orthotic device from any Illinois licensed prosthetist, licensed orthotist, or licensed pedorthist as required under the Orthotics, Prosthetics, and Pedorthics Practice Act.

A *customized orthotic device* is a supportive device for the body or a part of the body, the head, neck, or extremities, and includes the replacement or repair of the device based on the patient's physical condition as medically necessary, excluding foot orthotics. A *foot orthotic* is an in-shoe device designed to support the structural components of the foot during weight-bearing activities. A *licensed provider* is a prosthetist, orthotist, or orpedorthist licensed to practice in Illinois. A *prosthetic device* is an artificial device to replace, in whole or in part, an arm or leg and includes accessories essential to the effective use of the device and the replacement or repair of the device based on the patient's physical condition as medically necessary.

Coverage for prosthetic or custom orthotic devices is subject to the other general exclusions, limitations, and financial requirements of the policy, including coordination of benefits, participating provider requirements, utilization review of health care services, including review of medical necessity, case management, and experimental and investigational treatments, and other managed care provisions under terms and conditions that are no less favorable than the terms and conditions that apply to substantially all medical and surgical benefits provided under the plan or coverage. The policy, plan, or contract may require prior authorization for the prosthetic or orthotic devices in the same manner that prior authorization is required for any other covered benefit. Repairs and replacements of prosthetic and orthotic devices are also covered, subject to the co-payments and deductibles, unless necessitated by misuse or loss.

A policy, plan, or contract may require that, if coverage is provided through a managed care plan, the mandated benefits are covered benefits only if both of the following apply:

- The prosthetic or orthotic devices are provided by a licensed provider who is employed by a provider service that contracts with or is designated by the carrier, to the extent that the carrier provides in-network and out-of-network service.

- The coverage for the prosthetic or orthotic device is offered no less extensively.

This required coverage does not apply to accident only, specified disease, short-term hospital or medical, hospital confinement indemnity, credit, dental, vision, Medicare supplement, long-term care, basic hospital and medical-surgical expense coverage, disability income insurance coverage, coverage issued as a supplement to liability insurance, workers' compensation insurance, or automobile medical payment insurance.

Qualified Cancer Trials

According to 215 Ill. Comp. Stat. § 5/364.01, no individual or group policy of accident and health insurance issued or renewed in Illinois may be cancelled or nonrenewed for any individual based on that individual's participation in a qualified clinical trial.

Qualified cancer trials must meet all the following requirements:

- The effectiveness of the treatment has not been determined relative to established therapies.

- The trial is under clinical investigation as part of an approved cancer research trial in Phase II, Phase III, or Phase IV of investigation.

- The trial is approved by the federal Food and Drug Administration (FDA) or approved and funded by the National Institutes of Health, the Centers for Disease Control and Prevention, the Agency for Health Care Research and Quality, the U.S. Department of Defense, the U.S. Department of Veterans Affairs, or the U.S. Department of Energy in the form of an investigational new drug application or a cooperative group or center of any such entity.

- The patient's primary care physician, if any, is involved in the coordination of care.

HMOs are also required to provide this coverage.

Recognition of Domestic Partnership

According to an Executive Order from the Treasurer of Illinois and effective June 13, 2010, within the State Treasurer's Office (office), all policies, benefits, and rights that are afforded and available to spouses are likewise extended to domestic partners. Therefore, for the purposes of all office policies, including but not limited to sick leave, bereavement leave, FMLA, maternity/paternity leave, the Victim's Economic Security and Safety Act (VESSA), employment of relatives, and Executive Order 07-01, the term *spouse* will be interpreted to include domestic partners even if not required by state and/or federal law. Similarly, any references to children and step-children will be understood to refer to the children of a domestic partnership, regardless of biological or adoptive status. References to in-laws will be understood to refer to the family of an employee's domestic partner.

Rehabilitation Services

According to 215 Ill. Comp. Stat. § 5/367d, no claim may be denied under any group accident and health policy delivered or renewed in Illinois for treatment or services for rehabilitation following either a physical or mental illness rendered in a hospital solely because the hospital lacks surgical facilities.

Sexual Assault/Abuse Victims

Contracts or evidences of coverage issued by a health maintenance organization that provides benefits for health care services must, to the full extent of coverage provided for any other emergency or accident care, provide for the payment of actual expenses incurred — without offset or reduction for benefit deductibles or co-insurance amounts — for the following:

♦ In the examination and testing of a victim of sexual assault or abuse or an attempt to commit such offense as follows:

  • To establish that sexual contact did or did not occur.

  • To establish the presence or absence of venereal disease or infection.

♦ In the examination and treatment of injuries and trauma sustained by a victim of such offense.

Similarly, no policy of accident and health insurance delivered or issued for delivery to any person in Illinois that provides benefits for hospital or medical expenses based upon the actual expenses incurred, other than a policy that covers hospital and medical expenses for specified illnesses or injuries only, may contain any specific exception to coverage that would preclude the payment under the policy of actual expenses incurred:

♦ In the examination and testing of a victim of a sexual offense or of an attempt to commit such an offense:

  • To establish that sexual contact did or did not occur.

  • To establish the presence or absence of venereal disease or infection.

♦ In the examination and treatment of injuries and trauma sustained by a victim of such an offense.

Every policy of accident and health insurance that specifically provides benefits for routine physical examinations must provide full coverage for expenses incurred in the examination and testing of the victims.

No company authorized to transact health insurance in Illinois may deny, refuse to issue, refuse to renew, refuse to reissue, cancel, or otherwise terminate an insurance policy or restrict coverage of an individual because of any of the following:

♦ The individual has been the subject of domestic abuse.

♦ The individual has sought medical or psychological treatment for domestic abuse or protection.

♦ The individual has sought shelter from domestic abuse.

Shingles Vaccinations

A group policy of accident and health insurance or managed care plan must provide coverage for a vaccine for shingles that is approved for marketing by the FDA if the vaccine is ordered by a physician licensed to practice medicine in all its branches and the enrollee is 60 years of age or older. HMOs must also provide this coverage.

Temporomandibular Joint Disorder

According to 215 Ill. Comp. Stat. § 5/356g, every insurer that delivers or issues for delivery in Illinois a group accident and health policy providing coverage for hospital, medical, or surgical treatment on an expense-incurred basis must offer optional coverage for the reasonable and necessary medical treatment of temporomandibular joint disorder and craniomandibular disorder. This coverage must be offered for an additional premium and subject to the insurer's standard of insurability.

Benefits may be subject to the same pre-existing conditions, limitations, deductibles, co-payments, and co-insurance that generally apply to any other sickness. The maximum lifetime benefits for such conditions must be no less than $2,500.

Wellness Coverage

A group or individual policy of accident and health insurance or managed care plan that provides coverage for hospital or medical treatment on an expense incurred basis may offer a reasonably designed program for wellness coverage that allows for a reward, a contribution, a reduction in premiums or reduced medical, prescription drug, or equipment co-payments, co-insurance, or deductibles, or a combination of these incentives, for participation in any health behavior wellness, maintenance, or improvement program approved or offered by the insurer or managed care plan. The insured or enrollee may be required to provide evidence of participation in a program. Individuals unable to participate in these incentives due to an adverse health factor may not be penalized based upon an adverse health status.

A plan offering wellness coverage must:

- ◆ Give participants the opportunity to qualify for offered incentives at least once a year.

- ◆ Allow a reasonable alternative to any individual for whom it is unreasonably difficult, due to a medical condition, to satisfy otherwise applicable wellness program standards. Plans may seek physician verification that health factors make it unreasonably difficult or medically inadvisable for the participant to satisfy the standards.

- ◆ Not provide a total incentive that exceeds 20 percent of the cost of employee-only coverage. The cost of employee-only coverage includes both employer and employee contributions. For plans offering family coverage, the 20 percent limitation applies to cost of family coverage and applies to the entire family.

Dependent Care Coverage

No contract or evidence of coverage issued by a health maintenance organization that provides for coverage of dependents of the principal enrollee may contain any disclaimer, waiver, or other limitation relative to the eligibility or coverage of newborn infants of a principal employee from the moment of birth.

According to 215 Ill. Comp. Stat. § 5/356c, no policy of accident and health insurance providing coverage of hospital expenses or medical expenses or both on an expense-incurred basis that covers members of the insured's immediate family may contain any disclaimer, waiver, or other limitation of coverage relative to the hospital or medical coverage or insurability of newborn infants from the moment of birth.

Each contract, evidence of coverage, or policy of accident and health insurance must contain a provision stating that benefits must be granted immediately with respect to a newly born child from the moment of birth. The coverage for newly born children must include coverage of illness, injury, congenital defects, birth abnormalities, and premature birth.

Adopted Children

According to 215 Ill. Comp. Stat. § 5/356h, no individual or group policy of accident and health insurance which covers the insured's immediate family or children, as well as covering the insured, may exclude a child from coverage or limit coverage for a child solely based on any of the following:

♦ The child is an adopted child.

♦ The child does not reside with the insured.

A child who is in the custody of the insured, pursuant to an interim court order of adoption or, in the case of group insurance, placement of adoption — whichever comes first — vesting temporary care of the child in the insured, is an adopted child, regardless of whether a final order granting adoption is ultimately issued.

Autism Spectrum Disorders

According to 215 Ill. Comp. Stat. § 5/356z.14, a group or individual policy of accident and health insurance or managed care plan must provide individuals under 21 years of age coverage for the diagnosis of autism spectrum disorders and for the treatment of autism spectrum disorders to the extent that the diagnosis and treatment of autism spectrum disorders are not already covered by the policy of accident and health insurance or managed care plan. *Autism spectrum disorders* are pervasive developmental disorders as defined in the most recent edition of the Diagnostic and Statistical Manual of Mental Disorders, including autism, Asperger's disorder, and pervasive developmental disorder not otherwise specified. *Diagnosis of autism spectrum disorders* is one or more tests, evaluations, or assessments to diagnose whether an individual has autism spectrum disorder that is prescribed, performed, or ordered by a physician licensed to practice medicine in all its branches or a licensed clinical psychologist with expertise in diagnosing autism spectrum disorders.

Treatment for autism spectrum disorders includes the following care prescribed, provided, or ordered for an individual diagnosed with an autism spectrum disorder by a physician licensed to practice medicine in all its branches or a certified, registered, or licensed health care professional with expertise in treating effects of autism spectrum disorders when the care is determined to be medically necessary and ordered by a physician licensed to practice medicine in all its branches:

♦ Psychiatric care that is direct, consultative, or diagnostic services provided by a licensed psychiatrist.

♦ Psychological care that is direct or consultative services provided by a licensed psychologist.

♦ Habilitative or rehabilitative care that is professional, counseling, and guidance services and treatment programs, including applied behavior analysis, that are intended to develop, maintain, and restore the functioning of an individual.

♦ Therapeutic care, including behavioral, speech, occupational, and physical therapies that provide treatment in the following areas: self care and feeding, pragmatic, receptive, and expressive language, cognitive functioning, applied behavior analysis, intervention, and modification, motor planning, and sensory processing.

Terms of Coverage

Autism spectrum disorder coverage is subject to a maximum benefit of $36,000 per year and co-payment, deductible, and co-insurance provisions of a policy of accident and health insurance or managed care plan to the extent that other medical services covered by the policy of accident and health insurance or managed care plan are subject to these provisions. However, coverage is not subject to limits on the number of visits to a service provider.

Coverage for autism does not limit benefits that are otherwise available to an individual under a policy of accident and health insurance or managed care plan and autism coverage benefits may not be subject to dollar limits, deductibles, co-payments, or co-insurance provisions that are less favorable to the insured than the dollar limits, deductibles, or co-insurance provisions that apply to physical illness generally.

An insurer may not deny or refuse to provide otherwise covered services, or refuse to renew, refuse to reissue, or otherwise terminate or restrict coverage under an individual contract to provide services to an individual because the individual or their dependent is diagnosed with an autism spectrum disorder or due to the individual utilizing benefits provided by law.

Continued Treatment and Medically Necessary

Upon request of the reimbursing insurer, a provider of treatment for autism spectrum disorders must furnish medical records, clinical notes, or other necessary data that substantiate that initial or continued medical treatment is medically necessary and is resulting in improved clinical status. Care which is *medically necessary* is any care, treatment, intervention, service, or item which will or is reasonably expected to do any of the following:

+ Prevent the onset of an illness, condition, injury, disease, or disability.

+ Reduce or ameliorate the physical, mental or developmental effects of an illness, condition, injury, disease, or disability.

+ Assist to achieve or maintain maximum functional activity in performing daily activities.

When treatment is anticipated to require continued services to achieve demonstrable progress, the insurer may request a treatment plan consisting of diagnosis, proposed treatment by type, frequency, anticipated duration of treatment, the anticipated outcomes stated as goals, and the frequency by which the treatment plan will be updated.

When making a determination of medical necessity for a treatment modality for autism spectrum disorders, an insurer must make the determination in a manner that is consistent with the manner used to make that determination with respect to other diseases or illnesses covered under the policy, including an appeals process. During the appeals process, any challenge to medical necessity must be viewed as reasonable only if the review includes a physician with expertise in the most current and effective treatment modalities for autism spectrum disorders.

Note: Coverage for medically necessary early intervention services must be delivered by certified early intervention specialists.

Disabilities

Any group contract or evidence of coverage or accident or health policy that specifies that coverage for a dependent child terminates when the child reaches a specified limiting age must also specify that attainment of the limiting age does not terminate the coverage of a child incapable of self-sustaining employment because of mental retardation or physical disability and who remains dependent on the insured.

Extension of Coverage for College Students

Under 215 Ill. Comp. Stat. § 5/356z.11, a group policy of accident and health insurance or managed care plan amended, delivered, issued, or renewed in Illinois must continue to provide coverage for a dependent college student who takes a medical leave of absence or reduces their course load to part-time status because of a catastrophic illness or injury. This continuation coverage is subject to all of the policy's terms and conditions applicable to those forms of insurance. Continuation of insurance under the policy will terminate 12 months after notice of the illness or injury or until the coverage would have otherwise lapsed pursuant to the terms and conditions of the policy, whichever comes first, provided the need for part-time status or medical leave of absence is supported by a clinical certification of need from a physician licensed to practice medicine in all its branches.

Habilitative Services for Children

According to 215 Ill. Comp. Stat. § 356z.14, a group or individual policy of accident and health insurance or managed care plan must provide coverage for habilitative services for children under age 19 with a congenital, genetic, or early acquired disorder as long as all of the following conditions are met:

♦ A physician licensed to practice medicine in all its branches has diagnosed the child's congenital, genetic, or early acquired disorder.

♦ The treatment is administered by a licensed speech-language pathologist, licensed audiologist, licensed occupational therapist, licensed physical therapist, licensed physician, licensed nurse, licensed optometrist, licensed nutritionist, licensed social worker, or licensed psychologist upon the referral of a physician licensed to practice medicine in all its branches.

♦ The initial or continued treatment must be medically necessary and therapeutic and not experimental or investigational.

Habilitative services are occupational therapy, physical therapy, speech therapy, and other services prescribed by the insured's treating physician pursuant to a treatment plan to enhance the ability of a child to function with a congenital, genetic, or early acquired disorder. A congenital or genetic disorder includes, but is not limited to, hereditary disorders. An *early acquired disorder* refers to a disorder resulting from illness, trauma, injury, or some other event or condition suffered by a child prior to that child developing functional life skills such as, but not limited to, walking, talking, or self-help skills. Congenital, genetic, and early acquired disorders may include, but are not limited to, autism or an autism spectrum disorder, cerebral palsy, and other disorders resulting from early childhood illness, trauma, or injury.

Such coverage is subject to other general exclusions and limitations of the policy, including coordination of benefits, participating provider requirements, restrictions on services provided by family or household members, utilization review of health care services, including review of medical necessity, case management, experimental, and investigational treatments, and other managed care provisions. However, the coverage for children under age 19 does not apply to treatment of mental or emotional disorders or illnesses as covered under 215 Ill. Comp. Stat. Ann.§ 370 as well as any other benefit based upon a specific diagnosis that may be otherwise required by law.

Verification

Upon request of the reimbursing insurer, the provider under whose supervision the habilitative services are being provided must furnish medical records, clinical notes, or other necessary data to allow the insurer to substantiate that initial or continued medical treatment is medically necessary and that the patient's condition is clinically improving. When the treating provider anticipates that continued treatment is or will be required to permit the patient to achieve demonstrable progress, the insurer may request that the provider furnish a treatment plan consisting of diagnosis, proposed treatment by type, frequency, anticipated duration of treatment, the anticipated goals of treatment, and how frequently the treatment plan will be updated.

Unmarried Dependents

According to 215 Ill. Comp. Stat. § 5/356z.12a, beginning June 1, 2009, a group policy of accident and health insurance or managed care plan that provides coverage for dependents and that is amended, delivered, issued, or renewed after June 1, 2009, may not terminate coverage or deny the election of coverage for an unmarried dependent by reason of the dependent's age before the dependent's 26th birthday. A policy or plan subject to this section must, upon amendment, delivery, issuance, or renewal, establish an initial enrollment period of not less than 90 days during which an insured may make a written election for coverage of an unmarried person as a dependent under this section. After the initial enrollment period, enrollment by a dependent pursuant to this section must be consistent with the enrollment terms of the plan or policy.

The policy or plan subject to this section must allow for dependent coverage during the annual open enrollment date or the annual renewal date if the dependent, as of the date on which the insured elects dependent coverage under this subsection, has:

- A period of continuous creditable coverage of 90 days or more.

- Not been without creditable coverage for more than 63 days. An insured may elect coverage for a dependent who does not meet the continuous creditable coverage requirements of this subsection and that dependent must not be denied coverage due to age.

Military Personnel

A group policy of accident and health insurance or managed care plan that provides coverage for dependents and that is amended, delivered, issued, or renewed after June 1, 2009, may not terminate coverage or deny the election of coverage for an unmarried dependent by reason of the dependent's age before the dependent's 30th birthday if the dependent:

- Is an Illinois resident.

- Has served as a member of the active or reserve components of any of the branches of the U.S. Armed Forces.

- Has received a release or discharge other than a dishonorable discharge. To be eligible for coverage, the eligible dependent must submit to the insurer a form approved by the Illinois Department of Veterans' Affairs stating the date on which the dependent was released from service.

Note: Nothing in this section prohibits an employer from requiring an employee to pay all or part of the cost of coverage provided under this section.

Prescription Drug Coverage
Cancer

According to 215 Ill. Comp. Stat. § 5/270r, no HMO that provides coverage for prescribed drugs approved by the FDA for the treatment of certain types of cancer may exclude coverage of any drug on the basis that it has been prescribed for a type of cancer for which the FDA has not approved the drug. The drug must, however, be approved by the FDA and must be recognized for the treatment of the specific type of cancer for which it has been prescribed in any of the following reference compendia:

- American Hospital Formulary Service Drug Information.

- National Comprehensive Cancer Network's Drugs & Biologics Compendium.

- Thomson Micromedex's Drug Dex.

- Elsevier Gold Standard's Clinical Pharmacology.

- Other authoritative compendia as identified from time to time by the Federal Secretary of Health and Human Services.

If the drug has not been so recognized in the compendia, it must be recommended for that particular type of cancer in formal clinical studies, the results of which have been published in at least two peer-reviewed professional medical journals published in the United States or Great Britain. Coverage must also include medically necessary services associated with administering the drug.

Under Illinois law, coverage is not required for cancer treatment with any experimental or investigational drugs or any drug that the FDA has determined to be contraindicated (a situation in which a medication or treatment should not be administered) for treatment of the specific type of cancer for which it has been prescribed.

Contraceptives

According to 215 Ill. Comp. Stat. § 5/356z.4, an individual or group policy of accident and health insurance that provides coverage for outpatient services and outpatient prescription drugs or devices must provide coverage for the insured and any dependent of the insured covered by the policy for all outpatient contraceptive services and all outpatient contraceptive drugs and devices approved by the FDA.

An *outpatient contraceptive service* means consultations, examinations, procedures, and medical services provided on an outpatient basis and related to the use of contraceptive methods (including natural family planning) to prevent an unintended pregnancy.

Additionally, the required coverage may not impose any deductible, co-insurance, waiting period, or other cost-sharing or limitation that is greater than that required for any outpatient service or outpatient prescription drug or device otherwise covered by the policy.

Inhalants

A group policy of accident and health insurance or managed care plan that provides coverage for prescription drugs may not deny or limit coverage for prescription inhalants to enable persons to breathe when suffering from asthma or other life-threatening bronchial ailments based upon any restriction on the number of days before an inhaler refill may be obtained if, contrary to those restrictions, the inhalants have been ordered or prescribed by the treating physician and are medically appropriate. HMOs are also subject to this provision.

Organ Transplant Medication Notification Act

In accordance with the Illinois Pharmacy Practice Act, when a prescribing physician has indicated on a prescription "may not substitute," a health insurance policy or health care service plan that covers immunosuppressant drugs may not require or cause a pharmacist to interchange another immunosuppressant drug or formulation issued on behalf of a person to inhibit or prevent the activity of the immune system of a patient to prevent the rejection of transplanted organs and tissues without notification and the documented consent of the prescribing physician and the patient, or the parent or guardian if the patient is a child, or the spouse of a patient who is authorized to consent to the treatment of the person. Additionally, patient co-payments, deductibles, or other charges for the prescribed drug for which another immunosuppressant drug or formulation is not interchanged must remain the same for the enrollment period established by the health insurance policy or plan.

Mental Health Coverage

According to 215 Ill. Comp. Stat. § 5/370c, every insurer that delivers, issues for delivery, renews, or modifies group accident and health policies providing coverage for hospital or medical treatment or services for illness on an expense-incurred basis must offer to the applicant or group policyholder (subject to the insurer's standards of insurability) coverage for reasonable and necessary treatment and services for mental, emotional, or nervous disorders or conditions, other than serious mental illnesses, up to the limits provided in the policy for other disorders or conditions.

However, the insured may be required to pay up to 50 percent of expenses incurred as a result of the treatment or services, and the annual benefit may be limited to the lesser of $10,000 or 25 percent of the lifetime policy limit.

Each covered may select the physician licensed to practice medicine in all its branches, licensed clinical psychologist, licensed clinical social worker, licensed clinical professional counselor, or licensed marriage and family therapist (licensed medical professional) of their choice to treat their disorders.

The insurer must pay the covered charges of the licensed professional as long as both of the following apply:

♦ The policy covers the disorder or condition treated.

♦ The licensed medical professional is authorized by the state to provide the required services and in accordance with accepted principles of the applicable medical profession.

Applicable insurers must also provide policy coverage for treatment of serious mental illness under the same terms and conditions as coverage for hospital or medical expenses related to other illnesses and diseases. The required coverage must provide for same durational limits, amount limits, deductibles, and co-insurance requirements for serious mental illness as provided for other illnesses and diseases.

A *serious mental illness* is the following psychiatric illnesses, as defined in the most current edition of the *Diagnostic and Statistical Manual* (DSM) published by the American Psychiatric Association:

♦ Schizophrenia.

♦ Paranoid and other psychotic disorders.

♦ Bipolar disorders (hypomanic, manic, depressive, and mixed).

♦ Major depressive disorders (single episode or recurrent).

♦ Schizoaffective disorders (bipolar or depressive).

♦ Pervasive developmental disorders.

♦ Obsessive-compulsive disorders.

♦ Depression in childhood and adolescence.

♦ Panic disorder.

♦ Post-traumatic stress disorders (acute, chronic, or with delayed onset).

♦ Anorexia nervosa and bulimia nervosa.

However, coverage for treatment of serious mental illness **does not apply** to coverage provided to employees by employers who have 50 or less employees.

A group health benefit plan must meet all the following requirements:

♦ Provide coverage based upon medical necessity for the following treatment of mental illness in each calendar year:

• 45 days of inpatient treatment.

• 60 visits for outpatient treatment including group and individual outpatient treatment.

• For plans or policies delivered, issued for delivery, renewed, or modified after January 1, 2007, additional outpatient visits for speech therapy for treatment of pervasive developmental disorders. Theses supplementary outpatient visit will be in addition to speech therapy that is provided pursuant to the 60 visits for outpatient treatment including group and individual outpatient treatment.

- ◆ May not include a lifetime limit on the number of days of inpatient treatment or the number of outpatient visits covered under the plan.
- ◆ Must include the same amount limits, deductibles, co-payments, and co-insurance factors for serious mental illness as for physical illness.

Note: According to 215 Ill. Comp. Stat. § 5/356d, no claim may be denied under any group accident and health policy delivered or renewed in Illinois for treatment or services for mental illness or rehabilitation following mental illness rendered in a hospital solely because the hospital lacks surgical facilities.

Substance Abuse Coverage

According to 215 Ill. Comp. Stat. § 5/367, no policy of group accident and health insurance delivered in Illinois that provides inpatient hospital coverage for sicknesses — other than a policy that covers only specified sicknesses — may exclude from coverage the treatment of alcoholism.

According to 215 Ill. Comp. Stat. § 5/367d.1, no group policy of accident and health insurance that provides coverage for the treatment of alcoholism or other drug abuse or dependency on both an inpatient and outpatient basis may be issued, delivered, or amended in Illinois if it excludes from coverage services provided by persons or entities licensed by the Department of Alcoholism and Substance Abuse to provide alcoholism or drug abuse or dependency services.

Charges must otherwise be eligible for reimbursement under the policy, and the services provided must be medically necessary and within the scope of the licensure of the provider.

The substance abuse coverage requirements **do not apply** to arrangements, agreements, or policies authorized under Illinois' Health Care Reimbursement Reform Act of 1985, Limited Health Service Organization Act, or the Health Maintenance Organization Act.

Pre-Existing Conditions

According to Illinois Health Insurance Portability and Accountability Act, 215 Ill. Comp. Stat. § 97/20, a group health plan and a health insurance issuer offering group health insurance may, with respect to a participant or beneficiary, impose a pre-existing condition exclusion only under all of the following circumstances:

- ◆ The exclusion relates to a condition (whether mental or physical) for which medical advice, diagnosis, care, or treatment was recommended or received within the six-month period ending on the enrollment date.
- ◆ The exclusion extends for not more than 12 months (18 months in the case of a late enrollee) after the enrollment date.
- ◆ The period of any such pre-existing condition exclusion is reduced by the amount of creditable coverage applicable to the participant or beneficiary as of the enrollment date.

Genetic Information

Genetic information may not be treated as a pre-existing condition in the absence of a diagnosis of the condition relating to the genetic information.

Exceptions

HMOs that offer health insurance coverage in connection with a group health plan and that do not impose any allowable pre-existing condition exclusion may impose an affiliation period if the period is applied uniformly without regard to health-status-related factors, and the period does not exceed two months (three in the case of a late enrollee).

However, the pre-existing condition exclusion is **not** applicable to the following:

♦ A group health plan or health insurance issuer offering group health insurance coverage may not impose any pre-existing condition exclusion relating to pregnancy as a pre-existing condition.

♦ Certain newborns. A group health plan and a health insurance issuer offering group health insurance coverage may not impose any pre-existing condition exclusion in the case of an individual who, as of the last day of the 30-day period beginning with the date of birth, is covered under creditable coverage.

♦ Certain adopted children. A group health plan and a health insurance issuer offering group health insurance coverage may not impose any pre-existing condition exclusion in the case of a child who is adopted or placed for adoption before attaining 18 years of age and who, as of the last day of the 30-day period beginning on the date of the adoption or placement for adoption, is covered under creditable coverage. However, the exception does not apply to coverage before the date of the adoption or placement for adoption.

Note: These exceptions are no longer applicable to an individual after the end of the first 63-day period that the individual was not covered under any creditable coverage.

Providers

Podiatrists

The person entitled to benefits or person performing services under an individual or group policy of accident and health insurance, or a policy, contract, plan, or agreement for hospital or medical service or indemnity, wherever such policy, contract, plan, or agreement provides for reimbursement for any service provided by persons licensed under the Illinois Medical Practice Act of 1987, is entitled to reimbursement on an equal basis for such service when the service is performed by a person licensed under the Illinois Medical Practice Act of 1987 or the Podiatric Medical Practice Act of 1987.

This provision does not apply to any policy, contract, plan, or agreement in effect prior to September 19, 1969, or to preferred provider arrangements or benefit agreements.

Psychologists/Social Workers

Each insured that is covered for mental, emotional, or nervous disorders or conditions is free to select the physician licensed to practice medicine in all its branches, licensed clinical psychologist, licensed clinical social worker, licensed clinical professional counselor, or licensed marriage and family therapist of their choice to treat such disorders.

Woman's Principal Health Care Provider

According to 215 Ill. Comp. Stat. § 5/356r, an individual or group policy of accident and health insurance that requires an insured or enrollee to designate an individual to coordinate care or to control access to health care services must also permit a female insured or enrollee to designate a participating woman's principal health care provider.

The insurer or managed care plan must also provide the following written notice to all female insureds, to all new enrollees at the time of enrollment, and to all existing enrollees at least annually, as a part of a regular publication or informational mailing:

NOTICE TO ALL FEMALE PLAN MEMBERS: YOUR RIGHT TO SELECT

A WOMAN'S PRINCIPAL HEALTH CARE PROVIDER

Illinois law allows you to select a "woman's principal health care provider" in addition to your selection of a primary care physician. A woman's principal health care provider is a physician licensed to practice medicine in all its branches specializing in obstetrics or gynecology or specializing in family practice. A woman's principal health care provider may be seen for care without referrals from your primary care physician. If you have not already selected a woman's principal health care provider, you may do so now or at any other time. You are not required to have or to select a woman's principal health care provider.

Your woman's principal health care provider must be a part of your plan. You may get the list of participating obstetricians, gynecologists, and family practice specialists from your employer's employee benefits coordinator, or for your own copy of the current list, you may call [insert plan's toll-free number]. The list will be sent to you within 10 days after your call. To designate a woman's principal health care provider from the list, call [insert plan's toll-free number] and tell our staff the name of the physician you have selected.

Additionally, notice may be required if the plan requires that the primary care physician and the woman's principal health care provider have a referral arrangement with one another.

Discrimination Prohibited

According to 215 Ill. Comp. Stat. § 5/364, discrimination between individuals of the same class of risk in any of the following manners is prohibited:

- ♦ In the issuance of policies.

- ♦ In the amount of premiums or rates charged for any covered insurance covered.

- ♦ In the benefits payable.

- ♦ In any of the terms or conditions of an insurance policy.

- ♦ In any other manner whatsoever.

However, insurers are not prohibited from providing incentives for insureds to utilize the services of a particular hospital or person.

No company, in any policy of accident or health insurance issued in Illinois, may make or permit any distinction or discrimination against individuals solely because of handicaps or disabilities in any of the following manners:

- ♦ In the amount of payment of premiums or rates charged for policies of insurance.

- ♦ In the amount of any dividends or other benefits payable.

- ♦ In any other terms and conditions of the contract.

However, where the distinction or discrimination is based on sound actuarial principles or is related to actual or reasonably anticipated experience a distinction may be made.

Based on an individual's blindness or partial blindness, no company may:

- Refuse to insure or refuse to continue to insure.

- Limit the amount, extent, or kind of coverage available to an individual.

- Charge an individual a different rate for the same coverage.

With respect to all other conditions, including the underlying cause of the blindness or partial blindness, persons who are blind or partially blind are subject to the same standards of sound actuarial principles or actual or reasonably anticipated experience as are sighted persons. Refusal to insure includes denial by an insurer of disability insurance coverage because the policy defines disability as being presumed in the event that the insured loses their eyesight.

Coordination of Benefits

Employers, insurers, managed care plans, or third-party administrators may share the payment of expenses with another benefit plan sponsored by another employer, with the government through Medicare benefits, or with another type of insurance company through automobile or homeowners' insurance.

The state uses coordination of benefits language, following guidelines developed by the National Association of Insurance Commissioners (NAIC), to specify the order of benefit payments. Preserving cost-management initiatives such as deductibles and co-insurance is known as *maintenance of benefits*. Self-insured employee benefit plans are not required to adopt coordination of benefits language but most do specify how they will coordinate benefit payments with other plans.

Group accident and health insurance plans must specify how benefits will be coordinated. Small employer plans must follow the birthday rule when coordinating benefits for dependent children. *Small employer* means, in connection with a group health plan with respect to a calendar year and a plan year, an employer who employed an average of at least two but not more than 50 employees on business days during the preceding calendar year and who employs at least two employees on the first day of the plan year.

Order of Benefits

The following priorities apply when coordinating health benefit payments in Illinois:

- **Employee/Dependent.** Benefits will be paid first by the plan or policy that covers the individual on whose expenses the claim is based other than as a dependent will be determined before the benefits of a policy or certificate that covers the individual as a dependent.

- **Dependent Child/Birthday Rule.** Benefits for a dependent child whose parents are together will be paid first by the plan of the parent whose birthday comes first in the year. If both parents have the same birthday, benefits will be paid by the plan that has covered a parent longer. If one plan does not specify the birthday rule, benefits will be paid according to the order of benefits specified in that plan.

- **Dependent Child/Divorced or Separated Parents.** Benefits for a dependent child whose parents are divorced or separated will be paid first by the plan of the custodial parent, second by the plan of the spouse of the custodial parent, and third by the plan of the noncustodial parent. If a court decree states that one of the parents is responsible for the health care of the child, benefits will be paid by that parent's plan.

- **Active/Inactive Employee.** Benefits will be paid first by a plan or policy that covers the individual as an active employee before a plan that covers the individual as a retired or laid off employee. If only one of the plans specifies this rule, the standard is ignored.

- ◆ **Longer/Shorter Length of Coverage.** If the orders listed do not establish an order of benefits, coverage will be paid first by the plan that has covered the individual longer.

- ◆ **Continuation Coverage.** For an individual covered by two health benefit plans, HMO, or health insurance policies — one of which is a continuation plan under federal or state law — benefits will be paid first by the plan that covers the individual as an employee, member, or subscriber or as the employee's dependent and second under the continuation coverage. If only one of the two plans specifies this rule, this standard is ignored.

Maintenance of Benefits

A plan that pays benefits on a secondary basis may reduce benefits payable so that total benefits paid do not exceed expenses.

Medicare Coordination

The benefits of the plan that covers the person as an employee, member, or subscriber (or other than as a dependent) are determined before those of the plan that covers the person as a dependent, except that if the person is also a Medicare beneficiary the Medicare coverage is secondary to the plan covering the person as a dependent and primary to the plan covering the person as other than a dependent, such as a retired employee.

Utilization Review

Any preferred provider program, insurer, or administrator offering medical, dental, or hospital services must include utilization review (UR).

Same-Sex Domestic Partner Benefits

Per administrative order and effective since July 1, 2006, same-sex domestic partners of state employee's must be afforded the same health benefits as those received by married employees and their dependants. These benefits, to be extended to all state employees serving in agencies under the Governor's control, include health insurance, dental, and vision coverage.

A *domestic partner* is a person of the same sex who meets all of the following requirements:

- ◆ Has resided in the employee's household.

- ◆ Has had a financial and emotional interdependence with the employee, consistent with that of a married couple, for a period of not less than one year.

- ◆ Continues to maintain such arrangement consistent with that of a married couple.

All benefits will be administered in accordance with all applicable state and federal laws.

Health Care Continuation Law

Illinois' health care continuation law is located at 215 Ill. Comp. Stat. §§ 5/367.2 and 5/367e.

Illinois' health care continuation law covers all employers offering group accident and health insurance and requires the provision of continuation coverage.

Requirements

Under Illinois law, employers must offer continuation coverage to employees who have been continuously covered under a group plan for the three months before termination of employment.

The spouses and dependents of employees are covered if coverage is lost because of the retirement, termination of employment, or divorce of the covered employee. With respect to an employee who is involuntarily terminated between September 1, 2008 and the end of the period set forth in the federal American Recovery and Reinvestment Act of 2009, as amended, continuation must be available if the employee was insured under the group policy on the day prior to termination.

Within 10 days after the employee's termination, written notice of continuation rights must be presented to the employee by the employer. If the employee is unavailable, written notice must be mailed by the employer to the last known address of the employee within 10 days after the employee's termination. The employer must also send a copy of the notice to the insurer. The spouse or former spouse must notify the employer within 30 days of retirement, death, or divorce of a covered member. The employer must, in turn, notify the insurer of the event within 15 days of receiving the spouse's notice. Insurers then have 30 days after receiving the employer's notice to notify the spouse that coverage may be continued.

A terminated employee has 30 days following the later of the date of termination or the date the employee is presented or mailed written notice of continuation rights by either the employer or the group policyholder. In no event may this election period exceed 60 days. The insurer's notice to the spouse must include an election form and instructions for its return and the amount of monthly premium due and the spouse or former spouse must request continuation coverage within 30 days of receiving these instructions.

The insurer may not deny coverage to the employee due to the employer's failure to provide notice. In the event the employee contacts the insurer regarding continuation rights and advises that notice was not provided by the employer or group policyholder, the insurer must provide a written explanation to the employee of their continuation rights. Unless contrary to the federal American Recovery and Reinvestment Act of 2009 (ARRA), as amended, additional notice stipulations apply.

Disability of Dependent Child

As with regular coverage, a group plan that specifies that attainment of a specified age will terminate coverage of a dependent child must specify that this does not apply to a dependent child incapable of self-sustaining employment because of mental retardation or physical disability and who remains dependent on the child's parents. Insurers may require proof of disability and dependence two months before the child attains the limiting age and at any reasonable time thereafter.

Premiums for Continuation Coverage

Monthly premiums for continuation coverage are due in advance and may not exceed the group rate. Premiums due from a former spouse are the same as would be charged a current employee, plus the amount the employer would contribute toward the premium for a current employee.

After two years, the employer may charge an additional amount, not to exceed 20 percent for the costs of administration for coverage for a spouse who has attained age 55.

Termination of Continuation Coverage

Continuation privileges will terminate upon eligibility for Medicare, upon coverage in another group plan, failure to pay a required contribution, or on the date on which the group policy terminates.

Former spouses under 55 will lose coverage upon the first occurrence of one of the following:

 ♦ Failure to pay premiums when due, including any grace period allowed by the policy.

- When coverage would terminate under the terms of the existing policy if the employee and former spouse were still married to each other. However, the existing coverage will not be modified or terminated during the first 120 consecutive days subsequent to the employee spouse's death or to the entry of the judgment dissolving the marriage existing between the employee and the former spouse, unless the master policy in existence at the time is modified or terminated as to all employees.

- The date on which the former spouse first becomes, after the date of election, an insured employee under any other group health plan.

- The date the former spouse remarries.

- The expiration of two years from the date continuation coverage began.

Upon the termination of continuation coverage, the former spouse will be entitled to convert the coverage to an individual policy. Additionally, the continuation rights granted to former spouses who have not reached age 55 also include eligible dependents insured prior to the dissolution of marriage or the death of the employee.

Conversion to Individual Policy

Employees or members and their dependents who have been continuously covered for at least three months before termination of coverage by a group policy which provides hospital, medical, or major medical expense insurance and whose insurance terminates for any reason other than discontinuation of the policy or the member's failure to pay any required contributions are entitled to a converted policy. The surviving spouse of a deceased member is also eligible for coverage.

Notification of conversion rights must be included in the certificate of insurance. Written notice of conversion privileges must be given or mailed to the employee or member at the employee or member's last known address.

To request converted coverage, members must apply in writing to the insurer and pay the first premium within 31 days of termination or 15 days after receiving notice of conversion rights — whichever occurs later — but in no event later than 60 days following termination.

Premiums for Conversion Coverage

The initial premium for a converted policy must be determined according to the insurer's table of rates applicable to the age and class of risk of persons covered and the type of coverage provided.

Termination of Conversion Coverage

Coverage may terminate when an employee or member is covered or is eligible for coverage for similar benefits under another group plan or under Medicare. Additionally, converted coverage may be terminated when it would result in over insurance.

Duration of Conversion Coverage

Coverage will continue for twelve months after the member's insurance would otherwise have ceased due to termination of employment.

Penalties

In an insurer fails to notify a retired employee's spouse or former spouse of the right to continuation coverage, all premiums will be waived from the date the notice was required until the notice is sent.

Military Service Member Insurance Reinstatement

According to 215 Ill. Comp. Stat. § 5/368f , no Illinois resident activated for military service, as a result of the activation, will be denied reinstatement into the same individual health insurance coverage with the health insurer that the resident lapsed as a result of activation or becoming covered by the federal government-sponsored health insurance program. Such protections also apply to the activated resident's spouse or dependent who becomes eligible for a federal government-sponsored health insurance program, including the TriCare program providing coverage for civilian dependents of military personnel.

The Illinois resident has the right to reinstatement in the same individual health insurance coverage without medical underwriting, subject to payment of the current premium charged to other persons of the same age and gender that are covered under the same individual health coverage.

Except in the case of birth or adoption that occurs during the period of activation, reinstatement must be into the same coverage type as the resident held prior to lapsing the individual health insurance coverage and at the same or, at the option of the resident, higher deductible level. However, these reinstatement rights provided are not available to a resident or dependents if the activated person is discharged from the military under other than honorable conditions.

The health insurer with which the reinstatement is being requested must receive a request for reinstatement no later than 63 days following the later of deactivation or loss of coverage under the federal government-sponsored health insurance program. The health insurer may request proof of loss of coverage and the timing of the loss of coverage of the government-sponsored coverage in order to determine eligibility for reinstatement into the individual coverage. The effective date of the reinstatement of individual health coverage is the first of the month following receipt of the notice requesting reinstatement.

Note: All terms, conditions, and limitations of the individual coverage into which reinstatement is made apply equally to all insureds enrolled in the coverage.

Exceptions

The reinstatement provisions **do not apply** to any policy or certificate providing coverage for any of the following:

- Specified disease, specified accident, or accident-only coverage.

- Credit, dental, disability income, hospital indemnity, long-term care, Medicare supplement, vision care, or short-term nonrenewable health policy.

- Other limited-benefit supplemental insurance.

- Any coverage issued as a supplement to any liability insurance, workers' compensation, or similar insurance.

- Any insurance under which benefits are payable with or without regard to fault, whether written on a group, blanket, or individual basis.

Additionally, insurers are not required to reinstate the resident if the insurer requires residency in an enrollment area and those residency requirements are not met after deactivation or loss of coverage under the government-sponsored health insurance program.

Notification Requirement

All insurers must provide written notice to the policyholder of individual health coverage of their rights.

In lieu of the inclusion of the notice in the individual health insurance policy, an insurance company may satisfy the notification requirement by providing a single written notice through either of the following methods:

◆ In conjunction with the enrollment process for a policyholder initially enrolling in the individual coverage on or after July 20, 2006.

◆ Mailing written notice to policyholders, whose coverage was effective prior to July 20, 2006, no later than 90 days after July 20, 2006.

Contact Information

Illinois Department of Insurance

320 West Washington Street
Springfield, IL 62767-0001

Telephone: 217-782-4515
Fax: 217-782-5020
Internet: *http://insurance.illinois.gov*

Index

B

D

L

M

N

O

Q

R

S

Y

Z